Photo by Stanford Smith.

About the Author

Ken Wood has been a collector for more than half a century. A fascination with stamps from far off places sparked an interest in the lands from which they came. This has resulted in both *The Modern World* and his *Where in the World?* which deals with stamp-issuing entities of the past.

Born at Hastings, on England's south coast, near the site of the famous 1066 battle, Wood served in the British Army during World War II, spending several years in Egypt, Cyrenaica, and Malta as well as other Mediterranean and European areas.

After the war, he traveled widely, living in Guyana, Trinidad, and Canada, before settling with his wife Hilda in the United States.

Wood was editor of *Stamp Collector*, formerly *Western Stamp Collector*, from 1968 to 1980 and is currently its editor emeritus. He has been writing about the hobby for more than 25 years.

He is the author of the three-volume encyclopedia *This is Philately*, the philatelic atlas *Where in the World?* the handbook for new collectors *Basic Philately*, and *Post Dates*, a chronology of postal and philatelic events.

A Fellow of the Royal Philatelic Society, London, Wood is a holder of the Phoenix Award given by the Arizona State Philatelic Hall of Fame for service to philately. In 1974, he was named Distinguished Philatelist of the Year by the Northwest Federation of Stamp Clubs.

In 1979, the American Topical Association elected him to its Roll of Distinguished Topical Philatelists, and in 1984, he was named to the Hall of Fame of the Writers Unit #30 of the American Philatelic Society.

The Modern World
Today's Atlas for Stamp Collectors
by Kenneth A. Wood

Published by
Van Dahl Publications
Box 10,
Albany, OR 97321

For Hilda:

My companion on this trip around the world.

First edition, January 1987
Copyright © 1987 Van Dahl Publications

Library of Congress Cataloging in Publication Data

Wood, Kenneth A., 1926-
  The modern world.

Companion to: Where in the world? / K.A. Wood.
c1983.
    Bibliography: p.
    Includes index.
    1. Postage-stamps — Collectors and collecting — Maps.
I. Title. II. Title: Today's atlas for stamp collectors.
G1046.P8W57   1987   912   87-675089
ISBN 0-934466-10-6

All rights reserved. No part of this book
may be used or reproduced in any manner
whatsoever without written permission, except
in the case of brief quotations in critical
articles or reviews.

Printed in the United States of America.

Foreword

> So geographers, in Afric maps
> With savage pictures fill their gaps;
> And o'er unhabitable downs
> Place elephants for want of towns.
>   Jonathan Swift, *On Poetry*

My intention in compiling this atlas is to provide in a single volume, maps of all current stamp-issuing countries and their subdivisions that have stamps of their own, together with an outline of their geography, history, and economic status.

Produced in a similar format to *Where in the World?* which deals with entities that no longer exist or issue stamps, *The Modern World* can be either a companion volume to that atlas, or may be used alone by collectors whose interests lie in the area of today's stamps.

To collect stamps with only a minimal knowledge of their country of origin is to deprive oneself of much of the enjoyment our hobby offers. What is the location of a stamp-issuing entity? What are its relationships with nearby countries? And how have its location and neighbors affected its history and culture? It is the answer to such questions that can so greatly enhance our philatelic pleasure.

The world of stamps is one of great fascination and the more we know about the places from whence these tiny pieces of paper spring, the greater will be both our understanding of the world and our appreciation of those postal ambassadors from faraway places.

Won't you join me as we travel the world from the comfort of our favorite chair, striding, in our imagination, over mountain ranges in search of isolated principalities and skimming the oceans seeking remote desert islands?

        Kenneth A. Wood, FRPS,L

Arrangement and style

The arrangement of this atlas is conventional. Maps are grouped by continent or other recognized geographic area.

Preceding each section is a map of the area locating all current stamp-issuing entities. Maps are generally arranged alphabetically within sections, with one or two exceptions to permit full-page maps and related text to appear on facing pages.

Reference to the index will easily locate any desired country, even if it is sought under a name no longer in use, since the index is also a concordance of old and new country names.

Thus, if you seek Ceylon, you will be directed to it under its present name of Sri Lanka.

In general, I have followed the style of name spellings used by *The Times Atlas of the World,* seventh edition. Where alternative spellings exist, I have given preference to those likely to be most familiar to stamp collectors.

The text accompanying each map gives a concise, overall picture of the area. Climatic, geographic, historical, and economic information is presented in a standardized form to permit easy comparison with other areas.

Also included is a comprehensive listing of cities and towns that have had two or more names, or where several spellings are commonly used. This will be useful to collectors seeking to identify old place names found on postal markings.

To help identify a country's stamps, a typical recent stamp is illustrated within the text of each entity.

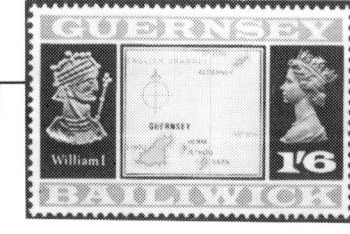

Contents

	Page
Foreword	v
Arrangement and style	vi
North America	1
Central America and Western Caribbean	11
Eastern Caribbean	22
South America	41
Europe	56
Africa	113
Southwest Asia	171
Asia	189
Australasia and Pacific Ocean	219
Antarctica	247
Old and new city and town names	249
References	254
Index	255

Appreciation

Anything as complex as a book has to be created by the combined work of many people. From those who help develop the project, to the production staff, it is a team effort.

This book as been no exception. Although it has kept me fully occupied for many months, there are others who have given their time and expertise. They too, must share in the pleasure of its completion.

A number of friends offered ideas, made suggestions, and helped in assembling the stamps that are illustrated and I am especially grateful to:
John M. Hotchner, Falls Church, Va.
Janet Klug, Pleasant Plain, Ohio.
Wally Miller, Westport, Wash.
William C. Norby, La Grange, Ill.
W.H. Sweitzer, Altoona, Pa.

At Van Dahl Publications I am indebted to Kyle R. Jansson for his editorial assistance and to James A. Magruder II for his confidence.

Production Manager Mona Conley, together with printing technicians Rachel Derksen, Anita Gourley, Teresa James, Corky Mason, Becky Rada, and Dana Buckentin worked smoothly as a team to make it all come together and deserve much credit for their expertise and remarkable patience.

Chief Photographer Warren Burgess of the *Albany Democrat-Herald* is responsible for the stamp and map photography. His talent and dedication are very much appreciated.

Thanks must also be extended to Jim Bristow of the *Salem Statesman-Journal* for his excellent work in producing the color separations for the cover.

Finally, my thanks go to Arlene Van Dahl, without whom it would not have been possible.

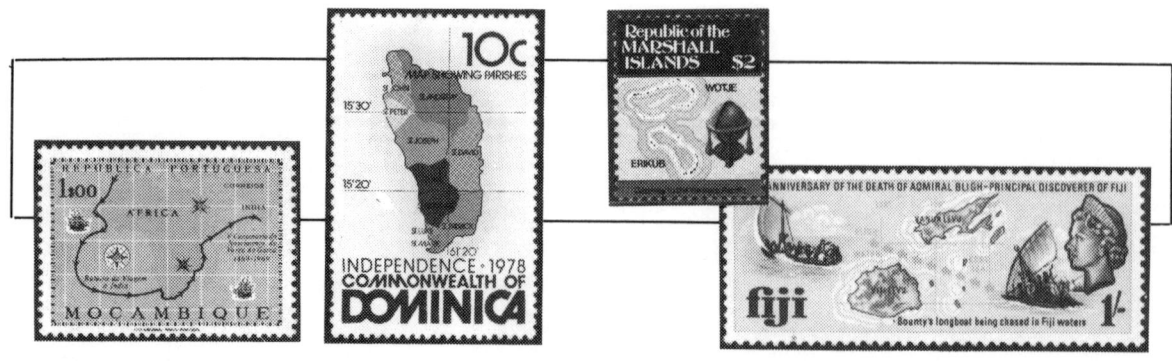

NORTH AMERICA

Stamp-issuing areas:

1. Bahamas
2. Bermuda
3. Canada
4. Mexico
5. St. Pierre and Miquelon
6. United States

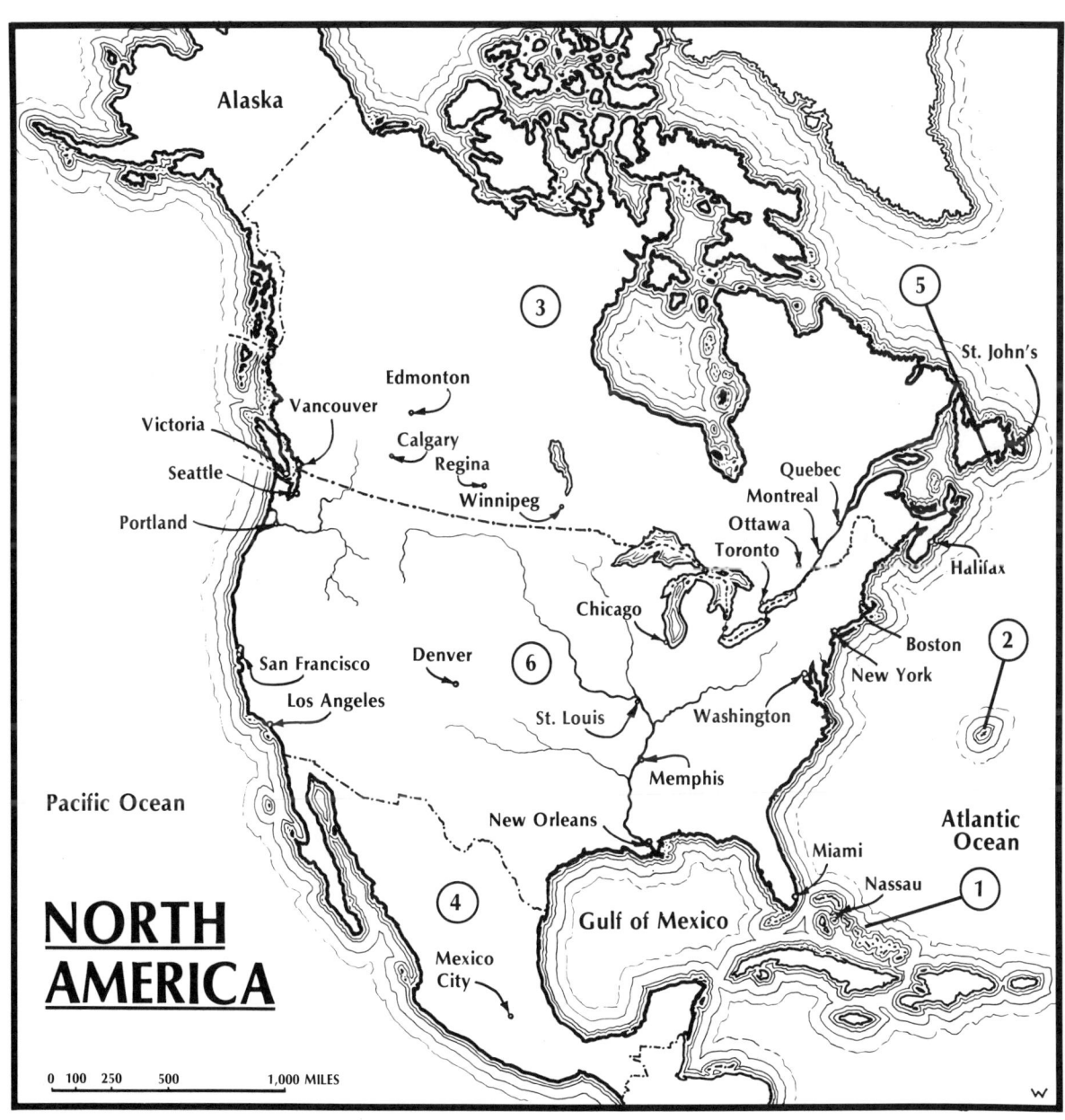

BAHAMAS, COMMONWEALTH OF

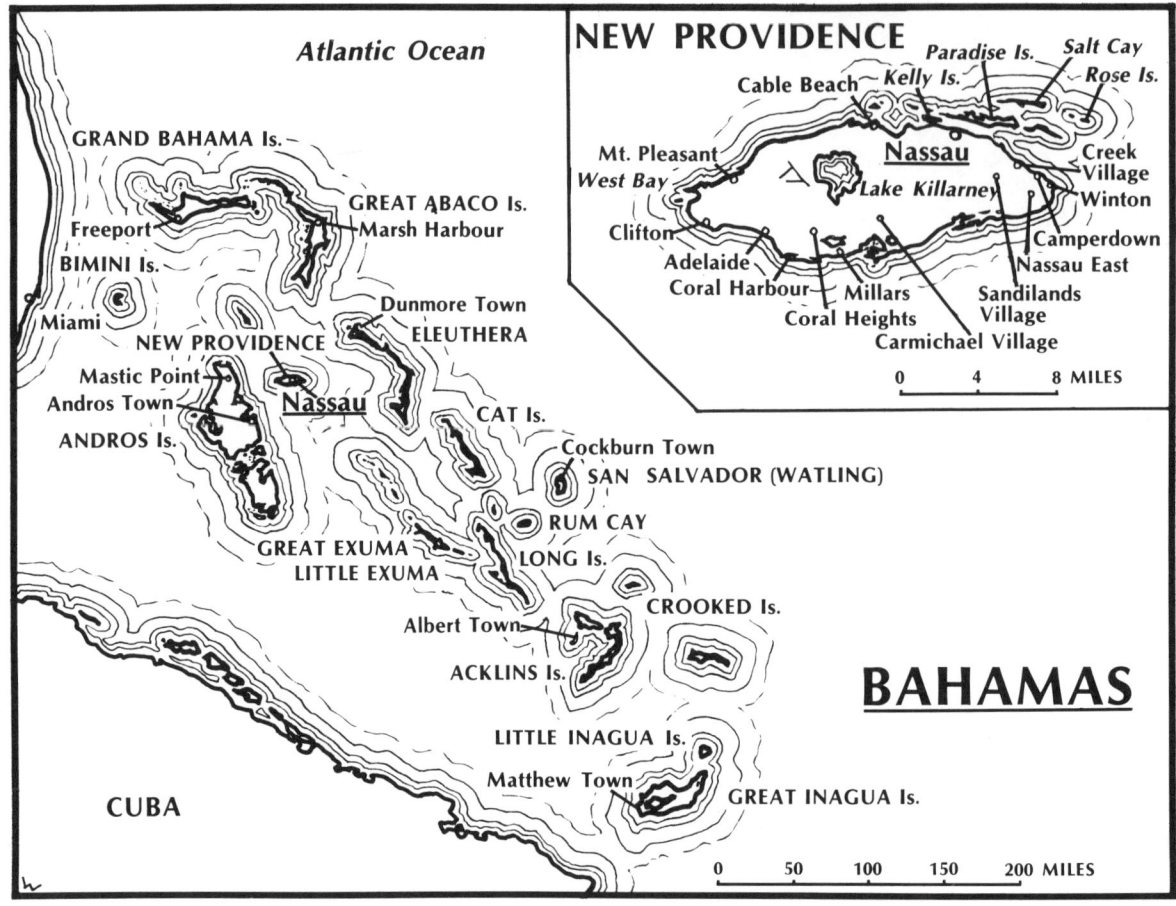

Area: 5,380 sq. miles
Population: 230,000 (1985)
Capital: Nassau
Currency: Dollar (100 cents)

A group of about 700 islands covering an area of 90,000 square miles off the coast of Florida in the Atlantic Ocean, the Bahamas is not part of the West Indies, despite being often so described.

Only about 30 islands are inhabited and there are some 2,000 cays and reefs scattered throughout the group.

The climate is subtropical with winter from December-April and summer from May-November. Summer temperatures range from 70-95 degrees F and 60-75 degrees F in winter. The 52-inch average annual rainfall occurs mostly between May and June, and September and October. Hurricanes are possible during June-November.

The Bahamas has been an independent member of the British Commonwealth since July 10, 1973.

The islands were discovered by Columbus in 1492, when he made his first landing in the New World, traditionally regarded to have been on San Salvador Island (Watling Is.). The original inhabitants were Arawak Indians.

English and Bermudan religious refugees made the first European settlement in 1647 on Eleuthera Island. The islands became a British colony in 1717.

A center of Confederate blockade running during the American Civil War, blockade running was also a Bahamain industry during Prohibition in the US.

Today, the main economic activities are tourism and international banking. The 1982 per capita income was $5,756. Oil refining and transshipment is important. There is little agriculture and most food is imported. Only 2% of the land is cultivated. Nassau and Freeport are the two chief ports.

Stamps were first issued in 1853 and were inscribed "INTERINSULAR POSTAGE" for domestic use. British stamps were used internationally until the 1860s. In recent years, stamps have been issued with increased frequency, although issues are still moderate by modern standards.

Philatelic Bureau: Postmaster General, GPO, PO Box N8302, Nassau, Bahamas.

BERMUDA

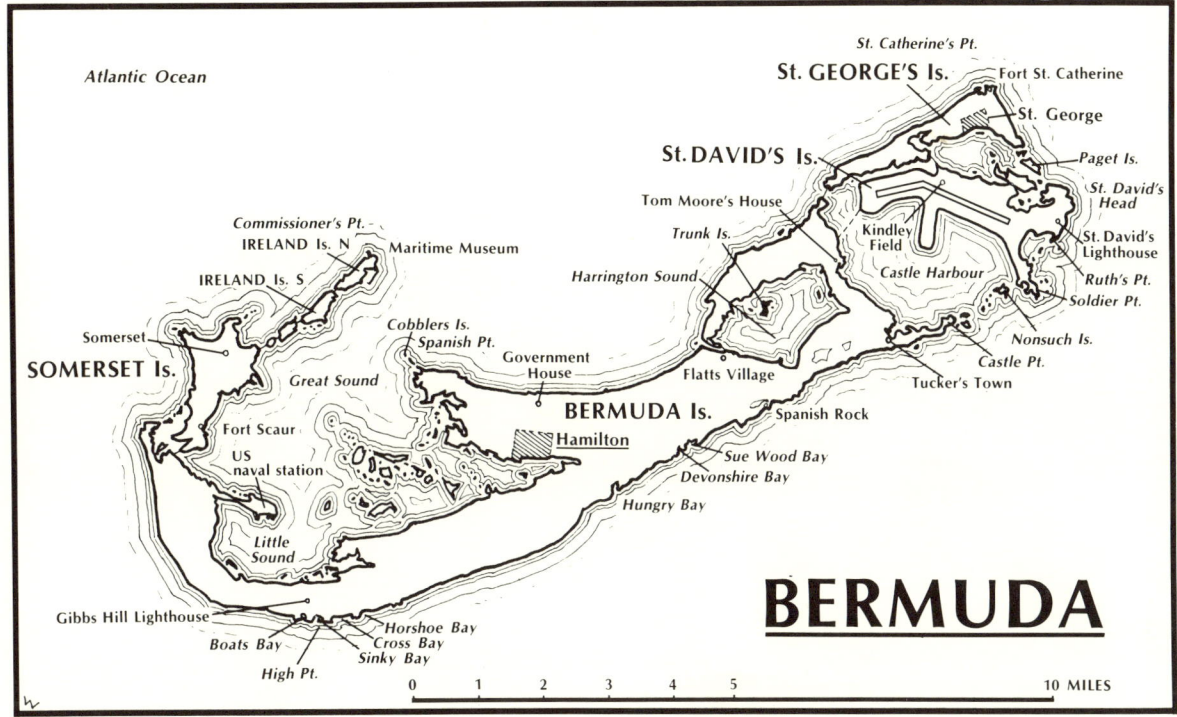

Area: 21 sq. miles
Population: 56,652 (1984)
Capital: Hamilton
Currency: Dollar (100 cents)

Bermuda comprises some 360 coral islands, only 20 of which are inhabited, located in the Atlantic 580 miles east of North Carolina.

The group is 24 miles long with an average width of less than one mile.

The climate is mild with summer temperatures rarely exceeding 90 degrees F and winter temperature seldom falling below 50 degrees F. Rainfall is distributed evenly throughout the year and averages about 60 inches annually. Few health hazards exist for visitors.

The population is approximately 59% black and 41% white. English is the language spoken and the literacy rate is 99%.

Although a British colony, now termed a dependency, Bermuda has internal autonomy. There is a governor appointed by the British monarch and the islands have the oldest legislative body of any British dependency, dating from 1620, and consisting of the House of Assembly and Legislative Council.

A prime minister is head of government and has a cabinet of 12 members appointed by him from members of the House of Assembly.

Bermuda's first political party, the Progressive Labour Party was formed in 1963 and in 1965, the United Bermuda Party came into being. A third party, the Bermuda Democratic Party was established in 1967.

Bermuda was discovered in 1503 by the Spanish sailor, Juan de Bermudez although he did not land because of the dangerous reef. In 1612, a group of 60 settlers arrived from Britain following the reports of Sir George Somers, who was wrecked there in 1609. The town of St. George was the first capital. It is the oldest continuous, English-speaking settlement in the Western Hemisphere.

Hamilton became the capital city in 1815.

Quite early in the 20th century, Bermuda became a popular tourist resort and today tourism is the major industry and source of income. There are numerous resort hotels.

There is little industry and most manufactured goods and food have to be imported. However, because of tourism, the economy is healthy.

The US has leased naval and air bases on the islands since WWII and there is a NASA tracking station there.

The first stamps used in Bermuda were the so-called Perot and Thies locals of 1848-1861. These are major rarities.

The first official government-issued stamps appeared in 1865. They depict the profile of Queen Victoria. Since then there has been a moderate flow of new stamps reflecting the islands' history, culture, and scenery. Current stamp-issuing policies are not excessive.

Philatelic Bureau: Bermuda Philatelic Bureau, GPO, Hamilton, Bermuda.

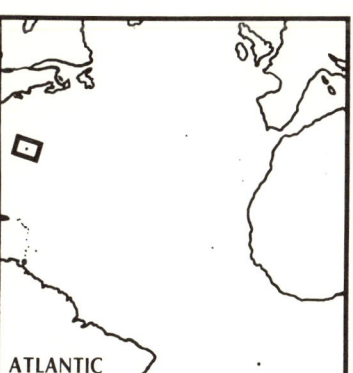

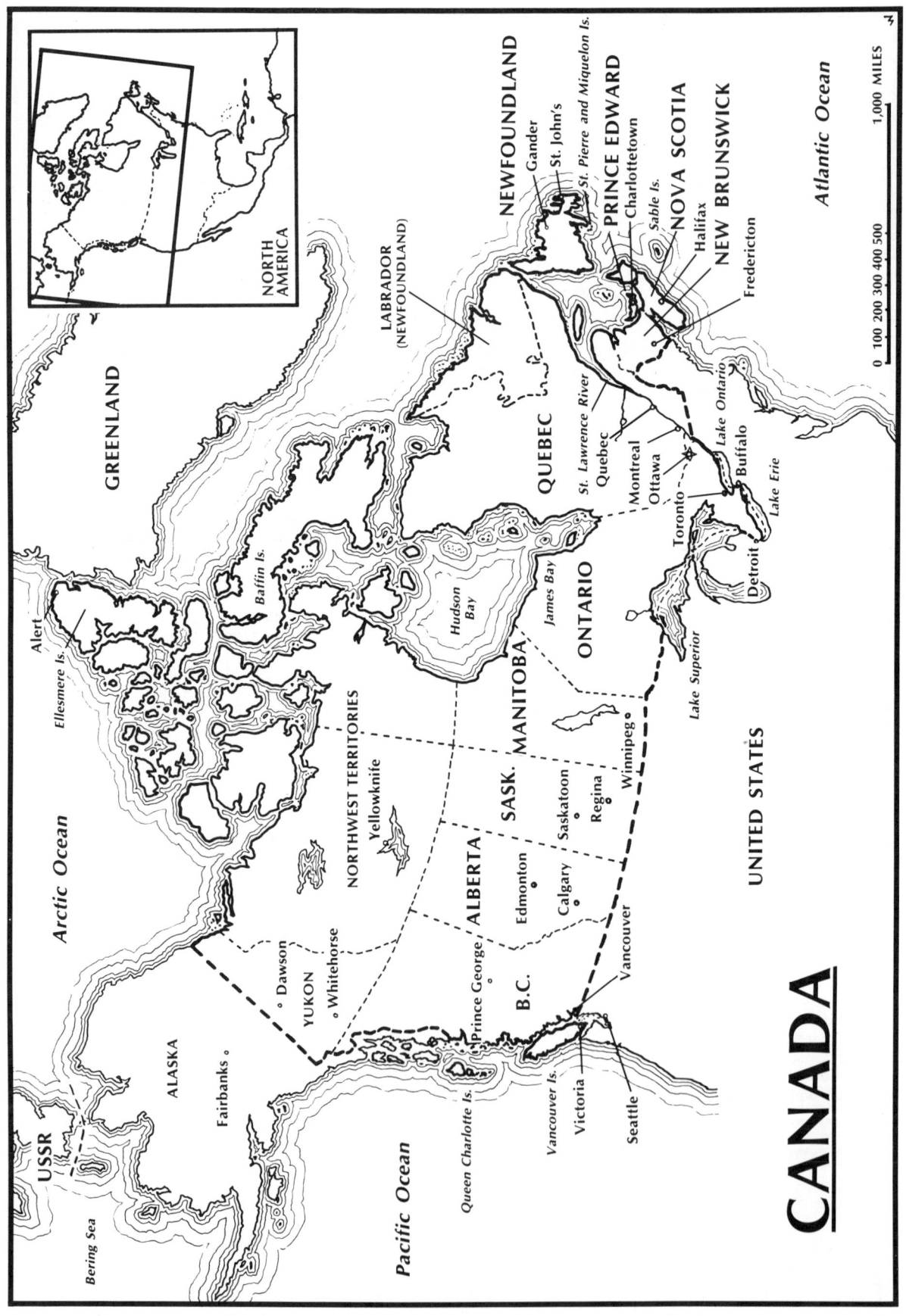

CANADA

Area: 3,849,670 sq. miles
Population: 25,262,500 (1985)
Capital: Ottawa
Currency: Dollar (100 cents)

Second largest country in the world after the Soviet Union, Canada stretches 3,223 miles from east to west and from near the North Pole to the US border. The southernmost part of Canada is actually located south of the latitude that forms the California-Oregon border.

The mainland coastline runs for 17,860 miles along the Pacific, Arctic, and Atlantic coasts.

The pre-Cambrian Shield, an area of ancient rock, extends from Labrador around Hudson Bay to the islands of the arctic. It is forested and dotted with lakes in the south and tundra in the north.

The Atlantic provinces in the east, including the island province of Newfoundland, are hilly, and on the mainland comprise a northern extension of the Applachian range.

Rolling prairies run west from the shield to the Rocky Mountains. This is the great wheat-growing area.

The west is rugged, with several north-south mountain ranges enclosing long valleys. The west coast is deeply indented and has numerous islands, the largest of which is Vancouver Island.

Canada's climate is continental, but varies widely, from mild and wet in southwestern British Columbia to arctic in the north. The prairies have short, hot summers and long, cold, but relatively dry, winters.

The climate in eastern Canada is more moderate than the prairies, but with greater precipitation, including heavy snow in winter.

Canada is made up of 10 provinces and two territories. These are Alberta, British Columbia, Manitoba, New Brunswick, Newfoundland, Nova Scotia, Ontario, Prince Edward Island, Quebec, and Saskatchewan. The territories are Yukon and the Northwest Territories.

Some of the provinces are former British colonies that once issued their own stamps. They are British Columbia, New Brunswick, Newfoundland, Nova Scotia, and Prince Edward Island.

French explorer Jacques Cartier is usually credited with discovering Canada in 1534, although John Cabot had sighted Newfoundland 37 years before in 1497. The Vikings seem to have been there before either.

Much of Canada's history is one of competition and conflict between the English and the French. The French established their colony of New France based on Quebec and Montreal, while the English settled the area of Nova Scotia.

Eventually, New France was taken by Britain and incorporated into what is now Canada. Although permitted to retain their language and culture, there has always been a degree of resentment on the part of the French and the two communities have co-existed in peace if not in complete harmony ever since. Today, Canada is officially bilingual.

The main British and French areas came to be called Upper Canada (Ontario) and Lower Canada (Quebec). The population of the English-speaking colonies was greatly boosted by the influx of United Empire Loyalists following the American Revolution and the independence of the 13 colonies.

Eventually Upper and Lower Canada united into the colony of Canada. Beginning in 1867, Confederation brought the other British colonies in to form the Dominion of Canada. Newfoundland held back and did not enter Confederation to become the 10th province until 1949.

After Confederation, the pace of westward expansion quickened and with the completion of the transcontinental railway, Canada was a unified nation.

With its system of government modeled on that of Britain, Canada became a self-governing dominion in the British Commonwealth in 1931. It severed the final legislative link in 1982, when it obtained the right to amend its constitution.

Canada's economic base is firm. The country is highly industrialized and is among the world's richest nations in natural resources.

Agriculture, along the southern strip where climatic conditions permit, is extensive and the prairies produce much of the world's wheat.

Ontario is the industrial and financial center of the country, although there has been much development in other areas, particularly the far west, in recent years.

The 1984 per capita income was $13,000 and the literacy rate is 99%.

Stamps were first issued for the colony of Canada in 1851. The country's philatelic heritage is rich and among collectors in the United States, is second in popularity only to that of their own country.

Canadian stamps have been issued in reasonable quantities and have maintained a high general standard of design and production quality.

Philatelic Bureau: Philatelic Service, National Philatelic Center, Canada Post Corporation, Antigonish, Nova Scotia, Canada, B2G 2R8.

The Canadian "Beaver" — first stamp of a new country.

Stamps of British colonies that are now part of Canada.

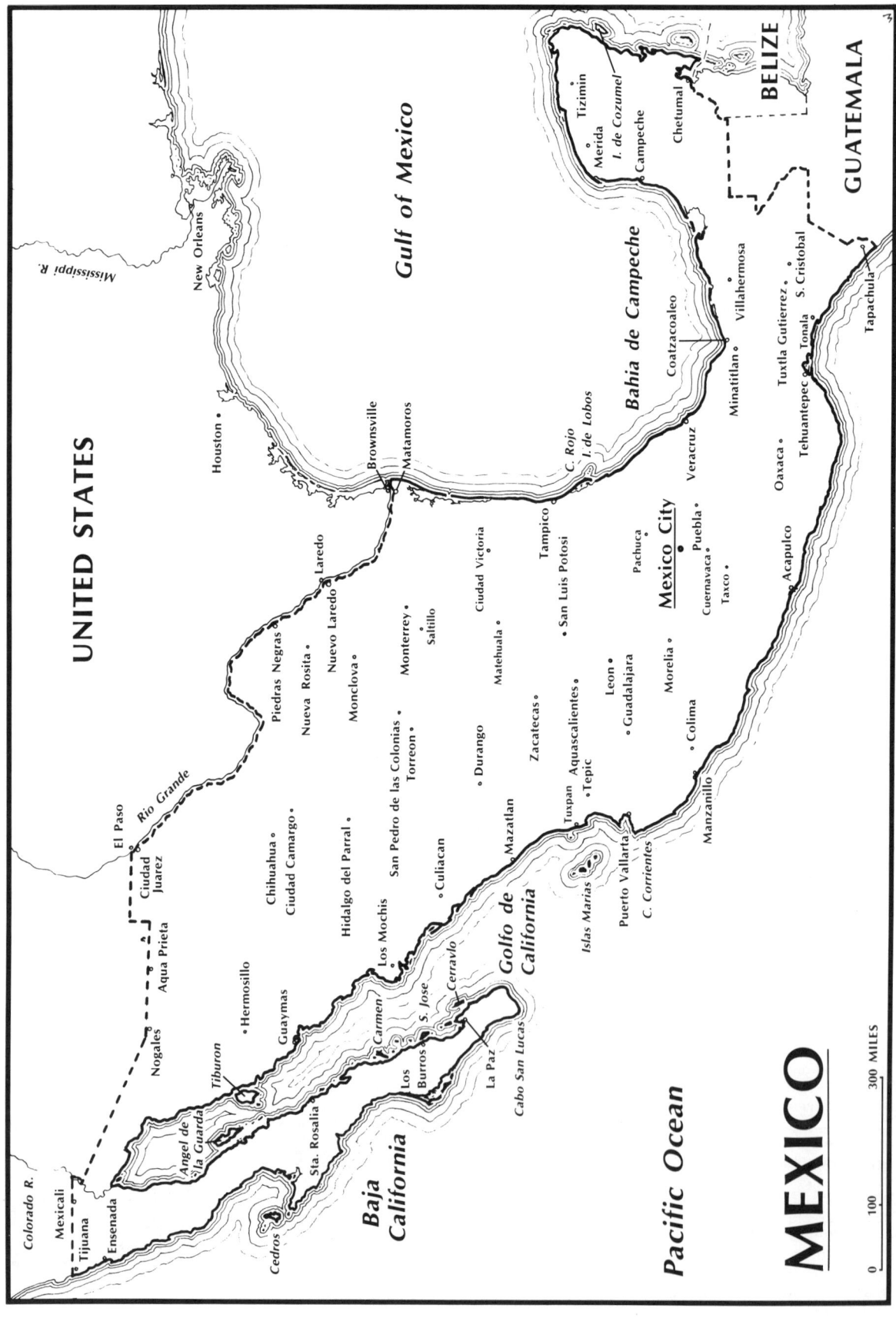

MEXICO, UNITED STATES OF

Area: 761,604 sq. miles
Population: 77,659,000 (1984)
Capital: Mexico City
Currency: Peso (100 centavos)

Mexico is a country with a varied topography that acts as a link between North and Central America.

From rain forest in the southern coastal regions to arid desert in the north, it incorporates many different climates.

A mountain range runs from the Isthmus of Tehuantepec northward. To the south of Mexico City it splits into the east and west ranges of the Sierra Madre Mountains. Between the two is the great central plateau. From an altitude of 8,000 feet at Mexico City, it drops to a low desert plain in the north.

Mexico's climate is influenced more by altitude than it is by latitude. Temperatures range from tropical in the coastal strips to cool at high altitude. For each 1,000 feet of altitude the average annual temperature drops about three degrees F.

The hottest area of Mexico is at the head of the Gulf of California, where the temperature often exceeds 110 degrees F.

Much of the country is dry and only a small portion receives rainfall adequate for agriculture to be possible.

Hurricanes are possible during June to November. They originate in both the Pacific Ocean and the Gulf of Mexico, although those from the Gulf of Mexico are generally the most severe.

Hernando Cortes conquered what is now Mexico for Spain between 1519-1521. When he arrived Cortes found a land where advanced Indian cultures had existed for many years. These had included the Olmec, Maya, Toltec, and the Aztec.

The Mayas, originally from Yucatan, had built great stone pyramids and devised their own calendar.

Tenochtitlan, now Mexico City, was founded in AD 1325 by the Aztecs, who created the empire that Cortes destroyed in his conquest.

For 300 years, until 1821, Spain ruled Mexico. The northern part of the country was not subjugated immediately, but by the end of the 16th century the Spanish had arrived in the present area of the US-Mexican border.

They began to move north and into Texas in an effort to forestall the French coming from the east in Louisiana and the Russians who were moving onto the west coast.

As Spain's influence waned in the New World, the colonial empire began to scent the possibility of freedom and on Sept. 16, 1810, Father Miguel Hidalgo proclaimed Mexican independence. The struggle lasted until Dec. 6, 1822, when the republic came into existence.

In the 1830s and 1840s there was war with Texas, which declared its independence from Mexico, and then with the United States.

The brief French-supported empire of Maximilian lasted only a few years until he was deposed and executed in 1867.

The early years of the 20th century included revolutions and unrest culminating in the constitution of 1917.

Gradually, social reform and development improved the lot of the population, although the country remained poor. The country's prospects brightened with the discovery of enormous oil resources. However the plunge in oil prices during the mid-1980s left the country in a state of financial crisis. The currency was devalued and the banks nationalized in attempts to stave off the collapse of the economy.

There is some industrialization, but massive social and economic problems are being caused by large-scale population moves into urban areas where it is proving impossible to provide either services or employment.

Agriculture remains important to the economy and employs 41% of the labor force. Tourism is also a major contributor to the nation's revenue.

The 1980 per capita income was $1,800 and the literacy rate in 1983 was 74%.

Stamps were first issued in 1856. Until 1884, Mexican stamps were overprinted with the names of the districts in which they were sold. This was a security measure designed to make it impossible for bandits to steal the stamps and sell them in other areas.

Over the years, Mexico has depicted much of its rich heritage on its stamps.

There have been many Official stamps, and during the fighting to drive out the French in the 1860s, provisional issues were released in liberated areas.

Local stamps have been issued in profusion during the various revolutionary activities.

Although a large number of Mexican stamps, both regular and air mail, have been issued, current stamp-issuing policies are moderate.

Philatelic Bureau: Departamento Filatelico, Edificio de Correos, 2° Piso, Tacuba 1, 06000 Mexico 1 D.F., Mexico.

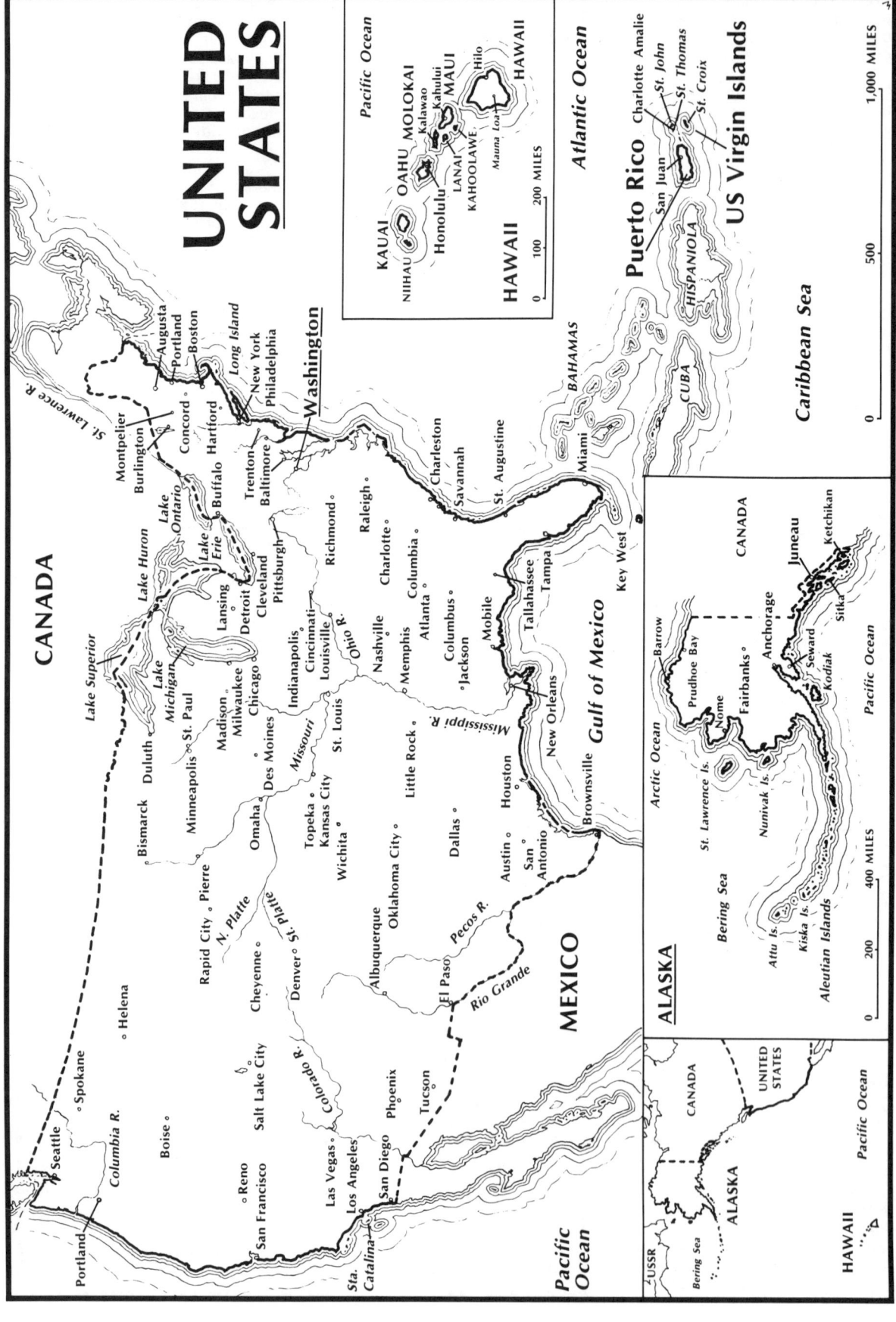

UNITED STATES OF AMERICA

Area: 3,623,420 sq. miles
Population: 238,631,000 (1985)
Capital: Washington, D.C.
Currency: Dollar (100 cents)

The United States includes 48 states in central North America, the states of Alaska and Hawaii, the District of Columbia, Puerto Rico, the US Virgin Islands, Guam, American Samoa, and the Trust Territory of the Pacific.

Its large size and varied topography includes just about every type of terrain and climate.

It ranges from the tropical humidity of the Gulf Coast in the south to the bleak tundra of the arctic, and from the fogs of the rocky New England coast to the blistering deserts of the southwest.

The continental climate is influenced mainly by the westerly wind stream, plus periodic surges of arctic and tropical air from north and south respectively.

The west coast is generally cool and wet, with up to 30 feet of snow falling in the western mountains during winter storms. To the east is a dry north-south belt, which includes the arid desert areas of the southwest. Here precipitation is much less than on the coast and temperatures can exceed 110 degrees F.

The midwest is cold in winter and often hot and humid in summer. The coldest temperature recorded in Minnesota is -59 degrees F. This can rise in summer to well over 100 degrees F. Precipitation ranges from 20-30 inches a year.

The southeast has a tropical climate with occasional intrusions of cold air from the north in winter, which can bring freezing temperatures. In the late summer and fall violent hurricanes can strike from the Atlantic and Gulf of Mexico.

The eastern and northeastern part of the country has a more moderate climate, although it can be hot and

The first US national stamps.

humid in summer and quite cold in winter.

Much of the population of the country is concentrated in the northeast, but in recent years, there has been a massive move into the west, southwest, and south.

Like many relatively new nations, the United States was born of revolution.

While native Americans had lived for centuries on the continent, its early history began in 1565 when Spain established the first European settlement on the mainland at St. Augustine, Fla. The first English settlement was at Jamestown in 1607. Soon, the Dutch and French had a foothold.

On the Atlantic coast the 13 British colonies became the focal point of North American development.

British attempts to control colonial trade and levy taxes caused resentment culminating in the 1776 American Revolution.

By 1788, the colonies were free and reasonably united. In that year, the Constitution was adopted and the new country was on its way to nationhood.

Alexander Hamilton established the first US bank and placed the country on a firm financial footing, although financial problems remained massive.

As the nation grew, it expanded westward. With the addition of the ex-French territory called Louisiana, Spanish California, and the Pacific Northwest, it soon reached from coast to coast.

During the mid-19th century conflict between the slave-owning states in the south and the northern states opposed to slavery erupted into a bloody civil war that threatened to destroy the nation. The war ended in defeat for the industry-lacking, cotton-dependent South and the Union was preserved.

After the war, economic progress was interspersed with depressions, but each time the country emerged stronger than before. The Spanish-American War of 1898, easily won new territory for the US in the Caribbean and western Pacific.

Although US participation in World War I was not extensive, it provided a much needed morale boost for the Allies.

The period between the two world wars was one of great prosperity followed by devastating depression, the effects of which were not removed until World War II gave the country its greatest economic boost to date.

This country emerged from the war richer and more prosperous than ever, while most of its allies were bankrupted and bled white by their efforts.

Since the war, the years have been marked by continual competition and periodic confrontation with the world's other superpower, the Soviet Union. The economic cycle of "boom and bust" continues, although the peaks are not as high nor the valleys as deep as in the 1880s and 1890s or the 1920s and 1930s.

The 1985 per capita income was $13,500 and the literacy rate is 99%.

The country's first national postage stamps were issued in 1847 and since then there has been a varied and interesting flow of stamps.

Many collectors have turned to the older stamps and to postal history. In this latter category, the US has a rich heritage and while much has been documented, there is still room for some fascinating research into the history of the US mail.

Philatelic Bureau: U.S. Postal Service, Philatelic Sales Branch, Washington, DC 20265, USA.

ST. PIERRE AND MIQUELON

Area: 93 sq. miles
Population: 6,041 (1982)
Capital: St. Pierre
Currency: Franc (100 centimes)

A final, tiny remnant of the French colonial empire in North America, the twin islands of St. Pierre and Miquelon, together with some small islets, lie a few miles off the southern coast of Newfoundland.

St. Pierre, with an area of 10 square miles has the bulk of the population and is the administrative and commercial center.

The landscape is bleak and bare with few trees. The climate is maritime, with an average winter temperature of 25 degrees F and a summer average of 60 degrees F.

Rainfall averages 60 inches a year. About 12% falls in winter as snow. Although there is much fog, there is also considerable sunshine during the winter and at midsummer.

The French first settled the islands in the early 17th century, attracted by the excellent cod fishing in the surrounding waters. They were expelled several times by the British, but the French gained the islands permanently in 1816 under the Treaty of Paris.

Governed as a colony until 1946, the islands then became a French Overseas Territory. In 1976, they were made a department of France.

Fishing rights in the adjacent waters were long a source of conflict with the British and the question was not settled until 1904. Fishing remains the major industry, although it no longer supports the population and large French government subsidies are required to keep

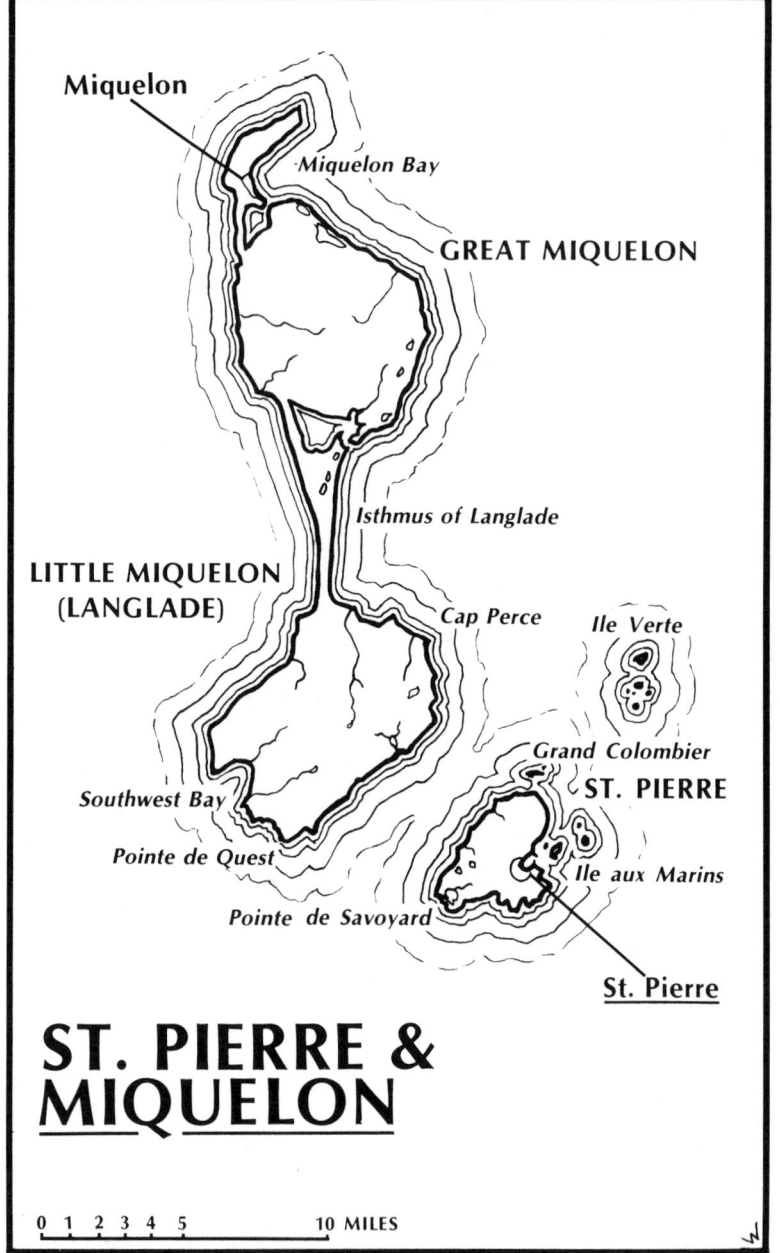

the economy healthy. There is a developing tourist industry.

Those of the inhabitants not employed in the fishing industry work in trade, commerce, or are engaged in government service. Primary education is free.

The population is generally descended from the inhabitants of the Atlantic coast of France.

Stamps were first issued in 1885 and followed the usual French colonial pattern. A moderate number of stamps was released. They are generally attractive and well engraved, reflecting the islands' economy, scenery, and history. In 1976, when French department status was achieved, the stamps of France went into use. On Feb. 4, 1986, the use of stamps inscribed for the islands was resumed.

Philatelic Bureau: St. Pierre and Miquelon Service Philatelique, 61-63 rue de Douai, 75436 Paris Cedex 09, France.

CENTRAL AMERICA & WEST. CARIBBEAN 11

Stamp-issuing areas:

1. Belize
2. Belize, Cayes of
3. Cayman Islands
4. Costa Rica
5. Cuba
6. El Salvador
7. Guatemala
8. Honduras
9. Jamaica
10. Nicaragua
11. Panama

CENTRAL AMERICA

BELIZE

Area: 8,860 sq. miles
Population: 158,000 (1984)
Capital: Belmopan
Currency: Belize dollar (100 cents)

Formerly the Crown Colony of British Honduras, Belize has a coastline fringed by an extensive barrier reef. The coastal strip is low and swampy, rising inland to low hills, the tallest of which is 3,680-foot Victoria Peak.

The climate is hot and humid inland, but tempered on the coast by prevailing winds off the sea.

Rainfall can be as high as 150 inches a year in the south, but averages a third of that in the north. Hurricanes occur and the capital was moved inland to Belmopan from Belize City to avoid them.

The first settlement was in 1638, when British logwood cutters arrived. Logwood was important in the making of dyes. Although the Spanish had taken little interest in the unattractive coast, they tried to expel the settlers, but without success.

The colony of British Honduras was formed in 1862 and administered from Jamaica. Guatemala has long claimed the area, but refused to take its case to the Court of International Justice. It was the population's desire to remain free of Guatemala that had prevented Britain from granting independence earlier, but on Sept. 21, 1981 the nation of Belize was created. However, Britain maintains troops in the country to protect it.

Sugar and timber are the main exports. The 1984 per capita income was $1,000. The 1985 literacy rate was 80%.

Stamps were first issued in 1866. Since independence there have been a large number of stamp issues, some of which are regarded as exploitive.

From May 30, 1984 to June 5, 1985 stamps were issued for the Cayes of Belize, several inhabited islands in the offshore barrier reef. These have not received catalog recognition.

Philatelic Bureau: Belize Philatelic Bureau, Private Bag #1, Belize City, Belize.

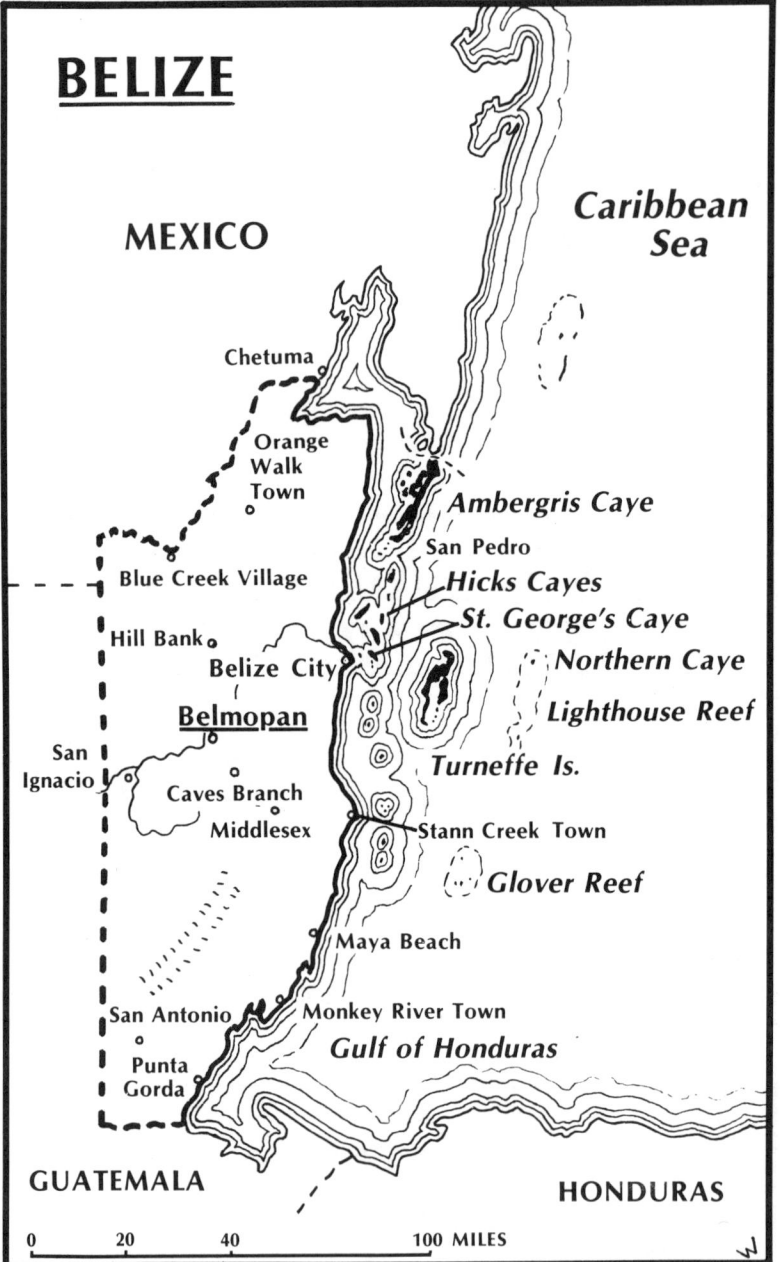

CAYMAN ISLANDS, DEPENDENCY OF

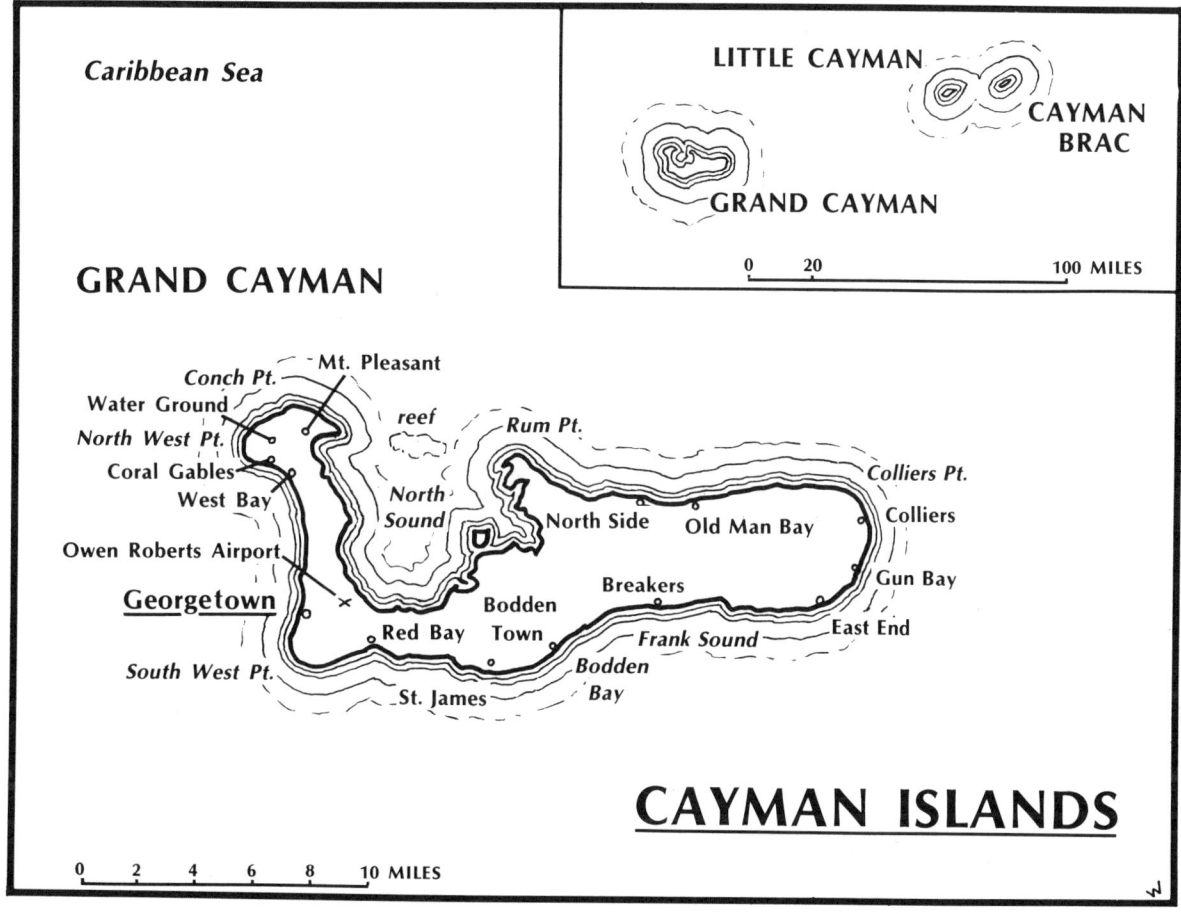

Area: 102 sq. miles
Population: 18,000 (1981)
Capital: Georgetown
Currency: Dollar (100 cents)

Named Tortugas by Christopher Columbus in 1503, for the large number of turtles he found there, the three Cayman Islands have become a tourist haven in recent years.

The main island is flat with some wooded areas. There is swamp in the central part and tropical vegetation. A coral reef protects the entrance to North Sound and the beaches are excellent.

Temperatures average 80-90 degrees F in the summer and about 10 degrees less in the winter. There is an average annual rainfall of about 60 inches. The islands have no rivers.

Cayman Brac is the most topographically dramatic of the three islands. It has cliffs rising to a central limestone plateau with pasture and coconut palms. There are dairy farms and beef cattle is raised. The island also grows fruits and vegetables.

None of the three islands were settled by Spain. They were annexed by Britain in 1655 and were colonized in 1741 from Jamaica. For many years, they were a haven for pirates and buried treasure has been found.

Administered from Jamaica, the islands achieved internal self-government in 1959.

Grand Cayman became a tax-free island in the 1970s and Georgetown is a free port. The island is an international banking center and many large banks have branches there.

Tourist facilities are good and there are excellent air services to the island.

Stamps were first issued in 1900 and until the mid-1930s were in the British Empire key type. In 1935, the beautiful King George V pictorial definitives were issued. These represented a high point in 20th-century British Empire stamp production with their attractive designs, rich coloring, and fine engraving. Few subsequent issues have come close to matching their quality.

Philatelic Bureau: Postmaster General, Philatelic Department, Georgetown, Grand Cayman, Cayman Islands.

COSTA RICA, REPUBLIC OF

Area: 19,653 sq. miles
Population: 2,693,000 (1984)
Capital: San Jose
Currency: Colon (100 centimos)

Known as the Switzerland of the Americas for its stable and democratic society, as much as for its mountain scenery, Costa Rica has a central mountainous area with low coastal strips on both Caribbean and Pacific coasts. The highest peaks reach to about 13,000 feet.

The climate varies according to altitude. The coasts are hot and humid, especially on the Caribbean side, with average high temperatures about 90 degrees F, dropping by about 20 degrees at the higher elevations, where the bulk of the population lives.

Christopher Columbus discovered the coast of Costa Rica on Sept. 18, 1502, during his last voyage.

The area was a Spanish colony from 1522 until 1821, when it became independent, but it was largely left alone and the inhabitants learned to fend for themselves. There then came a brief federation with Mexico and membership in the Central American Federation until that broke up in 1839.

Since then, the country has preferred to go it alone and this independence of spirit is still a characteristic of the "Ticos," as the Costa Ricans like to be called.

With an enviable reputation for stability in government and honesty in politics, Costa Rica claims the area's first free and honest elections, held there in 1890. It is still the most stable and developed country in an area not noted for either prosperity or democracy. The country has no armed forces.

The introduction of coffee and bananas in the 19th century provided a healthy base for the economy. Industries include fiberglass products, aluminum, textiles, and fertilizer, plus fishing, forest products, and tourism. In addition to coffee and bananas, sugar, cocoa, and cotton are grown.

The 1981 per capita income was $2,238 and the 1982 literacy rate was 90%.

The first stamps were issued in 1863 and feature the country's coat of arms.

Philatelic Bureau: Oficina Filatelica de Costa Rica, San Jose, Costa Rica.

CUBA, REPUBLIC OF

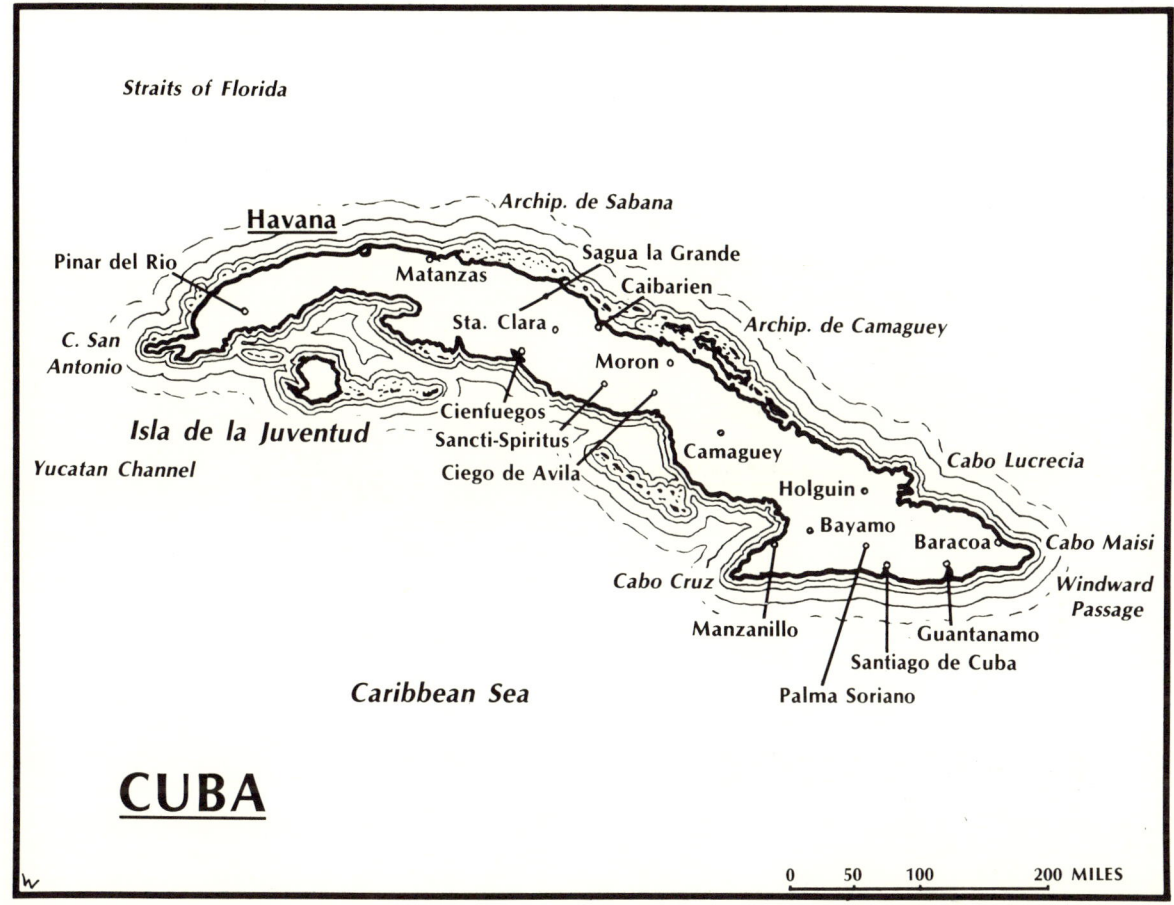

Area: 44,218 sq. miles
Population: 9,995,000 (1984)
Capital: Havana
Currency: Peso (100 centavos)

Cuba is the largest island in the Caribbean area. In addition to the Isle of Pines, there are about 1,500 adjacent keys and islets off its coast. Most of the island is low, rolling country, with some mountain areas. The highest are in the east, where peaks rise to 6,000 feet.

The average temperature in the summer is 80 degrees F, dropping to 70 degrees in winter. The annual rainfall averages 55 inches.

Christopher Columbus discovered Cuba on Oct. 28, 1492. The city of Havana soon became an important crossroads port between Spain and its Western Hemisphere colonies.

Settlement gradually spread throughout the island and as the enslaved native population was killed off, slaves had to be imported from Africa to work on the sugar plantations.

In 1895, a revolution against Spain began. The United States joined in on the side of the revolutionaries after an explosion sank the USS *Maine* in Havana harbor. On Dec. 10, 1898, Spain relinquished its hold on Cuba. After a period of US occupation, independence was proclaimed on May 20, 1902.

Political instability, with president following president, lasted until the late 1950s, when Fidel Castro took power. At first popular, he soon turned Cuba into a Communist state, suppressed all opposition and made the island a satellite of the Soviet Union.

Sugar dominates the economy. The 1981 per capita income was $840 and the 1983 literacy rate was 96%.

Cuba's first stamps were issued in 1855.

As part of a general economic embargo, the importation into the United States of Cuban stamps has been banned since July 8, 1963. This date was confirmed by the director of the Office of Foreign Assets Control, although it differs from the Feb. 7, 1962 date usually quoted.

Philatelic Bureau: Empresa de Correos, Prensa y Filatelia (COPREFIL), Box 100, Havana 1, Cuba.

EL SALVADOR, REPUBLIC OF

Area: 8,216 sq. miles
Population: 5,100,000 (1984)
Capital: San Salvador
Currency: Colon (100 centavos)

El Salvador comprises a coastal strip, a central plateau region intersected with valleys, and a mountainous northern area.

It is hot on the coast, subtropical in the central area, and cooler in the mountains. The average temperature at San Salvador is 73 degrees and 80 degrees on the coast.

From the 16th century, the country was part of the captaincy-general of Guatemala, which obtained independence from Spain in 1821. In 1823, it became one of the states of the Central American Federation, which also included Guatemala, Honduras, Nicaragua, and Costa Rica.

The federation broke up in 1839 and El Salvador assumed its present status. Today, the country is the smallest in Central America and the most densely populated.

Political instability has always prevented any real prosperity and relations with neighboring countries have often been strained.

A military coup gained power for the army in 1979, but it was unable to prevent civil war, which has raged in recent years.

An estimated 10,000 leftists supplied by the Soviet Union through Cuba, and by the regime in Nicaragua, gained control of some 25% of the country, despite the use of extreme right-wing death squads by the government.

In May 1984, there was a heavy voter turnout in presidential elections to elect moderate Jose Napoleon Duarte, who pledged to eliminate the death squads and restore order to the country. While the civil war has cooled recently, there has been a continuation of terrorist acts.

The economy is mainly agricultural with coffee, cotton, sugar, and corn being the main crops. The 1984 per capita income was $854 and the 1985 literacy rate was 62% (urban) and 40% (rural).

El Salvador's first stamps were issued in 1867. They depict the San Miguel volcano.

Philatelic Bureau: Direccion General de Correos, Departamento de Filatelia, El Salvador.

GUATEMALA, REPUBLIC OF

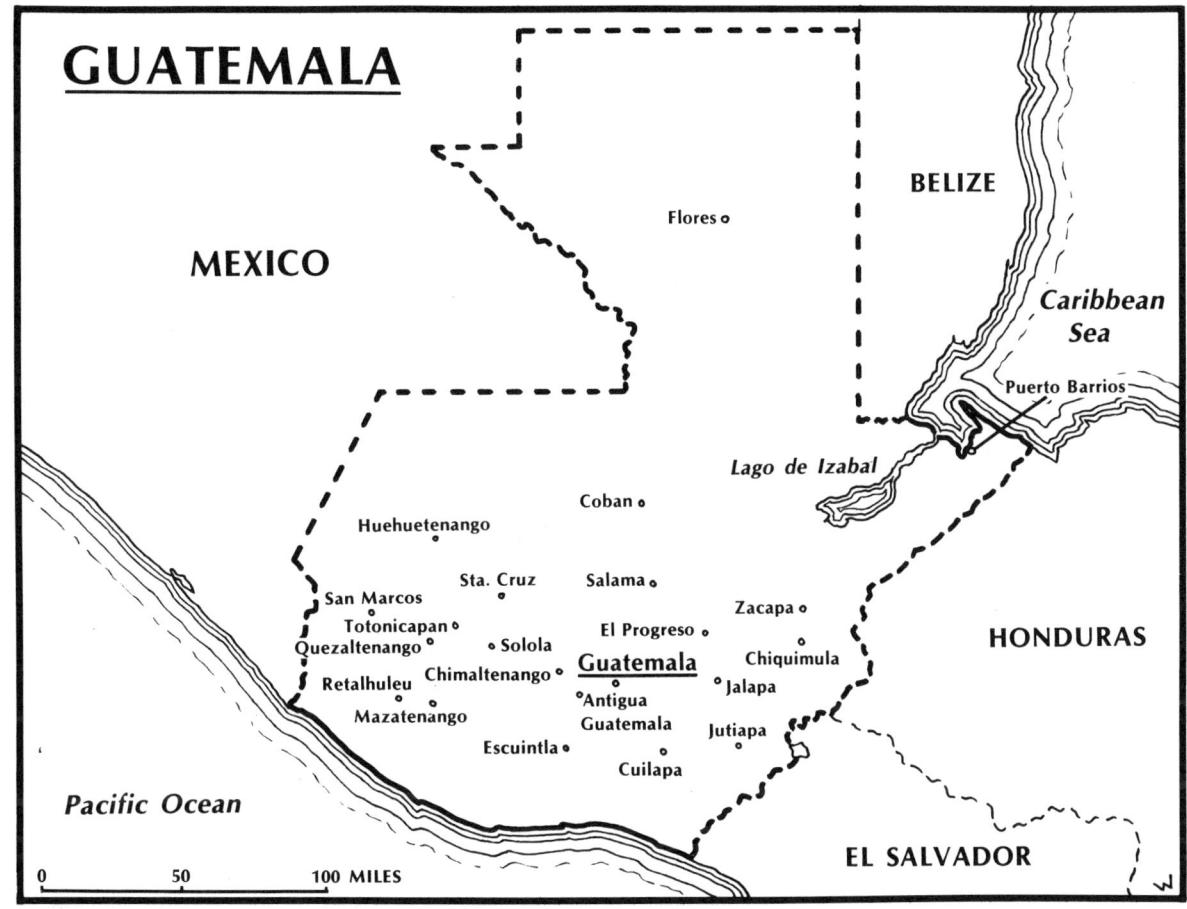

Area: 42,042 sq. miles
Population: 7,956,000 (1984)
Capital: Guatemala City
Currency: Quetzal (100 centavos)

Guatemala has its main coastline on the Pacific, with only a 50-mile coast on the Caribbean. Its capital city is located on a central plateau. There is a narrow coastal strip between the Pacific and a mountain range, but on the Caribbean side there are fertile valleys.

Rainfall can be as high as 200 inches a year along the Pacific mountain slopes and is also high on the Caribbean coast. Temperatures are reported to be moderate, although these vary according to location and altitude.

For more than a thousand years before the Spanish arrived in 1524, the Mayan Empire was an advanced culture in what is now Guatemala.

Indians are still the largest single ethnic group and to a large extent they retain their old customs. A total of 18 dialects is said to be in use.

The Spanish ruled until 1821, when the country declared its independence. But before it achieved final independence it spent a couple of years as part of the Mexican Empire.

It was also part of the shortlived Central American Federation until the federation broke up in 1839. Since then, a large number of governments have ruled and the presidents have mostly been military men who came to power through revolutionary activities. Political unrest continues and there has been much migration across the border into Mexico.

For years, Guatemala has laid claim to Belize, formerly British Honduras, and in 1971 issued a stamp featuring a map that showed Belize as part of Guatemala.

The economy is based on coffee, although sugar, bananas, and cotton are grown. Mineral resources include oil and nickel.

The 1984 per capita income was $1,085 and the 1984 literacy rate was 48%.

The first stamps were issued in 1871. The country's emblem, the quetzal bird, has been featured on many Guatemalan stamps.

Philatelic Bureau: Direccion General de Correos y Telegrafos, Departmento Filatelico, Guatemala City, Guatemala.

HONDURAS, REPUBLIC OF

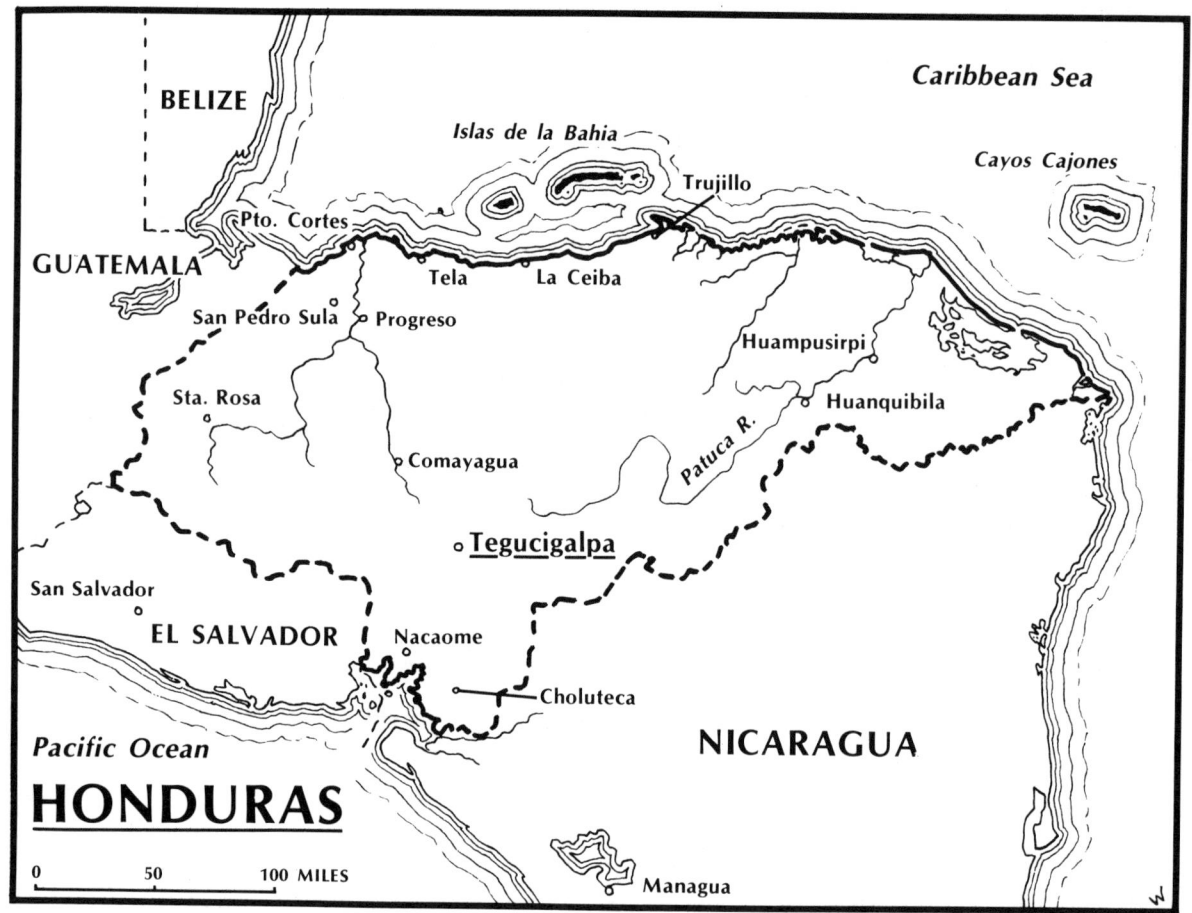

Area: 43,280 sq. miles
Population: 4,424,000 (1984)
Capital: Tegucigalpa
Currency: Lempira (100 centavos)

Honduras is crossed by two mountain ranges and has tropical lowlands on both the long Caribbean coast and the short, 40-mile Pacific coast. There is a plateau area between the mountains.

The climate is hot and humid on the coasts, but is more temperate at higher altitudes. The average temperature along the coasts is 80 degrees F. In the plateau area, annual average temperatures are about 70 degrees. At Tegucigalpa, high temperatures can reach 90 degrees. Rainfall varies considerably and some areas are subject to drought during the dry season.

Along with Guatemala, what is now Honduras, was the center of the Mayan Empire prior to the arrival of Europeans. But, by the time Christopher Columbus visited the coast in 1502, the Mayans had moved north to the Yucatan peninsula of Mexico. The first Spanish settlement was established in 1524.

In 1821, the area was annexed to the Mexican Empire. Two years later, Honduras joined the Central American Federation, which broke up in 1839.

Revolution and bickering with its neighbors have marked the history of the country.

A civilian government was elected in 1982. In recent years, the United States has provided considerable military aid and supplied advisors to help the country stand up to pressure from Nicaragua and to prevent that country from shipping arms to the rebels in El Salvador. Economic aid from the United States has been more than double the military assistance.

The chief export of Honduras is bananas. Other crops are coffee, corn, and beans. There is little industry, although textiles, cement, and some forest products are manufactured.

The 1982 per capita income was $590 and the 1984 literacy rate was 55%.

The first stamps were issued in 1866.

Philatelic Bureau: Departamento Filatelico, Direccion General de Correos, Tegucigalpa, D.C., Honduras.

JAMAICA

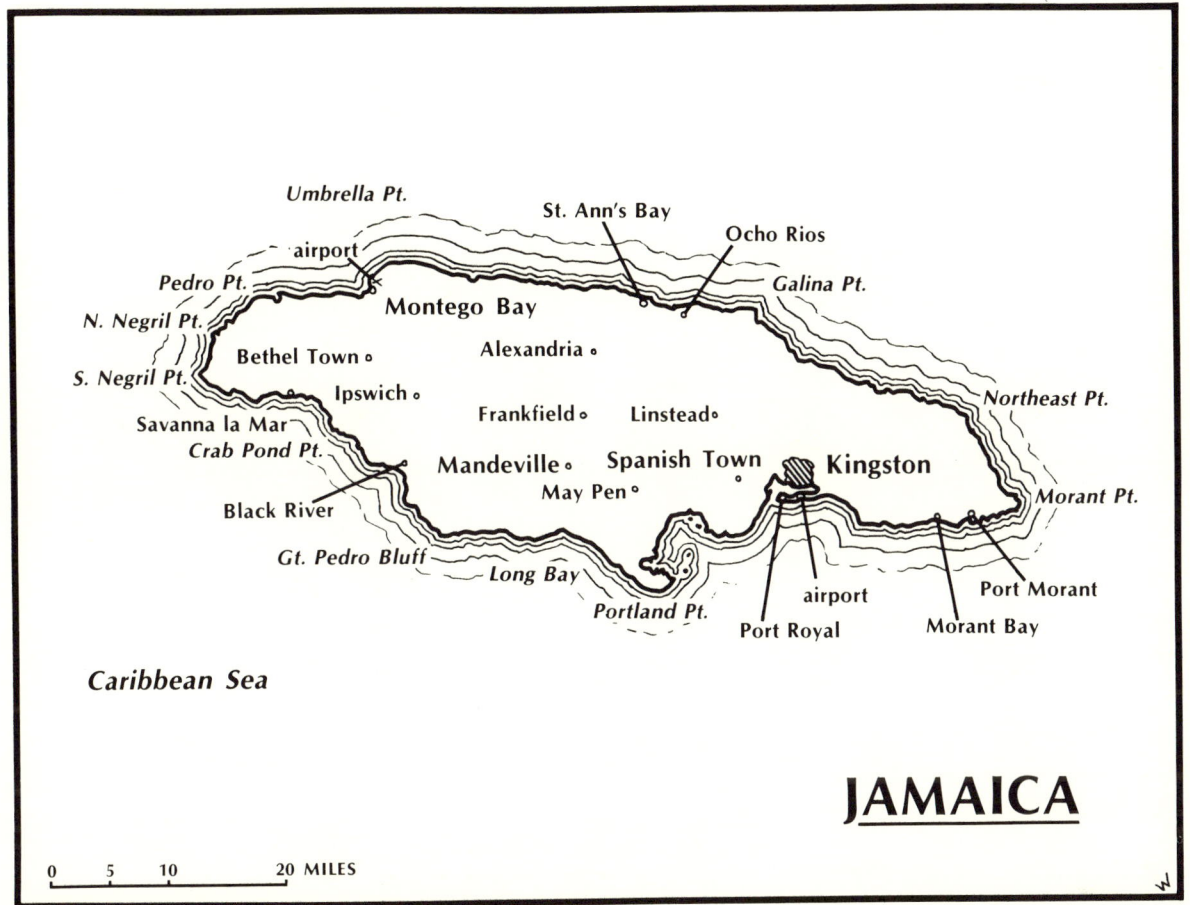

Area: 4,245 sq. miles
Population: 2,388,000 (1984)
Capital: Kingston
Currency: Dollar (100 cents)

The third-largest island in the Caribbean, most of Jamaica is covered by mountains. Its climate is warm and humid for most of the year, but cooler during the November-March period. During this cool period, along the north shore temperatures generally reach about 75 degrees F.

Rainfall varies sharply from up to 200 inches a year in some higher areas to almost none in the southwest. The island's annual average is 77 inches.

Hurricanes can occur and there have been devastating earthquakes. In 1907 an earthquake destroyed much of the capital city.

The original inhabitants were Arawak Indians, who were virtually exterminated by the Spanish settlers following the 1494 discovery of the island by Columbus. Thereafter, slaves were brought in from Africa. Their descendents now form about 80% of the population.

The British took the island from Spain in 1655 and it remained a British colony until receiving its independence on Aug. 6, 1962.

Slavery was abolished in 1838, some years before abolition in other areas.

During the 1930s the colony began to develop local political control and the political parties were formed that have played a major role in Jamaican affairs since independence. Adult suffrage was introduced in 1944.

From 1958 to 1961, Jamaica was a member of the shortlived West Indies Federation.

Sugar, cocoa, coffee, bananas, and coconuts are important to the economy, but bauxite is its mainstay, together with tourism, and Jamaican rum.

The 1981 per capita income was $1,340 and the 1984 literacy rate was 76%.

Stamps were first issued in 1860. Before that, British stamps had been used. In recent years, stamp issues have remained generally attractive and issue policies moderate.

Philatelic Bureau: Head Postmaster, Philatelic Bureau, GPO, Kingston, Jamaica.

NICARAGUA, REPUBLIC OF

Area: 49,291 sq. miles
Population: 2,232,000 (1985)
Capital: Managua
Currency: Cordoba (100 centavos)

Nicaragua has rugged mountains in the northern central portion, rising from coastal lowlands on both Pacific and Caribbean coasts. Between the Caribbean coastal plain and the mountains is an area of wooded, rolling hills.

The climate is tropical. The average temperature on the Pacific coast is about 80 degrees F and on the Caribbean coast it is 80-85 degrees. At higher elevations it is about 10 degrees lower.

On the northern Caribbean coast rainfall is about 255 inches a year, decreasing to 55 inches on the west coast plain.

Christopher Columbus landed on the east coast on Sept. 16, 1502, during his fourth voyage. In 1522, a force of 100 Spanish soldiers and four horses landed and crossed to the Pacific coast. They withdrew upon receiving a less-than-warm welcome from the local Indian inhabitants. Two years later they returned and remained in occupation for almost 300 years.

Following the end of Spanish rule, Nicaragua was united with Guatemala and Mexico. In 1826, it became part of the Central American Federation until the federation broke up in 1839.

After independence, the country gradually developed. With the discovery of gold in California, a transportation system across the country was established in 1852.

There have been periods of political instability and on several occasions US forces have been landed to maintain order.

The 1979 ouster of the Somoza government resulted in a leftist regime that is having a destabilizing influence on the area.

Industries include oil refining, textiles, and chemicals. Chief crops are bananas, cotton, coffee, sugar, cocoa, and rice. The 1980 per capita income was $804 and the 1982 literacy rate was 82%.

On May 6, 1985, as part of economic sanctions, the United States banned the importation of Nicaraguan stamps.

Philatelic Bureau: Division de Especis Postales y Filatelia, Telcor, Edificio Zacarias Guerra, 7 MO Piso, Apartado 325, Managua, Nicaragua.

PANAMA, REPUBLIC OF

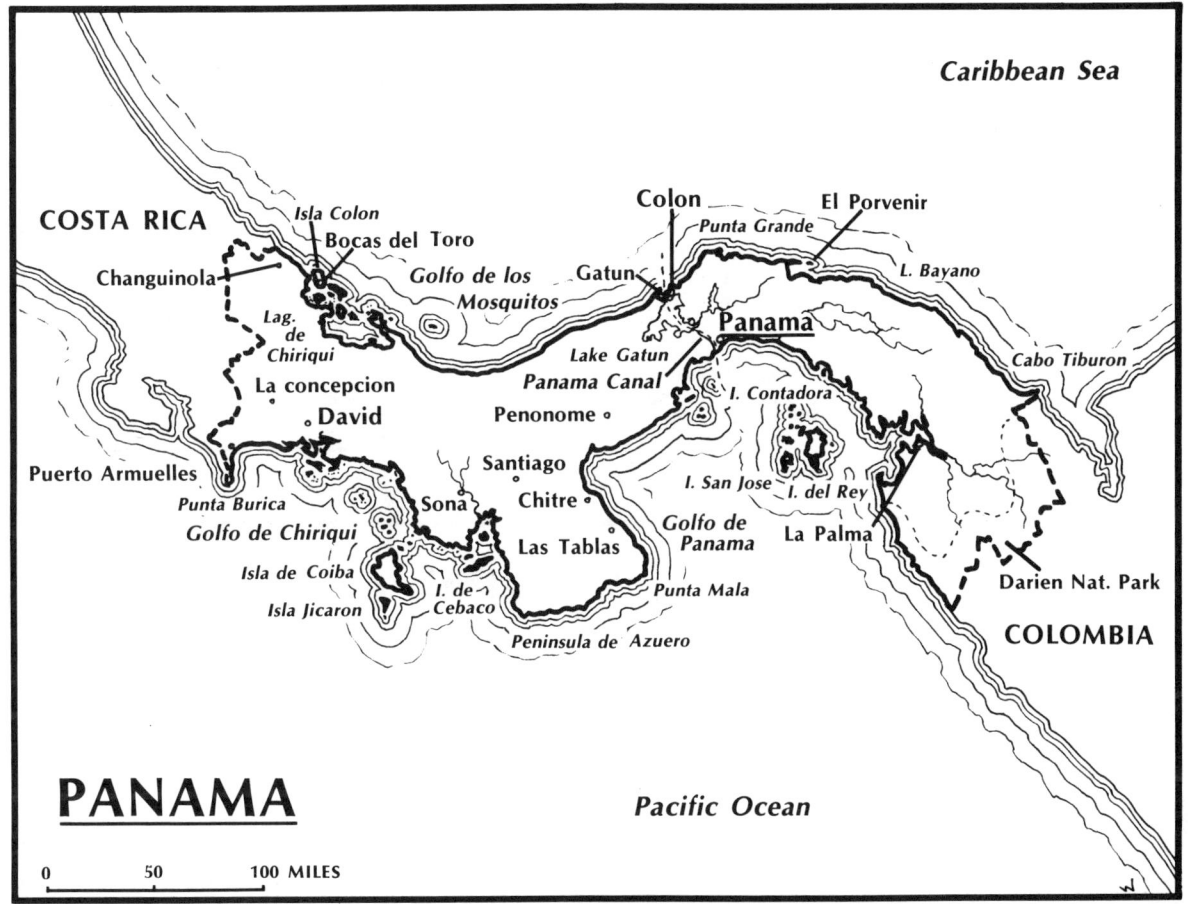

Area: 29,762 sq. miles
Population: 2,101,000 (1984)
Capital: Panama
Currency: Balboa (100 centavos)

Located in one of the world's strategic areas, Panama comprises the narrow isthmus that links North and South America and through which is cut the Panama Canal.

Mountains run along the backbone of the country, with the highest being 11,411 feet.

There are narrow coastal strips along Caribbean and Pacific shores. On the Caribbean it is mostly poorly drained with considerable mangrove swamps. A number of islands are located off the Pacific coast. Numerous rivers flow through the coast strips and into Lake Gatun. The eastern portion of the country is mostly rain forest.

Lowland temperatures average 80 degrees F, diminishing with altitude. Rainfall on the Caribbean coast ranges from 125-160 inches a year with the Pacific coast receiving 50-100 inches.

In 1718, Panama became part of the vice-royalty of New Granada and the isthmus was a vital link in the route to Spain for the treasure looted from Peru. Panama became the first European settlement on the American mainland.

In 1821, Panama proclaimed its independence from Spain and became part of Colombia. By 1903, Panama wanted to set up housekeeping on its own and the United States supported the breakaway from Colombia in return for acquiring rights for the projected Panama Canal, which went into operation in 1914. On Oct. 1, 1979, the United States handed the canal over to Panama and withdrew from the Canal Zone.

Political instability has done much to inhibit economic and social progress in Panama and the instability continues.

Oil refining and international banking are important to the economy, and bananas, pineapples, cocoa, coconuts, and sugar are the chief crops. No recent per capita income figure is available. The 1982 literacy rate was 85%.

Philatelic Bureau: Direccion General de Correos y Telecomunicaciones, Departamento de Filatelia, Apartado 3421, Panama 1, Panama.

EASTERN CARIBBEAN

Stamp-issuing areas:

1. Anguilla
2. Antigua
3. Aruba (Neth. Antilles)
4. Barbados
5. Barbuda (Antigua)
6. Bonaire (Neth. Antilles)
7. Curacao (Neth. Antilles)
8. Dominica
9. Dominican Republic
10. Grenada
11. Grenada Grenadines
12. Guadeloupe (uses French stamps)
13. Haiti
14. Martinique (uses French stamps)
15. Montserrat
16. Nevis
17. Puerto Rico (uses US stamps)
18. Redonda (Antigua)
19. Saba (Neth. Antilles)
20. St. Barthelemy (Guadeloupe)
21. St. Kitts
22. St. Lucia
23. St. Martin (Guadeloupe)
24. St. Vincent
25. St. Vincent Grenadines
    (incl. Bequia and Union islands)
26. Sint Eustatius (Neth. Antilles)
27. Sint Maarten (Neth. Antilles)
28. Trinidad and Tobago
29. Turks and Caicos (incl. Caicos Is.)
30. Virgin Islands, British
31. Virgin Islands (uses US stamps)

CENTRAL AMERICA

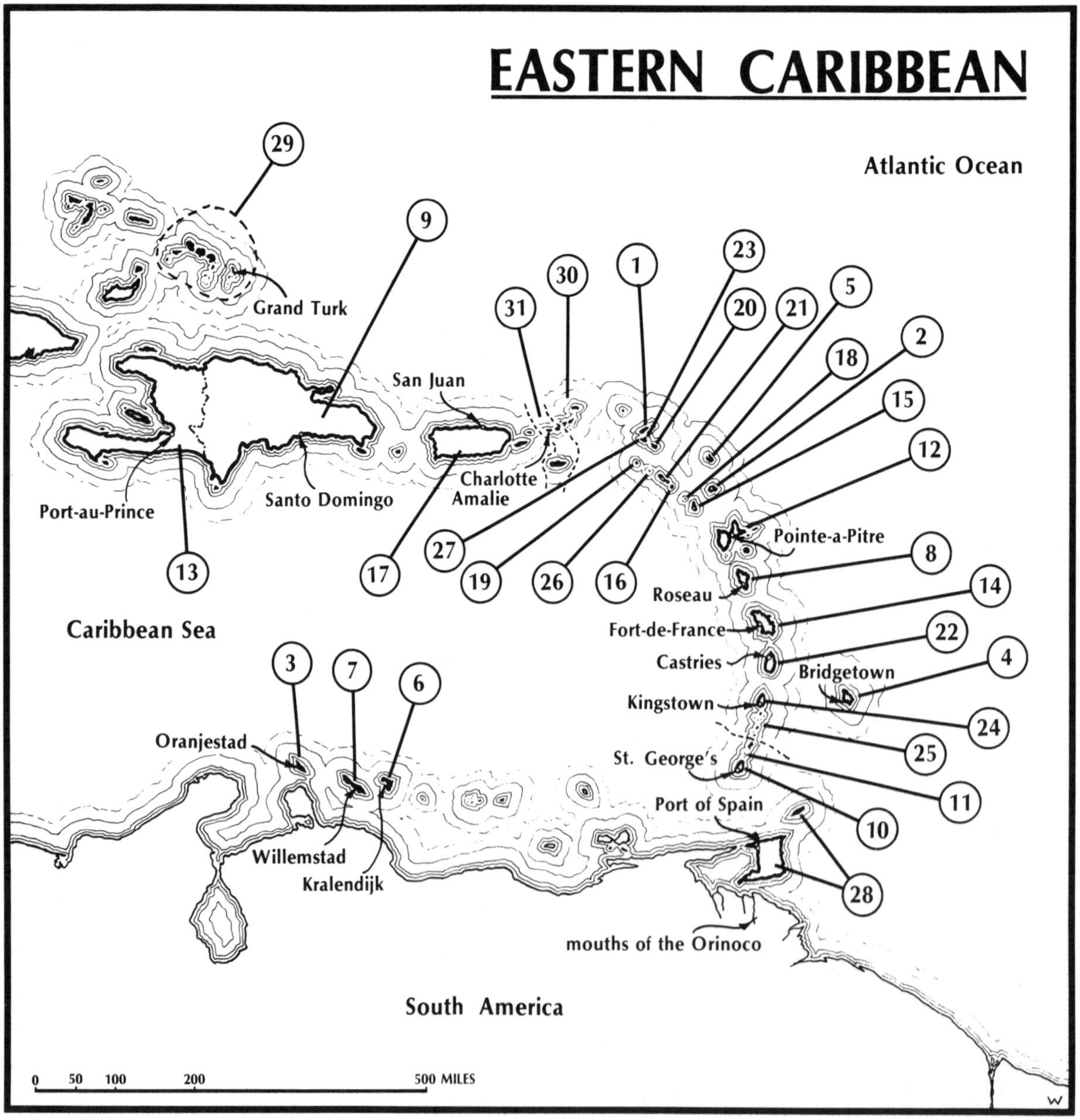

ANGUILLA

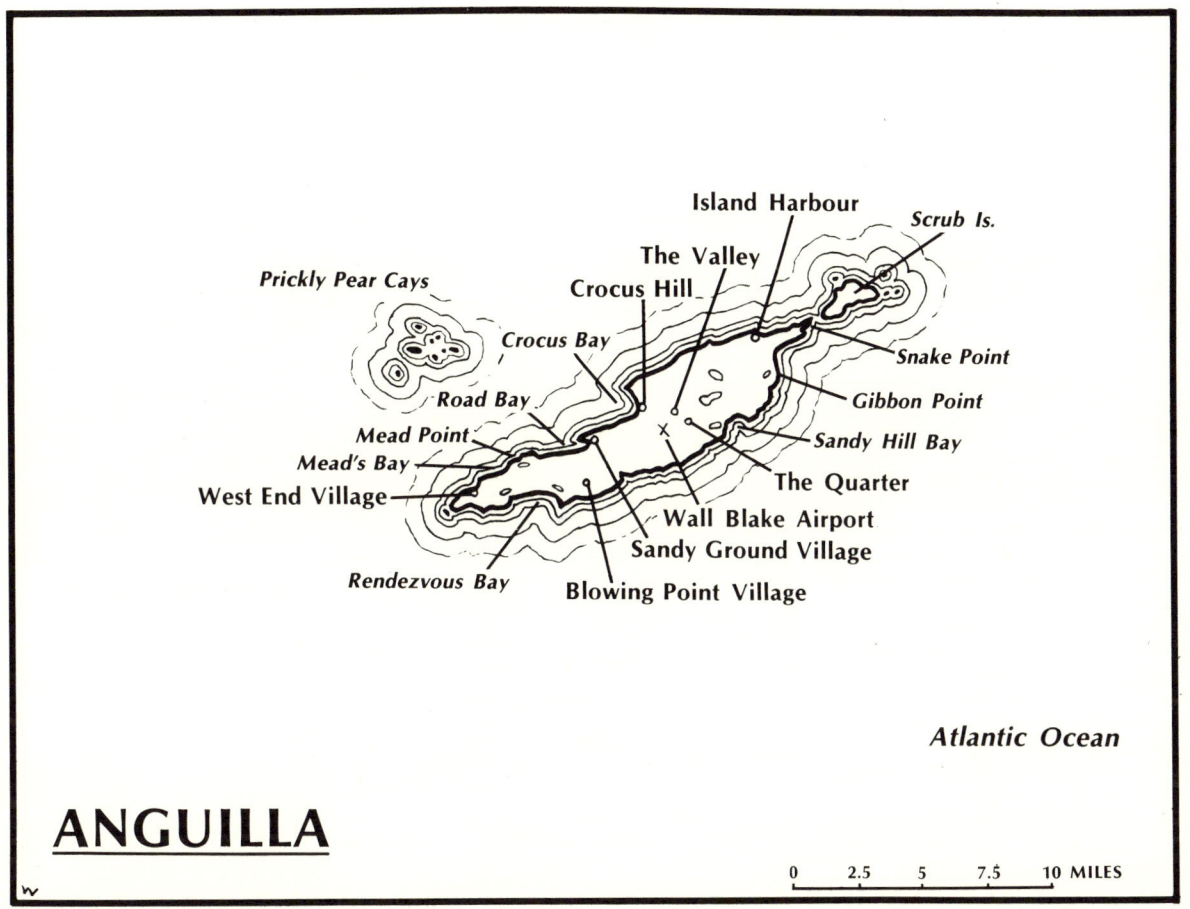

ANGUILLA

Area: 35 sq. miles
Population: 7,000 (1982)
Capital: The Valley
Currency: East Caribbean dollar (100 cents)

Anguilla is a bare, low-lying island about 60 miles north-northwest of St. Kitts in the Leeward Islands.

Columbus discovered Anguilla and other islands in the area in 1493, but it was colonized by Sir Thomas Warner of Great Britain in 1623. The island was administered from the British colony of St. Kitts from the 19th century.

In 1958, it petitioned for the dissolution of its political relationship with St. Kitts, but this was rejected by Great Britain.

In February 1967, together with St. Kitts, the island of Nevis, and the rock of Sombrero, Anguilla formed an internally self-governing unit in free association with the mother country.

However, a few months later, Anguilla, unhappy with what it regarded as its inferior position in the island-group's government and long discontented with its "poor relation" status, decided to break its ties. In May 1967, it proclaimed its independence from St. Kitts and expelled the representatives of the St. Kitts police force. A period of political stalemate followed.

After a British official, who had come to the island to explain that country's plans for the island's future, was forced to leave at gunpoint, British troops landed and a commissioner was installed to restore order and establish a local government.

In 1971, an act was passed giving the necessary powers to the commissioner to conduct the island's affairs and it settled down to a life of independence from its neighbors.

Cattle raising, salt production, and fishing are the main occupations, with boat building also being important.

Anguilla's name had first appeared on stamps in 1952, when stamps inscribed "St. Christopher-Nevis-Anguilla" were issued.

Stocks of stamps with this inscription that were on Anguilla at the time of independence were overprinted "Independent Anguilla," and these are rare, with only 100 sets possible.

Philatelic Bureau: The Postmaster, Dept. of Posts, The Valley, Anguilla, West Indies.

ANTIGUA AND BARBUDA

Area: 171 sq. miles
Population: 80,000 (1984)
Capital: St. John's
Currency: East Caribbean dollar (100 cents)

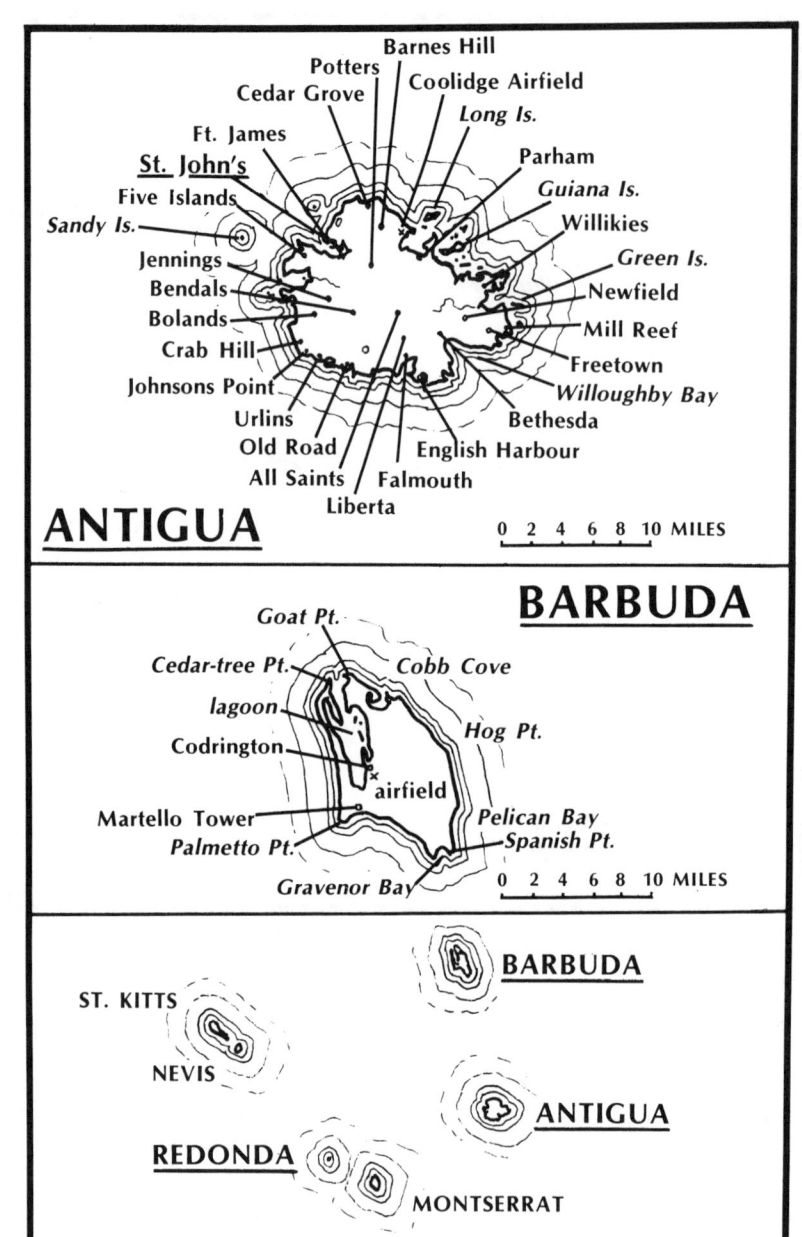

The country comprises the islands of Antigua and Barbuda, with the islet of Redonda.

Antigua is low-lying with an indented coastline. There are few trees and no rivers. Annual rainfall is about 44 inches.

Discovered in 1493 by Christopher Columbus, Antigua was settled by Britain in 1632. It remained a British colony until 1967, when associated state status was achieved. Independence came on Nov. 1, 1981.

Tourism is important in the economy. Crops include sugar and cotton. The old restored British naval base at English Harbour, where Admiral Horatio Nelson once served, is a popular attraction.

Stamps were first issued in 1862. A member of the Leeward Islands Federation, the federation's stamps were also used by Antiguans from 1890-1956 and replaced Antiguan stamps from 1890-1903. Issues have become more prolific in recent years.

Philatelic Bureau: Philatelic Bureau, GPO, St. John's, Antigua and Barbuda.

Barbuda: Barbuda is a low-lying island with an area of 63 square miles, some 25 miles north of Antigua. Its only settlement is Codrington. Fishing is the main occupation.

Colonized in 1628, the island was granted to the Codrington family in 1680, reverting to the crown in the 19th century.

Barbudan stamps were used briefly in 1922. They were re-introduced in 1968. Most of the numerous issues are stamps of Antigua overprinted.

Philatelic Bureau: Philatelic Bureau, GPO, Codrington, Barbuda, Antigua and Barbuda.

Redonda: A rock rising to 1,000 feet from the Caribbean 34 miles southwest of Antigua, it has an area of one half square mile and is uninhabited.

Phosphate deposits were worked there until 1916, when they were abandoned.

Stamps inscribed for the islet were introduced in January 1976. No official announcement was made by the Antiguan Post Office, although their only noted use has been from Antigua. They have not received catalog recognition.

Philatelic Bureau: Redonda Philatelic Bureau, Box 518, St. John's, Antigua and Barbuda.

BARBADOS

Area: 166 sq. miles
Population: 252,000 (1984)
Capital: Bridgetown
Currency: Dollar (100 cents)

Barbados is a relatively flat island with its highest point, Mount Hillaby, rising to 1,104 feet. Most of the island is covered with a coral limestone capping, and there is little surface water and no running streams. It is largely open country devoted to the growing of sugar.

The climate is tempered by ocean breezes and temperatures seldom exceed 90 degrees F. The average annual temperature is 75 degrees F.

The Arawak Indians are known to have inhabited the island, but when, in 1536, the Portuguese sailor, Pedro a Campos, landed he found it uninhabited. The Portuguese are said to have given it the name "Los Barbados" from the bearded fig trees found growing there.

The British landed in 1625 and claimed the island for King James. Two years later, the first settlement was founded and named Jamestown. A parliament was established in 1639.

By the mid-17th century Barbados was a thriving colony and because of its location "up wind" from the other West Indian islands, it escaped the fate of being tossed back and forth between the constantly warring European powers, and remained firmly British. Slaves on the island were freed in 1834. Independence came on Nov. 30, 1966, after a period of transition to self-rule.

One of the world's more densely populated areas, the island has a population of 90% African descent, 5% white, and 5% mixed.

While tourism is a major source of income, the economy is also bolstered by sugar, from which the famous Barbados rum is made. The

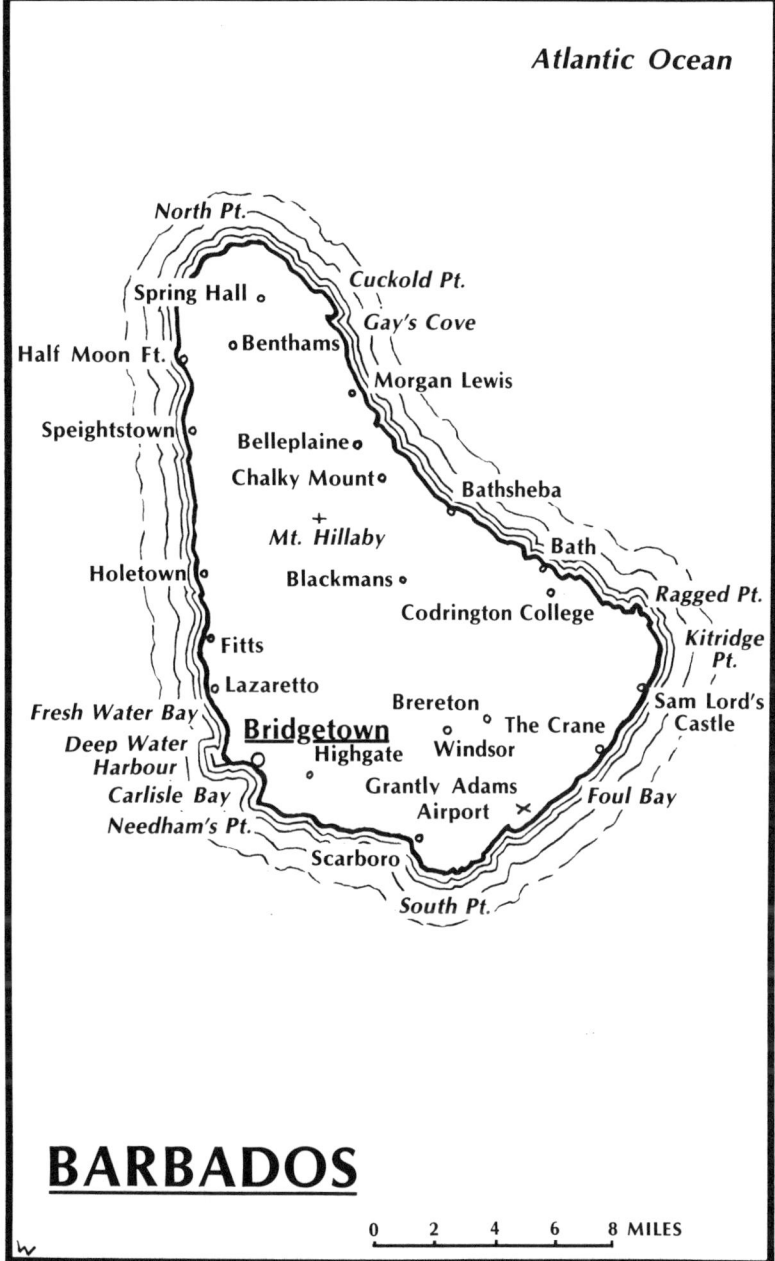

1982 per capita income was $3,040 and the 1984 literacy rate was 99%.

The island's postal history goes back to 1663, when a postal agency was established and a mail service linked the island with England.

An island Post Office was authorized in 1851. Post offices were in Bridgetown and 10 rural parishes the following year. The first stamps were issued in 1852.

Barbados had always been popular with collectors and its restrained and responsible stamp-issuing policies in recent years have ensured that it will continue to be widely collected.

Philatelic Bureau: Philatelic Bureau, GPO, Bridgetown, Barbados, West Indies.

DOMINICA, COMMONWEALTH OF

Area: 290 sq. miles
Population: 74,000 (1984)
Capital: Roseau
Currency: East Caribbean dollar (100 cents)

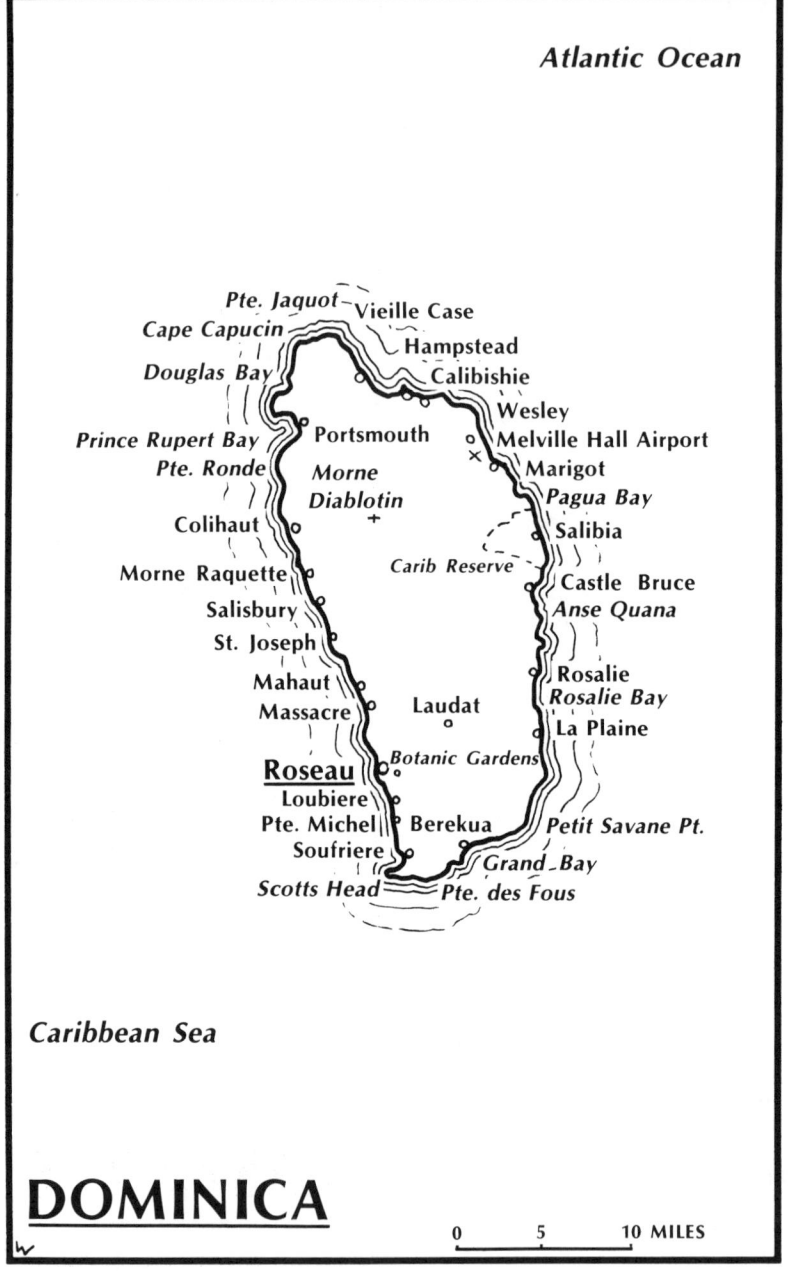

Dominica, pronounced "Dom-in-ee-ca," is situated between the French islands of Guadeloupe to the north and Martinique to the south in the Caribbean chain of the Lesser Antilles.

The island is mountainous and heavily forested. The climate is tropical, with sea-level temperatures ranging from 70-90 degrees F. Annual rainfall averages 112 inches, although the range is wide, being from 60 inches to more than 200. Hurricanes occur, the most recent being in 1979. The soil is rich and there are many streams.

Columbus discovered the island on Nov. 3, 1493 and named it Dominica because the discovery day was a Sunday. The ferocity of the native Carib Indians rendered foreign settlement impossible for a number of years. The island is still home to their last remaining descendants.

Desired by both British and French, Dominica changed hands several times, finally becoming British in 1805. Independence came Nov. 3, 1978. Until 1939, it was a member of the Leeward Islands federation. In that year it transferred to the Windward Island group.

Dominica is a botanist's paradise, covered as it is with a luxuriant

growth of tropical rain forest. The botanical gardens at Roseau is considered to be one of the finest in the Caribbean.

Although bananas are the chief crop, citrus and coconuts are important. Dominica limes are used to make the famous Roses lime juice.

Tourism is looming larger in the island's economy, although the island had been more popular and widely visited before the Canadian National Steamship passenger service by the popular "Lady" ships was discontinued. However, the introduction of air service has made the island easier to reach.

Dominica has had its own stamps since 1874, although it also used those of the Leeward Islands during the period it was part of that group.

Subsequent issues show much of the island's attractions, the 1938 definitive set being particularly attractive.

Philatelic Bureau: Postmaster, Stamp Order Division, GPO, Roseau, Dominica, West Indies.

DOMINICAN REPUBLIC

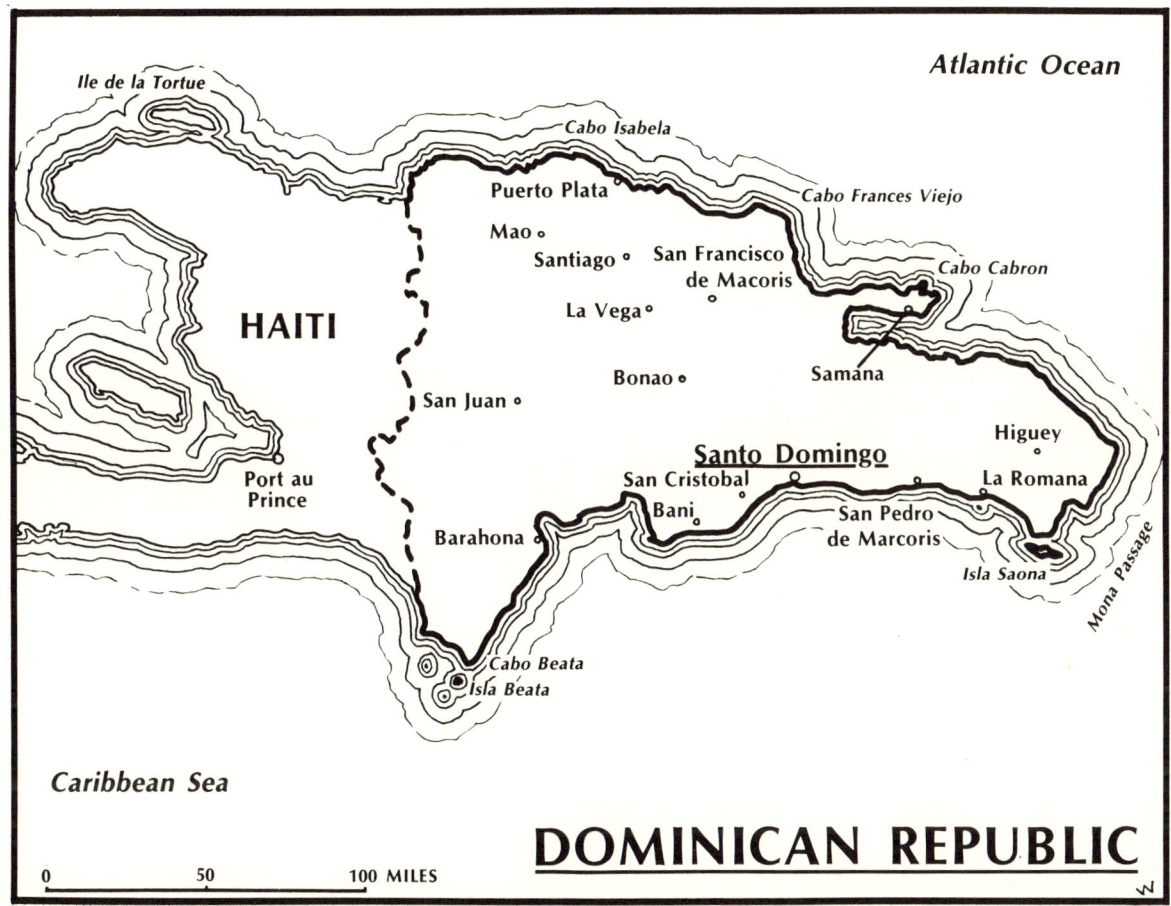

Area: 18,704 sq. miles
Population: 6,416,000 (1984)
Capital: Santo Domingo
Currency: Peso (100 centavos)

Occupying the eastern two-thirds of the island of Hispaniola in the Greater Antilles, the Dominican Republic has a coastline 1,000 miles long and shares a 195-mile border with Haiti.

There are mountains running along the center of the island with 10,206-foot Pico Duarte being the highest point in the Caribbean area.

The tropical climate is modified by trade winds and temperatures generally remain in the 70-85 degree F range. The climate cools as altitude increases. Rainfall averages 60 inches a year.

Columbus discovered Hispaniola in 1492. In 1502, the city of Santo Domingo was founded, making it the oldest European settlement in the Western Hemisphere.

Spain, ceded Haiti to France in 1677. It became independant in 1804 and in 1824, occupied the whole island. By 1844 an independence movement succeeded in gaining freedom for what then became the Dominican Republic. Spain returned to rule from 1861-65.

The country's economy collapsed and unrest caused the United States to send in the Marines in 1916 and establish a military government. This ended in 1924. From 1930 to his assassination in 1961, the dictator, Rafael L. Trujillo, exercised a brutal regime. There have been several coups since then and in 1965 the United States again sent in troops to prevent a Cuban-inspired Communist takeover.

Sugar, coffee, cocoa, tobacco, and rice are the chief crops. There is some light industry.

The 1980 per capita income was $1,221 and the 1981 literacy rate was 62%.

The Dominican Republic's first stamps in 1865 depicted the country's coat of arms. Since then, stamp issues have been prolific with a large number of air mail stamps.

Philatelic Bureau: Oficina Filatelica, Direccion General de Correos, Santo Domingo, Dominican Republic.

GRENADA, STATE OF

Area: 133 sq. miles
Population: 113,000 (1984)
Capital: St. George's
Currency: East Caribbean dollar (100 cents)

The smallest independent nation in the Western Hemisphere, Grenada is the most southerly of the Windward Islands. It is located at the botton of the chain of Lesser Antilles that runs in a great curve southeast and south from Puerto Rico to the coast of South America. The island is about 90 miles north of Trinidad.

Included in the State of Grenada are the southern portion of the Grenadines, a chain of small islands between Grenada and St. Vincent. The northern Grenadines are administered by St. Vincent.

Grenada is hilly, with Mount St. Catherine being the highest point at 2,757 feet. The south coast is indented with several good harbors, one of the most beautiful being at St. George's.

Volcanic in orgin, Grenada has a rich soil and a rainfall ranging from 60 inches along the coast to 200 inches in the mountains. This makes it ideal for agriculture and its tropic lushness has long justified its reputation as one of the most beautiful of all tropic islands.

Columbus discovered the island in 1498 and named it Concepcion. How it gained its present name is not known, although it is said that the Spanish re-named it at the end of the 1700s for the city of Granada in Spain.

Because of the desire of the warlike native Carib Indian population to remain on their island undisturbed, colonization was not successful for more than a century after its discovery by Europeans.

Eventually, the French established a settlement there after exterminating the Caribs and remained in possession until driven out by the British in the mid-1700s.

The Treaty of Paris in 1763 gave the island to Britain and except for a brief French occupation in the late 1700s, it remained British.

Following the failure of the sugar industry from a plague of ants and a devastating hurricane in 1780, nutmeg was introduced and Grenada soon became known as the Spice Isle. Nutmeg and cocoa cultivation made possible the elimination of the plantation system and the land came into the possession of many small independent farmers.

Until 1958, Grenada was governed as one of the Windward Island federation. It then joined the shortlived Federation of the West Indies, after the break-up of which it was granted associated state status with Great Britain. Full independence was achieved on Feb. 7, 1974.

In 1983, a military coup took over, murdering the prime minister, Maurice Bishop. US forces, together with contingents from six area countries, landed and overcame the Grenadian army and its Cuban advisors. The population welcomed the liberators and a democratic administration was established.

Grenada's economy depends on agriculture, with tourism making a major contribution. Since the period of political instability began, the number of tourists visiting the island was reduced. The economy is currently poor and the country faces a long, hard struggle to regain a measure of prosperity.

Grenada's first stamps appeared in 1861 and feature the beautiful Chalon Head portrait of Queen Victoria.

On July 12, 1937, Grenada became the first British colony to issue a King George VI definitive stamp, when it released the ¼d value depicting a portrait of the new king.

In recent years, Grenada has issued a massive number of stamps, many of which have no obvious national relevance. Together with a number of other Caribbean and African countries, it has issued many stamps depicting Walt Disney cartoon characters.

Philatelic Bureau: Postmaster General, GPO. St. George's, Grenada, West Indies.

Grenada Grenadines

The Grenadines form a chain of many small islands and islets stretching for 60 miles between Grenada and St. Vincent. The Grenada Grenadines comprise the portion of the chain south of Petit St. Vincent Island.

Carriacou is the largest of the Grenada Grenadines. Its chief town is Hillsborough. Cotton and cattle are raised on the island.

The waters around the Grenadines are ideal for sailing and they have become a popular vacation spot.

In 1973, Grenada started issuing stamps inscribed for the Grenada Grenadines, despite the fact that they are part of Grenada. Since then a large number of stamps have appeared. Many share a common theme with similar stamps inscribed for Grenada.

Philatelic Bureau: The same as for Grenada.

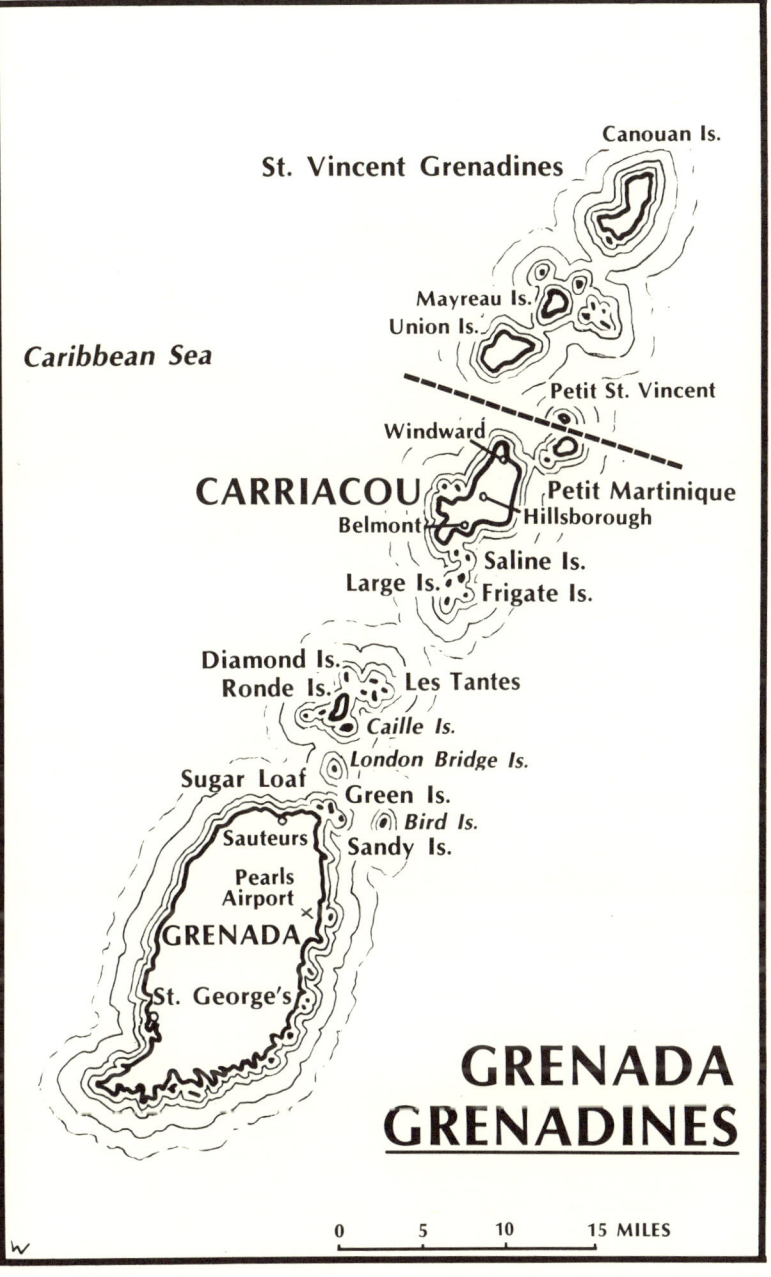

Grenada's beautiful Chalon Head issue and the first British Commonwealth King George VI stamp.

HAITI, REPUBLIC OF

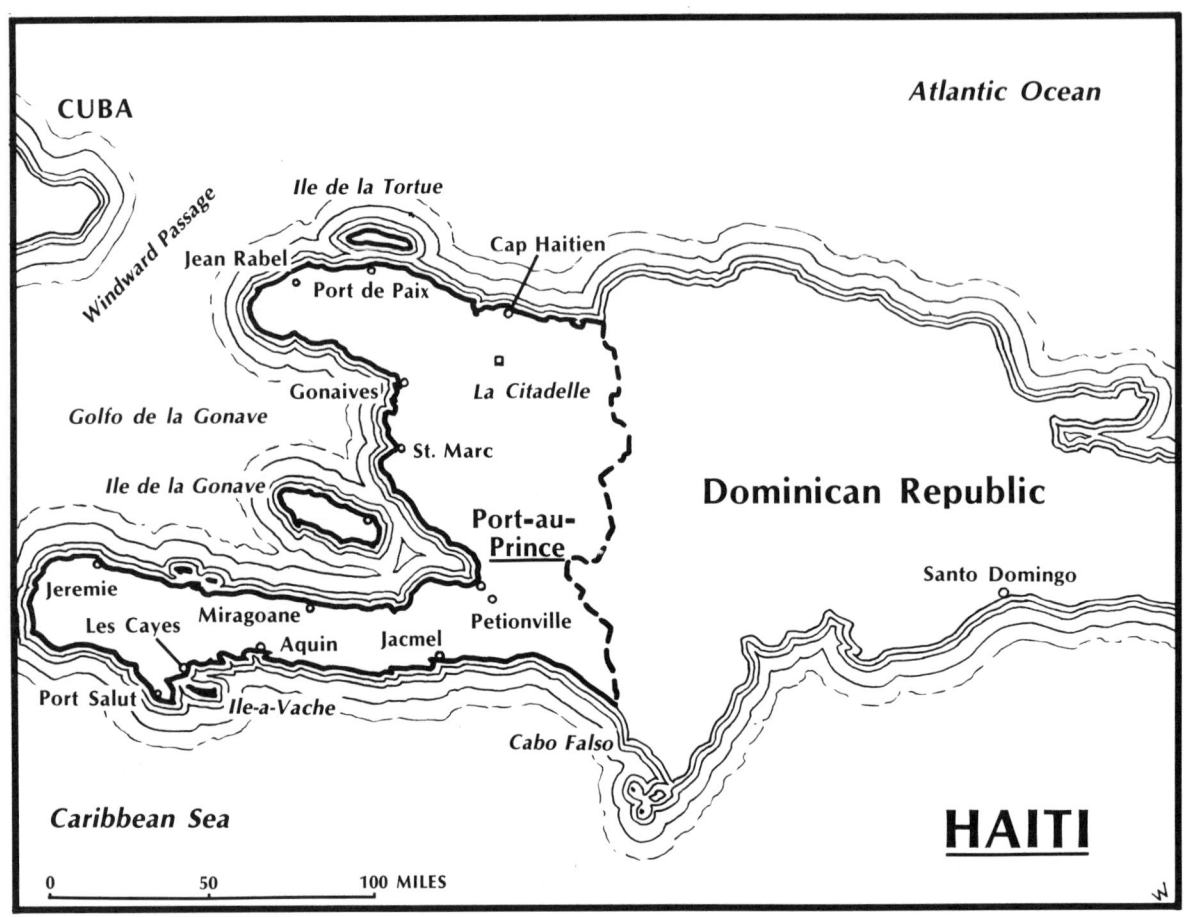

Area: 10,714 sq. miles
Population: 5,803,000 (1984)
Capital: Port-au-Prince
Currency: Gourde (100 centimes)

Haiti occupies the western third of the island of Hispaniola, which it shares with the Dominican Republic.

Cut off by mountains from the moist trade winds from the east, the country is mostly semi-arid. With its high population and two-thirds of its land area unsuitable for agriculture, and wracked by years of political corruption, Haiti is the poorest country in the Western Hemisphere. Temperatures are generally warm, averaging 70-90 degrees F all year.

Hispaniola was discoverd by Columbus in 1492. The western portion was a French colony from 1697. When slaves, led by Toussaint L'Ouverture, rebelled, the colony became independent in 1804.

The story of Haiti has been one of interracial conflict, political corruption, and inept government. In 1915, the United States occupied the country to restore order, but it was not welcomed and trouble continued. The occupation ended in 1934, but the economic state of the country did not improve.

Francois Duvalier made himself president for life in 1964 and was succeeded in 1971 by his son, who continued to rape the country until he was overthrown in 1986.

Despite the area of land not suitable for agriculture, Haiti has a rich variety of flora. Most tropical fruit grow wild as do cocoa and coffee. The forests abound in valuable hardwood and there are deposits of gold, silver, copper, iron, nickel, tin, and coal that remain undeveloped.

The chief crops are coffee, sisal, cotton, sugar, bananas, cocoa, tobacco, and rice. Tourism provides an important source of income and molasses and rum are produced.

The 1983 per capita income was a low $300 and the 1984 literacy rate was only 20%.

The country's first stamps were issued in 1881 and featured the Head of Liberty.

Since then stamp issues have been numerous with a large number of air mail stamps being released.
Philatelic Bureau: Office de Timbre, Box 3, Port-au-Prince, Haiti.

MONTSERRAT

Area: 32 sq. miles
Population: 11,600 (1980)
Capital: Plymouth
Currency: East Caribbean dollar (100 cents)

The British dependency of Montserrat, in the Lesser Antilles, is one of the Leeward Islands. It is located 27 miles southwest of Antigua and to the north of Guadeloupe.

Volcanic in origin, its highest point is 3,000 feet. The island's average temperature is 80 degrees F and rainfall is about 95 inches a year.

Montserrat was discovered by Columbus in 1493 and was named by him for a mountain in Spain. An Irish expedition authorized by Oliver Cromwell of England colonized it in 1632. To this day, one can detect an Irish brogue lurking within a West Indian accent.

Except for brief periods of French occupation in 1664-68 and 1782-84, Montserrat has remained a British colony.

In 1871, the island became part of the Leeward Island federation, which lasted until 1956. It joined the shortlived Federation of the West Indies in 1958, but this broke up in 1962.

Up to the 1950s, the island was served by Canadian National Steamship passenger service or by inter-island schooner. In recent years, the

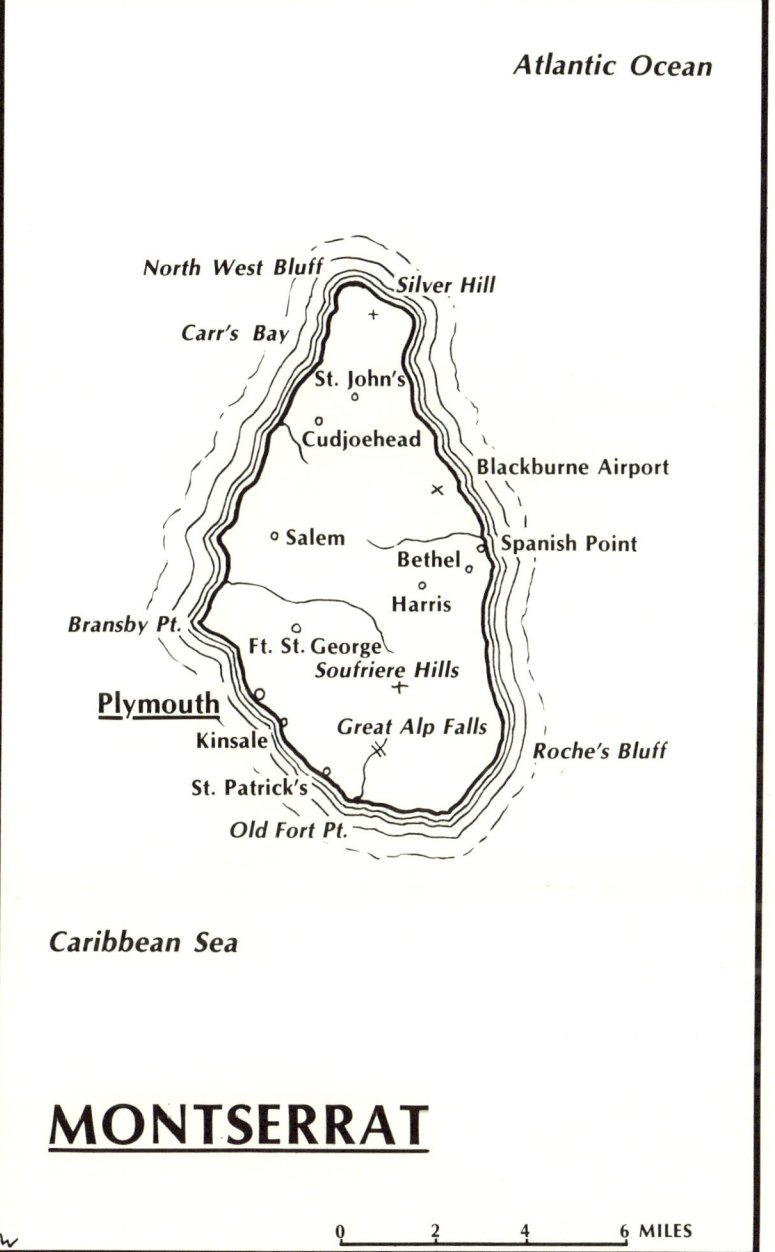

opening of an airport has once more made the island accessible to tourists.

Montserrat's first stamps were issued in 1876 and took the form of stamps of Antigua overprinted "MONTSERRAT."

The 1932 Tercentenary issue,

showing a view of the island off Plymouth has become an expensive modern classic.

From 1890 to 1956, stamps of the Leeward Islands were valid for use on the island and from 1890 to 1903, they replaced Montserrat stamps completely.

In recent years, stamp issues of Montserrat have become more numerous but policies are moderate when compared with those of some neighboring islands.

Philatelic Bureau: Montserrat Philatelic Bureau, GPO, Plymouth, Montserrat, West Indies.

NETHERLANDS ANTILLES

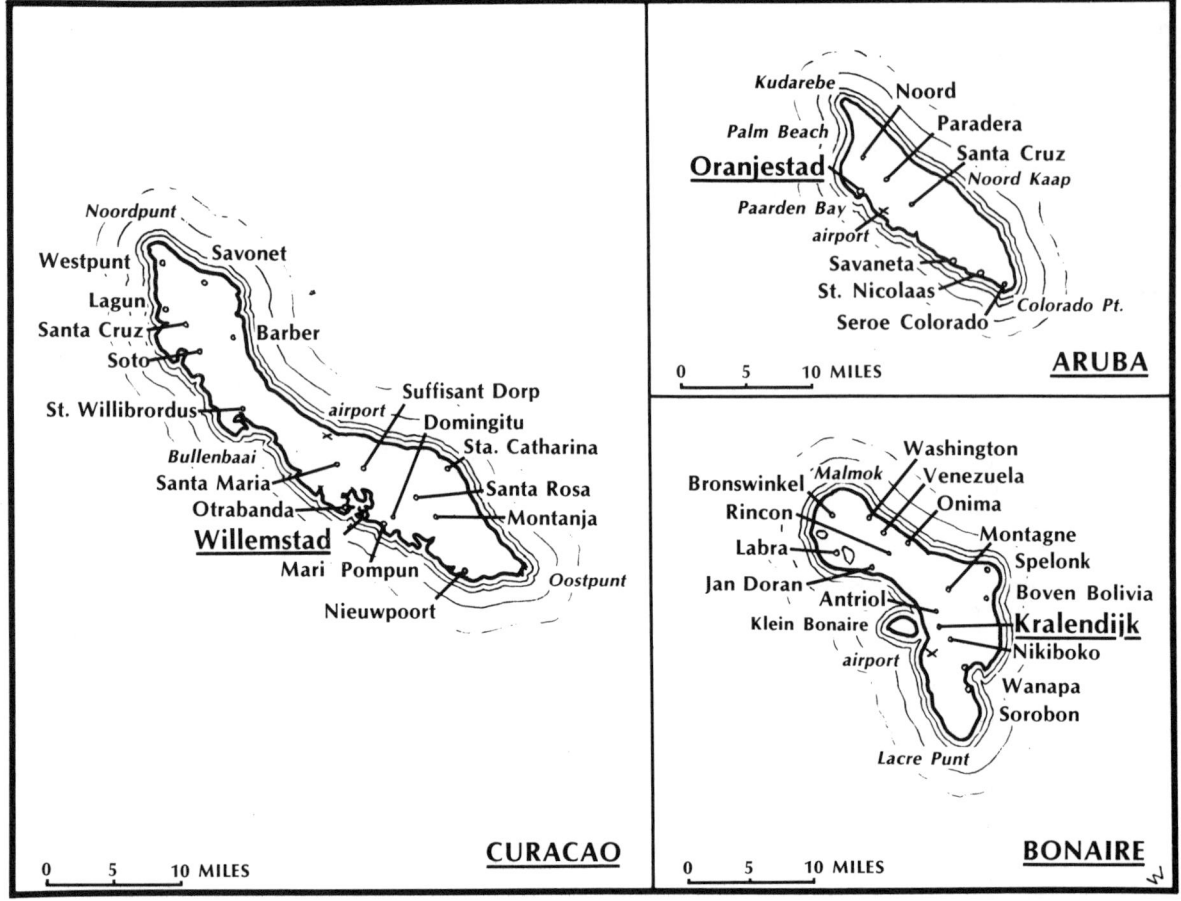

Area: 371 sq. miles
Population: 253,300 (1981)
Capital: Willemstad
Currency: Guilder (100 cents)

The Netherlands Antilles comprises a group of six Caribbean islands, three in the south off the coast of Venezuela (Curacao, Aruba, and Bonaire) and three in the north (St. Eustatius, Saba, and the southern third of St. Maartin). The country has equal status with the Kingdom of the Netherlands.

Alonso de Ojeda of Spain is credited with discovering the southern islands in 1499. The Spanish settled them in 1527, exterminating the Carib Indian population in the process, except on Aruba. The Carib Indians now form the majority of that island's population. The Dutch took over the islands in the mid-1600s when they came to work the salt deposits. Except for British occupation in 1800 and 1807-16, they have remained under Dutch control.

The discovery of oil in Venezuela and the construction of refineries on Curacao and Aruba gave the economy a much-needed boost. More recently, tourism and free port status for Willemstad have brought relative prosperity.

The Southern islands are low and dry. They are fringed with coral reefs. Annual average temperature is 80 degrees F. Rainfall of 20 inches or less a year renders vegetation sparse except for cacti and other drought-resistant species.

The northern group is volcanic in origin and thus more rugged than the three islands to the south. The islands were settled by Europeans in the mid-1600s. Sugar and cotton are grown on St. Eustatius and St. Maartin. Saba, with its very steep slopes and no harbor, has no economy of its own, except for the income of those working at the refineries in the southern islands and at sea.

Saba is the tip of an extinct volcano and is about five square miles in area. The chief town is Bottom, located not at the bottom of the crater, but some 800 feet up the side. Communications with the island have improved with the opening of an airstrip.

It was Fort Orange, on St. Eustatius, on Nov. 16, 1776 that gave the first salute by a foreign nation to the American Continental flag flown by the brig *Andrew Doria* of the Continental Navy. A stamp of the Netherlands Antilles was issued on Nov. 16, 1961 to mark the 185th anniversary of the event.

Stamps were first issued for the Netherlands Antilles in 1873 and were inscribed "Curacao" until the late 1940s, when the inscription was changed to "NED ANTILLEN" or "NEDERLANDSE ANTILLEN."

Philatelic Bureau: Philatelic Service Office, Postmaster, Willemstad, Curacao, Netherlands Antilles.

Aruba: The southern island of Aruba has long had its own political aspirations and beginning on Jan. 1,

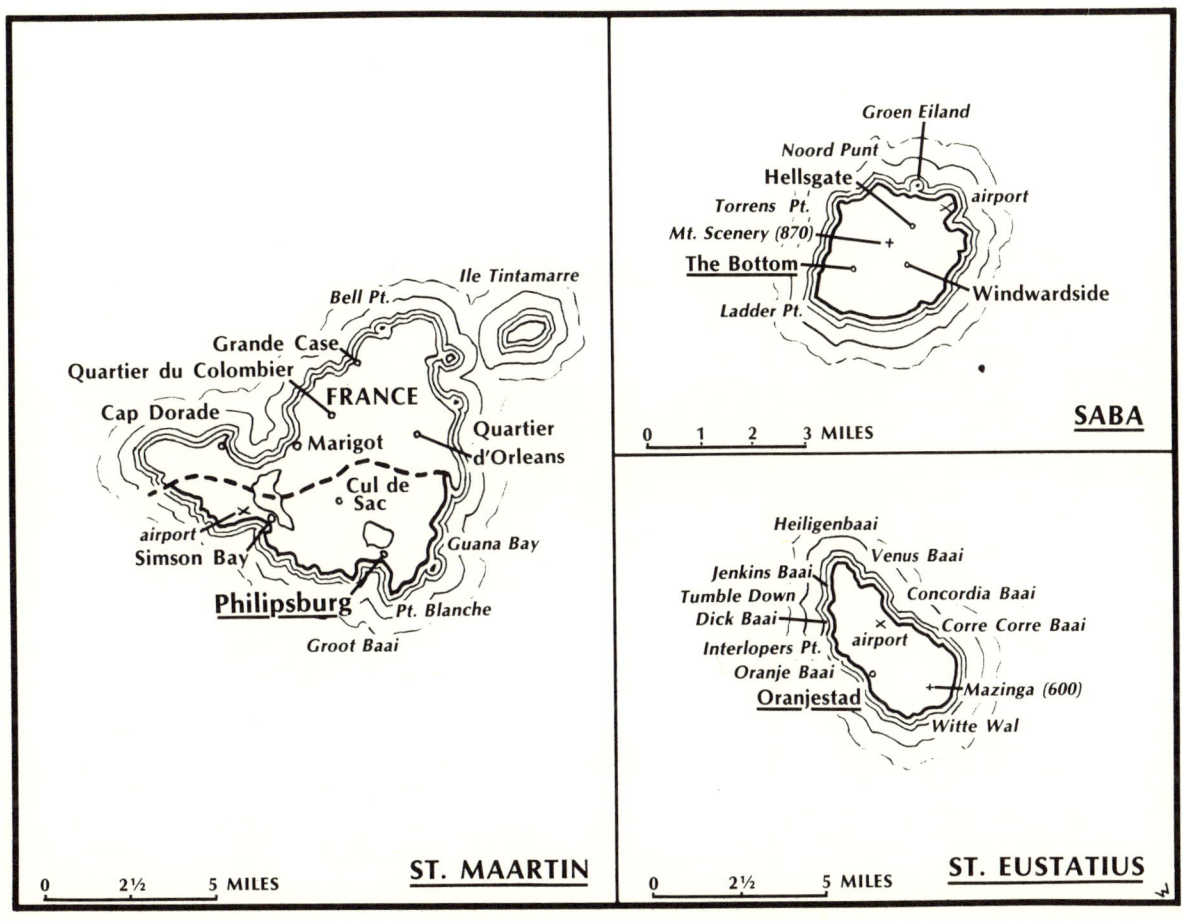

1986, it was given the privilege of issuing its own stamps.

This reflects a political change that is intended to give the island its independence in 1996.

Aruba has an area of 69 sq. miles and a population estimated at 66,500. The capital city is Oranjestad. The mainstay of its economy

is an oil refinery that processes oil from Venezuela. Tourism is also a source of income.

The island is mostly flat, with the highest point being 617 feet.

Philatelic Bureau: Philatelic Service, Post Office, Oranjestad, Aruba, West Indies.

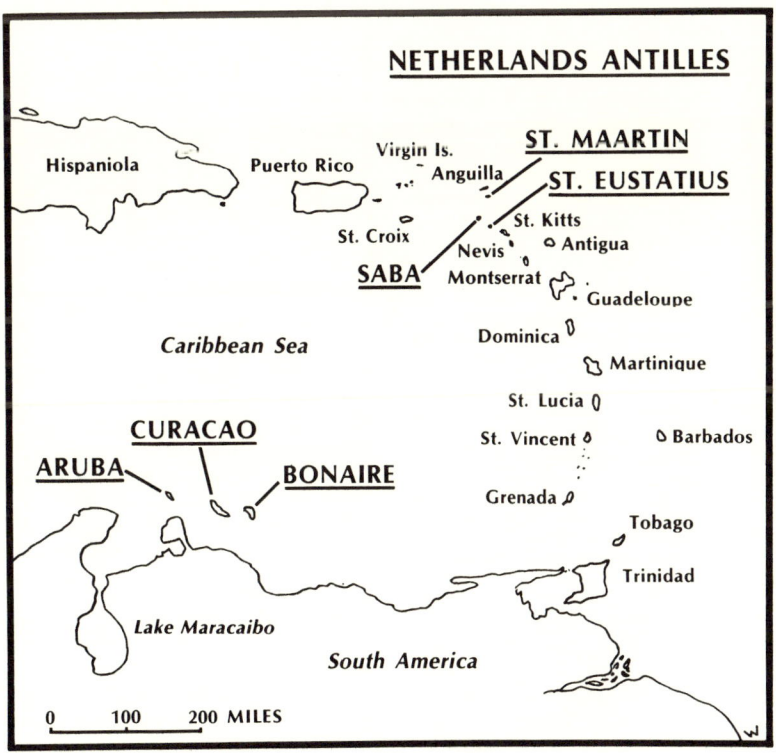

ST. KITTS-NEVIS (ST. CHRISTOPHER-NEVIS)

Area: 104 sq. miles
Population: 44,500 (1984)
Capital: Basseterre
Currency: East Caribbean dollar (100 cents)

The twin islands of St. Kitts-Nevis are located in the Leeward Islands at the northern end of the Lesser Antilles island chain. St. Kitts has an area of 68 square miles. With a rainfall of 55 inches a year, it has long been an important producer of sugar. The climate is moderate with temperatures ranging from 62-92 degrees F. The highest point is Mount Misery, which rises to 3,711 feet.

Nevis is separated from the southeastern tip of St. Kitts by a narrow channel. Its area is 36 sq. miles and the highest point is 3,596 feet. Cotton is its main product. Both islands are volcanic in origin.

The islands were first sighted by Columbus in 1493 and an English settlement was established on St. Kitts by Sir Thomas Warner in 1623.

From the 1950s until it broke away in 1967, the nearby island of Anguilla was administered from St. Kitts. Associated state status with Great Britain was achieved in 1967 and on Sept. 19, 1983, St. Kitts-Nevis became independent as the Federation of St. Kitts-Nevis, its formal title being the Federation of St. Christopher-Nevis.

The economy is based on sugar on St. Kitts and cotton on Nevis. Tourism is of growing importance. The 1980 per capita income was $920 and the 1984 literacy rate was 90%.

The first stamps for St. Kitts were issued in 1870 under the name of St. Christopher. These were replaced in 1890 by the general issue for the Leeward Islands and they remained in use until 1956, although stamps for St. Kitts-Nevis were issued beginning in 1903.

In 1952, the inscription was changed to include Anguilla and this continued until 1980, even though Anguilla had left to set up housekeeping on its own in 1967.

In 1980, separate postal administrations were set up for St. Kitts and Nevis and they issued their own stamps beginning on June 23 of that year.

Philatelic Bureau: St. Kitts Philatelic Bureau, GPO, Basseterre, St. Kitts, West Indies.

Philatelic Bureau: Nevis Philatelic Bureau, GPO, Charlestown, Nevis, West Indies.

ST. LUCIA

Area: 238 sq. miles
Population: 120,000 (1984)
Capital: Castries
Currency: East Caribbean dollar (100 cents)

St. Lucia is an island in the Windward group of the Lesser Antilles. It is located to the south of Martinique and north of St. Vincent.

Of volcanic origin, the island is well wooded, with fertile valleys, and many streams. Temperatures vary with altitude and range from 70 degrees F inland to 79 on the coast. Rainfall is about 50 inches a year on the coast rising to 120 inches in the interior.

In 1605, the British attempted the first settlement but they were driven off by the stout-hearted Carib Indians. In 1641, another attempt to colonize was also defeated. After the Indians were finally subdued, the island changed hands between Britain and France many times up to 1803, when Britain obtained final possession. It remained a British colony until 1967, when Associated State status with Great Britain was achieved. Independence came on Feb. 22, 1979.

Bananas, cocoa, coconuts, and citrus are the main crops. Tourism is gaining in importance as a revenue generator. The island has much scenic beauty, with boiling sulphur springs, fine beaches, and the dramatic tall rock formations known at the Pitons. Each rises more than 2,000 feet from southwest coast.

The flora and fauna is equally attractive and the St. Lucia parrot is one of the world's rarest birds.

There is no recent per capita in-

come figure. The 1984 literacy rate was 78%.

From its first stamp issue in 1860, St. Lucia was noted for its attractive and colorful stamps. The 1936 King George V pictorial definitives are especially beautiful. In recent years, the number of stamp issues has increased and the quality of production is not what it once was.

The subjects of some issues have no particular connection with the island.

Philatelic Bureau: Postmaster, GPO, Castries, St. Lucia, West Indies.

ST. VINCENT AND GRENADINES

Area: 150 sq. miles
Population: 138,000 (1984)
Capital: Kingstown
Currency: East Caribbean dollar
(100 cents)

Located in the Lesser Antilles, north of Grenada and south of St. Lucia, St. Vincent also includes the northern part of the Grenadines. It is one of the Windward Islands.

The island is volcanic and its highest point is the 4,018-foot active volcano, Soufriere. It erupted in 1821, 1902, and 1979, causing great damage.

St. Vincent has a tropical climate that varies with altitude. The temperature ranges from 67-90 degrees F and the rainfall from 50 inches on the coast to 150 inches in the mountains.

Although it is south of the normal hurricane path, several have hit the island, causing much damage.

It is not known exactly when St. Vincent was discovered by Europeans. The British and French fought over the island with resistance distributed impartially between them by the native Carib Indian population.

After changing hands a number of times, Britain finally gained title in 1783. The French continued to make mischief by assisting the Carib Indians to revolt, and they were not subdued until 1796, when the survivors were exiled to an island off Central America.

Portuguese and East Indian labor was introduced to work on the plantations following the abolition of slavery in 1834.

In 1958, the island joined the Federation of the West Indies, which broke up in 1962.

St. Vincent received Associated State status with Great Britain in 1969 and gained complete independence on Oct. 27, 1979.

Agriculture and tourism are the mainstays of the economy. Bananas are the main export and the island is the world's major supplier of arrowroot.

A poor island, its most recent available per capita income figure was $250 in 1979 and the 1981 literacy rate was 85%.

Stamps were first issued on May 8, 1861. Prior to this the stamps of Great Britain were used. The early stamps are highly regarded,

especially the 5/- issue of 1880, a handsome stamp featuring the seal of the colony.

The 1938 King George VI definitive issue is an attractive and colorful set.

In recent years, the stamps of St. Vincent have proliferated to an extraordinary extent, with stamps also being issued inscribed for the Grenadines and even for individual islands.

In 1984, St. Vincent achieved the distinction of issuing a total of 308 stamps, many of which featured subjects having no connection with the island.

Stamps inscribed for the Grenadines of St. Vincent first appeared in 1973 and for the islands of Bequia and Union in 1984. None have currently received catalog recognition.

Philatelic Bureau: Bureau Manager, St. Vincent Philatelic Services, GPO, Kingstown, St. Vincent, West Indies.

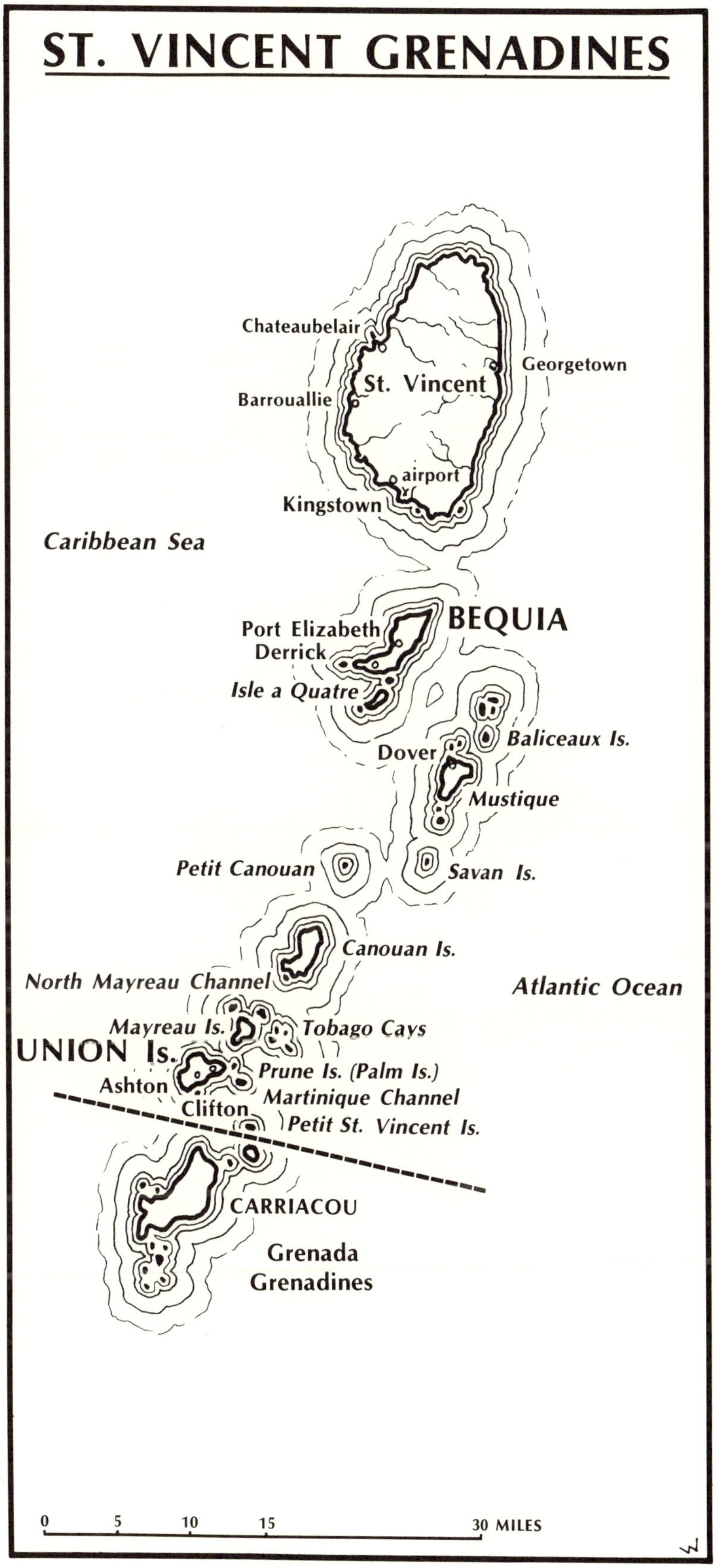

ST. VINCENT GRENADINES

TRINIDAD AND TOBAGO, REPUBLIC OF

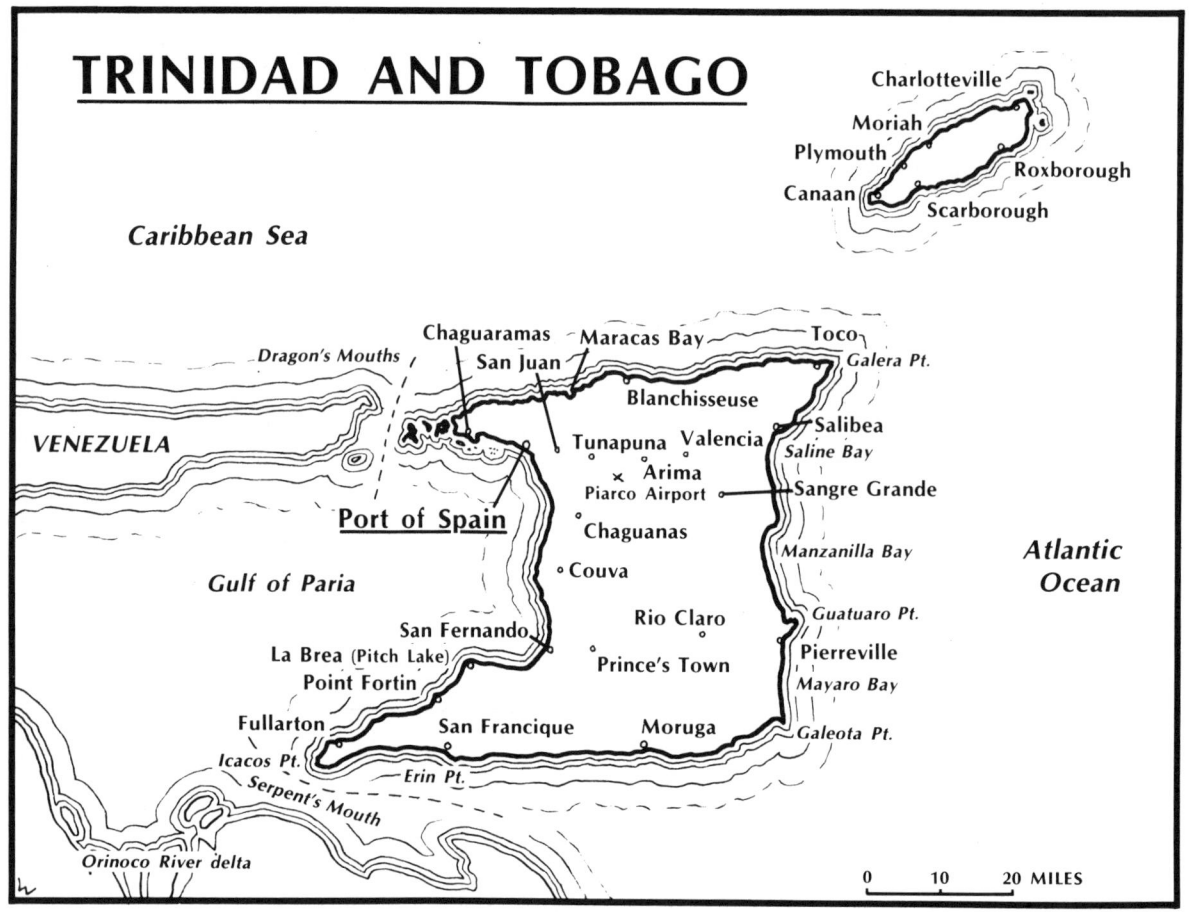

Area: 1,970 sq. miles
Population: 1,168,000 (1984)
Capital: Port of Spain
Currency: Dollar (100 cents)

The most southerly island in the Lesser Antilles, Trinidad is separated from mainland South America by a channel seven miles wide.

Trinidad is a geological extension of the mainland and shares much of its flora and fauna. The island is heavily wooded with three moderate mountain ranges crossing from east to west. The northern range is the highest, rising to 3,000 feet.

The climate is pleasant, with an average maximum temperature of 90 degrees F and a minimum of 70. Rainfall varies from 100 inches a year in the east to 70 in the west.

An interesting natural feature is the Pitch Lake, the contents of which has paved roads all over the island and around the world.

Columbus discovered and named Trinidad for three hills he sighted from the north in the 1490s. Spain did not settle it until 1577. Britain gained possession in 1797 and made it a crown colony. Independence came on Aug. 31, 1962.

Tobago is 19 miles northeast of Trinidad. It is a small island with an area of 116 sq. miles. With its miles of deserted, beautiful beaches, it is a popular vacation resort. Small farming is the main occupation. Initially a separate British colony, it merged in 1888 with Trinidad.

The most prosperous Caribbean country, Trinidad and Tobago has a diverse economy with large oil reserves and extensive refining facilities. Sugar, coffee, and cocoa are grown and rum is an important product. Tourism is a flourishing industry. The 1982 per capita income was $6,800 and the 1984 literacy rate was 96%.

Trinidad's government-issued stamps came in 1851. Tobago had its own stamps from 1858 to 1896. Since 1913, stamps have borne the names of both islands. Post-independence, stamp-issuing policies have been moderate.

Philatelic Bureau: Postmaster General, GPO, Port of Spain, Trinidad and Tobago.

TURKS AND CAICOS ISLANDS

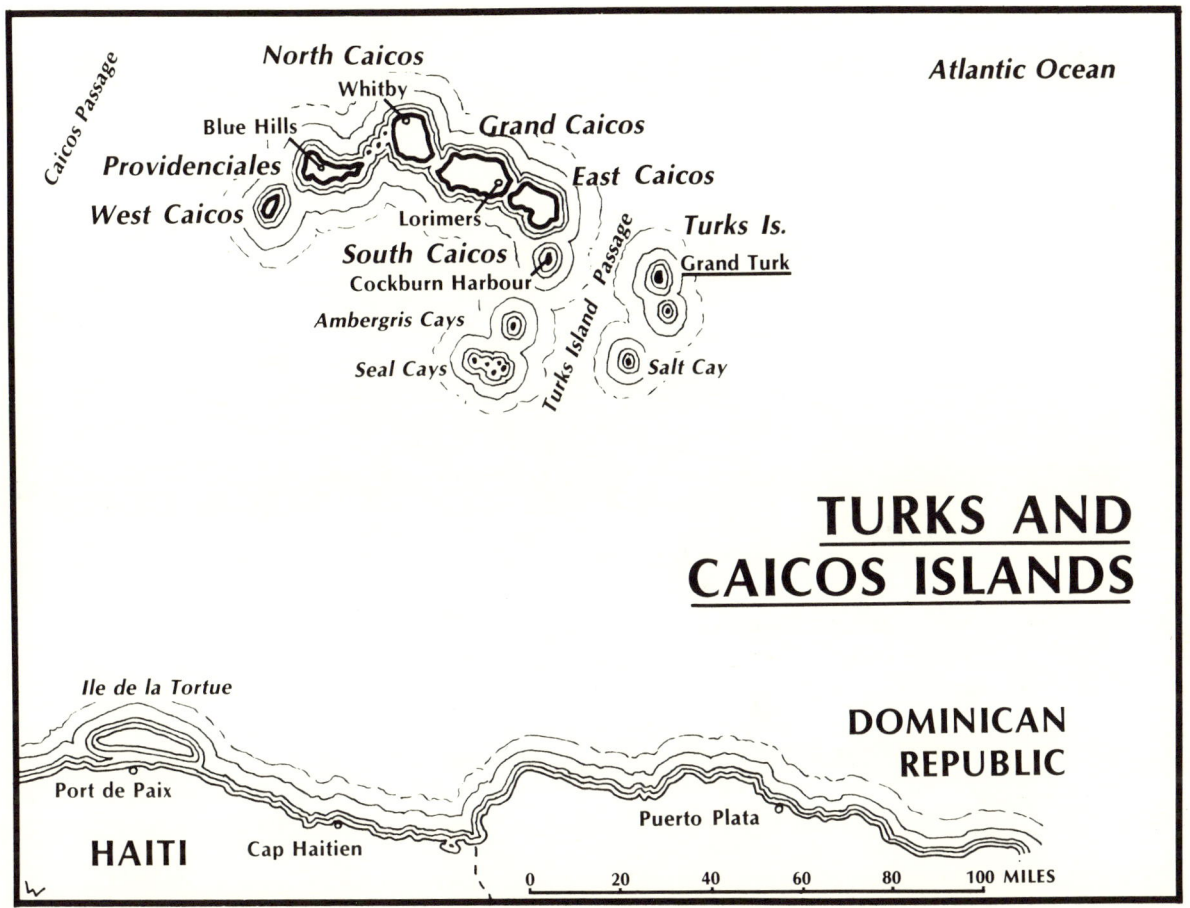

Area: 193 sq. miles
Population: 7,000 (1980)
Capital: Grand Turk
Currency: Dollar (100 cents)

The Turks and Caicos comprise two groups of small islands located to the southeast of the Bahamas and north of Hispaniola.

Although the climate is hot, it is tempered by trade winds. Temperatures range from 60-90 degrees F and rainfall averages 25 inches each year. The light rainfall results in periodic water shortages.

The islands are subject to frequent hurricanes.

Ponce de Leon, the first European visitor, came across the islands in 1512. In 1678, settlers from Bermuda established a salt trade with the American colonies, a venture that was maintained despite considerable harrassment by the French and Spanish.

At first administered by the Bahamas, the British Turks and Caicos were transferred to Jamaica in the mid-19th century and remained a dependency of that island until 1959. They became a British crown colony in 1962.

The making of salt by solar evaporation is still the main occupation, although there is some commercial fishing and tourism is becoming more important.

Even so, Britain has to supply the colony with considerable economic aid.

Stamps were first issued on April 4, 1867 and until 1900 were inscribed "Turks Islands." In that year, stamps were released inscribed "Turks and Caicos Islands" and these have continued up to the present.

Philatelic Bureau: Philatelic Bureau, Grand Turk, Turks and Caicos Islands.

Caicos Islands: On July 24, 1981, stamps began to appear inscribed for the Caicos Islands and these separate issues have continued.

Philatelic Bureau: Caicos Philatelic Bureau, South Caicos, Turks and Caicos Islands.

VIRGIN ISLANDS, BRITISH

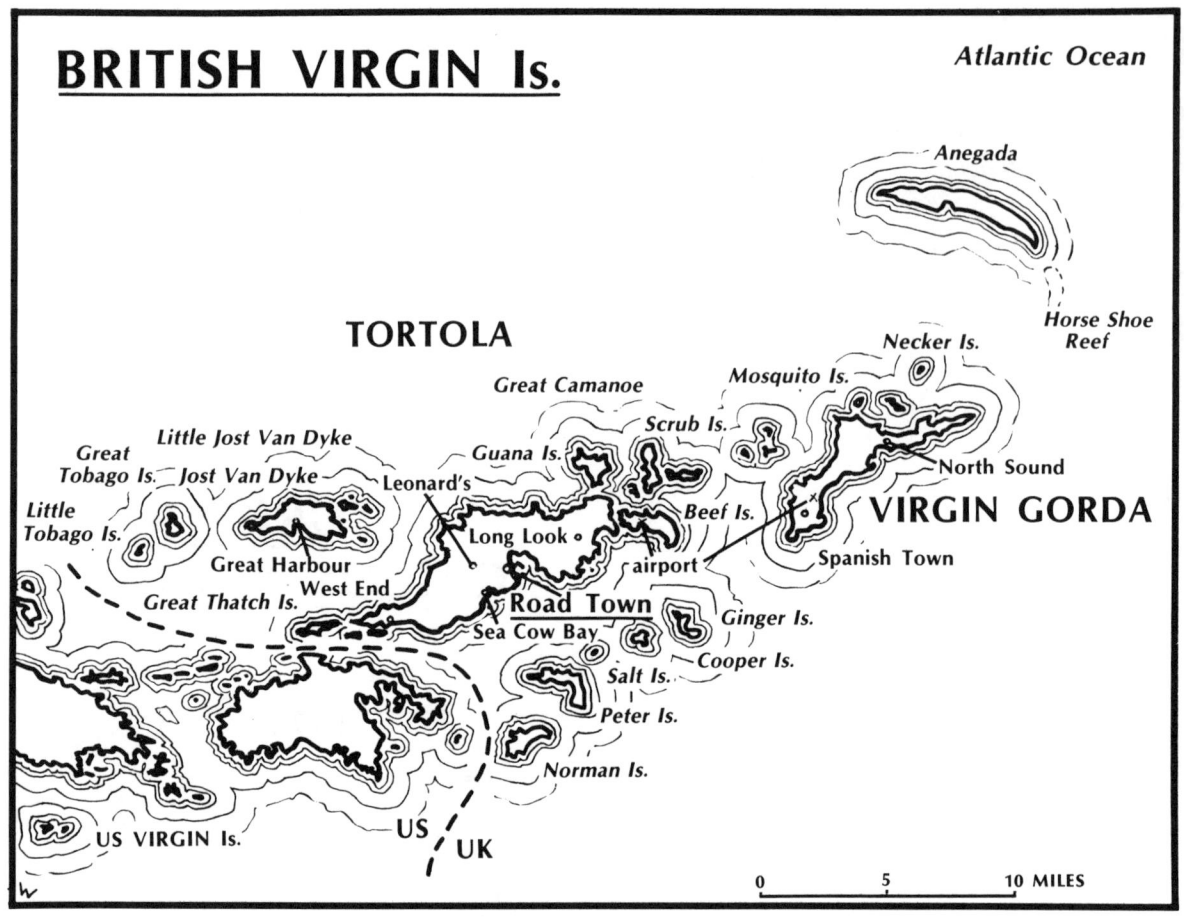

Area: 59 sq. miles
Population: 11,500 (1980)
Capital: Road Town
Currency: Dollar (100 cents)

The group of islands known as the British Virgin Islands is adjacent to the US Virgin Islands to the east of Puerto Rico. They are part of the Leeward Islands.

Although they have only a small land area, what they lack in size they more than make up in appeal for winter-escaping North Americans. The climate is extremely pleasant. Temperatures seldom go above 90 degrees F or drop below 65. Rainfall averages about 40 inches.

The islands were discovered by Columbus in 1493 and named by him "Las Virgenes" in honor of St. Ursula and her companions.

The British occupied Tortola in 1666 and have held it ever since. It had previously been the site of a Dutch Settlement established in 1648.

The islands comprise the main island of Tortola, plus Anegada, Virgin Gorda, Jost Van Dyke, and a number of smaller islands and islets.

Stock raising is an important occupation and there is some fishing. But tourism is the most important revenue source.

Stamps were first issued in 1866. Prior to this, stamps of Great Britain were used in the islands.

The British Virgin Islands has an important claim to philatelic fame in the form of a major rarity in the 1867 series. This is the "Missing Virgin" error. It is found — or rather, not found — on the 1/- denomination. The expensive variety had a blank space in the center where the figure of St. Ursula should appear.

However, it was not until the 1950s that BVI stamps generally began to get really eye-appealing, with issues depicting island scenes, flora and fauna, maps, and the romantic history of the area.

In addition to its own stamps, the islands also used stamps of the general issue for the Leeward Islands until they were discontinued in 1956.

Philatelic Bureau: The Postmaster, Philatelic Bureau, Road Town, Tortola, British Virgin Islands.

SOUTH AMERICA

Stamp-issuing areas:

1. Argentina
2. Bolivia
3. Brazil
4. Chile
5. Colombia
6. Ecuador
7. Falkland Islands
8. French Guiana (uses French stamps)
9. Guyana
10. Paraguay
11. Peru
12. Suriname
13. Uruguay
14. Venezuela

ARGENTINE REPUBLIC

Area: 1,065,189 sq. miles
Population: 30,097,000 (1984)
Capital: Buenos Aires
Currency: Austral

Argentina is South America's second-largest country after Brazil, and is four times the size of Texas.

Its topography varies from subtropical forest in the north to the bleak, barren land of Tierra del Fuego at the continent's southern tip and from the coastal lands in the east across the grassy ocean of the Pampas to the great wall of the Andes that runs down the country's western border with Chile.

Native inhabitants roamed the Pampas in the early 1500s, when the Spanish first arrived, but by the 19th century, nearly all had been exterminated.

Independence came in the early 1800s and Argentina prospered, becoming the most advanced nation in Latin America, but political instability plagued the country. Although the Peron regime in the 1940s and 1950s brought some order, the stability came at the expense of the economy. In recent years, military governments ruled with repression and great brutality.

The country is now struggling to repair its economy. In 1985, inflation had reached 850% and fiscal problems continue.

Philatelic Bureau: Seccion Filatelia, Correo Central, Local 55, 1000 Buenos Aires, Argentina.

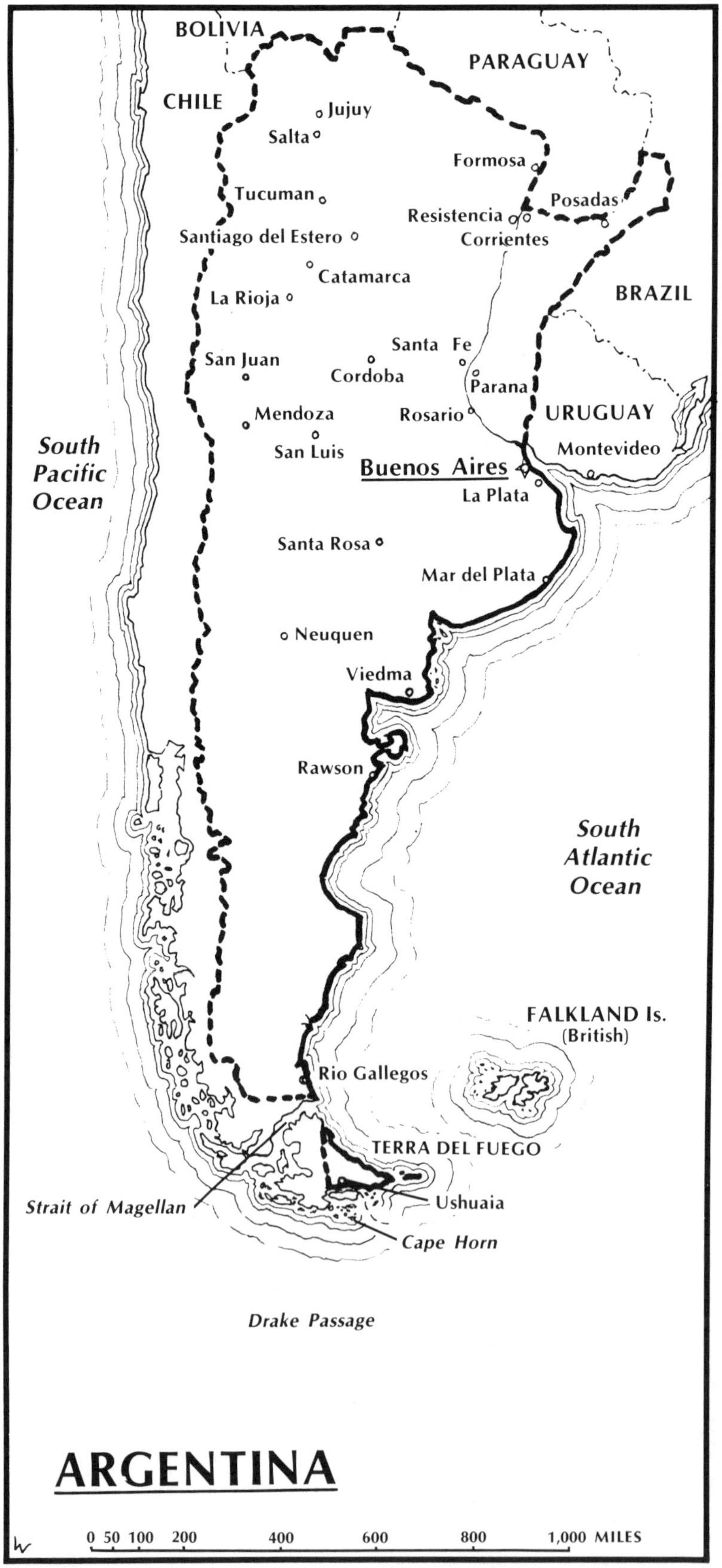

BOLIVIA, REPUBLIC OF

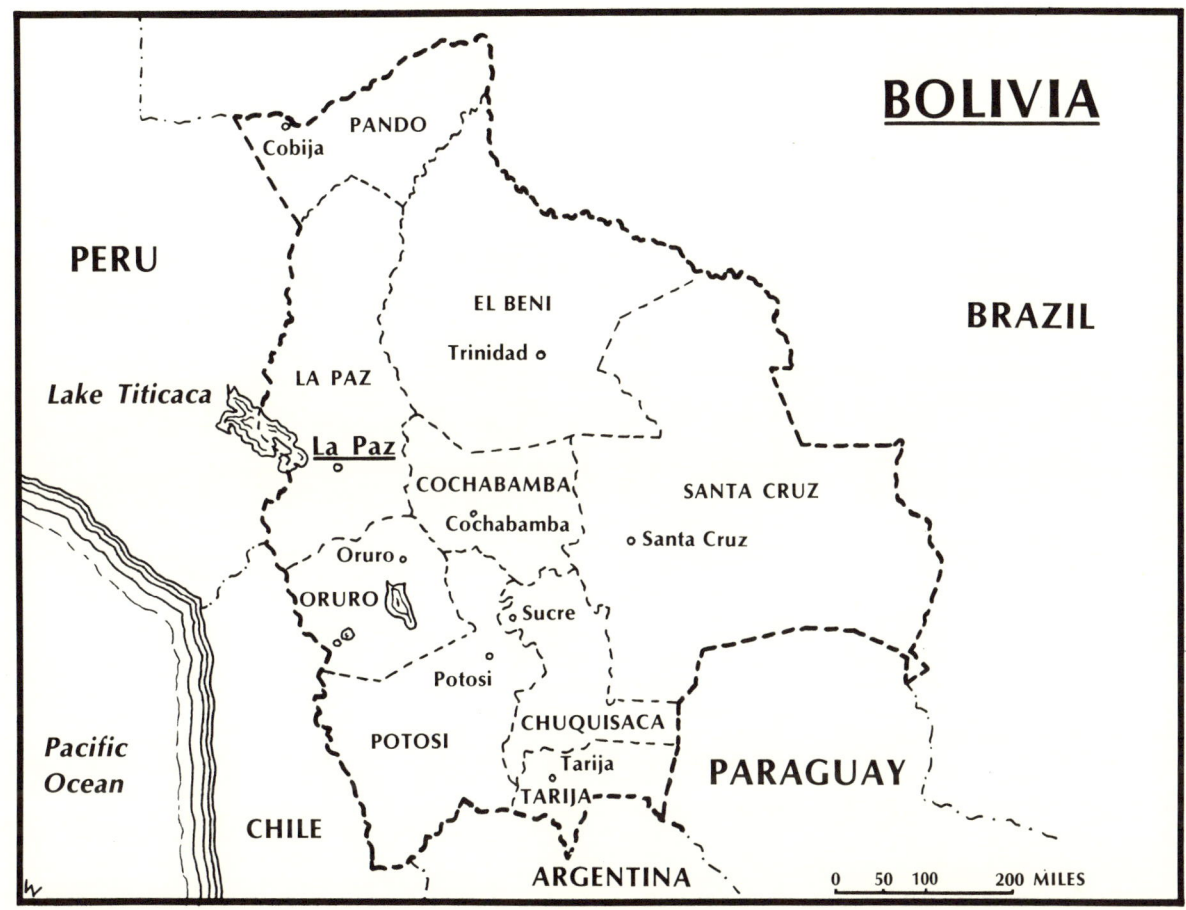

Area: 424,165 sq. miles
Population: 6,037,000 (1984)
Capital: La Paz (administrative)
Sucre (judicial)
Currency: New peso

Landlocked Bolivia comprises three geographic regions: The high plateau between two chains of the Andes Mountains, an area of rain forest on the eastern slopes, and Amazon lowlands.

Lake Titicaca, on the western border, at 12,500 feet is the world's highest lake on which there are steamships operating. La Paz, at more than 12,000 feet, is the world's highest capital city.

On the plateau, the climate is cool, with an average temperature of 50 degrees F. The temperature averages 70 degrees F on the eastern slopes.

A center of Inca culture, Bolivia was under Spanish rule from the 1530s until independence on Aug. 6, 1825. It is named for the South American liberator, Simon Bolivar.

The country has been plagued from the beginning with a continuing series of revolutions, counter revolutions, coups, and civil war. Ranging from lynching, to "suicide," to expulsion, the lot of Bolivian presidents has not always been a happy one.

Disputes with neighboring countries have also helped to keep the political pot boiling. In the 1879-84 war with Chile, Bolivia lost its seacoast and large areas of mineral-bearing land, and in more recent years, the 1932-34 war with Paraguay drained the economy.

By 1985, Bolivia's inflation rate was the world's highest and the foreign debt was more than $4 billion.

The 1982 per capita income was $570 and the 1983 literacy rate was 75%.

Bolivia's first stamps were issued in 1867, and subsequent issues have mirrored the country's political and economic fortunes. There have been numerous stamps depicting aircraft, emphasizing the role that aviation has played in a country where overland travel is still not easy.

Philatelic Bureau: Direccion Nacional de Correos, Seccion Filatelica, La Paz, Bolivia.

BRAZIL, FEDERATIVE REPUBLIC OF

Area: 3,286,470 sq. miles
Population: 134,400,000 (1984)
Capital: Brasilia
Currency: Cruzado

Taking up about half of South America, Brazil is the world's fifth largest country, after the Soviet Union, the United States, China, and Canada.

Its Atlantic coastline is 4,500 miles long and the country borders on every South American country except Ecuador and Chile.

There are several main geographic regions; the rain forest of the Amazon basin in the north, semiarid scrubland in the northeast, rolling plains in the central and southern portions with some mountain areas, and the coastal lands.

Most of the country is warm and humid. The average high temperature in Rio de Janeiro is 85 degrees F and the low is 65 degrees F.

The area that is now Brazil was discovered and claimed for Portugal in 1500 by the Portuguese navigator Pedro Cabral. Colonization began and the settlers gradually pushed their way inland.

There had been no Spanish opposition to the Portuguese settlement of the east coast of South America because the 1494 Treaty of Tordesillas between Spain and Portugal divided the New World between them. Everything west of a line running from north to south 100 leagues west of the Cape Verde Islands (370 leagues from 1506) was to be Spanish, with Portugal receiving everything east of the line.

This line intersected South America from the mouth of the Amazon south to Santos.

After the failure of a system of colonization involving a number of grants, in 1549 King John of Portugal appointed a governor general with headquarters at the capital city of Bahia (Salvador). Thus the colony grew as a unified area and settlement increased rapidly.

French and Dutch attempts to encroach upon the area added impetus to the Portuguese colony to remain a unified area rather than a series of isolated and separate settlements.

Restrictions by the Catholic Church on the use of native Indians as slaves on the large sugar plantations soon led to the importation of African slaves in large numbers and the impact of Africans on the culture of modern Brazil is marked. Slavery was not abolished until 1888.

During the Napoleonic Wars, Brazil achieved an unusual "first." It became the first colony to become the seat of government of the mother country, when Portuguese Regent Dom John took his court to Rio de Janeiro in 1808 to escape capture by Napoleon, who was then in the process of invading Portugal.

Growing unrest in Brazil persuaded him to return to Portugal and he left his son Dom Pedro, to act in his place. However, Dom Pedro's sympathies were with the colonists and he led the colony in a struggle for nationhood. By 1823, this was achieved and he became the new country's emperor.

After the second emperor was deposed in 1889, Brazil became the United States of Brazil, a name that was retained until 1967, when the present name was adopted.

As the country moved into its republican state, Brazil went through periods of unrest; president followed president and revolt followed revolt. Despite this the nation developed.

During World War I, Brazil's sympathies were with the Allies, and prompted by the sinking by Germany of several Brazilian ships, the country followed the United States into the war against the Central Powers. Brazil's military contribution was small, but as a source of food and natural resources, it was of great importance.

Brazil again sided with the Allies against Germany in World War II and sent an expeditionary force to help in the liberation of Europe.

Between the two world wars, Brazil's politics continued stormy until 1930 when, following a revolt, Getulio Vargas became president and virtual dictator. He ruled until 1945 and again from 1951-54, when he was forced from office. He is reported to have committed suicide when he realized the extent of the corruption in his regime.

Subsequent governments tended to be more oppressive. Censorship was imposed and opposition repressed.

Following 1977 US criticism of human rights violations in Brazil, relations between the two countries became strained. Since 1979, a more democratic policy has been followed.

In recent years, inflation has made the lot of the average Brazilian difficult and there is widespread malnutrition. In 1985, the foreign debt was $100 billion, the world's highest.

With a well-developed industrial base, Brazil has a varied economy. Industry produces steel, automobiles, chemicals, paper, and machinery. There is also some shipbuilding. Agricultural products include coffee (the world's largest producer), cotton, sugar, rice, and fruits. There is a wide variety of mineral resources, including diamonds.

The most recent per capita income figure is for 1978, when it was $1,523. The 1983 literacy rate was 75%

Philatelically, Brazil has a rich heritage. While most people think of nuts and coffee when they think of Brazil, most collectors think of "Bull's Eyes," the name for the first stamp issue. It consisted of three stamps released on Aug. 1, 1843. The "eye-like" effect of their design prompted their nickname. Brazil was the second country after Great Britain to release national adhesive postage stamps.

Its stamp-issuing history has reflected the country's political ups and downs, its geography, culture, and economic progress. A great number of stamps has been issued, but few are what collectors would regard as exploitive.

Philatelic Bureau: Empresa Brasileira de Correios e Telegrafos, Ed. Apolo, SCS, Quadra 13, Bl. A, Lote 36, 7° Andar, 70300 Brasilia DF, Brazil.

CHILE, REPUBLIC OF

Area: 292,135 sq. miles
Population: 11,655,000 (1984)
Capital: Santiago
Currency: Peso (100 centavos)

Chile is a long, narrow thread of a country with a 2,650-mile coastline along the west coast of southern South America. The average width is about 100 miles.

The climate is Mediterranean in the mid-portion, with desert in the north and forest in the south.

The western portion of Tierra del Fuego, with Easter Island and Juan Fernandes Island (Robinson Crusoe's island) in the Pacific belong to Chile.

A part of the Viceroyalty of Peru under Spain, the country was first settled by Europeans in 1541. It gained its independence in 1810.

Over the years, Chile prospered and became one of the continent's most advanced and developed countries. However, the brief Marxist regime of Salvador Allende Gossens led to economic chaos and the 1973 takeover by a military junta.

Industries include steel and textiles and there are extensive mineral resources, particularly copper. Agriculture is varied and there is an important wine industry.

Chile's first postage stamps were issued in 1853.

Current stamp-issuing policies are moderate and designs generally feature Chilean themes.

Philatelic Bureau: Departmento Filatelico, Subdireccion de Correos, Santiago, Chile.

COLOMBIA, REPUBLIC OF

Area: 440,831 sq. miles
Population: 28,248,000 (1984)
Capital: Bogota
Currency: Peso (100 centavos)

The only South American country with a coastline on both the Caribbean and Pacific, Colombia is a land of many valleys separated by rugged mountain ranges, which, until the coming of the airplane, greatly inhibited travel.

The country has three main areas. There is a flat coastal strip, central highlands, and eastern plains draining to the Orinoco and Amazon basins.

The climate ranges from hot and humid on the coast and the eastern plain to moderate and cool in the highlands. Bogota, at 8,630 feet, has an average high temperature of 65 degrees F and a low of 50 degrees F.

The area was made a Spanish colony in the mid-1500s with Bogota as its capital.

In 1717 Bogota became the capital of the Viceroyalty of New Granada that took in what is now Colombia, Venezuela, Eduador, and Panama.

Independence from Spain with Simon Bolivar as president was achieved in 1819 after several years of fighting. The new nation was known as the Republic of Greater Colombia. Venezuela and Ecuador broke away in 1830 and Panama became independent with US encouragement in 1903.

Colombia changed its name and political make-up several times, assuming its present name in 1886.

The 20th century opened on a scene of bloody civil war during which 100,000 people were killed. This was outdone by the period known as "The Violence" during the

1940s and 1950s, when up to 200,000 are said to have died. The country still faces many economic and social problems, including a very high birth rate.

Coffee is the mainstay of the economy. Other crops are rice, cotton, sugar, cotton, and bananas. Industrial production includes steel, cement, chemicals, textiles, and leather.

The 1981 per capita income was $1,112 and the literacy rate 82%.

The first stamps were issued in 1859 under the Granadine Confederation. Air mail stamps were first issued in 1919 for an experimental flight from Baranquilla to Puerto Colombia.

The country's dependence on the airplane for communications has resulted in a large number of air mail stamps.

Philatelic Bureau: Oficina Filatelica, Administracion Postal Nacional, Oficina 209, Edificio Murillo Toro, Bogota 1, Colombia.

ECUADOR, REPUBLIC OF

Area: 104,506 sq. miles
Population: 9,091,000 (1984)
Capital: Quito
Currency: Sucre (100 centavos)

There are three distinct geographical areas of Ecuador; the coastal plain, the highlands, and the eastern slope draining to the Amazon basin. Quito is located at 9,300 feet, while Guayaquil is the chief port and commercial center.

The hot and humid coastal region has temperatures from 65-90 degrees F and is the agricultural center. The highlands have spring weather year round with a temperature range of 50-70 degrees F.

There are several peaks above 16,000 feet, including *Cotopaxi,* the world's highest active volcano.

The Galapagos Islands, located about 600 miles west in the Pacific are also part of Ecuador. These are the islands, with their unusual fauna, that so intrigued Charles Darwin during his 19th century visit.

Although there have been ancient civilizations in the area, Ecuador's modern history begins with the coming of the Spanish in 1526.

Bartolome Ruiz landed there in that year, but settlement did not begin until 1532. Independence from Spanish rule came in 1819 and Ecuador became part of the Republic of Greater Colombia, which also included Colombia, Venezuela, and Panama.

The republic broke up in 1830 and the present independent state was born. Since then, the country's history has been one of revolution and there has been a succession of civilian and military dictatorships. The present democratic government dates from 1979.

Since the early 1970s, Ecuador's economy has been based on oil and falling prices have caused severe problems. The country is a large exporter of bananas and cocoa.

The 1983 per capita income was $1,428 and the 1984 literacy rate was 90%.

Ecuador's first stamp was issued in 1865. The country has been a prolific producer of stamps, especially air mails.

Philatelic Bureau: Departmento Filatelico, Museo Postal del Estado, Direccion General de Correos, Correo Central, Quito, Ecuador.

FALKLAND ISLANDS, BRITISH DEPENDENCY OF

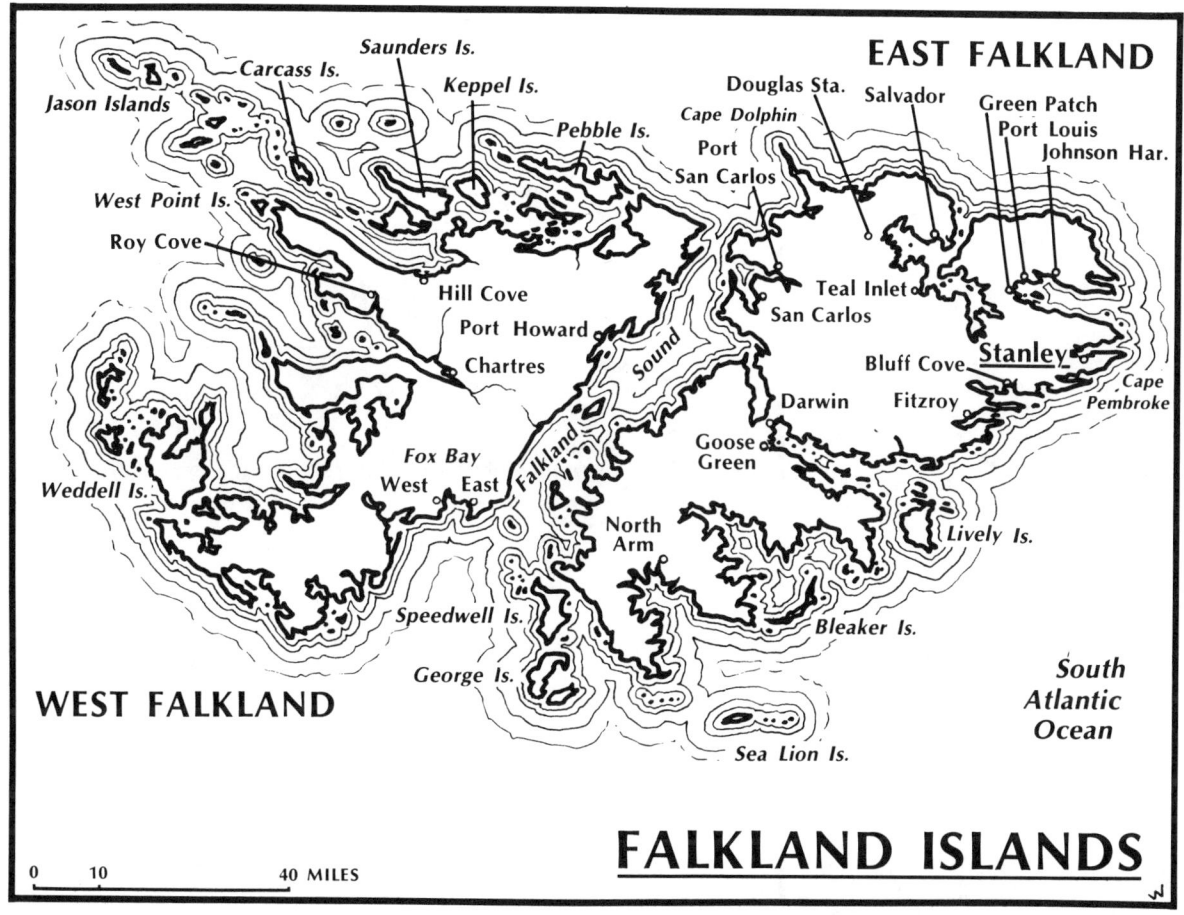

Area: 4,700 sq. miles
Population: 1,800 (1980)
Capital: Stanley
Currency: Pound (100 pence)

The Falkland Islands comprise about 200 islands in a tight group some 300 miles to the east of the southern tip of South America. The two main islands are East and West Falkland.

Hills rise to little more than 2,000 feet and for the most part the land is low, bare, and windswept. Peat is the chief source of fuel.

The natural vegetation consists mostly of grasses and attempts to introduce trees have failed.

The climate is cool and windy with an average temperature range of 36 degrees F in July to 49 degrees F in January. Frost can occur at any time of year. Stanley's rainfall is less than 30 inches a year, with generally light snowfall on about 50 days of the year.

The English navigator, John Davis, discovered the islands on Aug. 9, 1592, although a landing did not take place until 1690, when Captain John Strong named the islands for Viscount Falkland, then treasurer of the Royal Navy.

Subsequent to this, the French established a settlement but handed it over to Spain in 1766. In 1765, the British had built a fort at Port Egmont and formally claimed the islands. Spain and Britain competed for ownership until 1833, when the Spanish were evicted.

The islands became a crown colony on Feb. 29, 1892.

Britain held the islands unopposed until Argentine forces invaded and briefly occupied the islands in 1982. Within 2½ months they were expelled by a British task force.

Sheep are the backbone of the economy and wool is the main export. Recently, oil and gas deposits have been located in waters around the islands.

Stamps were first issued in 1878. The 1933 Centennial issue is considered to be one of the modern classic issues.

Recent stamps have maintained a high standard of design and production and they have retained their popularity among collectors. Although stamps have increased in number, issue policies have remained moderate.

Philatelic Bureau: Postmaster, Philatelic Bureau, GPO, Stanley, Falkland Islands.

GUYANA, COOPERATIVE REPUBLIC OF

Area: 83,000 sq. miles
Population: 775,000 (1984)
Capital: Georgetown
Currency: Dollar (100 cents)

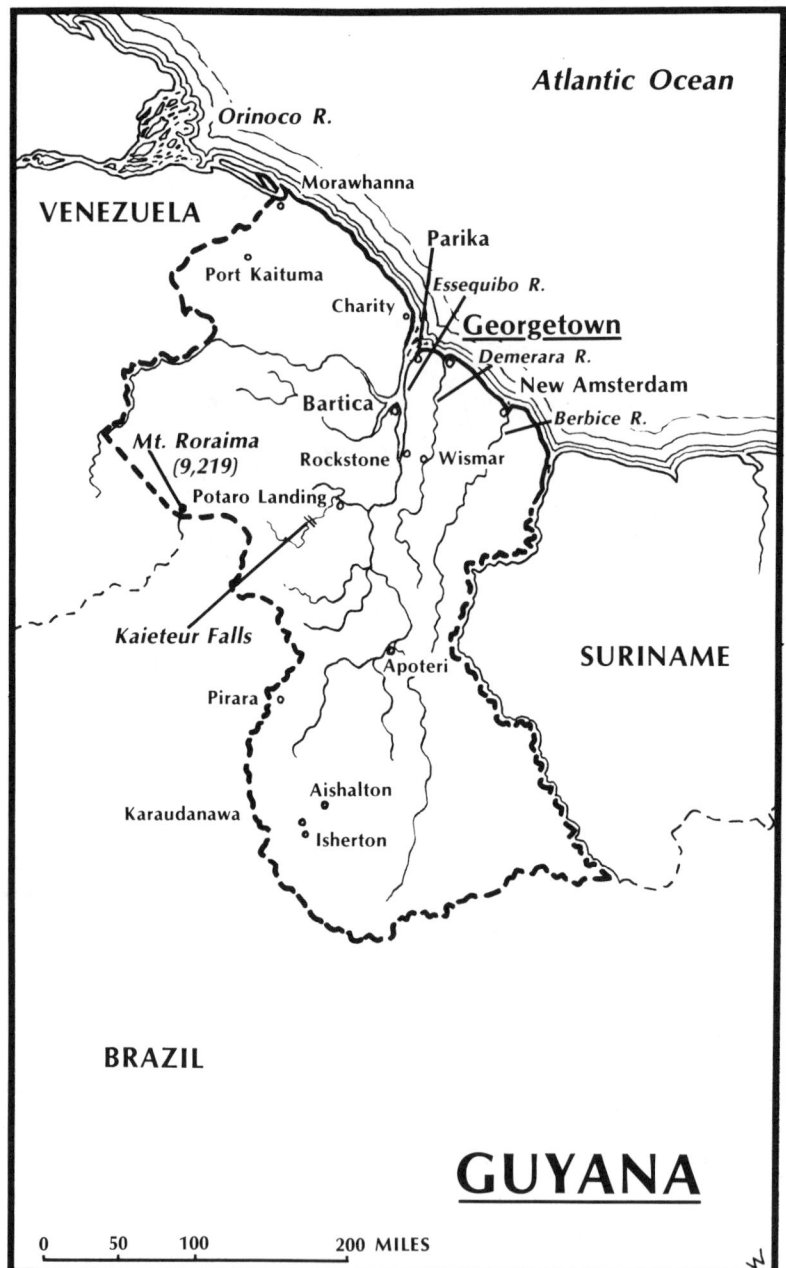

Formerly the colony of British Guiana, this little-known area has a coastal strip up to 40 miles in width, a large central rain forest zone, and open savannah in the extreme south.

The country is well watered by large river systems, which are used for transportation in the navigable lower reaches. The three major rivers are the Essequibo, the Demerara, and the Berbice. The Essequibo is joined near Bartica by the rivers Cuyuni and Mazaruni.

The climate is tropical and moist. Along the coast temperatures vary from 70-90 degrees F and they are 80-100 degrees in the interior. Rainfall can exceed 100 inches a year in some areas.

Columbus sighted the coast in 1498, but the flat coastal lands did not attract the seekers after gold and other treasure.

The Dutch were the first to settle in the late 1500s. Apart from a brief period of French occupation, control alternated between the Dutch and British. In 1814, it became a British colony. Gradual preparation for self-rule resulted in independence on May 26, 1966.

Tension between various racial elements has kept the political pot boiling and there has been much unrest and violence. The government nationalized most of the economy and the country remains depressed and undeveloped, with many once-efficient services in a deteriorated condition. Sugar is the traditional backbone of the economy, but rice and citrus are

grown. Mineral resources include bauxite and diamonds.

The 1983 per capita income was $457 and the 1985 literacy rate was 86%.

Guyana is famous in the philatelic world for its 1c magenta stamp of 1856, the only known copy of which was sold in 1980 for $850,000, the highest price ever paid for a single stamp off cover.

Stamps were first issued in 1850 and many of the early colonial stamps are expensive classics. In recent years, there has been an enormous flood of overprints and surcharges of every conceivable type and collector interest in the country's stamps is currently minimal.

Philatelic Bureau: Guyana Post Office Corporation, Robb St., Georgetown, Guyana.

PARAGUAY, REPUBLIC OF

Area: 157,047 sq. miles
Population: 3,623,000 (1984)
Capital: Asuncion
Currency: Guarani (100 centimos)

Landlocked Paraguay has access to the sea by water via the Parana-Paraguay river systems to the River Plate.

The Paraguay River splits the country into two very different regions. The eastern part is temperate with a mixture of rolling grassland and wooded country, while the western portion is sparsely inhabited swampy forest.

Temperatures at Asuncion range from 55 degrees F in winter to more than 100 degrees in summer.

Paraguay's population grew around its capital city, which was established Aug. 15, 1537. The Jesuits set up agricultural colonies in the area, which declined when they were expelled in 1767. Independence from Spain came in 1811.

By 1814 a republican government was in power. It isolated itself from the outside world, even to the extent of prohibiting traffic on the Paraguay River.

In 1864-70, the country fought in the disastrous War of the Triple Alliance with Argentina, Brazil, and Uruguay. It suffered a terrible defeat. At war's end half the population had been killed and the inhabitants numbered some 250,000, more than 200,000 of whom were women.

Since World War II, there has been political instability with right-wing factions exercising considerable oppression. The country became a haven for German war criminals.

Most of the workforce is engaged in agriculture and corn, wheat, cotton, peanuts, and tobacco are the main crops.

The 1983 per capita income was $1,600 and the 1984 literacy rate was 83%.

The first stamps were released in 1870 and subsequent issues followed a typical South American pattern.

The country's present philatelic reputation is very poor and an enormous quantity of gaudy items have been issued that are not recognized by the world's major stamp catalogs.

Philatelic Bureau: Oficina Filatelica, Direccion General de Correos, Asuncion, Paraguay.

PERU, REPUBLIC OF

Area: 496,220 sq. miles
Population: 19,157,000 (1984)
Capital: Lima
Currency: Sol (100 centavos)

The third-largest country in South America, Peru has three topographical areas. There is an arid coastal belt, the Andes Mountains that run up the spine of the country and rise to 22,200-foot Mount Huascaran, and the eastern lowlands that cover more than 50% of Peru and drain to the Amazon basin.

The climate is mild on the coast, while in the Andes it varies from temperate to frigid depending on altitude. The eastern portion is hot and humid with high rainfall.

Little is known of Peru's history before the Incas established an empire with their capital at Cuzco. By the 16th century, this empire reached from the source of the Amazon to the Pacific and from what is now Ecuador to Chile.

The Spanish arrived in the 1530s and set about plundering the Incas of their great store of gold and silver, carting it home to Spain in their galleons. The Incas were treated brutally and when uprisings occured, they were cruelly put down.

Jose de San Martin of Argentina began to lead Peru to independence from Spain in 1821. Peru gained its freedom when Simon Bolivar defeated the last Spanish forces at Ayacucho in December 1824.

Since then, Peru has been ruled by a succession of military and civilian dictators and coup has followed coup, with revolution and counter revolution thrown in for good measure.

Terrorism, unrest, and strikes have hurt the economy in recent years and inflation has added to the people's burden.

Minerals constitute Peru's main wealth. The 1979 per capita income was $655 and the 1978 literacy rate was 72%.

Communications are a problem in Peru. One rail line crosses the Andes and climbs to 15,693 feet to do so. It is the highest point reached by any standard-gauge railway.

Peru's first stamps came in 1857 in the form of two supplied by the Pacific Steam Navigation Co.

In common with many South American countries, Peru's air mail stamps have formed a large portion of the total stamp emissions, but with difficult land communications, the country early saw the advantages of air transport.

Philatelic Bureau: Chief, Philatelic Postal Museum, GPO, Lima, Peru.

SOUTH AMERICA

SURINAME

Area: 63,037 sq. miles
Population: 370,000 (1984)
Capital: Paramaribo
Currency: Guilder (100 cents)

Suriname's topography comprises three main areas. Like neighboring Guyana, the coastal strip is flat and often below sea level. Dikes are necessary in order to work the land. Most of the agriculture takes place along the coast. The central portion of the country is mixed forest and savannah, while the southern part is hilly and thickly forested.

The annual rainfall at Paramaribo averages about 90 inches and the year round temperature is about 70-90 degrees F.

Columbus sighted the coast of Suriname in 1498, but the low-lying land did not attract the seekers after gold and other riches. The first settlement was not made until 1651.

In that year the British established a settlement. Among the early arrivals were a number of Jews who, in 1665, built the first synagogue in the Western Hemisphere. The colony prospered, growing sugar, coffee, cocoa, and cotton.

Under the Treaty of Breda in 1667, the Netherlands received the area in exchange for what is now the city of New York.

After a period of neglect by the Dutch and occupation by Britain and France, the region finally became the colony of Dutch Guiana. On Dec. 15, 1954, it was made part of the Kingdom of the Netherlands and achieved complete independence on Nov. 25, 1975.

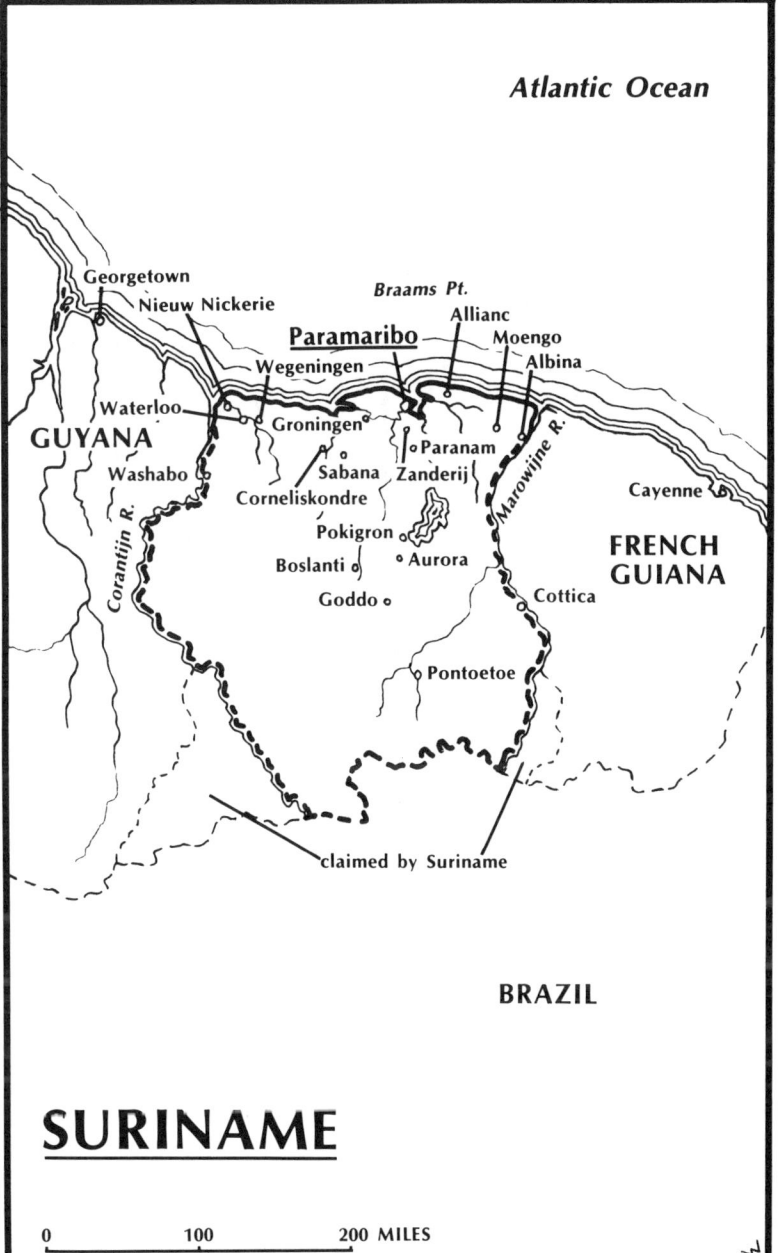

In February 1982, the National Military Council took over the country and the Netherlands cut off all aid.

Bauxite is the backbone of Suriname's economy. Rice, sugar, and fruit are the chief crops.

The 1981 per capita income was reported as $2,600 and the 1984 literacy rate was 65%.

Suriname's first stamps were issued in 1873 and they subsequently followed a pattern similar to those of the Netherlands.

Over the years, the country has issued a number of attractive issues picturing the people, culture, and scenery. There have been a large number of semi-postal issues.

Philatelic Bureau: Postal Administration, Philatelic Department, Paramaribo, Suriname.

URUGUAY, ORIENTAL REPUBLIC OF

Area: 68,040 sq. miles
Population: 2,926,000 (1984)
Capital: Montevideo
Currency: New peso

Uruguay is a land of rolling grasslands with some low hills. It has a temperate climate and freezing temperatures are virtually unknown. The average summer temperature is 71 degrees F and in winter it is 50 degrees F.

Rain falls throughout the year and there is no defined wet and dry season. The average annual rainfall is about 35 inches on the coast with decreasing amounts inland. Most rain falls in autumn.

European exploration of what is now Uruguay occurred during the early 1500s.

A lack of mineral wealth and a native population very much inclined to hang on to its territory, tended to discourage early attempts at colonization.

When the inhabitants were finally pacified by missionaries, the land became mostly cattle range and cattle raising has traditionally been the main occupation in the country.

The Spanish and Portuguese, and later the Brazilians, fought over the area and it became a sort of buffer state between Portuguese Brazil and Spanish Argentina.

Strangely, it was the British in 1807 — during the Napoleonic Wars when Spain was allied with France — who occupied the city of Montevideo and brought the people a taste for independence.

The British regime was less repressive than that of Spain and the local population was impressed.

Sadly, when independence did come in 1828, there were more than 40 years of internal strife before the people could set about building a country.

After a tumultuous beginning, the country settled down and by the turn of the century it was one of the world's more advanced societies. Its standard of living was the highest in South America and its government the most liberal.

In recent years, economic problems and severe inflation have caused social unrest and there has been a period of military rule.

Meat packing and wine loom large in the economy. Considerable grain is grown and other crops include citrus fruit and corn.

The 1980 per capita income was $2,780 and the 1978 literacy rate was 94%.

The first stamps were issued in 1856. They are the so-called Carrier Issues and are inscribed "DILIGENCIA."

Philatelic Bureau: Direccion Nacional de Correos, Departamento de Filatelica, Casilla de Correo 1296, Montevideo, Uruguay.

VENEZUELA, REPUBLIC OF

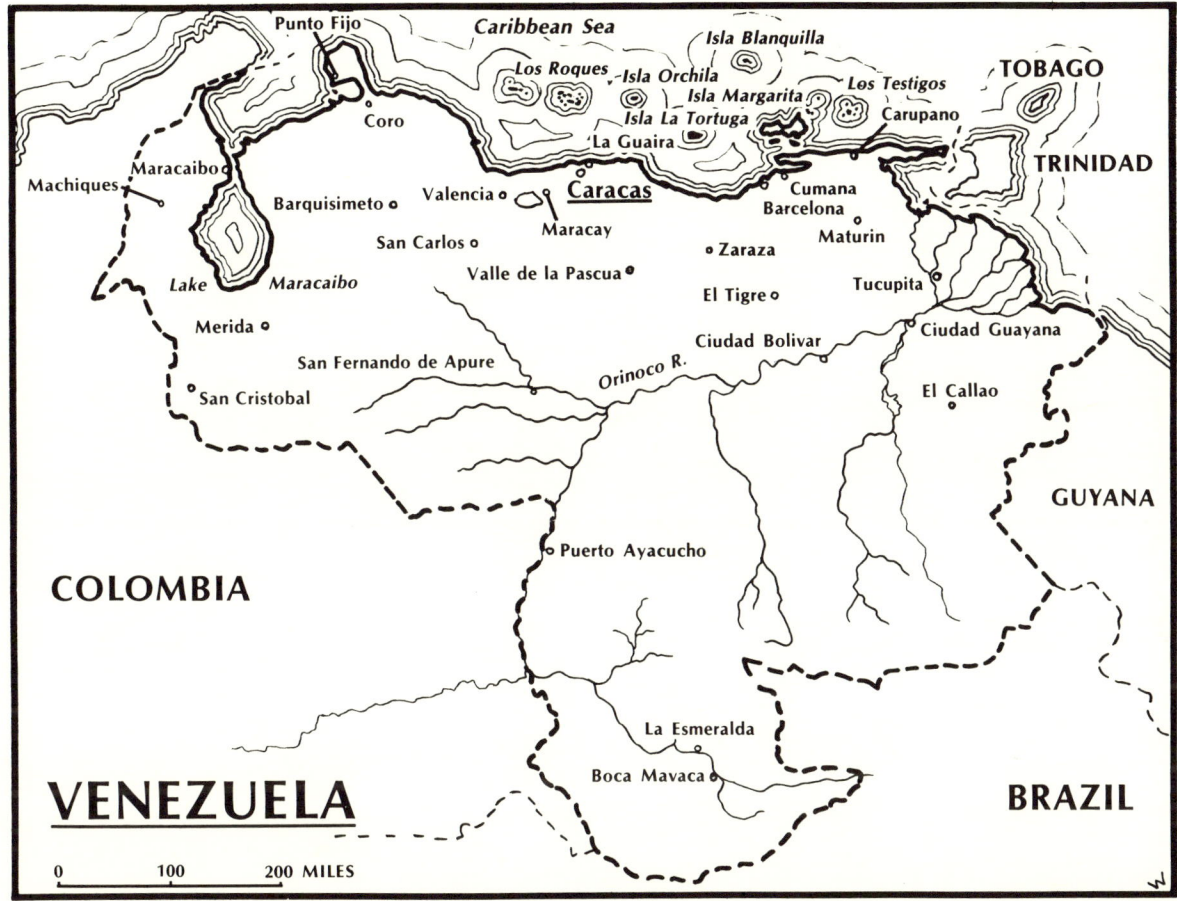

Area: 352,143 sq. miles
Population: 18,552,000 (1984)
Capital: Caracas
Currency: Bolivar (100 centimos)

Venezuela's name means "Little Venice" and it was given when early explorers saw native houses built on stilts over shallow Lake Maracaibo. The country has four topographical areas; the Andes and associated ranges in the northwest, the coastal strip including Lake Maracaibo in the west and the

Orinoco delta in the east, and the central plain and the high plateau to the south and east of the Orinoco River.

The climate varies with the region. The lowlands are hot and humid with an average temperature of 80 degrees F and the highlands are hot during the days and cool at night. Caracas, at 3,000 feet, has an average temperature of 70 degrees F.

Discovered by Columbus in 1498, Venezuela was a Spanish colony until 1821. From then to 1830, it was part of the Republic of Greater Colombia, when it assumed its present status.

Venezuela's history has been marked by political instability and a succession of dictators. In recent years a more democratic situation has prevailed.

Its large oil industry (it is the world's fifth largest producer) has suffered from lower prices and the economy is shaky. Other industrial products are steel, textiles, and paper. Crops grown include coffee, rice, fruit, and sugar.

Despite economic problems, the country is prosperous by South American standards and oil profits have been used to finance a national development program.

The 1982 per capita income was $4,716, although lower oil prices will undoubtedly have caused a more recent decline, and the 1984 literacy rate was 86%.

The first stamps of Venezuela were issued in 1859 and feature the country's coat of arms.

During the 1950s, a continuing series of several hundred stamps was issued depicting the coats of arms of the various districts of the country.

Philatelic Bureau: Direccion de Correos, Oficina Filatelica Nacional, Caracas, Venezuela.

EUROPE

Stamp issuing areas:

1. Aland Islands (Finland)
2. Albania
3. Alderney (UK)
4. Andorra
5. Austria
6. Azores (Portugal)
7. Belgium
8. Berlin, West (Germany)
9. Bulgaria
10. Cyprus (plus Turkish)
11. Czechoslovakia
12. Denmark
13. England (UK)
14. Faroe Islands
15. Finland
16. France
17. Germany, East
18. Germany, West
19. Gibraltar
20. Greece
21. Greenland
22. Guernsey (UK)
23. Hungary
24. Iceland
25. Ireland
26. Isle of Man (UK)
27. Italy
28. Jersey (UK)
29. Liechtenstein
30. Luxembourg
31. Malta
32. Monaco
33. Netherlands
34. Northern Ireland (UK)
35. Norway
36. Poland
37. Portugal
38. Romania
39. San Marino
40. Scotland (UK)
41. Spain
42. Sweden
43. Switzerland
44. USSR
45. Vatican City
46. Wales (UK)
47. Yugoslavia

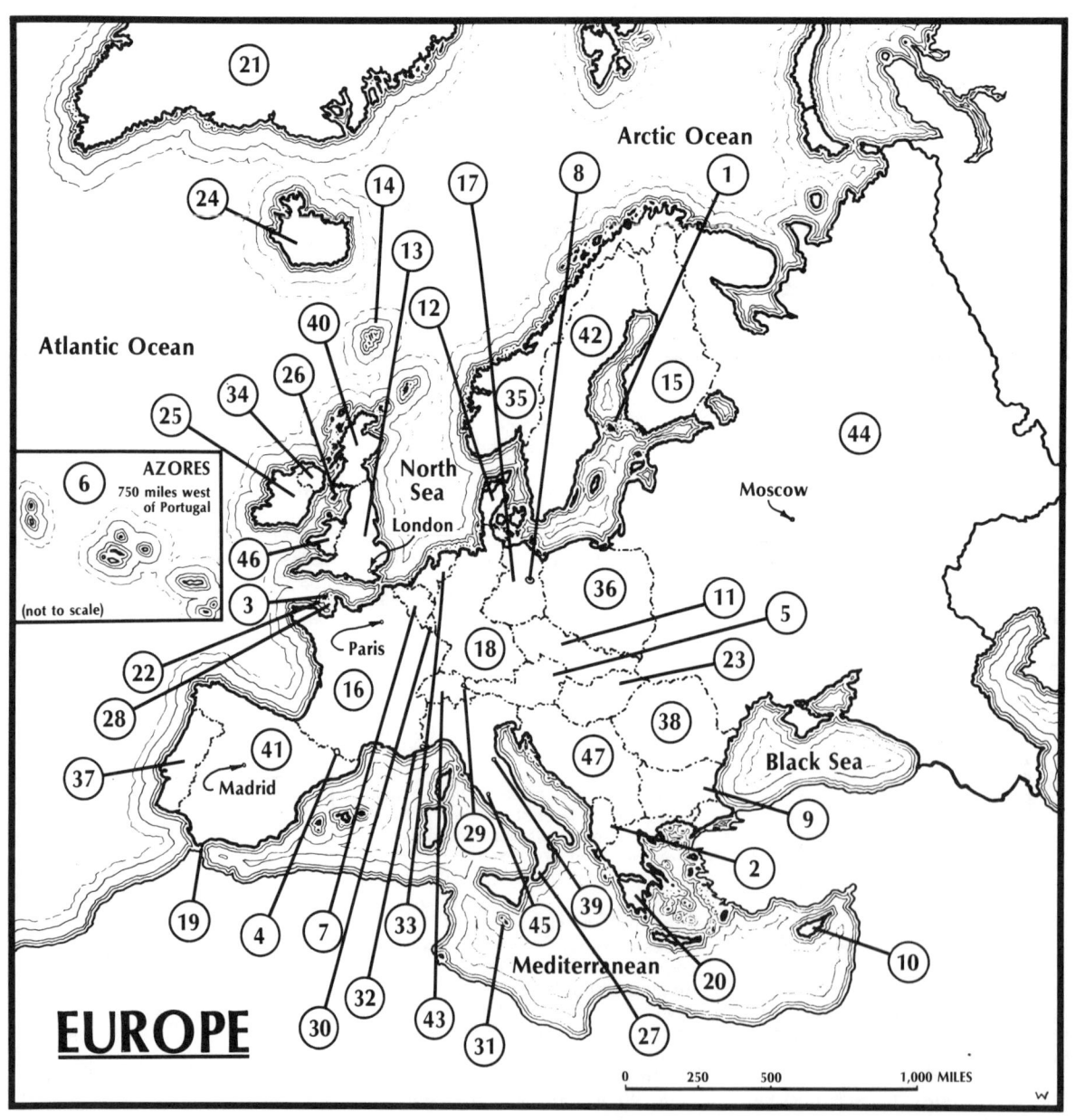

ALBANIA, SOCIALIST REPUBLIC OF

Area: 11,100 sq. miles
Population: 2,906,000 (1983)
Capital: Tirane
Currency: Lek (100 qintar)

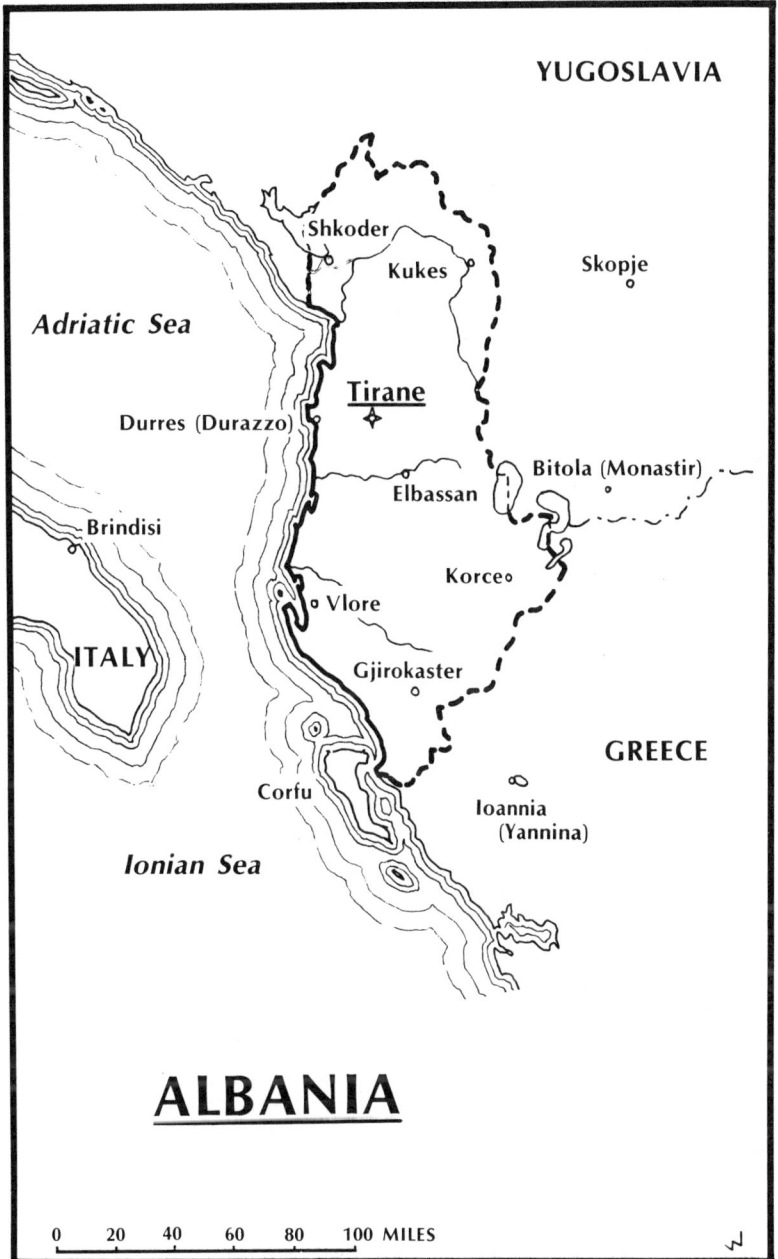

Albania's local name, Shqiperi, translates as "Eagle Country" and this well describes the small, mountainous land on the Adriatic Sea.

About one-fifth of the area is coastal plain and the rest is rugged, scrub-covered mountains. The only navigable river flows from Lake Scutari near Shkoder, to the Adriatic.

Hot summers and mild winters prevail along the coast, with temperatures ranging from a low of 40 degrees F in the winter to 83 degrees F in the summer. The interior is cooler.

For many years a tribal society, the people of Albania were once subjects of the Byzantine Empire. They later fell under Serbian domination before becoming part of the Ottoman Empire.

Independence came hard to Albania, but in 1912, the Turks yielded to a national uprising and on Nov. 28, independence was proclaimed. However, the fight for a national identity continued, as the Serbs and the Greeks sought to take territory from the new country. The situation was still chaotic when World War I broke out and Albania was occupied by various of the belligerents. During that conflict, the Balkan pot continued to boil as the Austro-Hungarian Empire lashed out in its death throes and the Ottoman Empire also was forced to relinquish its hold over the area.

During 1921, with many Albanians tired of waiting for the victors to solve the problem of Balkan boun-

daries, a congress was held in the country and a national government formed.

In 1939, Italy invaded and conquered Albania, turning it into an Italian province. When the Germans invaded the Balkans during World War II, they replaced the Italians and Albania inherited another master.

After the Germans had been driven out, the communists came to power and began a reign of terror, with summary executions of anyone opposed to their regime.

The country is poor. There is little industry and agriculture is restricted by lack of land. The 1979 per capita income figure was $830. The 1983 literacy rate was 75%.

Stamps were first issued in 1913 and were overprints on Turkish stamps.

Philatelic Bureau: Exportal, Rue 4 Shkurti, Tirane, Albania. Services provided are not known.

ANDORRA, PRINCIPALITY OF

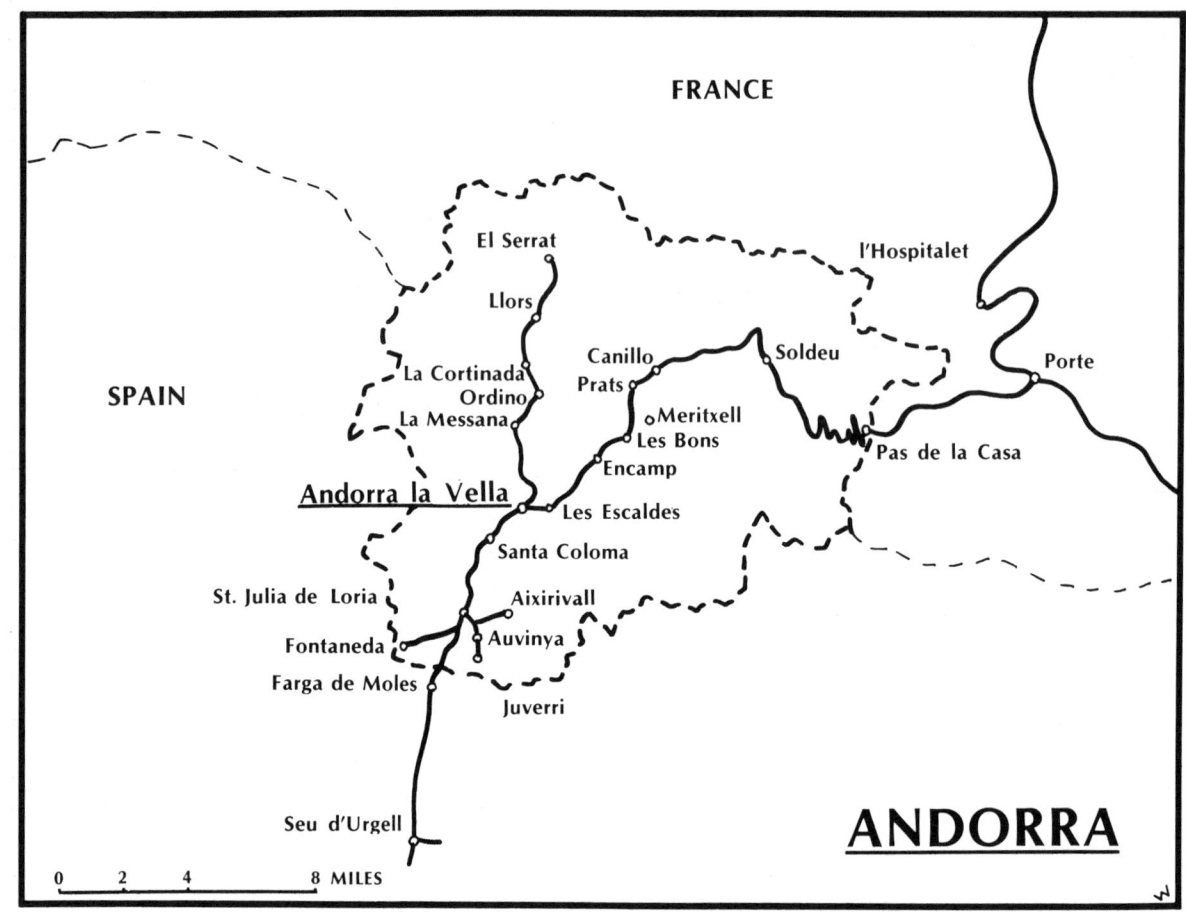

Area: 188 sq. miles
Population: 45,000 (1984)
Capital: Andorra la Vella
Currency: Franc (French), Peseta (Spanish)

Located high in the Pyrenees Mountains between France and Spain, Andorra's terrain is mostly vertical. The peaks rise to more than 9,000 feet and the population lives in six narrow valleys.

Summers are cool and dry, attracting many vacationers. Heavy snow over a six-month winter season makes Andorra a popular ski-resort area. There is good trout fishing in the many mountain streams.

Legend has it that in AD 806, Charlemagne drove the Moors from what is now Andorra and then personally thanked the inhabitants for their help.

In 1278, the French count of Foix and the Spanish bishop of Seo de Urgel agreed to act as co-princes of Andorra. That set a pattern of joint rule by France and Spain that has persisted to this day.

There is little agriculture, although sheep are raised and tobacco grown. A hydroelectric plant exports power to both Spain and France.

Philatelically, Andorra is unique. It has no postal administration of its own, but both France and Spain operate post services in the principality.

Despite this, the country needs no postage stamps for its internal use, since all domestic mail is carried free of charge. Stamps are only used on mail that is addressed outside the borders of the principality.

Postage stamps for Andorra were first issued by the Spanish Post Office in Andorra in 1928 and these were followed in 1931 by stamps issued by the French Post Office.

Philatelic Bureau (French): Service Philatelique des Postes et Telecommunications, 61-63 rue de Douai, 75436 Paris, France.

Philatelic Bureau (Spain): Direccion General de Correos, Servicio Filatelico International, Madrid 14, Spain.

Stamps of French (top) and Spanish Andorra.

AUSTRIA, REPUBLIC OF

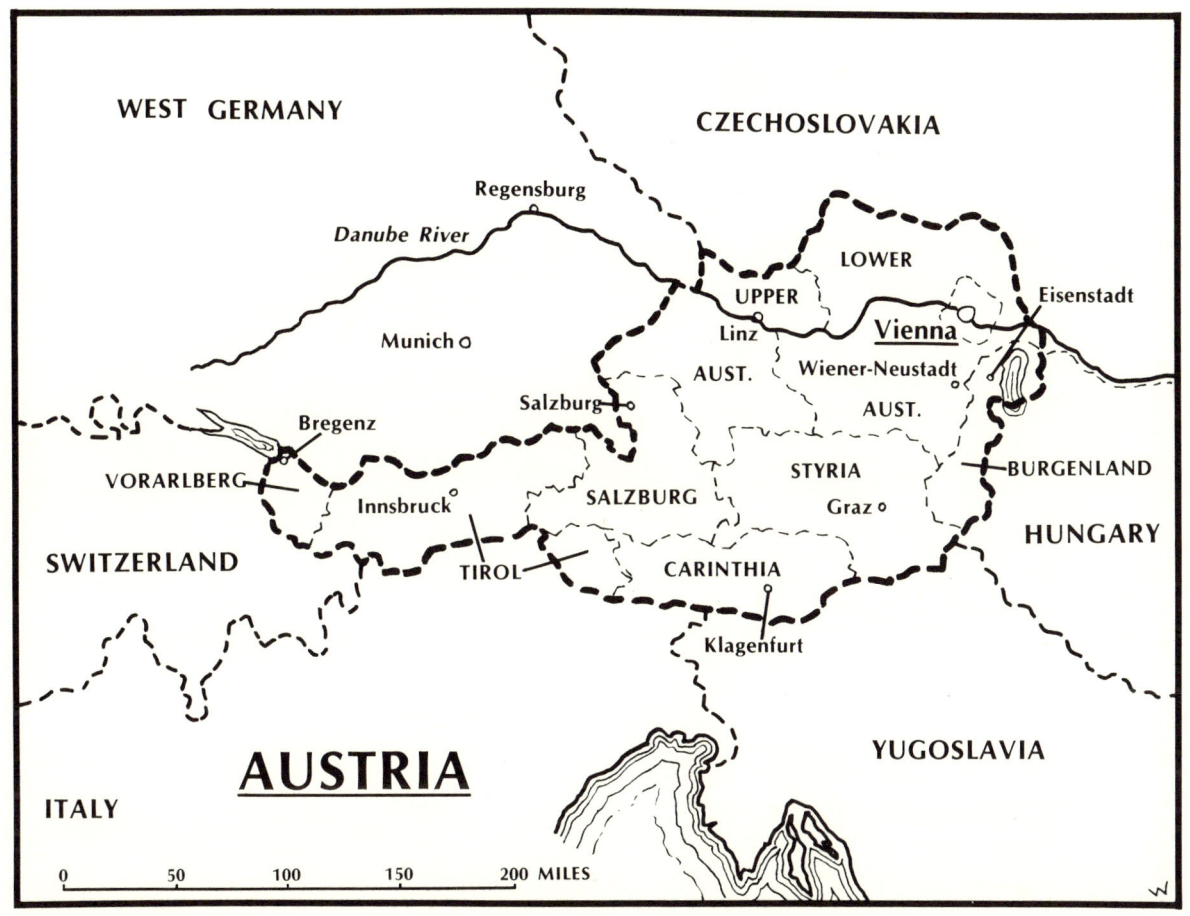

Area: 32,374 sq. miles
Population: 7,579,000 (1984)
Capital: Vienna
Currency: Schilling (100 groschen)

Now only a shadow of its former self, the Republic of Austria was once the dominant partner in an empire that included much of Eastern Europe and the Balkans.

The House of Habsburg (Hapsburg) developed as a power as early as the 14th century in much of what was later the Austro-Hungarian Empire.

The dual Austro-Hungarian monarchy was established in 1867 and existed in relative peace until the outbreak of World War I in 1914, when Austrian demands on Serbia following the assassination of Archduke Franz Ferdinand, the Habsburg heir and his wife Sophie at Sarajevo, triggered general war.

During the war, Austro-Hungary was allied with Germany and the Turkish Empire in a grouping known as the Central Powers.

The war proved the downfall of the Austro-Hungarian Empire and it collapsed, leaving a postwar Austria with about the same borders that it has today.

There was a dark period from 1938 to 1945, when Austria disappeared into the German Third Reich, to emerge at the end of World War II, beaten, battered, and occupied by the victorious allies.

Located at the crossroads of Europe and a bridge between East and West, Austria is a prosperous nation, pledged to neutrality.

Its spectacular mountain scenery and artistic and architectural heritage, makes it a country popular with tourists.

With an economy tied to the rest of Europe, Austria made a rapid recovery after World War II. It has a prosperous industrial base, producing steel, machinery, automobiles, glassware, textiles, and a range of other products. A number of agricultural crops are also important and mineral resources include iron, oil, coal, and copper.

The 1980 per capita income was $8,280 and the 1983 literacy rate was 98%.

The first stamps were issued in 1850. The country's postal history is long, varied, and interesting.

Philatelic Bureau: Oesterreichische Post, Briefmarkenversandstelle, A-1011 Vienna, Austria.

BELGIUM KINGDOM OF

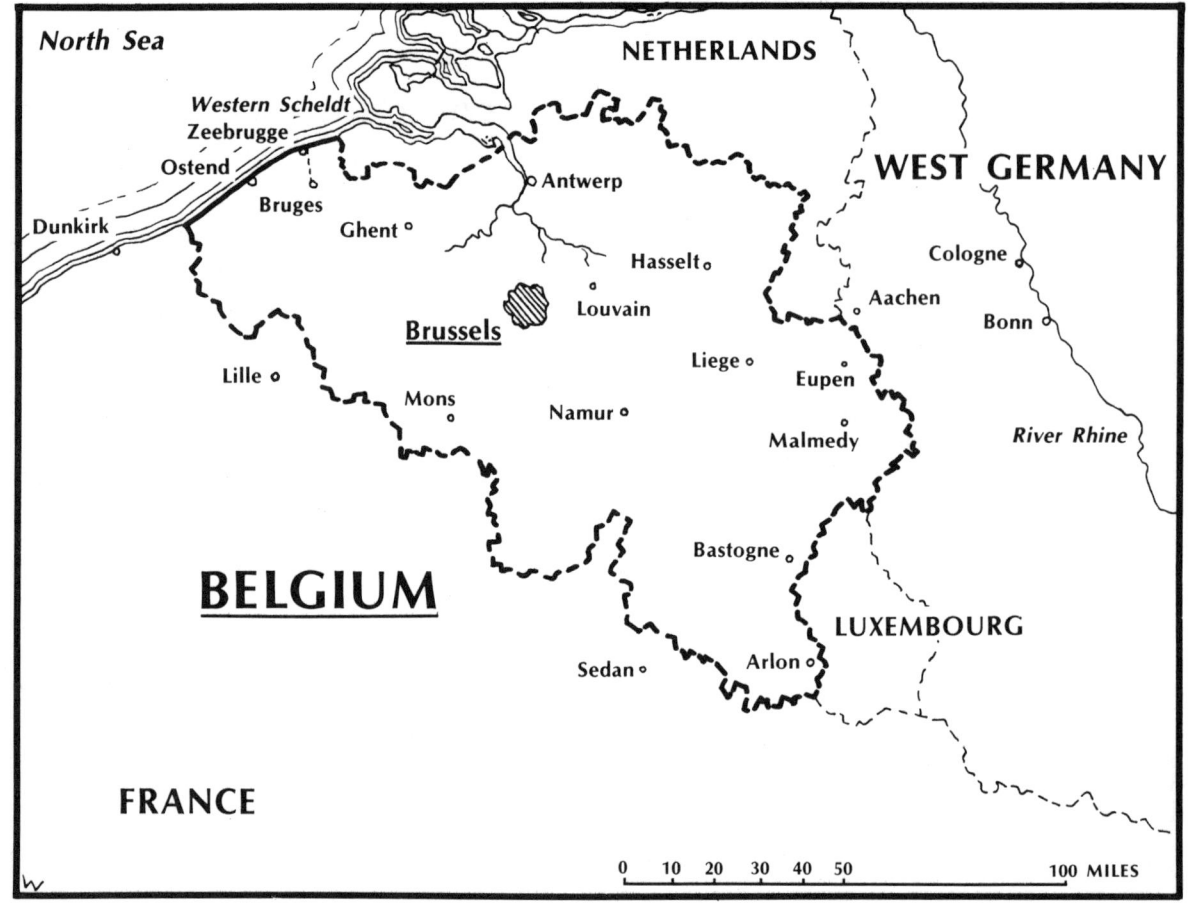

Area: 11,779 sq. miles
Population: 9,872,000 (1984)
Capital: Brussels
Currency: Franc (100 centimes)

Located in Western Europe, with a coastline on the North Sea, Belgium is mostly flat, with a hilly, wooded Ardennes region in the southeastern part.

The climate is cool, with an average high temperature in summer of 60 degrees F.

The country gets its name from an ancient Celtic people called the Belgae. The Roman province of *Gallia Belgiea* encompassed what is now Belgium plus a great deal more territory.

During the Spanish occupation, Belgium remained loyal to Spain while the Netherlands was fighting for its freedom.

Following years of war between France and Spain, Belgium remained a pawn in the power struggle and ended up belonging to Austria. Under the Austrians the country prospered. When Austria went to war with France, poor Belgium was once more occupied.

In 1815, the Congress of Vienna united Belgium with the Netherlands. Independence came in 1830 and Prince Leopold of Saxe-Coburg was made King of the Belgians.

Belgium again knew the invader's tread in 1914 and 1940. In both cases the invader was Germany and the country suffered brutal periods of occupation.

Unlike King Albert, who resisted the Germans in World War I and became a hero, Leopold gave up his country in 1940 and as a result, lost his throne when his country was freed.

An industrialized country, Belgium produces steel, chemicals, textiles, and glassware and is a diamond cutting center. Grains, potatoes, and sugar beet are important crops. The 1981 per capita income was $9,827 and the 1983 literacy rate was 98%.

Stamps were first issued in 1849. In the past, enormous surtaxes on its many semi-postal issues have raised the ire of collectors. Some amounted to as much as 40fr on a 5fr stamp.

Philatelic Bureau: Regie des Postes, Service des Collectionneur, Division 1.3.0.2., 1000 Brussels, Belgium.

BULGARIA, PEOPLE'S REPUBLIC OF

Area: 44,365 sq. miles
Population: 8,969,000 (1984)
Capital: Sofia
Currency: Lev (100 stotinki)

Bulgaria is located on the Balkan peninsula, with a coastline on the Black Sea. Its northern border with Romania is formed mostly by the Danube River.

The country's average elevation is 1,575 feet and summer temperatures range from 65-85 degrees F. Nights are cool. Precipitation averages 25 inches a year, with much of this falling as snow.

The first recorded mention of the Bulgars, who gave their name to the country, occurred in the fifth century AD. The early history of the area is one of tribal warfare and much coming and going of tribes.

Into this ebb and flow of the population moved the Turks. By 1400, the Turks began a domination that lasted for 500 years. Not until 1878 did the principality of Bulgaria win any measure of independence.

On Oct. 5, 1908, as Turkish power declined, Ferdinand, who had come to power in 1887, declared Bulgaria an independent kingdom, with himself as ruler.

In World War I, Bulgaria sided with the Central Powers and was defeated. In 1939, still hopeful of gaining back what had been lost in the past, Bulgaria again hitched its wagon to the German star, and again backed a loser.

As vengeful Soviet forces loomed on its borders, Bulgaria quickly switched sides and tried to eject the remaining Germans. Occupying the country, the Soviet Union held war crimes trials, killed 2,680 of those charged and imprisoned about 7,000.

Since then, the country has been firmly under Soviet control.

Industrial products include chemicals, metals, furs, motor vehicles, textiles, and wine. Fruit, corn, potatoes, and tobacco are grown. Lead, bauxite, coal, oil, and zinc are among Bulgaria's mineral resources.

The 1980 per capita income was $2,625 and the 1983 literacy rate was 95%.

The first Bulgarian stamps were issued in 1879.

Philatelic Bureau: Ministere du Transport et Communications, Service Philatelique Postal, 44 Rue Dencoglou, Sofia, Bulgaria.

CYPRUS, REPUBLIC OF

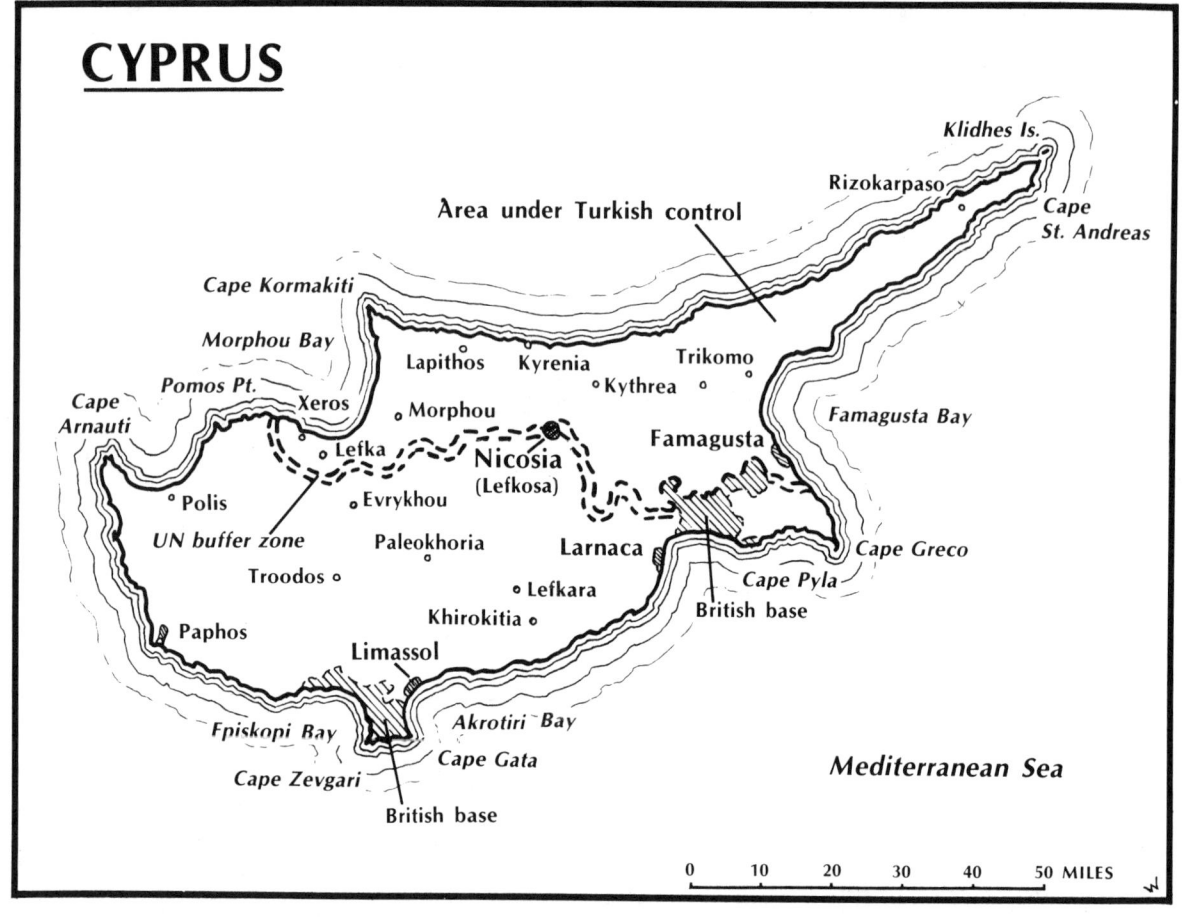

Area: 3,512 sq. miles
Population: 662,000 (1984)
Capital: Nicosia
Currency: Pound (100 cents)

Cyprus, the third largest island in the Mediterranean, is located in the northeast corner of that sea, about 40 miles off the shore of Turkish Asia Minor.

The island has mountains rising to 6,400 feet in the southwest and along the north coast. The climate is hot and dry during the summer and mild with some rain in winter. The average temperature is 70 degrees F and the rainfall each year is some 20 inches.

The history of Cyprus goes back to 1450 BC, when Egypt occupied it. The Greeks established a settlement soon after and the Phoenicians arrived about 800 BC.

Turkey ruled the island for 300 years until the Turkish-Russian War of 1877-78, when it persuaded Britain to administer the island. It became a British crown colony in 1925 and was given its independence on Aug. 16, 1960. Britain, Greece, and Turkey agreed to respect the new country, but clashes between the island's Greek and Turkish elements culminated in a Turkish invasion and occupation of the northern 40% of the island on July 20, 1974.

The Turkish-occupied area declared independence on Nov. 15, 1983 as the Turkish Republic of Northern Cyprus, but its declaration has not been recognized by other nations.

The 1983 per capita income was $3,986 and the 1984 literacy rate was 99%.

The first stamps were issued in 1880. Since independence, its stamps have had a distinctly Greek flavor. When the Turks set up a postal service in the north, its stamps looked very Turkish!

Philatelic Bureau: Philatelic Service, GPO, Nicosia, Cyprus.

For Turkish Cyprus: Turkish Republic of Northern Cyprus, Directorate of Postal Dept. (Lefkosa), Mersin 10, Turkey.

Stamps of Turkish Cyprus (right) and the republic (below).

CZECHOSLOVAK SOCIALIST REPUBLIC

Area: 49,350 sq. miles
Population: 15,466,000 (1984)
Capital: Prague
Currency: Koruna (100 haleru)

Czechoslovakia, in the heart of Central Europe, comprises Bohemia and Moravia in the west with Slovakia at its eastern end.

The west is a plateau surrounded by mountains; there is a hilly region in the center, and a mountainous region in the northeast with plains in the southeast. The climate is temperate, with cool summers and wet winters.

Until the end of World War I, the area that is now Czechoslovakia was part of the Austro-Hungarian Empire. Its independence was proclaimed on Oct. 30, 1918, but its life as an independent nation was brief.

By the late 1930s, a recovered and aggressive Germany began to foment unrest among the German minority in the country and then used it as an excuse to demand territory.

At the Munich conference in September 1938, Britain and France agreed to those demands in exchange for German promises not to make further trouble. Czechoslovakia paid a bitter price for that error of judgement. In March 1939, Germany invaded and occupied the entire country, setting up a brutal protectorate over Bohemia and Moravia and establishing a puppet regime in Slovakia.

The country was finally liberated by US and Soviet forces, but German occupation was exchanged for that of the Soviet Union. Now firmly under Soviet domination, Czechoslovakia made one more try for freedom in 1968. Soviet forces crushed the government and its military occupied the country. Since then, it has permitted no Czech opposition.

Although possessing the healthiest economy in the Soviet bloc, Czechoslovakia's standing as a developed industrial and technological nation has diminished under Soviet control. The 1980 per capita income was $5,800 and the 1981 literacy rate was 99%.

The first stamps were issued in 1918.

Philatelic Bureau: Artia Foreign Trade Corp., PO Box 790, Prague 1, Czechoslovakia.

DENMARK, KINGDOM OF

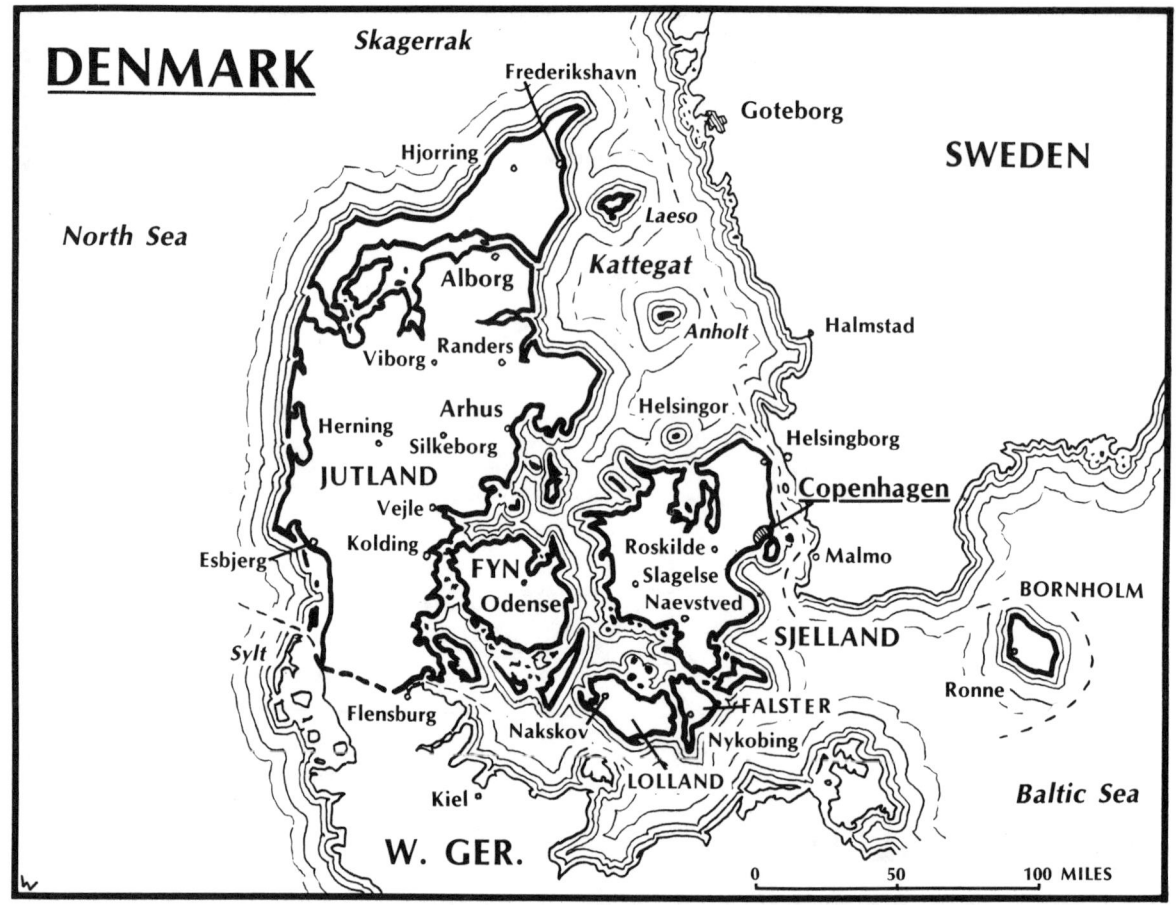

Area: 16,630 sq. miles
Population: 5,110,000 (1984)
Capital: Copenhagen
Currency: Krone (100 ore)

Denmark occupies a strategic location at the entrance to the Baltic Sea from the North Sea. It comprises the Jutland Peninsula and about 500 islands, some 100 of which are inhabited.

The land is flat and intensively

cultivated. It has a temperate climate, with winter temperatures from 20-40 degrees F and up to 70 degrees F in summer.

Denmark today is but a shadow of her former self. It was once a major power in Northern Europe and Scandinavia. Its territory extended into Norway and Sweden and across the North Sea to England, which it ruled until 1035.

During the late 1300s, Denmark was a leading Baltic power and acquired Iceland and the Faroes. In the 15th and 16th centuries, it was the dominant country in the Kalmar Union of Denmark, Norway, and Sweden.

By the 1800s, Denmark was engaged in colonizing Greenland, and establishing a colony in the West Indies. However, as a result of its support of Napoleon, Denmark had its fleet destroyed and lost Norway to Sweden.

During World War II, Great Britain and the US protected Danish interests in Greenland, Iceland, and the Faroes, while the country was occupied by Germany.

Greenland and the Faroes are still part of the Kingdom of Denmark.

The country has an industrial base making steel, machinery, textiles, furniture, and electronics, but it is for its dairy products that it is best known. Butter and bacon in particular are widely exported.

The 1980 per capita income was $12,956 and the literacy rate is 99%.

Stamps were first issued in 1851 and the country has always followed a most conservative stamp-issuing policy.

Philatelic Bureau: Postens Filateli Raadhuspladsen 59, DK-1550 Copenhagen, Denmark.

FAROE ISLANDS

Area: 540 sq. miles
Population: 45,000 (1982)
Capital: Torshavn
Currency: Krone (100 ore)

The Faroes is a group of self-governing islands in the Kingdom of Denmark.

They are mountainous and rugged, with high cliffs and indented coastlines. The islands are volcanic in origin and are the peaks of a submarine mountain range that stretches from Greenland to the British Isles.

Their name means "sheep islands" and this is appropriate, because of the large number of sheep raised there.

The climate is mild with stormy winters and cool summers. Winter temperatures seldom fall below 25 degrees F and fog is frequent throughout the year. Weather changes are sudden and it is said that, during a single day there can be snow, sunshine, rain, wind, calm, and fog!

The days are short in winter, but at midsummer there is about 20 hours of sunlight.

It is believed that the islands were discovered and settled by Vikings from Norway or the British Isles about AD 800-900.

They became part of Norway, and when Norway broke away from Denmark in 1814, the Faroes remained with Denmark.

Britain administered the islands on behalf of Denmark, when that country was under German occupation during World War II.

In 1948, the Faroes were granted self-government within the kingdom.

Fishing is the main activity of the

islanders and in proportion to the population, the Faroes has the world's largest fishing fleet.

Communications with the outside world are good and there is year-round air service, with car ferries operating to Iceland, Denmark, Norway, and Scotland six months of the year.

The first stamp for the Faroes was issued in 1919 and was a provisional issue during a stamp shortage. It was a surcharge on a Danish stamp.

The next stamps came in 1940-41, when Britain administered the islands on behalf of Denmark while it was under German occupation. They were also Danish stamps surcharged.

Modern regular stamp issues began on Jan. 20, 1975 and a modest stamp-issuing program has been followed.

Philatelic Bureau: Frimerkjadeildin, 3800 Torshavn, Faroe Islands.

FINLAND, REPUBLIC OF

Area: 130,150 sq. miles
Population: 4,874,000 (1984)
Capital: Helsinki
Currency: Markka (100 pennia)

Finland's name in Finnish is Suomen Tasavalta, meaning "Land of a Thousand Lakes." This is something of an understatement, since the actual total is closer to 60,000! Of Finland's land area, 12,190 square miles are occupied by lakes and the islands they contain.

Despite its northern location, Finland's climate is modified by the North Atlantic Current, the influence of the Baltic Sea, the great areas of forest, and the many bodies of water.

Most of the country is low and the average altitude is only 200-400 feet. There are some hills in the north rising to about 1,500 feet. The country's highest mountain is 4,300 feet and is located in the far north near the border with Norway. The country has great areas of peat bog.

The climate at Helsinki is similar to that of Boston in winter, but summers are cool, with the temperature seldom exceeding 75 degrees F. The growing season ranges from 170 days in the south to 110 days in Lapland. Annual precipitation is about 24 inches in the south and less in the north. About 33% falls as snow.

Finland has had a long association with Sweden dating back to the 12th century, when Sweden's King Eric introduced Christianity to the area.

By 1362, Finns were able to participate in the election of Swedish kings, which led eventually to the Swedish-Finnish Parliament. Finland was made a grand duchy of Sweden in 1581 and by the 1600s had become an integral part of the Swedish kingdom.

However, Swedish power had declined by the mid-1700s to the point where Russia was able to move in and annex part of the country.

In 1808, Alexander of Russia made Finland an autonomous grand duchy in the Russian Empire. The capital city was established at Helsinki (Helsingfors), and the country seemed to be moving forward towards eventual nationhood.

A setback came in 1899, when Nicholas II of Russia, reneged on his predecessor's word and tried to make Finland part of Russia. He made the Russian language compulsory, and forced Finns to serve in the Russian army. This fostered a growing nationalism and much resistance.

On the outbreak of World War I, Finland asked Germany for help in training Finns for a proposed revolution against Russia.

When Russia collapsed after the 1917 revolution Finland declared itself independent. A period of Civil war ensued until the Treaty of Brest-Litovsk in 1918 called for the removal of Russian troops from Finland.

Relations with the new Soviet Union were not good during the inter-war years and following Finnish refusal of Soviet demands, it invaded Finland on Nov. 30, 1939. After a valiant defense, the country

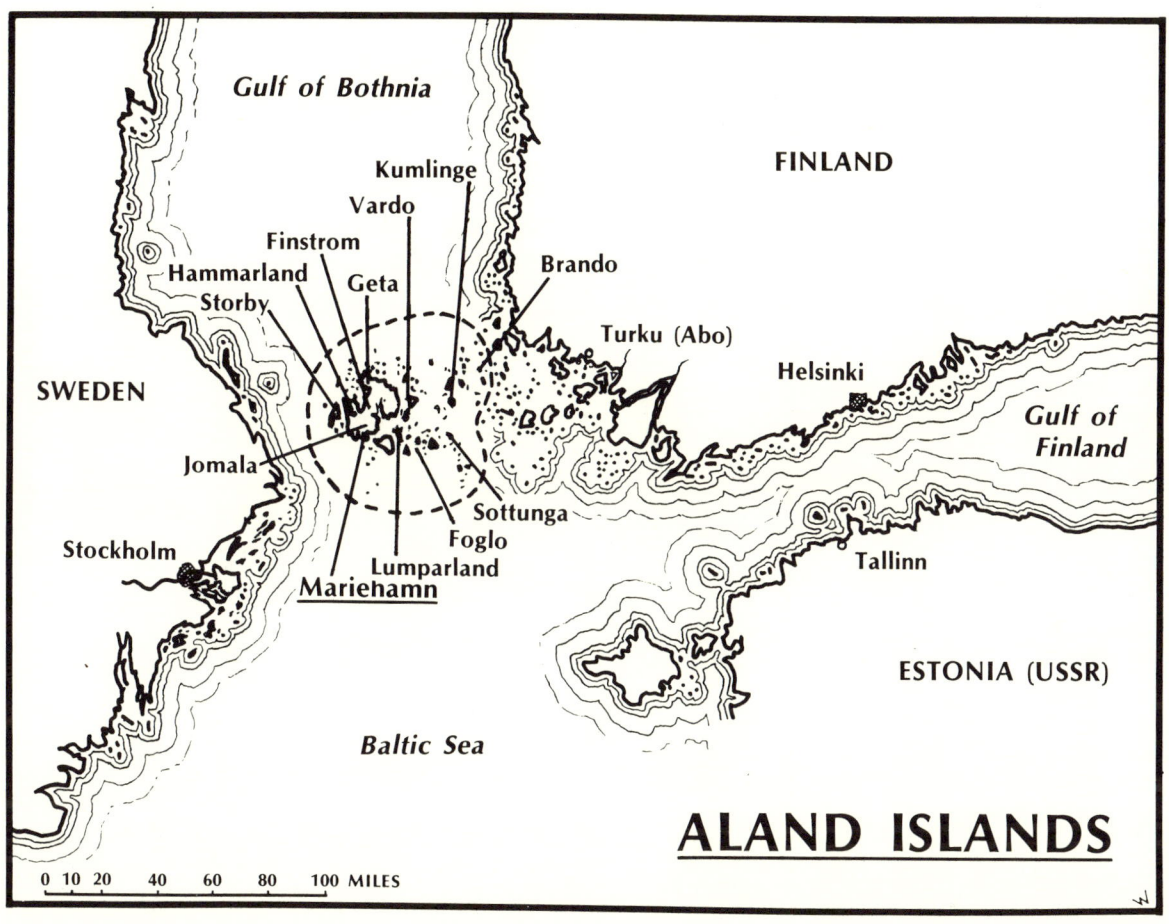

was crushed by Soviet might and a forced peace was signed on March 12, 1940.

This caused Finland to once again move into the German camp and during World War II it was allied with Germany. At war's end, the independent Finns managed to avoid the fate of Eastern European countries and retained their independence from Soviet domination.

The country is a member of the Nordic Group of Scandinavian countries and maintains good relations with all its neighbors, including the Soviet Union.

A normally prosperous nation, Finland's economy was affected by the worldwide recession and the surging energy prices during the 1970s. Forest products account for 40% of the country's exports. Industry includes steel, ship building, and textiles and there are deposits of copper. Grain and potatoes are grown and the dairy industry is important.

The 1980 per capita income was $10,447 and the literacy rate is 99%.

The first stamps were issued in 1856 under Russian control. Subsequent stamps are noted for their coarse rouletting, which makes perfect specimens extremely scarce.

The first stamps after independence feature the arms of the republic. The country has followed a conservative stamp-issuing policy.

Philatelic Bureau: General Direction of Posts and Telecommunications, Philatelic Section, Paasivourenkatu 3, PO Box 654, 00101 Helsinki 10, Finland.

Aland Islands: The Aland Islands are a group of about 6,500 islands and islets located at the entrance to the Gulf of Bothnia between Sweden and the southwestern tip of Finland.

With an area of 572 square miles, they are the smallest of the 10 provinces of Finland, but they possess an unusual amount of autonomy.

When Finland declared its independence, the Aland Islands voted in favor of union with Sweden. The granting of autonomy within the new country was a far as Finland would go.

On March 1, 1984, the islands began releasing their own postage stamps. Although Finnish stamps are valid in the Aland Islands, the Aland Island stamps cannot be used in the rest of Finland.

Philatelic Bureau: Philatelic Service, PO Box 100, 22101 Mariehamn, Aland, Finland.

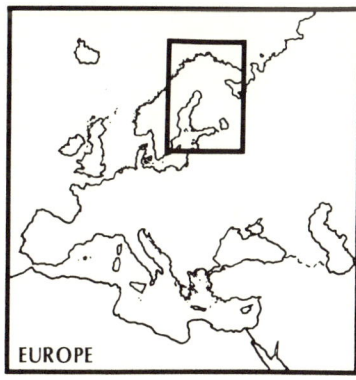

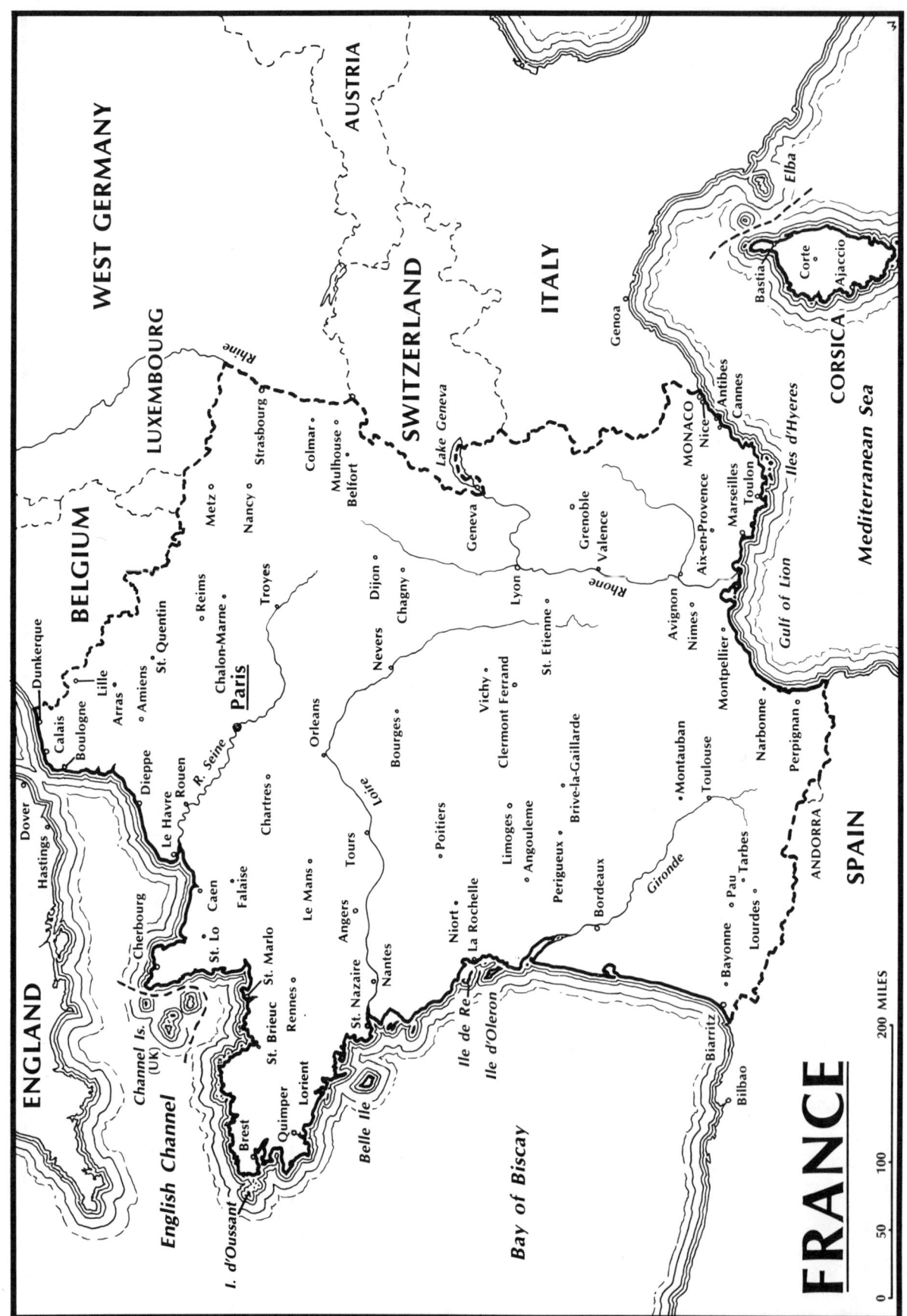

FRANCE, REPUBLIC OF

Area: 212,940 sq. miles
Population: 54,872,000 (1984)
Capital: Paris
Currency: Franc (100 centimes)

France is the largest country in Europe, with the exception of the Soviet Union. Much of it is flat or undulating plain and the rest is mountainous, especially the south, southeast, and east.

The climate is generally moderate with mild winters and cool summers, except in the south. There the climate is Mediterranean, with hot summers and warm winters.

Temperatures are usually more moderate near the coast. July average temperatures range from 60 degrees F on the English Channel coast to 72 degrees F in the south.

The northern and central areas receive 25-40 inches of rain each year, the Mediterranean coast may

The first French stamp.

get less than 20 inches, while in the mountains more than 80 inches can fall.

The first recorded date in the history of what is now France is 600 BC, when the Phoenicians founded the colony of Massilia, now Marseilles.

The Celtic tribes which inhabited the area of France called the country Gaeltachd — Land of the Gauls, the name adopted by the Romans, when they arrived. The first Roman incursions began about 120 BC, but it was not until 57-52 BC that Julius Caesar conquered Gaul.

The Romans ruled Gaul for about 500 years and following the fall of Rome, the Franks under Clovis took over much of the area. When Charlemagne came on the scene, he extended his domain far beyond the borders of modern France to lands of the Frisians, the Saxons, and to the Elbe River. Bavaria, much of Italy, and northern Spain came under his rule.

He was succeeded by his son, who became Louis I. Following his death, the Treaty of Verdun in AD 843 that affected the partition of Frankish territory did much to establish the form of modern France.

After years of diminished central power and fragmented rule, Louis VI, who came to the throne in 1108, succeeded in subduing feudal power and established a political base for extension of the kingdom.

In the 14th and 15th centuries, war with England was a normal state of affairs and English authority extended over a large part of what is now France.

During the 17th century, France reached the peak of its military power and cultural achievement. In 1682, Louis XIV occupied his great palace at Versailles and the overseas possessions were growing. But by century's end, the glory was waning and France emerged from the War of the Spanish Succession in 1713 as a second-rate power.

The lot of the people, particularly the overtaxed peasants, was hard and unrest began to grow. It culiminated on July 14, 1789 in the storming and capture of the Bastille. The bloody French Revolution was followed by the rise of Napoleon and the resulting Napoleonic wars that ended in French defeat at Waterloo.

The disastrous Franco-Prussian War of 1870-71 was another blow to French pride. Although with the help of its allies, France was victorious in World War I, it was at the cost of its manhood and the stage was set for the 1940 humiliation by the Germans.

After World War II, France tried to pick up the pieces. Although the days of empire were over, the country made desperate and ill-judged attempts to hang on to its colonies.

Now a member of the European Community, France is at peace with its neighbors.

A major industrial and agricultural power, France has a varied and extensive economic base, although it has been adversely affected by the worldwide recession.

The 1983 per capita income was $7,179 and the literacy rate is 99%.

The philately of France and its empire is popular, interesting and complex.

The first stamps were issued in 1849 and depict Ceres, the goddess of the harvest. Since then, it has released a stream of stamps depicting all aspects of French culture and history.

Mostly intaglio printed, French stamps are noted for fine engraving and colorful, high-quality production. The long-running French Art Series is a fine example.

Philatelic Bureau: Service Philatelique, 61-63 rue de Douai, 75436 Paris Cedex 09, France.

Some of the beautiful modern French stamps.

GERMANY, EAST AND WEST

Since 1949, Germany has been divided into two states; the Federal Republic of Germany (West Germany) and the German Democratic Republic (East Germany).

Prior to this, it had been the German Third Reich, a central European National Socialist dictatorship ruled by Adolf Hitler.

The history of Germany as a unified nation did not begin until the 19th century when Prussia defeated Austria in the 1866 Seven Weeks' War.

The peace treaty allocated four small north German states plus Schleswig-Holstein, to Prussia and excluded Austria from participation in Prussian affairs. This small beginning led in 1867 to the formation of the North German Confederation, which included 22 German states.

Chief architect of the confederation was the Prussian foreign minister, Prince Otto von Bismarck, who then proceeded to make agreements with the south German states of Bavaria, Baden, and Wurttemberg that placed their armies under Prussian control in case of war.

Prussia and the confederation administered a crushing defeat on France in the 1870-71 Franco-Prussian War, taking as the spoils of war most of the provinces of Alsace and Lorraine and imposing an indemnity of five billion francs.

While this victory gave a considerable boost to German nationalism and led directly to the 1871 formation of the German Empire under the Prussian monarch Wilhelm I, it also created a burning desire for revenge on the part of France. This was to have serious consequences for Germany in 1918.

The German Empire came into being on Jan. 18, 1871. It comprised 25 German states, 13 duchies and principalities, five grand duchies, four kingdoms, three free cities, and the territory taken from France in 1870-71. It covered 209,000 square miles and had a population of 41 million.

For the next 20 years, Bismarck devoted himself to making the German Empire supreme in Europe, socially, economically, and militarily.

His effort ended in 1888 when the egotistical and rather simple-minded Wilhelm II came to the throne. He dismissed Bismarck in 1890. This increasingly aggressive Germany under its new emperor caused Britain to ally itself with France and Russia and set the stage for World War I.

Following the assassination of the Austrian heir, Francis Ferdinand, at Sarajevo and the Austrian declaration of war on Serbia that came soon after, treaty obligations knee-jerked the European powers into the war.

When Germany was finally defeated in 1918, French desire for revenge for the 1871 humiliation resulted in harsh peace terms under the Treaty of Versailles.

France got Alsace-Lorraine back, but now the Germans felt humiliated at being beaten in battle. Their desire for revenge caused an even more terrible conflict within a generation.

In the 1920s, Germany was hard hit by inflation and economic bad times. Thus, when Hitler and his gang of street thugs came along in the early 1930s, his message of national rebirth appealed to a Germany longing for an opportunity to right the wrong it felt had been done to it.

Once in power, Hitler began to gear Germany for conquest and opened a reign of terror against any who opposed him, especially against the Jews, for whom he planned a hideous extermination.

Weakened by the cost of World War I, the other nations of Europe, as well as the United States, stood back, hoping that they would not become involved as Germany gnawed away on its neighbors, each time promising that it would be the last.

When Germany attacked Poland in 1939, even the appeasers had had enough and Europe again went to war.

For a while, Germany reigned supreme and terrorized Europe, but as Britain and the Soviet Union and later, the United States, gained strength, Germany declined. By 1945 it was battered and beaten.

Germany was divided into occupation zones for the United States, Britain, and the Soviet Union, with a zone also being given to France. These zones eventually evolved into today's two German states.

FEDERAL REPUBLIC OF GERMANY

Area: 95,975 sq. miles
Population: 61,387,000 (1984)
Capital: Bonn
Currency: Mark (100 pfennig)

The Federal Republic of Germany (West Germany) is the western part of the old German Third Reich and comprises the post-World War II British, French, and United States occupation zones.

The country is flat in the north and hilly in the center and west, rising to mountains in the south.

The climate is temperate and subject to frequent changes.

Temperatures range from an average of 65 degrees F in the summer to 30 degrees F in winter. Annual rainfall varies from 20 inches in the north to 80 inches in the southern mountains.

When Germany surrendered on May 8, 1945, the victors occupied zones previously agreed upon, and began to organize the shattered land and set up some form of government.

The new West German state started to exercise powers of self-government on Sept. 21, 1949, under a coalition government led by Chancellor Konrad Adenauer. The United States resumed diplomatic relations on July 2, 1951.

Full sovereignty was achieved on May 5, 1955, paving the way for membership on the North Atlantic Treaty Organization (NATO) and the Western European Union (CEPT).

The country made extremely rapid progress in rebuilding from the war and in getting its economy going. Considerable economic aid was given by the victors, and the country soon became a model for the other nations of Europe.

Today, West Germany is a highly developed, prosperous nation and an important member of the European Community.

Its economy is diverse, ranging from heavy industry to agriculture. The 1985 per capita income was $9,450 and the literacy rate is 99%.

Stamp issues are not excessive and stamp subjects have a West German relationship.

Philatelic Bureau: Versandstelle fur Postwertzeichen, Postfach 20 00, 6000 Frankfurt 1, Federal Republic of Germany.

GERMAN DEMOCRATIC REPUBLIC

Area: 41,825 sq. miles
Population: 18,718,000 (1984)
Capital: East Berlin
Currency: Mark (100 pfennig)

The German Democratic Republic (East Germany) is located mostly on the north European plain, which extends inland as far as the Leipzig area. There are mountains in the south.

The principal river is the Elbe, which has an area of fertile land along both banks for much of its length.

The country was proclaimed on Oct. 7, 1949. It was formed from the Soviet occupation zone and claims East Berlin as its capital. The US has not recognized the capital's location as it maintains that Berlin is part of the Soviet Union's Berlin occupation zone and not part of the general zone of occupation. Domestic and foreign policies of the country are those laid down by the Soviet Union.

In June 1953, there were worker's uprisings in East Germany. These were quickly crushed by Soviet authorities. Since then, there have been strict controls over the population and Soviet military forces remain.

East Germany became a member of the Warsaw Pact in 1956. Its economy is tied to that of the Soviet Union and other East European satellite countries.

In order to retain the most skilled and highly trained professional workers and cut back on the alarming number fleeing the country, the Berlin Wall was built in 1961. This was an attempt to bottle up the population and keep it isolated from Western influence.

The East German economy is the strongest in the Soviet bloc. Industries include steel, chemicals, machinery, textiles, and electrical. Important crops are grains, potatoes, and sugar beet.

The 1984 per capita income was $8,000 and the literacy rate is 99%.

Philatelic Bureau: VEB Philatelie Wermsdorf, Abt Export/ Import, Postfach 266, 7010 Leipzig, German Democratic Republic.

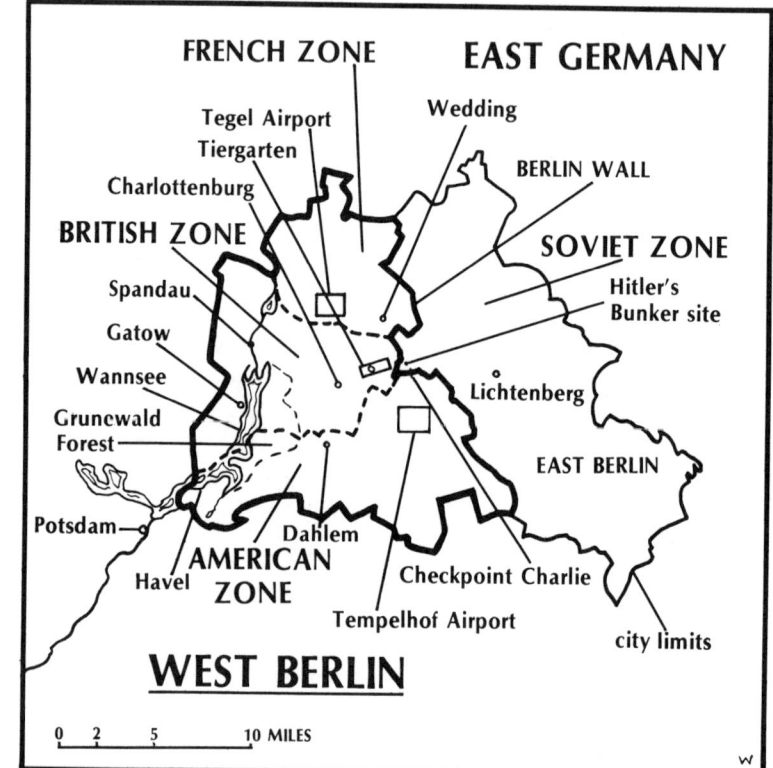

BERLIN

Area: 186 sq. miles
Population: 2,000,000
Currency: Mark (100 pfennig)

Berlin is located 110 miles within East German borders.

At the end of World War II, the city was not included in the general occupation zones, but was a separate area under the joint control of Britain, France, the Soviet Union, and the United States.

In 1948, the Soviet Union repudiated the agreement and refused to cooperate in joint administration of the city. It expelled the elected government of its area of Berlin and installed a Communist regime.

On June 24, 1948, the Soviet Union began a blockade of Western areas of the city in an attempt to force its former allies out. A massive airlift was mounted and kept the city supplied until the Soviet Union admitted defeat and re-opened the road and rail routes into the city.

Today, the British, French, and United States areas of West Berlin are an island in a sea of Communist territory, surrounded by the fortified Berlin Wall built by East Germany to prevent its citizens from fleeing to the West.

Stamps have been issued since 1948 for West Berlin. Many of the semi-postals bear designs similar to those of West Germany.

Philatelic Bureau: Versandstelle fur Postwertzeichen, Postfach 12 09 50, 1000 Berlin 12, Federal Republic of Germany.

GIBRALTAR

Area: 2.25 sq. miles
Population: 30,000 (1982)
Currency: Pound (100 pence)

Gibraltar is a British colony comprising a limestone peninsula jutting some 2.75 miles south from the coast of Spain at the entrance to the Mediterranean from the Atlantic and rising to a dramatic 1,398-foot peak. A narrow isthmus connects it to the mainland.

The climate is hot and dry in the summer. The average high temperature during August is 85 degrees F and the low is 70 degrees F. In January, the coolest month, the average high is 60 degrees F and the low is 50 degrees F. Annual rainfall is about 35 inches.

As one approaches the Strait of Gibraltar from the west by ship, the Rock looms impressively and is a distinctive reminder that the traveler is approaching warmer climes.

It gets its name from a corruption of Jabal al-Tarik (Mount Tarik), which honors the Muslim commander, Tarik ibn-Zaid, who captured it in AD 711.

Legend claims that it is one of the Pillars of Hercules. The other is said to be Mount Acho, on the African side of the eight-mile-wide entrance to the Mediterranean.

The Muslim occupation of the Iberian Peninsula ended in the 1460s and in 1501 Spain annexed Gibraltar.

British forces captured the Rock in 1704. They did not obtain immediate possession, since Dutch forces helped in the operation and both were fighting on behalf of Charles of Austria, whom they considered to be the rightful ruler of Spain.

British occupation of Gibraltar

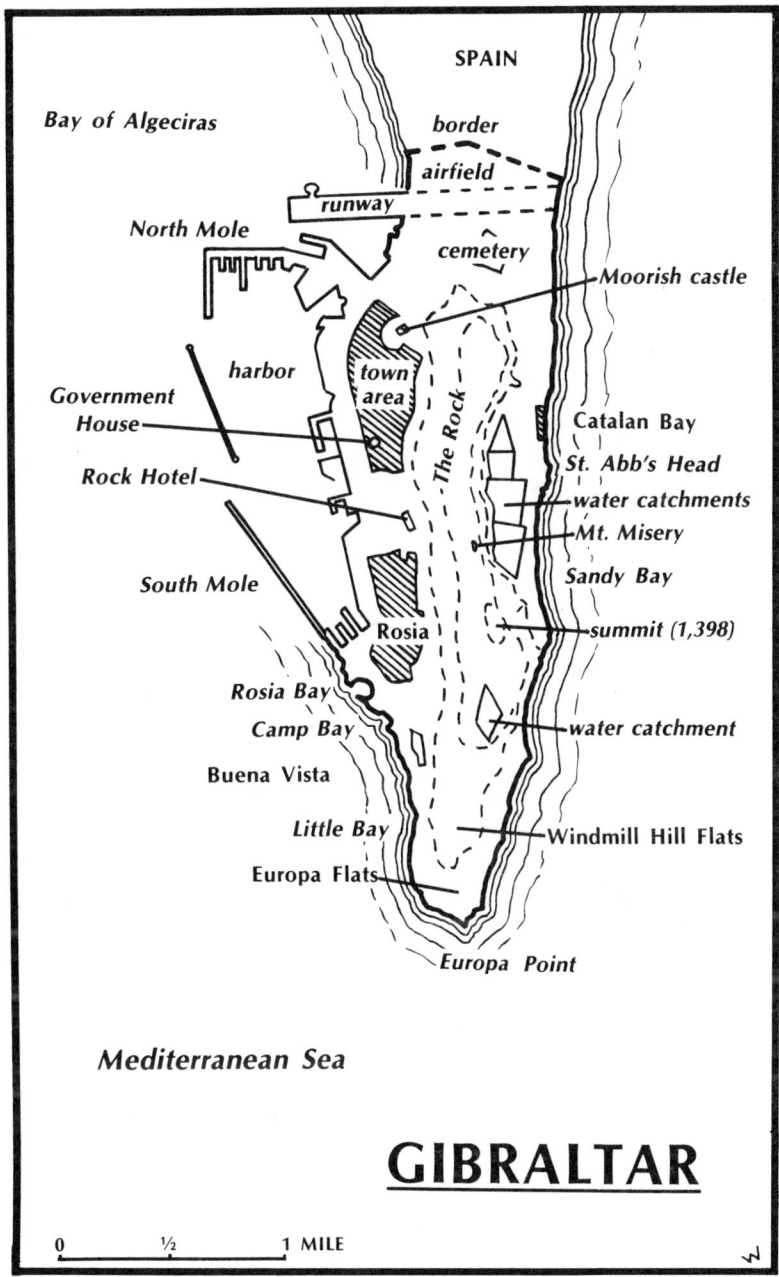

dates from 1711. Spain has long claimed the Rock and in 1779 began a four-year siege, which failed.

Gibraltar became a crown colony in 1830 and the opening of the Suez Canal made it an important link in Britain's chain of bases protecting its route to the East.

A referendum in 1967 resulted in only 43 votes of a total of 12,181 to join Spain. Since then, Britain has regarded the matter of sovereignty as closed.

The first stamps were issued in 1886 and were overprints on stamps of Bermuda. Prior to that, the colony used stamps of Great Britain.

Until 1931, only the monarch's profile appeared on the stamps, but in that year a set of pictorial stamps pictured the Rock.

Philatelic Bureau: Gibraltar Post Office, Philatelic Bureau, Box 5662, Gibraltar.

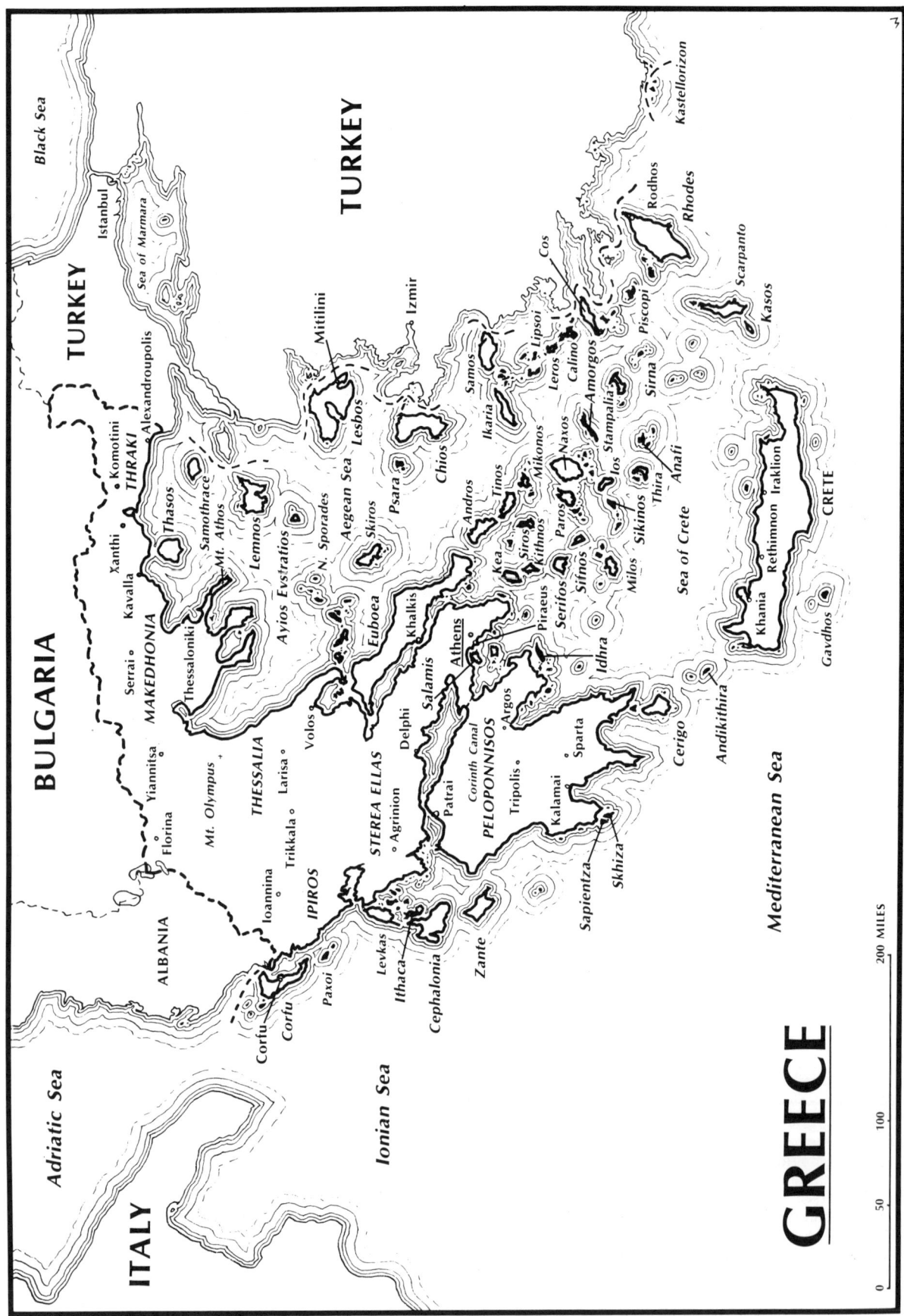

GREECE (HELLENIC REPUBLIC)

Area: 50,962 sq. miles
Population: 9,884,000 (1984)
Capital: Athens
Currency: Drachma (100 lepta)

Located at the extreme southeastern tip of Europe, at the end of the Balkan Peninsula, Greece is composed of a mainland area with a jagged coastline and a large number of islands, especially in the Aegean Sea between the Greek mainland and the Turkish shore of Asia Minor.

The main islands of Greece are Crete, Rhodes, Corfu, and the Dodecanese group.

The Greek climate is generally hot and dry during the summer, with average sea-level temperatures of about 80 degrees F. Winters are colder in the north with an average January temperature at Thessaloniki of 40 degrees F. It is about 10 degrees F warmer in the south, but very much colder in the mountain areas.

At Corfu, on the west coast, January temperatures average 50 degrees F.

Rainfall is heavier in the north, with Thessaloniki receiving about 20 inches a year and Athens, further south, getting about 15 inches. Corfu's annual average rainfall is 50 inches.

The cradle of much of Western culture and civilization, the area that is now Greece was at the height of its achievements in art, architecture, philosophy, mathematics, drama, and literature about 500 BC.

It was during this time that the state of Athens enjoyed its golden age.

Their moment of glory waning, the Greek states came under Roman domination in the second century BC. In its turn, Rome's power dwindled and by AD 400, the area was part of the Byzantine Empire.

After the fall of Constantinople (Istanbul) in 1453, Greece came under the control of the Ottoman Empire of the Turks.

It remained a Turkish dominion until the 1820s, when a war for independence began. Out of this struggle, the modern Greek state emerged to inherit the glory of ancient Greece.

The Treaty of Adrianople in 1829 established an independent Greece. It was a tiny country, about one third its present size. This was less than the Greeks had hoped for and the peace brought a period of unrest and economic hard times. In 1832, it is reported that the Greek treasury contained about $300!

In 1833, Britain, France, and Russia installed a monarchy in Greece. Otto of Bavaria was made king and ruled for 30 years until he was deposed. He was replaced by a member of the Danish royal family who became George I.

Several Balkan wars in the years before World War I resulted in territorial gains for Greece, including Crete and areas of Macedonia and Thrace.

When world war broke out in 1914, Greece was exhausted and remained neutral until 1917, when it entered the conflict on the side of the Allies. As war booty, Greece obtained even more territory from Turkey.

The modern political history of Greece has been marked by the struggle between monarchist and republican. Periods of royal rule have alternated with republican administration.

The 1939 invasion and occupation of Albania by Italy resulted in guarantees of protection for Greece from Britain and France.

This did not prevent Italy from invading Greece from Albania, but the aggression backfired as the Greeks drove the Italians out and occupied a quarter of Albania!

The Italian humiliation was avenged by Germany in April 1941, when it occupied the Balkans and extended that occupation to the island of Crete. Until October 1944, when the Germans retreated, Greece suffered under a harsh occupation and famine was widespread.

After liberation, the various resistance groups began to fight each other for control of the country and fearing a Communist takeover, Britain sent in forces to support the government. The immediate threat was foiled but the unrest broke into civil war in 1948-49. Massive aid to build up the country's economy gradually brought a measure of stability.

In recent years, the situation in Cyprus has kept old hatreds alive between Greece and Turkey, Greek relations with the United States have been cool in the 1980s, and there have been disagreements over NATO and Cypriot policies.

Greece became a member of the European Community on Jan. 1, 1981.

The economy was hurt by rising energy prices in the 1970s and inflation has been high. The 1980 per capita income was $4,590 and the literacy rate is 95%.

Greek philately is rich and varied. Its first stamps came in 1861 and set the tone. They are the Hermes Heads, one of the world's popular classic issues. The original issue is complex and interesting and some famous collections have been made of it.

Greek mythology has provided the subjects for numerous Greek stamps as has its fight for independence from Turkey.

Modern Greek stamps are colorful and have a distinctive character that makes them instantly recognizable.

Philatelic Bureau: Greek Post Office, Philatelic Service, 100 Aiolou St., Athen, 131, Greece.

Some typical stamps of Greece.

GREENLAND (KALAALLIT NUNAAT)

Area: 840,000 sq. miles
Population: 51,000 (1982)
Capital: Godthab (Nuuk)
Currency: Krone (100 ore)

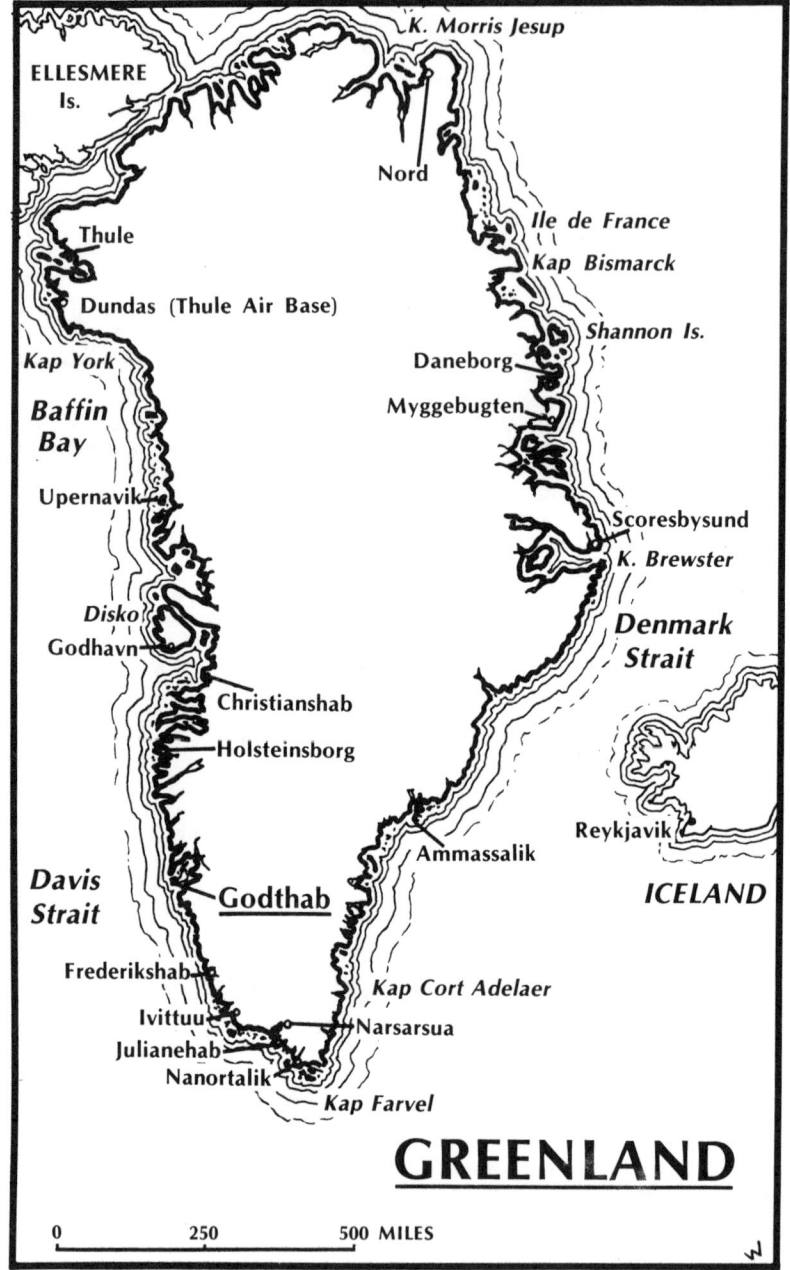

Greenland is the world's largest island. Of its 840,000 square-mile area, however, all but 130,000 square miles is covered by ice having an average thickness of 1,000 feet.

The climate is polar, although the Gulf Stream modifies the temperatures slightly in the southwest. Along the coasts and in the southwest, frost seldom occurs in June, July, or August. On the interior ice plateau it is always cold.

Average temperatures there in February of -53 degrees F and of 13 degrees F in July have been recorded. The lowest recorded temperature was -85 degrees F and the highest in summer was 27 degrees F.

Annual precipitation is 40 inches in the south, dropping to 8 inches in the north.

A range of mountains runs down the east coast, with its highest point being 12,139-foot Mount Gunnbjorn. A similar range runs along the west coast, having peaks of from 5,000-6,000 feet.

The first settlement in Greenland was made in AD 986 by Eric the Red. It was located just to the north of Julianehab. A second colony was established near Godthab. The settlements thrived and in 1261 became linked to Norway.

Climatic changes in the 1400s made life difficult in Greenland and contact with the colonists was lost. Their fate remains unknown.

Recolonization did not begin until 1721, when Hans Egede, a missionary, arrived at Godthab.

When Norway and Denmark split up in 1814, Greenland remained with Denmark.

In 1941, the United States signed an agreement with the Danish minister in that country whereby the United States would assume responsibility for the protection of Greenland while Denmark was under German occupation. A US air base is still maintained at Thule.

Greenland became part of the kingdom of Denmark in 1953 and achieved home rule on May 1, 1979.

Much of the population is dependent on hunting and fishing for its livelihood. Only a small area in the southwest corner of the island can be used for agriculture. Here some sheep are raised and grass is grown for winter fodder.

Stamps were first issued in 1938 and have a distinctly Danish flavor. Issue policies have been extremely modest.

Philatelic Bureau: Gronlands Postvaesen, 100 Strandgade, PO Box 100, DK-1004 Copenhagen, Denmark.

HUNGARIAN PEOPLE'S REPUBLIC

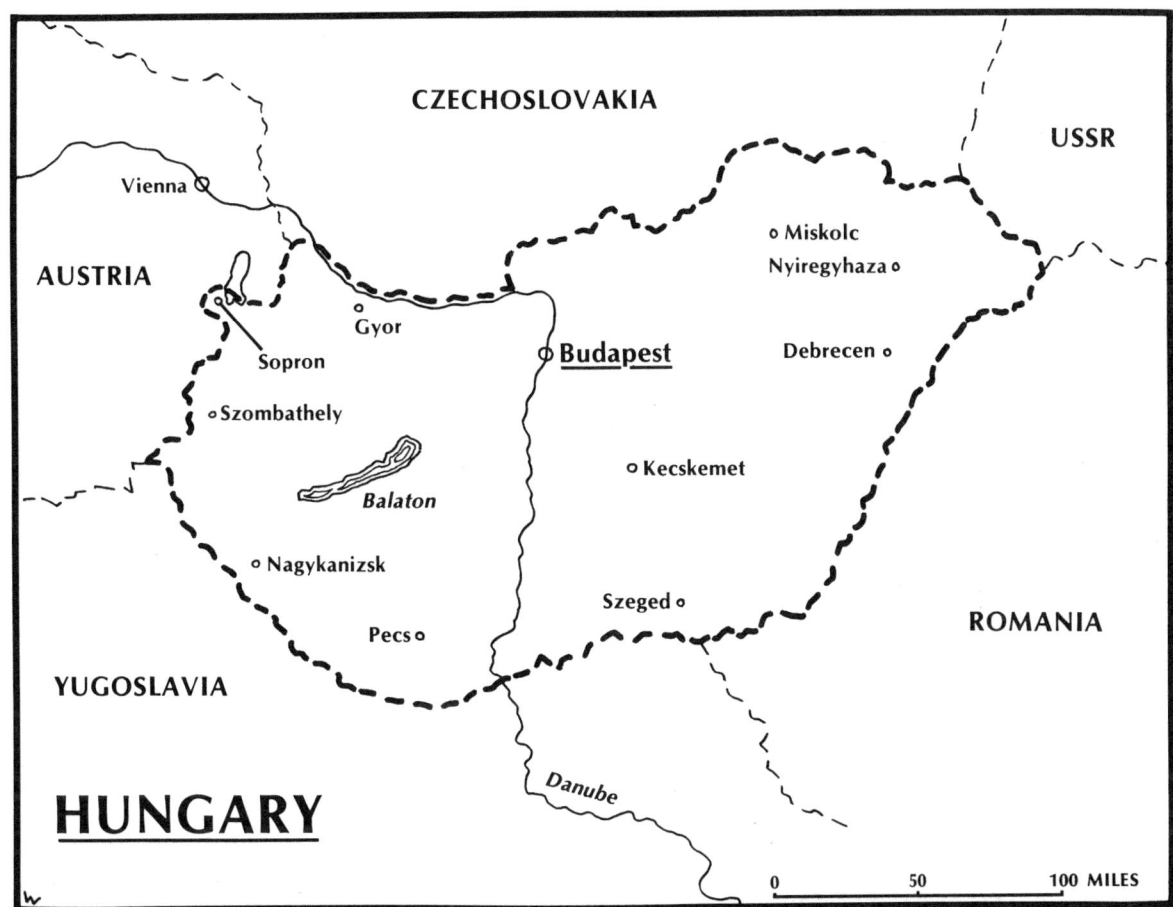

Area: 35,919 sq. miles
Population: 10,681,000 (1984)
Capital: Budapest
Currency: Forint (100 filler)

Hungary is mostly flat with an area of hills running from the northeast to the west central part of the country.

In terms of climate, the country is located in an area of transition between the extremes of the east and the more moderate weather prevailing in Western Europe.

During the long, hot summers there are strong hot and dry winds that cause problems of erosion in exposed agricultural areas.

The seasons are of about equal length. The average temperature for the country is 31 degrees F in January and 71 degrees F in July. Precipitation averages about 25 inches a year.

The Romans ruled over what is now Hungary during the heyday of their empire. About AD 1000 Magyars overran the Slav and Germanic settlers. During the 15th-17th centuries, the Turks regularly invaded the area, following which came Austrian domination, when Hungary was made part of the Austro-Hungarian Empire.

The dual monarchy was set up in 1867 and ended with defeat in World War I.

Allied with Germany in World War II, Hungary was again defeated. After the war it became a satellite of the Soviet Union.

An uprising against Soviet domination in 1956 was put down with Soviet forces. Many Hungarians were killed and thousands fled the country. Soviet troops are still stationed there.

The 1982 per capita income was $4,180 and the literacy rate is 98%.

Stamps were first issued in 1871 under the dual monarchy. From the beginning, stamp issues have been frequent. Its early stamps were found in great profusion in the albums of young collectors some 50 years ago.

Since 1945, stamp issues have become very prolific, with numerous commemorative, semipostal, and air mail stamps being released.

Philatelic Bureau: Philatelia Hungarica, PO Box 600, Budapest 1373, Hungary.

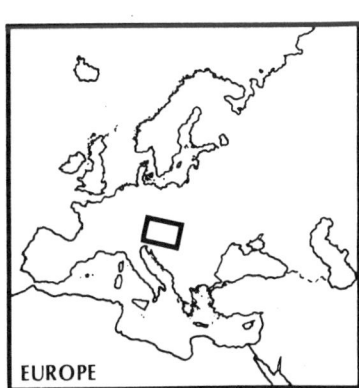

ICELAND, REPUBLIC OF

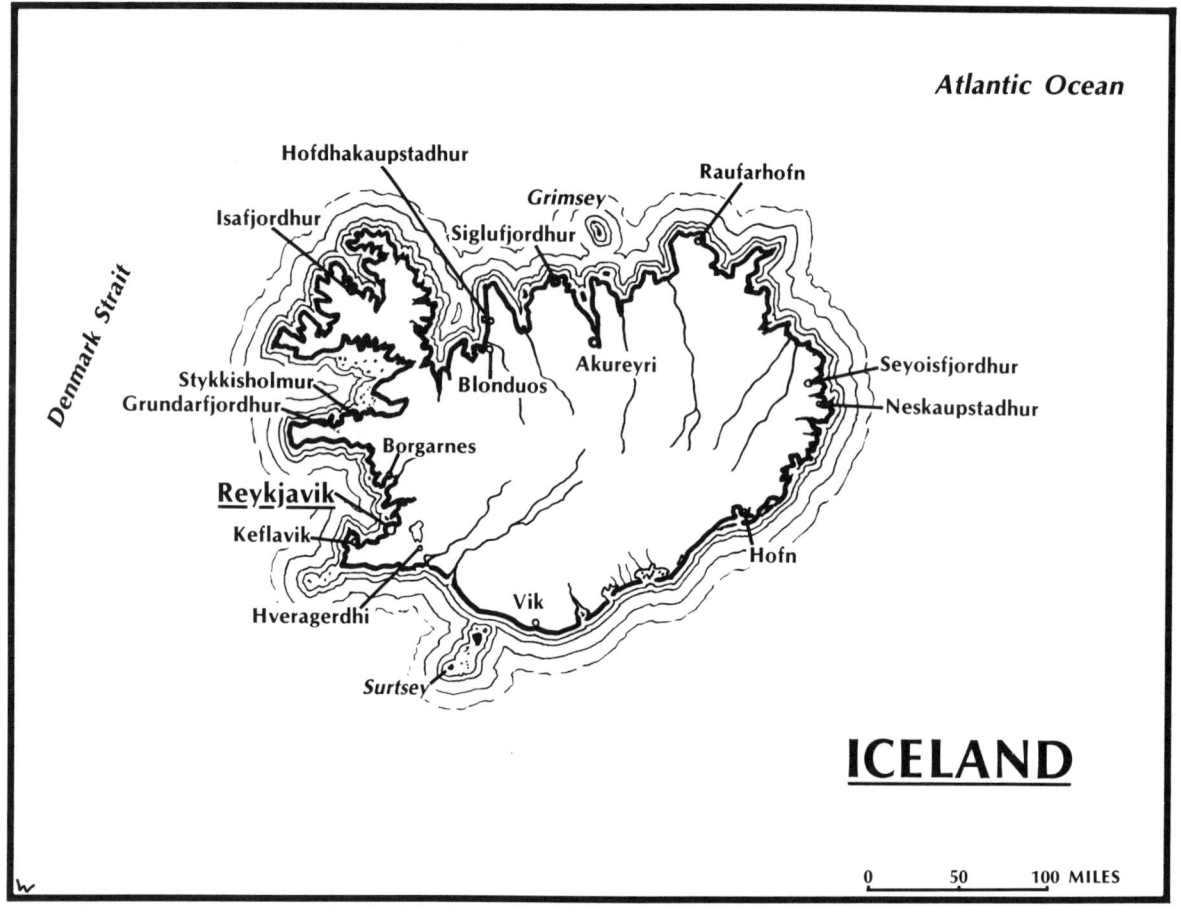

Area: 39,769 sq. miles
Population: 239,000 (1984)
Capital: Reykjavik
Currency: Krona (100 aurar)

Located off the east coast of Greenland and just below the Arctic Circle, Iceland is a young volcanic island with hot springs, glaciers, lava deserts, and mountains. The highest rises to 6,600 feet. Most of the population is concentrated in the southwest.

The climate is modified by the Gulf Stream and at Reykjavik, the January average temperature is 30 degrees F. In July it rises to 52 degrees F. Summers are damp and winters windy.

Iceland possesses the world's oldest surviving parliament, the Althing, established in AD 930, when the island became a republic. Independence continued until 1262. In that year, Iceland came under Norwegian sovereignty.

It became a possession of Denmark when that country brought Norway under its crown in the 14th century. The last links with Denmark were not severed until 1941.

Home rule came in 1903 and in 1918 Iceland was recognized as a sovereign state united with Denmark under a common monarch.

In 1940, British forces occupied the island to protect it from German aggression when Germany invaded Denmark. The United States took over in 1941.

Iceland became a fully independent republic on June 17, 1944. Currently, it is the only NATO member country with no military forces of its own.

The country's economy is based on fishing and fish products account for about 80% of its exports. Some aluminum is produced and crops include potatoes, turnips, and hay for winter fodder.

Thermal hot springs on the island have been harnessed and are a source of free heat for much of the capital city.

The latest per capita income figure is $9,000 and the literacy rate is 99.9%.

The first stamps were issued in 1873 and bear a family resemblance to contemporary issues of Denmark.

Generally, stamps of the island are attractive and its moderate stamp-issuing policy makes the country popular with the world's collectors.

Philatelic Bureau: Frimerkjasalan, Postboks 1445, Reykjavik, Iceland.

IRELAND (IRISH REPUBLIC)

Area: 27,137 sq. miles
Population: 3,575,000 (1984)
Capital: Dublin
Currency: Pound (100 pence)

The Irish Republic occupies Ireland except for Northern Ireland, a small area in the northeast that is part of the United Kingdom.

The island is mostly a central rolling plain surrounded by a band of coastal highlands. The climate is modified by the Atlantic Ocean and is mild and wet. Temperatures average 40 degrees F in winter and 60 degrees F in summer. It rarely goes below freezing or above 75 degrees F.

The earliest known inhabitants of Ireland lived there about 6000 BC and were of a stone-age culture. About 2000 BC, tribes arrived from southern Europe, bringing a culture that used gold ornaments and built large stone monuments.

In 400 BC, the warlike Celts invaded the island establishing a society dominated by priests called druids.

A turning point in Irish history was the AD 432 arrival of St. Patrick, who in 30 years, converted the island to Christianity. This introduced a rich period in which the art of illumination, metalwork, and sculpture flourished.

During the 1100s, English influence began to make itself felt when King Henry II started a struggle between the two people that continues to this day.

Ireland was part of the United Kingdom from 1800 to 1920, when the Irish Free State was formed. The six mostly Protestant northern counties opted to remain within the United Kingdom.

Links with Britain were gradually severed and in 1948, the country left the British Commonwealth and proclaimed itself a republic.

Recently, the republic and the United Kingdom agreed to cooperate to reduce tension in Northern Ireland, but the situation remains unstable as the two religions show no sign of ending their conflict.

Ireland has little industry and the economy is still based on agriculture, which employs 29% of the workforce.

The 1984 per capita income was $4,750 and the literacy rate was 99%.

Ireland's first stamps were issued in 1922 and were overprints on stamps of Great Britain. Stamp-issuing policies are moderate.

Philatelic Bureau: The Controller, Philatelic Bureau, GPO, Dublin 1, Ireland.

ITALY (ITALIAN REPUBLIC)

Area: 116,303 sq. miles
Population: 56,998,000 (1984)
Capital: Rome
Currency: Lira (100 centesimi)

Italy is one of the world's most distinctively shaped countries. Long and boot-shaped, it projects from southern Europe as it aims its toe at the island of Sicily.

In addition to the peninsula, Italy comprises the large islands of Sicily and Sardinia, plus a number of smaller islands in the surrounding waters of the Ligurian Sea, the Tyrrhenian Sea, the Adriatic, and the Mediterranean. Much of the peninsula is mountainous.

The climate ranges from hot in the south to cool in the mountainous northern area. There are considerable variations even within short distances and distinctions between winter and summer range widely.

As the center of the Roman Empire, and later, of the Renaissance, Italy has a rich cultural heritage.

The period from 500 BC to AD 500 was one in which Rome ruled most of the Western world, including the greater part of Europe, England, the Balkan Peninsula, the Near East, and northern Africa.

The glories of empire remain in the form of impressive fragments of Roman architecture, including roads and aquaducts.

During the Middle Ages, the Italian peninsula comprised a large number of city states and small states, all constantly in a state of flux and often at war.

Not until the mid-19th century did unification become a possiblility. At that time, the Kingdom of Sardinia under King Victor Emmanual II, gained extensive lands on the mainland, including the states of Parma, Modena, Romagne, and Tuscany. These were unified and on March 17, 1861, Victor Emmanuel was proclaimed king of the new nation of Italy. The remaining states joined the kingdom by 1870.

During World War I, Italy, which had been allied with Germany and the Austro-Hungarian Empire, changed sides and entered the war in 1915 as an ally of Great Britain and France.

Fascism, personified by Benito Mussolini, gained control of Italy following the war. Mussolini soon began his march to empire, setting an example that was to be more efficiently followed by Adolf Hitler, who regarded the comic-opera dictator as an idol to be imitated. The two countries soon became allies.

But Mussolini's empire proved to be a cardboard one and his army collapsed under the pressure of small, ill-equipped British forces in the early years of World War II. Italy itself required considerable shoring up by Germany.

In the years between the wars, Italy was an industrial country, with a great technological ability to build fine automobiles and aircraft. Indeed, Italy built one of the world's first strategic bombing forces during World War I.

Italian automobiles were once regarded as among the world's best built and most advanced.

Since World War II, Italy has declined as a world power and there has been much political instability with many changes of government.

Leftist terrorists have been responsible for many murders, bombings, and kidnappings. More recently, Moslem fanatics have operated there with relative impunity.

Economically, Italy made great progress in recovering from the effects of World War II and until the escalation of oil prices in the mid-1970s was healthy and growing. Since then, inflation and recession have severely disrupted the economy.

The most recent per capita income figure is $6,914 and the literacy rate is 98%.

The first stamps of Italy could be regarded as the last issue of Sardinia, as they comprised perforated versions of former Sardinian stamps.

Much of Italy's culture and history can be found depicted on its stamps. Its postal history is long and interesting, ranging from the glories of medieval Venice to the development of air mail.

Italy was in the forefront of early aviation and was the first nation to release offical government air mail stamps. These stamps came in 1917 and took the form of overprints on special delivery stamps to frank mail carried on air mail routes between Turin and Rome and Naples and Palermo in Sicily.

After Mussolini was overthrown in 1943, he was rescued by Hitler and installed in a northern Italian government under the name of the Italian Socialist Republic. Stamps were created for this puppet state by overprinting Italian stamps.

Italy can claim the honor of issuing the world's first stamp to depict a jet aircraft. This was the 1945 air mail issue showing the Caproni-Campini CC2 aircraft of 1940.

In recent years, Italian stamps have been relatively moderate in number and modest in face value.

Philatelic Bureau: Ufficio Principale Filatelico, via Mario de Fiori, 103/A, 00187 Rome, Italy.

A selection of Italian stamps.

LIECHTENSTEIN, PRINCIPALITY OF

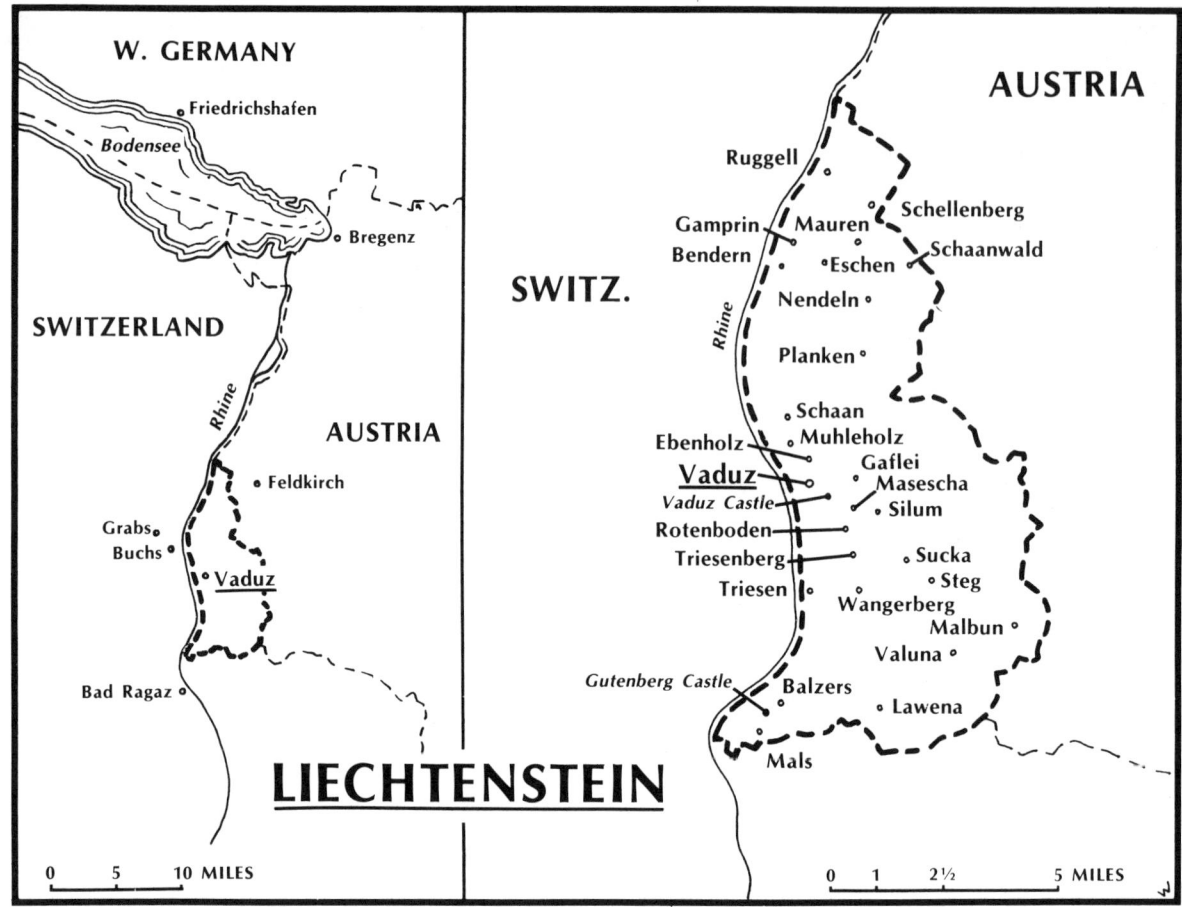

Area: 62 sq. miles
Population: 27,000 (1984)
Capital: Vaduz
Currency: Swiss franc (100 rappen)

Liechtenstein is located in the mountain range that runs across southern Switzerland and into Austria.

The only non-mountainous area lies along the Rhine River that forms the principality's western border. It comprises about one third of the total land area.

The climate is alpine, with cool summers and cold, snowy winters.

The principality dates from 1719, when the lordships of Schellenberg and Vaduz combined to form the present state. The line of succession has remained unbroken since then.

The ruling prince appoints the head of a government consisting of 15 elected members.

In 1866, Liechtenstein withdrew from the Germanic Confederation and disbanded its army.

Until 1919, the principality was allied with Austria, but is now included within the Swiss customs union.

Taxes are low and a number of foreign corporations have headquarters in Liechtenstein. Considerable light industry has been developed in recent years and one third of the population comprises foreign workers.

The official language of the country is German and the literacy rate is 99%.

From 1912, when stamps were first issued, until the end of World War I, the stamps of Liechtenstein were obviously of Austrian origin.

During 1920-21, the principality took over its own postal affairs. It then tarnished its philatelic reputation by dumping a large number of canceled-to-order stamps on the market.

Nowadays, the fact that it has become more conservative, while most other countries have greatly increased their stamp output, makes it appear to be one of the more responsible stamp-issuing entities.

Today, the country is widely collected and its stamps are admired for the beauty of their design and the high quality of their production.

Philatelic Bureau: Official Philatelic Service, FL-9490, Vaduz, Liechtenstein.

LUXEMBOURG, GRAND DUCHY OF

Area: 1,034 sq. miles
Population: 366,000 (1984)
Capital: Luxembourg City
Currency: Franc (100 centimes)

Luxembourg's name is said to derive from the early form, Lucilinburhuc, meaning "Little Fortress."

There are two main regions, a hilly, forested extension of the Ardennes in the north and the northern part of the French Lorraine Plateau, a rolling area of open country in the south, averaging 1,000 feet in altitude.

The climate is in between the maritime type of northwestern Europe and the more severe weather common to the interior of Europe. The average monthly temperature at Luxembourg City runs from 32 degrees F in January to 63 degrees F in July. Rainfall is about 40 inches in the southwest, dropping to 25 inches in the east.

Luxembourg became an independent state in AD 963. About 1060, Conrad, a descendent of Count Siegfried of the Ardennes, took the title of Count of Luxembourg. In 1354, the state became a duchy.

After undergoing a number of associations with other European countries, Luxembourg was split up in 1831, with the larger portion going to Belgium to form the present province of Luxembourg in that country. The smaller area remained and is today's Grand Duchy of Luxembourg. It was not until 1839, that the grand duchy recognized this detachment of most of its territory, and 1839 is still considered as the beginning of the modern state.

Until 1867, Luxembourg was administered from the Netherlands.

The Treaty of London of that year guaranteed its neutrality and vested sovereignty in the House of Nassau.

Germany violated Luxembourg's neutrality on 1914 and again in 1940. Since its liberation in 1944, its economy has recovered and it is now a member of the BENELUX union with Belgium and the Netherlands.

The economy is based on its steel mills, which provide 90% of its exports. Wine is also an important product.

The 1981 per capita income was $10,444 and the literacy rate is 99%.

Luxembourg released its first stamp in 1852 and dangerous reprints exist. Its moderate stamp-issuing policies over the years, have made Luxembourg popular and widely collected.

Philatelic Bureau: Direction des Postes, Office des Timbres, PO Box L-2020, Luxembourg City, Luxembourg.

MALTA

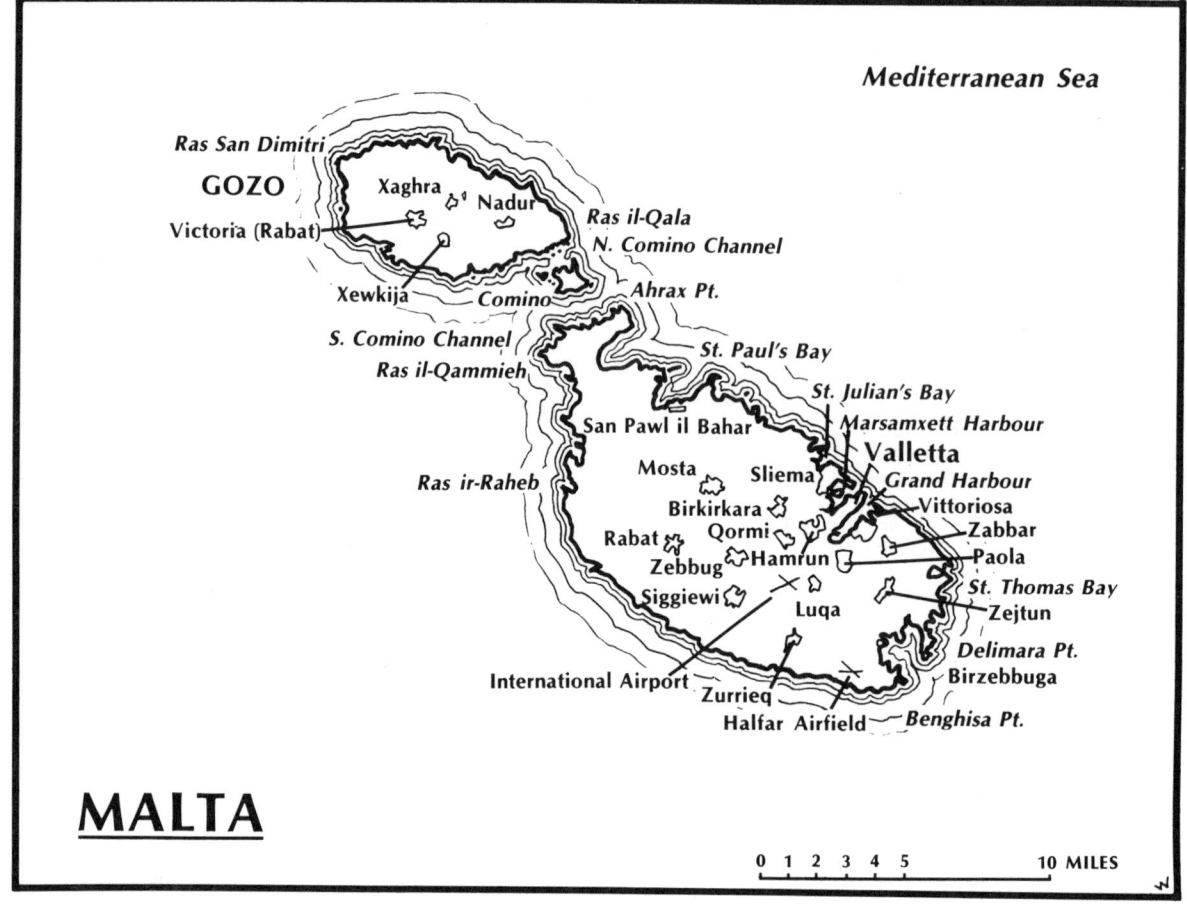

MALTA

Area: 122 sq. miles
Population: 356,000 (1984)
Capital: Valletta
Currency: Pound (100 cents)

The islands that comprise Malta are rocky with low hills on which terraced fields of poor soil have been made for the growing of grain and vegetables, mostly potatoes, onions, and beans. There are no rivers.

The climate is generally hot and dry in summer and wet and cool in winter. It is almost always windy. The monthly average temperature at Valletta varies from 55 degrees F in January to 80 degrees F in July. High temperatures can exceed 100 degrees F in summer and there can be frost in winter. The annual rainfall is about 20 inches.

The coast is indented and rocky with stretches of sandy beach.

In about 1000 BC, the Phoenicians established ports and trading settlements on Malta and were followed by the Carthaginians. The islands became part of the Roman Empire about 200 BC. It was during the Roman period, in AD 60, that St. Paul was wrecked on Malta at a spot still called St. Paul's Bay.

The islands were occupied by Arabs in 870, and later became a colony of Sicily. They were granted to the Knights of St. John of Jerusalem in the 1500s.

The French, under Napoleon, occupied Malta in 1798, but the islanders appealed for help to the British, and in 1799 Nelson drove the French out. Subsequently, Malta became a British colony and an important naval base.

Malta's bravery during German World War II attacks gained the population the George Cross, the only time a medal has been given to an entire country.

Internal self-government came in 1961 and on Sept. 21, 1964, Malta became independent.

Utilization of the extensive shipyard facilities built by the British and a growing tourist traffic are important to the islands' economy. The most recent per capita income figure is $2,036 and the 1981 literacy rate was 83%.

The island's stamps have been popular with collectors since they were first issued in 1860.

Philatelic Bureau: Philatelic Bureau, GPO, Auberge d'Italie, Valletta, Malta.

MONACO, PRINCIPALITY OF

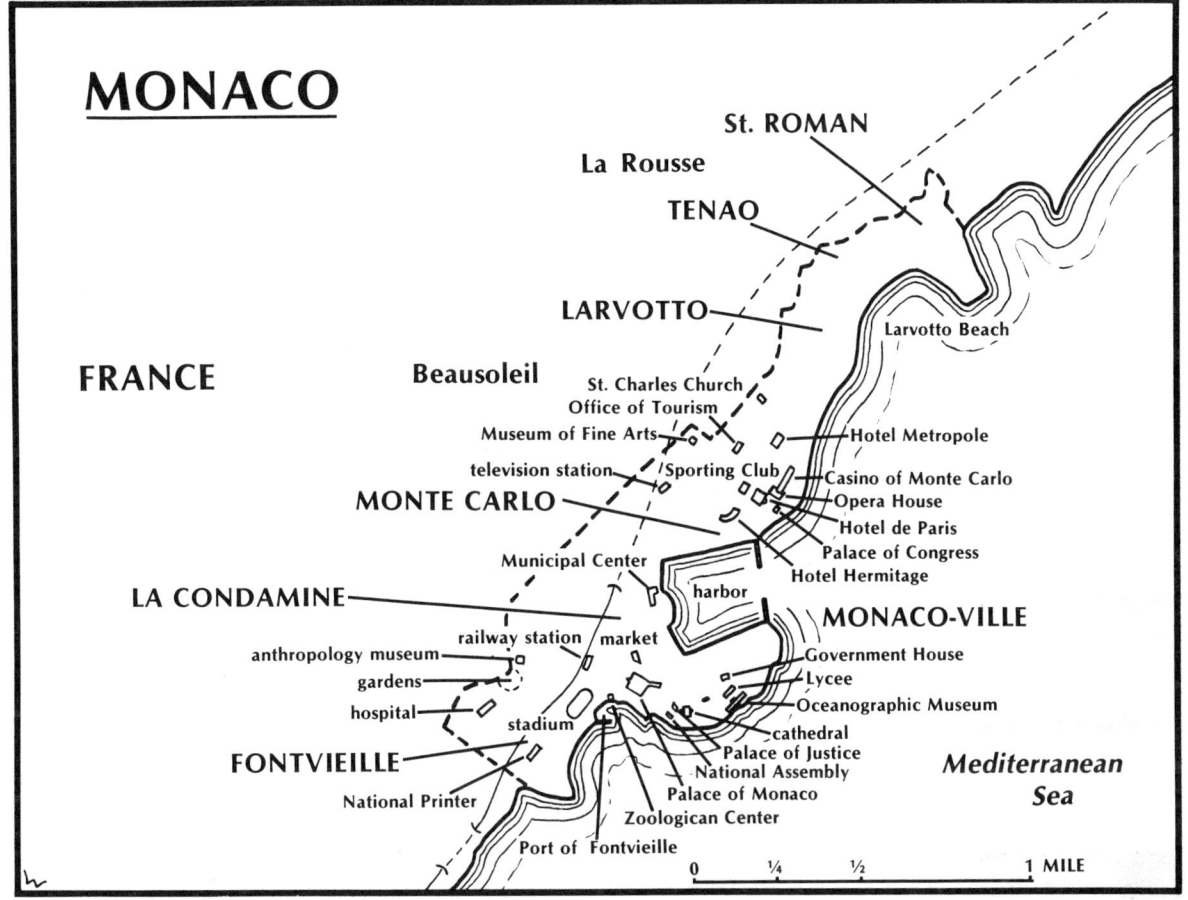

Area: .73 sq. mile
Population: 28,000 (1984)
Capital: Monaco-Ville
Currency: Franc (100 centimes)

Monaco is the world's second smallest state after the Vatican. It is situated on the south coast of France about nine miles east of Nice.

The principality is noted for its beautiful scenery and sunny climate. The average minimum temperature in winter is 48 degrees F and the average maximum in summer is 78 degrees F.

A Phoenician temple and later a Greek temple to the god Heracles stood on the headland of Monaco.

The House of Grimaldi has ruled Monaco almost continuously since AD 1070. In the early days, the ruler was entitled to two percent of the cargo of all ships passing within sight of the fortified town. It must have been satisfying to lie in the sun and watch the ships go by!

From 1793 to 1814, France dispossessed the Grimaldi family and annexed Monaco. Over the years, France has acquired portions of the principality, which was once more extensive than it is today.

A July 17, 1918 treaty with France provided for French protection and established that the policy of Monaco would not differ from that of France in the areas of political, military, naval, and economic interests.

Prince Rainier III, the present ruler, ascended the throne in 1949.

In contrast to popular belief, only four percent of Monaco's income is derived from its famous casino. Most, about 55%, comes from tourism, with 25-30% from the principality's industry, which includes chemicals, precision instruments, and plastics.

The first stamps were issued in 1885. The quantity of stamps issued in relation to postal requirements has gained the principality a widespread reputation for releasing them to augment its revenue by sales to collectors.

Philatelic Bureau: Office des Emissions de Timbres-Postes, Department de Finances, Principality of Monaco.

NORWAY, KINGDOM OF

Area: 125,057 sq. miles
Population: 4,145,000 (1984)
Capital: Oslo
Currency: Kroner (100 ore)

Norway, Land of the Midnight Sun, of scenic fjords, and the world's oldest stamp design still in use, is a narrow country running the length of the Scandinavian peninsula's west coast.

Its deeply indented, rugged, 2,125-mile coastline gives the country some of Europe's most spectacular scenery. The island group named Svalbard, 370 miles to the north is also part of Norway. Its area is 23,957 square miles.

Norway's interior is mountainous, interspersed with valleys and lakes. Much of the land is forested and only three percent is cultivated.

The modifying effect of the Atlantic Gulf Stream gives Norway a climate that belies its northern location. It has weather warmer than that of lands much further south.

On the western coast at Bergen, the average temperature in January is 35 degrees F and in July it is 57 degrees F. Oslo's average January temperature is 25 degrees F, rising to 65 degrees F in July.

The highest temperature ever recorded at Oslo is 95 degrees F. Even at Karasjok in the far north, a high temperature of 88 degrees F has been recorded. At North Cape, mainland Norway's most northerly point, there is an average of 190 days a year on which freezing temperatures are recorded.

Between May and August, the sun never completely sets at North Cape, while in the south, the long twilight gives no total darkness during the same period.

In winter, at North Cape, the sun does not rise above the horizon for more than two months. In the south at midwinter there are 17½ hours of darkness at night.

The greatest annual precipitation is in the mountains, where more than 100 inches can fall. This drops to 40 inches in the extreme south.

Norway has a history that reaches back into the mists of its Viking past. Its early inhabitants explored far beyond the reaches of the then-known world, even to the east coast of North America.

Between AD 800 and 1050, they settled in Greenland, Iceland, the Faroes, the Isle of Man, Scotland, Ireland, England, and France.

Harald I is generally regarded as the man who united Norway about AD 900, but others claim that Olaf II (AD 1015-1030) first ruled over the country.

There have been many rulers down the years and the thread of succession is a tangled one.

In 1397, the kingdoms of Sweden, Denmark, and Norway joined in the Union of Kalmar and for the next 400 years a weak Norway was ruled by Denmark.

During that period, the country declined and the Black Death ravaged it further. Both Sweden and Denmark were more powerful, and when Sweden pulled out of the union in the early 1500s, Denmark made a virtual province of Norway.

As a result of defeat in the Napoleonic wars, when Denmark allied itself with France, Denmark was forced to give up Norway to Sweden.

Norway objected to being given away and declared its independence. Although the attempt failed and Norway was forced to bow to Swedish will, a measure of independence was attained, including the right to have its own military forces, customs, and government. But it was not until 1905 that Norway became a kingdom in its own right.

After achieving its freedom and with a progressive and liberal government, Norway soon became one of the most advanced countries in Europe.

It succeeded in remaining neutral in World War I, and tried to do the same in World War II. In 1940, however, Germany invaded Norway and a new word was introduced into the English language — "quisling," meaning "traitor."

Vidkun Quisling was head of the Norwegian Nazi Party and his name soon became an epithet applied to all traitors as the Germans made him head of a Norway in captivity.

During the war, the government of Norway operated from London until May 9, 1945, when liberation came. Quisling was captured, tried, convicted, and hanged.

After the war, Norway abandoned its traditional neutrality and is now a member of NATO and the European Community, despite a 1957 Soviet threat that "it might have to pay dearly" for its behavior.

Norway's diverse economy, with industry powered by abundant hydroelectric resources, one of the world's largest merchant fleets, and North Sea oil, provides the country with a very high standard of living. The 1980 per capita income was $12,432 and the literacy rate is 99%.

The first Norwegian stamps were issued in 1855. The country has always followed a modest stamp-issuing policy and it has always been popular with collectors.

The Post Horn definitive design was first issued on Dec. 25, 1871 and, with minor modifications, is still in use today.

Country designations used by Norway on its stamps include both "NORGE" and "NOREG."

Philatelic Bureau: Postens Filatelitjeneste, Postboks 1085 Sentrum, Oslo 1, Norway.

A selection of Norwegian stamps. The famous posthorn design is seen on the left.

NETHERLANDS, KINGDOM OF THE

Area: 16,464 sq. miles
Population: 14,437,000 (1984)
Capital: The Hague
Amsterdam
Currency: Guilder (100 cents)

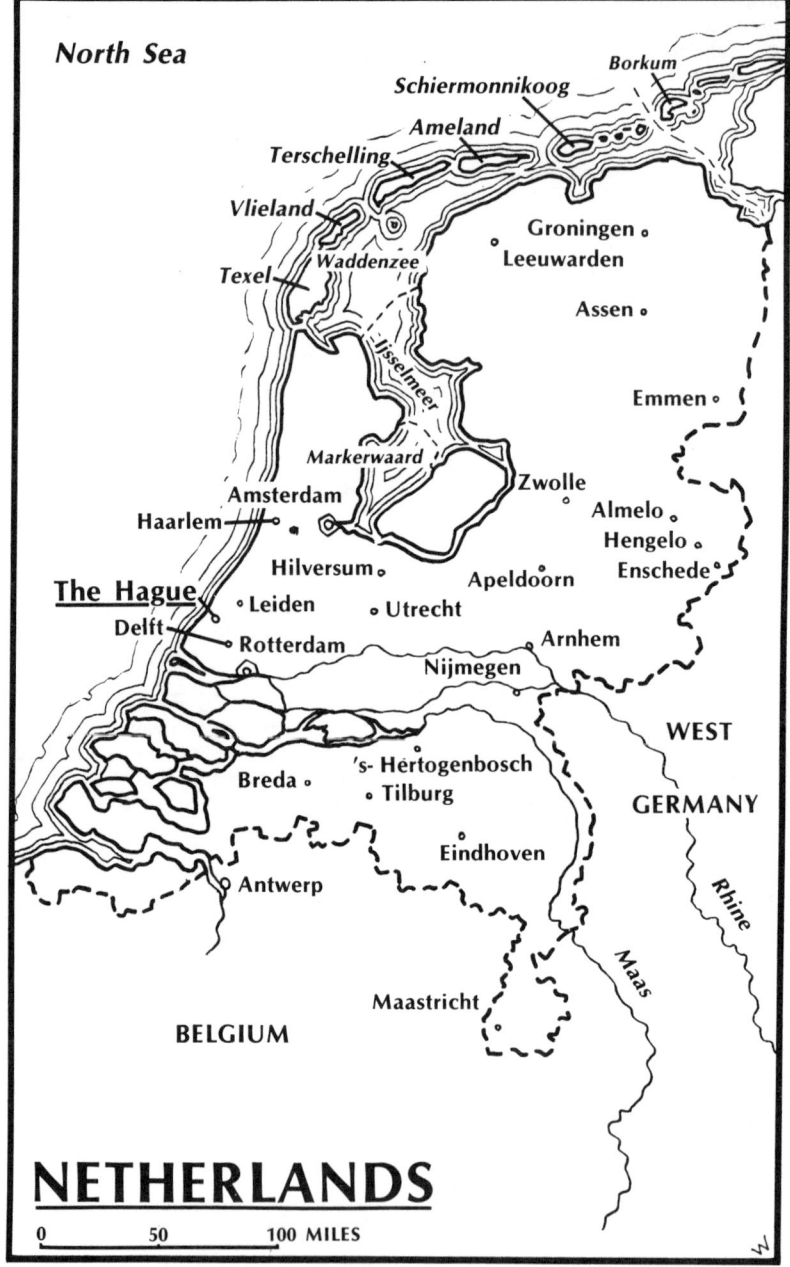

Most of the Netherlands is low and flat, with much of the area being below sea level. There are some low hills rising to about 1,000 feet in the southeastern portion of the country.

A large part of the country's land area had been reclaimed from the sea and is enclosed with an elaborate system of dikes.

The climate is cool and damp. Summer temperatures seldom exceed 75 degrees F. Winters are long, with damp, cold winds sweeping in off the North Sea. The average winter temperature is about 32 degrees F. Rainfall averages 25-30 inches a year.

In 55 BC, Julius Caesar made the area of the Netherlands part of the Roman Empire. After the fall of Rome, Charlemagne added it to his territory. Subsequently, the Netherlands, which then included Belgium and Flanders, was split among Europe's nobility until it eventually came under the Spanish crown.

During the 17th century, the country became a powerful colonial nation and its navy won great respect. During the 1700s, Dutch power waned and Napoleon conquered the area, making his brother Louis king.

Following the defeat of Napoleon in 1815, the Congress of Vienna made the Netherlands a kingdom under William I. In 1830, Belgium broke away from the kingdom and set up housekeeping on its own, with Prince Leopold of Saxe-Coburg as King Leopold I.

The Netherlands remained neutral during World War I, but suffered greatly under a brutal German occupation during World War II. This experience, plus the aggressive behavior of the Soviet Union after the war, decided the

Dutch to abandon neutrality. The nation has been a strong supporter of NATO and the European Community.

The Netherlands' economy has a broad base and includes such varied elements as shipping, heavy industry, diamond cutting, bulb raising, and tourism.

The 1983 per capita income was $9,175 and the 1984 literacy rate is 98%.

The first stamps were released in 1852 and since then the country has pursued a relatively modest stamp-issuing policy.

Philatelic Bureau: Netherlands Post Office Philatelic Service, PO Box 30051, 9700-RN Groningen, the Netherlands.

POLAND (POLISH PEOPLE'S REPUBLIC)

Area: 120,727 sq. miles
Population: 36,887,000 (1984)
Capital: Warsaw
Currency: Zloty (100 groszy)

Poland, a nation whose borders have been adjusted many times, currently has a coastline on the Baltic Sea and is located on a large plain that stretches from central Europe to the Ural Mountains, deep in the Soviet Union. The Carpathian Mountains form the southern border with Czechoslovakia.

The climate features cold winters and mild summers. The winters are most extreme when influenced by strong winds out of the east. Temperatures remain below freezing for at least two months in the winter in the west and three months in the east. Rivers freeze and even harbors on the Baltic are icebound for varying periods.

Warsaw has an average temperature in January of 27 degrees F and in July of 66 degrees F. Precipitation ranges from 20-30 inches a year, falling mostly as snow in winter months.

Poland was a great power in the 14th to 17th centuries, but was divided between Austria, Prussia, and Russia in the 18th century.

It did not regain its freedom until the end of World War I; a freedom that was to last only until 1939, when Germany and the Soviet Union invaded the country and carved it up between them. In their World War II occupation area, the Germans murdered some six million Poles, about half of them Jews.

At the end of the war, despite the existence of a recognized Polish government-in-exile in London, the Soviet Union installed its own puppet regime and made Poland a satellite country.

Despite unrest and the desire of Poles to run their own country, the Soviet Union remains firmly in control.

Poland's economy is poor, although the country has considerable heavy industry and mineral resources. The 1982 per capita income was $4,670 and the literacy rate is 98%.

The first stamp issue was in 1860 under Russian control. Since World War II, stamp issues have been extensive and a great mass of canceled-to-order material has been exported to the West.

Philatelic Bureau: Ars Polona, PO Box 1001, 00-950 Warsaw, Poland.

PORTUGAL, REPUBLIC OF

Area: 36,390 sq. miles
Population: 10,045,000 (1984)
Capital: Lisbon
Currency: Escudo (100 centavos)

Portugal is located in the extreme southwest part of Europe and shares the Iberian Peninsula with Spain.

The Azores and Madeira, two island groups in the Atlantic Ocean, are also part of metropolitan Portugal. The mainland is divided by the Tagus Valley into a mountainous northern area, with lowlands to the south.

The climate is mild, with moist winters and dry summers. Sea-level temperatures in January average 48 degrees F in the north, increasing to 52 degrees F in the south.

Lisbon receives about 24 inches of rain each year, while Porto gets about 45 inches.

Portugal was once the Roman province of Lusitania. Following the fall of Rome, the area became part of Spain. In AD 1143, Portugal became an independent kingdom under King Alfonso I.

Beginning in the early 15th century, Prince Henry the Navigator made Portugal one of the world's greatest maritime powers. Gradually its explorers spun their web across the world and by 1490, Bartholomeu Dias had sailed around the Cape of Good Hope and opened a route to the riches of the East.

An agreement with Spain gave Portugal all the New World lands for a distance of 100 leagues (later 370 leagues) west of the Azores and Cape Verde Islands. This brought Brazil into the Portuguese Empire.

As it must to all empires, decline came to Portugal's and in 1580, Spain defeated Portugal to begin

what the Portuguese call The Sixty Years' Captivity. In 1640, the country regained its freedom.

An end to the monarchy came in 1910 when a revolution created the republic.

Years of political instability have rendered the economy shaky. There is some light industry and the country is the world's major exporter of cork. Mineral resources include tungsten, uranium, and iron. Crops are grains, grapes, olives, rice, and potatoes. Wine is an important product.

The 1984 per capita income was $1,930 and the 1985 literacy rate was 80%.

Stamps were first issued in 1885 and the country has a varied and interesting philatelic history.

Philatelic Bureau: Philatelic Office, Av. Casal Ribeiro 28-2°, 1096 Lisbon Codex, Portugal.

PORTUGAL — AZORES

Area: 888 sq. miles
Population: 292,000 (1975)
Capital: Ponta Delgada
Currency: Escudo (100 centavos)

The Azores is a group of nine volcanic islands about 800 miles west of Lisbon. They are part of Portugal and comprise the districts of Ponta Delgada, Angra do Heroismo, and Horta.

The climate is mild, with sea-level temperatures ranging from 48 degrees F in January to 82 degrees F in July. There are often strong west winds in winter and mild breezes from the northeast in summer.

The islands are believed to have been discovered about 1427 by the Portuguese explorer Diogo de Silves. The first settlement was made in 1432 on Santa Maria.

The Azores resumed issuing stamps on Jan. 2, 1980. Stamps had previously been issued from 1868-1931, and for Horta and Ponta Delgada in the 19th century.

Since the islands are now an integral part of Portugal, philatelic sales are the most likely explanation for the resumption of stamp issues.

Philatelic Bureau: Philatelic Office, Av. Casal Ribeiro 28-2°, 1906 Lisbon Codex, Portugal.

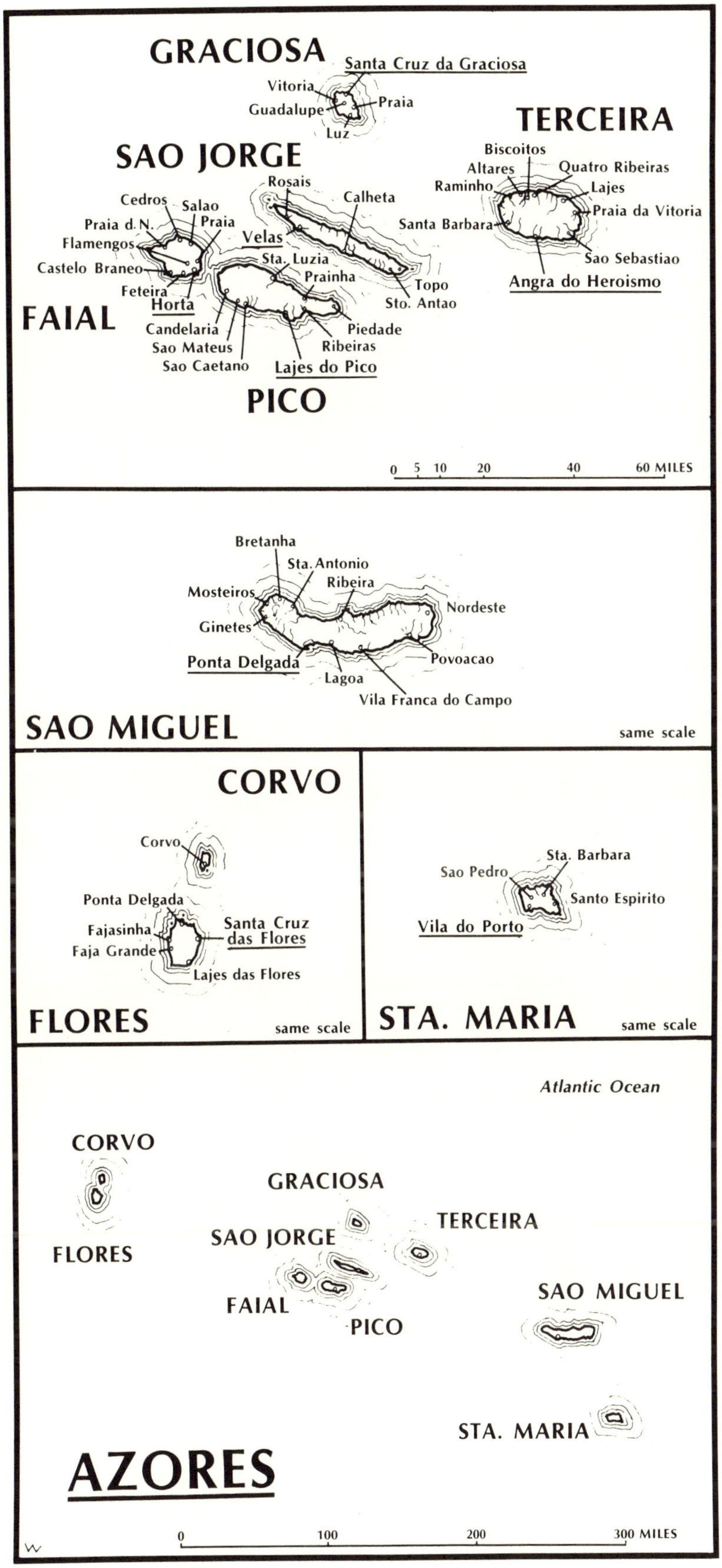

PORTUGAL — MADEIRA

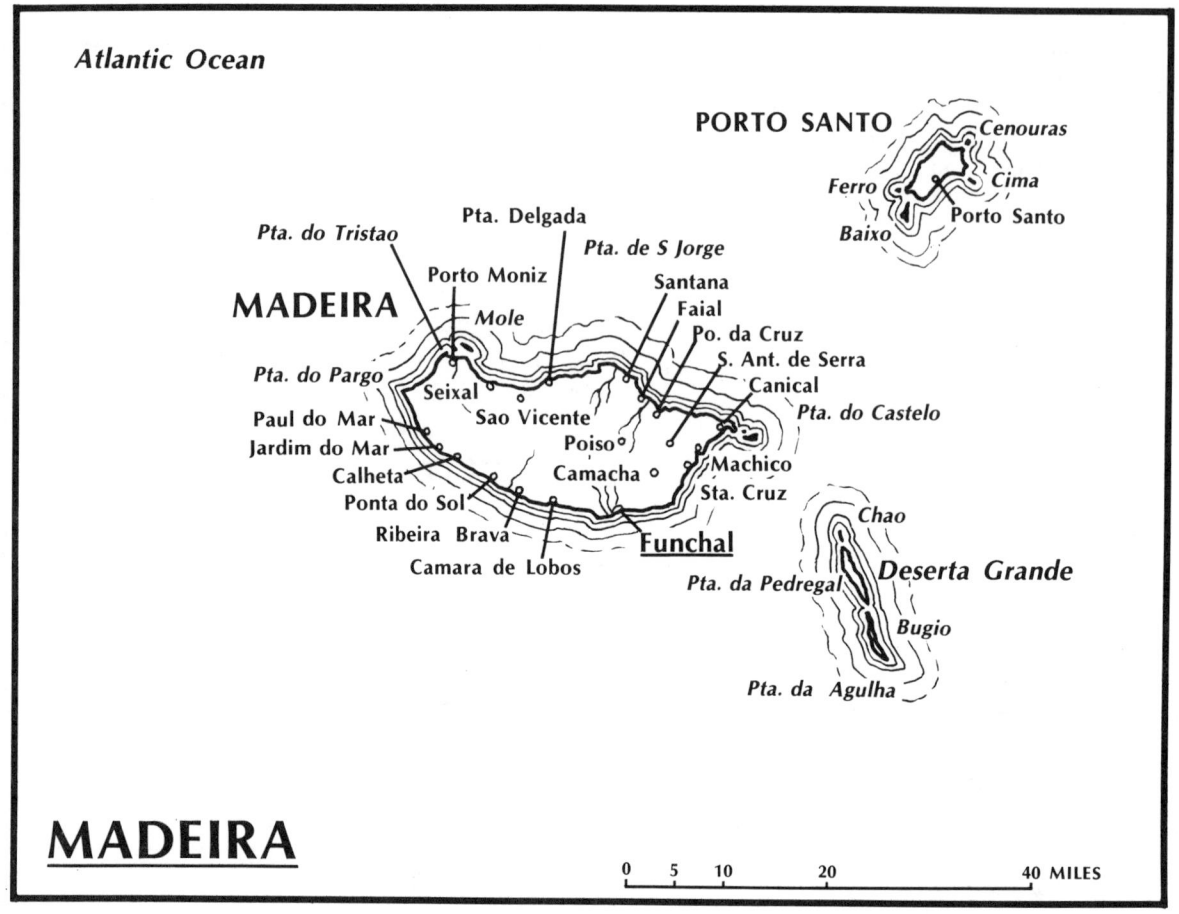

Area: 307 sq. miles
Population: 270,000 (1976)
Capital: Funchal
Currency: Escudo (100 centavos)

Located about 360 miles off the African coast and 535 miles from Lisbon, Portugal, Madeira is a group of islands that is part of that country.

The climate is mild and healthy, with an average annual temperature of 65 degrees F at Funchal. Frost is unknown. Rainfall ranges from

under 25 inches at Funchal to 80 inches on the northern slopes.

Believed to have been discovered by the Phoenicians, the islands were colonized by Prince Henry the Navigator of Portugal in the mid-1400s. The thick forest covering the island was burned off and the fires are said to have burned for years. Sugar was planted and a wine industry developed.

The British occupied the islands for a brief period in 1801 and again from 1807-14.

Although wine dominates agricultural exports, sugar and bananas are still important and there is a considerable fishery. Tourism is important.

Embroidery was introduced in 1850 by an Englishwoman and employs about 40,000 people. The value of embroidery products has exceeded the value of wine as an export.

The Madeira islands are currently enjoying a philatelic revival, with the resumption on Jan. 2, 1980 of their own stamps after many years of postal anonymity.

Stamps had been first issued from 1868-1898, when stamps of Portugal were resumed. These were used until 1980, with the exception of an issue in 1928-29 to raise funds for a museum. Their use was obligatory on certain dates during both years.

Since the islands are part of Portugal, there appears no political reason for the resumption of stamp issues and philatelic sales are the likeliest reason.

Philatelic Bureau: Philatelic Office, Av. Casal Ribeiro 28-2°, 1906 Liston Codex, Portugal.

ROMANIA, SOCIALIST REPUBLIC OF

Area: 91,700 sq. miles
Population: 22,683,000 (1984)
Capital: Bucharest
Currency: Leu (100 bani)

It is through Romania that the Danube River comes to the end of its journey into the Black Sea. The country occupies much of the basin of the Danube, which also forms most of its southern border with Bulgaria.

Romania's climate is mostly continental, with long cold winters lasting from December to March, hot summers, and long autumn seasons. Spring is very short with winter merging almost directly into summer.

The January average minimum temperature at Bucharest is 20 degrees F and the average maximum temperature in July is 85 degrees F.

Modern Romania was formed from the two principalities of Moldavia and Walachia.

Walachia was created in 1330 and Moldavia in 1349. By the 16th century both were under Turkish control and they turned to Russia in the 18th century for help in easing their lot. In 1774 Russia defeated Turkey and obtained better treatment for the two provinces.

Moldavia and Walachia united in 1862 and in 1881 became the independent Kingdom of Romania under Carol I.

Beaten by Hungary in World War I, Romania gained large territories in the peace settlement. During World War II, the country allied with Germany, taking an active part in the German invasion of the Soviet Union. At the end of the war, Soviet forces occupied Romania and turned it into a Soviet satellite.

It has been one of the more outspoken and independent satellites, though, and actually spoke out against the Soviet invasion of Czechoslovakia in 1968.

Romania's economy is diversified and includes steel, machinery, oil products, chemicals, and textiles. There are reserves of oil, natural gas, and coal. Tourism is of growing importance.

The 1980 per capita income was $5,250 and the literacy rate is 98%.

Romania's first stamps were issued in 1865.

Philatelic Bureau: ILEXIM, 13 Decembrie St. No. 3, PO Box 136-137, Bucharest, Romania.

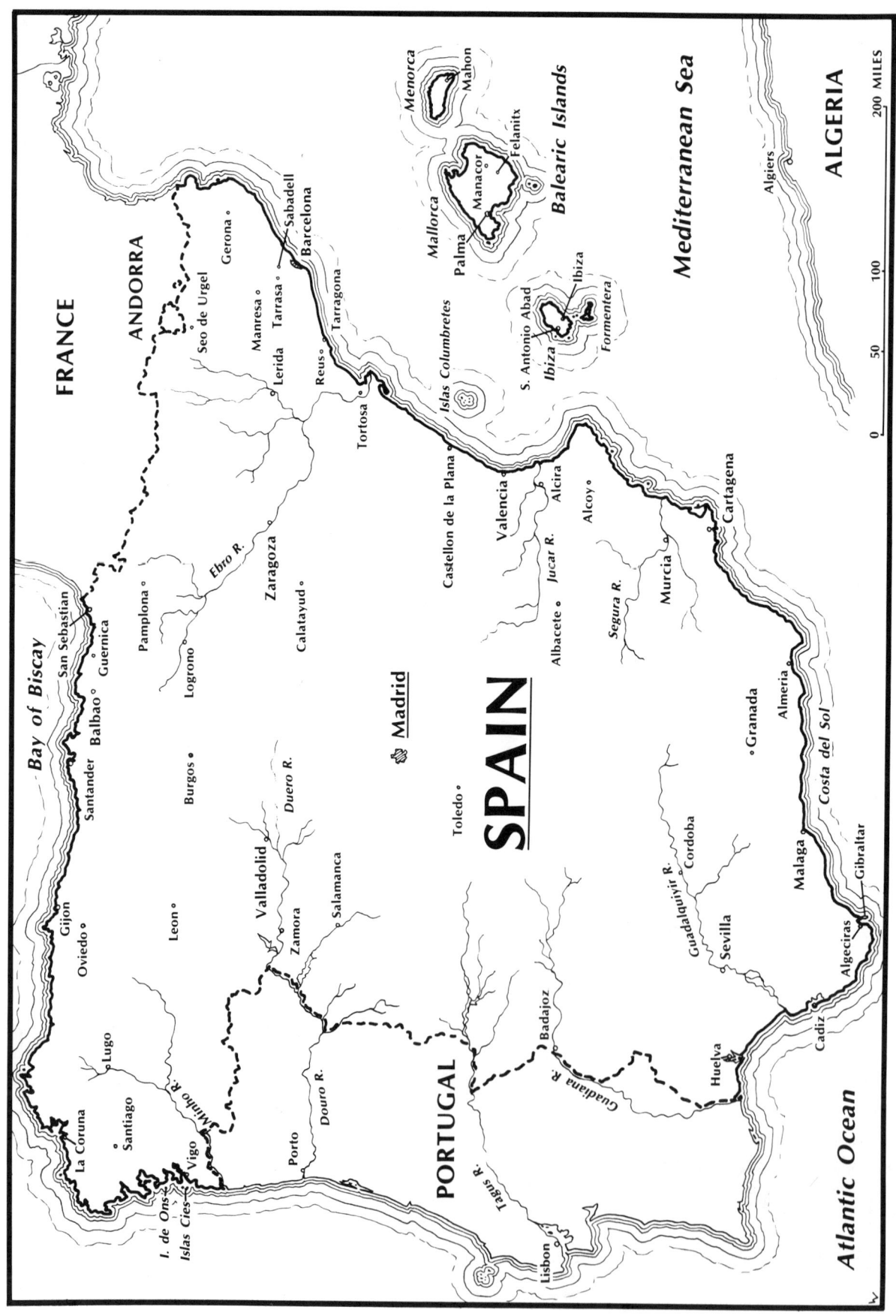

SPAIN (SPANISH STATE)

Area: 195,988 sq. miles
Population: 38,435,000 (1984)
Capital: Madrid
Currency: Peseta (100 centimos)

Spain currently comprises the Iberian Peninsula except for Portugal, the Balearic Islands, Canary Islands, and the Moroccan enclaves of Ceuta and Melilla.

The mainland area consists mostly of high plateau rising from the sea. This is divided into smaller areas by mountain ranges and rivers.

Most of the country is arid with large temperature extremes and receives less than 20 inches of rain a year. An exception occurs in the northwest, where there is a moderate climate with only a small temperature range and relatively high rainfall. As an example, Santiago receives an average of 65 inches of rain each year, while Almeria, on the Mediterranean coast, gets only about 10 inches.

The capital city of Madrid is located at the country's center. Its altitude is about 2,000 feet, making it Europe's highest capital city.

The early history of the Iberian Peninsula was marked by a series of incursians. From the Mediterranean came the Phoenicians, Greeks, and Carthaginians. The Celts and Romans came overland from Europe.

The Romans came to stay and not until the seventh century did the last of the Roman strongholds on the southern coast fall to the invading Visigoths. The Moors swept in from the sea in AD 711 and within a few years had driven the Visigoths far to the north.

Efforts to expel the Moors lasted more than 700 years and not until 1492, the year that Columbus discovered the Western Hemisphere, did Spain overcome the last Moor resistance and unite under Ferdinand and Isabella.

During the 1500s, Spain became the world's most powerful nation. It built up a great empire in the New World, looting it of its treasure and enslaving the native population. It also occupied the Netherlands and considerable territory in Germany and Italy.

With the defeat by the English of the "invincible Armada" in 1588, the power of Spain in Europe began to wane.

Napoleon invaded the Iberian Peninsula and installed his brother Joseph on the Spanish throne (1808-1814). Spain was restored to independence largely as a result of the Duke of Wellington's Peninsula War against the French.

During the 19th century, the Spanish colonial empire in the Americas gained its freedom. At the end of the century, the Spanish-American War of 1898 eliminated the last Spanish colonies in the Americas, when the United States took Cuba and Puerto Rico.

Political instability continued in Spain until the mid-1930s, when it erupted into a bloody civil war as a Spanish general, Francisco Franco began, with the help of Germany and Italy, to take over the country. By 1939, he had become ruler of Spain. His fascist dictatorship lasted until his death in 1975.

Spain remained neutral in World War II despite German overtures to join the Axis against the Western Allies.

On Franco's death, Prince Juan Carlos was made king. He restored democratic institutions and brought Spain out of its fascist period. Spain's first free elections since 1936, were held June 15, 1977.

During the 1960s and up to the mid-1970s, Spain experienced strong economic growth and was ranked as the world's ninth largest industrial power. Since then, the economy has declined and in 1985 the unemployment rate was 18.6%, the highest in Europe.

Industry is diverse, ranging from shipbuilding to textiles. There are extensive mineral resources including oil, uranium, lead, iron, copper, zinc, and coal.

The 1979 per capita income was $5,500 and the literacy rate is 97%.

Spain, which issued its first stamps in 1850, began in 1930 an outstanding period of Spanish stamp design and production. The first issue in this period was a spectacular set honoring the painter Goya and reproduced some of his paintings, including the famous *La Maja Desnuda,* which raised a few conservative eyebrows, but delighted a whole generation of young collectors! That issue and the following Columbus issue remain highlights of Spanish stamps.

Recent intaglio-printed stamps have also been attractive, but the photogravure produced stamps have suffered from being printed on a poor quality coated paper that neither stands up to handling nor does justice to the subjects imprinted on it.

Among the best of modern issues are the Castles series and the ships set.

Philatelic Bureau: Direccion General de Correos, Servicio Filatelico Internacional, Madrid 14, Spain.

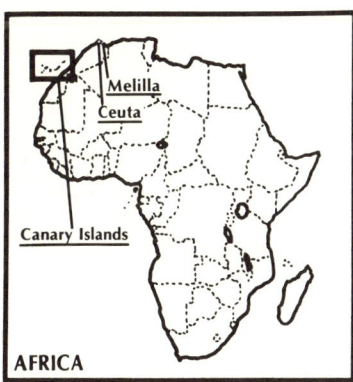

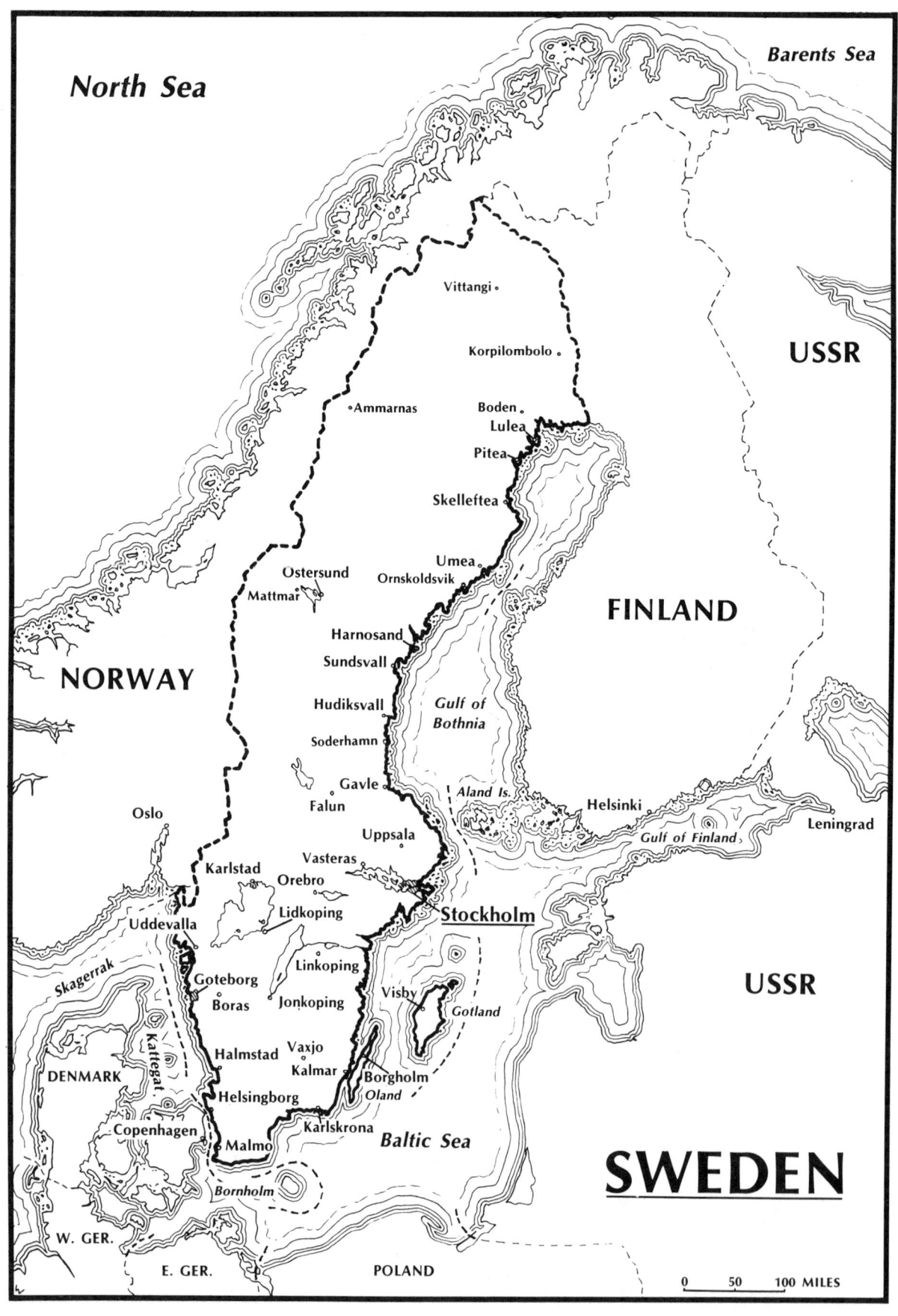

SWEDEN, KINGDOM OF

Area: 179,900 sq. miles
Population: 8,335,000 (1984)
Capital: Stockholm
Currency: Krona (100 ore)

Sweden shares the Scandinavian Peninsula with Norway and fronts on the Gulf of Bothnia, the Baltic Sea, and the Kattegat. The country is long and has an average width of 250 miles.

Its climate is generally similar to that of New England despite being in the same latitude as Alaska and the southern portion of Greenland. This is because of the modifying effect of the Atlantic Gulf Stream. Even so, winter lasts about six months.

There is a large variation in the hours of daylight between winter and summer. At Stockholm in winter, the sun rises at 9 a.m. and sets at 3 p.m. Midsummer days last from 2:30 a.m. to 9 p.m.

The country tends to be rolling to flat in the southern and central areas. Mountains are found in the northern part, mostly along the border with Norway. There are a number of rivers that run across the country from the mountains in the west to the Gulf of Bothnia and the Baltic Sea.

Temperatures vary according to location. Stockholm has a January average of 28 degrees F and a July average of 62 degrees F. At Haparanda, at the northern end of the Gulf of Bothnia, the average January temperature is 13 degrees F and for July is 61 degrees F.

Southern Sweden receives between 20-30 inches of precipitation each year. North of Haparanda this drops to less than 20 inches, most of which falls as snow.

The Gulf of Bothnia freezes during the winter and ports are closed from mid-November to mid-May. Stockholm and the other Baltic ports are not usually closed.

Swedes have called Sweden home for some 5,000 years, longer than any other European people. A Viking society dominated its early history and their travels carried them as far as the Black Sea.

About AD 800, English, Danish, and German monks introduced Christianity and in AD 1003, the first Swedish king was baptized.

After about 1100, the Viking type of society was replaced by a feudal system.

Before the end of the 12th century Sweden conquered Finland and Denmark attacked Sweden to begin a long series of wars between two countries.

In 1397, the Union of Kalmar united Sweden, Denmark, and Norway. But even during this period Danes were fighting Swedes. The union came to an end in the early 1500s.

In the 16th century, Sweden entered a period of expansion, even to the point of occupying parts of Estonia and Poland. After 1600, Sweden was engaged in war with Poland and the Hapsburg armies in Germany.

In 1638, a Swedish settlement was established near Wilmington, Delaware, which the Dutch took over in mid-century.

Swedish armies invaded Russia and defeated Peter the Great at Narva in 1700. They were beaten in 1709 at Poltava, and after this, Sweden's power declined and the heyday of its European incursions ended. Sweden lost Finland to Russia in 1809, but at the end of the Napoleonic Wars, received Norway. This proved something of a headache, since Norway badly wanted its own independence, something it achieved in 1905.

During the 19th century most of the institutions of modern Sweden came into being and the country entered a period of industrialization.

Sweden remained neutral during World Wars I and II and benefited greatly from trade with the warring nations.

The country remains determined to go it alone and still follows a policy of armed neutrality. In recent years it has protested numerous violations of its territorial waters and airspace by the Soviet Union.

The Swedish economy is diverse and well developed, ranging from shipbuilding to the making of automobiles. It has a technologically advanced aviation industry, designing and building many of its own military aircraft.

Mineral resources include iron, copper, gold, silver, zinc, and lead.

Forest products account for a quarter of the country's exports and the country is almost self-sufficient in food production.

The 1980 per capita income was $14,621 and the literacy rate is 99%.

Sweden's first stamps were issued in 1855. After Great Britain, Sweden was the first country to use perforated stamps, the first issue being perforated 14.

Most Swedish stamps are intaglio printed and are noted for the fine quality of their design and engraving. Modern stamps are produced either in coil or booklet formats.

Only a few semi-postal or air mail stamps have been released.

Philatelic Bureau: PFA Postens Frimarksavdelning, S-105 02 Stockholm, Sweden.

SAN MARINO, MOST SERENE REPUBLIC OF

Area: 24 sq. miles
Population: 23,000 (1984)
Capital: San Marino
Currency: Lira (100 centesimi)

Tiny San Marino claims to be the oldest state in Europe. It is enclaved in north central Italy, about 12 miles from the shores of the Adriatic Sea.

It is a mountainous state, with the three peaks of 2,300-foot Mount Titano, each capped by a castle, being its highest points. The three peaks are San Marino's best-known landmark and are featured on the state's coat of arms and several of its stamps.

The climate is moderate and about 35 inches of rain fall each year.

According to legend, San Marino was founded in the fourth century AD by a Christian stone cutter, a native of the island of Arb (Rab), who left nearby Rimini because of religious persecution.

In the ninth century its recorded history began when a monastery existed there. A community grew up around it and a small state developed.

In 1862, during the formation of the unified Kingdom of Italy, a treaty was concluded. It has been renewed at intervals ever since. During World War II, the country managed to remain neutral, although it was heavily bombed.

Universal male suffrage came in 1909, but women did not receive the vote until 1960.

All citizens able to bear arms are required to do so from age 16-55.

The economy of San Marino is based on agriculture and the raising of livestock. There is some light industry. Cheese is an important product.

Tourism is the state's largest money maker and many thousands of tourists visit each year. Hotels and restaurants have been built to serve them and there is considerable demand for gold and silver articles and pottery.

Postage stamps are included in lists of San Marino's most important exports, although the country is not such a prolific producer as in the past.

San Marino released its first stamps in 1877. During the 1960s a large number of different issues appeared, many having subjects with no San Marino connection and obviously made for philatelic sale.

More recently, the flood has diminished and current stamp-issuing policies are relatively modest.

Philatelic Bureau: Philatelic Office, 47031 Republic of San Marino.

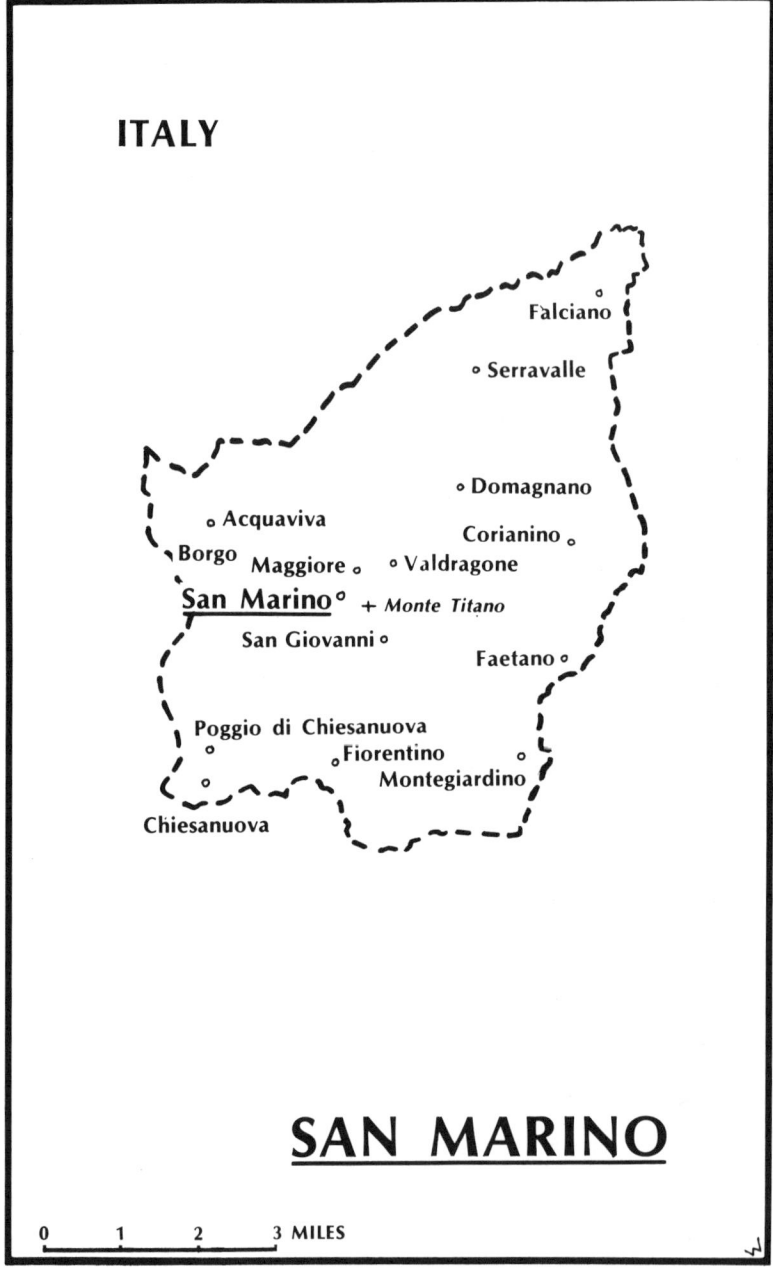

SWITZERLAND (SWISS CONFEDERATION)

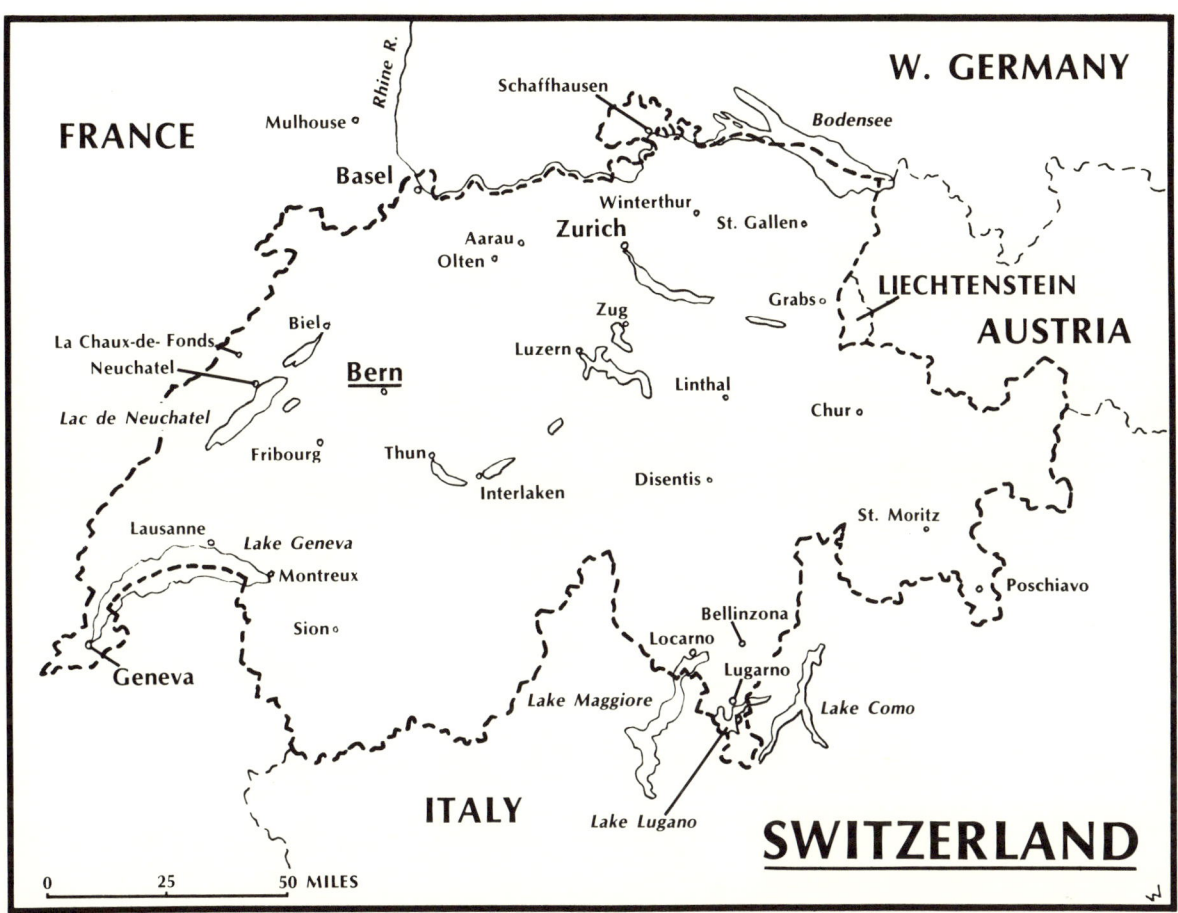

Area: 15,941 sq. miles
Population: 6,500,000 (1984)
Capital: Bern
Currency: Franc (100 centimes)

A federal republic of 23 cantons, Switzerland is located at the meeting point of northern and southern Europe. It is also Europe's watershed. The Rhine River that flows to the north rises there, as does the Rhone, which flows south through France to the Mediterranean. Both the River Inn, which flows into the Danube and the Ticino, which becomes the Italian River Po, have their sources in Switzerland.

The Alps, an extensive mountain range, runs across the southern part of the country and the Jura Mountains are located along the western and northwestern borders. The two ranges enclose much of the country in the center as a plateau area. The highest point in Switzerland is 15,200-foot Mount Rosa.

The climate varies with altitude, with average January temperatures ranging from 32 degrees F at Basel (900 feet) to 16 degrees F at Santis (8,200 feet). Bern receives about 40 inches of precipitation each year.

The country was part of the Roman Empire until the fourth century AD. After Rome fell, Teutonic tribes made numerous invasions. The area became part of Charlemagne's empire and later came under German domination.

Independence dates from 1315 with the birth of the Swiss Confederation after the Battle of Morgarten, when the Swiss defeated the Hapsburg army.

Switzerland's policy of permanent neutrality began in the early 1500s and it has not fought a foreign war since then, although it defended itself from French invasion in 1798.

The Swiss economy is varied and ranges from international banking to dairy products and chocolate. Instrument making, drugs, and tourism are also important.

The 1984 per capita income was $14,408 and the literacy rate is 99%.

The first stamps were the cantonal issues for Zurich (1843), Geneva (1843), and Basel (1845). Federal stamps came in 1850.

Philatelic Bureau: Philatelic Service PTT, Zeughausgasse 19, CH-3030 Bern, Switzerland.

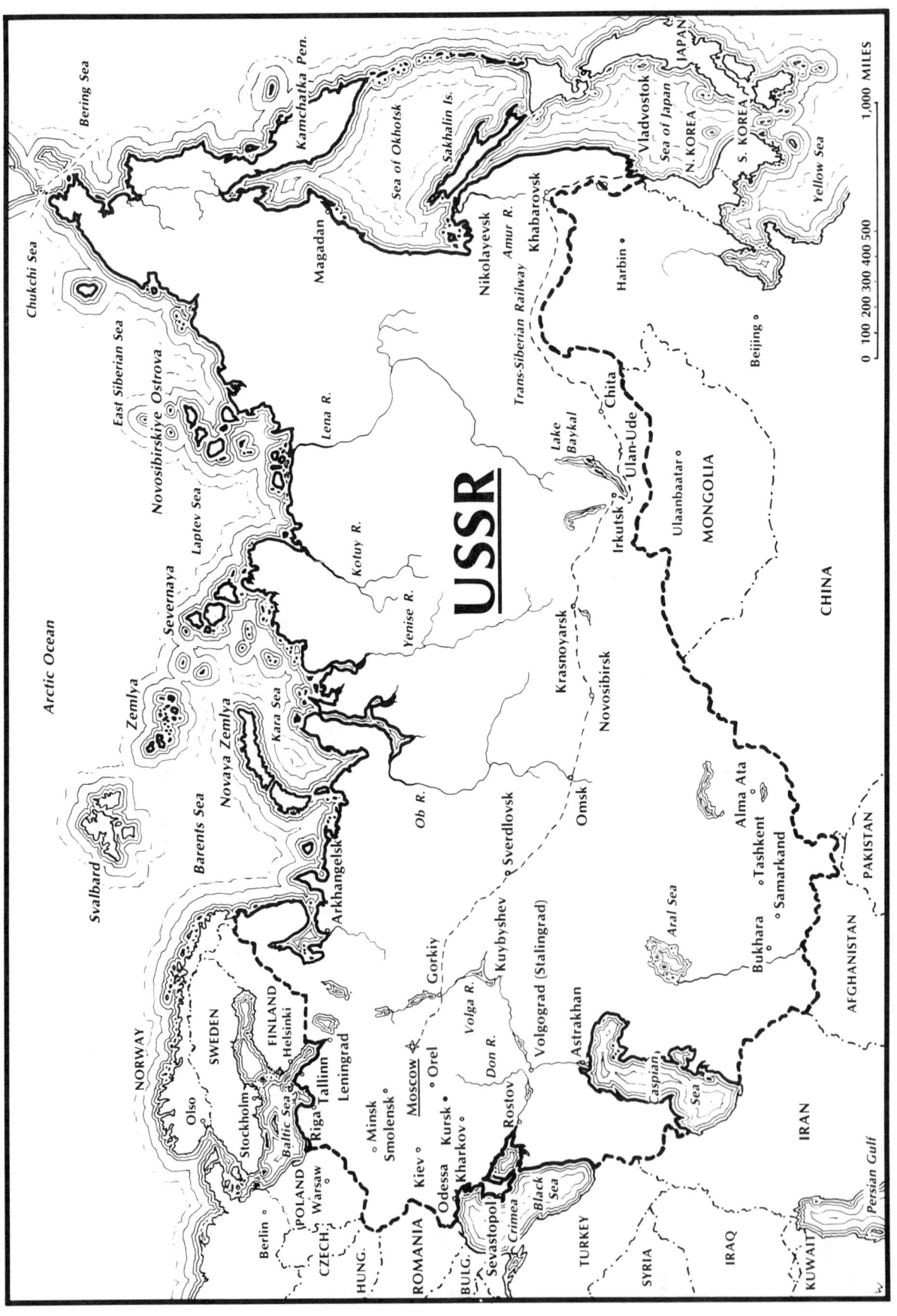

UNION OF SOVIET SOCIALIST REPUBLICS (USSR)

Area: 8,649,500 sq. miles
Population: 272,500,000 (1983)
Capital: Moscow
Currency: Ruble (100 kopecks)

The Soviet Union is a federation of 15 republics, the largest of which is the Russian Soviet Federated Socialist Republic. It contains more than 50 percent of the country's total population and 75 percent of its area.

About 20 percent of the USSR is mountainous. Mostly, the mountains are located along the southern border of the country, forming a natural barrier to communications.

The highest peak is 24,590-foot Mount Communism in the Pamir Mountains, near where Afghanistan and China meet.

In the Caucasus Mountains, between the Black Sea and the Caspian, Mount Elbrus rises to 18,480 feet, the highest point in Europe.

Running for more than 20,000 miles along the Arctic and Pacific coasts of the Soviet Union is a deeply indented coastline. It is the longest of any country.

Because much of its coast is frozen in winter, the Soviet Union has few year-round outlets to the ocean. Apart from Black Sea ports, two exceptions are Murmansk on the Kola Peninsula and Petropavlovsk near the tip of the Kamchatka Peninsula. Other ports, including the large naval base at Vladivostok, are kept open in winter with ice breakers.

The main river is the Volga, which runs for 2,500 miles from north of Moscow to the Caspian Sea. It is the largest European river and drains almost one third of the Soviet Union in Europe.

The Caspian Sea, which is on the border between Europe and Asia, is the world's largest lake. It has an area of 170,000 square miles.

The great expanse of the Soviet Union includes all types of climates except tropical. The one outstanding feature, to which most of the country is subject, is the length and severity of the winter season. In some northern areas it can run from September to May and almost half of the country has a six-month winter.

Notable exceptions are the Caucasus and Crimea, which enjoy subtropical conditions. The south coast of the Crimea on the Black Sea, has a mild Mediterranean-type climate and is the country's resort area.

In contrast, the Verkhoyansk Region of Yakutsk ASSR is known as the land of perpetual frost, where temperatures of -90 degrees F have been recorded.

The country's hottest area is in Turkmen SSR on the border with Iran and Afghanistan. Here, temperatures as high as 105 degrees F can occur and the July average is 85 degrees F.

In Moscow, the temperature can fall to -40 degrees F in winter and the city has a July average of 64 degrees F. The maximum temperature recorded in the city is 99 degrees F. The first snow falls on Moscow in October and before the thaw comes in April, it can reach a depth of 4-5 feet. Rainfall averages 20-25 inches each year.

The history of the Soviet Union began with the Russian Revolution of 1917, although there had been unrest for a number of years prior to that.

The first Russian state had been founded around Novgorod and Kiev in the ninth century AD by Scandinavians, but it was Peter the Great (1682-1725) who founded the Russian Empire in 1721.

During the 19th and early 20th centuries modern Western ideas began to spread through the country, while the rulers tried to keep the people in a state of virtual bondage. The regime began to fall apart after the defeats by Japan in 1905 and the Germans during World War I.

In 1917, the Russian boiler, its safety valve tied down by the government, exploded. The czar and his family were murdered and, within a short time, a communist regime was established under Lenin.

After Lenin's death in 1924, Stalin took power, maintaining his rule with terror, a series of brutal purges, mass executions, and exile to work camps for all who opposed him.

When Germany invaded the Soviet Union in 1941, the Communists came close to defeat, but with courage and massive aid from the United States and Great Britain, the Germans were driven back. The Soviets occupied eastern Germany by the end of the war.

After the war, the Soviet Union concentrated on expanding its domination over its Eastern European neighbors. It occupied the independent nations of Latvia, Lithuania, and Estonia and made them part of the Soviet Union, an occupation that the United States has never recognized.

During the past 40 years, the cold war between the Soviet Union and the West has alternated between periods of mutual suspicion and of outright confrontation, including the Berlin Blockade, the invasions of Czechoslovakia and Hungary, the Cuban missile affair, the invasion of Afghanistan, and the interference in Poland.

Most of the USSR's industry is state-owned and its heavy industry is second only to that of the United States. The 1976 per capita income was $2,600 and the literacy rate is 99%.

The stamps of the Soviet Union have been released in enormous quantities and it is without question the most prolific of all stamp-issuing nations. Much of its output is exported to the West in canceled-to-order form as a means of acquiring hard currency.

Philatelic Bureau: Philatelic Department, V/O Mezhdunarodnaya Kniga, Moscow 121200, USSR.

UNITED KINGDOM

Area: 94,222 sq. miles
Population: 56,023,000 (1984)
Capital: London
Currency: Pound (100 pence)

The United Kingdom comprises England, Northern Ireland, Scotland, and Wales, and is located on two main islands off the coast of northwestern Europe. At its closest point, across the Strait of Dover, the French coast is just 22 miles distant.

England is mostly rolling country with ranges of low hills. Scotland is composed of hills near the border, the Lowlands in the central area and the Highlands in the north. Wales is almost all hilly with mountains in the north, and Northern Ireland is generally open agricultural country.

The climate is influenced by the Gulf Stream and is more moderate than that of the nearby European mainland.

In England, the weather is variable and subject to sudden and frequent changes. Long periods of settled weather are rare.

English temperatures in winter show little variation between north and south. Newcastle in the north, London, and Gloucester in the west, all have a January average temperature of 40 degrees F. In the south, the average July temperature is 62 degrees F, two degrees less than in the north, mainly because of solar heating during slightly longer days.

Rain falls throughout the year and ranges from 30-40 inches a year in the west to 20-25 inches in the east.

Celtic-speaking people from Europe inhabited England when the Romans first visited in 55 BC. The Roman conquest did not begin until AD 43 and within four years they occupied the country.

During their time in England, the Romans built Hadrian's Wall across the north of the country to keep out the warlike Picts, established more than 50 cities and towns, and built a network of roads.

However, Roman culture had little impact on the native population and

UNITED KINGDOM

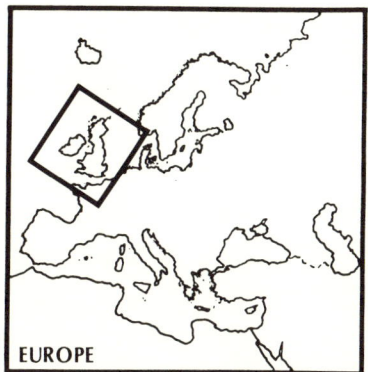

when the Romans left in 409-10, only the roads, the walls, and Christianity that had been introduced by the soldiers, remained.

A period of tribal turmoil ensued with invasions from the north and across the North Sea from Europe by various peoples. The surviving Britons were mostly driven into mountain strongholds in Wales.

Alfred the Great, who ruled during the 800s, was able to consolidate the kingdom and organize a form of government.

The Norman Conquest of 1066 introduced a new era and forever changed the face of England.

Henry II (1133-1189), the first of the Plantagenets, added territory in France to the kingdom and began the conquest of Ireland.

On June 15, 1215, King John was forced to sign the Magna Carta, a document that became the foundation stone of English liberty.

Henry VIII's break with the Roman Catholic Church and the onset of the great Elizabethan age saw England's flowering as a great nation.

Elizabeth I (1533-1603) became Queen of England and Ireland in 1558 and she inspired her subjects to great achievements. With the 1588 defeat of the Spanish Armada, Britain replaced that country as a colonizing power and ruler of the seas.

When James VI of Scotland succeeded to the English throne in 1603 and became King James I of England, the two countries united and the country assumed essentially its present form, with the exception of Ireland, only the northern six counties of which remain in the kingdom. The legislative union of Britain and Ireland dates only from Jan. 1, 1801, when the United Kingdom of Great Britain and Ireland came into being (Wales had become linked with England in 1284, and in 1707 England and Scotland made their marriage official, adopting the name of Great Britain with the Union Jack as their flag).

A civil war from 1642 to 1649 resulted in a republican form of government under that humorless man, Oliver Cromwell. The monarchy was restored in 1660.

With the exception of that interlude, Britain enjoyed peace and a time of development unmatched across the English Channel.

At the end of the 18th century, the Industrial Revolution began and it changed the face of Britain more than any political or military revolution.

It led to a period of decline in agriculture as the population moved to the new industrial centers and the country came to depend on the new colonies for food. This dependence almost caused disaster during the two world wars.

Nevertheless, for a number of years, Britain led the world in industrial technology, British-built trains ran on foreign rails, British machinery powered the growing factories of the world, and British ships ruled the waves. During the Victorian age, Britain became the world's leading power and her empire the most extensive ever seen.

This was an age of stability. The empire was secure and many of the colonies were already being groomed for eventual independence.

The advance of technology increased its tempo as the new century dawned and with Queen Victoria still on the throne, the good time seemed endless.

But war clouds loomed in Europe as the various powers became enmeshed in the tangle of treaty obligations and in 1914 came catastrophe for Britain. World War I cost the country a generation of its best men and left the nation weakened and apathetic.

In 1920, Ireland broke away except for the six northern counties that chose to remain in the United Kingdom.

The period between the two world wars was a time of drift. The nation watched as a newly re-armed Ger-

UNITED KINGDOM

many again sought to dominate its neighbors. It stood by with the rest of the world as Germany gained such power that it is almost certain that if Hitler had landed in Britain immediately after the fall of France, he would have become another William the Conquerer. Fortunately, the people could not stand the thoughts of jackboots trampling the landscape and perked up just in time, to fight on alone for a year while others girded their loins.

At the end of the war Britain was drained, almost bankrupted by the cost of buying what it needed to wage war, and reduced to a secondary power. As the colonial empire was given its freedom, Britain withdrew from the seat of world power.

In recent years there has been something of a resurgence, although the economy has been hurt, first by the surge in energy costs and later by the worldwide recession. In 1973, Britain became a member of the European Community.

The economy is diverse, covering all types of heavy and light industry. Agriculture has grown although the country must still import much of what it needs.

The 1979 per capita income was $7,216 and the literacy rate is 99%.

Britain's important place in the philatelic world will always be secure and as the first country to introduce the postage stamp in 1840, her postal heritage is great.

Following long years of drabness. British stamps have improved since the 1960s and are now colorful and generally well produced. Issue policies are moderate. Although a number of portions of the United Kingdom have set themselves up in the post office business, complete with their own stamp issues, the area is popular with collectors.

Philatelic Bureau: British Post Office Philatelic Bureau, 20 Brandon St., Edinburgh, Scotland, EH3 5TT, United Kingdom.

THE CHANNEL ISLANDS

Although not formally part of the United Kingdom, the Channel Islands of Jersey, Guernsey, Alderney, and Sark, together with several smaller islands, have been British crown dependencies since the reign of King John.

They are the remnants of English possessions in France and were part of the Dukedom of Normandy.

The climate is mild and snow and frost are rare. A long growing season makes the islands ideal for the growing of early vegetables for the British market. Jersey and Guernsey dairy cattle are world famous.

Tourism is important to the island's economies.

The Channel Islands were the only British soil to be occupied by the Germans during World War II.

Jersey and Guernsey have their own postal services and issue postage stamps. Alderney also issues its own stamps, although Guernsey, of which it is part, operates the postal service.

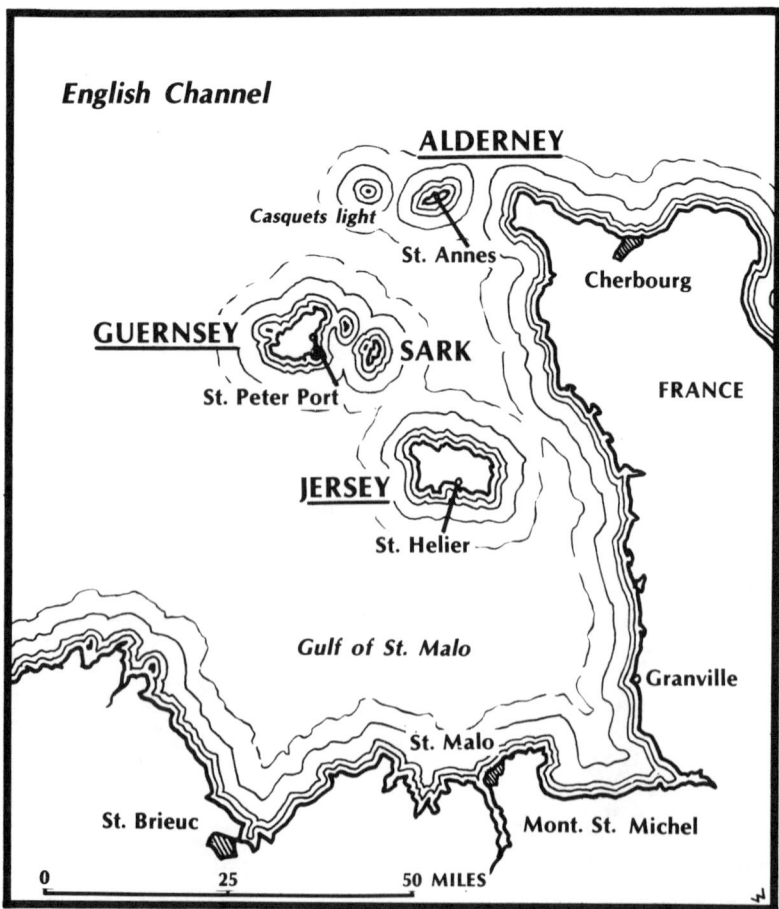

GUERNSEY

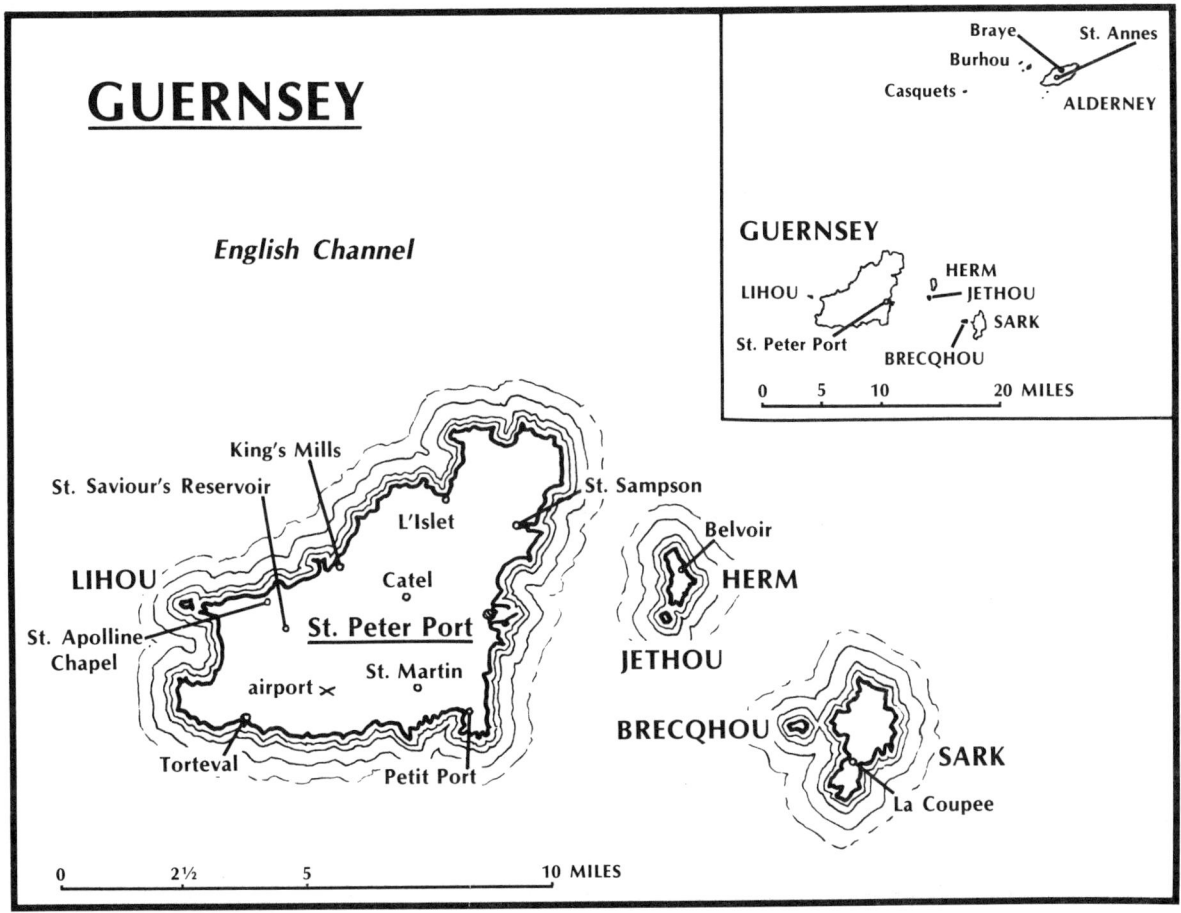

Area: 30 sq. miles
Population: 54,256 (1976)
Capital: St. Peter Port
Currency: Pound (100 pence)

The Baliwick of Guernsey includes the islands of Guernsey, Alderney, Brechou, Herm, Jethou, and Sark.

The islands are thought to have been colonized from the mainland of Normandy about the 11th century AD and were almost completely integrated into the social and political structure of Normandy.

After the Norman conquest, the king of England was also Duke of Normandy and this brought the islands into contact with England.

When Normandy was lost to the French, the islands remained under the control of England and were annexed to the English crown in 1254. They were permitted to retain their Norman laws and culture.

The islands were badly battered over the years as England and France fought their many wars.

A lieutenant governor officiates as the personal representative of the sovereign, although government is by a legislative body known as the States of Deliberation.

Because the Baliwick of Guernsey is not part of the United Kingdom, and is attached directly to the crown, it is not affected by acts of the parliament at Westminister, unless specifically named therein.

At the time of the French surrender to Germany in 1940, many of the islanders were evacuated to the United Kingdom. The Germans occupied the islands until the end of the war.

The economy is based on dairy cattle, market gardening, and tourism. The dairy industry occupies the southern part of the island, with most market gardening being done in the north.

Stamps were issued during the German World War II occupation and in 1958 the British Regional stamps were released.

Guernsey's own stamps began on Oct. 1, 1969, when the independent Guernsey Postal Administration came into being.

Alderney began its own stamp issues on June 14, 1983, although postal services remain in the hands of the Guernsey Post Office.

Philatelic Bureau: States Philatelic Bureau, Head Post Office, Guernsey, Channel Island, Great Britain.

For Alderney: Philatelic Bureau, Post Office Headquarters, Smith Street, Guernsey, Channel Islands, Great Britain.

JERSEY

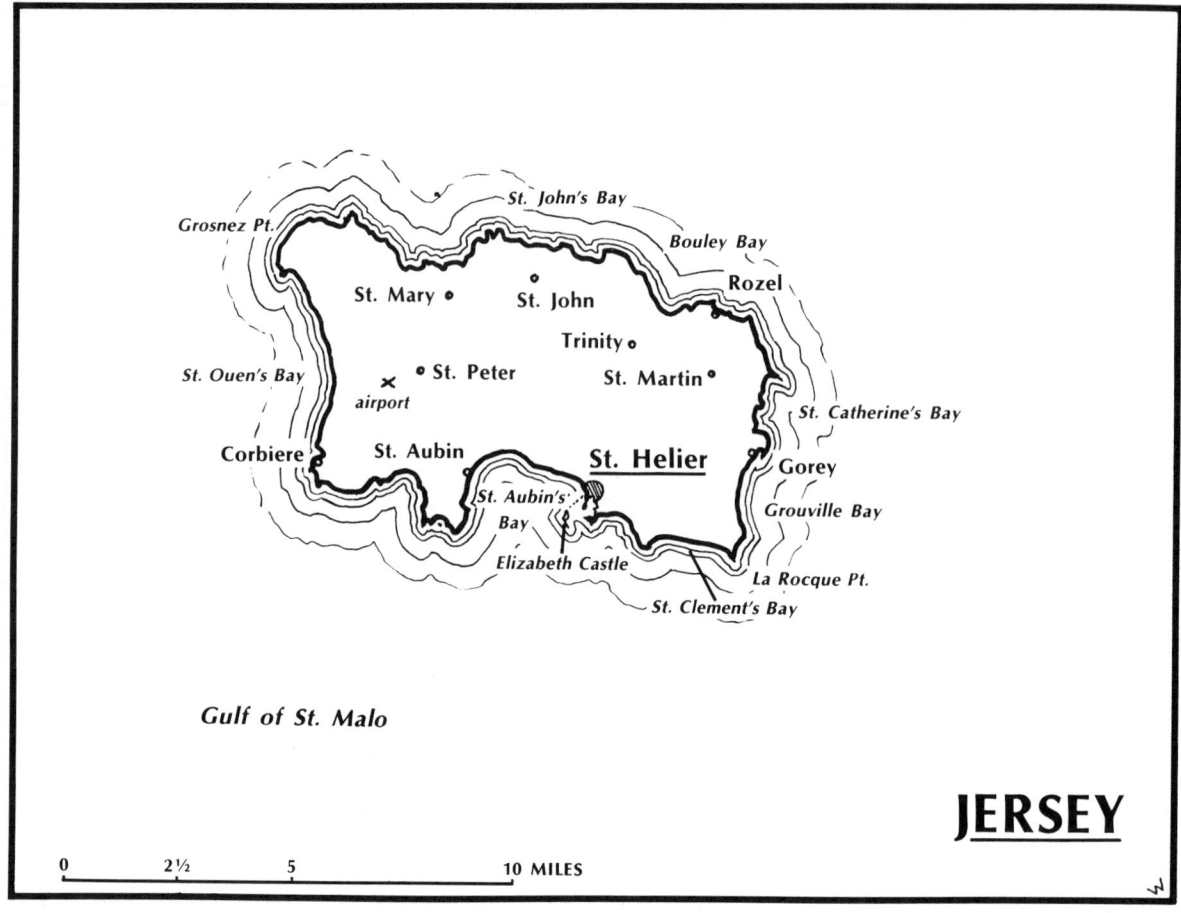

Area: 45 sq. miles
Population: 74,382 (1977)
Capital: St. Helier
Currency: Pound (100 pence)

The Baliwick of Jersey is the largest of the English Channel Islands. It is located south of Guernsey and about 12 miles west of the French Cotentin Peninsula. Like Guernsey, it is not part of the United Kingdom, but is attached directly to the British crown as a crown dependency.

Mostly a plateau, falling off to the south, Jersey enjoys more hours of sunshine than Guernsey. There is an average of about 2,000 hours of sunshine each year. The average annual temperature is 52 degrees F.

The history of Jersey followed the same course as that of Guernsey and its form of government developed along the same lines. Dominated by an aristocracy, it was less active in trade and commerce than its neighbor. The De Carteret family controlled the island and it is due to it that Jersey held firm for King Charles during the civil war of the mid-1600s.

The legislative body, called the States of Jersey, assumed its full power to govern in 1771. Proceedings are conducted in French, which is the official language. Family feuds tore island society apart during the 18th and 19th centuries, but the island grew rich, mostly from the Newfoundland fisheries and smuggling.

The dairy industry is extensive and the small Jersey cow is famous for its rich milk. It is the only breed allowed on the island since 1789 and even Jersey cows that have left the island are not permitted to return, so strictly is the breed protected.

As in Guernsey, there is much market gardening and early potatoes, harvested in May for the British market are an important crop. Flowers, tomatoes, and vegetables are widely grown.

The island is a popular tourist resort. Air service is excellent and sea ferries run frequent services from the south coast of England and from French ports.

Stamps were issued in Jersey during the German World War II occupation and in 1958, British Regional stamps were issued for the island.

Jersey gained its own stamp issues with the inauguration on Oct. 1, 1969 of its own postal service. Since then, there has been a regular release of commemorative stamps mostly related to local history, events, and scenery.

Philatelic Bureau: The Jersey Post Office, Philatelic Bureau, PO Box 304, Jersey, Channel Islands, Great Britain.

ISLE OF MAN

Area: 227 sq. miles
Population: 61,000 (1982)
Capital: Douglas
Currency: Pound (100 pence)

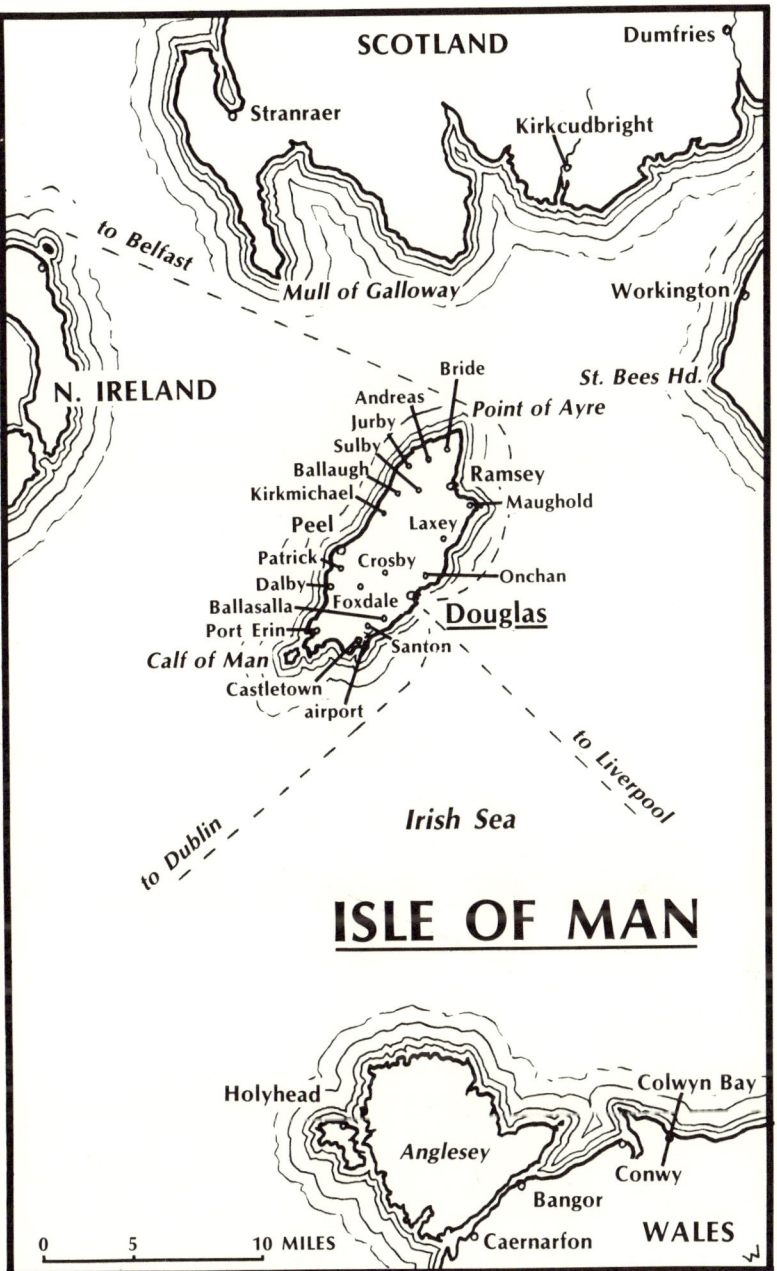

The Isle of Man is not part of the United Kingdom, but is a crown possession with considerable self government. Its status is similar to that of the Channel Islands.

The island is about 30 miles long by 10 miles wide. There is a central area of hills with 2,034-foot Snaefell being the highest point. The landscape is generally treeless.

A small island off the southern tip, the Calf of Man, is a bird sanctuary administered by the Manx National Trust.

The climate is mild. The February average temperature is 41 degrees F and that for August is 58 degrees F. About 41 inches of rain fall each year. There is considerable fog, but snow and frost are rare.

About AD 800, Scandinavians began to visit the island. First they came to loot, but they soon began to settle. The system of government they established remains today in the form of the Tynwald parliament.

The British monarch appoints a lieutenant governor as head of government. The parliament comprises two houses, which usually sit separately, but on occasion they come together to form a Tynwald.

During the 1700s, the island was a smuggling center since the importation into the island of spirits and tobacco was duty free. With a fast cutter, a skillful crew could make a good living ferrying such contraband across the narrow strip of water to the English coast.

To suppress this traffic, the British government in 1765 passed an act to enable it to buy the sovereignty of the island for the British Crown for £70,000.

The origin of the strange three-legged emblem that is the device of the island is not known. Its first appearance is believed to be on the village cross of Kirk Maughold dating from about 1375. It is also seen on the 1395 shield of Sir William la Scrope, king of Man, and on the Manx sword of state in about 1450.

Food is extensively produced and sheep graze on the hills. Produce is exported. Manx tweed and woolen goods are also produced.

The first stamps for the island were the British Regional issues of 1958. They were the Wilding portrait stamps, and changed in 1971 to the Machin design.

In 1973, postal autonomy was introduced and the island began to operate its own postal service and issue its own stamps on July 5.

Philatelic Bureau: Philatelic Bureau, PO Box 10M, Douglas, Isle of Man, Great Britain.

UNITED KINGDOM: NORTHERN IRELAND

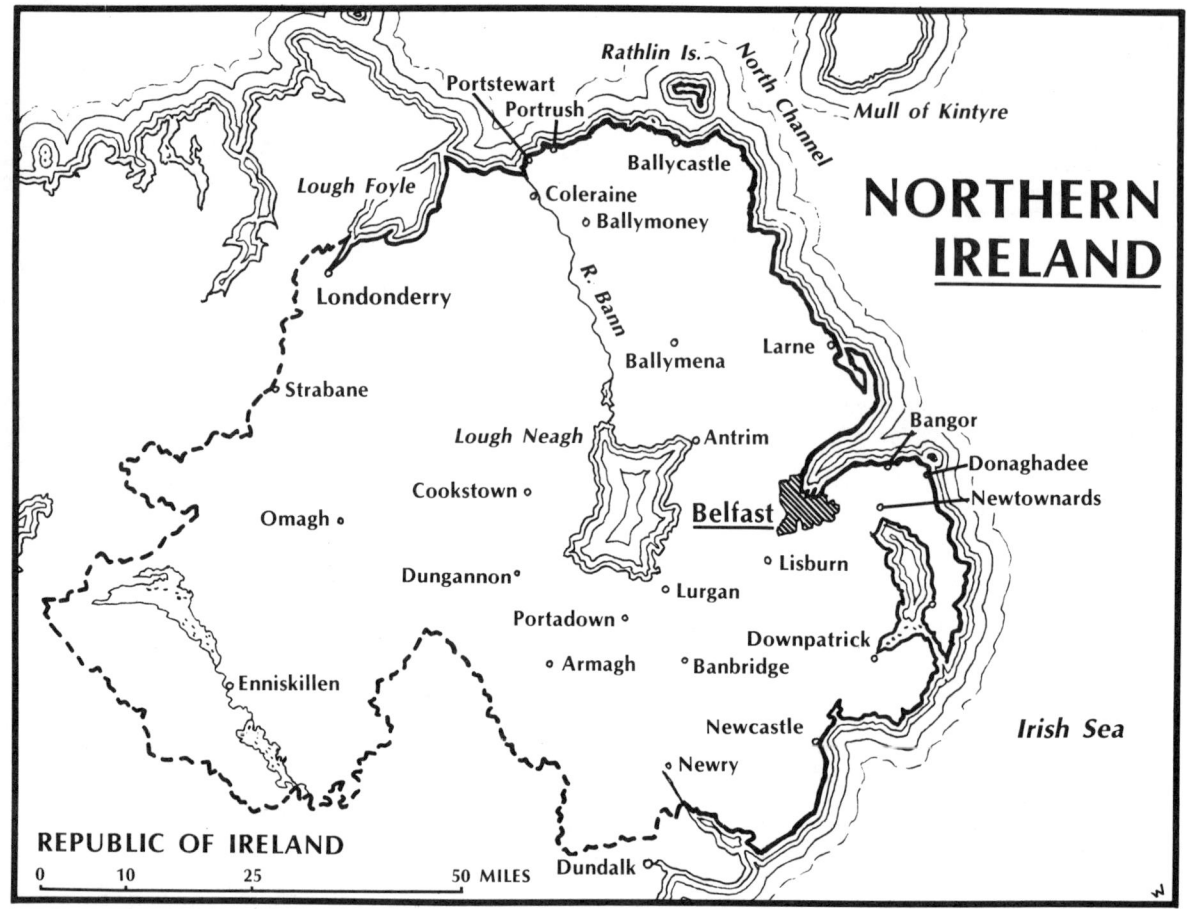

Area: 5,463 sq. miles
Population: 1,490,230 (1981)
Capital: Belfast
Currency: Pound (100 pence)

Northern Ireland is part of the United Kingdom and comprises the mainly Protestant six northern counties that decided to remain within the UK when the rest of Ireland opted for independence in 1920.

The country is mostly low lying and flat, with Lough Neagh, the largest lake in the British Isles, in the center. In the northwest there are the Sperrin Mountains, with the Mourne Mountains in the southeast.

The climate is mild and damp throughout the year. The average annual temperature is 50 degrees F. January and July average temperatures are 40 and 58 degrees F respectively. Annual rainfall ranges from more than 40 inches in the north to about 30 inches in the south.

The Republic of Ireland has always refused to accept the partition of Ireland, but Northern Ireland has likewise always refused to consider a reunion. The reasons are a general fear of both Catholic domination of what would then be a Protestant minority and of a reduction in the relatively high standard of living since industrialized Northern Ireland is considerably more prosperous and developed than the republic.

In recent years, Northern Ireland had been wracked by increased violence between Catholic and Protestant.

Northern Ireland's economy is based on industry, especially shipbuilding, although linen manufacture is important. It has increasingly diversified and includes light engineering, synthetic fibers, and electronics.

Northern Ireland's first stamps appeared in 1958 and took the form of the British Regional (now called "Country") issues. They were the Wilding portrait design, which was changed in 1971 to the Machin design. The stamps feature the Red Hand of Ulster emblem.

They are sold at post offices in the region for which they are intended to be used, but are valid for postage throughout the UK.

Philatelic Bureau: British Post Office Philatelic Bureau, 20 Brandon St., Edinburgh, Scotland, EH3 5TT, United Kingdom.

UNITED KINGDOM: SCOTLAND

Area: 30,405 sq. miles
Population: 5,117,145 (1981)
Capital: Edinburgh
Currency: Pound (100 pence)

Scotland, a former kingdom, is part of the United Kingdom. It occupies the northern part of Britain and includes a large number of islands, especially off the west coast, as well as the Orkney and Shetland groups to the north.

There are three major areas on the mainland; the rolling southern uplands along the border with England, the central Lowlands, and the rugged Highlands in the north.

The coastline is deeply indented, with long, narrow inlets, called lochs and broad inlets, called firths. The former occur mostly on the west coast and the latter on the east coast.

The Scottish climate, like that of the rest of the British Isles, is modified by the ocean and, in the southwest, by the Gulf Stream. Seasonal variations are small with cool summers and moderate winters.

Scotland was known in antiquity as Caledonia and among its inhabitants was a warlike race called the Picts, who offered stout resistance to the invading Romans. They caused the Romans to build Hadrian's Wall across the north of England to keep them out. Portions of it can still be seen.

It came together as one kingdom in about AD 1018 under Malcom II. Edward I of England brought Scotland under English suzerainty. This intrusion brought about a Scottish alliance with France in 1295 and began a long association with that country.

Scotland's economy is varied, ranging from heavy industry to the production of whiskey. Whiskey is the prime export. Glasgow is the UK's most important ship-building and industrial center.

A wide range of textiles, including tweeds, woolens, silks, and linens, are produced. Fishing is also a major factor in the economy, with herring and cod being caught in quantity. The Orkney and Shetland groups of islands have become centers of the North Sea oil industry.

Scotland has had its own

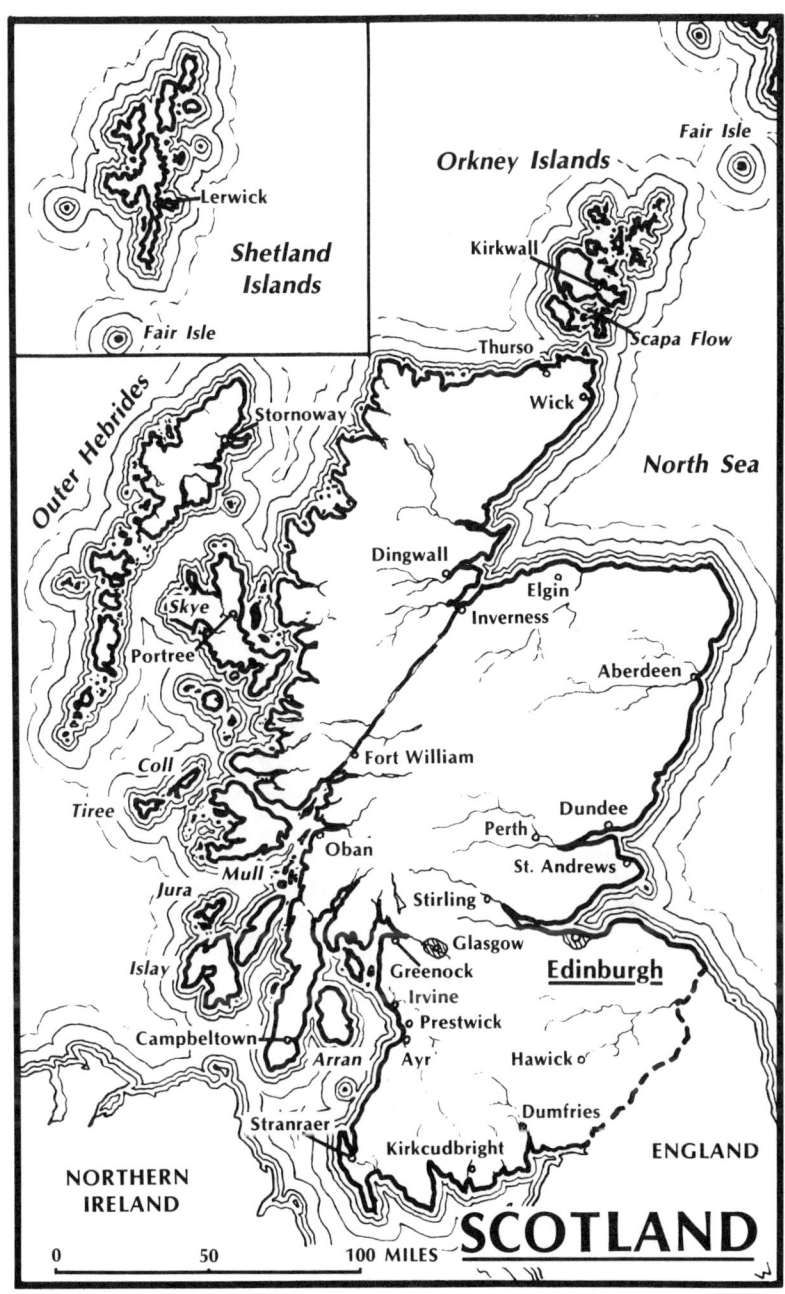

Regional (now called "Country") stamps since 1958. The first were in the Wilding portrait design, but in 1971 the Machin design was introduced. These are on sale at post offices in Scotland and are available to collectors from the British Post Office's philatelic bureau.

A number of recent UK aerogrammes have had various Scottish themes.

Philatelic Bureau: British Post Office Philatelic Bureau, 20 Brandon St., Edinburgh, Scotland, EH3 5TT, United Kingdom.

UNITED KINGDOM: WALES

Area: 8,016 sq. miles
Population: 2,790,000 (1981)
Capital: Cardiff
Currency: Pound (100 pence)

The Principality of Wales is administered with England as one unit. It occupies an area projecting into the Irish Sea from the western portion of Great Britain. It includes the island of Anglesey, off the northern tip of Wales, separated by the Menai Strait. Also included is the former county of Monmouthsire.

The country is almost completely mountainous, with the most rugged area in the north. This includes Snowdon, at 3,560 feet, the highest point in England and Wales.

The climate, like that of England, is mild and moist. The average January and July temperatures are 42 and 60 degrees F respectively. Rainfall ranges from 100 inches a year in the northern mountains to about 30 inches in some coastal areas.

The Romans subdued the tribes of Wales between AD 69-79. Following the Roman retreat from Britain, the Celtic inhabitants of England fled west before Anglo-Saxon invaders and eventually merged with the tribes in the Welsh mountains.

An English army conquered Wales in 1062-64 and William the Conquerer later persuaded the Welsh to recognize him as their king. Not until 1284, however, did King Edward I annex Wales to England as a principality.

Then, in a master-stroke of public relations, he had his son made Prince of Wales. Since then, the eldest son of the British monarch has been made Prince of Wales. Prince Charles, heir to the British throne, currently holds the title.

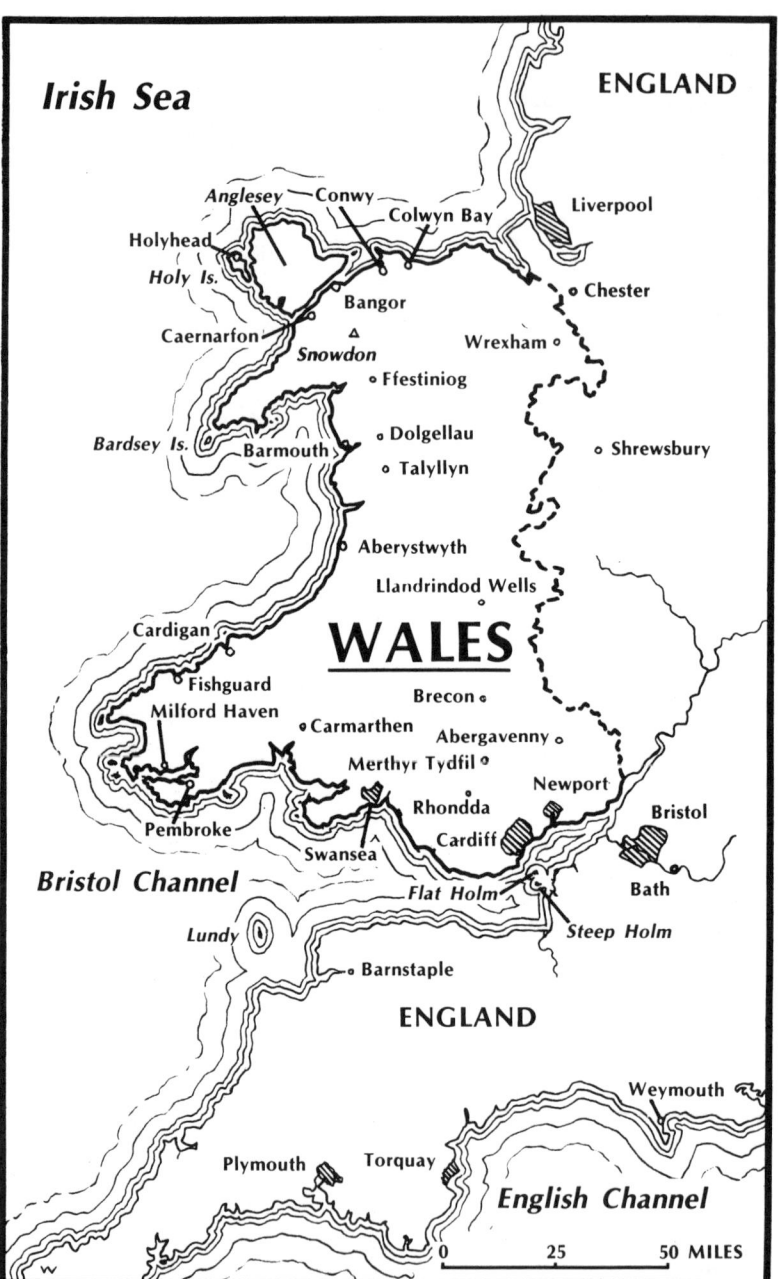

English is the official language of Wales, although about 20 percent of the population speaks both English and Welsh and some 32,000 speak only Welsh.

Mining is the backbone of the Welsh economy. Coal is the most valuable resource of the area, although some lead, uranium, copper, zinc, and manganese are mined. Welsh slate is famous and has roofed buildings around the world.

The first stamps for Wales were issued in 1958 and were in the British Regional (now called "Country") stamps. They bear the Wilding portrait of Queen Elizabeth II, and were replaced in 1971 by the Machin design. They feature the Welsh dragon emblem.

These stamps are sold at post offices in Wales but are valid for postage throughout the United Kingdom.

Philatelic Bureau: British Post Office Philatelic Bureau, 20 Brandon St., Edinburgh, Scotland, EH3 5TT, United Kingdom.

VATICAN CITY, STATE OF

Area: 108.7 acres
Population: 1,000 (1984)
Capital: Vatican
Currency: Lire (100 centesimi)

The Vatican City, headquarters of the Roman Catholic Church and residence of the pope, is located on the right bank of the Tiber River, in the city of Rome, capital of Italy.

The state, which has extraterritorial status, includes St. Peter's Basilica, the Vatican Palace, museums, archives, a number of ecclesiastical buildings, and the Vatican gardens.

It has its own radio station, railway depot, and post office.

The population is of various nationalities, mostly Swiss and Italian. Citizenship is generally granted only to those who live there by reason of their office or employment and, with some exceptions, to their families.

In 1871, the Italian Parliament passed a law which assured the pope's spiritual freedom, provided him an income, and gave special status to the Vatican City. However, Pope Pius IX and his successors refused to acknowledge these laws and decided to regard themselves as prisoners in the Vatican.

Not until Feb. 11, 1929, did the Holy See and the Italian Government sign an agreement known as the Lateran Treaty that resolved the dispute.

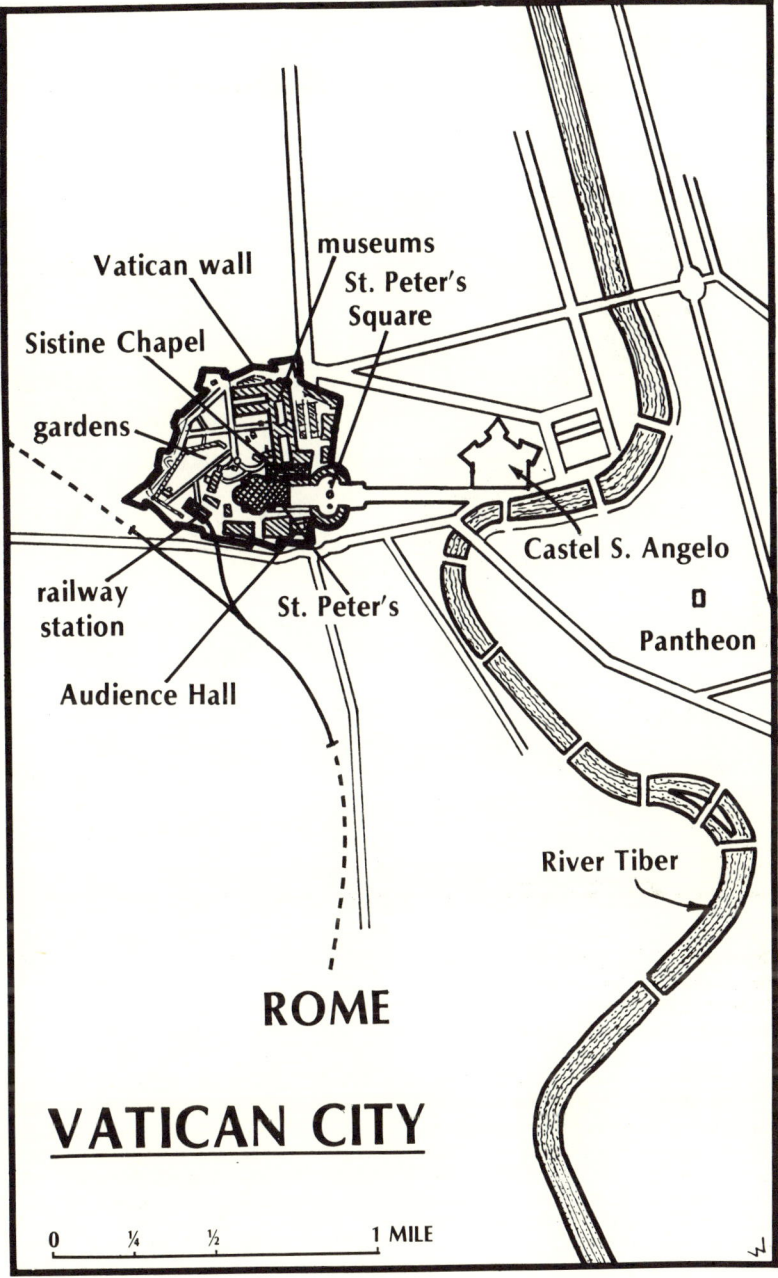

The Vatican City maintains a 75-man Swiss Guard under a colonel for ceremonial duties and has a modern civilian security force.

It mints its own coinage and the Vatican Post Office issues postage stamps.

A permanent observer at the United Nations, the Vatican maintains diplomatic relations with many countries and is a member of the Universal Postal Union and the International Telecommunications Union.

The United States restored formal relations with the Vatican in 1984 after the US Congress repealed an 1867 ban on diplomatic relations.

The present sovereign of the Vatican is the Supreme Pontiff John Paul II, Karol Wojtyla, a native of Poland and the first non-Italian to be elected pope in more than 450 years.

The Vatican issued its first postage stamps on Aug. 1, 1929, following the Lateran Treaty. Since then, a moderate flow of stamps has been released with designs featuring religious themes, art, and architecture.

Philatelic Bureau: Ufficio Filatelico, Governatorato, Vatican City.

YUGOSLAVIA, SOCIALIST FEDERAL REPUBLIC OF

Area: 98,766 sq. miles
Population: 22,997,000 (1984)
Capital: Belgrade
Currency: Dinar (100 paras)

Yugoslavia was formed after World War I from the former Kingdom of Serbia and several other Balkan states. The country is mountainous, except for an interior plain covering about one third of the area and running from Zabreb southeast in an oval shape to Nis.

The climate is generally moderate, but varies with location and altitude. On the coast, winters are warm and summers hot. Average temperatures are 45 degrees F in January and 75 degrees F in July. In the central plains a more continental climate prevails. The average January temperature is 30 degrees F and in July is 75-80 degrees F.

When the Austro-Hungarian Empire collapsed at the end of World War I, the Kingdom of Serbs, Croats, and Slovenes was created from the already independent states of Serbia and Montenegro, plus several areas newly liberated from the Austro-Hungarian Empire.

The new country faced a major problem just to stick together, the peoples of the Balkans never having been noted for brotherly love, and its prospects seemed dim. But it existed until 1941, when the Germans invaded and occupied it.

During the occupation, which was marked by great brutality, strong resistance movements developed. One of the leaders of the freedom fighters was Josip Broz Tito and after the liberation, he came to power, creating a communist government. He ruled until his death in 1980.

The economy is diverse and includes some heavy industry. A Yugoslav-built automobile has recently been introduced to the US market. Tourism is an important source of income.

The latest per capita income figure is $3,109 and the literacy rate is 90 percent.

The stamps of Yugoslavia are issued in more restrained quantities than in other Eastern European areas and the subjects are of Yugoslav-related significance.

Philatelic Bureau: Jugomarka, Palmoticeva 2, Belgrade, Yugoslavia.

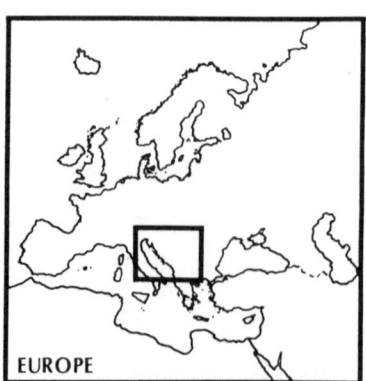

AFRICA

Stamp-issuing areas:

1. Algeria
2. Angola
3. Ascension
4. Benin
5. Botswana
6. Burkina Faso
7. Burundi
8. Cameroon
9. Cape Verde
10. Central African Republic
11. Chad
12. Comoros
13. Congo
14. Djibouti
15. Egypt
16. Equatorial Guinea
17. Ethiopia
18. Gabon
19. Gambia
20. Ghana
21. Guinea
22. Guinea-Bissau
23. Ivory Coast
24. Kenya
25. Lesotho
26. Liberia
27. Libya
28. Madagascar
29. Madeira (Portugal)
30. Malawi
31. Mali
32. Mauritania
33. Mauritius
34. Morocco
35. Mozambique
36. Namibia (SWA)
37. Niger
38. Nigeria
39. Rwanda
40. St. Helena
41. St. Thomas and Prince
42. Senegal
43. Seychelles
44. Sierra Leone
45. Somalia
46. South Africa
47. Sudan
48. Swaziland
49. Tanzania
50. Togo
51. Tristan da Cunha
52. Tunisia
53. Uganda
54. Zaire
55. Zambia
56. Zil Elwannyen Sesel
57. Zimbabwe

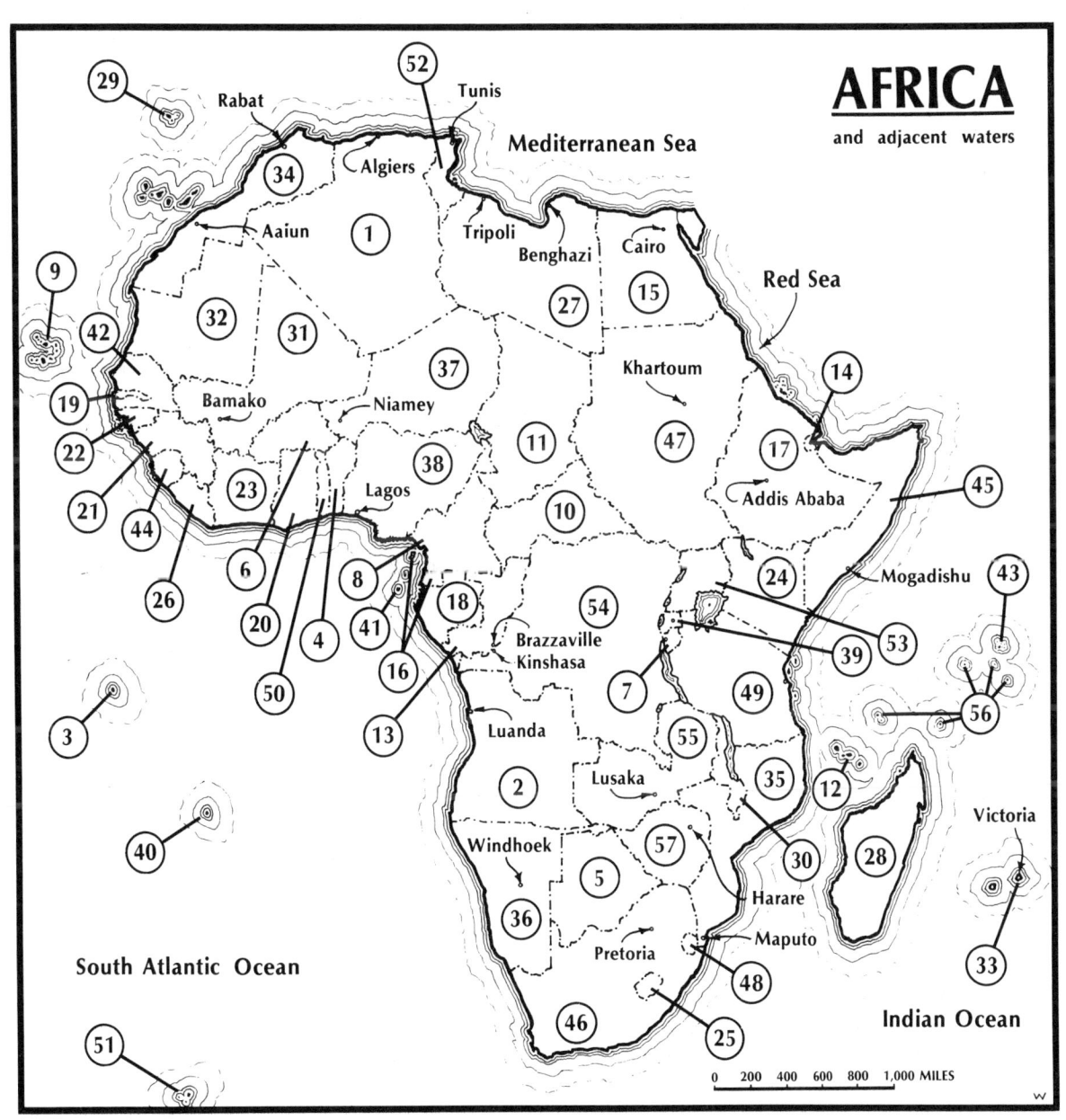

ALGERIA, DEMOCRATIC AND POPULAR REPUBLIC OF

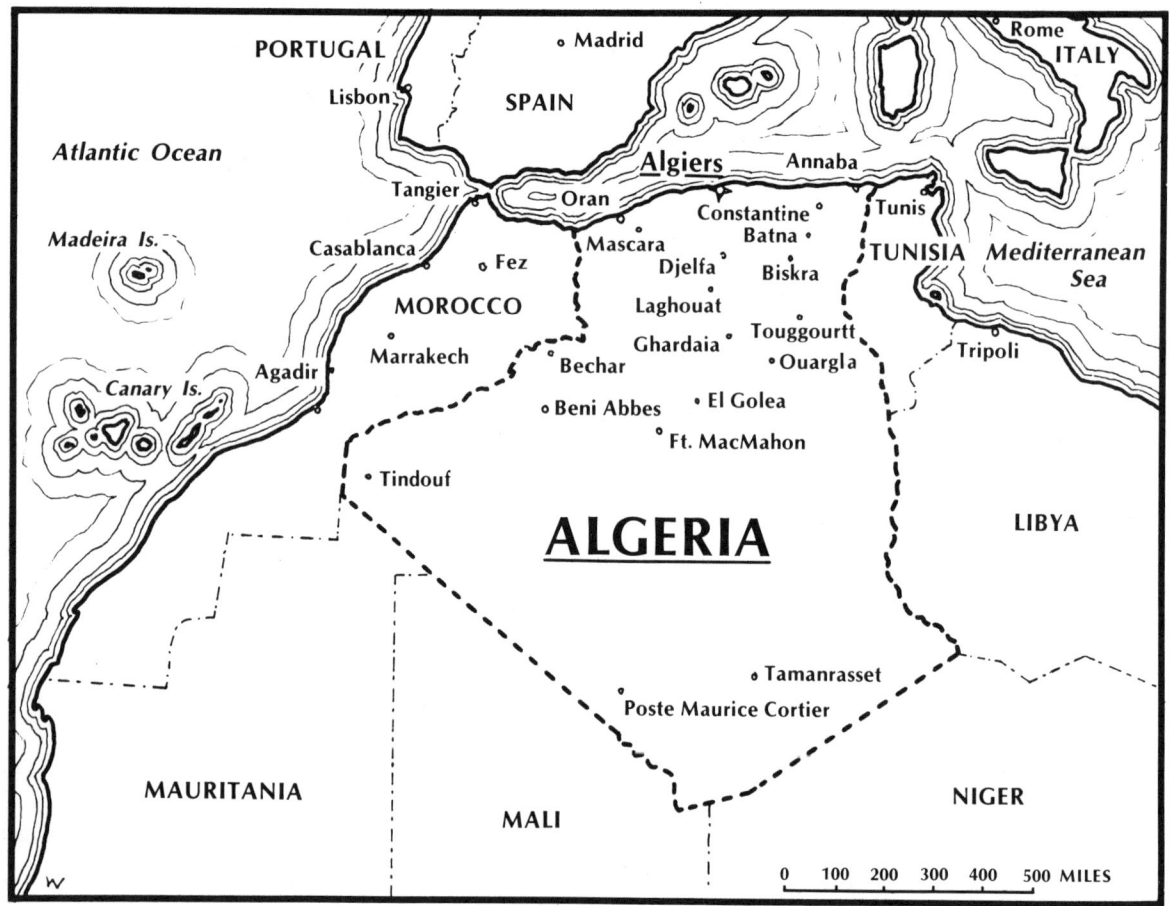

Area: 918,497 sq. miles
Population: 21,351,000 (1984)
Capital: Algiers
Currency: Dinar (100 centimes)

With a 640-mile coastline on the Mediterranean, Algeria stretches south deep into the Sahara Desert across two ranges of the Atlas Mountains. The mountains divide the country into three zones; a coastal strip in which most of the population lives and to which most agriculture is confined, a 3,000-foot arid plateau between the two mountain ranges, and the vast Sahara Desert in the south.

The climate varies in these zones. On the coast, summers are hot with little rain and winters cool with rain. The plateau area has a desert climate ranging between extremes of heat and cold, and the Sahara zone is hot with sandstorms occurring with some frequency.

Many cultures have occupied the area of Algeria, including the Phoenicians, Romans, Byzantines, Arabs, Turks, and French. Islam and the Arabic language came to the area with the Arabs. The Turks came in the mid-1500s. French colonization began in 1830 and large numbers of French settlers occupied the coastal area.

Second-class status of the local population sparked a nationalist movement in the 1950s and a brutal civil war ensued. This resulted in the French expulsion and independence was proclaimed July 5, 1962.

The current one-party socialist regime is struggling with a poor economy made worse by dependence on oil. There is much unemployment. The per capita income in 1982 was $1,951 but the oil-price slump will have reduced this.

Primary education is free and compulsory to age 13 and the literacy rate is 46%.

Stamps were first issued in 1924. They were French stamps overprinted "ALGERIE." Colonial-era issues are attractively engraved and mostly feature scenes of the country. With independence, Islamic influence became stronger and stamp designs are now more stylized and symbolic. Issue policies are moderate.

Philatelic Bureau: Recevuer Principal des Postes, Alger RP, Algeria.

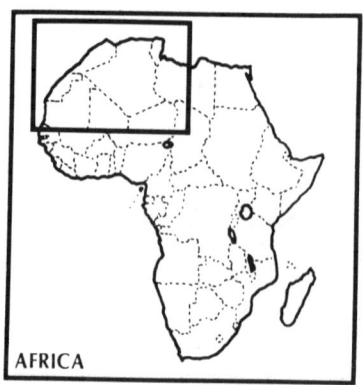

ANGOLA, PEOPLE'S REPUBLIC OF

Area: 481,351 sq. miles
Population: 7,770,000 (1984)
Capital: Luanda
Currency: Kwanza (10 leweys)

Larger than Texas and California combined, Angola is a country with a shaky government supported by the Soviet Union and strong Cuban military forces.

The bulk of the country lies to the south of the Congo (Zaire) River, but there is a small enclave called Cabinda to the north, separated by the river and a strip of Zaire territory. Cabinda, with timber and oil resources is currently seeking independence from Angola.

The main part of Angola comprises a narrow coastal strip rising to a large plateau ranging from 3,000-5,000 feet in elevation.

The climate is hot and humid on the coast and varies from the same to cool and dry with occasional freezing temperatures on the plateau. Most of the population lives in the west and north.

Resources include iron, diamonds, copper, timber, and oil. Main crops are coffee and bananas. Only 2% of the land is arable and there is no significant industry.

Discovered by the Portuguese explorer Diogo Cao in 1483, early relations with the local inhabitants were good and the Portuguese were made welcome. With the development of the slave trade, relations declined and until the 1800s, forced labor for Portuguese plantations in Brazil was the territory's main export.

Colonial settlement did not begin in Angola until the 20th century.

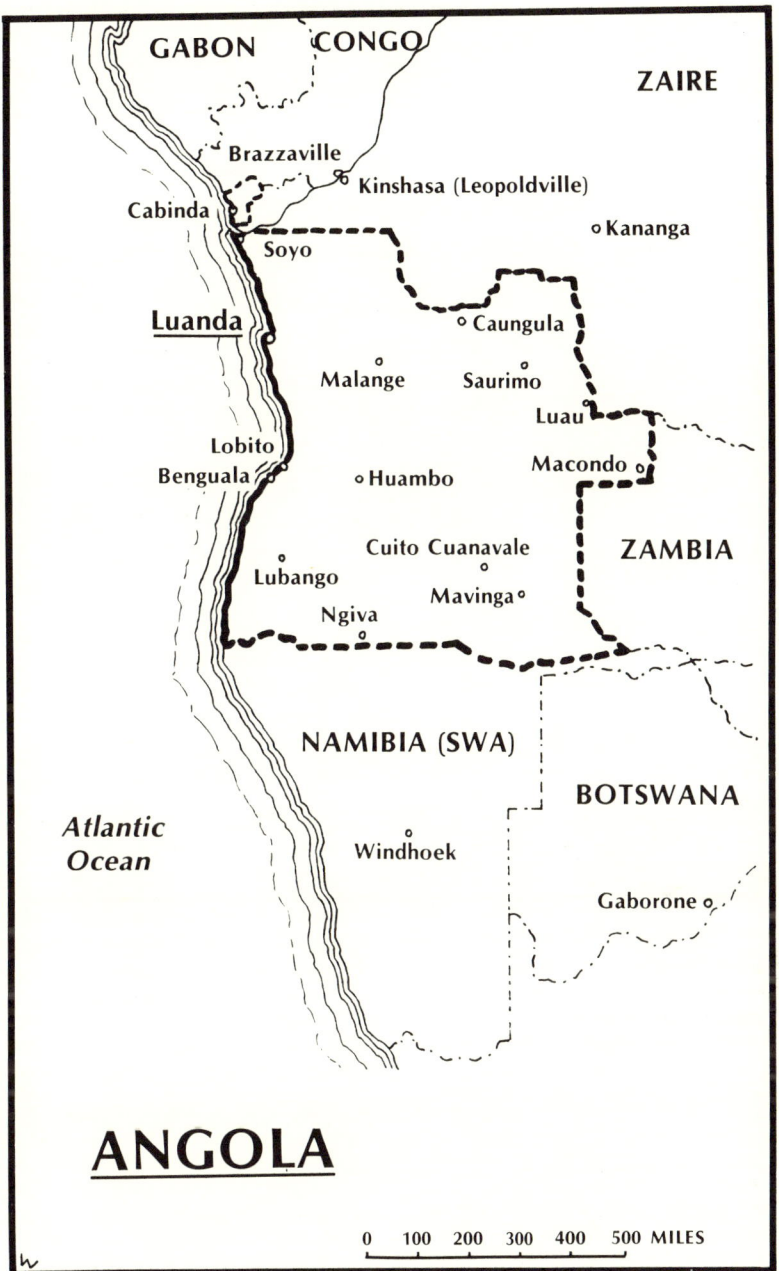

Demands for independence led to civil war in the 1960s and freedom came in 1974. Internal strife, fostered by support for the various factions by the Soviet Union, China, and the United States led to economic ruin. The country is still in a state of chaos. There are no reliable economic statistics.

The first stamps were issued in 1870 and subsequent issues followed the Portuguese colonial pattern. The later stamps were well produced and colorful and were popular with collectors. With independence, came more political, symbolic designs having a strong socialist flavor. Issue policies are moderate.

Philatelic Bureau: Centro Filatelico de Angola, Lda, C.P. 2688, Luanda, Angola.

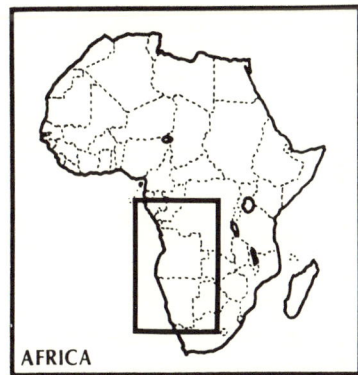

ASCENSION

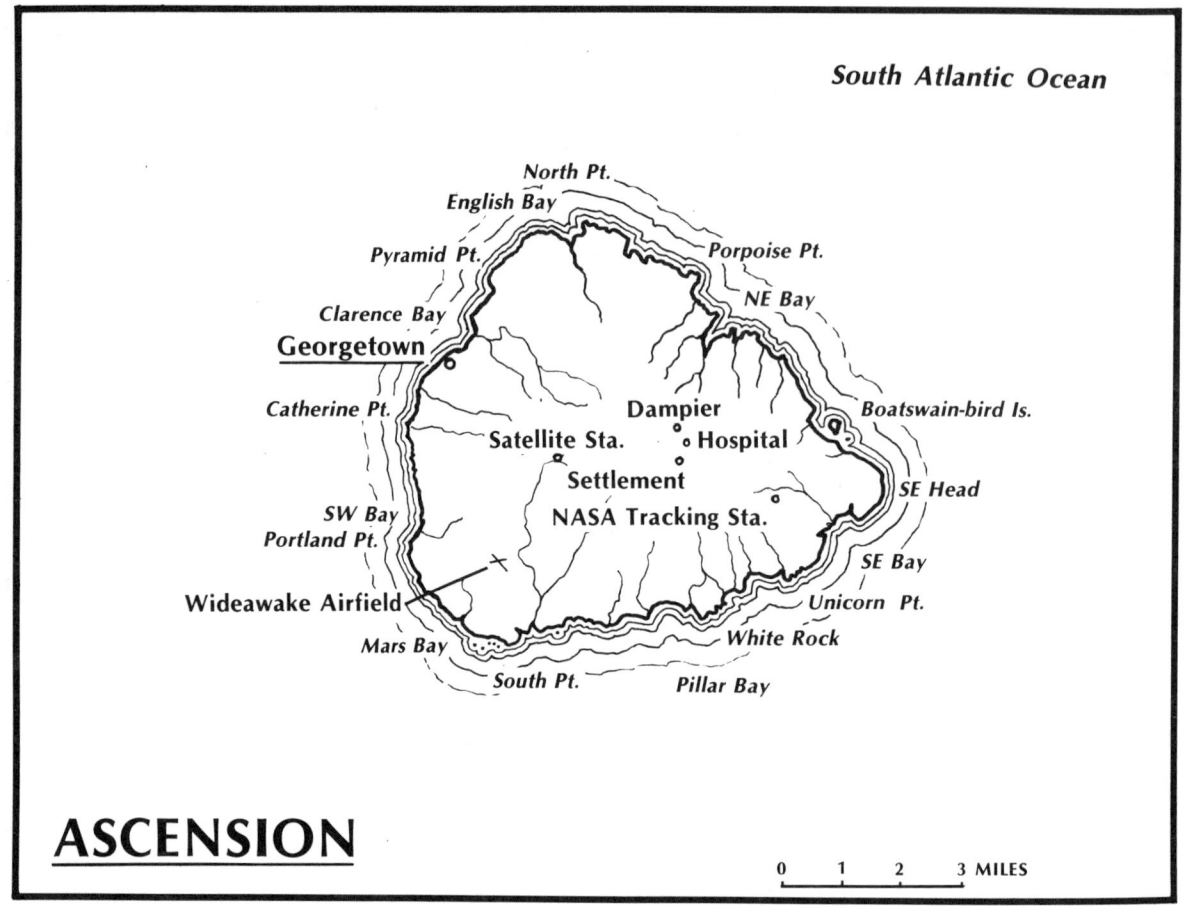

Area: 34 sq. miles
Population: 1,179 (1976)
Capital: Georgetown
Currency: Pound (100 pence)

Volcanic activity created the tiny island of Ascension located in the South Atlantic Ocean, some 700 miles northwest of St. Helena, from which it is administered.

The island is bare of vegetation except for a small area at the peak of 2,870-foot Green Mountain. The climate is mild and healthy with average annual rainfall ranging from six inches on the coast to 25 inches at the higher elevations. Prevailing winds are from the southeast.

The island was discovered on Ascension Day 1501 by the Portuguese explorer Joao da Nova Castella. It was uninhabited until 1815, when a British force arrived to garrison the island to prevent its use as a base from which to rescue Napoleon from his exile on St. Helena. The British Admiralty administered the island until 1922, when it was made a dependency of St. Helena.

Today, the island is a radio and satellite communications center for Great Britain and the United States. It is the site of the first British overseas satellite communications station established in 1966.

Wideawake Airfield, a large base on the island, was built during World War II as a staging point for aircraft flying between North America, Africa, and the Far East.

In his autobiography, *Global Mission,* General "Hap" Arnold describes a stopover on Ascension in 1943 and notes that about 2,000 aircraft had stopped on their way to war during the previous year. It was an important base during the 1982 Falkland Islands War.

The island's first stamps were issued in 1922 and are stamps of St. Helena overprinted "ASCENSION."

In 1934, a beautiful set of King George V pictorial definitives was issued featuring scenes of the island.

In recent years, stamp issues have increased in frequency and in view of the small population, philatelic sales must be a consideration.

Philatelic Bureau: Postmaster, Jamestown, St. Helena, South Atlantic.

BENIN, PEOPLE'S REPUBLIC OF

Area: 43,483 sq. miles
Population: 3,910,000 (1984)
Capital: Portonovo
Currency: CFA franc (100 centimes)

Located in West Africa, Benin was the Republic of Dahomey until Nov. 30, 1975. It had previously been the French colony of Benin until 1895, when it became part of the colony of Dahomey.

Benin is mostly flat with dense vegetation. The coastline runs for 75 miles along the Bight of Benin. The climate is hot and humid with a long rainy season (March-July) and a short one (September-November) on the coast and one lasting from June to October in the interior.

Although the capital is Portonovo, some government functions are performed in the city of Cotonou.

The area came under French control in the 1890s. Prior to this it had been an absolute monarchy, deriving its power in no small measure from the use of fierce female warriors in its army.

The French colony of Benin was merged into the colony of Dahomey in 1895. It later joined French West Africa and became the independent Republic of Dahomey on Aug. 1, 1960.

The country has had an unsettled history since independence and there have been a number of coups. In 1974, the government embarked on a Marxist-Leninist course and this continues.

The economy is based on agriculture, although production of major crops has declined. Exports include palm oil, cotton, coffee, and peanuts. Drought in the more arid north has had an adverse effect on the economy.

The per capita income was $310 in 1982 and literacy in 1984 was a low 11%.

Stamps were first issued in 1892 in the form of the French colonial

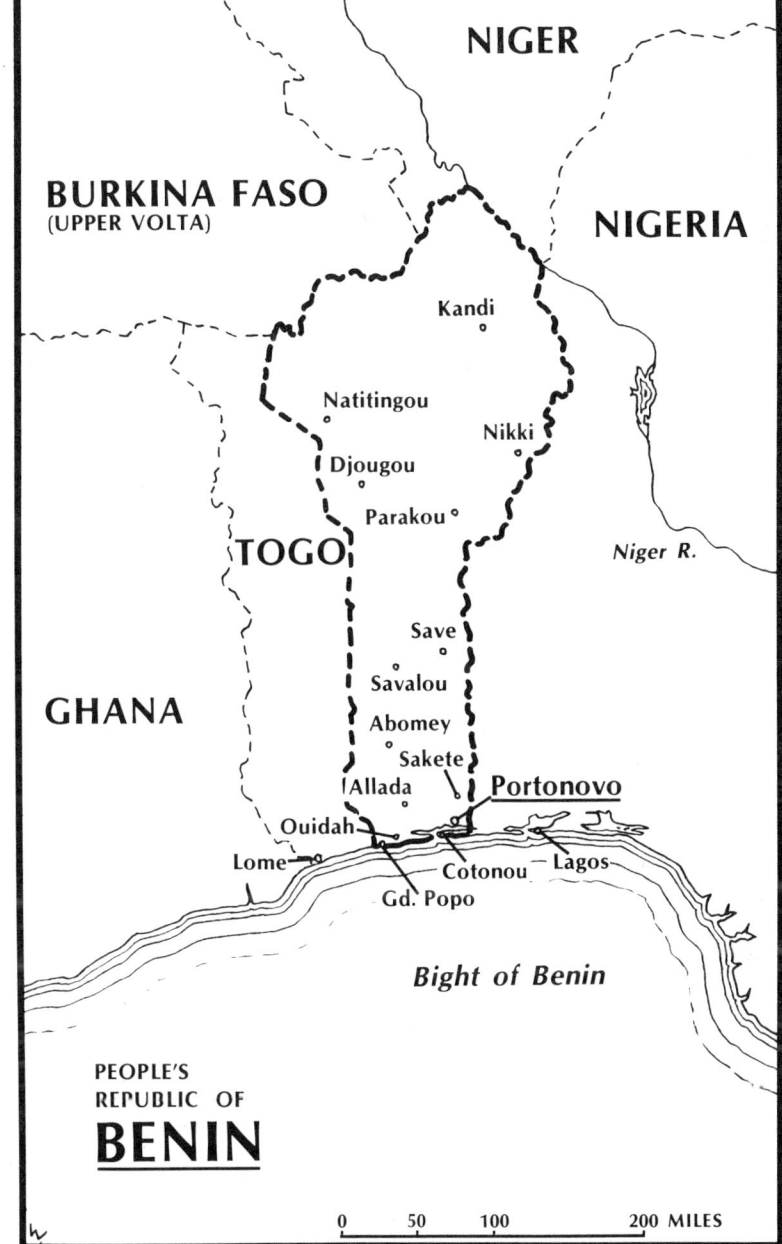

Commerce and Navigation key type inscribed "BENIN." Following the merger with Dahomey, Benin used stamps of that colony until 1945, when stamps of French West Africa went into use until independence in 1960.

The first stamps of the People's Republic of Benin appeared on Dec. 8, 1975.

Philatelic Bureau: Office des Postes et Telecommunications, Direction des Services Postaux et Financiers, Cotonou, People's Republic of Benin.

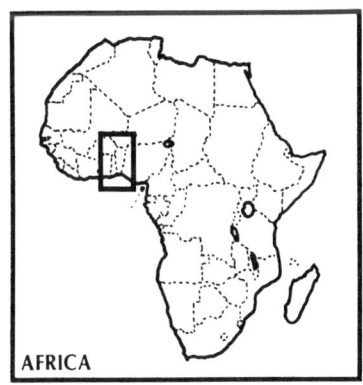

BOTSWANA, REPUBLIC OF

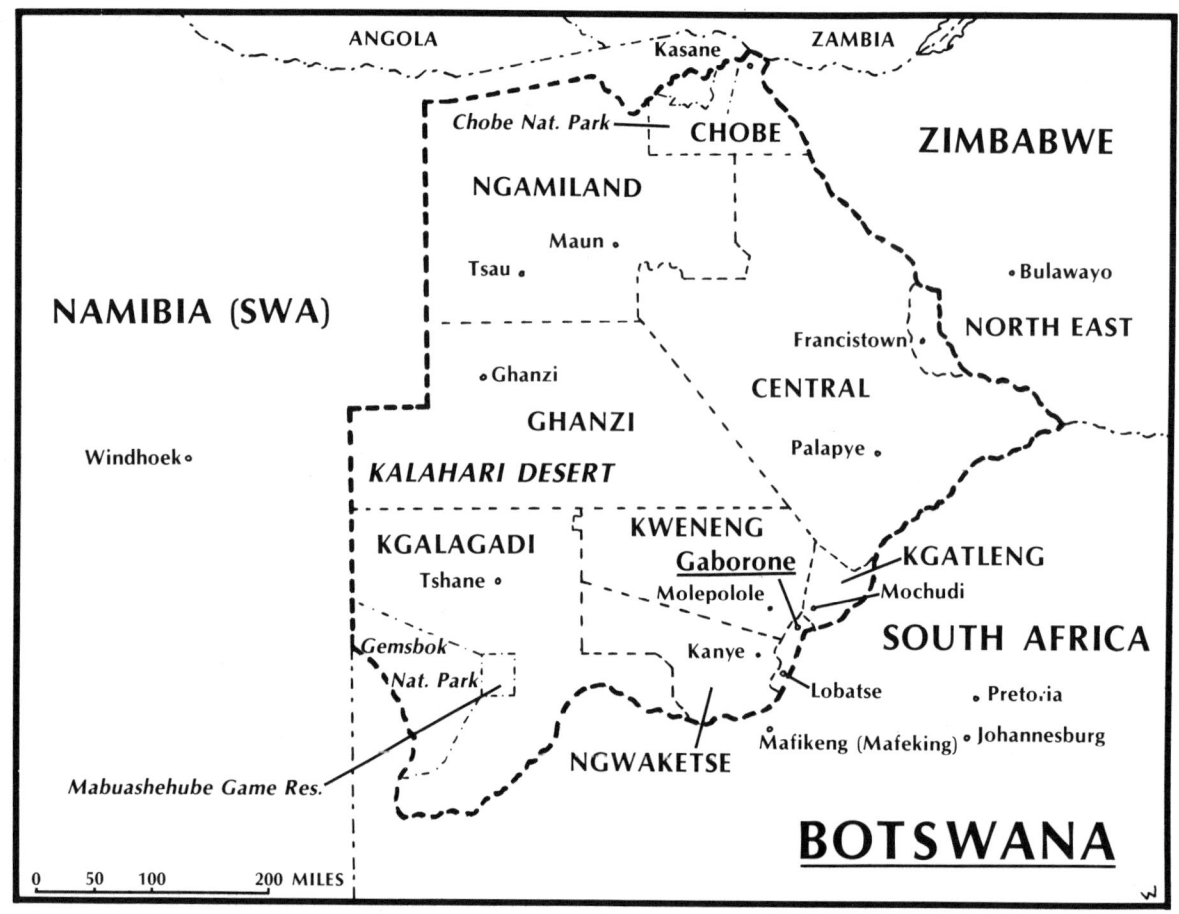

Area: 231,804 sq. miles
Population: 1,038,000 (1984)
Capital: Gaborone
Currency: 1 Pula (100 thebe)

The area of southern Africa that is now Botswana is a large tableland containing the Kalahari Desert and having an average altitude of 3,000-4,000 feet. It is rich in wildlife and there are several national parks devoted to its preservation.

The climate is subtropical. Average annual rainfall varies from nine inches in the south to 25 in the north. May to September is generally rainless. Temperatures range from below freezing in winter to more than 100 degrees F in summer. Agriculture is confined mostly to the north.

Tribal warfare raged among the native population at the time of the first contact with European missionaries early in the 19th century.

Following the discovery of gold and the resulting incursions by Boers from the Transvaal, the population appealed to the British for help. In 1885, the area was made a British protectorate. The southern portion became the Crown Colony of British Bechuanaland and later joined the Cape Province to become part of South Africa, while the northern part was the Bechuanaland Protectorate, now Botswana.

When the Union of South Africa was created in the early 1900s, Bechuanaland Protectorate asked to be excluded and it was gradually developed to run its own affairs.

Full independence came on Sept. 30, 1966, when the present name was adopted.

Cattle is the mainstay of the economy and the Botswana Meat Commission claims to be Africa's largest meat exporter. Minerals, including diamonds, are also of growing importance. The 1984 per capita income was $544 and the 1983 literacy rate was 30%.

The Bechuanaland Protectorate issued its first stamps in 1888. They were overprints on stamps of British Bechuanaland. Various overprints followed until 1932, when a series depicting cattle was issued.

With independence, the stamps of Botswana went into use. Issue policies are moderate.

Philatelic Bureau: Department of Posts and Telegraphs, Philatelic Bureau, P.O. Box 700, Gaborone, Botswana.

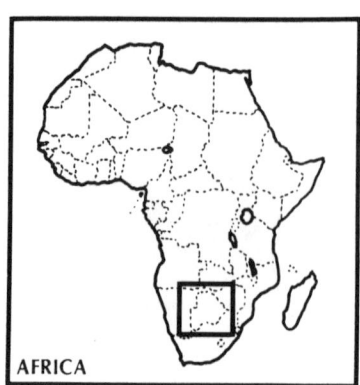

BURKINA FASO, REPUBLIC OF

Area: 105,869 sq. miles
Population: 6,733,000 (1984)
Capital: Ouagadougou
Currency: CFA franc (100 centimes)

Previously known as Upper Volta, landlocked Burkina Faso is located on a plateau area that is part of the West African savannah region.

The climate is hot. Average annual rainfall ranges from 40 inches in the south to 10 in the north. High temperatures are 90-100 degrees F, dropping to 70-80 degrees F at night. Rain falls from May to October.

The French gained control over the area in the 1890s and the colony of Upper Volta was created from parts of the colony of Upper Senegal and Niger in 1919. It existed until 1932, when it was divided among French Sudan, Ivory Coast, and Niger. In 1947, it was reconstituted as a French Overseas Territory.

Semi-autonomous status was achieved on Dec. 11, 1958 and full independence came on Aug. 5, 1960. The name was changed to Burkina Faso on Aug. 4, 1984.

In recent years, drought has stricken the country and it is one of Africa's poorest. Deposits of manganese exist but they are not developed. There is no industry. The per capita income in 1981 was $180 and the 1984 literacy rate was a low 7%.

The country is presently ruled by a president. The constitution has been suspended, the legislature disbanded, and political parties abolished.

Stamps were first issued for Upper Volta in 1920. They are overprints on stamps of Upper Senegal and Niger.

In recent years there have been numerous stamp issues, many of which are devoted to topical subjects having no relationship to the issuing country.

Philatelic Bureau: Service Philatelique, Office des Postes et Telecommunications, Ouagadougou, Burkina Faso.

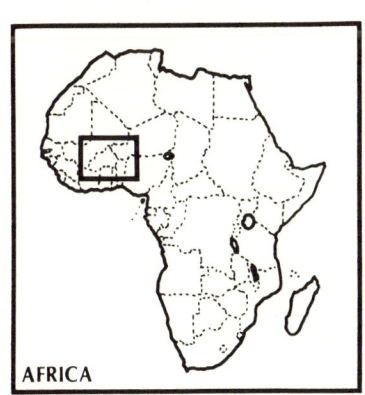

BURUNDI, REPUBLIC OF

Area: 10,759 sq. miles
Population: 4,691,000 (1984)
Capital: Bujumbura
Currency: Franc (100 centimes)

With its western border on the Great Rift Valley, Burundi lies on a plateau with mountains rising to 9,000 feet. The landscape is rolling and the climate moderate.

The average temperature at the capital is 73 degrees F, but frost occurs at the higher altitudes. The main dry season is from May to September. The White Nile has its southernmost source in Burundi.

A feudal society existed prior to the arrival of Europeans. This persisted and was only abolished in 1977.

The area was made part of German East Africa in the 1890s and was occupied by Belgian forces from the Congo in 1916. After World War I, Belgium was given a League of Nations Mandate over the area called Ruanda-Urundi, which also included what is now Rwanda.

Following World War II, this area became a United Nations Trust Territory, also under Belgian administration. Independence was achieved on July 1, 1962.

The economy is agricultural and extremely shaky, with famine a threat whenever crops are not adequate. Coffee is the main export.

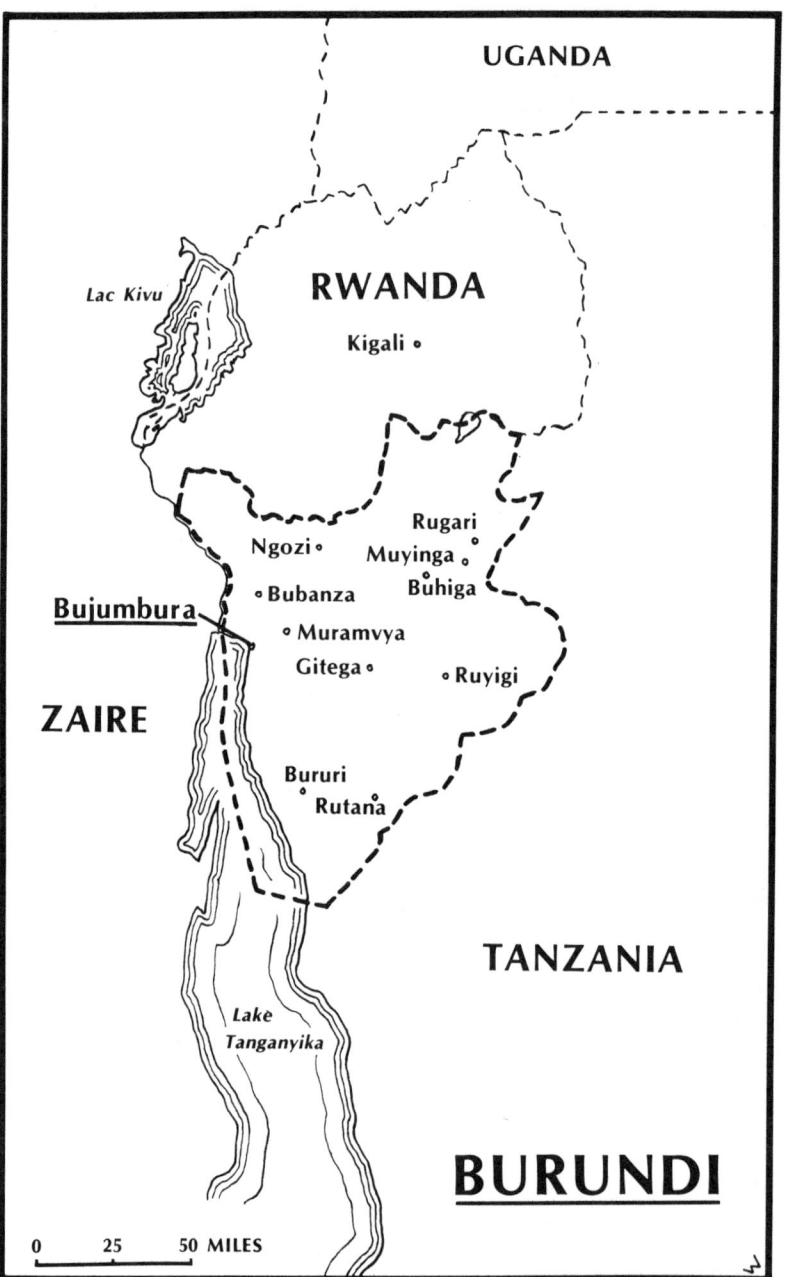

The per capita income in 1982 was $235 and the 1983 literacy rate was 25%.

The poor economy has not been helped by internal strife. Although the present regime is pledged to reconcile differences and increase productivity, its success has not been great.

The Belgian administration issued the first stamps in 1924 under the name of Ruanda-Urundi. These continued until July 1, 1962, when stamps of Burundi appeared. Since then, an enormous quantity of stamps featuring every conceivable subject has been released and the country's philatelic reputation is poor.

Philatelic Bureau: Agence Philatelique du Burundi, Boite Postale 45, Bujumbura, Burundi.

CAMEROON, UNITED REPUBLIC OF

Area: 179,558 sq. miles
Population: 9,506,000 (1984)
Capital: Yaounde
Currency: CFA franc (100 centimes)

The geography and climate of Cameroon are varied. There is equatorial rain forest in the south, a high plateau in the mid-portion, mountainous forest in the west, and savannah in the north.

High temperatures and humidity exist on the coast, ranging to arid conditions in the north. At the inland capital city, high temperatures are 85-90 degrees F with lows of 65-70.

Located at what is called the "crossroads of Africa," Cameroon is one of the area's more stable and prosperous countries. Both English and French are official languages and the University of Yaounde is Africa's only university to teach courses in both languages.

The first European contact was with the Portuguese in the 16th century and it was not long afterwards that the slave trade flourished along the coast. Mission settlements were established during the mid-1800s and Germany gained control of the area in 1885.

The German colony of Kamerun was captured by the British and French during World War I. After the war, it was divided and administered as League of Nations mandates by the two countries and from 1946 as United Nations trusteeships. The French portion became independent on Jan. 1, 1960. In 1961, the northern part of the British portion opted to join Nigeria, with the south joining the Republic of Cameroon.

Political stability has made possible considerable development and

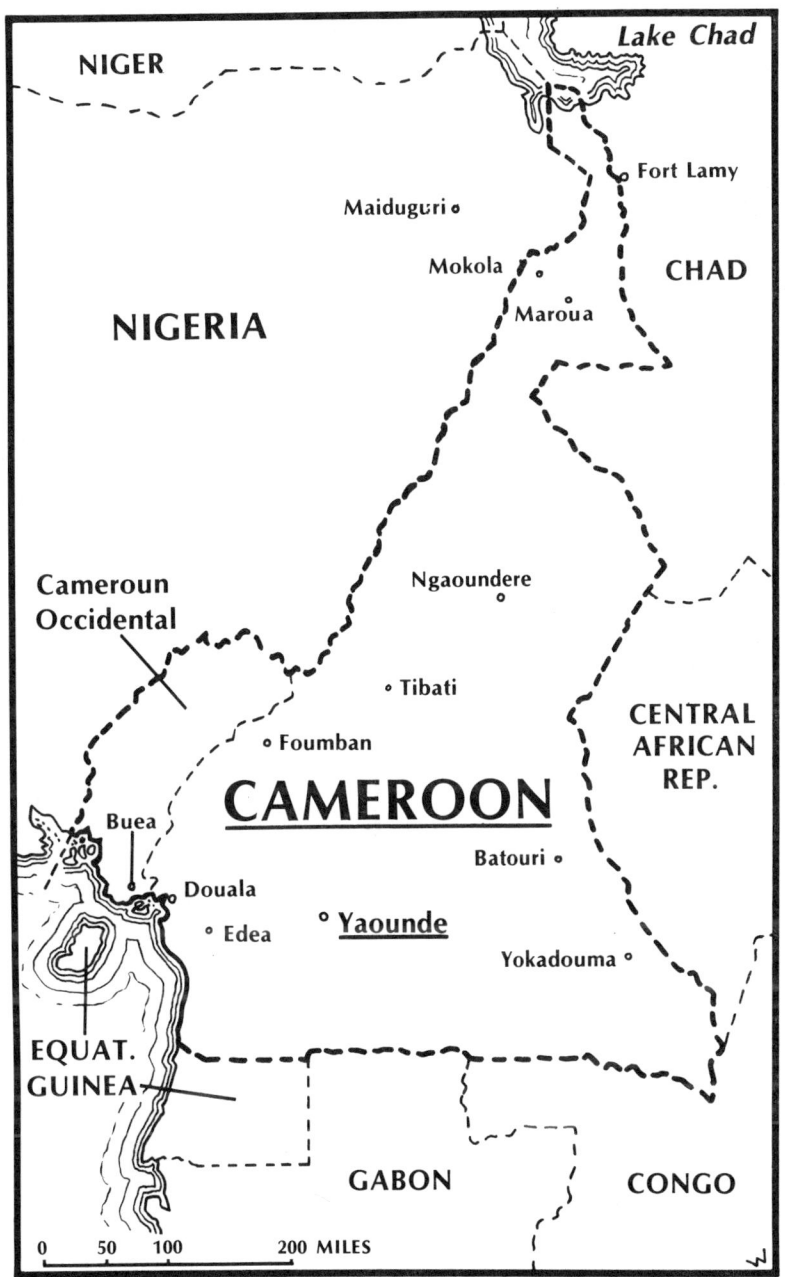

the economy is in better shape than those of neighboring countries. Aluminum processing is an important industry and cocoa, coffee, peanuts, tea, bananas, cotton, and tobacco are grown. Other resources include timber and oil. The 1979 per capita income was $628 and the literacy rate in 1978 was 34%.

Stamps were issued under the German administration, beginning in 1897. British and French occupation overprints followed the World War I takeover. French colonial issues continued in the French area until independence.

Although there have been a considerable number of new stamp issues in recent years, these have not been excessive by central African standards.

Philatelic Bureau: Receveur General des PTT, Yaounde, Cameroon.

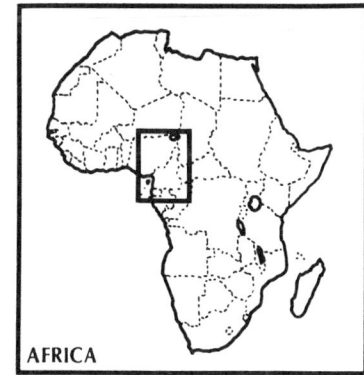

CAPE VERDE, REPUBLIC OF

Area: 1,557 sq. miles
Population: 300,000 (1984)
Capital: Praia
Currency: Escudo (100 centavos)

The volcanic islands of the Cape Verde group are located about 385 miles off the coast of West Africa. They have a temperate climate with little seasonal variation. The annual temperature range is from 80 degrees F in September to 71 degrees F in February. Rain is scarce and erratic, with the capital city recording only about nine inches a year. There are periods of drought and famine is not uncommon.

Little vegetation grows except in interior valleys. Blowing sand from the Sahara can form a 'fog' and has caused much erosion on the islands.

Portuguese settlers arrived in 1492 and the islands became a colony of Portugal. The islands' location and the several fine harbors brought initial prosperity and they were once a commercial and trading center of some importance. A cable station was established in 1875.

In 1951, the islands became an overseas province of Portugal and independence was granted on July 5, 1975.

Today, the economy is poor. The islands have few natural resources and subsistence agriculture is a major occupation. Fishing and income from workers overseas are important to the economy. Bananas, coffee, and sugar cane are grown and exported when adequate rainfall

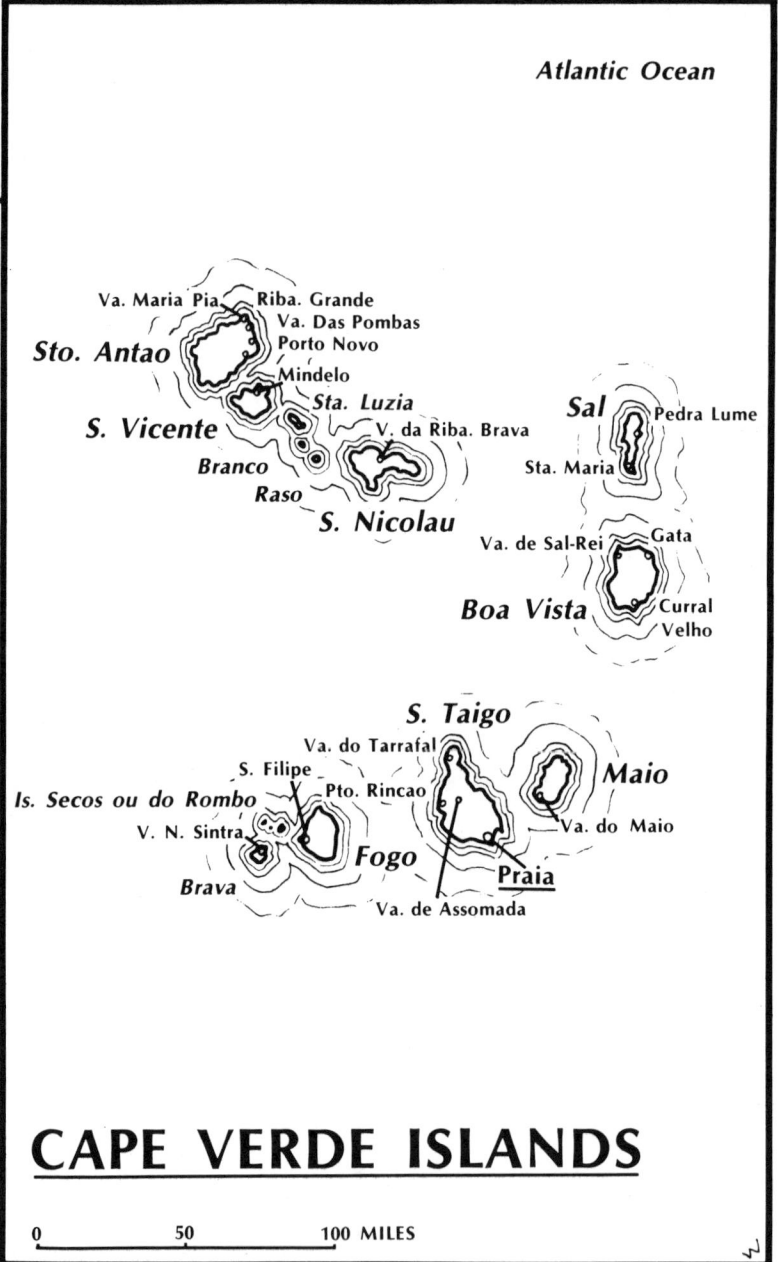

permits. During a recent drought only 4% of the islands dietary staple, corn, was produced.

There are plans to develop the fishing industry, and ship repair facilities and a plant for refining oil are being considered by the government. Tourism is another possible way to boost the economy, but there are few current facilities for visitors.

The 1980 per capita income was $300 and the 1984 literacy rate was 37%.

Stamps were first issued in 1877 and followed the usual Portuguese colonial pattern. Since independence, stamp-issuing policies have not been excessive.

Philatelic Bureau: Direccao dos Servicos de Correios e Telecomunicacoes, Praia, Cape Verde.

CENTRAL AFRICAN REPUBLIC

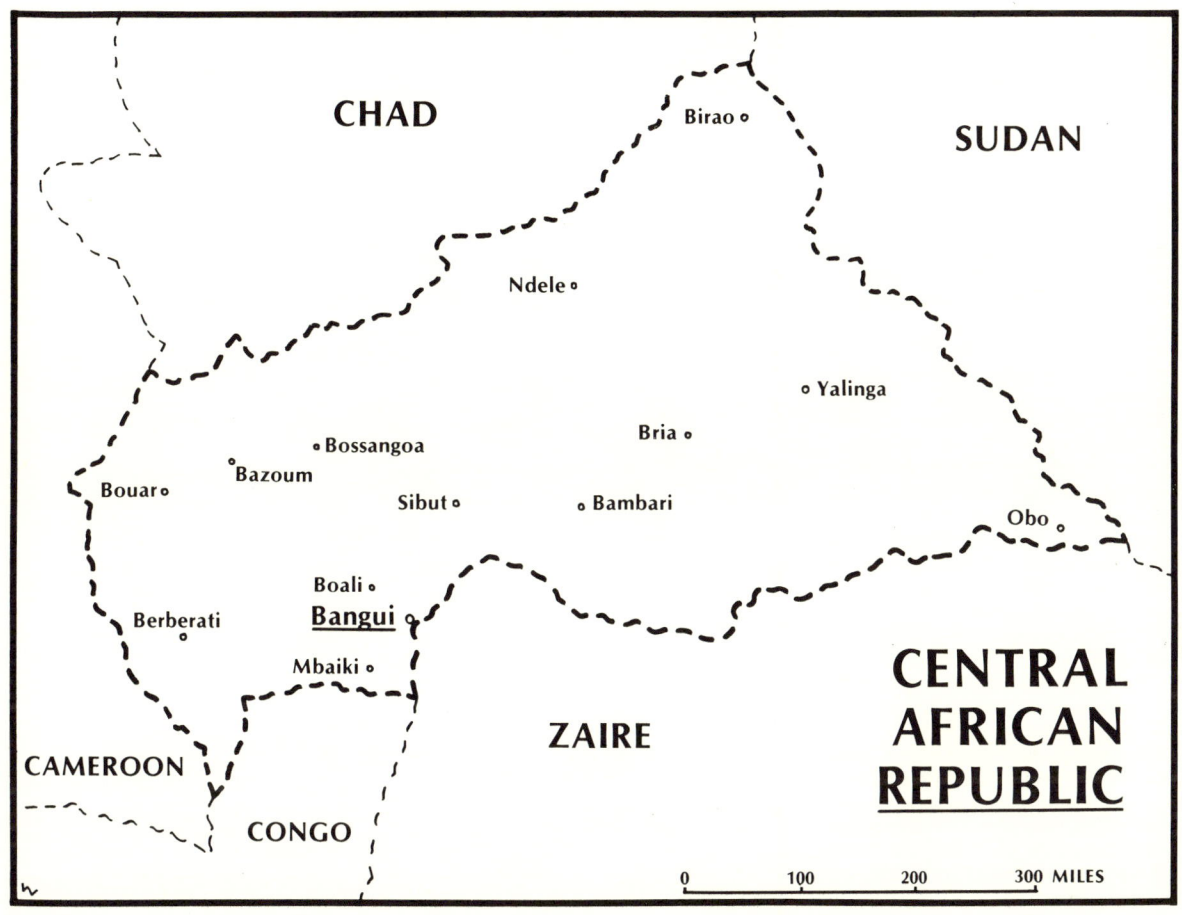

Area: 241,313 sq. miles
Population: 2,585,000 (1984)
Capital: Bangui
Currency: CFA franc (100 centimes)

Located at about the geographic center of Africa, the Central African Republic is some 400 miles from the

ocean on a large plateau averaging about 2,000 feet in elevation.

In the north the country drains into Lake Chad and in the south into the Congo (Zaire) River system. The north is semidesert, while there is a tropical rain forest in the south, where the rainfall averages 70 inches a year. Average annual temperatures at Bangui range from 80-90 degrees F.

The country has been described as a vast zoo and the elephant's last refuge. The elephant population is estimated at 30,000.

The French controlled the area from the late 19th century and it was originally the colony of Ubangi-Shari before becoming part of French Equatorial Africa. The status of autonomous republic as the Central African Republic was achieved on Dec. 1, 1958, with full independence on Aug. 13, 1960.

For a brief period in the 1970s, during the brutal regime of the self-proclaimed "Emperor" Bokassa, the country was called the Central African Empire.

An unstable politcal climate has inhibited economic growth and the country is poor, although there are mineral resources. Diamonds are the chief export. Crops include cotton, coffee, and peanuts. The 1982 per capita income was $310 and the 1983 literacy rate was 20%.

Stamps were issued under the various colonial groupings. Central African Republic stamps appeared in 1959. A considerable number of stamps has been issued in recent years.

Philatelic Bureau: Service Philatelique des PTT, Bangui, Central African Republic.

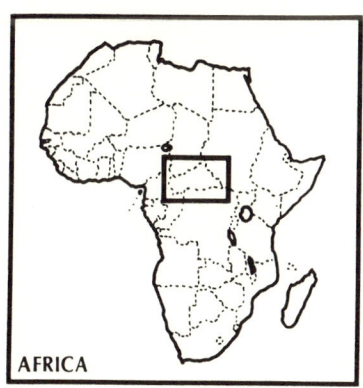

CHAD, REPUBLIC OF

Area: 495,752 sq. miles
Population: 5,116,000 (1984)
Capital: Ndjamena
Currency: CFA franc (100 centimes)

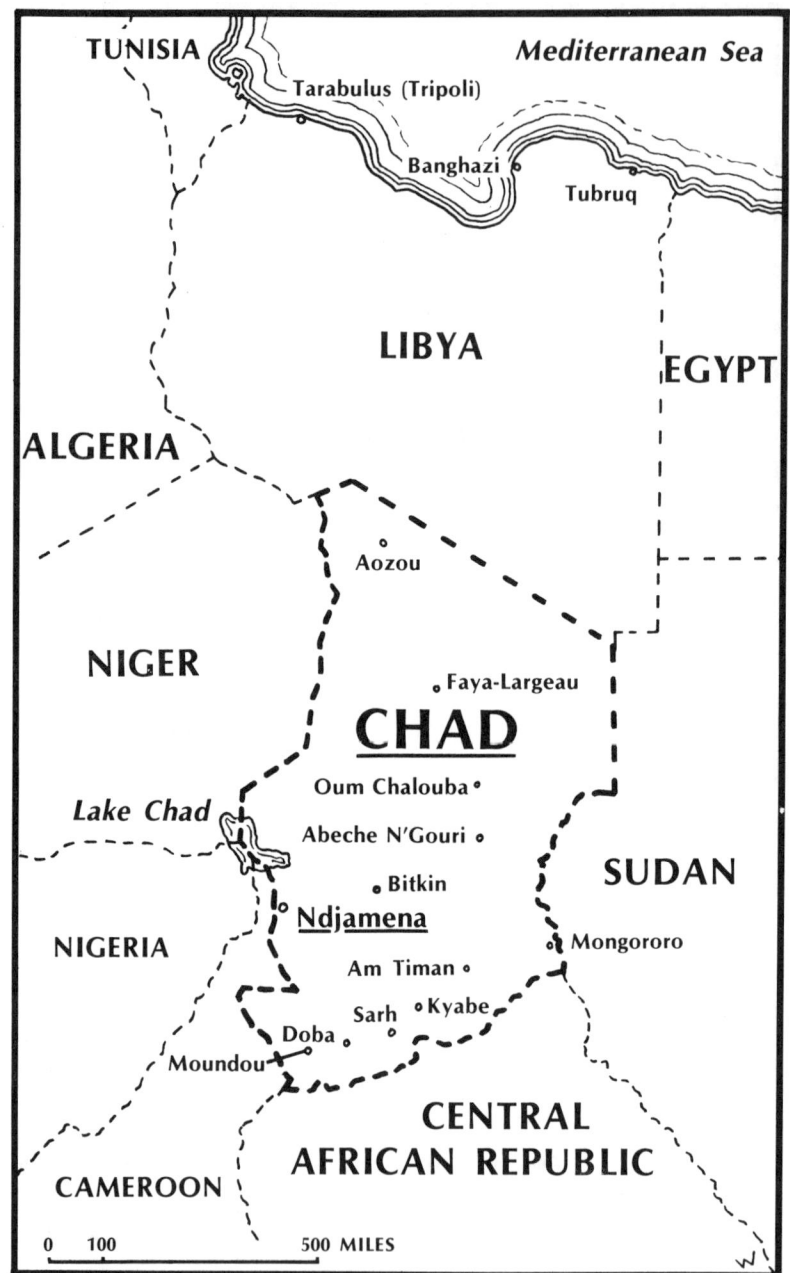

One of the world's poorest nations, Chad lies between two cultures — Islam coming from the north across the Sahara Desert, and that of central Africa.

With an elevation of 750 feet at Lake Chad, the land rises in the north to desert mountains reaching almost 12,000 feet, with rolling savannah country in the south. Although there is an average rainfall in the south of 50 inches, the north is generally dry and the climate has been compared to that of Arizona.

Chad has been a crossroads between Arabs and the Negroid tribes of central Africa since ancient times and there have been organized societies in the Lake Chad area for more than 1,000 years.

The northern population is largely nomadic.

Religions practiced by the people of Chad include Islam, Christianity, and the traditional beliefs.

French authority over the area was established during the 1890s and it became a dependency of the colony of Ubangi-Shari. It was made a separate colony in 1920 and later, a component of French Equatorial Africa. Autonomous status in the French Community came in 1959 and full independence was achieved on Aug. 11, 1960.

In recent years, Libya has interfered in Chad's affairs and its troops entered the country in 1980. They were withdrawn later, but Libya backed a rebel movement in

Chad that prompted France to send troops in 1983 to assist the government.

Chad's economic situation is serious and recent droughts have caused widespread starvation. More than 90% of the population is engaged in subsistence food production. The natural resources are not developed and the country is suffering from its isolated, landlocked position, as well as its poor soil and harsh climatic conditions.

The 1976 per capita income was only $73 and the 1978 literacy rate was 15%.

Stamps were first issued for Chad in 1922. They are stamps of Middle Congo overprinted "TCHAD."

A large number of stamps has been issued in recent years. Many dating from the 1970s are not recognized by the major catalogs.

Philatelic Bureau: Receveur General de PTT, Ndjamena, Chad.

COMOROS, FEDERAL ISLAMIC REPUBLIC OF THE

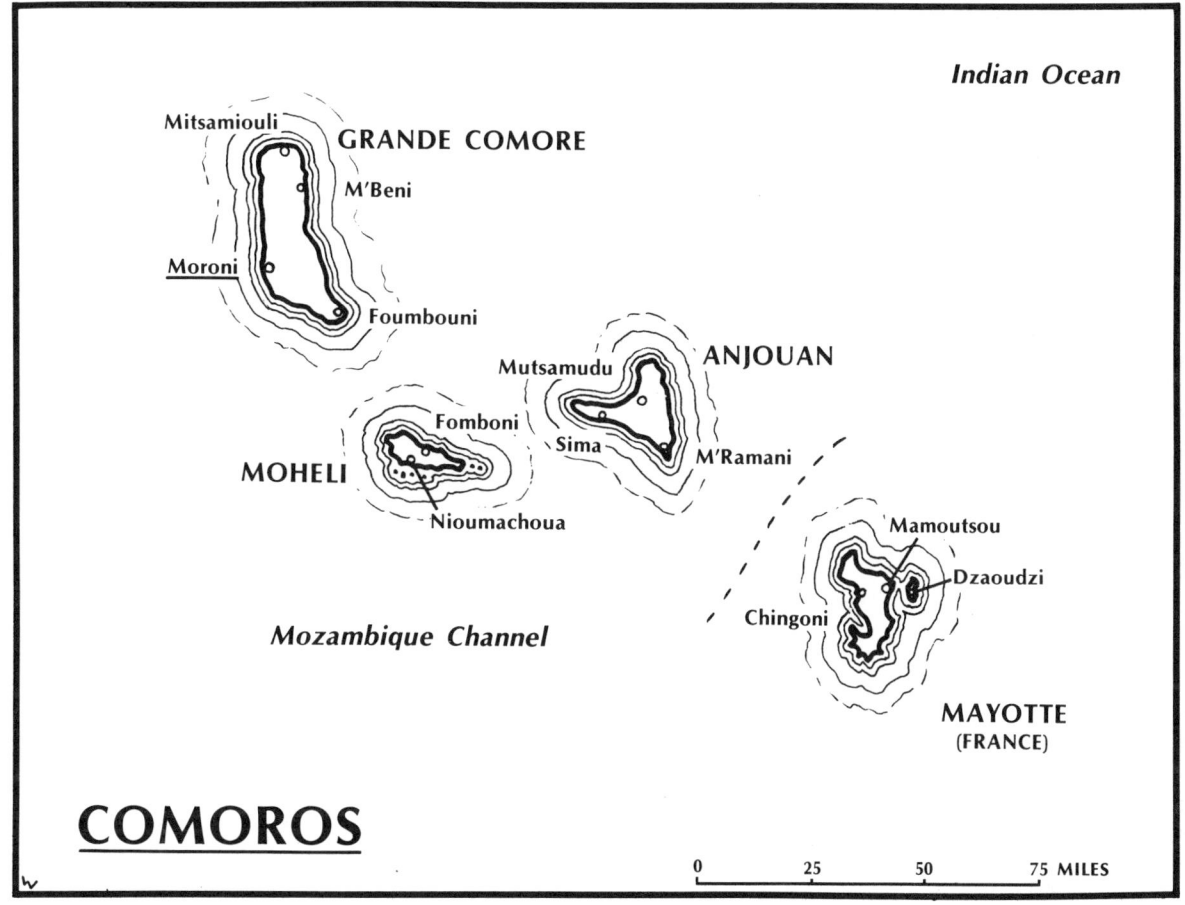

Area: 688 sq. miles
Population: 445,000 (1984)
Capital: Moroni
Currency: CFA franc (100 centimes)

The independent Comoro islands comprise the islands of Grande Comore, Moheli, and Anjouan. They are located in the Mozambique Channel off the northern part of Madagascar and midway between that island and the African coast.

The fourth island, Mayotte, elected to remain French when the group was granted independence. It is Christian, whereas in the other islands Islam is the official religion.

The climate is tropical and temperatures range from an average in December of 82 degrees F to a low in July of 73 degrees F. Rainfall is varied and each year the islands can receive from 39 to 118 inches.

The capital city of Moroni is located on the island of Grande Comore.

The English sailor, James Lancaster, is believed to have been the first European to visit the islands in about 1591. They were subsequently dominated by Arab influence.

France took possession of Mayotte in 1843. The sultans of the other islands came under French protection in 1886 and French colonial stamps were issued for each island.

From 1914 to 1947, the Comoros were administered from Madagascar and in the latter years they became an overseas territory of France.

The islands became independent on July 6, 1975.

Perfume is the chief industry and the raising of perfume plants is the main agricultural activity. Other crops include vanilla and copra. The 1982 per capita income was $240 and the literacy rate was 15%.

When the islands were administered from Madagascar from 1914 to 1947, they used the stamps of that island. Stamps for use in the group were first issued in 1950.

Since independence, in common with other ex-French colonies, stamp issues have proliferated, although not to the same degree as some of the African nations.

Philatelic Bureau: Direction General des PTT, Service Philatelique, Moroni, Comoro Islands.

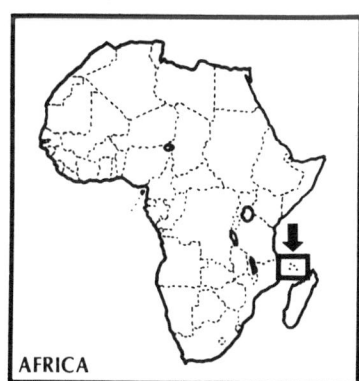

CONGO, PEOPLE'S REPUBLIC OF THE

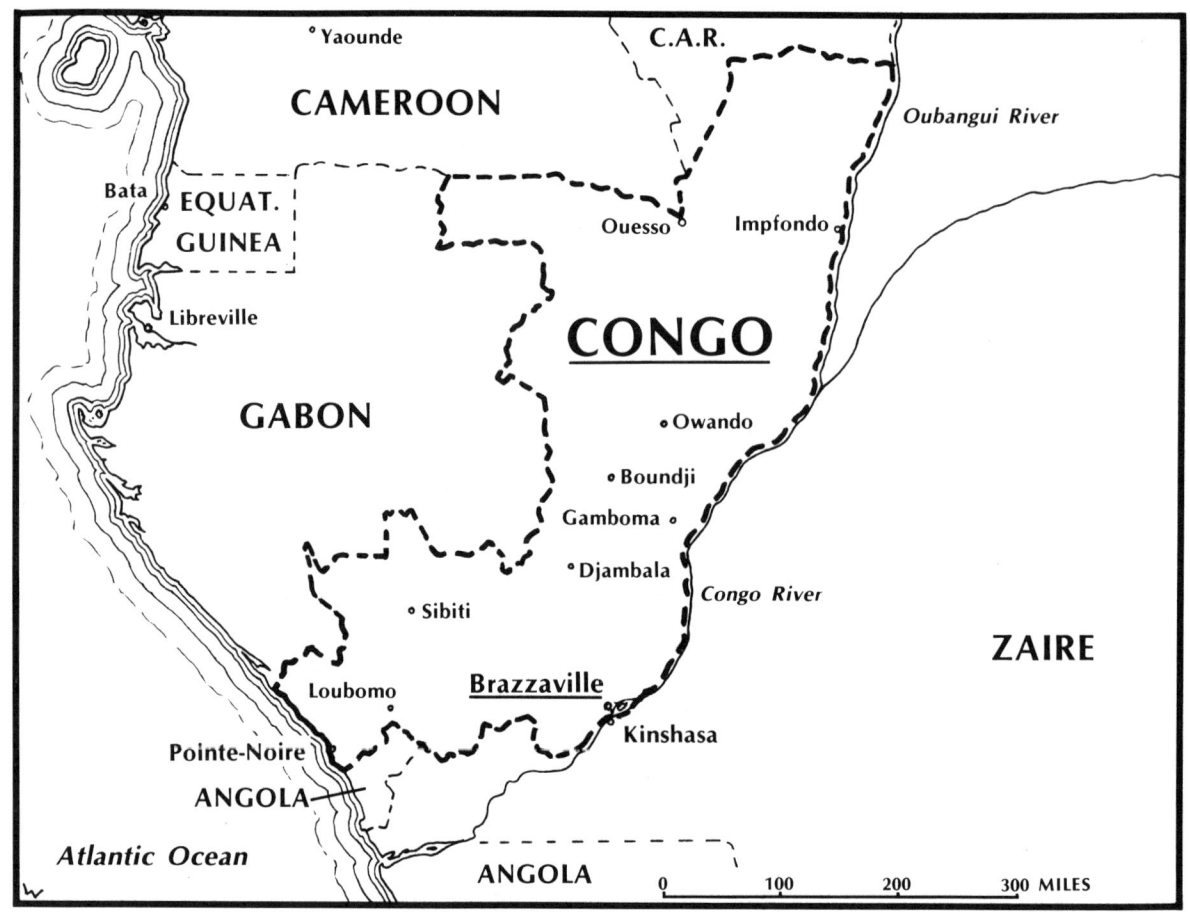

Area: 132,046 sq. miles
Population: 1,745,000 (1984)
Capital: Brazzaville
Currency: CFA franc (100 centimes)

Formerly the French colony of Middle Congo, then part of French Equatorial Africa, the Congo ex-

tends more than 800 miles from its short Atlantic Ocean coastline inland along the north banks of the Congo (Zaire) and Oubangui rivers.

Much of the country is rain forest and the climate is humid. The average annual temperature is 75 degrees F and rainfall is from 45 to 80 inches a year.

The French gained control of the area in 1883. In 1910, it became part of French Equatorial Africa, after a period as the colony of Middle Congo. On Aug. 15, 1960, the Congo achieved full independence.

There has been considerable instability in government with several coups. Currently the government has strong Marxist leanings and relations with the Soviet Union have been strengthened. Despite a proclaimed nonaligned policy, the Congo sides with the Communist states on virtually all international issues.

The economy is weak. Tropical timber is an important export, but there is minimal light manufacturing and no heavy industry. Mineral resources include oil, potash, natural gas, lead, copper, and zinc. Palm oil, cocoa, coffee, and tobacco are grown.

The 1978 per capita income was $500 and the 1980 literacy rate was 80%.

Under French administration, stamps were issued inscribed for Middle Congo from 1907-1933 and subsequently stamps of French Equatorial Africa were used until independence.

Since independence, stamp issues have been extensive and a number of issues during the 1970s are not recognized by major catalogs.

Philatelic Bureau: Direction General des PTT, Service Philatelique, Brazzaville, People's Republic of the Congo.

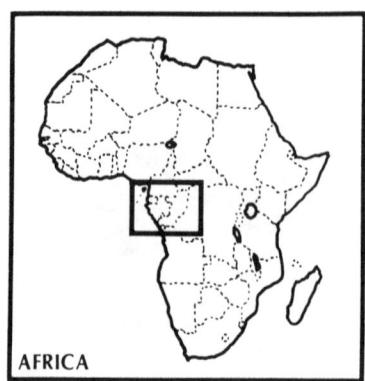

DJIBOUTI, REPUBLIC OF

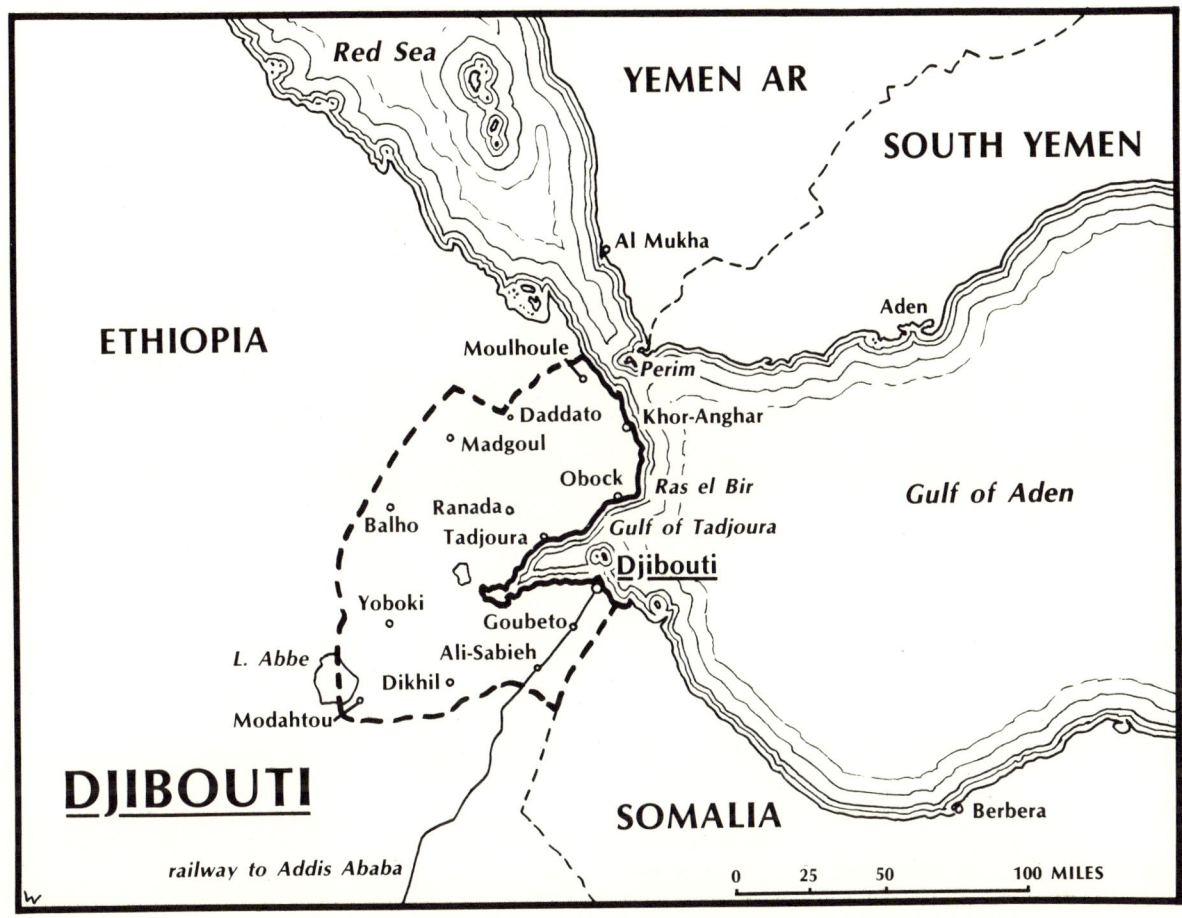

Area: 8,996 sq. miles
Population: 289,000 (1984)
Capital: Djibouti
Currency: Franc (100 centimes)

Composed mostly of bare, arid desert, this small corner of Africa was an unlikely candidate for nationhood. Having to import virtually everything it needs, Djibouti is positioned precariously between two countries periodically warring; Ethiopia and Somalia.

The country is noted for its heat

and lack of rain. The average maximum temperature in summer is 104 degrees F and the winter minimum is 73 degrees F. There is usually only about five inches or less of rainfall each year, and thus little vegetation except for desert scrub.

The inhabitants are nomadic, raising sheep, goats, camels, and some cattle.

The area's strategic location at the southern end of the Red Sea attracted French attention and by 1862 it had gained control of the town of Obock.

By 1888, the colony of French Somali Coast was established. The name was changed to the French Territory of Afars and Issas in 1967, these being the names of the two ethnic groups. Independence was granted on June 27, 1977.

There are no significant natural resources except for marine salt, a small quantity of which is exported. Trade is important and Djibouti is the ocean terminal of a railway to Ethiopia. French aid is the main support of the economy.

The 1982 per capita income was $180 and the 1981 literacy rate was 20%.

Stamps were first issued for the French settlement at Obock in 1892 and were used until 1894 when stamps were issued for the colony of French Somali Coast following removal of the seat of government to Djibouti.

The 1967 name change was reflected in the stamps and since independence, stamps have been inscribed for the new country.

Philatelic Bureau: Office des Postes et Telecommunications, Djibouti, Republic of Djibouti.

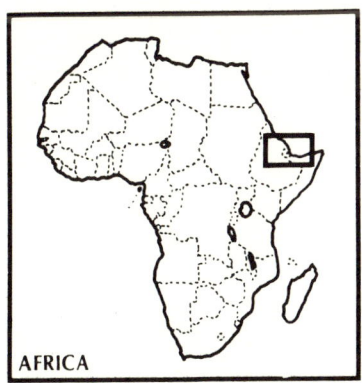

EGYPT, ARAB REPUBLIC OF

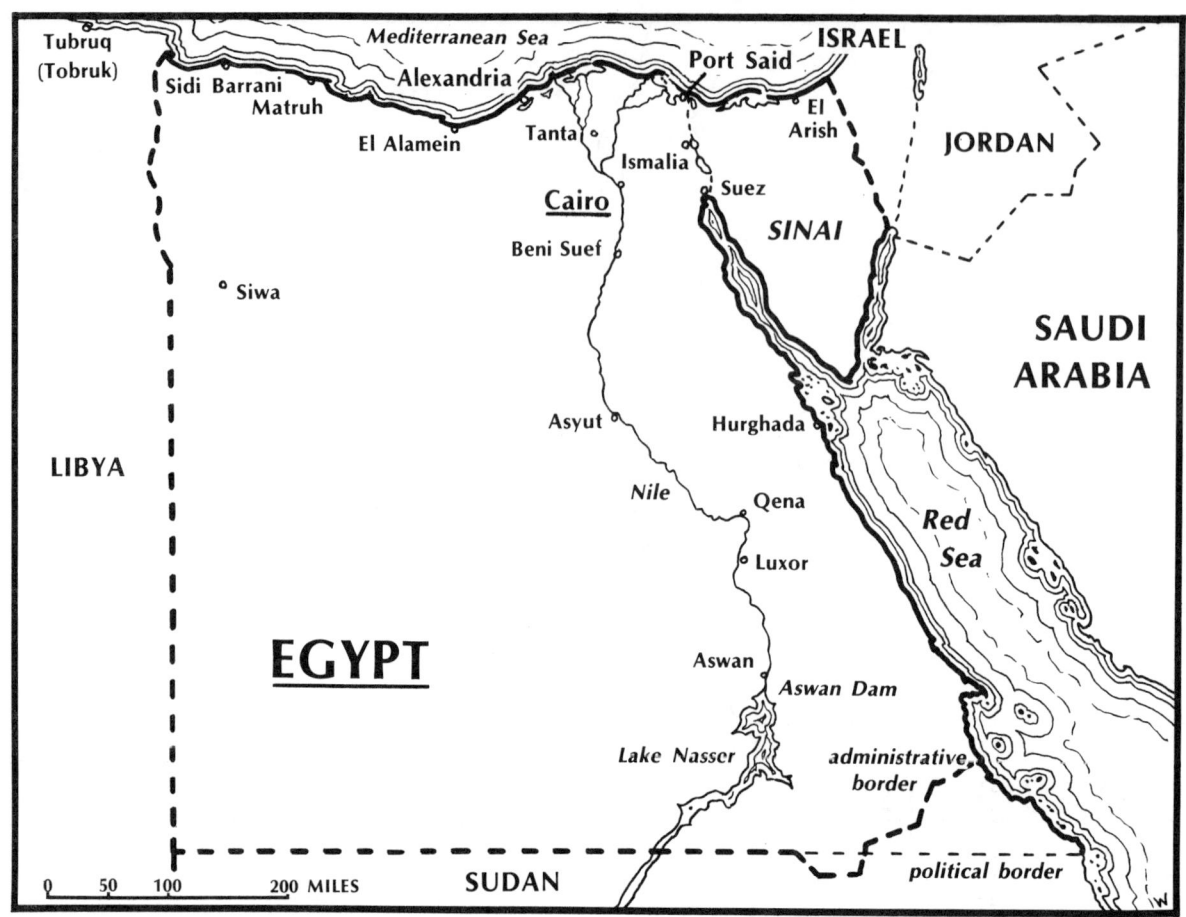

Area: 386,650 sq. miles
Population: 47 million (1984)
Capital: Cairo
Currency: Egyptian pound

Egypt has long been one of the world's crossroads and has a recorded history dating back some 6,000 years. About 3,200 BC it was a kingdom extending south deep into Africa and north to present-day Syria. Decline, followed by Asian invaders set the pattern for subsequent rule by Greeks, Romans, Byzantines, Arabs, and Turks.

The Turks occupied Egypt until World War I, when they were expelled by the British, who assumed responsibility for the country's welfare until 1922. Partial autonomy was granted then and the sultan became King Fuad.

Despite the danger of German attack in World War II and massive British efforts to defend the country, Egypt remained neutral.

With the 1952 ouster of King Farouk, Egypt became a republic. Brief federations with Syria and Libya proved unsuccessful and today the country is an oasis of moderation in a Middle East torn by conflict and hatred.

The Suez Canal drew Egypt to the center of the modern world, although periods of closure during recent wars with Israel have rendered it of much less global importance.

Industrial products include textiles, chemicals, and petrochemical products. Egypt is one of the world's largest producers of cotton. Other crops include fruits, grain, vegetables, and sugar. Mineral resources are oil, gypsum, iron, and manganese.

The climate is warm and dry. Rainfall is restricted to the Mediterranean coast, where about eight inches falls each year. In Cairo, the annual rainfall is about one inch a year and the summer temperature ranges from 70-100 degrees F. Winter temperatures are about 40-65 degrees F.

Egypt's early stamps are attractive, well produced, and popular. Recent issues stress national propaganda and are largely symbolic in design.

Philatelic Bureau: Philatelic Office, Cairo, Egypt.

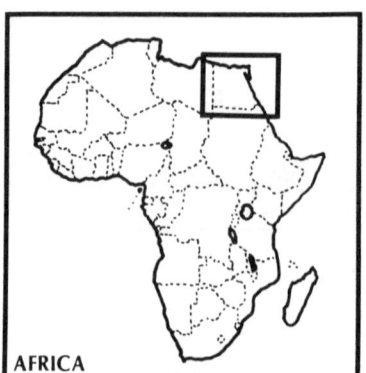

EQUATORIAL GUINEA, REPUBLIC OF

Area: 10,832 sq. miles
Population: 275,000 (1984)
Capital: Malabo
Currency: Ekuele

Equatorial Guinea comprises the former Spanish African colonies of Rio Muni on the mainland, the island of Fernando Po (now Bioko), and the smaller islands of Annobon, Corisco, and Elobey.

The climate varies between the islands and the mainland area but is generally hot and humid. The average temperature at Malabo is 80 degrees F.

Bioko was discovered by the Portuguese in the mid-1400s and ceded to Spain in 1778. The area in its present form was established in 1909 as Spanish Guinea, although Spanish colonial stamps were issued for the various segments at different times. Independence was granted on Oct. 12, 1968.

Since then the country has suffered the brutal 11-year regime of

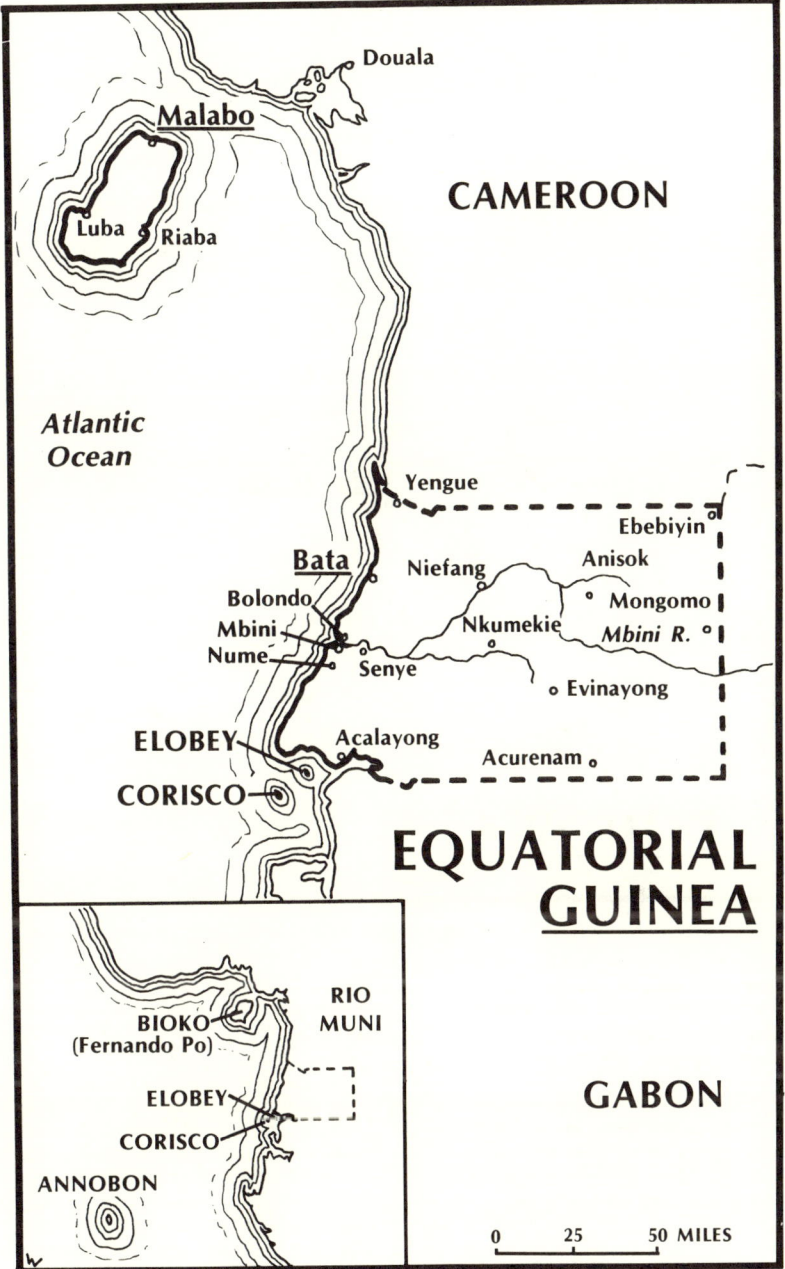

Maise Nguema Biyogo, during which it is estimated that up to one third of the country's inhabitants fled. He was overthrown in 1979.

The country is poor and the economy remains shattered by the loss of most skilled workers.

Cocoa, coffee, and timber are the main exports. There is no industry and natural resources are insignificant and undeveloped. The 1983 per capita income was $250 and the 1984 literacy rate was 55%.

Whatever philatelic popularity the area had under the Spanish administration completely vanished as the new country embarked on a policy of releasing as many stamps as possible in as many forms as the promoter could devise and bearing as large a variety of subjects as could be imagined. None of these confections are listed in the major catalogs and it is extremely doubtful that they were ever on sale at post offices in the country.

In recent years, the flood has ceased, although few collectors are interested in the philately of the country.

Philatelic Bureau: Oficina Filatelica de la Direccion General de Correos, Malabo, Republic of Equatorial Guinea.

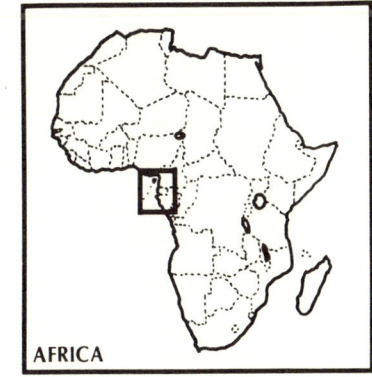

ETHIOPIA

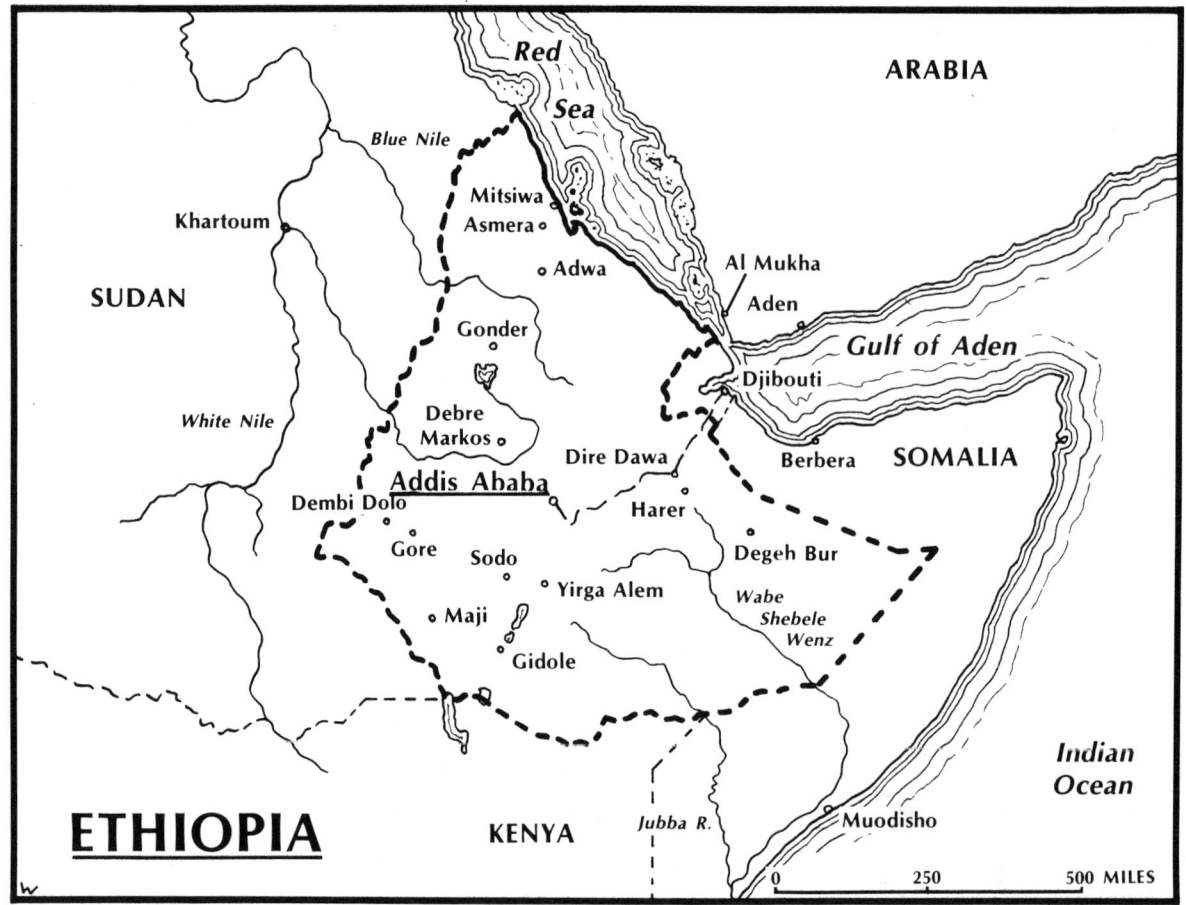

Area: 472,400 sq. miles
Population: 31,998,000 (1984)
Capital: Addis Ababa
Currency: Birr (100 cents)

The oldest independent nation in Africa and one mentioned by Herodotus as early as the fifth century BC, Ethiopia possesses but a shadow of its former glory, with a

failing economy and areas stricken by famine.

Most of the country is high plateau varying from 6,000-10,000 feet. The average maximum temperature at Addis Ababa (elevation 8,000 feet) is 80 degrees F and the low is 40 degrees F.

Independent until the Italian invasion and occupation of 1936, the country was liberated by Britain in 1941. Emperor Haile Selassie, who had ruled since 1930, except for the Italian occupation period, was deposed in 1974. A socialist state was proclaimed and opposition violently suppressed.

Since then there has been a succession of coups and uprisings. Soviet advisors and Cuban troops helped defeat neighboring Somalia over a border dispute.

The present Marxist regime has close ties with the Soviet Union, but it is the West that is supplying vast amounts of humanitarian aid to the areas suffering drought and famine. The country has suffered also from an emphasis on military strength at the expense of the economy. In 1980 the per capita income was a low $117. The 1984 literacy rate was only 15%.

Until Ethiopia gained Eritrea in 1952, its sole link with the outside world was the railway from Addis Ababa to Djibouti. However, unrest in Eritrea has probably rendered it less useful as an outlet.

Stamps were first issued by Ethiopia in 1894 and, except for the Italian occupation period, have been issued ever since.

Philatelic Bureau: Ethiopian Postal Service, Philatelic Section, P.O. Box 1112, Addis Ababa, Ethiopia.

GABONESE REPUBLIC

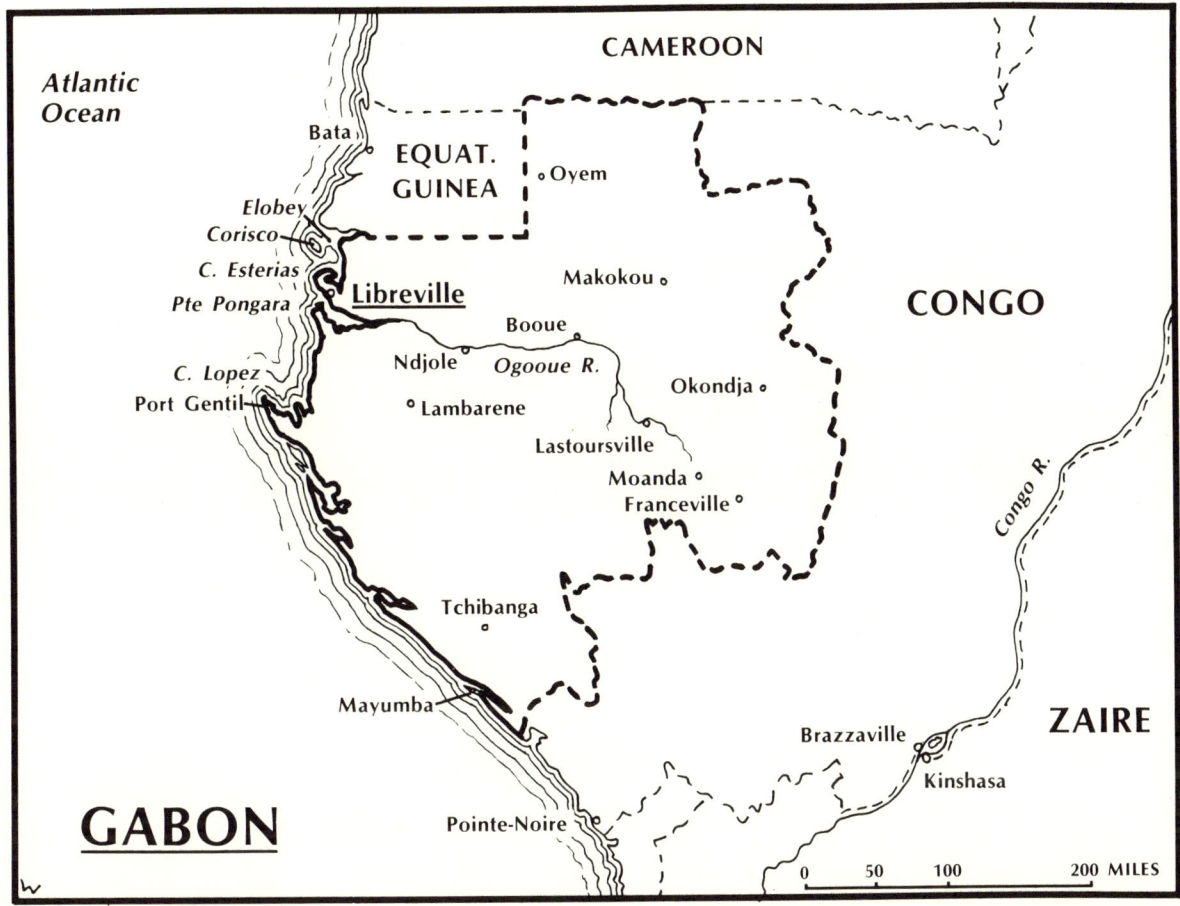

Area: 102,317 sq. miles
Population: 958,000 (1984)
Capital: Libreville
Currency: CFA franc (100 centimes)

One of the most prosperous nations in black Africa, Gabon was first visited by Portuguese merchants in the 15th century.

Most of the country is covered by rain forest and the climate is hot and humid. Annual rainfall at Libreville is more than 100 inches.

By the late 1830s, the French had exerted the most influence in the

area, but it did not become a colony until the early 1900s, although they had occupied it in 1885.

In 1934, it became part of French Equatorial Africa and achieved the status of an autonomous republic in the French Community on Nov. 28, 1958. Full independence came on Aug. 17, 1960.

The country owes its present prosperity to good natural resources, enlightened government policies with resulting foreign investment, and a policy of economic development by evolution rather than by revolution. These policies have paid off in a 1981 per capita income of $2,974 and a 1983 literacy rate of 65%.

The petrochemical industry is the chief source of income. Other mineral resources include manganese, uranium, iron, and natural gas. Crops grown are cocoa, coffee, rice, peanuts, and bananas. Timber resources are also extensive.

The first stamps of Gabon were the general issue of the French colonies handstamped "GAB" and surcharged. They were issued in 1886. In 1904, stamps of the Commerce and Navigation key type were released inscribed "GABON." The first pictorial issue appeared in 1910.

Since independence stamp issues have increased considerably, but are still fairly moderate when compared with the stamps of other countries in the area.

Philatelic Bureau: Service Philatelique, Direction General des PTT, Libreville, Gabon.

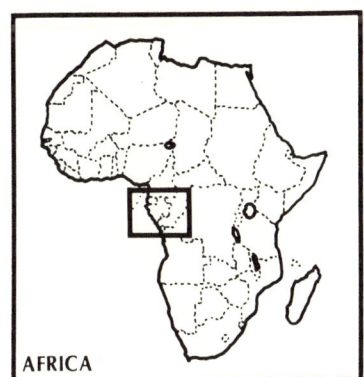

GAMBIA, REPUBLIC OF THE

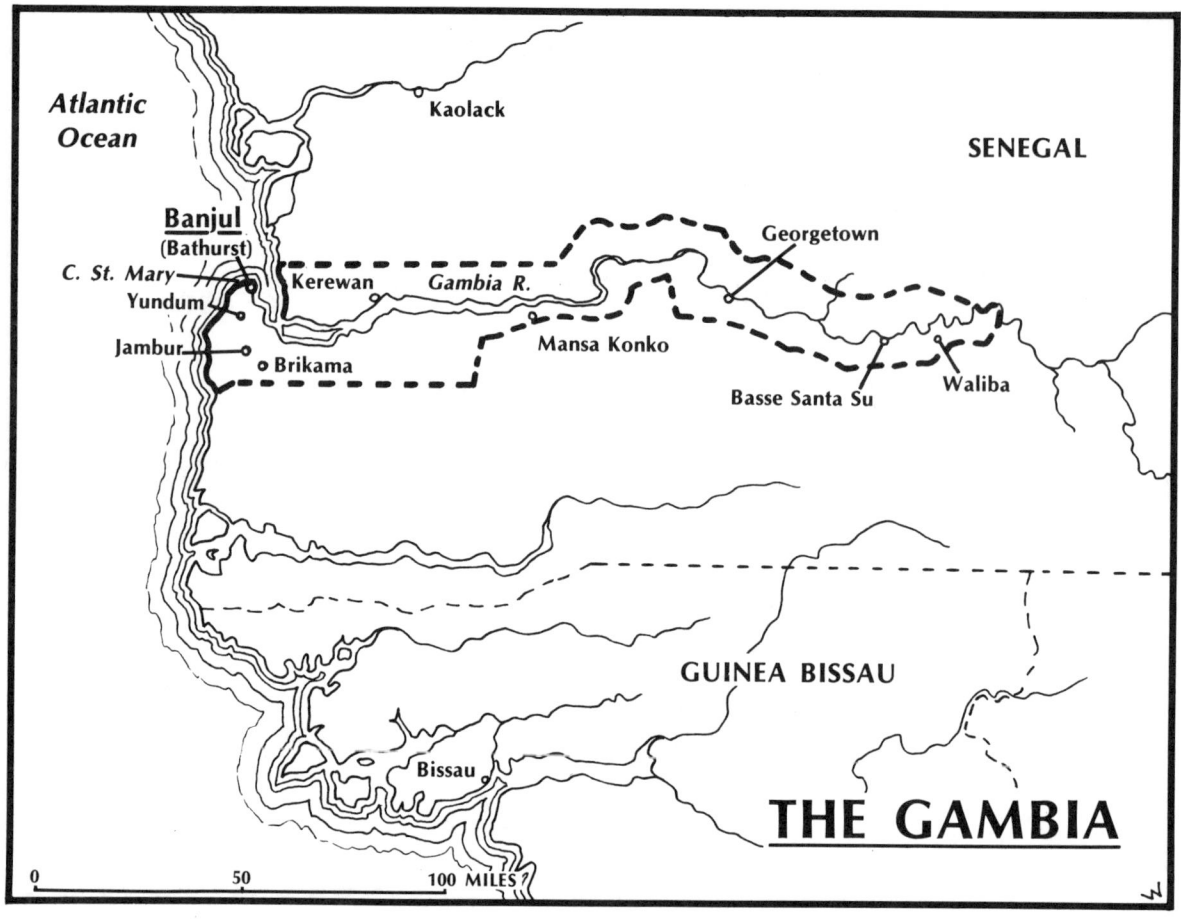

Area: 4,361 sq. miles
Population: 695,886 (1983)
Capital: Banjul
Currency: Dalasy (100 bututs)

The Gambia is a narrow country extending for about 200 miles along both banks of the Gambia River in West Africa. Its width varies from 7-20 miles.

The climate is subtropical with 30-55 inches of rain a year falling only during the summer months. Temperatures average from 60-110 degrees F but daily temperatures exceed 90 degrees F from April to June.

The country is claimed to be Africa's only functioning democracy and is noted for its honest elections. It was Britain's first colony in Africa and trading rights there had been sold to British merchants by the Portuguese as early as 1588.

Conflict with France for control of the area continued through the 18th century, with Britain gaining final possession under the Treaty of Versailles in 1783. It was made a colony in 1843. Internal self-government was granted in 1963 and full independence came on Feb. 18, 1965. It became a republic on April 24, 1970.

There has been some political unrest and a coup was attempted in 1981. Close ties exist with the Republic of Senegal.

Tourism is the chief source of income and the economy is mostly agricultural, with peanuts being the main export. The 1981 per capita income was $330 and the 1982 literacy rate was 12%.

The first stamps, issued in 1869, are the beautiful "cameos," or embossed heads of Queen Victoria.

A moderate stamp-issuing policy has been continued following independence and stamp subjects generally relate to the country.

Philatelic Bureau: Postmaster General, GPO, Banjul, The Gambia.

The Gambia's beautiful cameo.

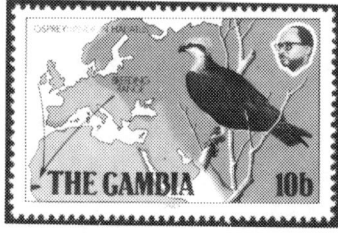

AFRICA

GHANA, REPUBLIC OF

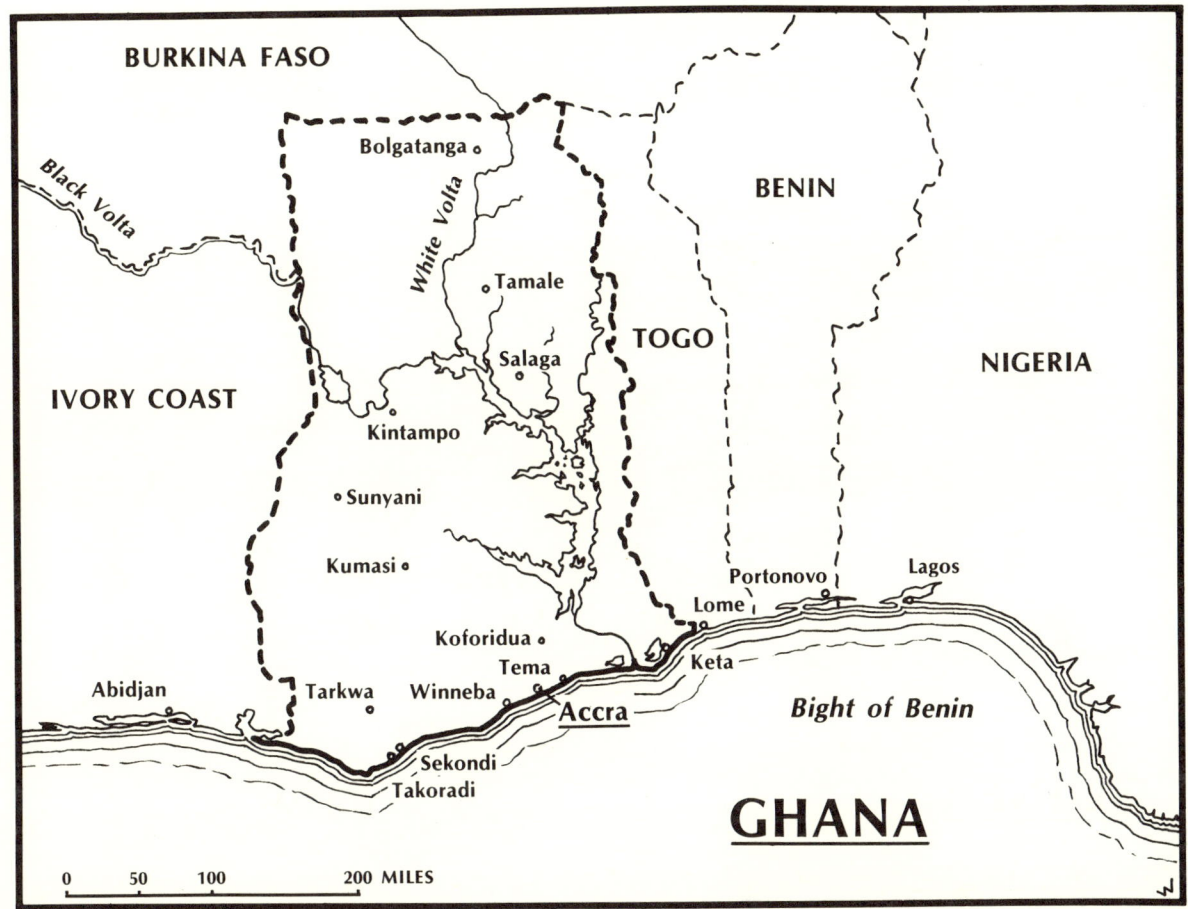

Area: 92,098 sq. miles
Population: 13,804,000 (1984)
Capital: Accra
Currency: Cedi (100 pesawas)

From its low coastal plain, the country of Ghana, formerly the British colony of the Gold Coast, rises to a belt of rain forest, which gives way to the northern savannah region.

The coast is warm and fairly dry, the forest area hot and humid, and the savannah is hot and dry. Rainfall on the coast averages about 33 inches a year. Temperatures at Accra range from 75-100 degrees F.

The Portuguese were the first Europeans to arrive in the area, setting up a trading post. The first British merchants came in 1553, followed by the Danes, Dutch, and Germans.

Britain bought out Danish interests and made the Gold Coast a colony in 1874. By the 1900s, the area had assumed its present form except for the addition of the British mandate area over the former German colony of Togoland that had been taken during World War I, and which became part of the colony following a 1956 plebiscite. The Gold Coast became independent on March 6, 1957 under the name of Ghana.

The dictatorial and corrupt regime of President Nkrumah was overthrown in 1966 and further coups in 1972, 1978, 1979, and 1981 have done little to ensure the health of Ghana's economy, which is not good. The 1980 per capita income was $420 and the 1983 literacy rate was 30%.

The country has valuable natural resources including gold, manganese, diamonds, and bauxite. There is considerable timber. Cocoa is the chief crop and the main export.

Stamps were first issued in 1875. Following independence, the country became very popular among collectors in the United States until the 1961 sale of remainders canceled-to-order with postal cancels. Its popularity vanished then and it is not widely collected today.

Philatelic Bureau: Philatelic Bureau, Department of Posts, Accra, Ghana.

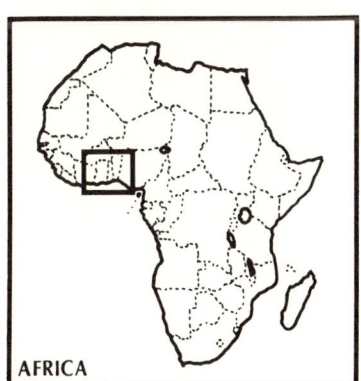

GUINEA, REPUBLIC OF

Area: 94,925 sq. miles
Population: 5,579,000 (1984)
Capital: Conakry
Currency: CFA franc (100 centimes)

Located on the "bulge" of West Africa, Guinea has four geographic zones: A coastal strip, a pastoral

area, plateau land, and a forest zone. The rivers Niger, Gambia, and Senegal all have their origins in Guinea.

There are two climatic areas. Most of the country, including the coast, is subtropical with high temperatures and humidity. Conakry's annual average temperature is 85 degrees F for a high and 74 degrees F for a low. Annual rainfall is 169 inches. The inland area has a greater variation of temperature.

France gained control over what is now Guinea in the late 19th century. It eventually became part of the federation of French West African colonies. Reforms after World War II gave more power and responsibility to Africans and Guinea was the only French colony to reject membership in the French Community, opting for complete independence on Oct. 2, 1958.

A militant and oppressive regime with close ties to the Soviet Union under Sekon Toure followed. The military took control after his death in 1984.

Rich in natural resources, including one third of the world reserve of high-grade bauxite, the country has considerable unrealized potential for development. The 1980 per capita income was $293 and the 1983 literacy rate was 48%.

Stamps were first issued by French Guinea in 1892. French West African stamps were used from 1944 to 1958. Since then, there have been numerous stamp issues.

Philatelic Bureau: Agence Philatelique, Boite Postale 814, Conakry, Republic of Guinea.

GUINEA-BISSAU, REPUBLIC OF

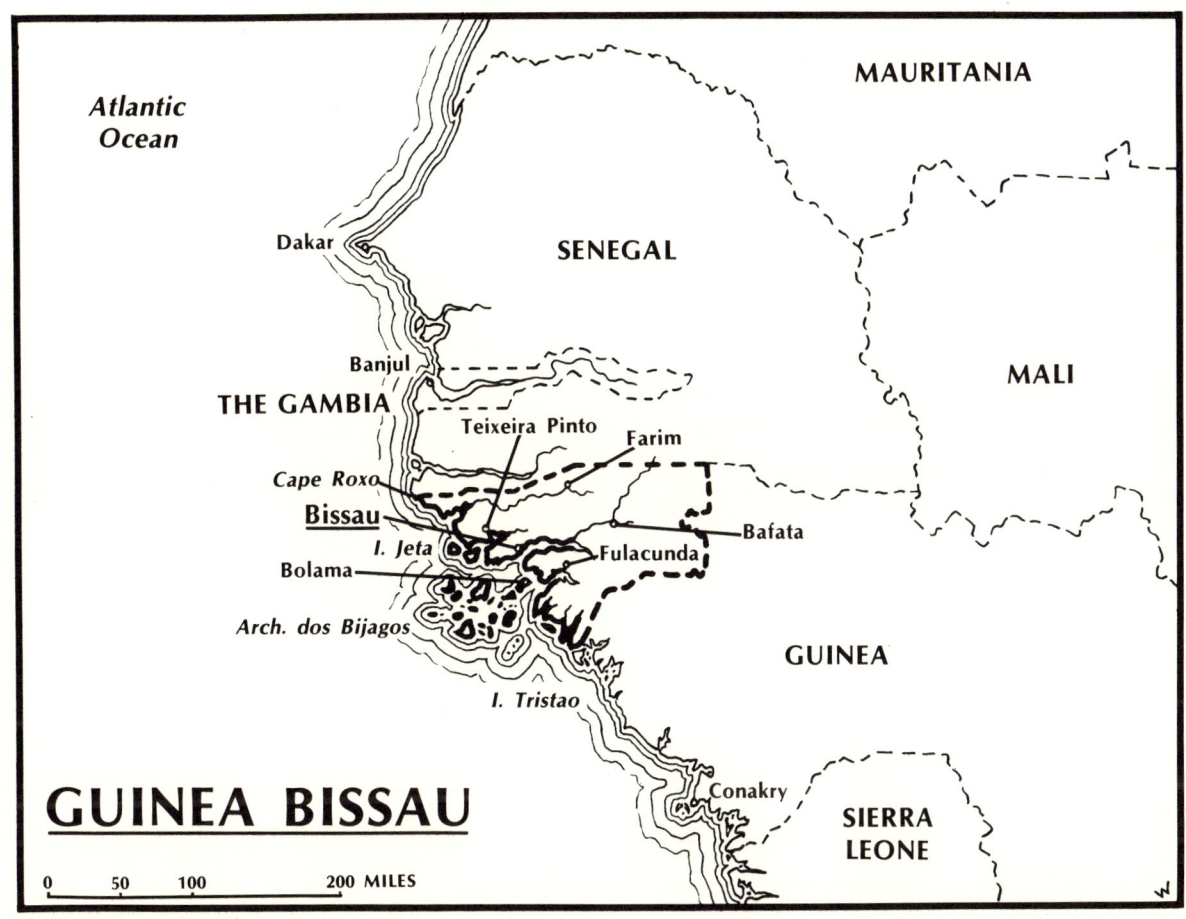

Area: 13,948 sq. miles
Population: 842,000 (1984)
Capital: Bissau
Currency: Peso (100 centavos)

Most of Guinea-Bissau is low coastal swampland, rising to savannah inland. Elevations do not exceed 1,000 feet.

The climate is tropical with an average temperature of 77 degrees F. During the dry season, which lasts from December to May, a dry dust-laden wind can blow from the Sahara Desert. Bissau's annual rainfall is 70 inches.

The Portuguese landed in the area in 1446, but few trading posts are known to have existed before 1580. The slave trade was soon the major activity. By the early 19th century, when slaves ceased to be an important commodity, Bissau became the main commercial center.

Portuguese colonial rule was established in the 1880s and the area was known as Portuguese Guinea. Bolama was the first capital city, but the administrative center was moved to Bissau in 1941.

In 1952, the colony became an overseas province of Portugal. This did not satisfy the aspirations of the inhabitants and independence was gained on Sept. 24, 1973 after a long and bloody struggle with Portugal, which tried hard to resist the desire for freedom. Portugal did not recognize the new nation until Sept. 10, 1974.

The country is poor, with an economy dependent on agriculture. Peanuts, cotton, and rice are the main crops. Mineral deposits include bauxite.

The 1979 per capita income was $170 and the 1982 literacy rate was a low 9%.

Stamps were first issued for Portuguese Guinea in 1881. Since independence, there have been numerous stamps issued. Many that were issued during the 1970s have not gained catalog recognition.

Philatelic Bureau: Direccao dos Servicos dos Correios, Telegrafos e Telefones, Bissau, Guinea-Bissau.

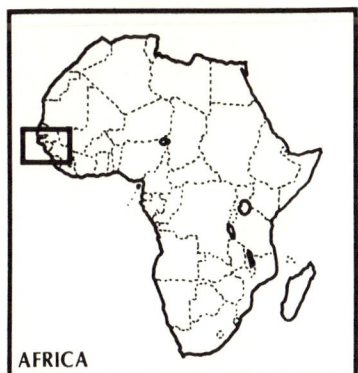

IVORY COAST, REPUBLIC OF

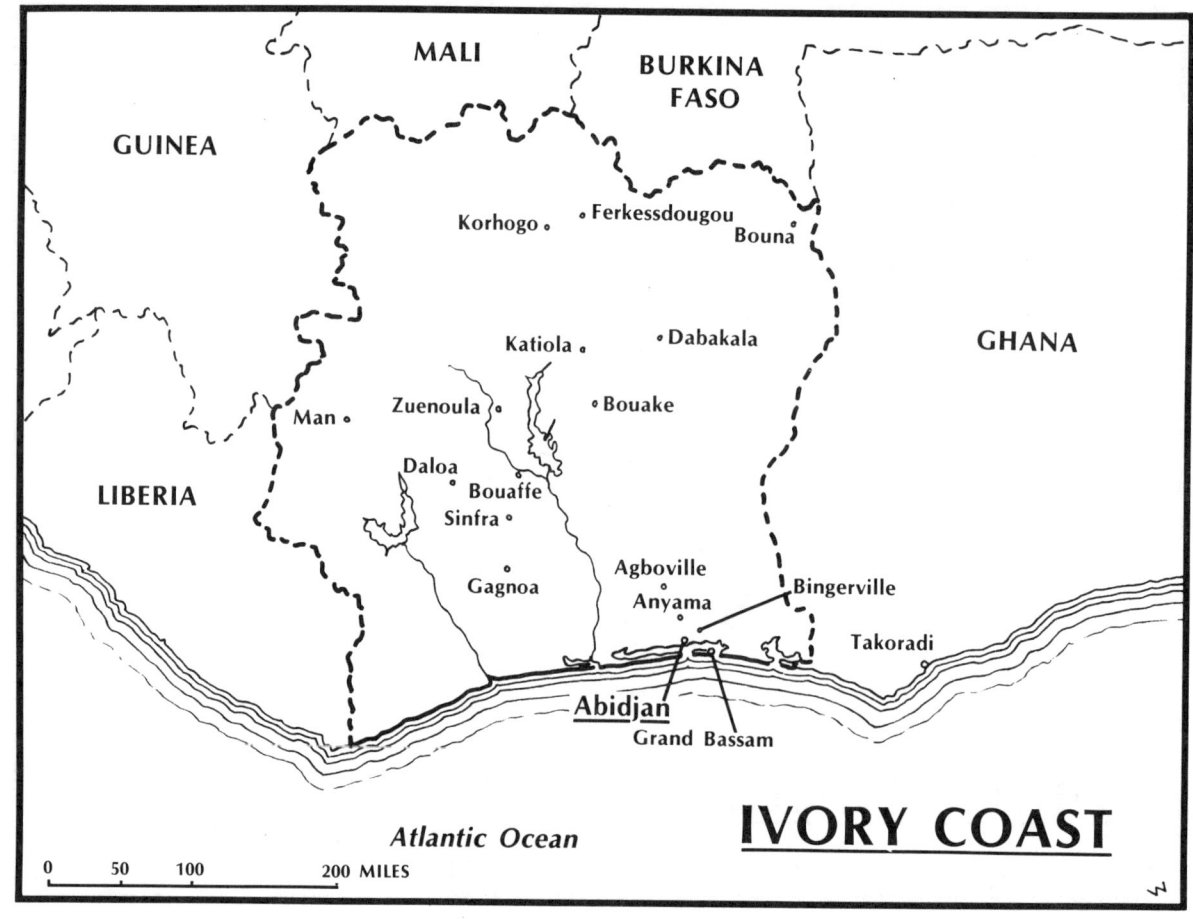

Area: 124,503 sq. miles
Population: 9,178,000 (1984)
Capital: Abidjan
Currency: CFA franc (100 centimes)

A lack of good landing places along the coast protected what is

now the Ivory Coast from exploitation by early European traders and the area was left to its own devices.

In 1700, the French set up a trading post at Abidjan and by the 1840s had obtained a protectorate over the area. They gradually extended their influence inland. Even so, it was not fully under French control until 1915, although it had been made a colony in 1893.

The area later became a unit of French West Africa until 1958, when it achieved the status of an autonomous republic in the French Community. Full independence came on Aug. 7, 1960.

Political stability and close ties with the West have permitted the mainly agricultural economy to flourish and the country is one of black Africa's more prosperous.

Coffee, cocoa (Ivory Coast is the world's third largest producer of both), and tropical hardwoods are the main exports, but other crops are being developed. The opening of the Vridi Canal that made Abidjan a deep-water port stimulated trade.

The 1984 per capita income was $1,100 and the 1983 literacy rate was 24%.

Stamps were first issued in 1892 for the colony. From 1944 to independence, the stamps of French West Africa were used. Since independence, stamp production has been relatively heavy and few popular topics have been left unpictured.

Philatelic Bureau: Office des Postes et Telecommunications, Direction des Services Postaux, Service Philatelique, Abidjan, Ivory Coast.

KENYA, REPUBLIC OF

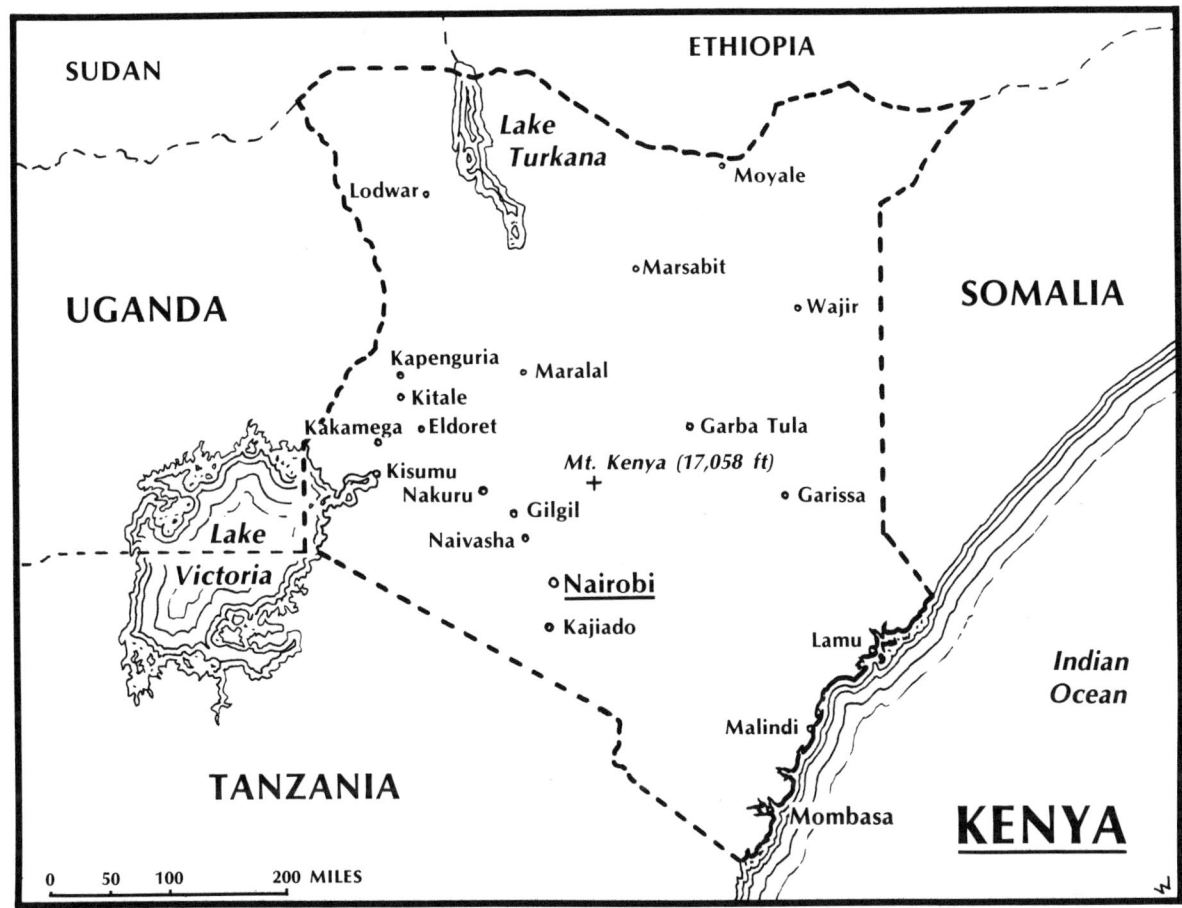

Area: 224,081 sq. miles
Population: 19,362,000 (1984)
Capital: Nairobi
Currency: Shilling (100 cents)

Although arid and semi-desert in the north, it is the moderately tropical climate, beautiful beaches along the coast, and its wealth of wildlife that has made tourism Kenya's main economic activity.

The Great Rift Valley in the west and towering, 17,000-foot Mount Kenya in the center of the country dominate its topography. Much of the country is plateau ranging from 3,000-10,000 feet in elevation and the climate there is cool. Along the coast the average temperature is 80 degrees F and at Nairobi (altitude 5,400 feet), the average maximum is 77 degrees F and the minimum 57 degrees F.

There are indications that man has roamed Kenya for more than two million years and it is a rich area for anthropological research.

Arabs traded with the area and took slaves as early as the 8th century.

The British established the East African Protectorate in 1895 and the moderate climate soon attracted many white settlers. Kenya became a colony in 1920. It was grouped with Uganda and after World War I, with Tanganyika, for administrative purposes.

Independence was achieved on Dec. 12, 1963 after a bloody uprising.

Tourism is the mainstay of the economy. Crops include coffee, tea, and cotton. There are some mineral resources. The 1981 per capita income was $196 and the 1978 literacy rate was 40%.

Stamps were first issued under the name of British East Africa in 1890 and from 1935-63 were inscribed for Kenya, Uganda, and Tanganyika. Since independence, stamp-issuing policies have not been excessive.

Philatelic Bureau: Philatelic Bureau, P.O. Box 30368, Nairobi, Kenya.

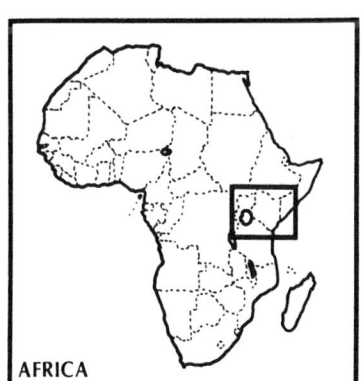

LESOTHO, KINGDOM OF

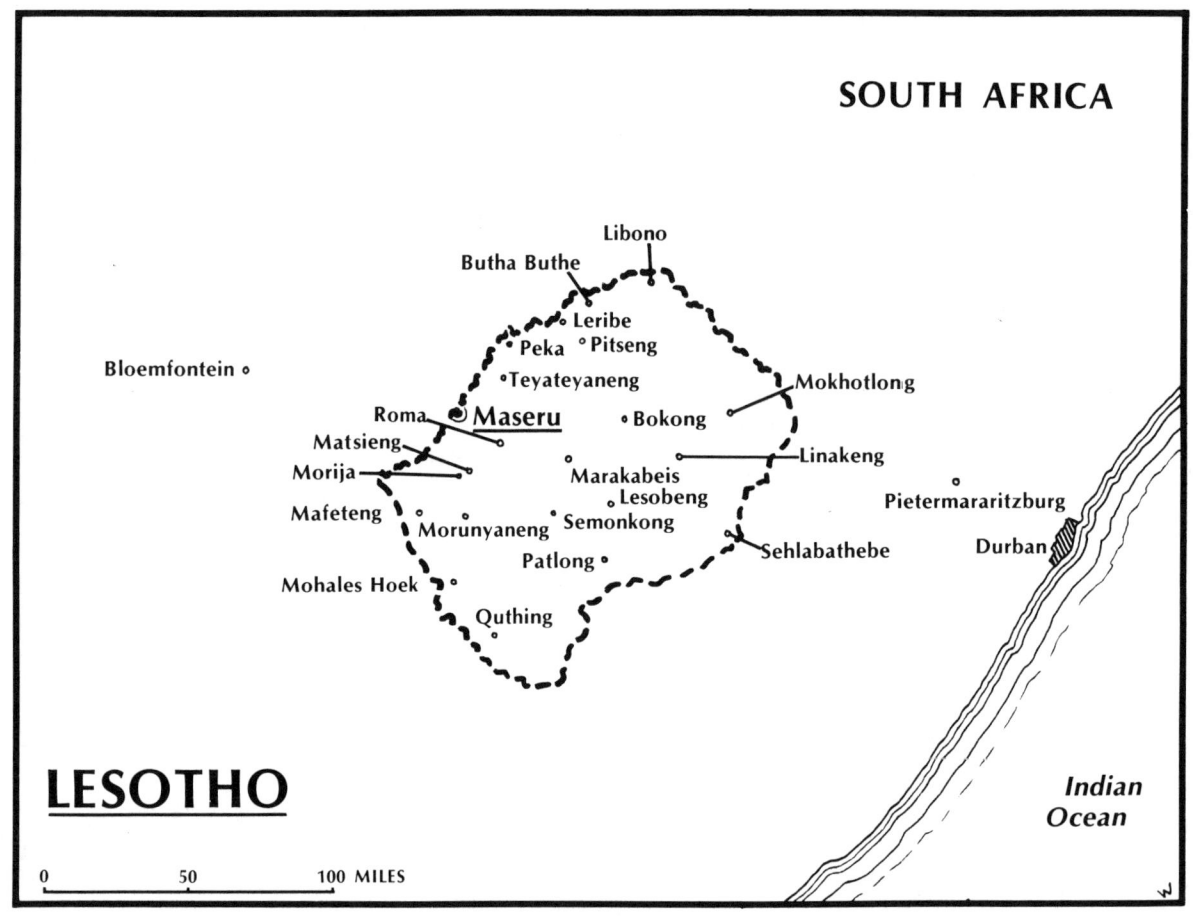

Area: 11,716 sq. miles
Population: 1,474,000 (1984)
Capital: Maseru
Currency: Maloti (100 sente)

Enclaved within the Republic of South Africa, a quarter of Lesotho is classed as lowland ranging from

5,000-6,000 feet in elevation. The rest is mountainous, rising to 11,000 feet.

Temperatures run from 90 degrees F in summer to 20 degrees F in winter. They can go as low as 0 degrees F in winter in the mountain regions.

Formerly the British colony of Basutoland, Lesotho had been taken under British protection in 1868 at the request of the inhabitants, who feared Boer incursions.

The British succeeded in preventing the incorporation of Basutoland into South Africa and gradually granted greater powers of self-government, grooming the colony for independence. This came on Oct. 4, 1966.

With a subsistence agriculture economy, Lesotho is largely dependent on South Africa and most of its income derives from its citizens working in that country. More than 50% of the male workforce earns its living in South Africa. The 1979 per capita income was $355 and the 1984 literacy rate was 65%. Together with Botswana and Swaziland, Lesotho is a member of a customs union with South Africa.

There are only about 9,000 acres of land in the country under cultivation and soil erosion is a national problem.

Economic aid is provided by Great Britain, the United States, and the World Bank. In some areas, pack animals constitute the sole means of transportation, although roads are being constructed. There is one rail line, running from Maseru to a point in South Africa on the line from Bloemfontein to Natal.

Stamps were first issued for Basutoland in 1933. Before that, the stamps of South Africa had been used. Since independence, stamp issues have increased in number, but are not excessive.

Philatelic Bureau: Philatelic Bureau, P.O. Box 413, Maseru, Lesotho.

LIBERIA, REPUBLIC OF

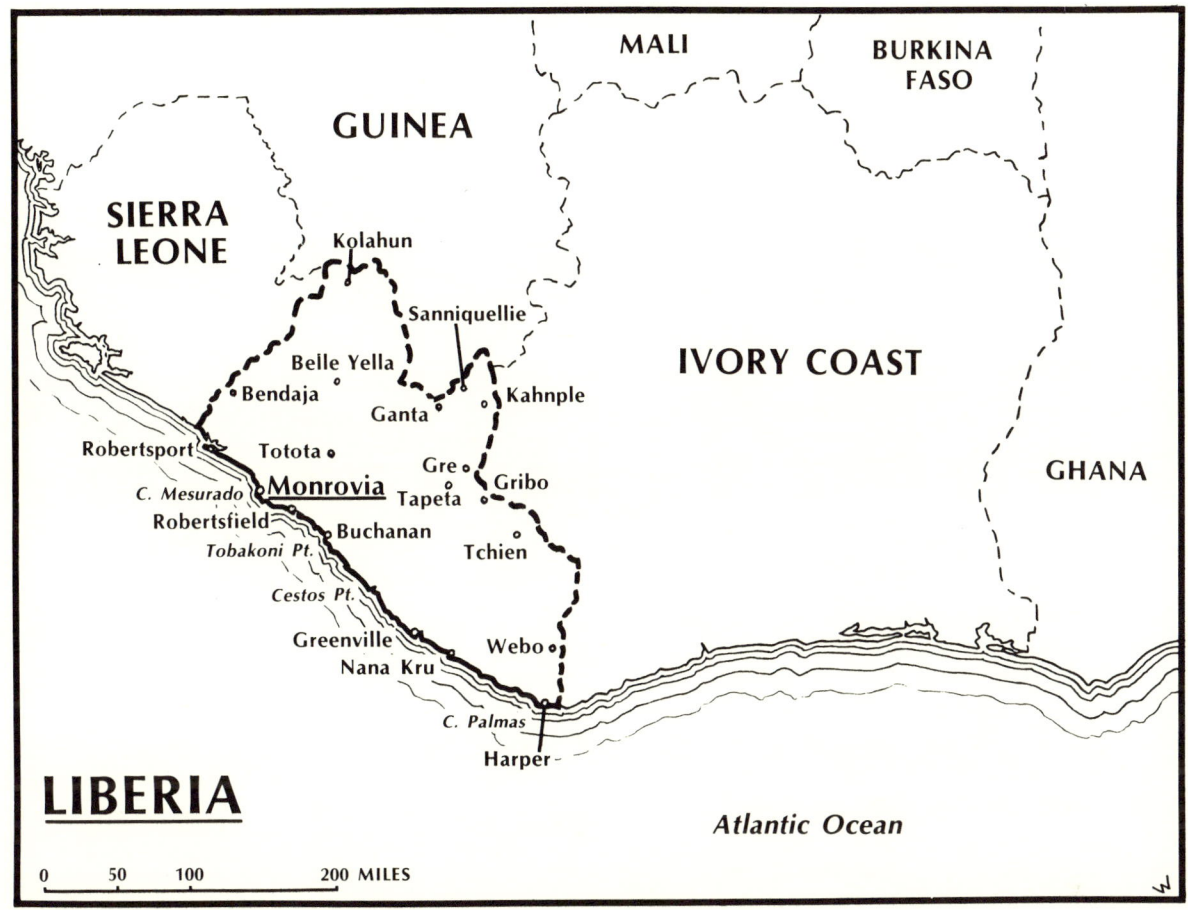

Area: 38,250 sq. miles
Population: 2,180,000 (1984)
Capital: Monrovia
Currency: Dollar (100 cents)

The interior of Liberia rises from a coastal plain in the southern portion of West Africa's "bulge" in a series of plateaus. Mountains seldom rise above 3,000 feet.

The climate is hot and humid and the country is forested. About 200 inches of rain fall annually on the coast and the average annual temperature is 80 degrees F.

The Portuguese explored the coast in the 1400s and some trade developed between the local natives and European merchants.

In 1816, the American Colonization Society received a charter from the US Congress to establish settlements for freed slaves on the coast of what is now Liberia. The first was at Monrovia in 1822. On July 26, 1847, Liberia became Africa's first republic under a constitution modeled on that of the United States.

Ironically, in a country set up as a haven for freed slaves, as late as the 1930s, the League of Nations found that there was truth in charges of brutal treatment and actual slavery being practiced on the country's plantations. The scandal led to the resignation of the president.

On April 12, 1980, a coup overthrew the government and killed the president. An army sergeant, Samuel Doe, made himself president.

The country's economy was once dominated by rubber, but its importance declined after World War II. There is some light industry and the chief crops are rice, coffee, cocoa, and sugar. Mineral resources include iron, diamonds, and gold. Timber is also important.

The 1982 per capita income was $400 and the 1984 literacy rate was 24%.

Realizing early the possible income from the sale of stamps to collectors, by the turn of the century there was a flow of pretty stamps picturing Liberian flora and fauna.

Philatelic Bureau: Liberian Philatelic Agent, Ministry of Posts and Telecommunications, Monrovia, Liberia.

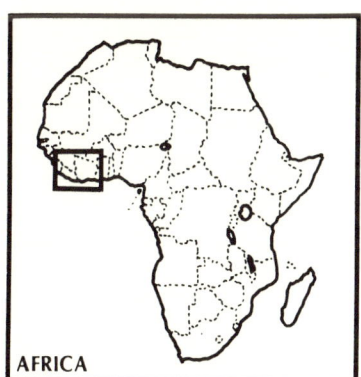

LIBYA

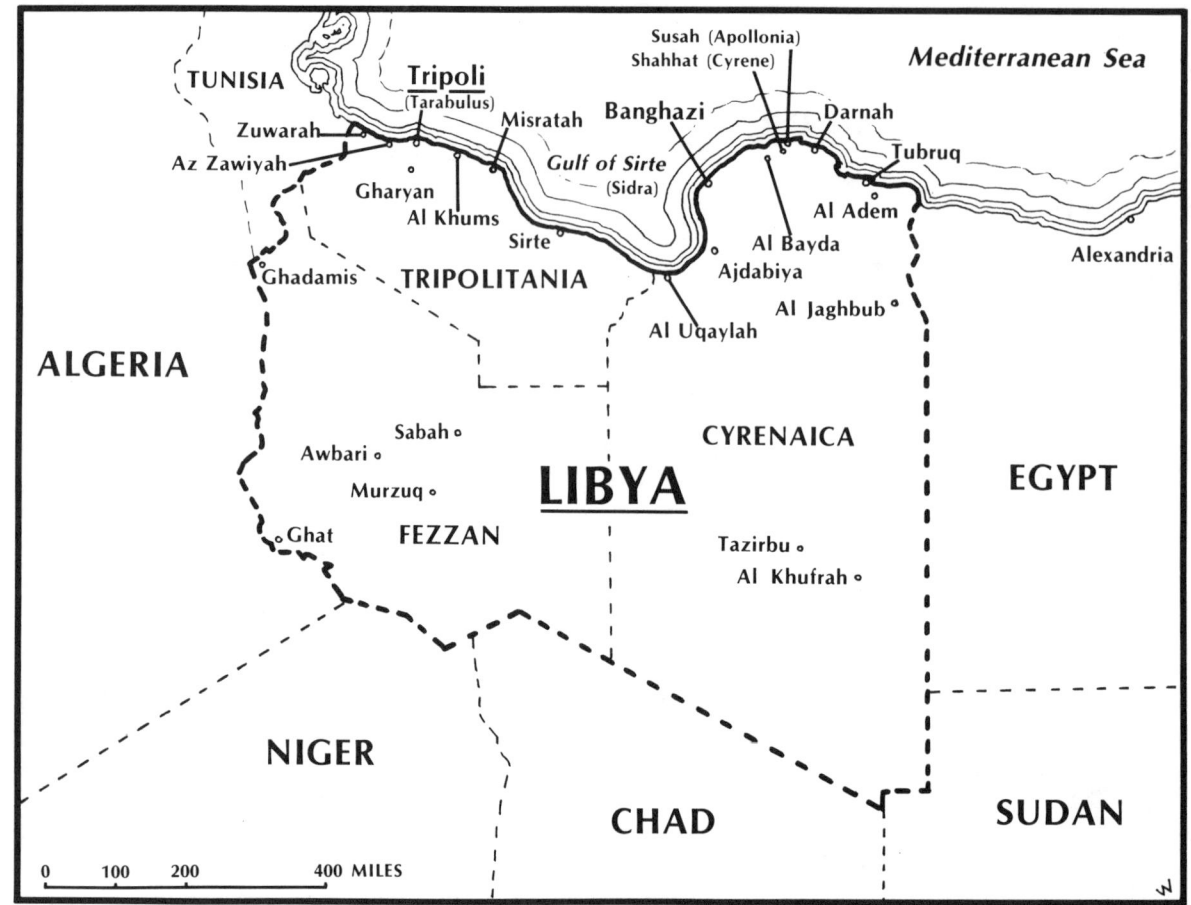

Area: 679,536 sq. miles
Population: 3,684,000 (1984)
Capital: Tripoli
Currency: Dinar (1,000 dirham)

About 90% of Libya is desert, with only a coastal strip, an area in the bulge of Cyrenaica and around several interior oases, being suitable for cultivation. The interior is hot and dry, with erratic rainfall every few years.

Along the coast, summer temperatures reach 90 degrees F and humidity can be high, although

the climate is generally pleasant except when a hot, dry, sand-laden wind blows from the south.

Until liberation from Italian occupation by Britain during World War II, Libya had a long history of foreign domination. Phoenicians, Carthaginians, Greeks, Romans, Arabs, Turks, and Italians, all had occupied the area. Today, little remains of their presence, except for the magnificent Greek and Roman ruins along the coast, such as those at Cyrene.

After World War II, Britain established King Idris on the throne and with the discovery of large oil reserves, the future seemed bright. The revolution of 1969 and the taking of power by Col. Khadafy have converted the country to a center of violence and a haven for terrorists. Libya's acts of war and terrorism against its neighbors have made it a source of continuing unrest in the area.

The economy, once rich, has suffered from government policy and the slump in oil prices. Industry includes carpet making, textiles, and shoes. Crops are dates, olives, citrus, grapes, and tobacco. The 1981 literacy rate was 40%.

Stamps were first issued in 1912 under the Italian administration. Independent issues began in 1951. In recent years, stamp issues have been very extensive. Subjects are mostly of a political and propaganda nature. Following the Jan. 7, 1986 imposition of economic sanctions on Libya by the United States, the importation of Libyan stamps into the United States was prohibited. At the time of publication, this ban was still in effect.

Philatelic Bureau: Service Philatelique, Direction General des PTT, Tripoli, Libya.

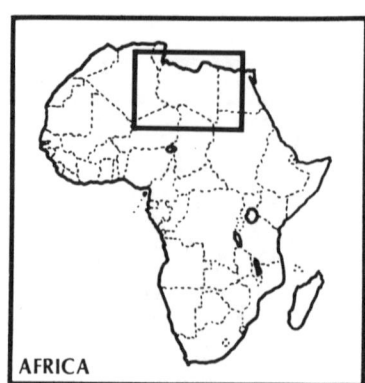

MADAGASCAR, DEMOCRATIC REPUBLIC OF

Area: 228,880 sq. miles
Population: 9,645,000 (1984)
Capital: Antananarivo
Currency: Franc (100 centimes)

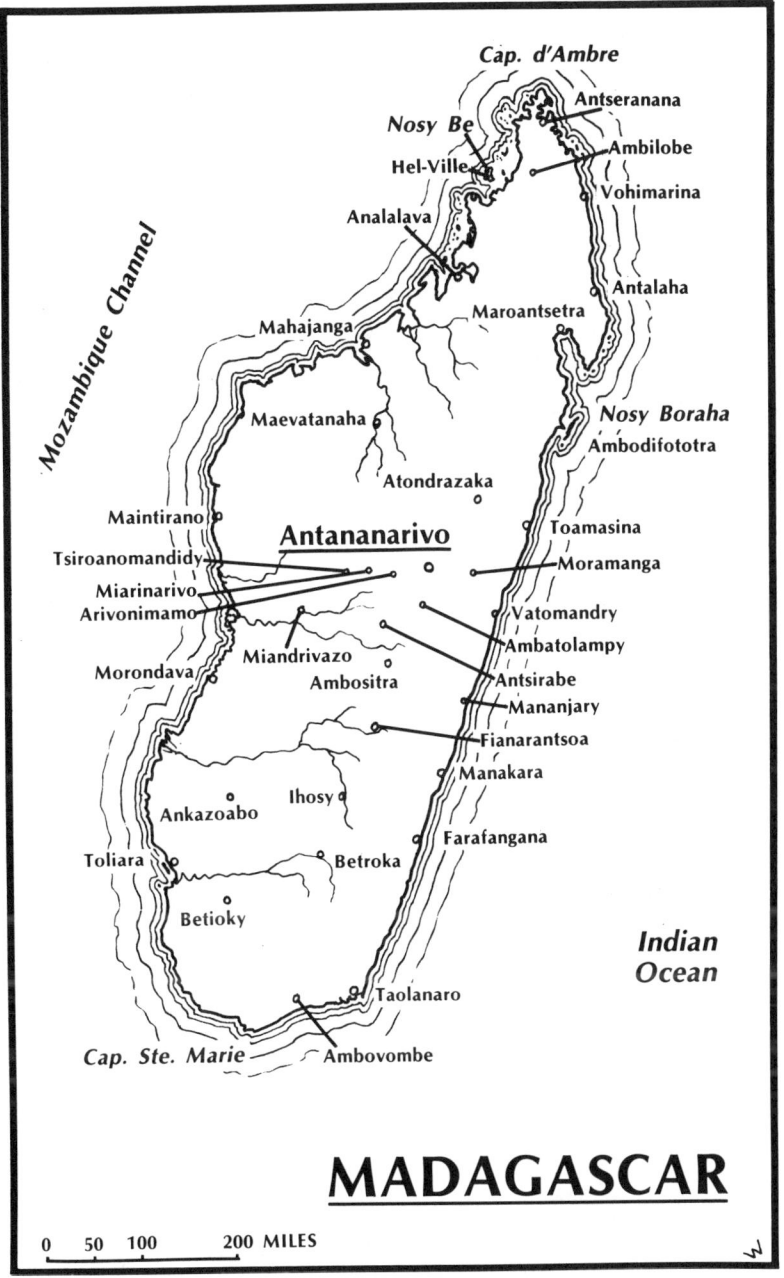

Madagascar, the world's fourth-largest island, comprises a hot and humid coastal belt and an interior plateau with an average elevation of 2,500-6,500 feet. The plateau's climate is temperate with distinct warm and cool seasons. Rainfall is heaviest along the east coast, which is exposed to the trade winds of the Indian Ocean.

The original inhabitants came from the areas of Malaysia and Indonesia about 2,000 years ago. Although the Portuguese arrived in the 1500s, the Arabs had trading posts there from the seventh century.

The French imposed a protectorate over the island in 1885 and made it a colony in 1896. After the fall of France in World War II, Britain occupied it to protect it from Japanese aggression, handing it over to the Free French in 1943.

A 1947 uprising by the population, which had long resented the French presence, was put down after bitter fighting. Independence within the French Community was granted on Oct. 14, 1958. Full independence was achieved on June 26, 1960. In recent years, the government has become repressive and moved closer to the communist bloc.

Although there are some mineral resources, the economy is mainly agricultural and the chief crops are

coffee, vanilla, spices, sugar, tobacco, and peanuts.

The 1982 per capita income was $279 and the 1984 literacy rate was 53%.

Stamps were first issued for Madagascar in 1889. For a brief period in the 1880s there was a British consular mail service that also had its own stamps.

Dependencies of Madagascar that had their own stamps for various periods under French rule include Diego Suarez, Nossi-Be, St. Marie de Madagascar, and the Comoro Islands.

Since independence stamp-issuing policies have been similar to those of former French African colonies, with a considerable number of stamps being issued. Stamps are inscribed "Reboblika Demokratika Malagasy."

Philatelic Bureau: Service Philatelique, Direction General des PTT, Antananarivo, Madagascar.

MALAWI, REPUBLIC OF

Area: 45,747 sq. miles
Population: 6,829,000 (1984)
Capital: Lilongwe
Currency: Kwacha (100 tambala)

Malawi is located along part of Africa's Great Rift Valley, which cuts through Lake Nyasa (Lake Malawi).

Most of the country is plateau with elevations rising to 8,500 feet in the north and 3,500 feet in the south. The southern tip of the country is only about 200-300 feet above sea level.

The climate is subtropical. It is hot and humid along the lake and in the extreme south, but can drop as low as 40-50 degrees F at night on the plateau during the cool months.

Man's presence in the area has been established at least one million years ago, but David Livingstone's arrival in 1859 was the first important contact with Europeans. In 1878, a Scottish company, the African Lakes Co., was formed to supply the growing number of missions, and European settlements soon followed.

In 1891, Britain established an administration over the area and in 1907 formed the Nyasaland Protectorate. It joined with Northern and Southern Rhodesia in 1953 as the Federation of Rhodesia and Nyasaland, which lasted for 10 years before being disbanded in 1963. Malawi was formed as an independent nation from the Nyasaland Protectorate on July 6, 1964.

Textiles and farm implements are the main industries and tea, tobacco, sugar, and coffee, the chief crops. The 1979 per capita income was $220 and the 1983 literacy rate was 25%.

The first stamps used in the area were those of British Central Africa. In 1908 stamps inscribed "Nyasaland Protectorate" were released. Since independence, stamp issues have increased, but by African standards, have not been excessive.

Philatelic Bureau: Post Office Philatelic Bureau, P.O. Box 1000, Blantyre, Malawi.

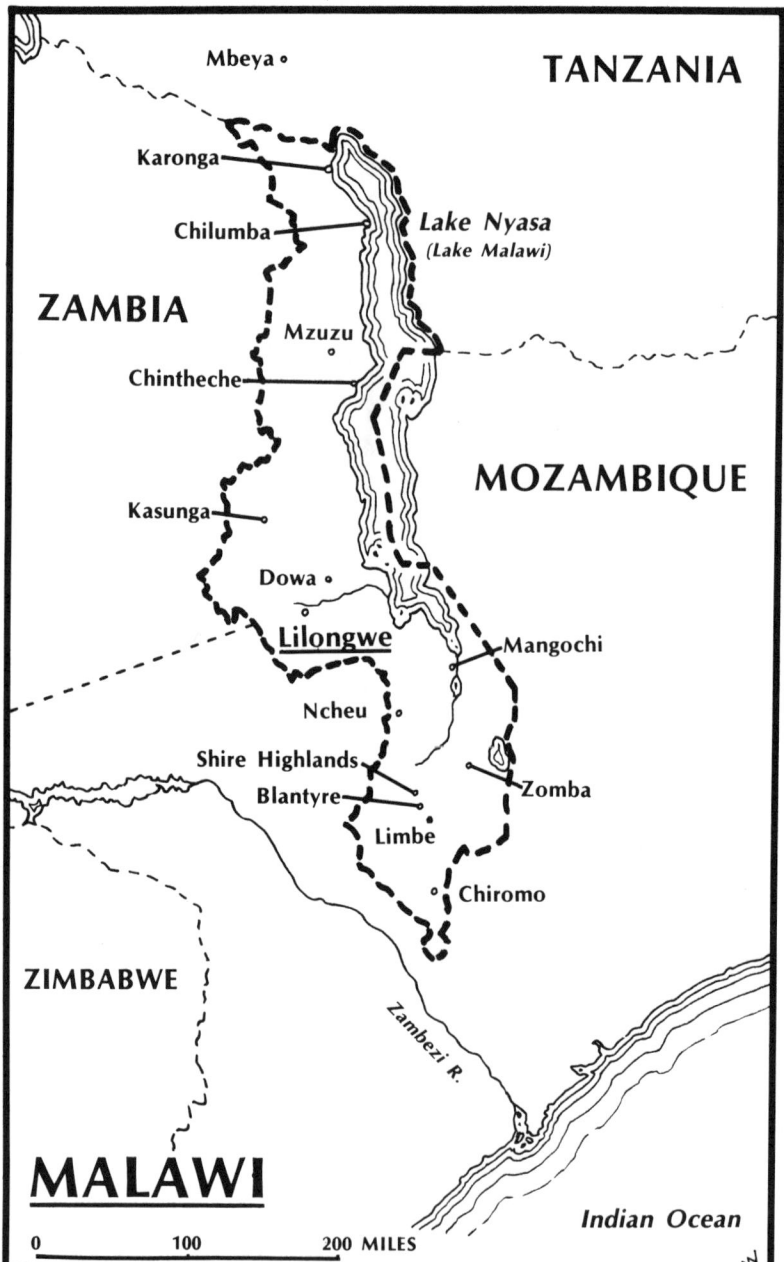

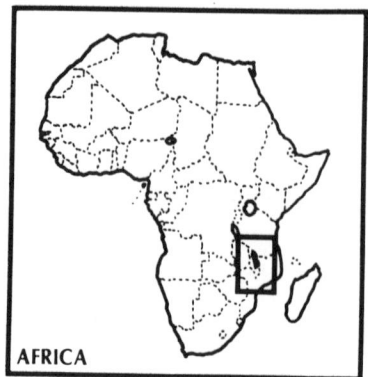

MALI, REPUBLIC OF

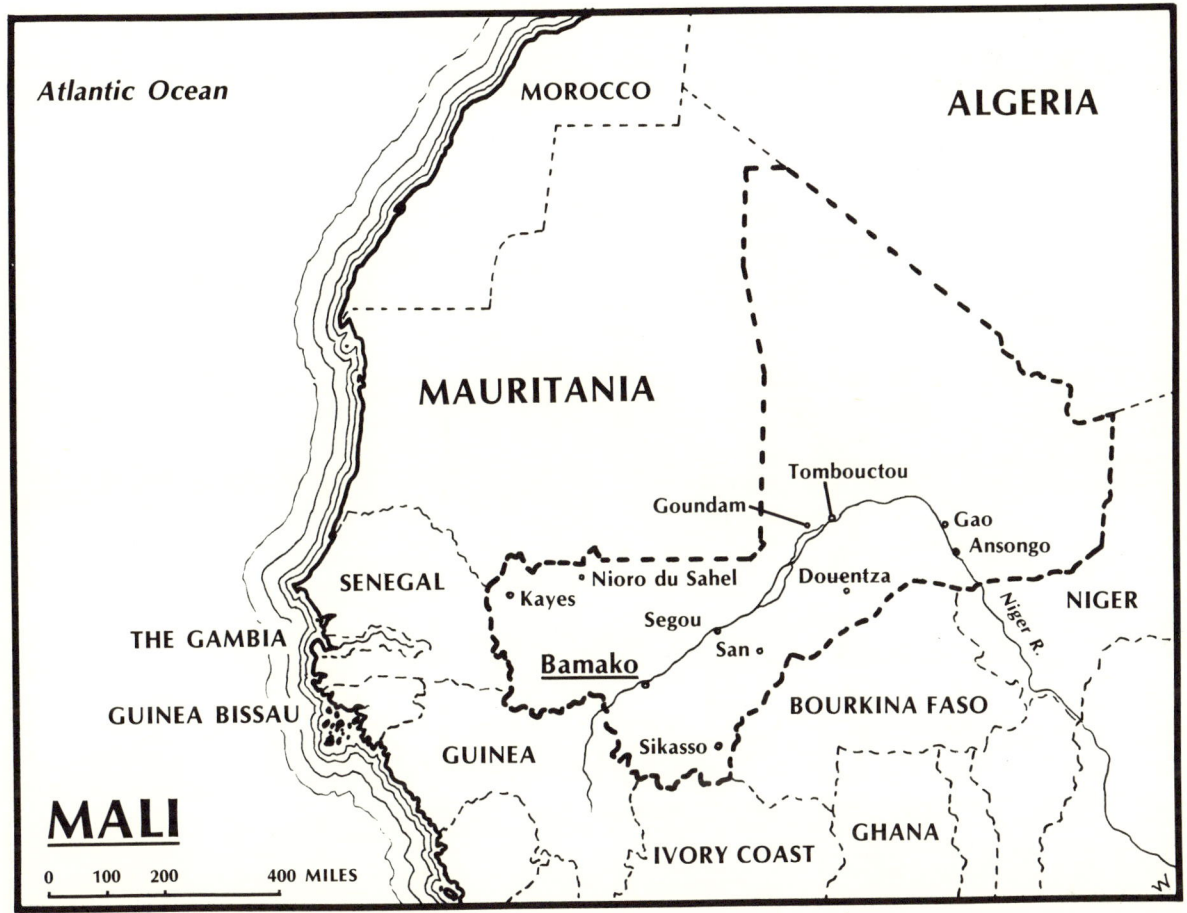

Area: 478,841 sq. miles
Population: 7,562,000 (1984)
Capital: Bamako
Currency: Franc (100 centimes)

The landlocked West African country of Mali is mostly dry savannah with the northern portion being in the Sahara Desert.

The northern climate is hot and almost completely rainless, while the south has a short season when rain may fall from June to September.

Timbuktu (Tombouctou), one of Africa's more romantic and mysterious cities, is located in Mali. The ancient city is the southern terminus of the trans-Saharan caravan route and was at the height of its prosperity during the 16th century when it is said to have had a population of one million. Its most recent recorded population figure is about 107,000.

It was across the Sahara that Islam came to the area and today the country is 90% Moslem.

French influence began to make itself felt in the area about 1880. It became the colony of French Sudan and then a unit in French West Africa.

In 1958, it achieved independence as the Sudanese Republic and joined with Senegal to form the Federation of Mali. The federation broke up within a year and the Republic of Mali was created on Sept. 22, 1960.

In recent years, drought and famine have stricken the country and the economy has been shattered. In the 1973-74 drought alone, some 100,000 people are said to have died of starvation. The 1981 per capita income was $140 and the 1984 literacy rate was a low 10%.

Stamps were first issued in 1894, but in 1899 the colony was divided among neighboring French colonies. Reformed after World War I, stamps were again issued in 1921. In 1944, stamps of French West Africa went into use until independence in 1958.

Since independence, stamp issues have been extensive with few popular topics unrepresented.

Philatelic Bureau: Service Philatelique, Direction General des PTT, Bamako, Mali.

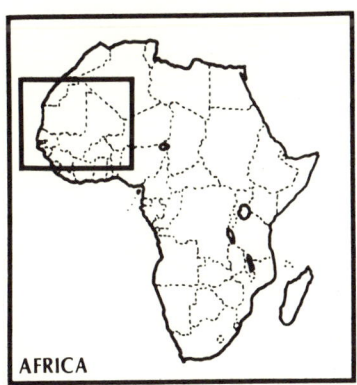

MAURITANIA, ISLAMIC REPUBLIC OF

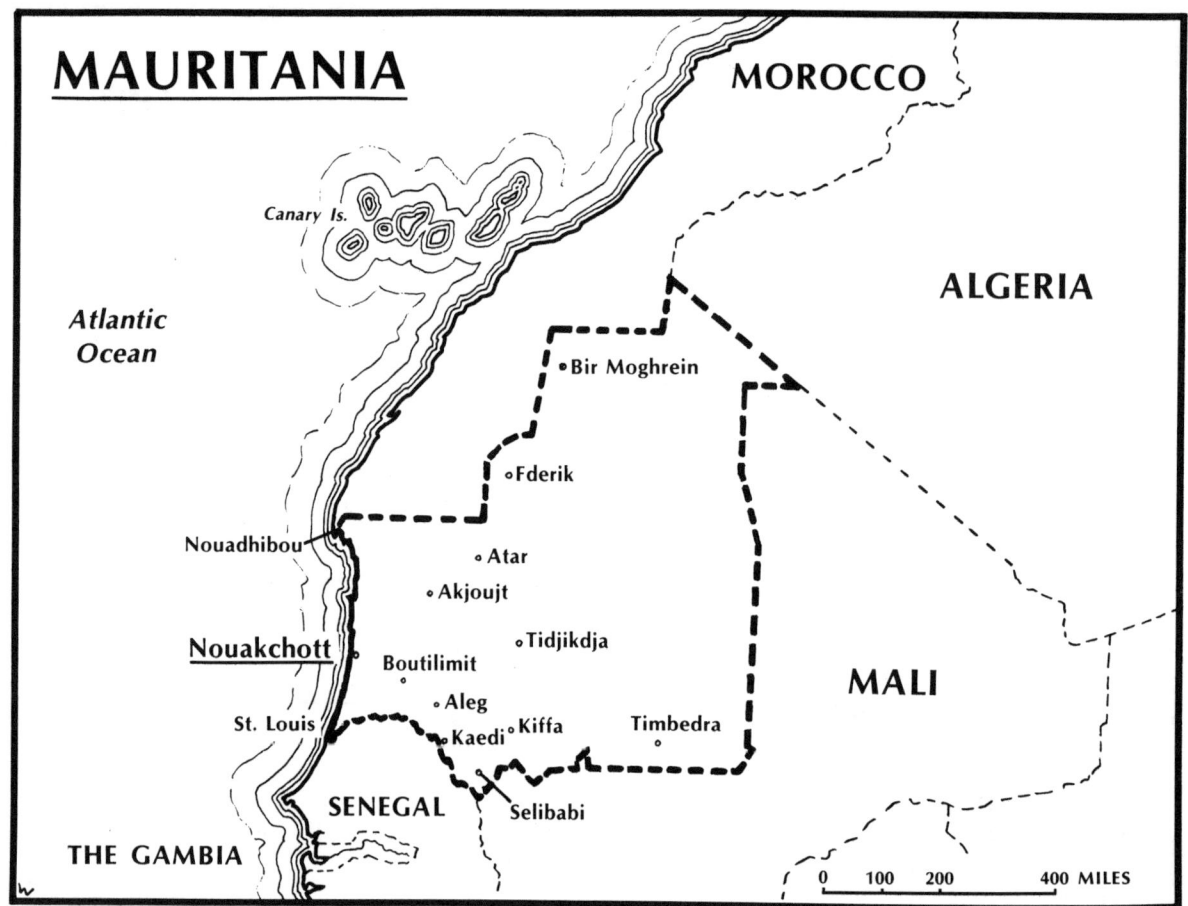

Area: 419,229 sq. miles
Population: 1,632,000 (1984)
Capital: Nouakchott
Currency: Ouguiya

A dry, arid country, Mauritania has been wracked by famine in recent years. Except for a southern strip along the Senegal River there is little agriculture, most of the land being dry, rocky plateau. A large portion is in the Sahara Desert.

The climate is hot and dry, except for the southern strip, which is more humid, and the small rainfall occurs mostly in this area. Temperatures usually exceed 100 degrees F, but nights are cool. In the south, there is less variation between day and night temperatures.

Early inhabitants were Berbers from the north who came during the third and fourth centuries seeking pasture for their herds in a land less arid than it is today. Trade routes were established and Islam spread into the area.

The French arrived and began to take over in the late 19th century, but Mauritania did not become a colony until 1920. It was not fully under French control until the 1930s and even then government was largely through tribal chiefs. It became part of French West Africa until 1946, when it was made an overseas department of France.

Autonomy in the French Community was achieved in 1958 and on Nov. 28, 1960 full independence came. The capital city was transferred to Nouakchott from St. Louis, which is now located in Senegal.

In 1980, Mauritania was forced to relinquish to Morocco its claim to the southern part of the former Spanish Sahara.

Dates and grain are the chief crops and there are some mineral resources. The 1984 per capita income was $466 and the 1985 literacy rate was 17%.

Stamps were first issued in 1906. They were used until replaced by those of French West Africa. Since independence there has been a large number of stamp issues. Many picture topics popular among collectors. Some have little or no connection with Mauritania.

Philatelic Bureau: Service Philatelique, Direction General des PTT, P.O. Box 99, Nouakchott, Mauritania.

MAURITIUS

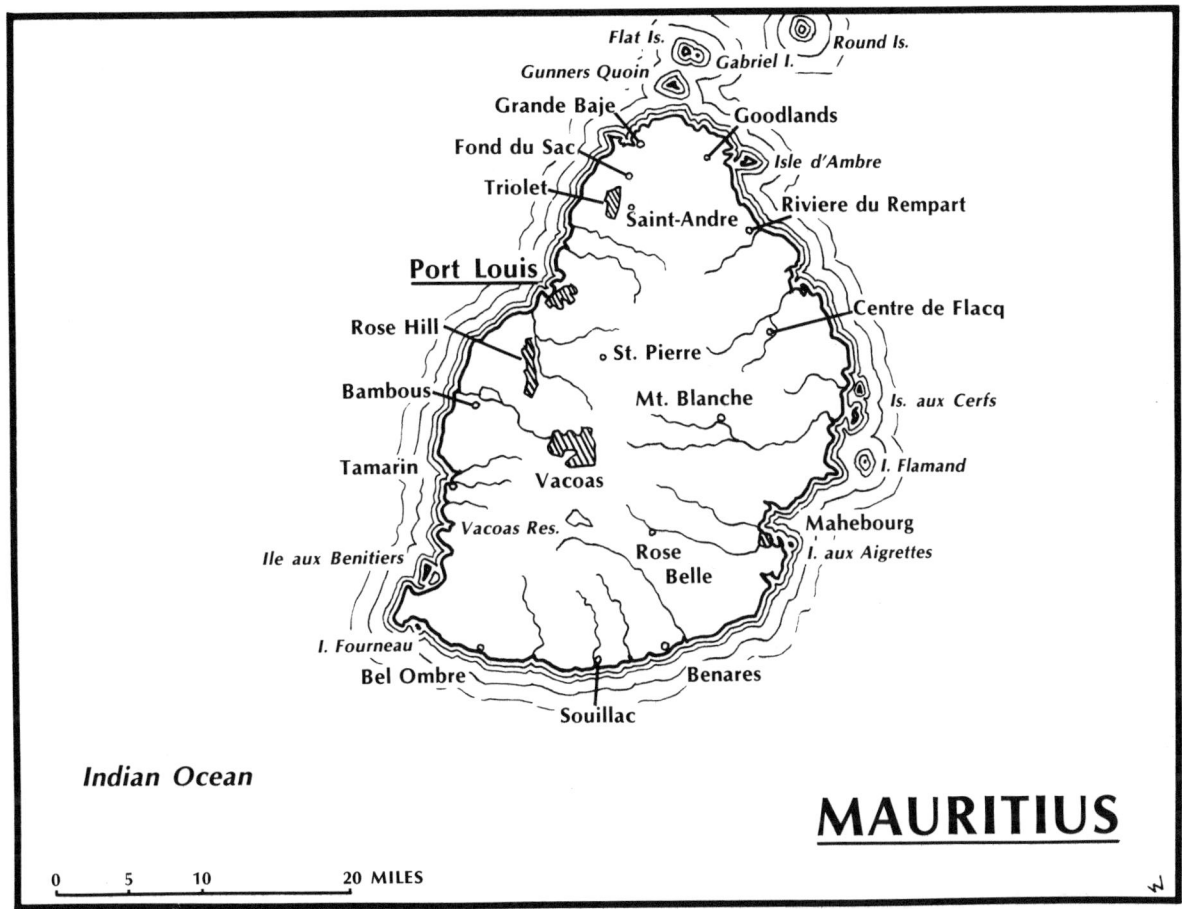

Area: 787 sq. miles
Population: 1,018,000 (1984)
Capital: Port Louis
Currency: Rupee (100 cents)

The volcanic island of Mauritius is located about 500 miles east of Madagascar in the Indian Ocean.

There is a central plateau enclosed by a rim of mountains. Although humid, the climate is not unduly hot. The average annual high temperature is 75 degrees F on the coast and 67 degrees F inland. Annual rainfall can be as high as 200 inches.

First visited by the Portuguese in the 16th century, the Dutch established a settlement in 1638 and named the island for Prince Maurice of Nassau. It was abandoned in 1710.

The French arrived in 1715, renaming the island Ile de France. In 1810 during the Napoleonic wars, the British captured it and retained it under the Treaty of Paris. They permitted the inhabitants to retain their French institutions and language.

After the abolition of slavery in 1833, an influx of indentured labor from India for the sugar industry changed the island's cultural makeup. With self-government and later independence, Indians came to dominate politics. Independence was granted on March 12, 1968.

Sugar and tea are the chief crops, although low sugar prices in recent years have had an adverse effect on the economy. Tourism is becoming an important source of income. The 1981 per capita income was $1,052 and the 1982 literacy rate was 61%.

Mauritius looms large in philatelic lore for its famous 1d and 2d "POST OFFICE" stamps of 1847. These were the first stamps issued in a British colony.

The story is that Joseph Barnard, a Port Louis jeweler who engraved the designs, made a mistake by inscribing them "POST OFFICE" instead of "POST PAID."

However, it seems much more likely that he merely copied the inscription already in use on the handstamp postmarkers of the Mauritius Post Office. Even so, the stamps are among philately's crown jewels.

Philatelic Bureau: Department of Posts and Telegraphs, GPO, Port Louis, Mauritius.

MOROCCO, KINGDOM OF

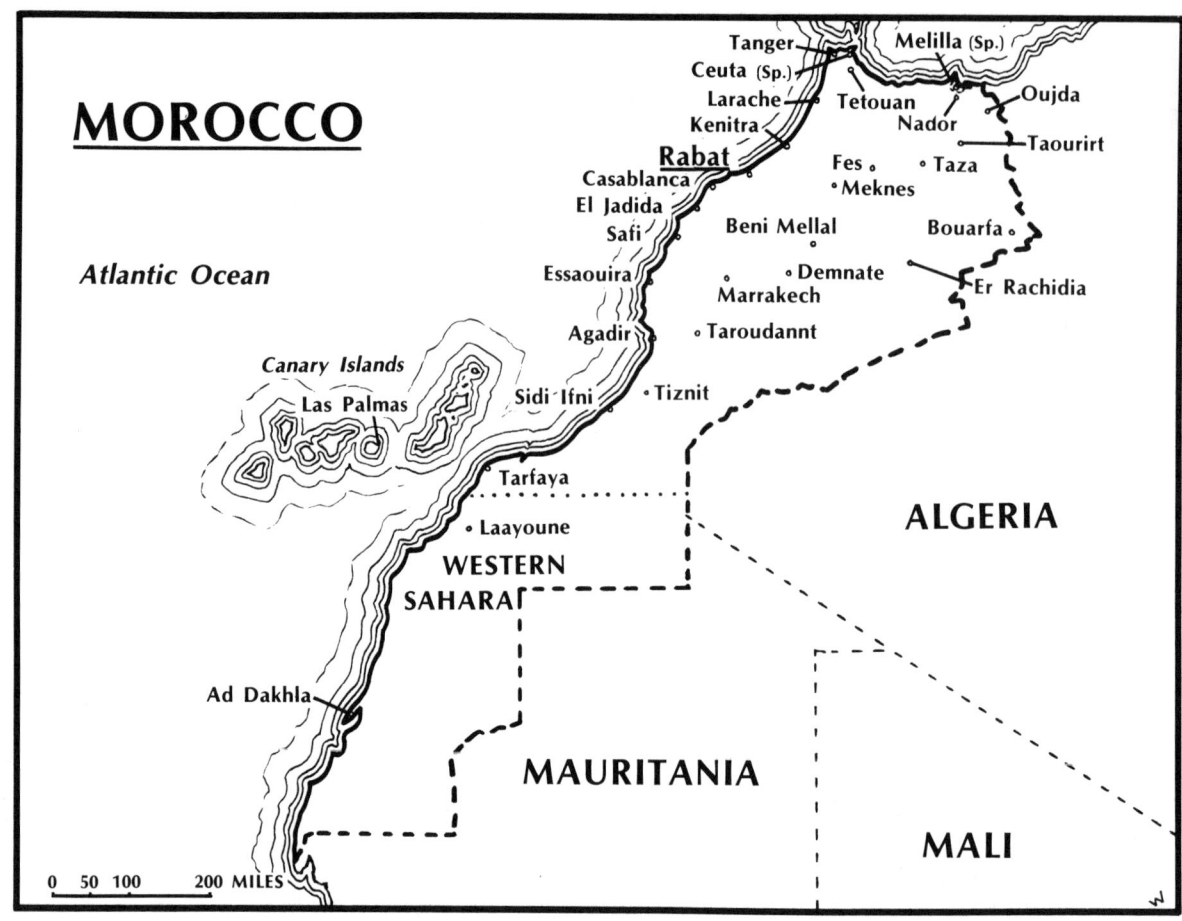

Area: 171,117 sq. miles
Population: 23,565,000 (1984)
Capital: Rabat
Currency: Dirham (100 centimes)

Morocco comprises the former French and Spanish protectorates, Spanish Sahara, plus the enclaves of Ifni and the Tangier International Zone. Spanish enclaves still exist at Ceuta and Melilla.

The country has a coastal plain where most of the population lives, separated by mountains from the interior plateau that merges into the Sahara Desert. The northern coastal plain is the country's major agricultural area.

The climate is semitropical. Temperatures are not high on the coast, but there is considerable humidity. Inland of the mountains there is a great variation between day and night temperatures. The Mediterranean coast is mild and sunny.

Once the center of a large Berber empire in North Africa, Morocco came under French and Spanish control in the early 20th century. Britain permitted French influence to grow in exchange for a free hand in Egypt.

Tribal uprisings were common during the French protectorate, which took in most of Morocco, except for the small Spanish area in the north.

Morocco became independent on March 2, 1956. On April 14, 1976, most of Spanish Sahara was annexed and the rest was obtained from Mauritania shortly thereafter. The United Nations has not recognized the annexation and refers to the area as Western Sahara.

Morocco's economy is based on agriculture with some light industry — carpets, clothing, leather goods, etc. Tourism is of increasing importance. Crops include dates, fruit, grain, and grapes. The 1981 per capita income was $800 and the 1978 literacy rate was 24%.

Stamps have been issued for the various colonial areas and many British stamps were overprinted and surcharged for use at the British post offices in various cities.

Since independence stamps have followed a pattern typical of Moslem countries, with designs largely symbolic in character.

Philatelic Bureau: Ministere des PTT, Division Postale, Rabat, Morocco.

MOZAMBIQUE, PEOPLE'S REPUBLIC OF

Area: 308,650 sq. miles
Population: 13,413,000 (1984)
Capital: Maputo
Currency: Metical

Comprising an area of coastal lowland, with two interior plateau zones, Mozambique has a tropical climate, except in the high plateau around 3,000 feet. Rainfall is uncertain and, in 1984, severe drought was responsible for many deaths from starvation.

The first European visitor to what is now Mozambique was Vasco da Gama in 1468. He found that there were already Arab trading posts operating.

By the 1500s, the area was under Portuguese control and was made a colony. Independence was granted on June 25, 1975, after a bloody 10-year war against colonial domination.

Since then, the government has pursued a Marxist course, with many thousands of skilled people leaving. The country is economically dependent on South Africa.

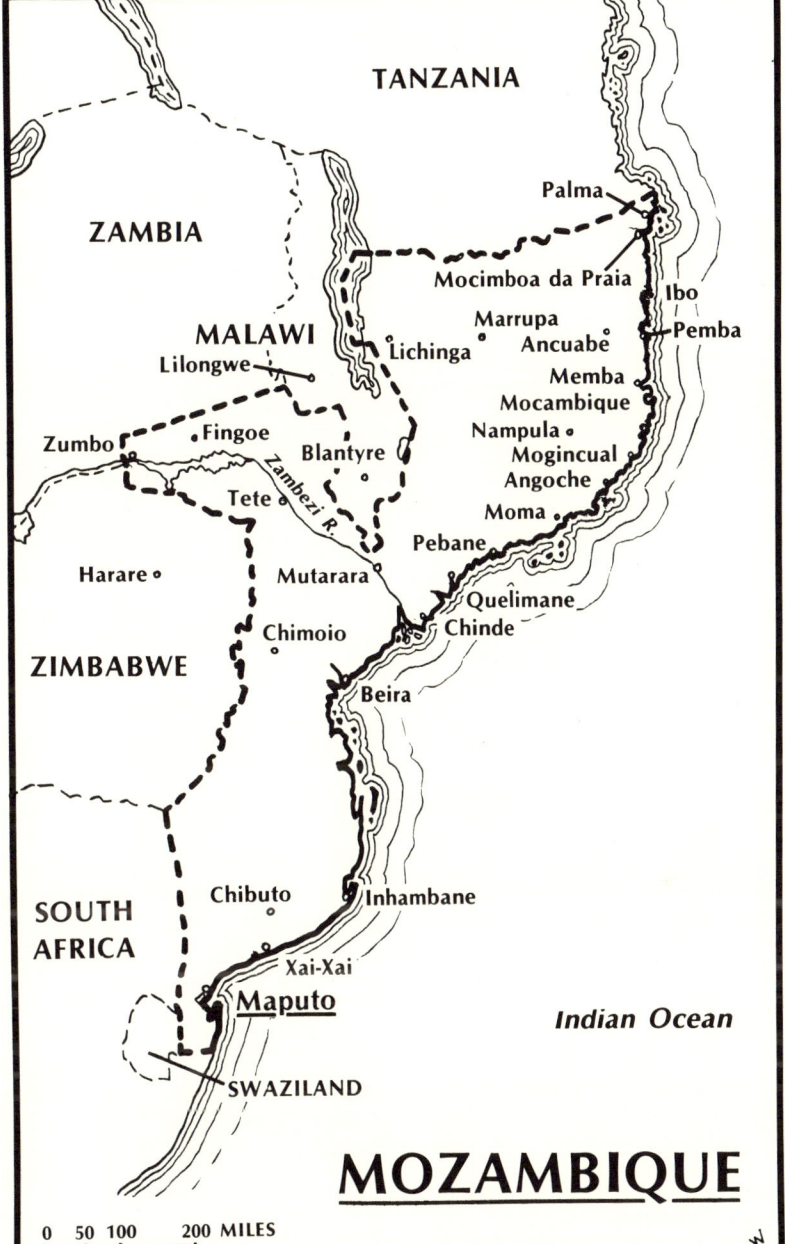

The economy is shaky, with subsistence agriculture being the chief occupation of the population.

There are mineral resources, including coal and bauxite, but the government's policies are discouraging the foreign investment necessary to develop them.

Stamps were first issued in 1877 and followed the usual Portuguese colonial style. More popular among past generations of collectors were the colorful issues of the Mozambique Co. and the Nyassa Co., two private companies that were granted rights over large areas of the colony.

They ran them almost like private countries and seemed well aware of the value of philatelic sales of their stamps.

Since independence, stamp issues have been plentiful but not excessive by African standards.

Philatelic Bureau: Philatelic Services, Box 4444, Maputo 1, Mozambique.

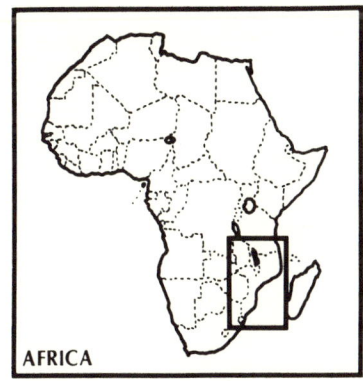

NAMIBIA (SOUTH-WEST AFRICA)

Area: 318,827 sq. miles
Population: 1,038,000 (1982)
Capital: Windhoek
Currency: Rand (100 cents)

Most of Namibia is high plateau with an average elevation of 3,500 feet. There is a strip of coastal desert, while an area of the eastern portion is part of the Kalahari Desert.

The climate is hot and dry with an average annual rainfall of 22 inches in the north, six inches in the south, and two inches on the coast. At Windhoek, the temperature averages 86 degrees F for a high in summer and 69 degrees F in the cool months.

The first Europeans to visit the area were the Portuguese in the 15th century. Exploration by British and Dutch traders and missionaries took place during the 19th century. In 1878, the British annexed Walvis Bay and a surrounding 484-square-mile area to Cape Province. This has since been made part of the Republic of South Africa.

In 1883, a German merchant claimed the coastal region for Germany and until World War I, the area was a German colony. Following the war, the League of Nations gave South Africa a mandate over the area. When the United Nations tried to convert it to a trust territory after World War II, South Africa refused to recognize UN authority and continues to occupy what is now the international territory of Namibia.

Opposition by the inhabitants to South African rule has been severe-

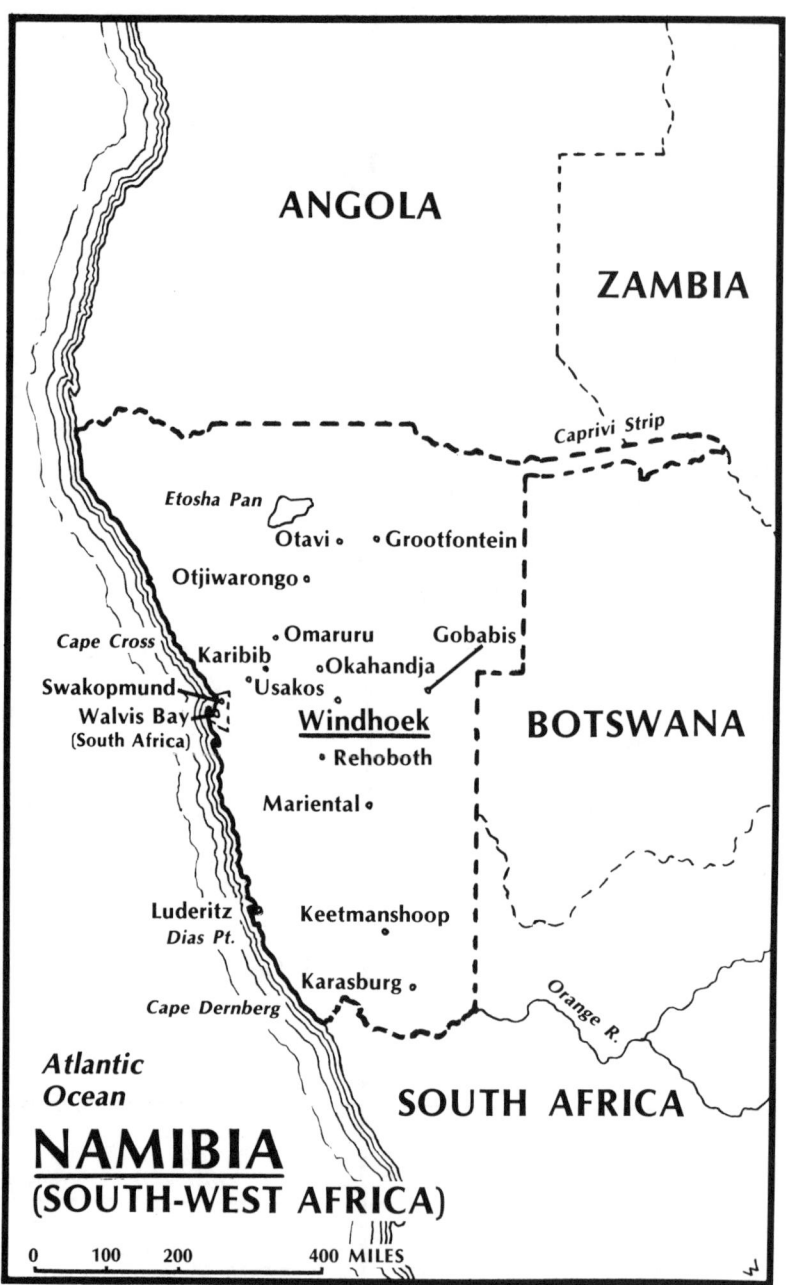

ly put down, with punishment reported to include public floggings.

Namibia is rich in mineral resources and one of the world's largest producers of diamonds. Copper, lead, zinc, tin, silver, and uranium are among the other more important minerals found there.

Most of the population is engaged in livestock raising and subsistence agriculture, the latter taking place in the northern areas.

Stamps were first issued under German rule in 1897. The first issues of South-West Africa appeared on Jan. 2, 1923 and were overprints on stamps of South Africa. Today, stamps are issued by South African authorities inscribed "SWA."

Philatelic Bureau: Philatelic Services and INTERSAPA, GPO, Pretoria, South Africa.

NIGER, REPUBLIC OF

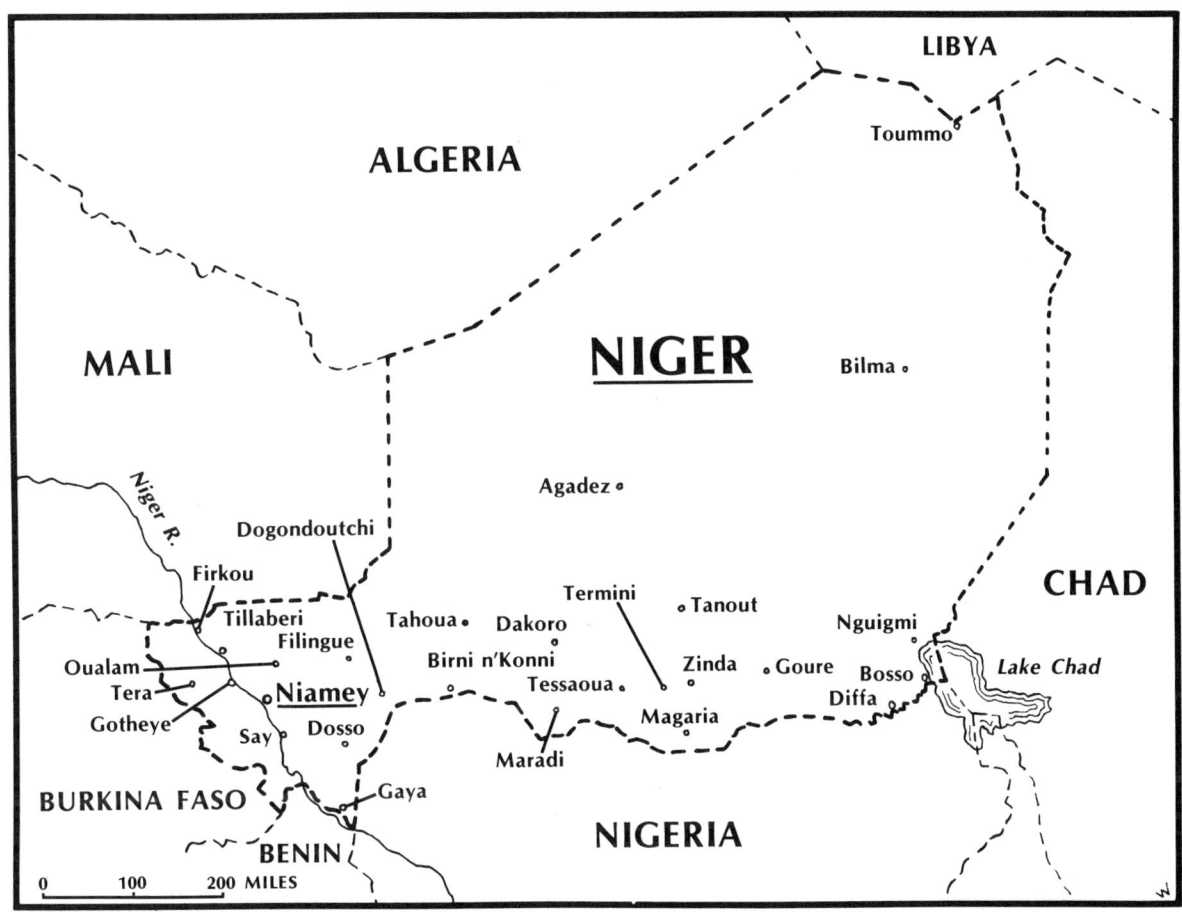

Area: 459,100 sq. miles
Population: 6,284,000 (1984)
Capital: Niamey
Currency: CFA franc (100 centimes)

Niger is located on the southern border of the Sahara Desert. It is mostly barren and rocky with some savannah. The climate is hot and dry

with an annual rainfall of about 4-30 inches, mostly in June-September. However, two thirds of the country receives less than four inches of rain each year.

Most of the population is concentrated in the south along the Niger River, the only part of the country where agriculture is possible.

The first Europeans arrived during the 19th century and French influence began to make itself felt around the turn of the century. First a French military territory, the area was not made a colony until 1922. The desert Tuaregs had put up a stiff fight in defense of their country.

Niger later became a unit of French West Africa. After World War II, a weakened France relaxed its grip on its colonial empire and on Dec. 4, 1958 Niger became an autonomous republic within the French Community. Full independence came on Aug. 3, 1960.

Niger's economy has been devastated by drought in recent years and lack of water is the country's greatest problem.

Peanuts are the chief official export and cattle sold unofficially across the borders to neighboring countries is said to make up 30-40% of all exports. Mineral resources include uranium, of which Niger is reported to have one fifth of the world's known reserves.

The 1981 per capita income was $475 and the 1984 literacy rate was 8%.

Stamps were first issued in 1921 and followed the usual French colonial pattern. Stamps of French West Africa were used from the 1940s until 1959. At that time, the republic issued its own stamps.

Since independence, stamps have been issued in great profusion. Many have subjects quite unrelated to the issuing country.

Philatelic Bureau: Service Philatelique, Direction General des PTT, Niamey, Niger.

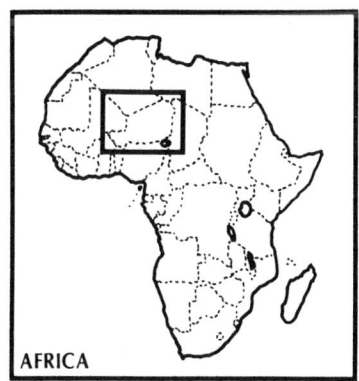

NIGERIA, FEDERAL REPUBLIC OF

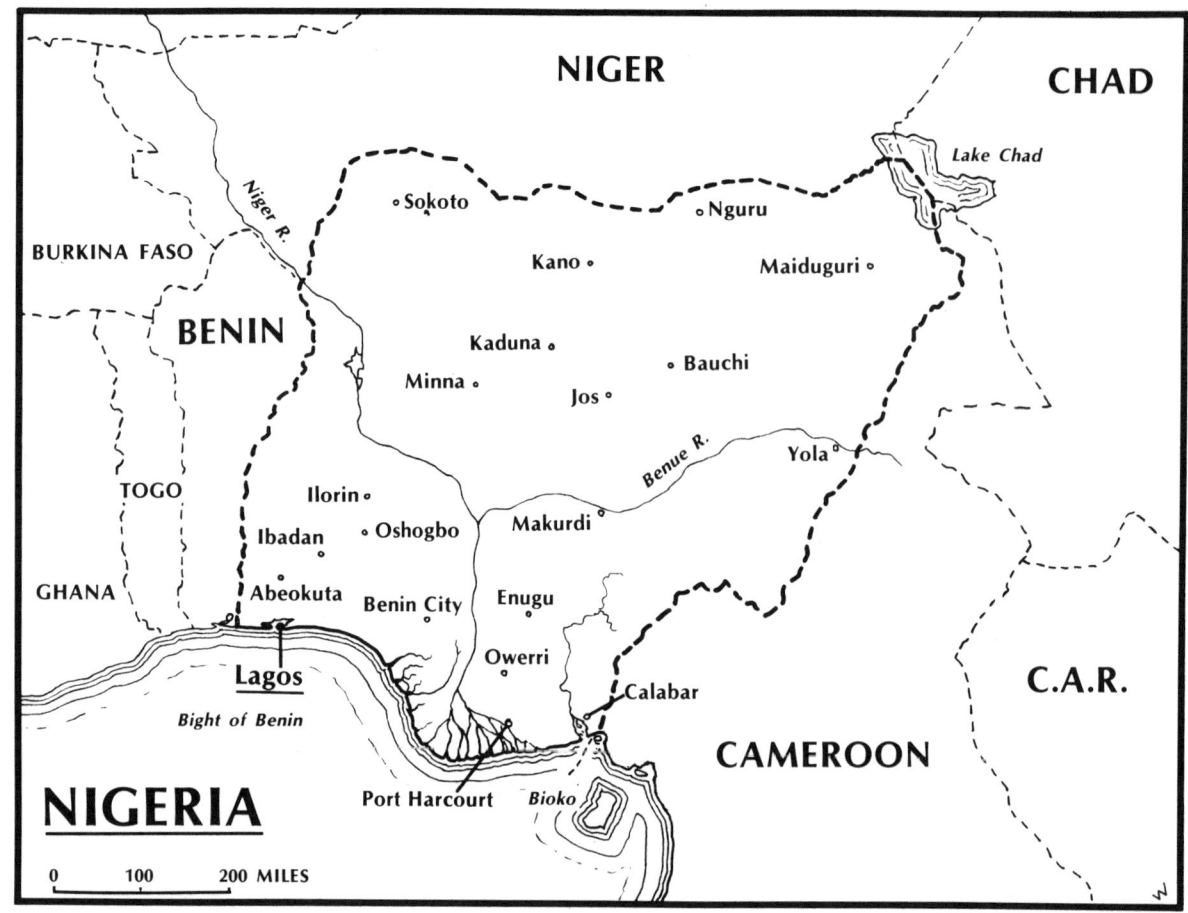

Area: 356,700 sq. miles
Population: 88,148,000 (1984)
Capital: Lagos
Currency: Naira (100 kobo)

Nigeria has a varied topography, ranging from semi-desert in the north to mangrove swamps along the coast. North of the coastal region there is an area of rain forest, beyond which is a dry plateau 6,000-7,000 feet in height. This comprises open woodland and savannah.

The annual rainfall runs from 150 inches along the coast to 25 inches or less in the north.

The area's history goes back far beyond the period of European colonization. Deposits of iron ore were being worked and terra cotta artworks produced by the Nok culture more than 2,000 years ago. The northern city of Kano can trace its history back to AD 1100.

European contacts were first made with advanced cultures in the south in the 15th and 16th centuries. Later, the slave trade decimated the native cultures.

In the late 19th century, British influence grew following the abolition of slavery as a result of British efforts. Several colonial areas developed, which were united in the colony of Nigeria in 1914. Independence was granted on Oct. 1, 1960 and the republic formed on Oct. 1, 1963.

In 1967, the eastern region proclaimed itself the Republic of Biafra and a bloody 2½-year civil war ensued before the revolt was put down. The political situation has remained unstable with several coups and a military regime currently in power.

Nigeria's vast oil reserves have dominated the economy, but the recent decline in prices has had an adverse effect and the economy is not healthy. Cocoa is the main export crop. The 1980 per capita income was $750 and the 1984 literacy rate was about 30%.

Stamps were first issued for the united colony in 1914.

Since independence, stamp-issuing policies have been moderate.

Philatelic Bureau: Nigerian Philatelic Service, GPO, Tinubu Street, PMB 12647, Lagos, Nigeria.

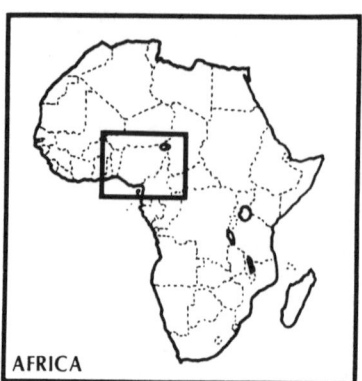

RWANDA, REPUBLIC OF

Area: 10,169 sq. miles
Population: 5,836,000 (1984)
Capital: Kigali
Currency: Franc (100 centimes)

Rwanda is mostly grassy uplands located between the Nile and Congo drainage systems. The Great Rift Valley is on its western border.

Despite Rwanda's location almost on the equator, the elevation modifies the climate and in the west the average daily temperature is 73 degrees F. Annual rainfall is about 31 inches a year but is heavier in the west than the east.

The area's recorded history goes back some 1,000 years, when Tutsi cattle breeders arrived there and dominated the local inhabitants.

German influence began in the 1890s and it became a part of German East Africa. During World War I, Belgian troops from the Congo occupied the area. At the end of the war, Belgium received a League of Nations mandate over what was

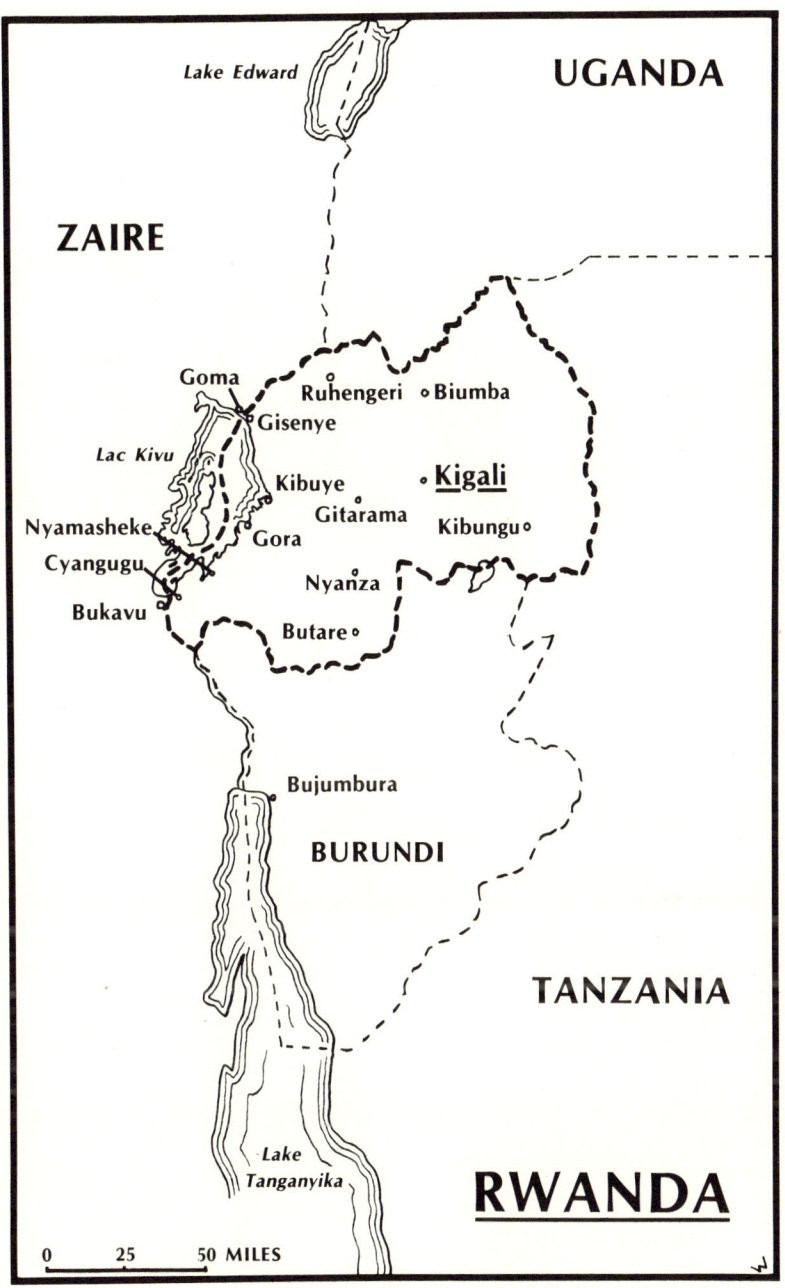

then known as Ruanda-Urundi and is now the two nations of Rwanda and Burundi.

Internal autonomy was granted to Rwanda on Jan. 1, 1962 with full independence coming on July 1, 1962.

The country is one of Africa's most densely populated at 573 per square mile and is heavily cultivated. There is much soil erosion and periods of drought make famine a constant threat. Most of the population is engaged in subsistence agriculture.

Coffee and tea are the chief export crops and mineral deposits include tin and gold. The 1982 per capita income was $250 and the 1983 literacy rate was 37%.

Stamps of Rwanda were first issued in July 1962. Since then, there have been hundreds of stamps released, many of which have designs quite unconnected with the country.

Philatelic Bureau: Direction General des PTT, Kigale, Rwanda or Agences Philateliques Gouvernementales, Chaussee de Waterloo 868/870, 1180 Brussels, Belgium.

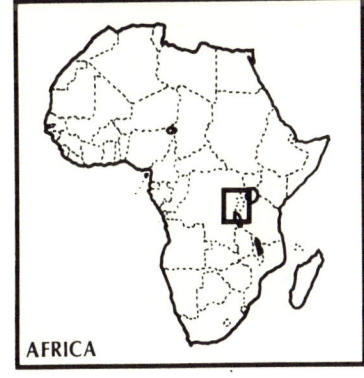

ST. HELENA, CROWN COLONY OF

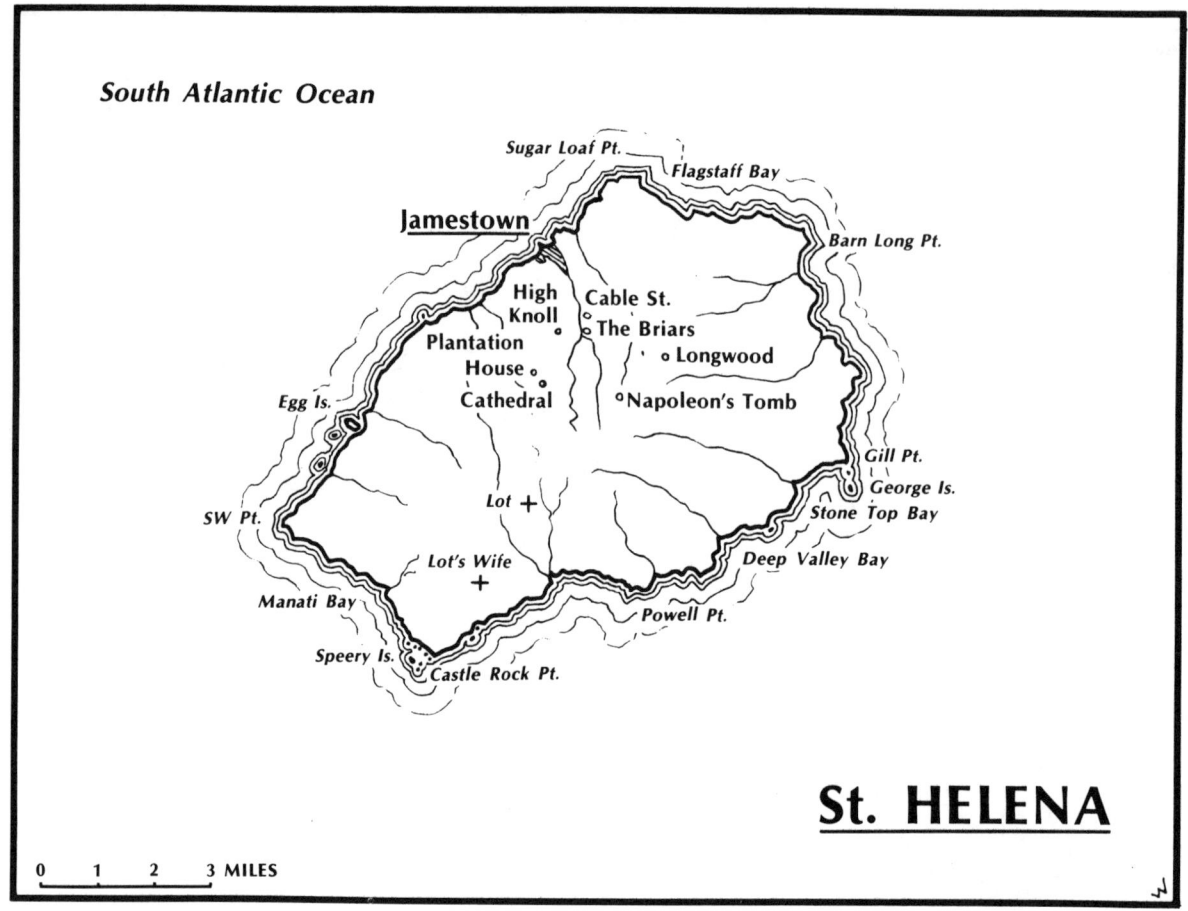

Area: 47 sq. miles
Population: 5,300 (1981)
Capital: Jamestown
Currency: Pound (100 pence)

St. Helena is a volcanic island in the South Atlantic, about 1,150 miles off the African coast. Its highest point is 2,800-foot Diana

Peak and the tall twin rocks named Lot and Lot's Wife are known for their distinctive appearance.

There is only a small area of level ground located at about 1,600 feet. The island's only landing place is at James Bay.

The climate is modified by trade winds and the cold South Atlantic Current. Summer temperatures run from 65-90 degrees F and 55-85 degrees F in winter. Temperatures are reduced at higher altitudes. Rainfall likewise varies from eight inches a year at sea level to about 30 inches in the higher regions.

The Portuguese sailor, Joao da Nova Castella, discovered and named the island on May 21, 1592. During the late 1500s several English explorers visited and in 1654, the East India Co. established a settlement on the island. Ousted briefly by the Dutch in 1673, the island has been British ever since. The astronomer Edmund Halley lived there from 1676-78 and built an observatory.

In 1815, St. Helena became famous when Britain chose it as the place of exile for the Emperor Napoleon, who lived there until his death in May 1821.

From about 1879, as steam gradually replaced sail, ships found less reason to call there and the island declined in importance. Boer prisoners of war were held there from 1899-1902 during the South African War.

In 1922, the island of Ascension was made a dependency and in 1938, Tristan da Cunha also became a dependency.

Stamps were first issued for St. Helena in 1856. They are an attractive design featuring a profile of Queen Victoria. During its stamp-issuing life, the island has followed a moderate policy and this continues, although there are more issues now than in the past.

Philatelic Bureau: Postmaster, Jamestown, St. Helena, South Atlantic.

ST. THOMAS AND PRINCE, DEMOCRATIC REPUBLIC OF

Area: 372 sq. miles
Population: 89,000 (1984)
Capital: Sao Tome
Currency: Dobra (100 cents)

The two volcanic islands of St. Thomas and Prince are located off Gabon on Africa's west coast. The larger, St. Thomas, rises to 6,600 feet.

The climate is tropical with an average annual temperature of 80 degrees F, which modifies to the high 60s at higher altitudes. Rainfall varies from 200 inches on the southwest slopes to about 40 in northern areas at low elevation.

Discovered by the Portuguese in the 1470s, a Portuguese settlement was established on St. Thomas in 1493. This was followed in 1500 by one on Prince. By the mid-1500s, with the help of African slave labor, the islands had become large sugar producers.

As sugar declined at the beginning of the 19th century so did the islands' economies. In the early 1800s coffee and cocoa were introduced as replacement crops and by 1908, St. Thomas was one of the world's largest producer of cocoa.

Despite the Portuguese abolition of slavery in 1876, labor conditions remained bad on the islands, with

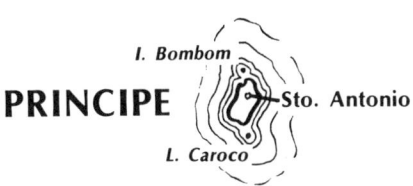

much abuse by plantation managers. As late as 1953 there were riots over bad conditions and many workers killed. The anniversary of what has become known as the Batepa Massacre is a national holiday.

Independence was achieved on July 12, 1985 after a period of transitional government.

Agriculture remains the base of the economy and there is some commercial fishing. There is a potential for a tourist industry with climate, scenery, and location all being favorable. However, hotel and transportation facilities are not yet adequate.

The 1981 per capita income was $300 and the 1983 literacy rate was 50%.

Stamps were first issued in 1869 and followed the usual Portuguese colonial pattern. Many recent stamp issues have not received catalog recognition.

Philatelic Bureau: Direccao dos Correios e Telecommunicacoes, Seccao Filatelica, Sao Tome, St. Thomas and Prince.

SENEGAL, REPUBLIC OF

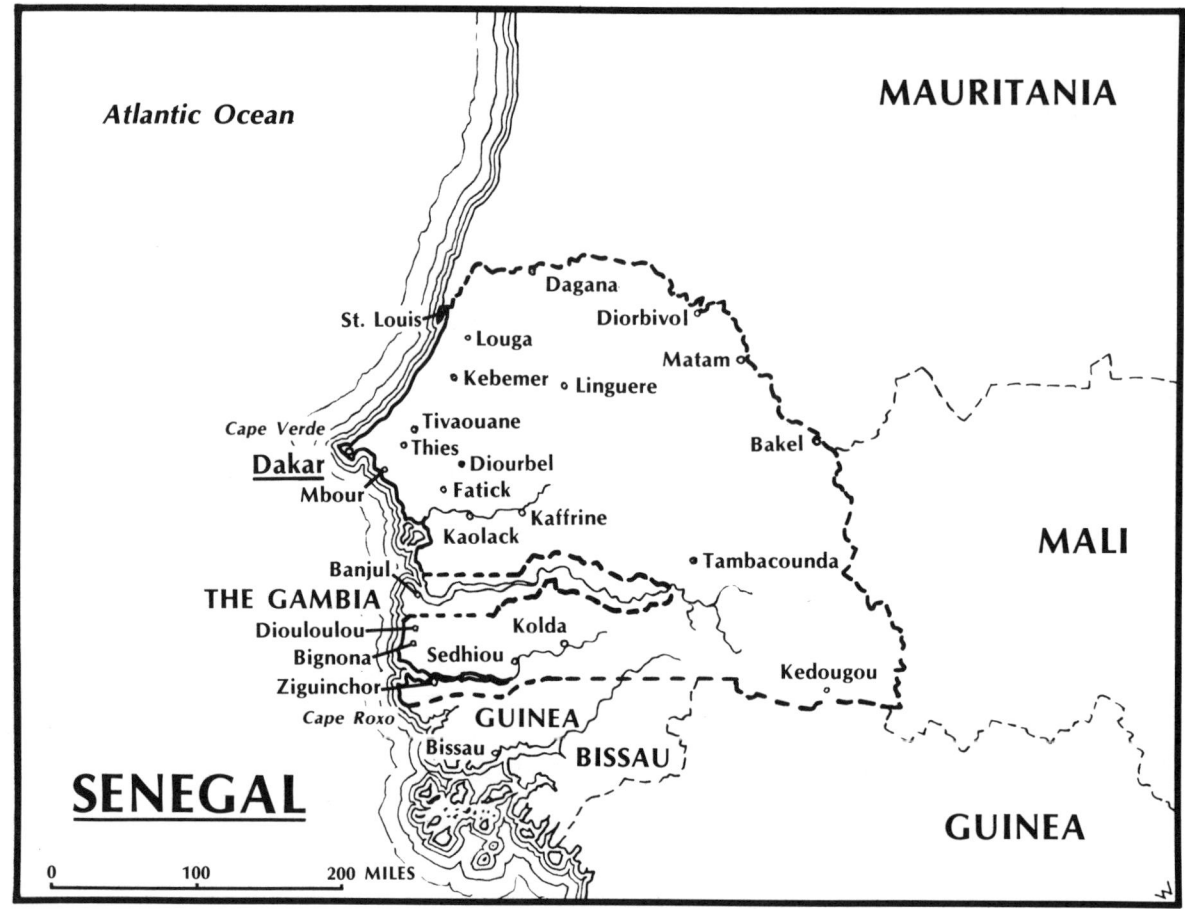

Area: 75,995 sq. miles
Population: 6,541,000 (1984)
Capital: Dakar
Currency: CFA franc (100 centimes)

Most of Senegal is low rolling savannah with swamp or rain forest along the southern coast. The capital city of Dakar is on a long peninsula jutting into the Atlantic from the "bulge" of West Africa.

The city has an average annual temperature of 85 degrees F with an average minimum of 54 degrees F. The city's annual rainfall is about 24 inches.

The Portuguese were the first Europeans to arrive during the 15th century, but French influence has been strong since the 17th century. France administered the area as a protectorate from the 19th century until 1920, when it became a colony. Senegal was a unit of French West Africa and Dakar was the colonial federation's capital.

Self-government came in 1958 as a republic in the French Community and it joined with the Sudanese Republic to form the Federation of Mali in 1960. Senegal withdrew from the federation on Aug. 20, 1960 and has been a republic since then.

Senegal is considered to be the most democratic of the ex-French West African colonies. In 1981, it entered into a confederation with The Gambia, in which the two countries retained their independent status but adopted joint defense and fiscal policies.

The economy is agricultural and peanuts are the main export crop. In recent years drought has caused famine and the country is poor. The 1975 per capita income was $342 and the 1984 literacy rate was a low 10%.

Stamps were first issued in 1887 and continued in the traditional French colonial pattern. From 1944 to independence, stamps of French West Africa were used.

Since independence, stamp issues have followed the usual trend of African countries, although there have not been quite so many stamps released as there have been from other ex-French colonies in the area.

Philatelic Bureau: Office des Postes et Telecommunications du Senegal, Bureau Philatelique, Dakar, Senegal.

SEYCHELLES, REPUBLIC OF

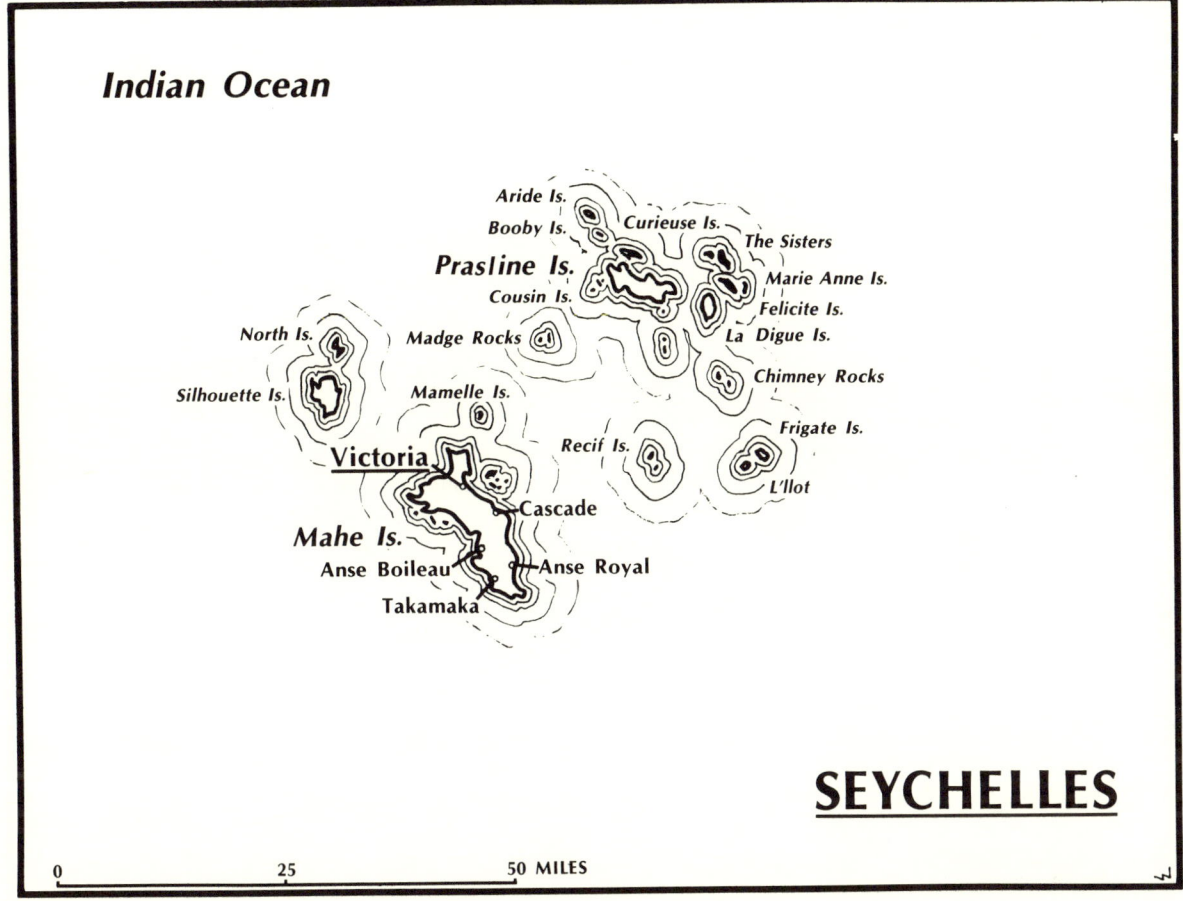

Area: 171 sq. miles
Population: 66,000 (1984)
Capital: Victoria
Currency: Rupee (100 cents)

The Seychelles comprise a main island group plus a number of coral islands and atolls scattered to the south over the Indian Ocean. The latter are known as Zil Elwannyen Sesel, or Outer Islands (q.v.).

The main island group is rocky, with granite mountains rising to

3,000 feet. The climate is pleasant and healthy, although humid. Rainfall is 90 inches a year at Victoria on the island of Mahe, with up to 140 inches annually in the mountains. Temperatures range from 75-85 degrees F. There is a cool season from May to September.

The uninhabited islands appeared on Portuguese charts from the early 1500s, but were not settled until the French took possession in the mid-1700s. They were taken by Britain in 1794 and retained under the 1814 Treaty of Paris. First administered from Mauritius, the Seychelles became a crown colony on Aug. 31, 1903.

In 1965, the Outer Islands were made part of the British Indian Ocean Territory. When independence was granted on June 29, 1976, those islands were restored to the Republic of Seychelles. Socialists ousted the president only a year after independence and in 1979 turned the country into a one-party state.

Subsistence agriculture and fishing are important occupations and some copra, vanilla, and spices are produced. The economy is improving, but recent statistics indicate that fully 49% of the labor force is occupied in government, with only 19.4% employed in industry and commerce, and 18.5% in agriculture.

The 1981 per capita income was $1,030 and the 1983 literacy rate was 60%.

Stamps were first issued in 1890. Since independence, a moderate stamp-issuing policy has been followed.

Philatelic Bureau: Philatelic Bureau, P.O. Box 60, Victoria, Mahe, Seychelles, Indian Ocean.

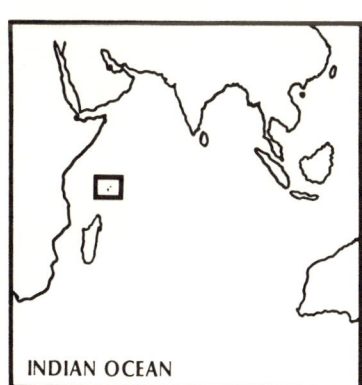

SIERRA LEONE, REPUBLIC OF

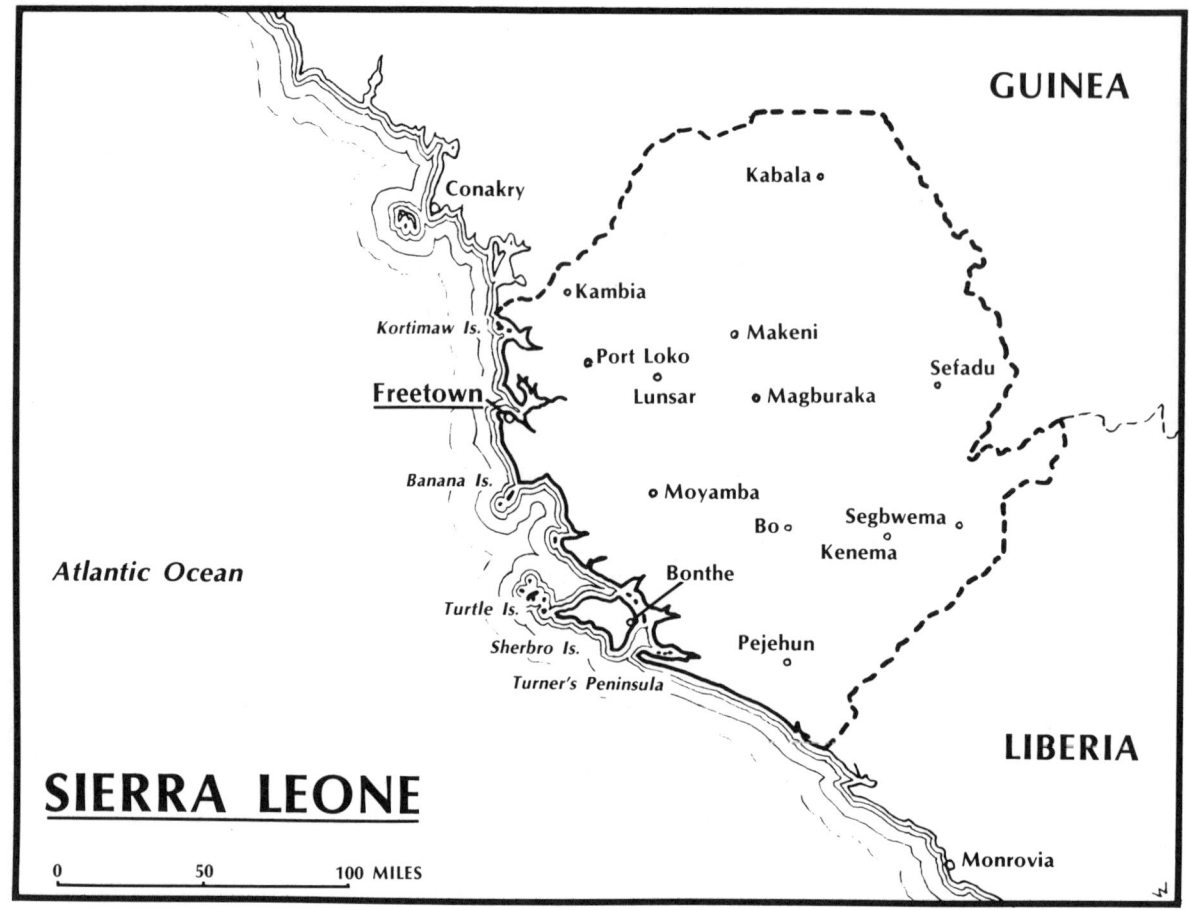

Area: 27,699 sq. miles
Population: 3,805,000 (1984)
Capital: Freetown
Currency: Leone (100 cents)

Located on the southern bulge of West Africa, Sierra Leone has a coastal belt of mangrove swamps with wooded uplands in the interior rising to 6,390-foot Bintumani, the tallest mountain in West Africa.

The climate is tropical, with an average high temperature of 80 degrees F. This drops to an average low of 75 on the coast and 60 inland.

Annual rainfall can reach 200 inches along the coast. The dry season is from November to April.

The Portuguese sailor Pedro de Cinta gave the land its name in 1460. It translates as "Lion Mountain."

The first English arrived in 1562 and Sir Francis Drake came to the area in 1580.

In 1787, the first freed slaves from Britain and black refugees from the American colonies settled there and the city of Freetown was established as their home. The crown colony of Sierra Leone was formed in 1808 and under British rule, it became the educational center of British West Africa.

After a gradual self-government and grooming for self-rule, independence came on April 27, 1961. It became a republic in 1971 and was proclaimed a one-party state in 1978.

The economy has deteriorated in recent years and the country is poor and in debt. An agricultural land, cocoa and coffee are the chief crops. Mineral resources include diamonds and bauxite.

The 1980 per capita income was $176 and the 1984 literacy rate was 15%.

The first stamps were issued in 1859. Of the colonial issues, the 1933 Wilberforce issue is a British Commonwealth classic. Soon after independence, there came a period during which large numbers of free-form, self-stick stamps were issued. This resulted in a loss of collector interest and the country is not philatelically popular despite a return to more conservative policies.

Philatelic Bureau: Postmaster General, GPO, Freetown, Sierra Leone.

SOMALI DEMOCRATIC REPUBLIC (SOMALIA)

Area: 246,300 sq. miles
Population: 6,393,000 (1984)
Capital: Muodisho (Mogadishu)
Currency: Shilling (100 centesimi)

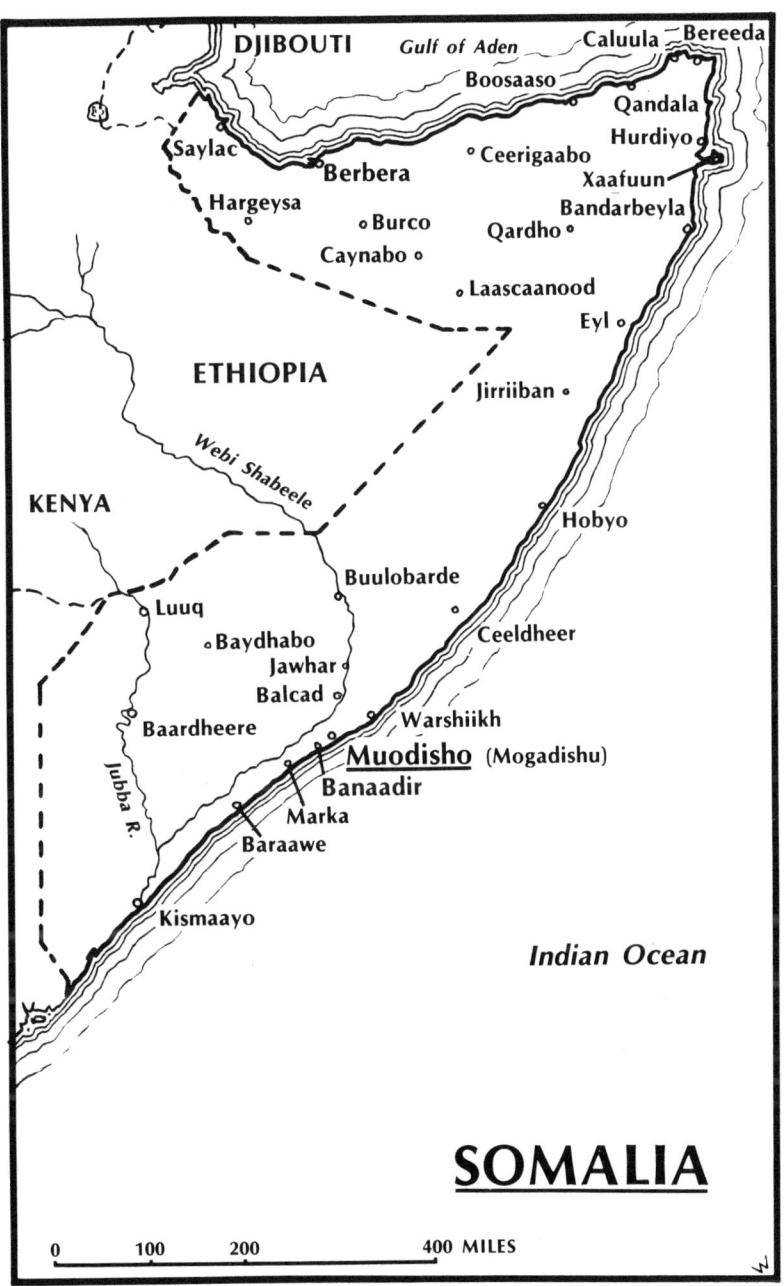

Somalia occupies the easternmost portion of Africa. It has a 1,700-mile coastline running from Djibouti at the foot of the Red Sea, to Kenya in the south.

It is mountainous and arid in the north, with peaks rising to some 7,000 feet, while the south is low and flat. The small area suitable for agriculture is in the south.

The country's climate is hot and rainfall erratic. Average high temperatures range from 85-105 degrees F and lows run from 60-80 degrees F, although the coastal climate is generally more moderate and not unpleasant.

The country was formed in 1960 from the British-administered Somaliland Protectorate and the ex-Italian colony of Italian Somaliland.

Arabs from Yemen founded a sultanate in the area in the seventh century AD and their influence gradually spread down the coast to Zanzibar.

In the late 19th century the British presence grew and the protectorate was established. The Italians took the area to the south and formed a colony after subduing the inhabitants.

For a brief period during World War II, Italy invaded and occupied the British protectorate. It was soon liberated and the Italians expelled from East Africa completely.

The gradual transformation to independence began with the British military administration and after the war the United Nations formed a trusteeship over the area until independence came on July 1, 1960.

In 1969, a revolutionary group took over. Severe drought and a war with Ethiopia have drained the economy. Natural resources are not large although there are deposits of iron, tin, bauxite, and uranium.

Crops include sugar and bananas, with livestock being the main export.

The 1983 per capita income was under $500 and the 1984 literacy rate a low 5%.

Stamps were issued by both the British and Italians in the areas they controlled. Since independence, stamp issues have been moderate.

Philatelic Bureau: Philatelic Service, Ministry of Posts and Telecommunications, Mogadishu, Somali Democratic Republic.

SOUTH AFRICA, REPUBLIC OF

Area: 435,868 sq. miles
Population: 31,698,000 (1984)
Capital: Pretoria (administrative)
Cape Town (legislative)
Bloemfontein (judicial).
Currency: Rand (100 cents)

South Africa, located at the southern tip of Africa, was formed by the 1910 merger of the British colonies of the Cape of Good Hope, Natal, the Transvaal, and the Orange River Colony. The two latter areas had been the independent Boer states of the Transvaal and the Orange Free State prior to the Anglo-Boer war of 1899-1902.

The country has a moderate climate, with sunny days and cool nights. There is a narrow coastal strip, but the interior is a plateau ranging from 3,000-6,000 feet in height. The average mean temperature in the south is 62 degrees F and in the north at Johannesburg, it is 61 degrees F. Rainfall varies from about five inches a year on the west coast to 40 inches in the east.

Cape of Good Hope

The Portuguese were the first to visit the Cape in 1486, but there was no settlement until 1652, when the Dutch East India Company set up a "refreshment station" there.

The French occupied the Cape from 1781-84 and the British took it from 1795-1803, when it was returned to the Dutch under the Treaty of Amiens. By the end of the century, there were settlements of Dutch and Germans throughout the Cape area.

Britain took the Cape again during the Napoleonic Wars and retained it under the Treaty of Vienna of 1814.

By 1836, many Boer farmers, angered at the loss of their slaves caused by the British abolition of slavery, and wishing to escape British rule, moved north of the Orange River.

SOUTH AFRICA & HOMELANDS

1. Bophuthatswana
2. Ciskei
3. Transkei
4. Venda

The colony annexed Natal in 1843, Griqualand West in 1871, part of the Transvaal in 1877, and British Bechuanaland in the 1890s. Natal was made a separate colony in 1856. The chief city is Cape Town.

The first stamps of the Cape of Good Hope came on Sept. 1, 1853. They were the famous Cape Triangulars and are claimed to be the world's first stamps in this shape. It is said that the shape was selected so that illiterate postal workers could distinguish outgoing mail from that coming into the colony!

Natal

Although the Portuguese had been the first Europeans to see the coast of Natal and named it *Terra Natalis*, they did not claim or settle it.

The British Navy charted the coast in 1822-23. In 1843, after considerable conflict between natives, traders, and Boers, they annexed it to the Cape of Good Hope. In 1856, it became a colony. The chief city is Durban.

War with the native population, especially the Zulu War of 1879, kept the colony in a state of turmoil.

Then, in 1881, during the first Anglo-Boer War, came an invasion of Boers, which bruised British pride by causing a number of engagements to be "played at home," as it were.

During the second Boer War, the Boers bloodied the nose of the British Army by bottling it up in the embarrassing siege of Ladysmith, a wound not soothed until 1900, when the Boers were finally driven out.

Natal first issued stamps in 1857 and continued until union in 1910, but the most memorable are the beautiful Chalon Heads of 1860-74.

The Transvaal

Named for its location north of the Vaal River, the Transvaal is the site of a Boer settlement that became the South African Republic and was recognized by Britain in 1852.

Hostile natives, who objected to their country being taken from them, and bickering within Boer ranks led to virtual bankruptcy and Britain was persuaded to annex the republic in 1877.

However, in 1880, the Boers defeated the British at Majuba and once again decided to run their own country.

Following the Boer defeat in the second Anglo-Boer War of 1899-1902, it became a British colony and remained so until the Union of South Africa was formed in 1910. Chief cities are Pretoria and Johannesburg.

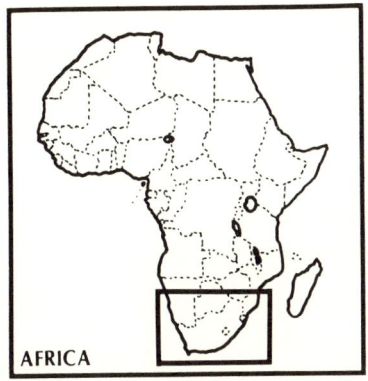

Stamps were first issued in 1869 and continued under the various occupations and administrations until regular colonial stamps were issued after it became a colony. These were used until the 1910 union.

Orange River Colony

In 1836, the Great Trek from the Cape of Good Hope colony brought Boer settlers to the area north of the Orange River, where they formed a settlement called Transorangia.

The British, who felt a responsibility to both Boer and native in-

habitants, found it impossible to administer the area properly. In 1848, they annexed it and proclaimed the Orange River Sovereignty.

After six years it reverted to Boer control and was named the Orange Free State.

In 1899, it joined the other Boer republic, the Transvaal, against the British in the second Anglo-Boer War. Following the Boer defeat in 1902, it became the Orange River Colony. The chief city is Bloemfontein.

Stamps were first issued in 1868 and continued through the British occupation and the colonial period until 1910, when the Union of South Africa was formed.

The Republic

When the Union of South Africa came into being on May 31, 1910, it was as a dominion of the British Empire. But in 1934, under the Statute of Westminister, it became a sovereign state within the empire.

At the outbreak of World War I, there was considerable pro-German sentiment on the part of the Boer population, but it was overcome and South African forces expelled the Germans from South-West Africa.

South Africa was granted a League of Nations mandate over the area, and its continuing occupation of what is now Namibia (q.v.) has brought international condemnation upon South Africa in recent years.

Since World War II, the growing official policy of imposing second-class status on the vast black majority has generated repugnance in the world community and opposition from fellow members of the British Commonwealth caused South Africa to withdraw from that community and become a republic on May 31, 1961.

In recent years, white control has slipped noticeably and the country seems on the brink of a bloody civil war. Hundreds of blacks have been killed and repressive measures have been taken by the regime to suppress all opposition.

South Africa has a strong industrial base. It is by far Africa's most highly developed and most properous country.

It is the world's largest producer of gold and diamonds and has large reserves of other minerals including copper, platinum, and uranium, lacking only oil.

The 1982 literacy rate was 98% for whites and 50% for blacks.

The first stamps were issued in 1910 and from 1926 to 1952 stamps were inscribed alternately in the two official languages, English and Afrikaans. Stamps are now inscribed simply "RSA."

The stamps of South Africa and its homelands, plus SW Africa were embargoed by the US Treasury Department on Oct. 2, 1986.

Philatelic Bureau: Philatelic Services, GPO, Pretoria 0001, South Africa.

The Homelands

After World War II, South Africa's apartheid policy became official. In 1959, it introduced the so-called "Bantustans" or "homelands" system. The first of these to obtain its own stamps was Transkei on Oct. 26, 1976.

Three others so far are Bophuthatswana (Dec. 6, 1977), Venda (Sept. 13, 1979), and Ciskei (Dec. 4, 1981).

None of the homelands have received international recognition and the stamps have no validity in the international mails. Some usage is said to be tolerated.

SUDAN, DEMOCRATIC REPUBLIC OF THE

Area: 966,757 sq. miles
Population: 21,103,000 (1984)
Capital: Khartoum
Currency: Egyptian pound (100 piastres)

Africa's largest country, the Sudan's lifeline is the Nile river, which flows from south to north some 2,300 miles through the country.

A land of extremes, it has arid, rocky desert with virtually no rain in the north and tropical forest in the south. At Khartoum, the average maximum temperature exceeds 100 degrees F for 10 months of the year and is about 90 degrees F during the other two. Temperatures drop considerably at night.

A coptic country until Arabs brought Islam in the 1400s, the Sudan was conquered and unified by Egypt in the 1820s. Towards the end of the 19th century the self-styled "Mahdi" (leader of the faithful) led his dervishes in a rebellion that resulted in the murder of the British administrator, General Gordon, at Khartoum. An 1898 campaign by Anglo-Egyptian forces defeated him and the two countries established a condominium government that lasted until the 1950s.

In 1953, after King Farouk of Egypt was ousted, Britain and Egypt agreed to a three-year transition period for Sudanese independence, and the country became independent on Jan. 1, 1956.

Since then, there has been much instability and coups have toppled

the government on several occasions. Policies have vacillated between East and West. Libya has not neglected to keep the political pot boiling, and in 1981 and 1984 was accused of bombing Sudanese towns.

The economy is poor and the country has been wracked by drought and famine. Cotton is the chief export and the Sudan is the principal world source of gum arabic. The 1982 per capita income was $370 and the literacy rate was 20%.

The Sudan will always have a place in the hearts of stamp collectors for its popular "Camel Postman" stamp design. It was first issued in 1898 and the last example was released in 1954.

Since independence, stamps have been mostly political in nature and symbolic in design.

Philatelic Bureau: Philatelic Office, Posts and Telegraphs, Public Corp., Khartoum, Sudan.

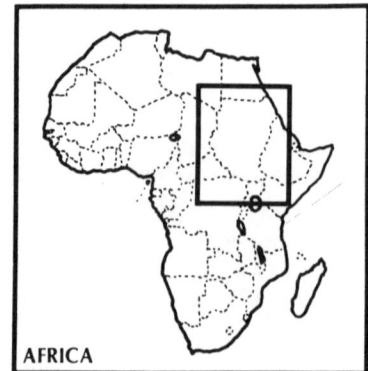

SWAZILAND, KINGDOM OF

Area: 6,704 sq. miles
Population: 651,000 (1984)
Capital: Mbabane
Currency: Emalangeni (100 cents)

Swaziland is surrounded by South Africa and Mozambique. It possesses a royal dynasty that has ruled for at least 400 years.

The country has a varied topography and climate, ranging from temperate highlands to subtropical lowlands. Rainfall varies from up to 90 inches in the western mountains to 20-30 inches in the lowlands. Temperatures are from an average high of 75 degrees F in the lowlands to 60 degrees on the high plateau.

The Swazi people were settled in Zululand during the mid-1700s but were gradually pushed north. By the 1800s they were finally established in what is now Swaziland.

Contact with the British first came when the Swazi ruler asked for protection from Zulu raids. This was provided and Swazi independence guaranteed.

There was a period of South African administration, but after the Boer War, Britain resumed its role of protector and a gradual process of preparation for independence began. This was speeded up after World War II, when South Africa intensified its policy of racial discrimination and there seemed a danger that Swaziland might fall under South African domination. Full independence was granted on Sept. 6, 1968.

The king assumed full power in 1973 and repealed the constitution. Parliament's authority was reduced to that of advisor.

Swaziland is one of the more prosperous of new African countries.

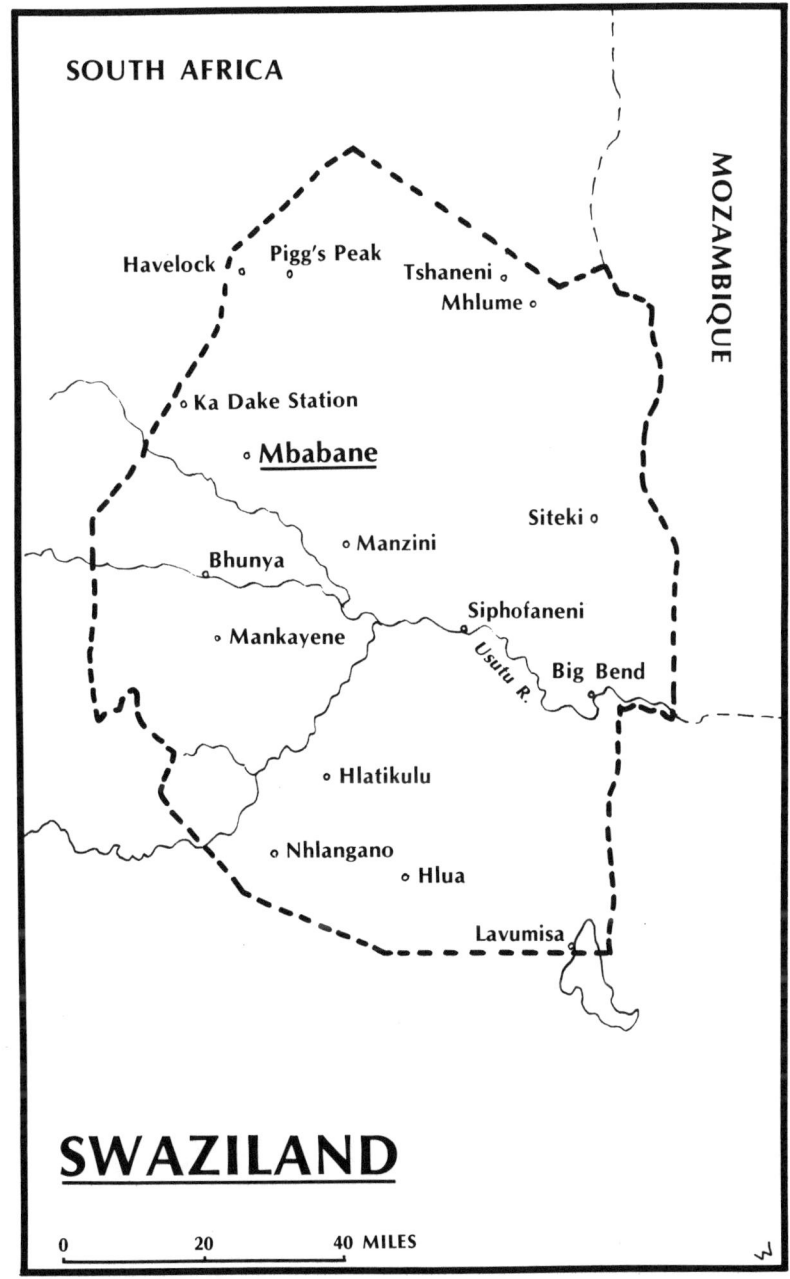

Mineral resources include iron, coal, and asbestos. Cotton, rice, pineapples, sugar, and citrus are important crops.

In the past several years, there have been a number of secondary industries established, mostly on several new industrial estates. These make plastic containers, furniture, beer, soft drinks, paint, and clothing.

Tourism is also becoming more important as a source of revenue. Additional hotels and other facilities for visitors are being build.

The 1981 per capita income was $840 and the 1983 literacy rate was 65%.

Stamps were first issued in 1889. Since independence, a moderate stamp-issuing policy has been followed.

Philatelic Bureau: Swaziland Stamp Bureau, Department of Posts and Telecommunications, Box 555, Mbabane, Swaziland.

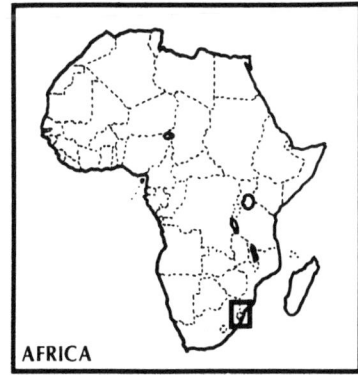

TANZANIA, UNITED REPUBLIC OF

Area: 364,886 sq. miles
Population: 21,202,000 (1984)
Capital: Dar es Salaam
Currency: Shilling (100 cents)

Comprising the former British mandated area of Tanganyika and the Sultanate of Zanzibar, Tanzania has a hot and humid coastal strip; a hot, arid central plateau region; a high lake area in the west; and temperate highlands. The climate varies greatly between these various areas.

Mount Kilimanjaro, Africa's tallest mountain, is located on the border with Kenya.

Some of the oldest known remains of man's ancestors have been found in the area and discoveries by Dr. Richard Leakey indicate that East Africa may well have been man's earliest home.

Arab slavers and European explorers began to visit the interior early in the 19th century, but the coastal area had been familiar to Arab traders since the 8th century. Persian and Indian settlers arrived in the 12th century.

By the 1500s, the Portuguese claimed ownership of the coastal region, but were driven out by the 18th century.

In 1871, the Scottish missionary-explorer, David Livingstone, was "found" in the interior by the American journalist Henry Stanley.

German colonial activities began in the 1880s and the colony of German East Africa was soon formed.

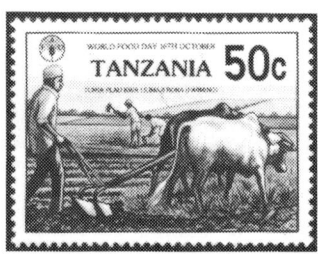

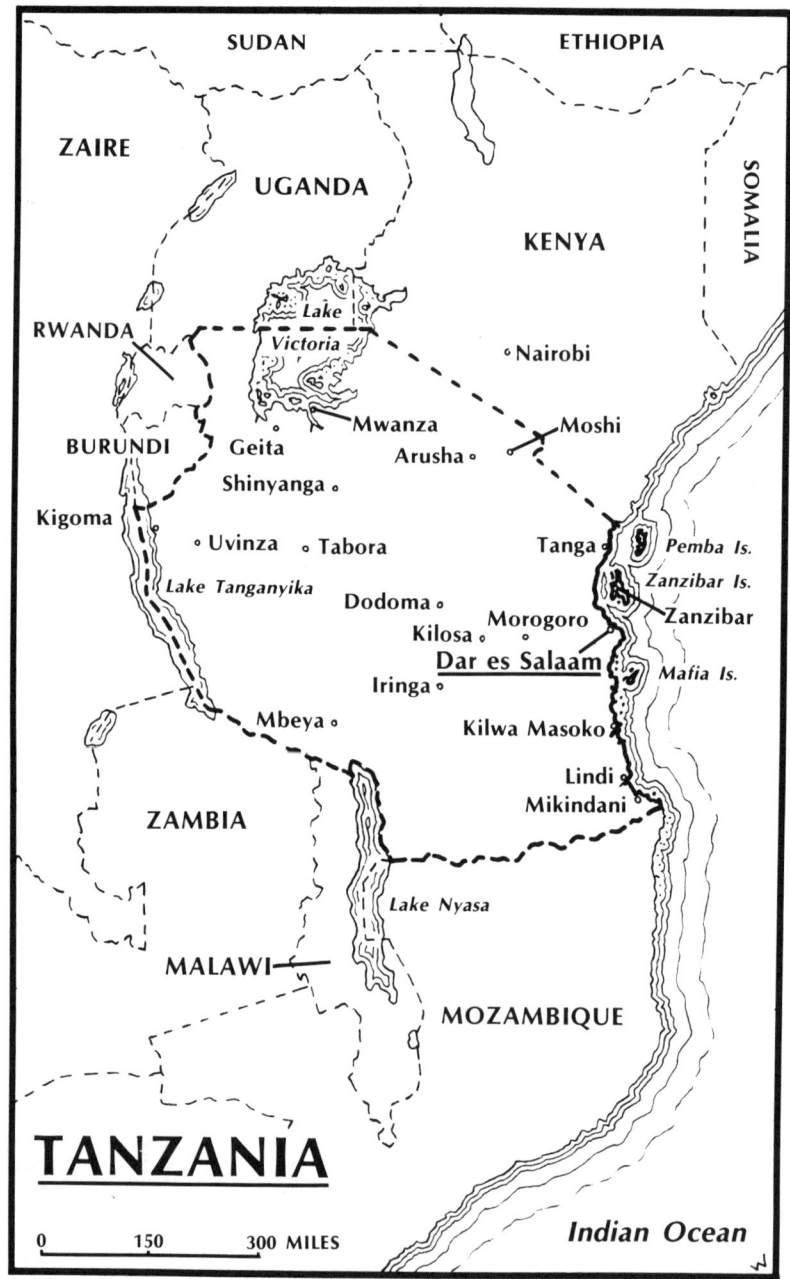

During World War I, Britain took the area and it was made a League of Nations mandate. Independence was granted on Dec. 9, 1961 and the area united with Zanzibar on April 26, 1964.

Zanzibar was an Arab sultanate from the 19th century and a base for slavers. Not until 1876 was Britain able to put an end to the slave trade there. The sultanate was a British protectorate from 1890 to independence on Dec. 19, 1963.

Tanzania has deposits of diamonds, gold, and nickel. Crops include cotton, coffee, tea, and tobacco. Zanzibar's spices are world famous and it exports most of the world's cloves.

The 1982 per capita income was $240 and the 1984 literacy rate was 66%.

Stamps were first issued in 1893 for German East Africa and in Zanzibar in 1895. Since independence, stamp-issuing policies have not been excessive.

Philatelic Bureau: Tanzania Posts and Telecommunications, Department of Posts, Stamp Bureau, Box 2988, Dar es Salaam, Tanzania.

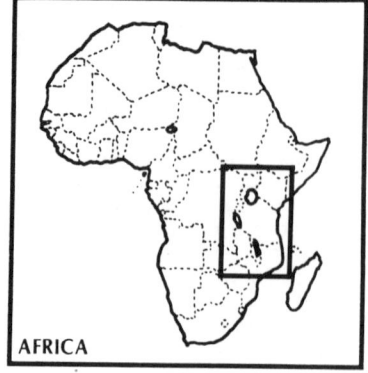

TOGO, REPUBLIC OF

Area: 21,853 sq. miles
Population: 2,926,000 (1984)
Capital: Lome
Currency: CFA franc (100 centimes)

A long, narrow West African country, Togo is mostly savannah, with a range of forested hills running through it.

Its climate is humid in the south with temperatures of from 75-90 degrees F and 65-100 degrees F in the north.

During the 15th and 16th centuries, Portuguese explorers and traders visited the coast of Togo. The subsequent development of the slave trade soon gave the area the name of "The Slave Coast."

In the 1880s, German influence grew and that country proclaimed a protectorate over the coastal region. German control was soon extended inland and it became a colony.

Britain and France occupied Togo during World War I, and after the war the League of Nations divided the ex-colony and gave mandated areas to the two countries. This arrangement was continued by the United Nations after World War II.

In 1957, the British area voted to join the colony of the Gold Coast in becoming the independent country of Ghana. The French area chose independence and became a republic on April 27, 1960.

Agriculture is the basis of the economy and the chief crops are coffee, cocoa, and rice. There is some industry, mainly textiles and the making of shoes.

The 1981 per capita income was $350 and the 1984 literacy rate was 18%.

Stamps were first issued by the

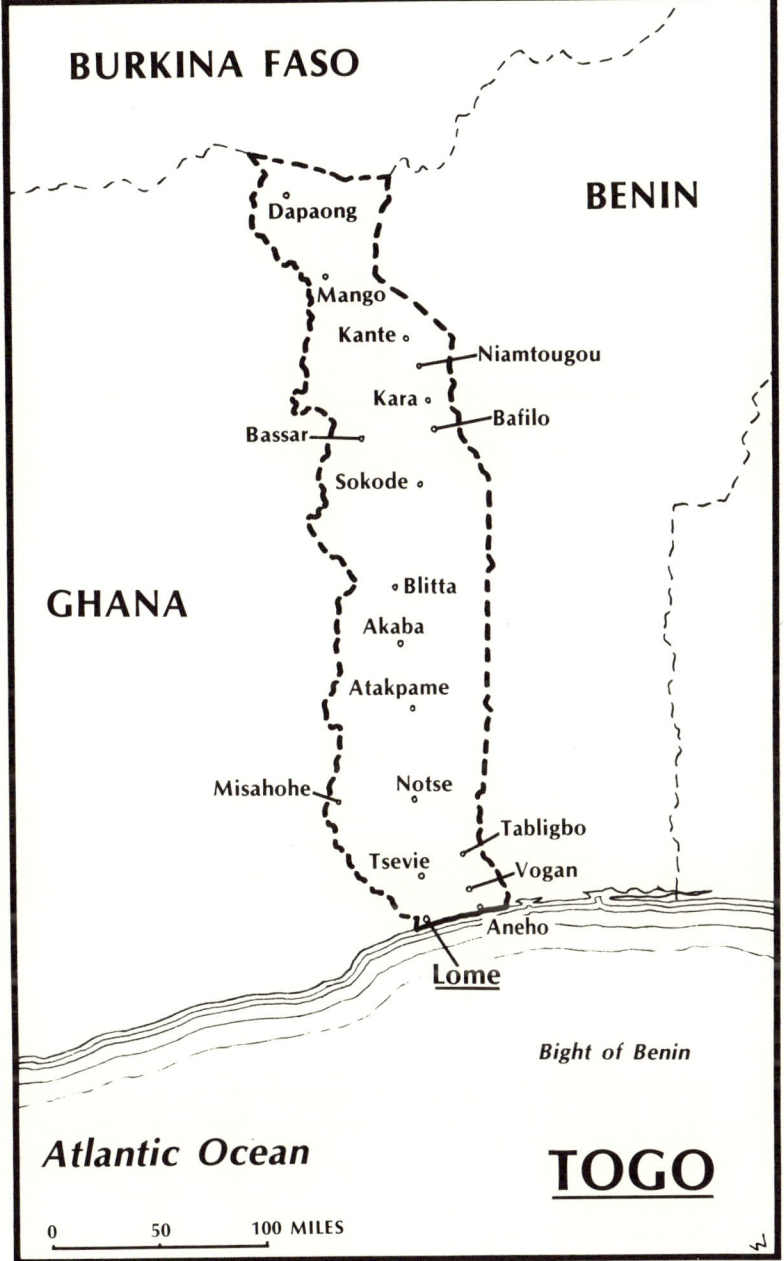

German administration in 1897. Occupation stamps were issued by the Anglo-French occupation forces. These consisted of German colonial stamps overprinted in English "TOGO/ Anglo-French/ Occupation," and separately in French.

Stamps in the French colonial tradition were used in the French mandate area and those of Gold Coast were used in the British portion.

Since independence, stamp issues have been extremely prolific. Many of the more exploitive issues, such as the high-value gold foil "stamps," have not received catalog recognition.

Philatelic Bureau: Direction General des Postes et Telecommunications, Service Philatelique, Lome, Togo.

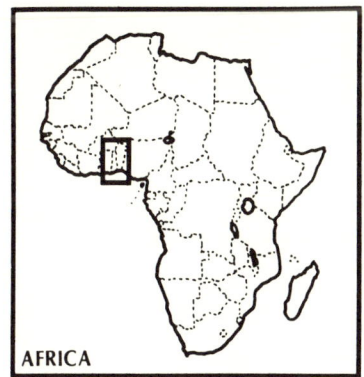

TRISTAN DA CUNHA, DEPENDENCY OF

Area: 40 sq. miles
Population: 292 (1973)
Capital: Edinburgh
Currency: Pound (100 pence)

Tristan da Cunha comprises a group of three volcanic islands; Tristan da Cunha, Inaccessible, and Nightingale, together with the islets

of Stoltenhoff and Middle, and Gough Island located about 250 miles to the south-southwest.

Tristan da Cunha is the only inhabited island in the group. It has a central volcanic cone about 6,750 feet in height.

The climate is mild, with an average high temperature of 65 degrees F and a low of 50 degrees F. About 65 inches of rain falls each year at Edinburgh and frost is unknown.

The islands were discovered by the Portuguese admiral, Tristao da Cunha in 1506. The Dutch unsuccessfully attempted a settlement in 1656.

In 1816, Britain annexed the islands and garrisoned them for a short period to prevent their use as a base by privateers. In 1938, they were made a dependency of St. Helena.

A naval weather and radio station operated there during World War II, and true to Royal Navy tradition Tristan da Cunha was commissioned as HMS *Atlantic Isle*.

The 1961 volcanic eruption forced the evacuation of the island and the population was taken to the United Kingdom. Most islanders found it impossible to adjust to such a different way of life and returned to the island in 1963, when the volcanic activity had ceased.

Fishing for crawfish and the growing of potatoes are the main occupations.

The first stamps were issued in 1952 and consist of the contemporary stamps of St. Helena overprinted "TRISTAN/ DA CUNHA." Since then, island scenes and activities, as well as its history have been subjects of stamp issues.

Philatelic Bureau: Postmaster, Jamestown, St. Helena, South Atlantic.

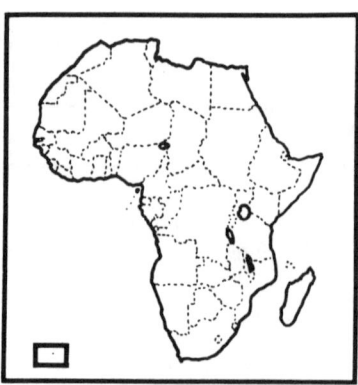

TUNISIA, REPUBLIC OF

Area: 63,378 sq. miles
Population: 7,202,000 (1984)
Capital: Tunis
Currency: Dinar (1,000 millimes)

Tunisia has a 1,000-mile coastline on the Mediterranean and is divided into a fertile northern portion, a central coastal plain, and a semi-arid plateau that merges south into the Sahara Desert.

The north has a Mediterranean climate with mild but wet winters and hot summers. In the south, the weather is hot and dry all year.

The area occupied by Tunisia has a long history. It is the site of Carthage, the capital city of the civilization that tried to fight both Greece and Rome. The Romans finally won in 146 BC, but the fame of Carthage lives on.

The Romans continued to develop the area and the surviving remnants of their work indicate a state of prosperity not equaled since. Islam came to Tunisia in AD 670, but it was some years before the country was completely converted. The Turks had taken over and ruled by the 16th century and Tunisia remained part of the Ottoman Empire for several hundred years.

By the 1880s, France had replaced the Turks and it became a French protectorate in 1883. The French brought a new energy to replace the ineptness of the Turks and there was considerable development.

After World War I, the voice of nationalism began to be heard in the

land but the French were not listening. Pressure built as a weakened France tried to re-assert its control after World War II. However, France was unable to control the demands for freedom and was forced to withdraw. Tunisia became independent on March 20, 1956.

The economy is varied, with textiles, oil, and tourism predominating. Crops include grain, dates, olives, citrus, figs, and grapes.

The 1983 per capita income was $844 and the 1984 literacy rate was 62%.

Stamps were first issued in 1888 by the French. Subsequent issues followed the usual French colonial pattern.

Since independence, stamp issues have not been excessive.

Philatelic Bureau: Service Philatelique des PTT, Bureau Directeur de Tunis Recette Principale, Tunis, Tunisia.

UGANDA, REPUBLIC OF

Area: 93,104 sq. miles
Population: 14,268,000 (1984)
Capital: Kampala
Currency: Shilling (100 cents)

Uganda is located on the equator and comprises a plateau 3,000-6,000 feet above sea level. A chain of mountains called *The Mountains of the Moon* rising to more than 16,500 feet form part of the western border with Zaire. Lakes also form much of the country's borders.

The climate is modified by altitude. The northeast is arid with less than 20 inches of rain a year, increasing to about 50 inches in the west and southwest.

Arab traders arriving in the 1830s found African kingdoms with political establishments several centuries old in the area that is now Uganda.

British explorers searching for the headwaters of the Nile followed in the 1860s. Captain John Speke was the first. He reached Lake Victoria in 1862. British influence grew until a protectorate was proclaimed in 1894. Uganda remained under British administration until independence was granted on Oct. 9, 1962.

In 1971, Idi Amin seized power and his barbaric seven-year reign was marked by a brutality that sickened the civilized world. The

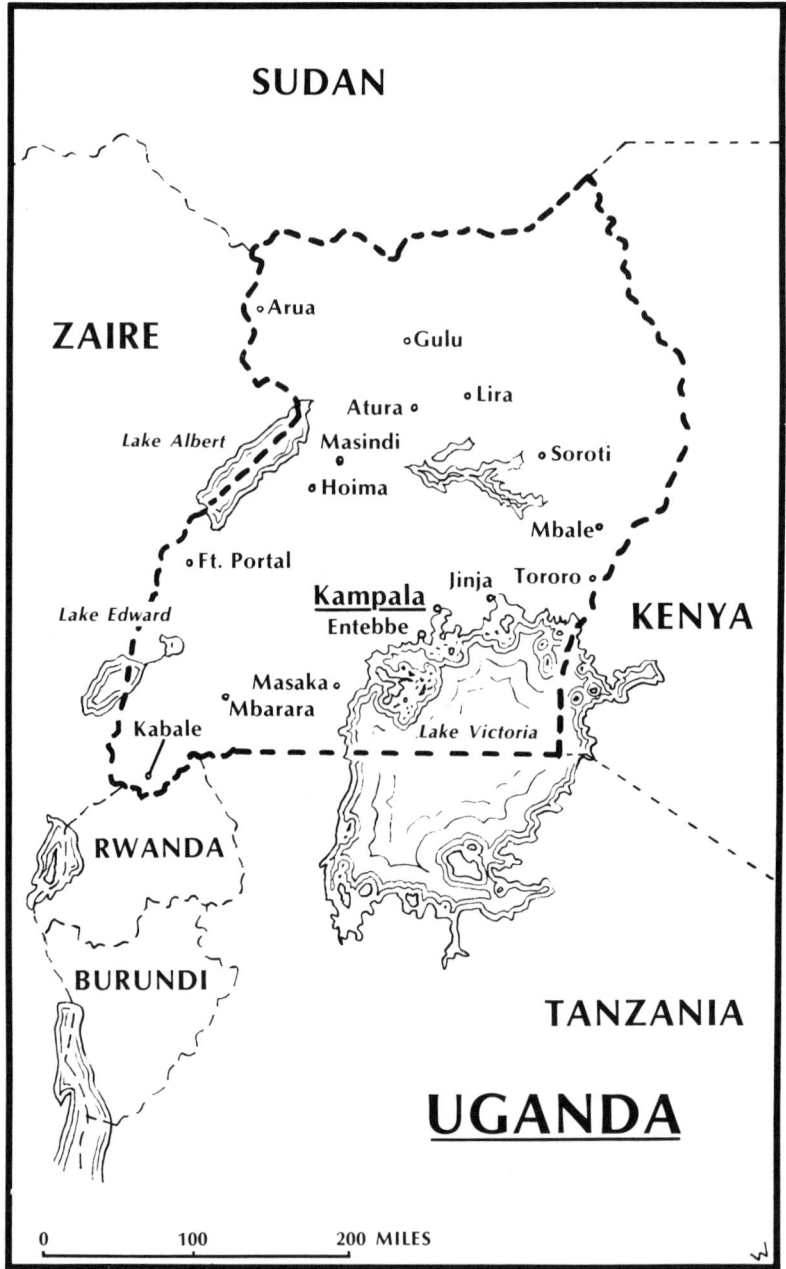

degree of his corruption and his crimes against humanity outlined at the 1977 Commonwealth Conference caused Western nations to end aid to the regime.

The economy, wrecked by Amin, remains in chaos. Coffee, cotton, tea, peanuts, bananas, and sugar are grown and there are cobalt and copper deposits. Recent statistics on the per capita income and literacy rate are lacking, but in 1976 the per capita income was $240 and in 1978 the literacy rate was 25%.

The first stamps were the famous typewritten stamps created in 1895 by the Rev. Ernest Miller. At various times, Uganda has shared stamp issues with Kenya and Tanganyika and later, with the East African Postal and Telecommunications Administration. It has had its own stamps exclusively since 1977.

Philatelic Bureau: Uganda Posts and Telecommunications Corp., Dept. of Posts, Stamp Bureau, Box 231, Kampala, Uganda.

ZAIRE, REPUBLIC OF

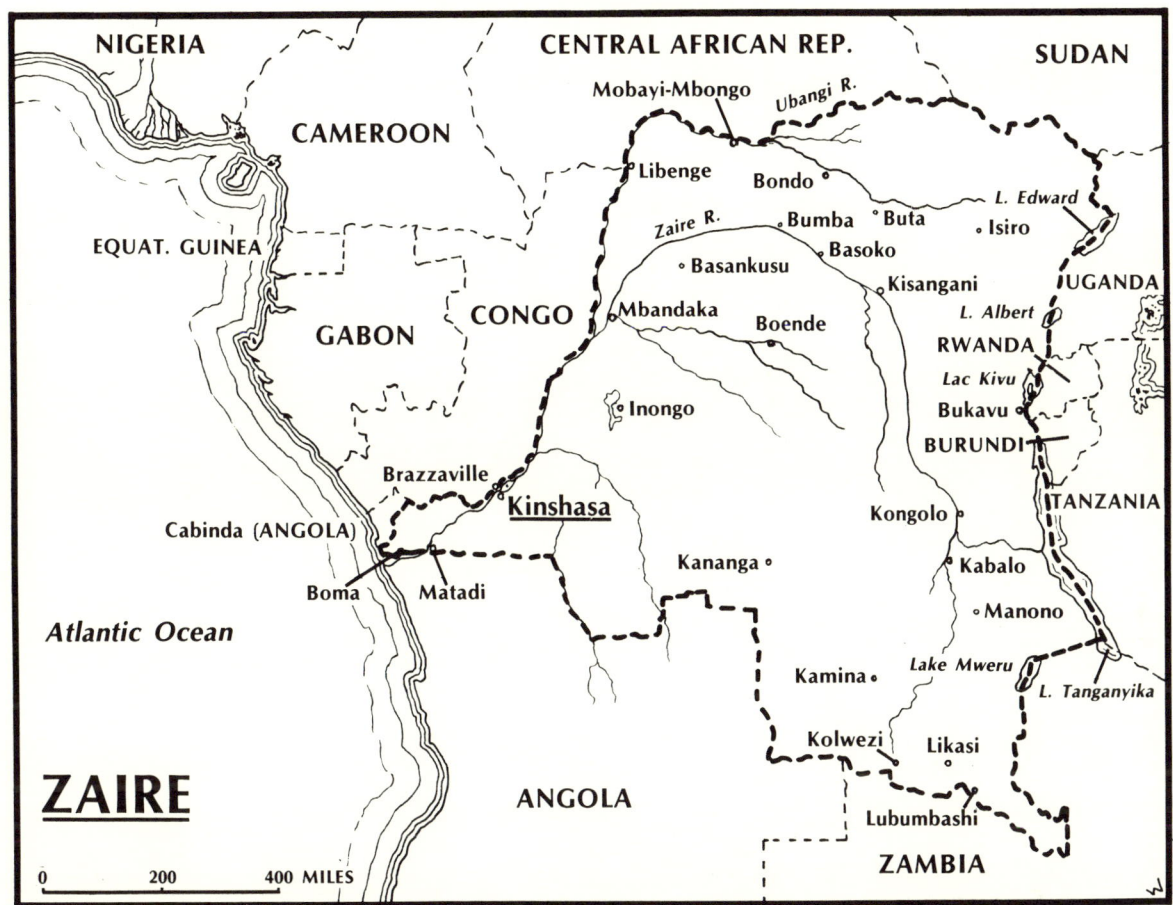

Area: 905,365 sq. miles
Population: 32,158,000 (1983).
Capital: Kinshasa
Currency: Zaire (100 ma-kuta)

Mostly comprising the Congo (Zaire) River basin, Zaire was formerly known as the Congo Democratic Republic and before that, the Belgian Congo.

The name was changed to Zaire on Oct. 27, 1971. It is a Kikongo word meaning "river."

There is a very short Atlantic coastline at the mouth of the Congo (Zaire) River and the large, low-lying central area is covered with tropical rain forest. There are uplands to the west, savannah in the south, and grasslands in the northwest. The eastern region is mountainous.

The climate is generally hot and humid with an average annual rainfall of 42 inches.

King Leopold II of Belgium laid claim to the area in 1885 after employing the American journalist Henry Morton Stanley to explore it, and what is now Zaire became Leopold's personal kingdom under the name of Congo Free State. Abuse of native workers led to international condemnation and in 1907 it was ceded to Belgium as the colony of the Belgian Congo.

Independence came on June 30, 1960. Since then, political instability, violence, and rebellions have been common. This has prevented the development of a healthy economy and the country is poor despite being rich in mineral resources. There are no recent figures, but in 1975 the per capita income was $127 and the 1980 literacy rate was 40% for men and 15% for women.

Since independence, stamp issues have been frequent and subjects have run the gamut of topics popular with collectors.

From 1960-63, the rebel province of Katanga issued stamps. Although not all catalogs recognize them, they appear to have been tolerated in the international mails.

Philatelic Bureau: Bureau Philatelic, Box 1981, Kinshasa 1, Zaire, or Agences Philateliques Gouvernementales, Chaussee de Waterloo 868/ 870, 1180 Brussels, Belgium.

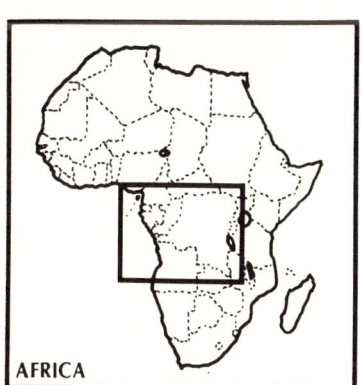

ZAMBIA, REPUBLIC OF

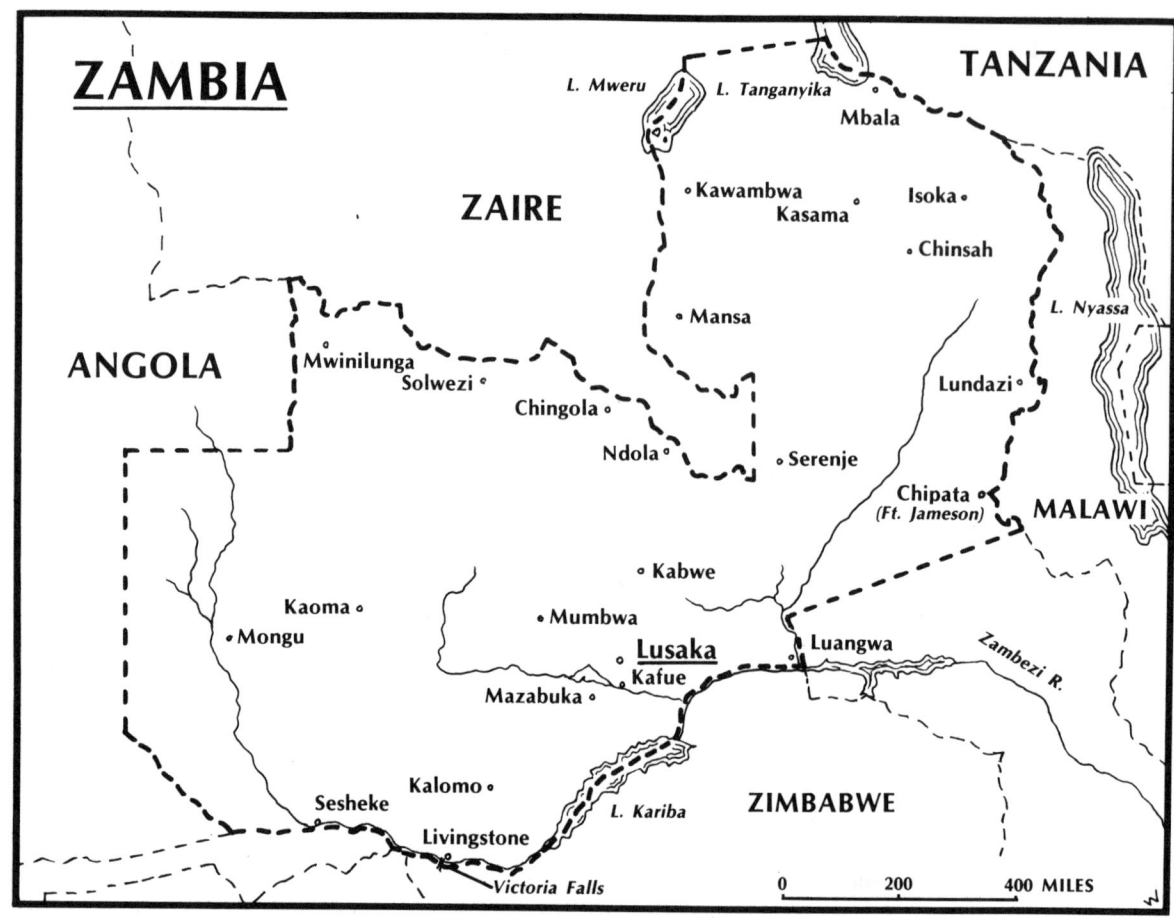

Area: 290,586 sq. miles
Population: 6,554,000 (1984)
Capital: Lusaka
Currency: Kwacha (100 ngwee)

Zambia is mostly high plateau ranging from 3,000-4,000 feet in elevation. It drains in the north to the Congo (Zaire) River system and in the south to the Zambezi River.

The famous Victoria Falls are on the Zambezi River near the city of Livingstone.

The climate is subtropical with maximum temperatures from 80-100 degrees F in summer and minimums ranging from 45-55 degrees F in winter. Rainfall averages about 30 inches a year.

With the possible exception of Portuguese explorers, the area was not visited by Europeans until the mid-19th century, when David Livingstone came upon Victoria Falls in 1855.

Cecil Rhodes obtained mineral rights and brought British influence in 1888. The area was administered by the British South Africa Co. until 1924, when what is now Zambia was made the British Protectorate of Northern Rhodesia.

In 1953, Northern and Southern Rhodesia and Nyasaland joined to form the Federation of Rhodesia and Nyasaland in 1953. It broke up in 1963.

Northern Rhodesia became independent as the Republic of Zambia on Oct. 24, 1964.

The economy is based on copper and Zambia is the world's third-largest producer after the United States and Canada. The decline in copper prices and recent drought have hurt the country's economy and caused famine.

The 1982 per capita income was $570 and the 1984 literacy rate was 54%.

Stamps were first issued in the area in 1890 and depict the coat of arms of the British South Africa Co. They are listed in the catalogs under Rhodesia.

In 1905, a very handsome set was issued depicting Victoria Falls that proved popular with collectors.

Since independence, Zambia's stamp-issuing policies have been moderate and responsible.

Philatelic Bureau: Philatelic Bureau, Box 1857, Ndola, Zambia.

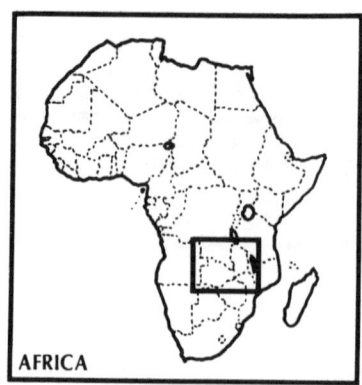

ZIL ELWANNYEN SESEL

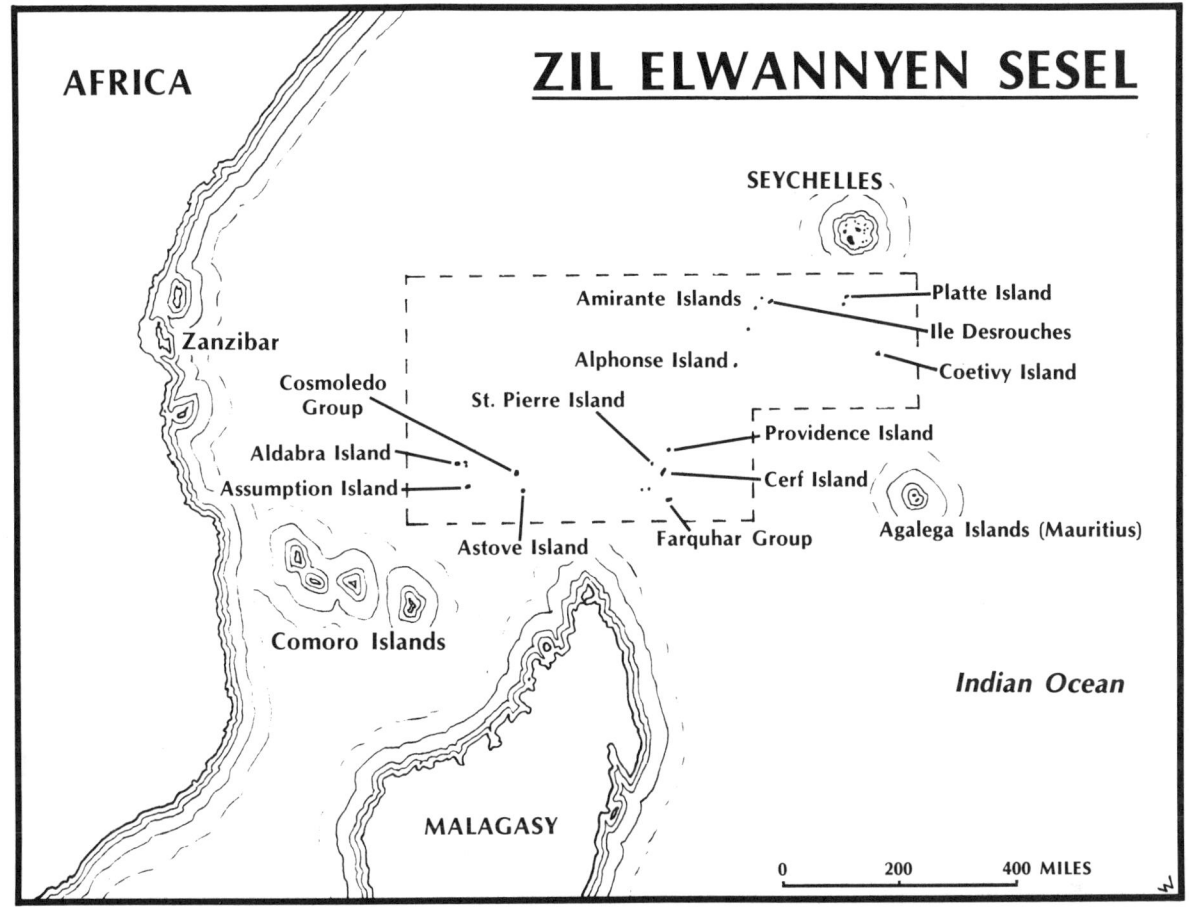

Population: 3,000

Zil Elwannyen Sesel is the name given to the so-called "Outer Islands" of the Seychelles that are located to the south of the main group.

Prior to the independence of the Seychelles on June 29, 1976, the outer islands had been administered as part of the British Indian Ocean Territory. When the Seychelles became independent, the islands were made part of the new republic.

They comprise some 25 coral islands and atolls, including the island groups of Amirante, Farquhar, and Aldabra. Nine islands are inhabited. Guano, copra, timber, and tortoise shell are main sources of income.

Stamps were first issued for the islands on June 20, 1980.

Although the official announcement of the stamps stated that for some years, the outer islands had been without postal service, there seems no reason why this could not have been provided by the Seychelles Post Office, using the country's own stamps. The prospect of multiple stamp sales must be considered as the main reason for their release. They are not recognized by all catalogs.

Since the stamps were first issued, the spelling of their inscription has been changed twice. The first spelling used was "Zil Eloigne Sesel." This was subsequently changed to "Zil Elwagne Sesel," and later changed again to the present spelling of "Zil Elwannyen Sesel."

Philatelic Bureau: Philatelic Bureau, P.O. Box 60, Victoria, Mahe, Seychelles, Indian Ocean.

ZIMBABWE

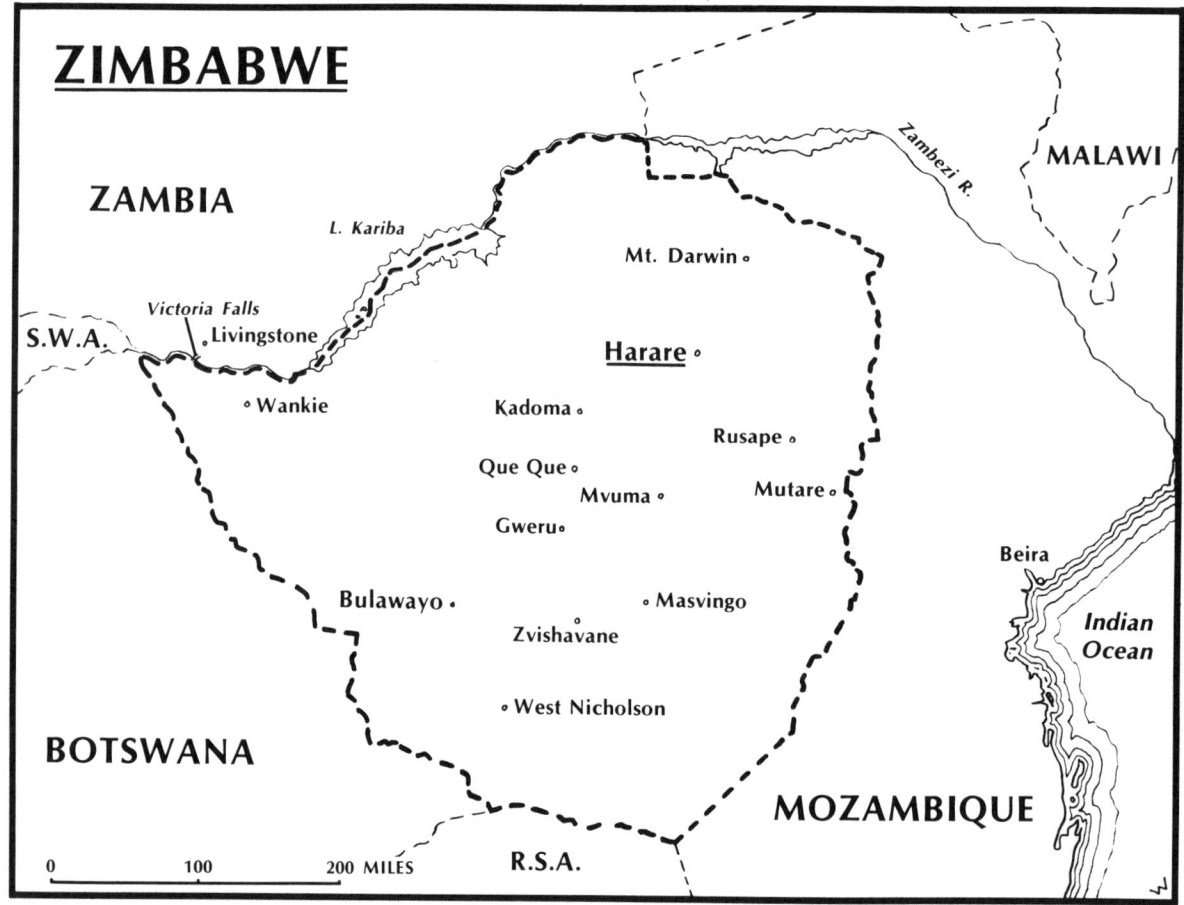

Area: 150,873 sq. miles
Population: 8,325,000 (1984)
Capital: Harare
Currency: Dollar (100 cents)

Formerly the British colony of Southern Rhodesia, Zimbabwe is mainly high plateau from 3,000-4,000 feet in elevation, with a 4,000-5,000-foot strip running diagonally across the country from northeast to southwest.

The climate is subtropical and varies with altitude. Maximum summer temperatures are from 80-100 degrees F and minimum winter temperatures are from 35-45 degrees F. Rainfall generally is about 30 inches a year.

There is evidence of a culture dating back to the 9th to 13th centuries in Zimbabwe. The Portuguese in the 16th century were the first European visitors.

Cecil Rhodes was active in bringing commercial development when he obtained mineral rights from tribal chiefs in 1888.

The British colony of Southern Rhodesia was formed in 1923, after the white population had rejected union with South Africa.

On Nov. 11, 1965, the colony declared its own independence, but the international community did not recognize the declaration because the black majority played no part in the rebel government. After a period of unrest and virtual civil war, Great Britain, by a miracle of diplomacy, brought the rebel colony to the point at which free elections could be held.

On April 18, 1980, the new country of Zimbabwe was born.

There is some industrial development, but the country's wealth is in its mineral resources, which include chromium, gold, nickel, copper, iron, and coal.

There are no up-to-date figures on per capita income, but the 1980 literacy rate was 45%.

Philatelic Bureau: Posts and Telecommunications Corp., Box 4220, Harare, Zimbabwe.

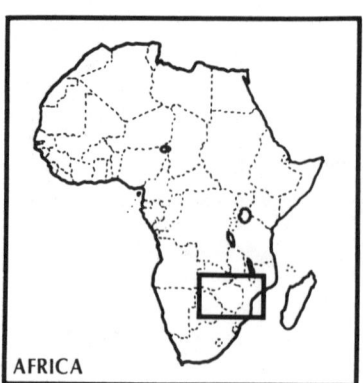

SOUTHWEST ASIA

Stamp-issuing areas:

.1 Afghanistan
.2 Bahrain
.3 Iran
.4 Iraq
5. Israel
6. Jordan
7. Kuwait
8. Lebanon
9. Oman
10. Pakistan
11. Qatar
12. Saudi Arabia
13. Syria
14. Turkey
15. United Arab Emirates
16. Yemen Arab Republic
17. Yemen, PDR

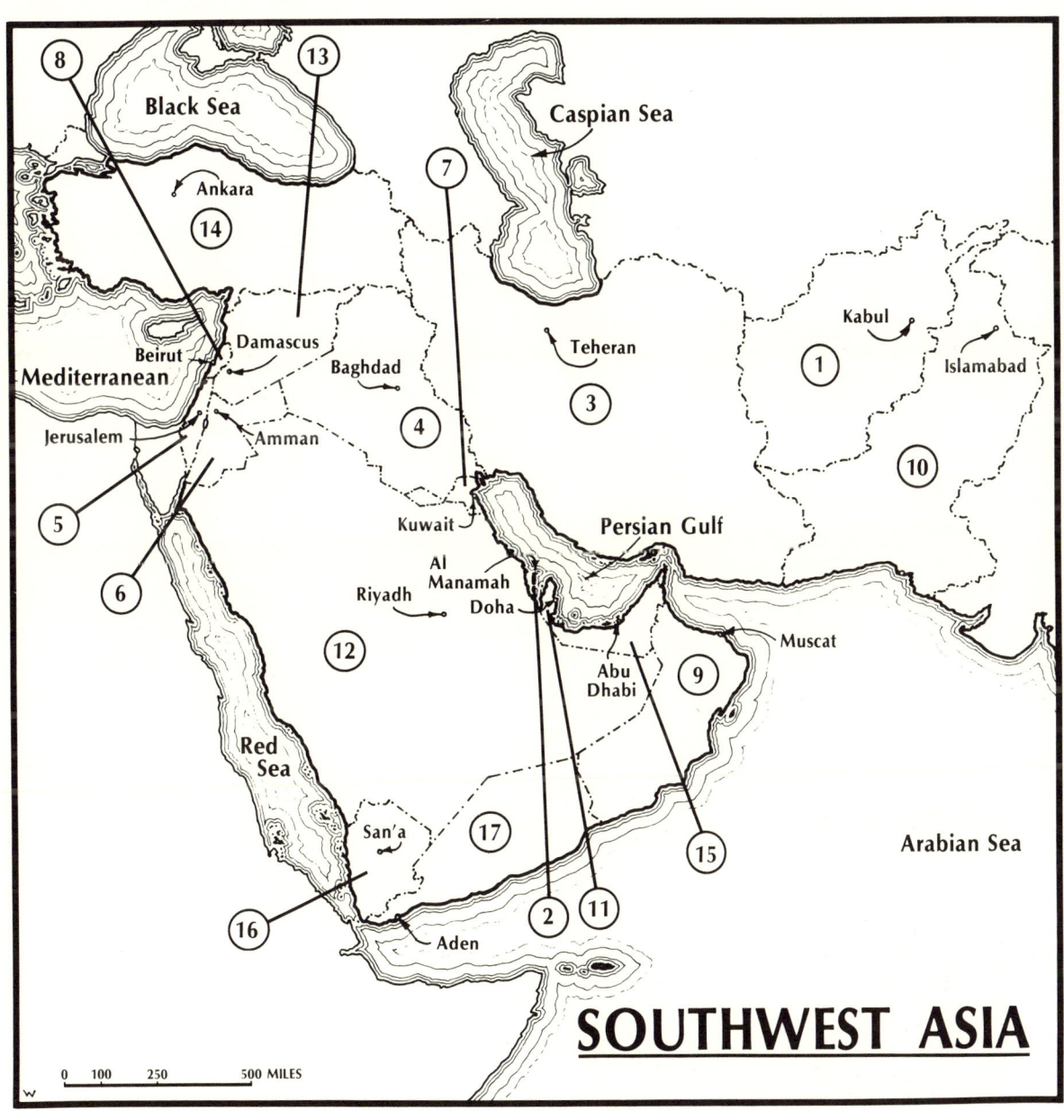

AFGHANISTAN, DEMOCRATIC REPUBLIC OF

Area: 251,772 sq. miles
Population: 14,448,000 (1984)
Capital: Kabul
Currency: Afghani (100 pouls)

Afghanistan has often suffered for its strategic location at what has been called the crossroads of central Asia, and it is still suffering.

The country is composed of a series of mountain ranges rising to 25,000 feet, between which are small valleys watered by mountain streams.

The climate is cold in winter and hot in summer, with extensive variations in both time and place. At Kabul, the temperature can rise 40 degrees F between sunrise and noon. The city's average January temperature is 32 degrees F. At Jalalabad, temperatures up to 115 degrees F have been recorded. Rainfall is light and does not usually exceed 15 inches a year.

Afghanistan has always been in the path of invaders, from Alexander the Great in 328 BC to today's Soviet forces.

Over the years many intruders followed Alexander, including Scythians, Turks, Arabs, Persians, Ghengis Kahn, Tamerlane, and the Moghuls. In 1747, Ahmad Shah Durrani formed a unified kingdom.

The monarchy ruled until 1973, when it was overthrown in a coup and replaced by a republican form of government. Pro-Soviet leftists took over in a bloody 1978 coup. However, they were not sufficiently subservient and the Soviet Union invaded the country in 1979.

The inhabitants have resisted strongly and the conquest is still stalled, despite large numbers of Soviet troops, estimated at up to 100,000.

The country's economy is poor and the 1978 per capita income was $168. The 1982 literacy rate was 10%.

Stamps were first issued in 1871. These are the famous Tiger's Heads that were canceled by having a piece torn from them. In recent years stamp issues have not been frequent.

Philatelic Bureau: Director of Posts, Philatelic Section, Kabul, Afghanistan.

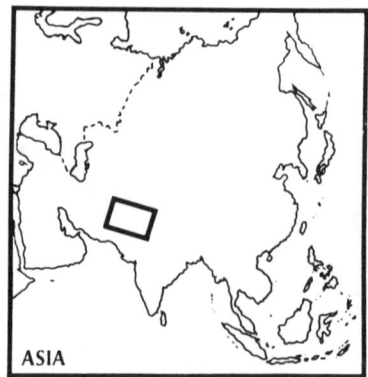

BAHRAIN, STATE OF

Area: 258 sq. miles
Population: 409,000 (1984)
Capital: Al Manamah
Currency: Dinar (1,000 fils)

Bahrain is an emirate in the Persian Gulf made rich by oil. It is located off the coast of Saudi Arabia, near the peninsula of Qatar.

The main island is mostly a low plateau with a high point of only 445 feet and is connected by causeways to two adjacent islands. Saudi Arabia has completed a 15-mile causeway to connect Bahrain with the mainland.

The climate is hot and humid. Temperatures commonly reach 106 degrees F and the humidity ranges from 70-80% except during a brief winter season. Less than four inches of rain falls each year.

Bahrain has long been an important commercial and trading center and is mentioned in the literature of the Assyrians, Persians, Greeks, and Romans.

Captured by the Portuguese in 1521, it was taken by Persian in 1602 and held by that country until 1783.

In the 19th century, Britain took action on several occasions to protect the islands from being taken by Oman, Turkey, Persia, and Egypt.

By 1861, Britain had agreed to protect the islands on a permanent basis in exchange for a promise by the sheik to refrain from war, acts of piracy, or the practice of slavery.

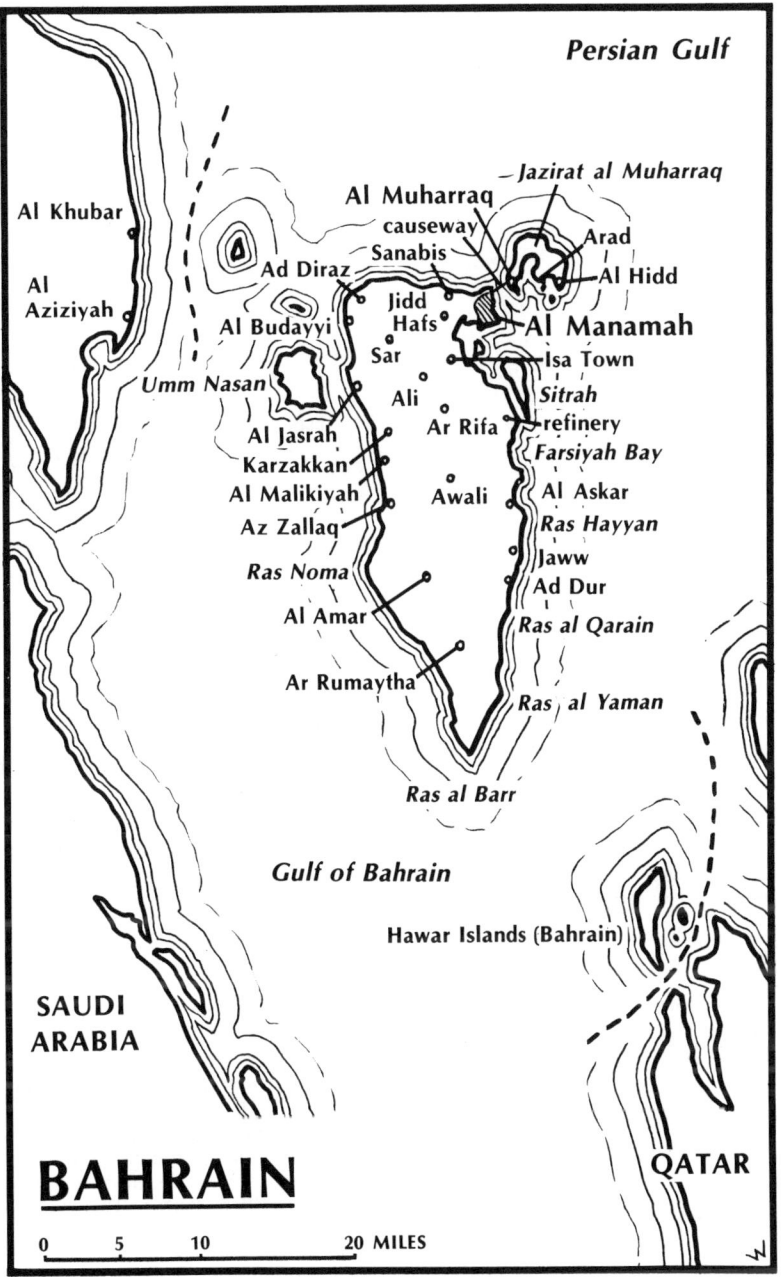

When Britain announced it would end its Persian Gulf presence in 1971, Bahrain joined with other Gulf states in an attempt to form a union of Arab emirates in the area. The union was not successful.

Bahrain then decided to become an independent country and did so on Aug. 15, 1971.

Before the discovery of oil in the early 1930s, Bahrain's economy was based on pearl fishing. Fortunately, as this declined in the face of competition from the cultured pearl industry, oil more than took up the slack. In fact, it made Bahrain rich.

As its own oil supplies become depleted, Bahrain is making another major adjustment in its economy. It is now a major international banking center and has a large aluminum smelting plant.

The 1980 per capita income was $6,315 and the 1982 literacy rate was 40%.

Bahrain's first stamps were issued in 1933 and were Indian stamps overprinted and used by the Indian postal administration, which operated Bahrain's postal service. Since independence it has followed a moderate issue policy.

Philatelic Bureau: Philatelic Bureau, Postal Directorate, Box 1212, Bahrain, Persian Gulf.

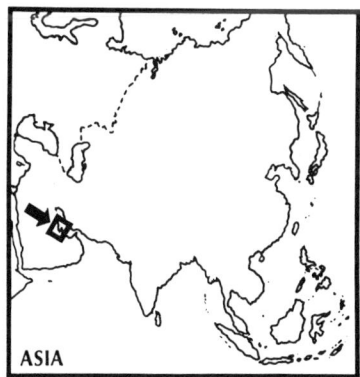

IRAN, ISLAMIC REPUBLIC OF

Area: 636,363 sq. miles
Population: 43,280,000 (1984)
Capital: Tehran
Currency: Rial

An area of arid plains and highlands surrounded by a rugged mountain rim, most of Iran's population lives in the north, around Tehran and along the Caspian shore. About 70% of the land area, mostly the desert and mountains of the south, is almost uninhabited.

Tehran has a July average temperature of 85 degrees F and maximum summer temperatures can reach 110-115 degrees F.

Along the Persian gulf and southern coasts, it is cooler, although the humidity is generally high. Northern Iran is cold in winter and at Tabriz, the average January temperature is 29 degrees F.

Rainfall is variable and erratic. It ranges from four inches a year in the low interior basins to more than 40 inches along the Caspian coast.

The history of Iran ranges from the glory of the Persian Empire about the fifth century BC to the poverty ridden chaos that has existed since the 1979 revolution.

The Arabs brought Islam to Persia in AD 700 and during the Middle Ages, both Turks and Mongols took their turns at ruling the country.

British influence was strong in the country beginning the 19th century. During World War II a route through the country passed massive amounts of supplies to the Soviet Union from the United States and Britain. In 1946, despite an agreement to respect Iran's territory, the Soviet Union unsuccessfully attempted to take over the Azerbaijan region of Iran.

In recent years, under the rule of the Shah, there was economic and social progress. Literacy grew and the lot of women improved. But his rule was autocratic.

A regime took power in 1979 under Ayatollah Ruhollah Khomeini that proved even more autocratic and repressive. Under it, the country has become almost medieval. The economy is in chaos and the country is warring with Iraq.

The first stamps were issued about 1870. Recent issues have been largely political and propagandistic.

Philatelic Bureau: Philatelic Bureau, General directorate of Posts, Tehran, Iran.

IRAQ, REPUBLIC OF

Area: 167,924 sq. miles
Population: 15,000,000 (1984)
Capital: Baghdad
Currency: Dinar (1,000 fils)

Iraq covers territory ranging from 10,000-foot mountains along the northern border with Turkey and Iran, to reed-covered swamps at the head of the Persian Gulf.

Much of the country is influenced by the twin river systems of the Euphrates and Tigris, the waters of which irrigate large areas of the two fertile valleys through which they flow. Lower Iraq is subject to severe flooding by both rivers.

A large part of western Iraq is desert.

Historically known as Mesopotamia, Iraq was the site of Sumerian, Babylonian, and Parthian cultures.

Baghdad became a center of government in the eighth century AD and by 1638 was a frontier outpost of the Ottoman Empire.

The area became a British mandated territory after the World War I defeat of Turkey and was made independent in 1932.

Ruled as a constitutional monarchy until 1958, Iraq has since been in a state of turmoil as coup has followed coup.

On Sept. 22, 1980, Iraqi aircraft attacked Iranian airfields and Iranian aircraft retaliated. Since then the two countries have been involved in a bitter war, with heavy ground fighting along the border resulting in many casualties on both sides.

Oil is still the basis of Iraq's economy, although dates are an important export.

The 1981 per capita income was $2,410, although this has dropped in recent years. The literacy rate is 70%.

Following a post-World War I period during which British occupying forces overprinted and surcharged Turkish stamps, special stamps for Iraq were issued beginning in 1923.

Recent stamps have had a strong political theme. Designs are mostly symbolic.

Philatelic Bureau: Posts and Savings Administration, Stamp Department, Philatelic Bureau, Baghdad, Iraq.

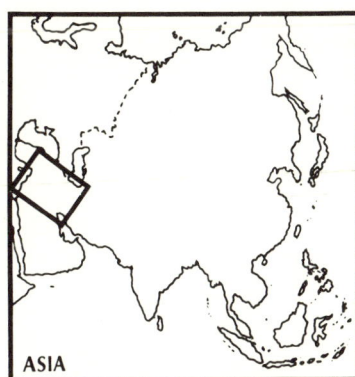

ISRAEL, STATE OF

Area: 7,850 sq. miles
Population: 4,024,000 (1984)
Capital: Jerusalem
Currency: Shekel (10 agorot)

Israel has four geographic regions; the coastal strip, central mountains, the Rift Valley of the Jordan River, and the Negev Desert.

The climate is temperate, except in the Negev, which is hot. On the coast the average winter maximum temperature is 60-65 degrees F. Rainfall is about 30 inches a year in the north, 20 inches in the central area, and less than eight inches in the Negev.

Israel was created May 14, 1948 from the area of the Ottoman Empire taken by British forces in World War I and mandated to Britain by the League of Nations after the war.

It has been in a constant state of war with its Arab neighbors.

On March 26, 1979, Israel and Egypt signed a peace treaty ending 30 years of war, although other Arab countries have condemned Egypt.

Industries include aviation, munitions, textiles, electronics, diamond cutting, plastics, and drugs. Citrus fruit, olives, and cotton are important crops.

The 1983 per capita income was $5,609 and the 1984 literacy rate was 88% (Jewish) and 48% (Arab).

Stamps were first issued during the British mandate period.

Philatelic Bureau: Ministry of Communications, Philatelic Services, Tel Aviv-Yafo 61 080, Israel.

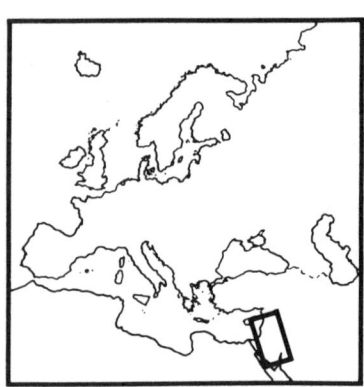

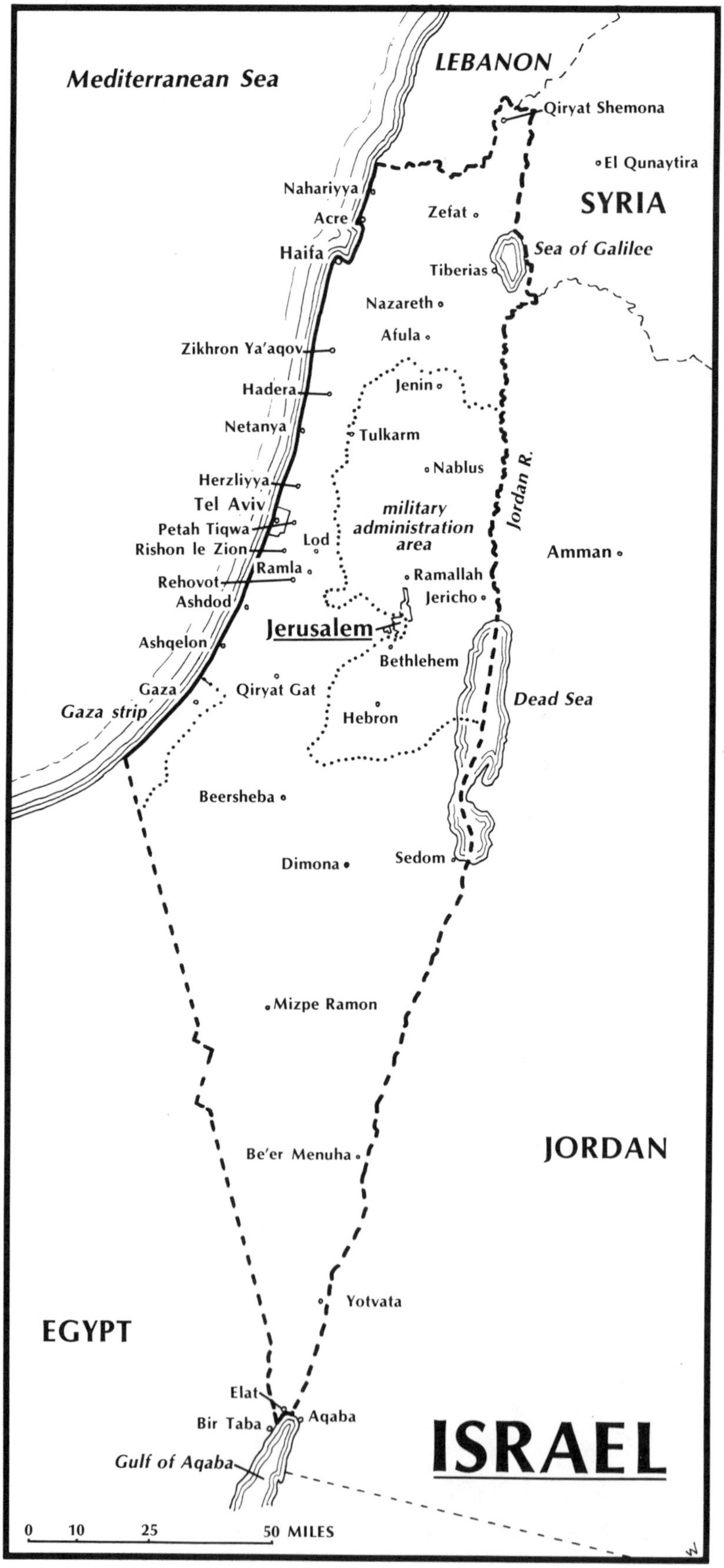

JORDAN, HASHEMITE KINGDOM OF

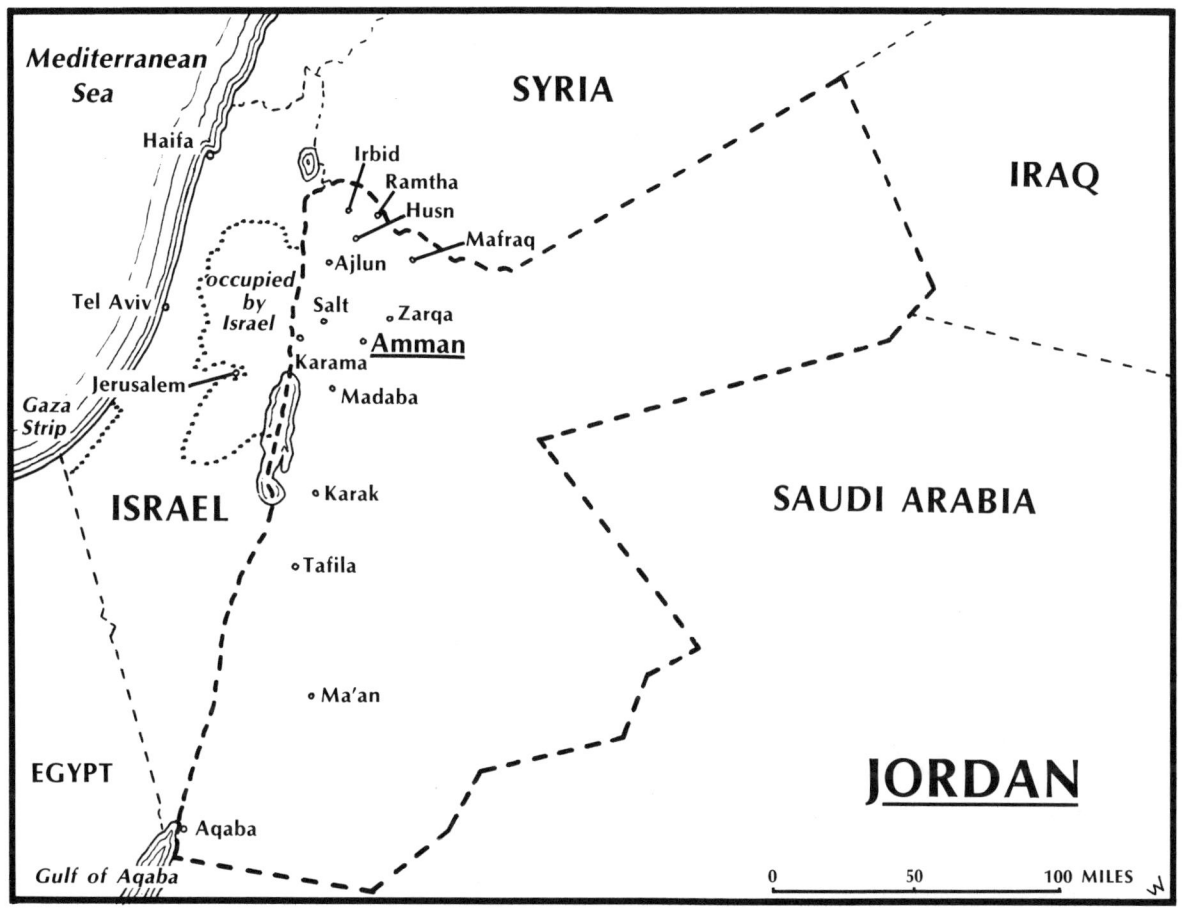

Area: 37,297 sq. miles
Population: 2,689,000 (1984)
Capital: Amman
Currency: Dinar (1,000 fils)

Jordan is mostly arid desert. Only about 12% of its area is agricultural, located mostly immediately to the east of the Jordan River and the Dead Sea, where the rainfall is moderate.

The rainy season is from November to March and the rest of the year is very dry.

Amman has an average January temperature of 50 degrees F and 90 degrees F in August.

Jordan has an outlet to the sea via the port of Aqaba.

The country was part of the Ottoman Empire from the 16th century. British forces freed the area during World War I. After the war it was made a British mandated territory by the League of Nations and in 1922 the autonomous state of Transjordan was created.

When Israel was formed, the West Bank of the Jordan River and the old city of Jerusalem was added to the kingdom, which changed its name to Jordan. This territory was subsequently lost to Israel in the 1967 war, which resulted in a large number of refugees from across the river into Jordan.

The Palestinian resistance movement then gained considerable power in Jordan and began to prove a threat to the security of the country, especially since it regarded parts of both Israel and Jordan as its rightful land.

In 1970, open conflict broke out, with the Palestinians being covertly aided by Syria. A Syrian tank force, disguised as a Palestinian force, entered Jordan. It withdrew as the Jordanian army gained control of the situaion and the Palestinians were expelled from the country. The army was created from the famous British-trained Arab Legion.

The country's economy is not extensive. Textiles are made and olives and grains are grown. Tourism is important and there is some light industry at Aqaba.

The first stamps were issued during the British mandate period. The country's stamp-issuing policy has been moderate and stamp subjects have been Jordan related.

Philatelic Bureau: Ministry of Communications, Philatelic Section, PO Box 71, Amman, Jordan.

KUWAIT, STATE OF

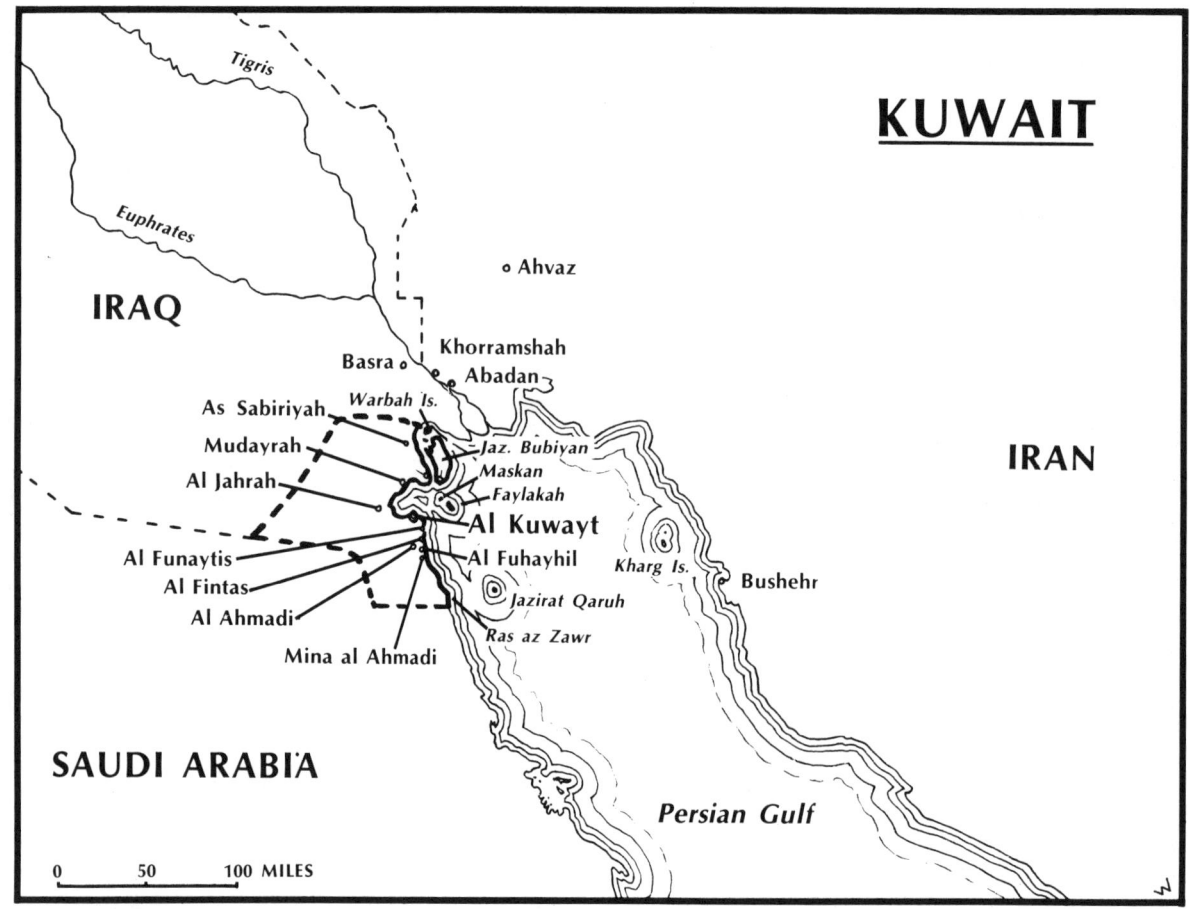

Area: 6,532 sq. miles
Population: 1,758,000 (1984)
Capital: Al Kuwayt
Currency: Dinar (1,000 fils)

Kuwait is located at the northwestern corner of the Persian Gulf. It occupies a mainland area and several islands in the gulf. The name is said to be derived from the word "kut," meaning "small fort."

With the exception of a small oasis at Al Jahrah, the country is pure desert.

The climate is hot, with summer temperatures reaching 130 degrees F. Rainfall is usually less than four inches a year, falling mostly in winter.

Kuwait's modern history began in 1740, when the city of Kuwait was established by people from the area of Qatar.

In the late 1770s, the British operated their Aleppo-Persian Gulf mail service from Kuwait, while the terminus at Bushire was occupied by the Persians.

In 1899, Kuwait signed a treaty with Great Britain that provided for protection and British handling of Kuwait's foreign affairs. The treaty was in effect until 1961, when Britain withdrew and Kuwait became independent.

Oil, discovered in the 1930s, is the only source of Kuwait's wealth. By the Mid-1970s Kuwait was one of the world's richest countries, with a per capita income in 1975 of $11,430. Although the recent decline in oil prices has reduced the level of prosperity somewhat, the country is still well off.

Oil profits have provided free medical services, free education, and a wide range of social services for Kuwait's people. There are no taxes, except for customs duties. The 1983 literacy rate was 71%.

Although there is little or no agriculture, there is some commercial fishing.

Stamps inscribed "Kuwait" were issued in 1958. Previously stamps of India had been used, then Indian stamps overprinted "Kuwait."

On Feb. 1, 1959, Kuwait became responsible for its own postal affairs.

A relatively large number of stamps has been issued in recent years.

Philatelic Bureau: Director, Post Office Department, Philatelic Bureau, Safat Post Office, Kuwait.

LEBANON, REPUBLIC OF

Area: 3,950 sq. miles
Population: 2,601,000 (1984)
Capital: Beirut
Currency: Pound (100 centimes)

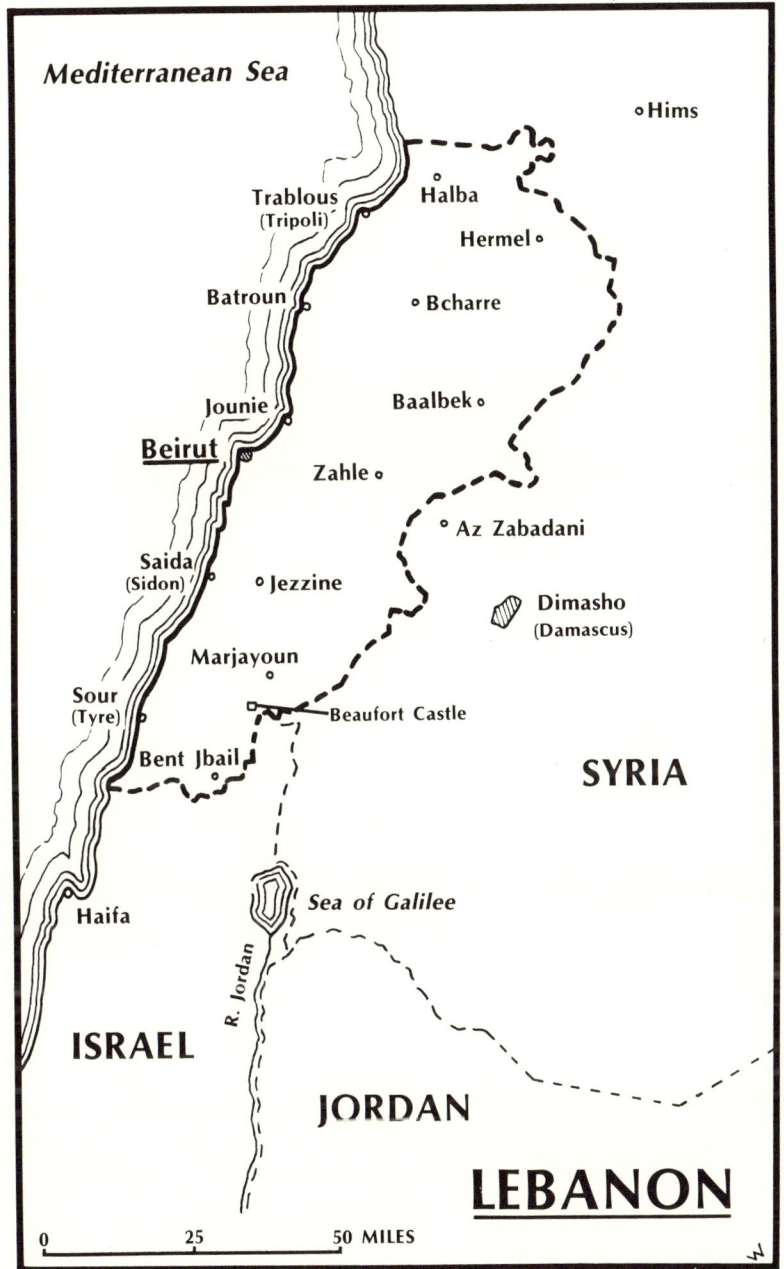

An unhappy country torn by religious strife, barbaric terrorism, and violated by its neighbors, Lebanon is composed of a coastal strip backed by mountain, the fertile central Bekaa Valley, and more mountains along the border with Syria.

The climate is similar to that of California and varies with altitude and location. On the coast, summers are hot and winters mild, with an average annual rainfall of 30-40 inches. Temperatures average 60 degrees F in January and 90 degrees F in July. In the Bekaa Valley, they vary from a 50 degree F average in January to 90 degrees F in July. Rainfall there runs from 15-25 inches a year.

Lebanon was the home of the Phoenicians, who used it as a base for their extensive maritime civilization from about 2700-450 BC. The ruins at Baalbek are famous.

For many years the area was dominated by the Turks as part of the Ottoman Empire, but was liberated during World War I.

After the war, the League of Nations mandated it to France. Although the mandate called for an independent Lebanon, France refused to leave and considerable unrest resulted. Partial autonomy was granted in 1927, but it was not until 1943 that Lebanon became independent.

Since 1975, the country has been in an almost continuous state of civil war between Christian and Moslem, aggravated by Palestino terrorist elements, which have used the country as a base for attacks on Israel.

In 1982, Israel invaded southern Lebanon forcing the Palestinians to leave the country.

The 1983 per capita income was $1,150 and the 1984 literacy rate was 75%.

The stamps of Lebanon date from 1924, when French stamps were issued overprinted "GRAND LIBAN." Various overprints continued until 1925, when a set picturing local scenes was issued.

Most stamps of Lebanon have been air mail issues, although in recent years few stamps of any kind have been issued.

After the 1975-76 hostilities, when the civil war cooled for a while, pre-war stocks of stamps were overprinted with a security net design in a number of variations, because of the existence of large quantities of looted stamps.

Philatelic Bureau: Receveur Principal des Postes, Service Philatelique, Beirut, Lebanon.

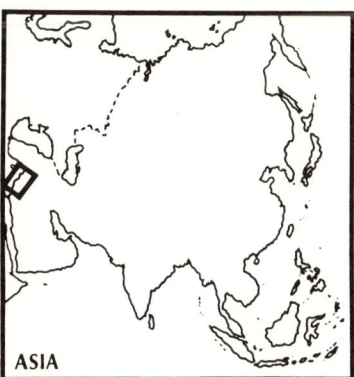

OMAN, SULTANATE OF

Area: 120,000 sq. miles
Population: 1,009,000 (1984)
Capital: Muscat
Currency: Rial (1,000 baizas)

Located in a strategic position at the mouth of the Persian Gulf, Oman comprises a large area facing on the Gulf of Oman and the Arabian Sea, plus a small portion at the tip of the Musandam Peninsula on the Strait of Hormuz. This area is separated from the rest of Oman by territory of the United Arab Emirates.

A long stretch of Oman's border with the UAE and Saudi Arabia is undefined.

The climate is hot. Average high and low temperatures for January are 65 and 77 degrees F, and for June are 84 and 94 degrees F. Rainfall varies between 1½ and 3½ inches a year.

The area's first contact with Europeans was in 1508, when the Portuguese occupied parts of the coast. They stayed until 1650.

By 1832, the ruler of Muscat and Oman had built an impressive empire, reaching as far as East Africa and the island of Zanzibar, with extensive settlements along the coast of Persian and what is now Pakistan.

There had been a long history of association with Great Britain, going back to a 1798 treaty of friendship. A new treaty was signed in 1951 and recognized Muscat and Oman as a fully independent state.

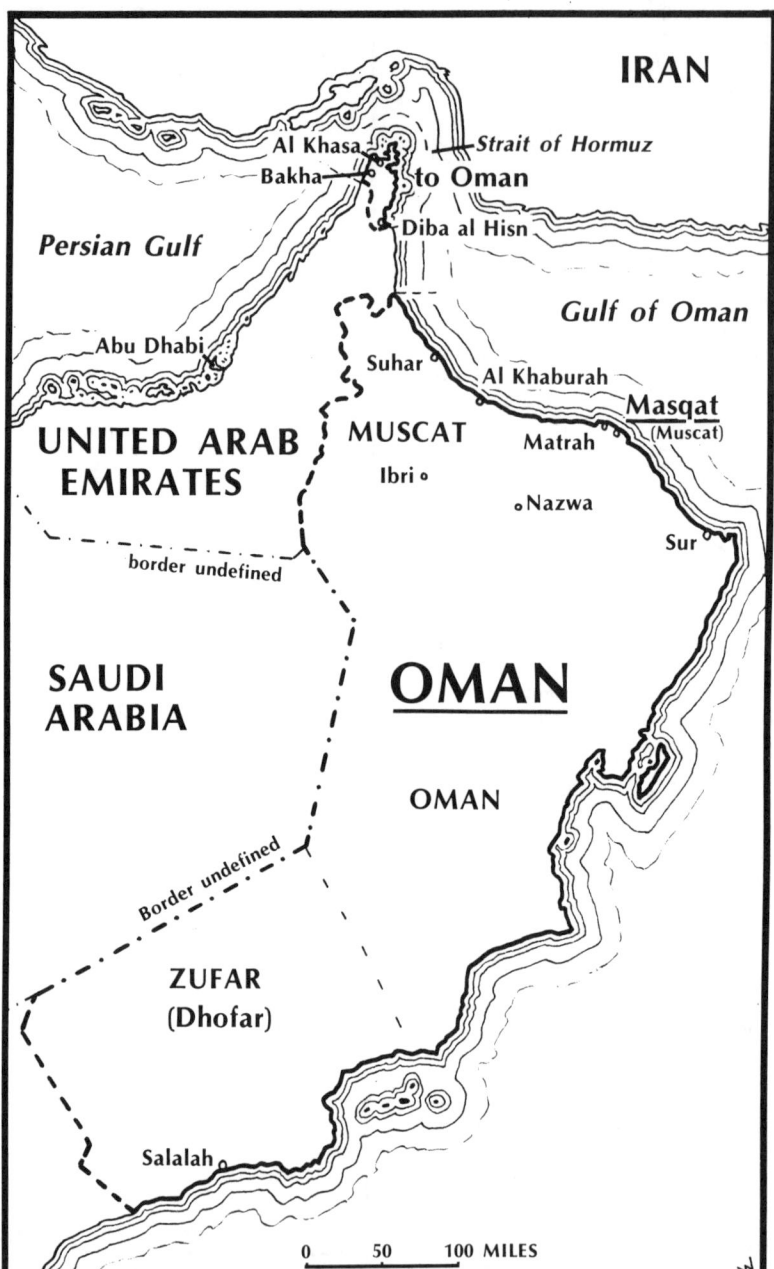

In 1964, a revolutionary movement developed in Dhofar Province, in the southern part of the country. Supported by several Communist states, its admitted purpose was to overthrow all the Persian Gulf area governments. Labels were created inscribed "State of Oman" and "Oman Imamate State." These had no postal validity. The revolution was defeated in 1975 with British help.

In 1970, Muscat and Oman assumed its present name and the country instituted social reforms.

Oil comprises about 95% of Oman's exports. Dates are the most important crop. There is no recent per capita income figure. In 1975 it was $2,400. The 1983 literacy rate was 20%.

Until 1947, Oman's postal service was administered from British India and Indian stamps were used. Pakistan stamps were used in 1947-48, when British stamps surcharged for the British Postal Agencies in Eastern Arabia went into use.

Philatelic Bureau: Philatelic Bureau, Department of Posts, Telegraphs, and Telephones, Muscat, Oman.

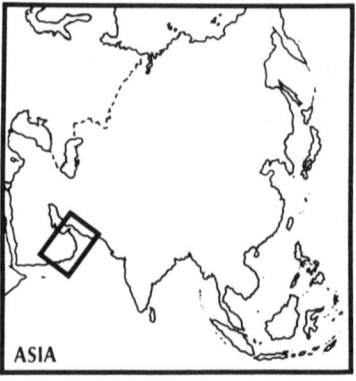

PAKISTAN, ISLAMIC REPUBLIC OF

Area: 310,524 sq. miles
Population: 96,628,000 (1984)
Capital: Islamabad
Currency: Rupee (100 paisa)

Pakistan is one of the two countries carved out of British India in 1947. It is a Moslem country, whereas the other country, India, is primarily Hindu.

Stretching for 1,000 miles from the Arabian Sea to the Himalayan foothills, Pakistan has the Indus River for its backbone and source of fertility for the central valley that comprises the largest part of the country. Arid areas exist, especially in the west.

The climate is generally hot and dry on the coast, cooling in the northern upland regions. Temperature variations are wide, ranging from freezing in the mountains to 120 degrees F on the coast. Rainfall throughout the country averages under 10 inches a year.

The area has a long history and was the center of the Indus Valley civilization that flourished about 4,000-2,500 BC.

In subsequent years, invasions from the west gave the country a culture that differed from that of the rest of the Indian sub-continent. The Arabs introduced Islam in the eighth century AD. Moslems came to rule much of India until the coming of the British in the early 19th century and the resurgence of Hinduism.

Under Mohammad Ali Jinnah, the Dominion of Pakistan came into being in 1947 at the time India received its independence. It became a republic in 1956.

Pakistan comprised two areas, 1,000 miles apart, West Pakistan (the present country) and East Pakistan. The latter area, which was located at the head of the Gulf of Bengal, rebelled in 1971 and gained its independence as the country of Bangladesh.

The country's economy is not strong, although some industrialization has taken place. The 1980 per capita income was $280 and the 1984 literacy rate was 24%.

Stamps of India were used until independence, when Pakistani stamps were issued. Issue policies have been moderate.

Philatelic Bureau: Pakistan Philatelic Bureau, GPO, Karachi, Pakistan.

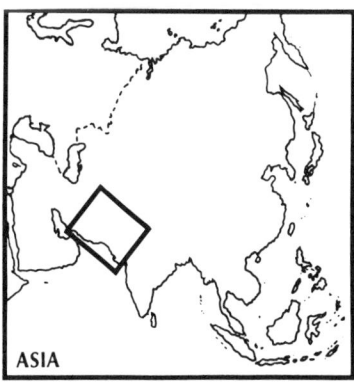

QATAR, STATE OF

Area: 4,247 sq. miles
Population: 276,000 (1984)
Capital: Doha
Currency: Riyal (100 dirhams)

Qatar, pronounced "gutter," is a peninsula jutting in to the Persian Gulf from the Saudi Arabian coast, adjacent to the United Arab Emirates.

It is mostly flat and barren, with little rain and temperatures reaching 120 degrees F in the summer. Humidity is high.

Only about half of the population is indigenous, with the rest being immigrants from Egypt, Iraq, Oman, and the United Arab Emirates. Qatar also has refugees from Palestine, Iran, India, and Pakistan.

Bahrain ruled Qatar until 1872, when the Turks took control, making it part of their Ottoman Empire.

With the defeat of Turkey in World War I and its withdrawal from the area, Great Britain signed a 1916 treaty with Qatar, taking responsibility for the country's defense and foreign affairs. A further treaty in 1934 expanded Britain's protection. Britain's withdrawal from the Persian Gulf resulted in Qatar's independence on Sept. 3, 1971.

Oil was discovered in 1940, but was not exploited until after World War II. Since then, the enormous revenues from oil exports have brought about great changes and something of a population explosion. As recently as 1960, the population was estimated at 60,000. The population is now more than four times that figure.

From a poverty-stricken village, Doha has become a modern city, with a water system using distilled sea water.

A steel mill has been built and there are modern port facilities at Doha. Before the development of oil resources, the traditional occupations were pearl diving, fishing, and nomadic stock raising.

Despite the harsh climate and lack of soil, agriculture has been brought to the stage where Qatar is now an exporter of fruit and vegetables to other Gulf countries.

The 1982 per capita income was $35,000, the world's highest. The 1985 literacy rate was 60%.

The British established a postal service at Doha in 1950 and at Umm Said (Musay'id) in 1956. Initially, stamps of the British Postal Agencies in Eastern Arabia were used. In 1957, British stamps overprinted "QATAR" and surcharged in local currency were issued.

The first stamps inscribed for Qatar were issued in 1961.

Philatelic Bureau: Philatelic Bureau: Department of Posts, Doha, Qatar.

SAUDI ARABIA, KINGDOM OF

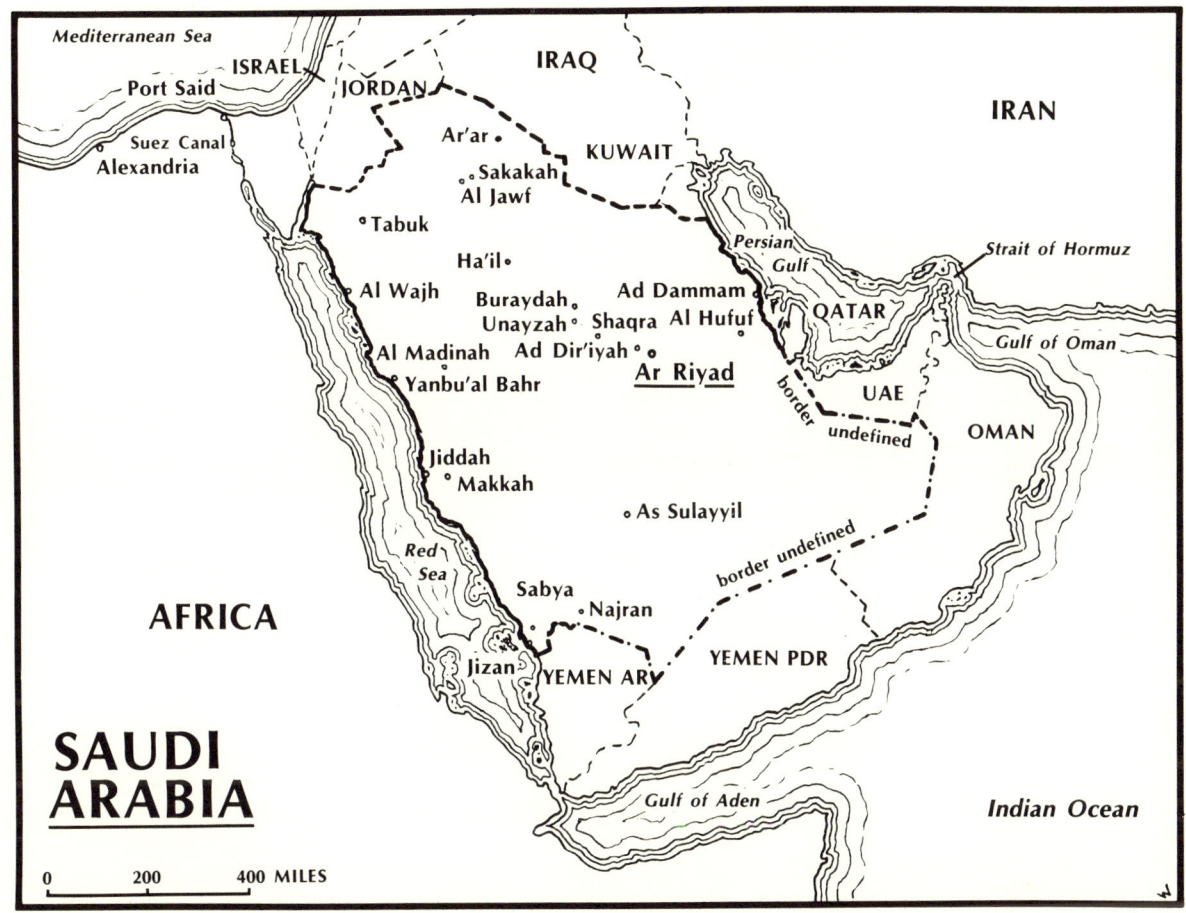

Area: 830,000 sq. miles
Population: 10,794,000 (1984)
Capital: Ar Riyad
Currency: Riyal (100 halalas)

Occupying about 80% of the Arabian Peninsula, Saudi Arabia is the focal point of the Moslem world, because the holy cities of Mecca and Medina are located within its borders.

From a range of mountains running along the Red Sea coast, the land slopes to the east and the Persian Gulf. It is mostly desert and in the south is the famous Empty Quarter, a great area of sand too arid for any life to exist.

There are no rivers in the country and rainfall does not exceed four inches a year except in the southwest mountains bordering on the Red Sea, where up to 30 inches can fall annually. This is the location of the country's highest mountains, rising to more than 9,000 feet.

Temperatures often go above 120 degrees F and humidity along the coast can be high. In winter, freezing temperatures can occur in the central and northern areas.

The country's modern history begins with the conquest by Nejd of the Kingdom of Hejaz, which had become independent in 1916. Both had been part of the Ottoman Empire until World War I.

Hejaz comprised the area bordering on the Red Sea and included the holy cities of Mecca and Medina, while Nejd consisted of the larger eastern part of what is now Saudi Arabia.

In 1926, both areas were incorporated into the Kingdom of Hejaz and Nejd, which in 1932 became the Kingdom of Saudi Arabia.

Oil is the basis of the economy and the country is estimated to possess one quarter of the known world oil reserves. Crops include dates, and grains. There are deposits of gold, silver, and iron.

The 1979 per capita income was $11,500, although this is believed to have dropped considerably as a result of the reduction in oil prices. The 1978 literacy rate was 15%.

Stamp issues have not been excessive. Beginning in 1975, their inscription was changed from "Saudi Arabia" to "K.S.A."

Philatelic Bureau: Division of Posts and Telegraphs, Philatelic Station, Ar Riyad, Saudi Arabia.

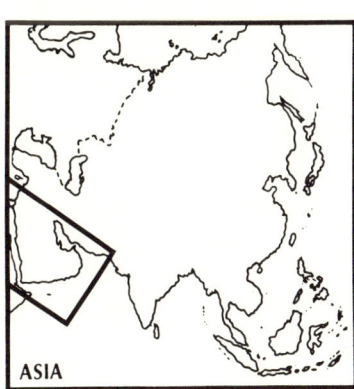

SYRIAN ARAB REPUBLIC

Area: 71,500 sq. miles
Population: 10,075,000 (1984)
Capital: Damascus
Currency: Pound (100 centimes)

Syria is divided into several geographic areas. There is the coastal mountain region, the Euphrates River valley that runs from the north to the southeast, mountains in the south, and a desert area in the east.

The climate is hot, with average summer temperatures exceeding 80 degrees F. Rainfall is about 30 inches a year on the coast, reducing to less than 10 inches in the eastern desert.

The area now comprising Syria possessed an advanced culture around the city of Ebla as early as 2,500-2,400 BC.

Syria came under the rule of the Turks and remained part of the Ottoman Empire for 400 years until World War I.

The French received a mandate over Syria from the League of Nations after the war, but the country did not receive its independence until it was occupied by British and Free French forces in 1941. French troops finally left in 1946.

Since then, Syria has several times attacked Israel and has given refuge to various terrorist organizations. It has been supported by the Soviet Union.

There is some oil production, but reserves are expected to diminish within a few years. Apart from oil, exports include cotton, grains, textiles, wool, vegetables, and tobacco. There are no recent per capita income figures. The 1981 literacy rate was 65%.

The first Syrian stamps were those of France overprinted "T.E.O." (Territoires Ennemis Occupes) released in 1919. During the 1930s, stamps were issued showing many of Syria's scenic and historic attractions.

A brief union with Egypt from 1958-61 produced stamps in similar designs but in different currencies for the two countries.

Philatelic Bureau: Establissement des Postes et des Telecommunications, Service Philatelique, Damascus, Syria.

TURKEY, REPUBLIC OF

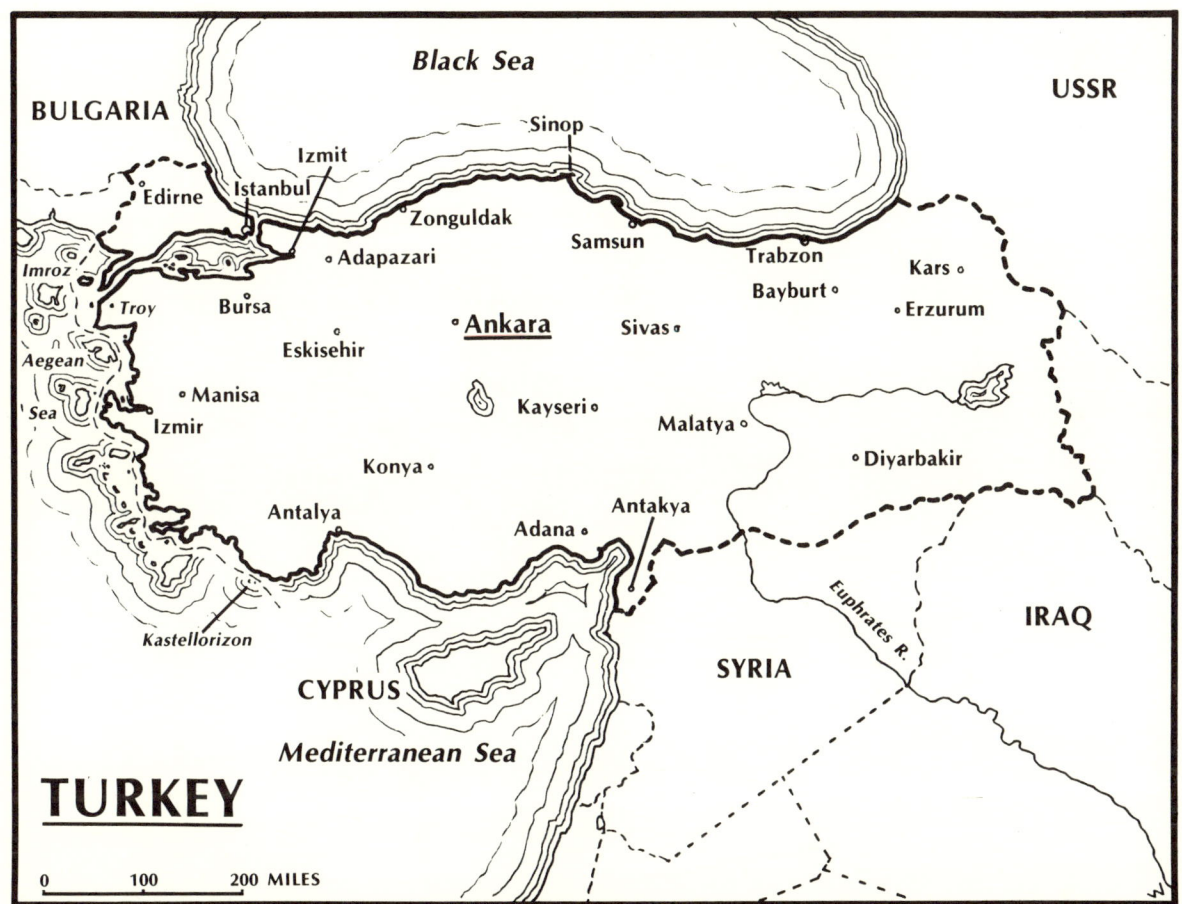

Area: 300,948 sq. miles
Population: 50,207,000 (1984)
Capital: Ankara
Currency: Lira (100 kurush)

Located partly in Europe and partly in Asia, Turkey is one of the world's crossroads countries. Through its Bosphorus, Sea of Marmara, and Dardanelles must pass all the sea traffic between the Black Sea and the Mediterranean.

The coastal areas on the Black Sea, Aegean, and Mediterranean receive sufficient rain for tea to be grown in the northeast, tobacco in the west, and cotton in the south. The interior of Turkish Asia Minor is mostly plateau in the west and wheat is grown there. In the east, the land is more mountainous and agriculture is limited.

At the peak of its glory, the Ottoman Empire of the Turks had been master of North Africa, Egypt, southeastern Europe, and western Asia.

In 1453, it had taken Constantinople (Istanbul), for 1,000 years the capital of the Byzantine Empire, and the Turks had surged into the Balkans, even obtaining a toehold on the Italian "boot," at Otranto.

The Turkish tide began to ebb after the 1571 defeat by Spain and the Papal States of the Turkish fleet at the Battle of Lepanto, although the Turks went on to occupy Tunis. Despite its decline, the creaking empire managed to survive well into the 20th century and came to an end as an ally of Germany and Austria in World War I.

After the war, a new leader emerged. He was Kemal Ataturk and he finally led his country out of the Middle Ages and made it a modern republic.

Turkey remained neutral in World War II, only declaring War on Germany in February 1945, when it was plain that the war was over.

Although much more progressive than in the past, Turkey is still a poor country with considerable political instability. The economy is shaky and in 1984, the per capita income was $1,000 and the 1985 literacy rate was 70%.

The first stamps were issued in 1863.

Many stamps have been issued, although current policies are moderate.

Philatelic Bureau: Direction Generale des PTT, Dept. des Postes, Section de Timbres, Ankara, Turkey.

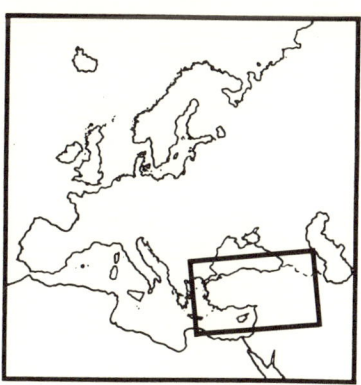

UNITED ARAB EMIRATES

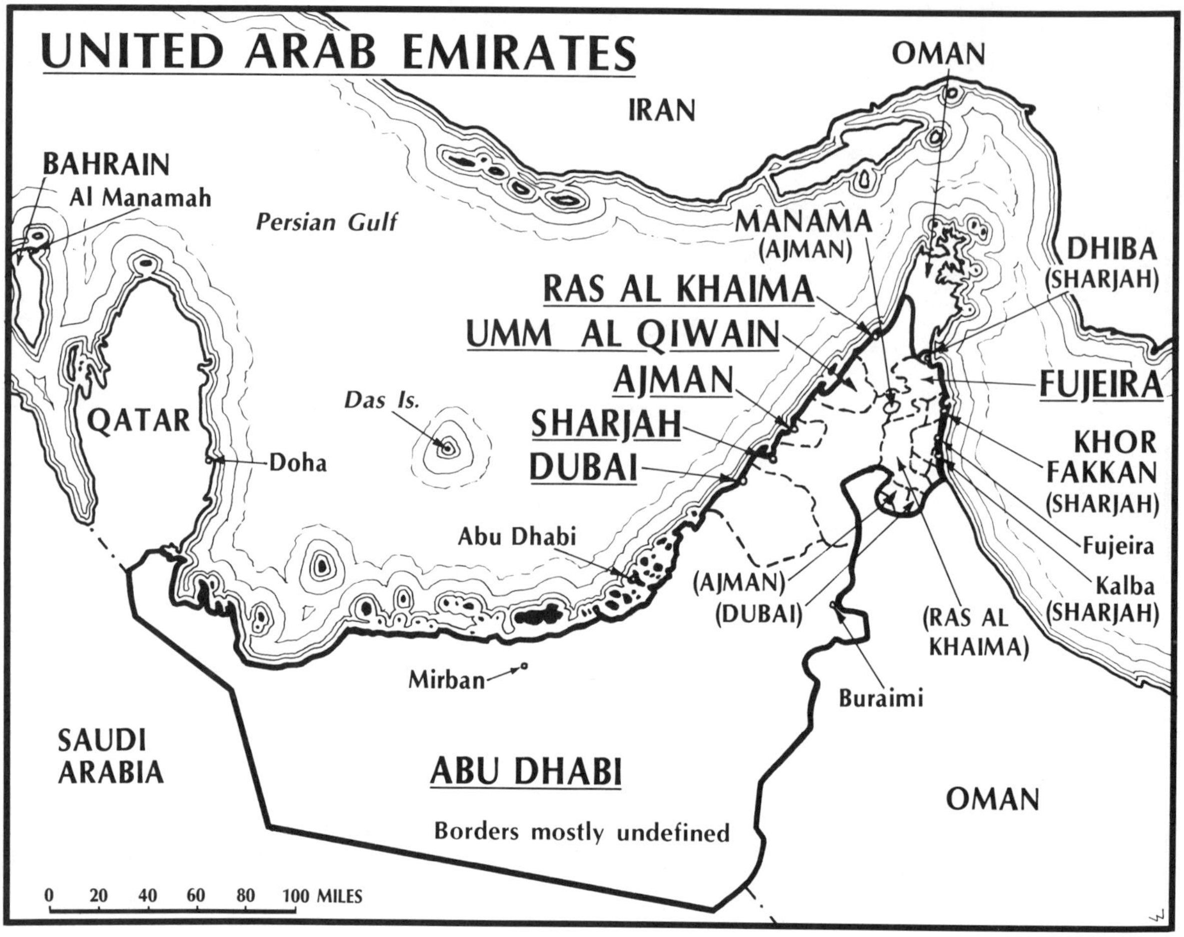

Area: 32,000 sq. miles
Population: 1,523,000 (1984)
Capital: Abu Dhabi
Currency: Dirham (100 fils)

The United Arab Emirates is a federation of seven sheikdoms located on the south side of the Persian Gulf.

The flat, arid coast of the UAE runs eastward from the base of the Qatar Peninsula for about 400 miles, almost to the tip of the peninsula at the entrance to the gulf. There is also a short coastline on the Gulf of Oman.

The Persian Gulf coast has a number of low islands. Inland, the coastal strip becomes a sea of sand dunes that merges into the Empty Quarter of Saudi Arabia. In the east, there are mountains that draw an annual rainfall of about 15 inches and this makes possible some agriculture.

Temperatures on the Persian Gulf coast commonly reach 120 degrees F.

Formerly called the Pirate Coast, the area was a haven for pirates. Their activities led to an 1819 British campaign that curbed them. In 1820, the various sheiks along the coast signed an undertaking not to engage in maritime terrorism.

After Britain announced that it would withdraw from the affairs in the area in 1971, the sheikdom attempted various federations without success and two, Bahrain and Qatar, decided to become independent on their own. The other seven, comprising Abu Dhabi, Dubai, Sharjah, Ajman, Umm al Qiwain, Ras al Khaima, and Fujeira, joined to form the United Arab Emirates in 1971.

Oil is the base of the economy and with an estimated per capita income of $24,000, the UAE is one of th world's richest nations. International banking is a growing source of income.

The first stamps were issued in August 1972. Previously, each sheikdom had issued its own stamps.

Philatelic Bureau: Philatelic Bureau, GPO, Dubai, United Arab Emirates.

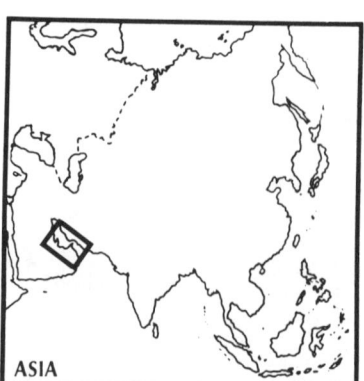

YEMEN ARAB REPUBLIC

Area: 77,200 sq. miles
Population: 4,890,000 (1984)
Capital: San'a
Currency: Rial (40 bogaches)

Fabled land of the Queen of Sheba, the Yemen Arab Republic has a hot, arid coastal strip about 40 miles wide, although the mountainous interior is generally well watered and surprisingly fertile. It is one of the most productive agricultural areas in the entire Arabian Peninsula.

There are mountains that rise to 12,000 feet and San'a, the capital city, is located at an altitude of 7,000 feet. It has a maximum summer temperature of about 85 degrees F. Frosts occur and snow has been recorded.

Site of the ancient and rich Kingdom of Sheba, the area was once a prosperous trade link between India and Africa.

The Turks were an important factor in Yemen from the 16th century and were in complete control for various periods, most recently from 1872-1918, when the Ottoman Empire finally crumbled.

The Imam Yahya, believed a descendant of the Imam al Hadi Yahya, who ruled in the ninth century AD, was left in control by the retreating Turks.

The Imam Yahya's son, Imam Ahmas, ruled from 1948-1962, when he was reported to have been assassinated. His heir, Imam Mohamad al-Badr retreated to the mountains under pressure from a revolutionary group and a bloody civil war began.

Egypt sent troops to aid the rebels and Saudi Arabia supported the royalists. The fighting lasted to 1970 and a total of 150,000 people are said to have died in the conflict.

Peace was finally made and royalists and republicans began to work to put their country together again. Even so, there has been considerable political unrest and in 1974 an army group seized power. Its leader was assassinated in 1977.

The country's economy is poor. There are some oil reserves, but no industry except for some textiles and cement. About three quarters of the labor force is engaged in agriculture, growing wheat, cotton, coffee, and the narcotic, gar. The earnings of workers in foreign countries sent back to families is an important source of revenue.

The most recently available per capita income figure is $475. The 1985 literacy rate was 20%.

Stamps were first issued for domestic use in 1926 and for international use in 1930.

Philatelic Bureau: Ministry of Communications, Philatelic Bureau, GPO, San'a, Yemen Arab Republic.

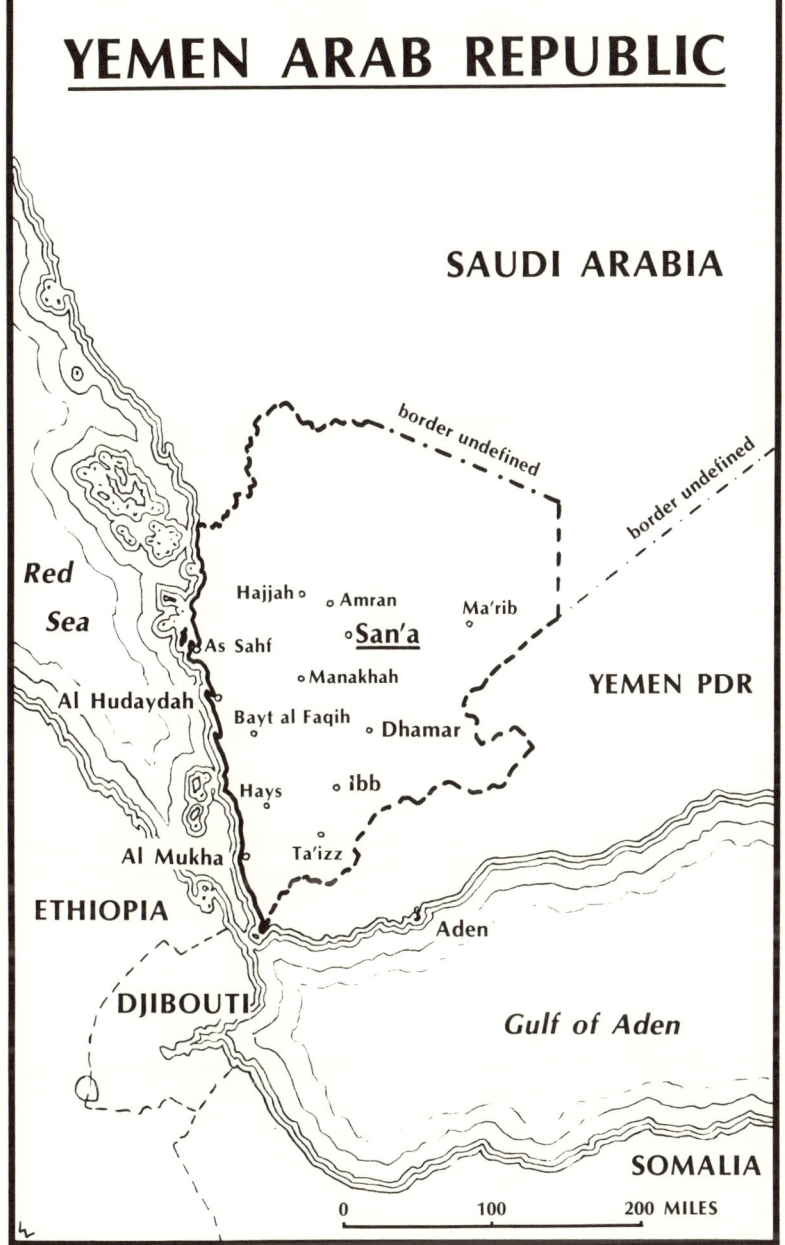

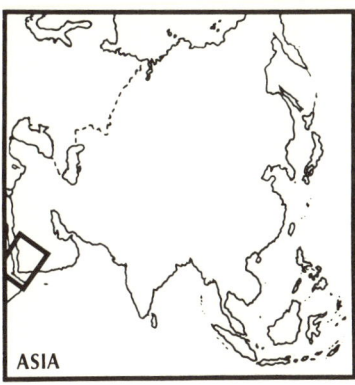

YEMEN, PEOPLE'S DEMOCRATIC REPUBLIC OF

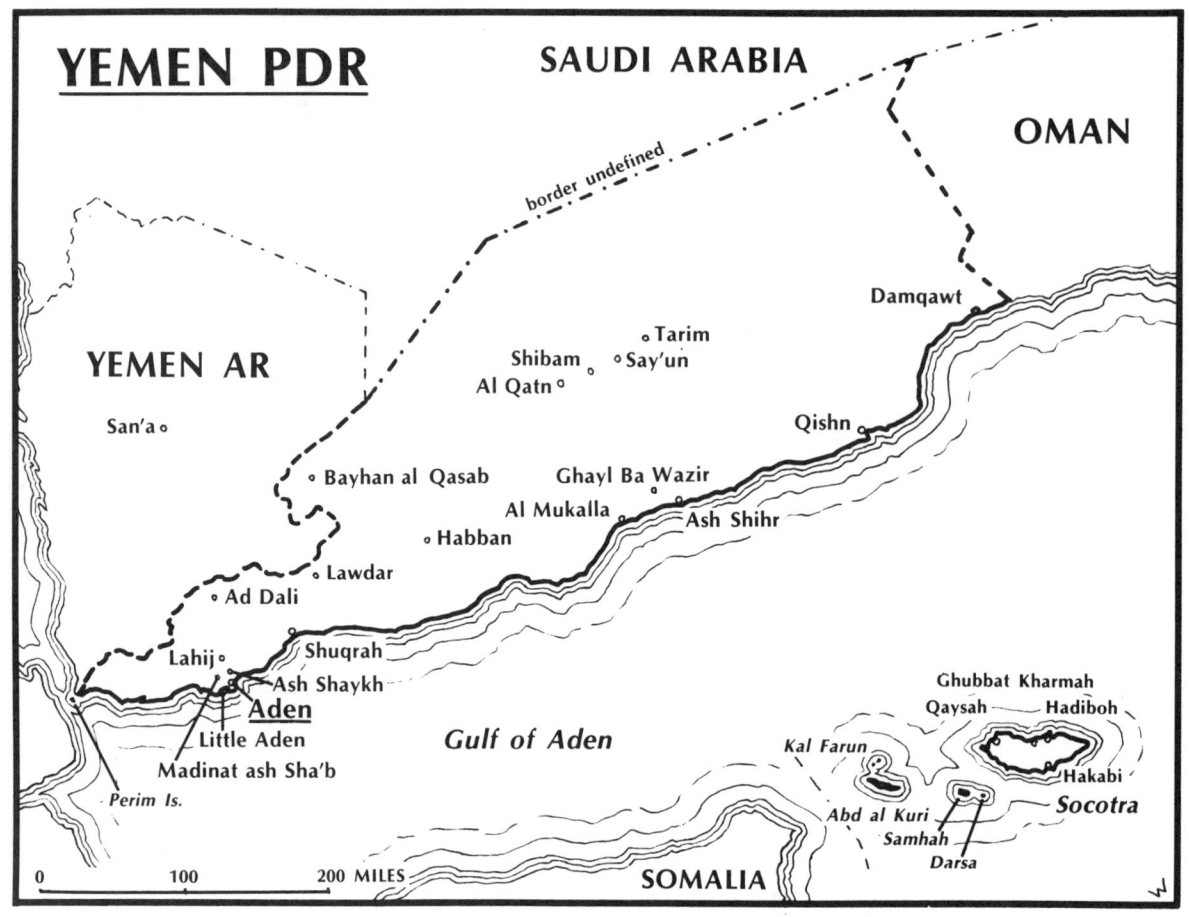

Area: 130,540 sq. miles
Population: 2,147,000 (1984)
Capital: Aden
Currency: Dinar (1,000 fils)

The most important part of the People's Democratic Republic of Yemen is the former British crown colony of Aden, once one of the world's largest coaling stations.

Today, Aden is the capital of a poor, barren, and unstable land.

In addition to the large area on the southern coast of the Arabian Peninsula, the country includes the islands of Socotra and Perim.

Along the coast the land is flat and arid, while the interior is mountainous and rugged.

The climate is very hot and summer temperatures often exceed 130 degrees F. Average rainfall is under three inches a year.

Aden was a fishing village in 1839 when it was taken by the British.

As steam began to power much of the world's shipping, the village developed into a coaling station. When the Suez Canal opened in 1869, Aden assumed even greater importance, because of its location on the main route to India and the East.

Until 1937, it was administered from India. In that year Britain made it a crown colony. The surrounding area became the Aden Protectorate and Britain made agreements with the various sheikdoms in the area.

The crown colony and protectorate achieved a degree of self rule in 1963 as the Federation of South Arabia, but when independence was promised, internal warfare broke out as the various factions strove to gain power.

The area became independent on Nov. 30, 1967. Since then there has been much unrest and overthrowing of governments. Open warfare with neighboring countries has also occurred and there has been support from the Soviet Union.

There is little industry and cotton is the main export. The latest available per capita income is $310 and the 1980 literacy rate was 39%.

Stamp issues have not been extensive since independence.

Philatelic Bureau: Director General of Posts and Telegraphs, GPO, Aden, People's Democratic Republic of Yemen.

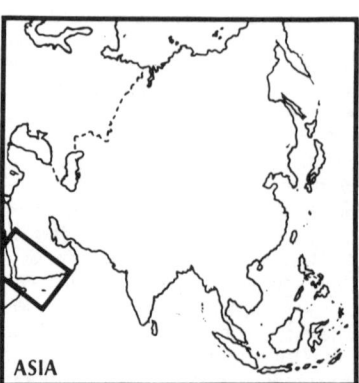

ASIA

Stamp-issuing areas:

1. Bangladesh
2. Bhutan
3. Brunei
4. Burma
5. Cambodia
6. China, People's Republic of
7. China (Taiwan)
8. Christmas Island
9. Cocos (Keeling) Islands
10. Hong Kong
11. India
12. Indonesia
13. Japan
14. Korea, North
15. Korea, South
16. Laos
17. Macao
18. Maylasia
19. Maldive Islands
20. Mongolia
21. Nepal
22. Philippines
23. Singapore
24. Sri Lanka
25. Thailand
26. USSR in Asia
27. Vietnam

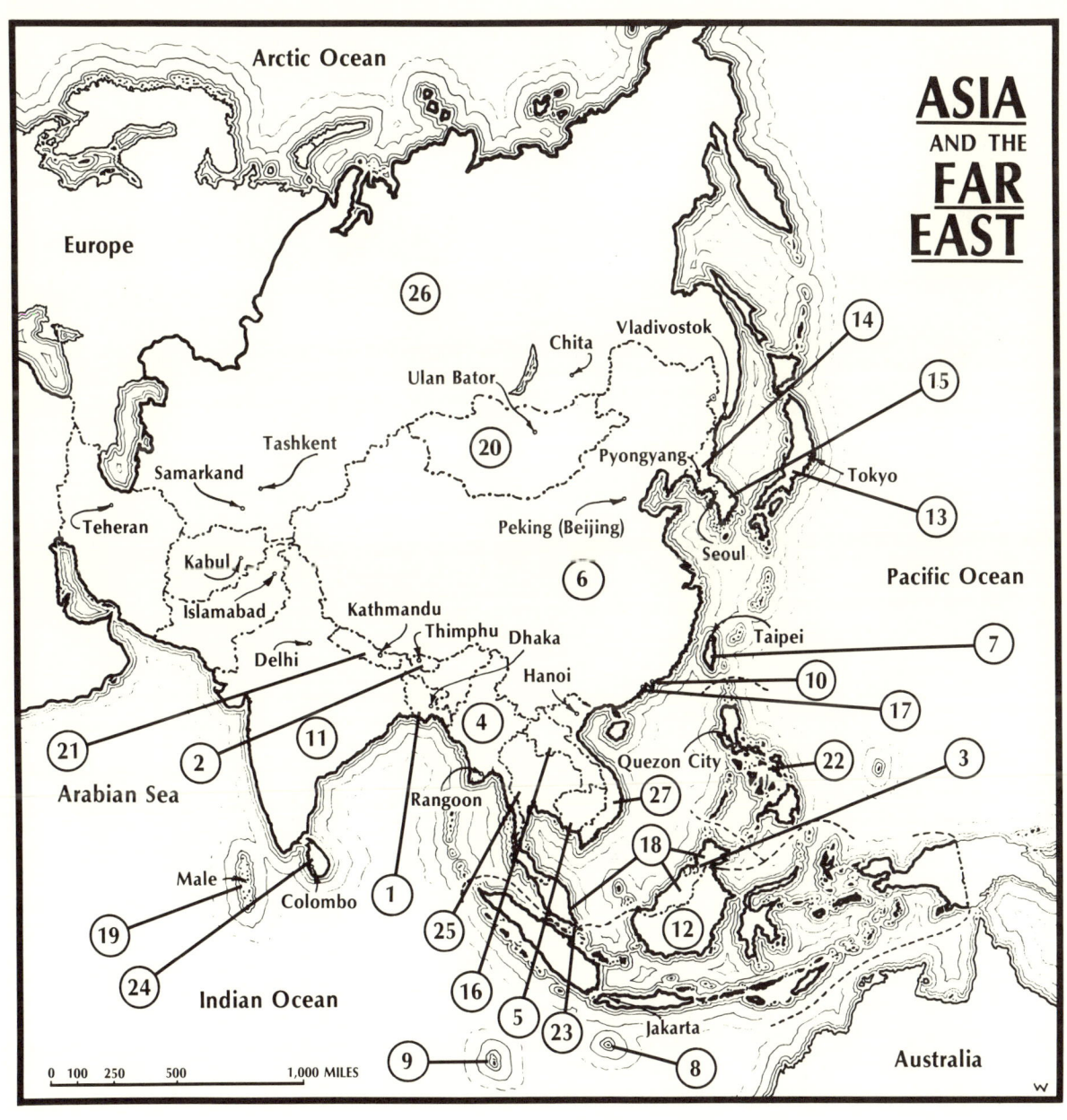

BANGLADESH, PEOPLE'S REPUBLIC OF

Area: 55,183 sq. miles
Population: 99,585,000 (1984)
Capital: Dhaka (Dacca)
Currency: Taka (100 paisas)

A land subject to the natural disasters of storm and flood, Bangladesh was a politically conceived area carved out of eastern India at the time of the 1947 partition.

It is the world's eighth most heavily populated country.

The name translates as "Bengal Nation," and it comprises an irregularly shaped country at the head of the Bay of Bengal. The land is mostly alluvial plain at the junction of two great rivers, the Ganges and the Brahmaputra. The coastal land is generally delta swamp through which the many river branches find their way to the sea.

There is no geographical significance to the country's borders and their position was based on the religious distribution of the population.

Bangladesh has a hot, monsoon climate. The average temperature is 84 degrees F. The rainfall is high and averages 85 inches a year.

The area has been under Moslem rule since about AD 1200, although it remained remote and to an extent, independent.

When British influence began to make itself felt in the 18th and 19th centuries, development began. Many of the country's civil engineering works; bridges, canals, roads, drainage projects, etc., date from the 19th century.

Friction between Hindu and Moslem had existed for years and, in 1947, when India was partitioned between Hindu and Moslem, what is now Bangladesh was made an isolated, eastern part of Moselm Pakistan, separated from the main part of the country by hundreds of miles of Hindu-dominated territory.

Unrest, caused by dissatisfaction with the remote rule of Pakistan, led to open civil war and in 1972 eastern Pakistan broke away and proclaimed itself the independent People's Republic of Bangladesh.

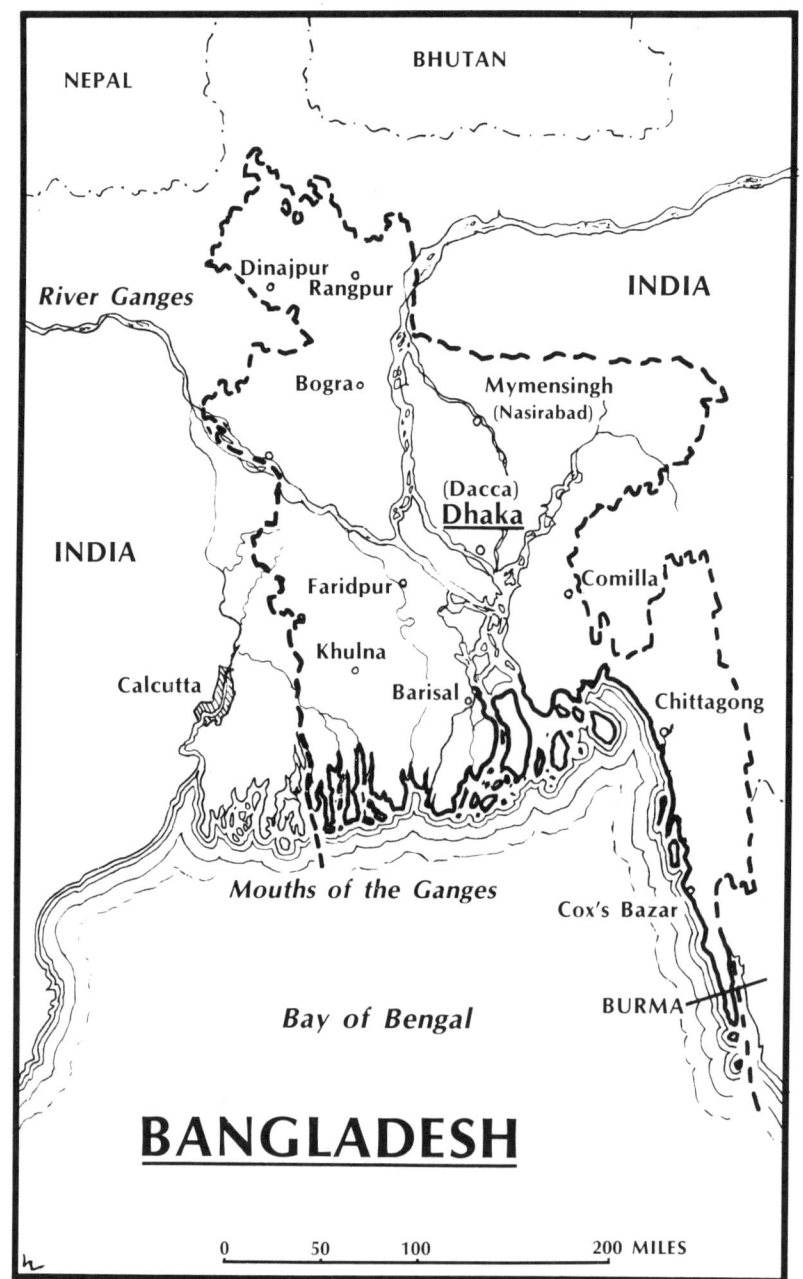

Once dependent on jute, the economy has been hard hit by dwindling demand and worldwide recession. There is a small textile industry, but 74% of the labor force is employed in agriculture. The 1983 per capita income was $119 and the 1984 literacy rate was 25%.

Stamps were first issued on July 29, 1971. Issue policies have been moderate.

Philatelic Bureau: Senior Postmaster, Philatelic Bureau, GPO, Dacca, Bangladesh.

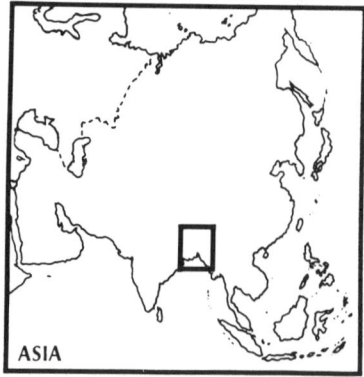

BHUTAN, KINGDOM OF

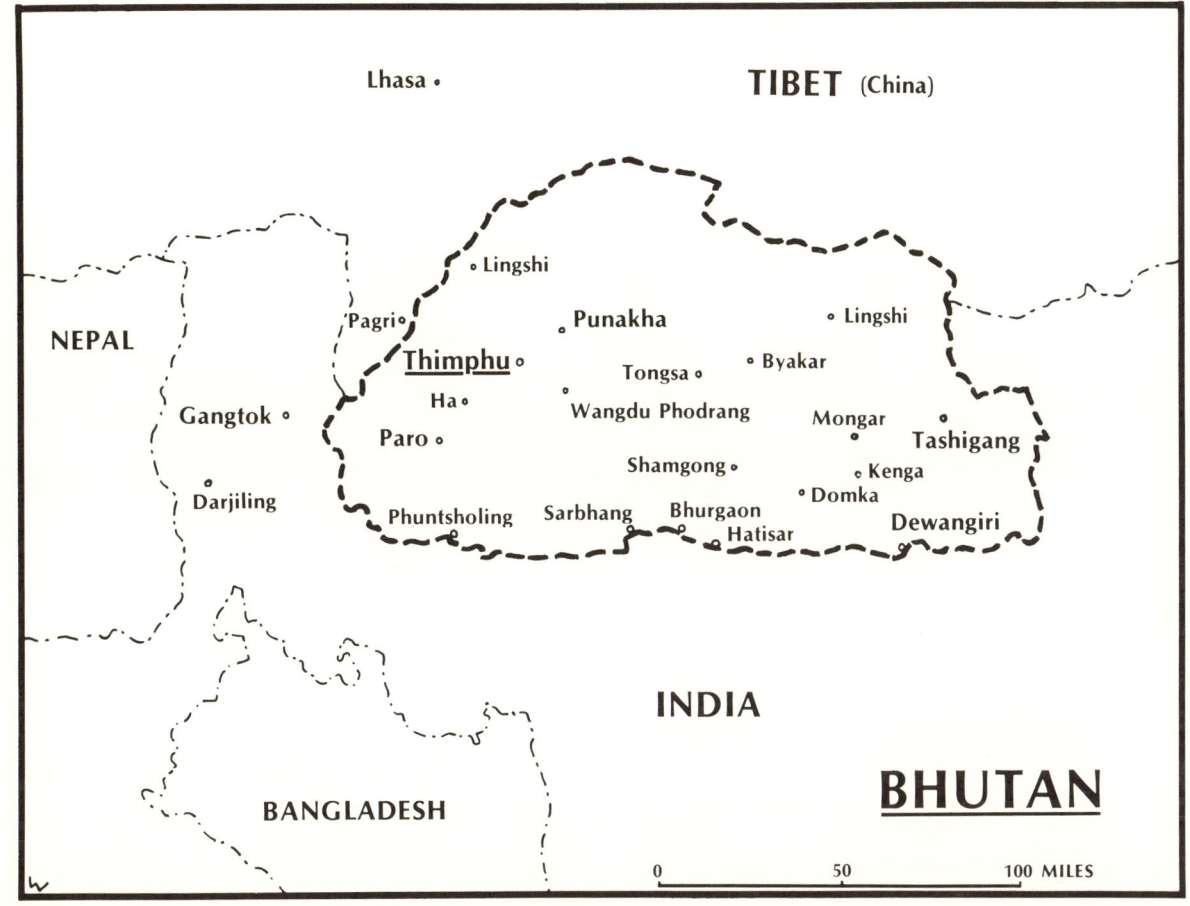

Area: 17,800 sq. miles
Population: 1,417,000 (1984)
Capital: Thimphu
Currency: Ngultrum (100 chetrum)

The Kingdom of Bhutan is an isolated country tucked away in the fastness of the Himalayas.

In the north, mountains rise to 24,000 feet. In the center and south there are thickly populated valleys at about 5,000-9,000 feet.

The climate varies with altitude. It is subtropical in the south, while the northern valleys are temperate.

Bhutan is heavily forested and the rugged mountain barriers make access difficult. Rainfall is heavy to moderate, with up to 300 inches a year falling in the subtropical region, declining to 40-60 inches in the cooler areas.

Severe Himalayan storms give the country its local name — Land of the Thunder Dragon.

Bhutan came under Tibetan control in the 16th century. Over the years ministers of the kings became powerful, reducing the rulers to figureheads.

In 1885, the king requested Chinese aid in controlling his ministers and this was done. To combat the threat of Chinese control of the country, one of the ministers encouraged the British. He eventually became king and British influence grew strong.

A treaty between Britain and Bhutan was signed in 1910 under which Bhutan remained independent and Britain assumed responsibility for the country's foreign affairs.

When India gained its own independence it took over this protective role. There is now airline service between the two countries and roads link them.

Agriculture is the basis of the economy and crops include rice, corn, and wheat. The 1981 per capita income was $100 and the 1983 literacy rate was a low 5%.

Stamps were first issued in 1962 and except for a period during the 1960s and 1970s when all kinds of exploitive gimmicks were released, issues have been relatively restrained. But given the low literacy rate, issues must be far in excess of postal requirements.

Philatelic Bureau: Philatelic Officer, Philatelic Bureau, GPO, Phuntsholing, Bhutan.

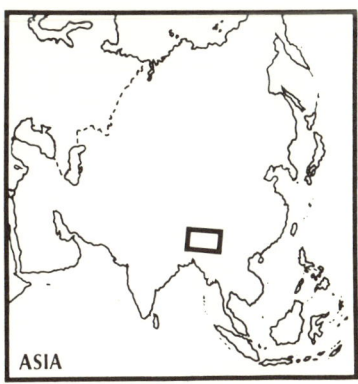

BRUNEI (STATE OF BRUNEI DARUSSALAM)

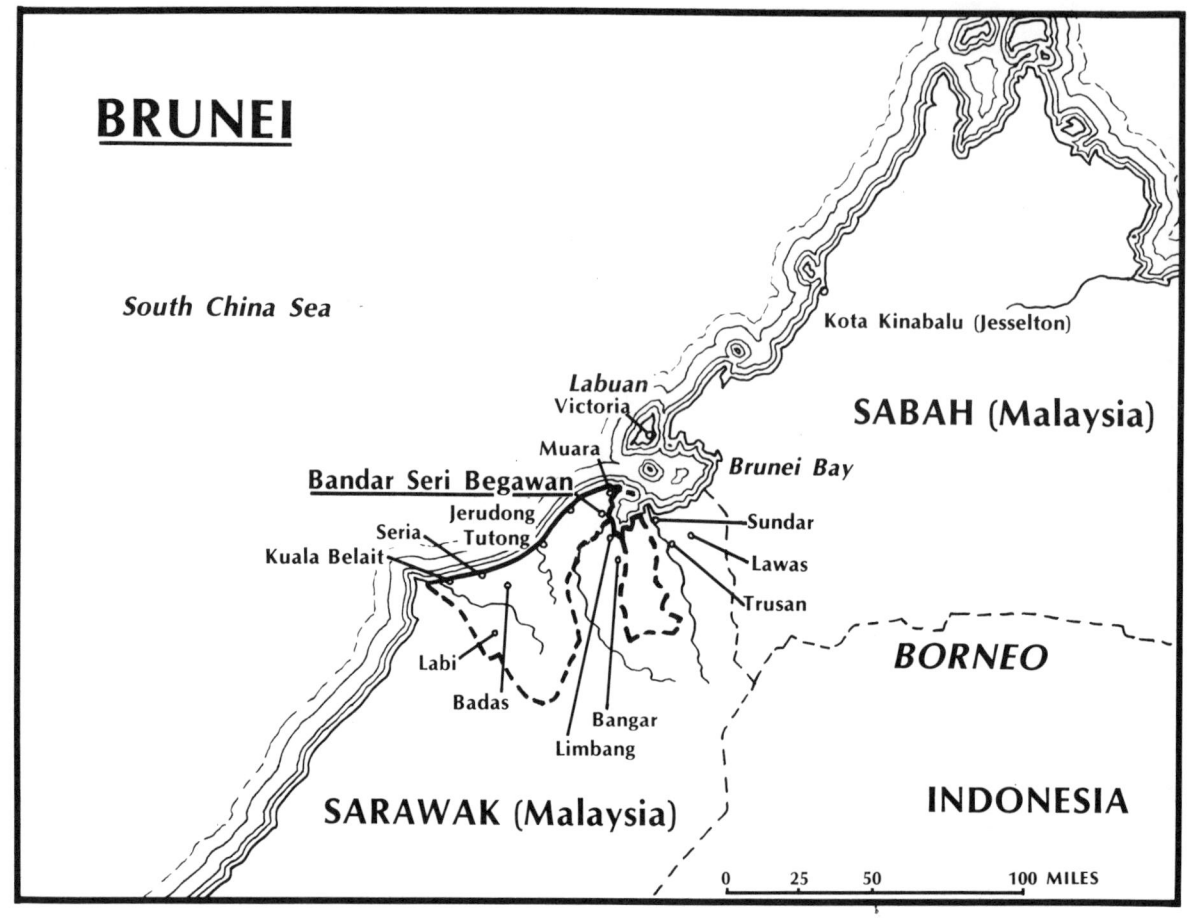

Area: 2,226 sq. miles
Population: 218,000 (1984)
Capital: Bandar Seri Begawan
Currency: Dollar (100 cents)

Comprising two enclaves on the northwest coast of Borneo, Brunei is but a shadow of its former self.

The land alternates between hills and swamp in the larger western enclave, while in the eastern area, mountains rise to 6,000 feet in the interior.

The climate is tropical. Average temperatures vary between 75-85 degrees F. Rainfall is high. About 100 inches fall each year on the coast and there is up to 200 inches a year in the interior.

Sultan Mohammed (1405-15) introduced Islam to Brunei. The present sultan is a direct descendant.

In 1521, when Magellan called there, the sultanate controlled almost all of Borneo and many surrounding islands.

Britain extended protection against pirates in the late 1800s and appointed a British resident as administrator.

After the 1941-45 Japanese invasion and occupation, the British resumed their administration and guided the country towards self-rule. Because Brunei suffered so much destruction at the hands of the Japanese, a great deal of rebuilding had to be done. It now has the largest mosque in the Far East, a sports stadium, and an Olympic swimming pool.

Undreamed of prosperity came with the development of oil deposits that had been discovered in the 1920s. Offshore fields went into production and Brunei became the third-largest producer in the British Commonwealth.

Revenue from oil far exceeded expenditure and provided free pensions for the old and disabled and free education for children.

The country became fully independent on Jan. 1, 1984. The 1981 per capita income was $22,000.

Stamps were first issued in 1895 and feature a star and landscape. The Scott catalog does not list them.

Philatelic Bureau: Postal Services Department, GPO, Bandar Seri Begawan, Brunei.

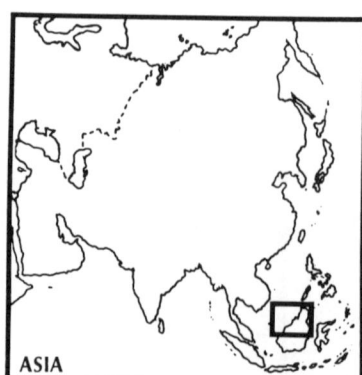

BURMA, SOCIALIST REPUBLIC OF THE UNION OF

Area: 261,288 sq. miles
Population: 36,196,000 (1984)
Capital: Rangoon
Currency: Kyat (100 pyas)

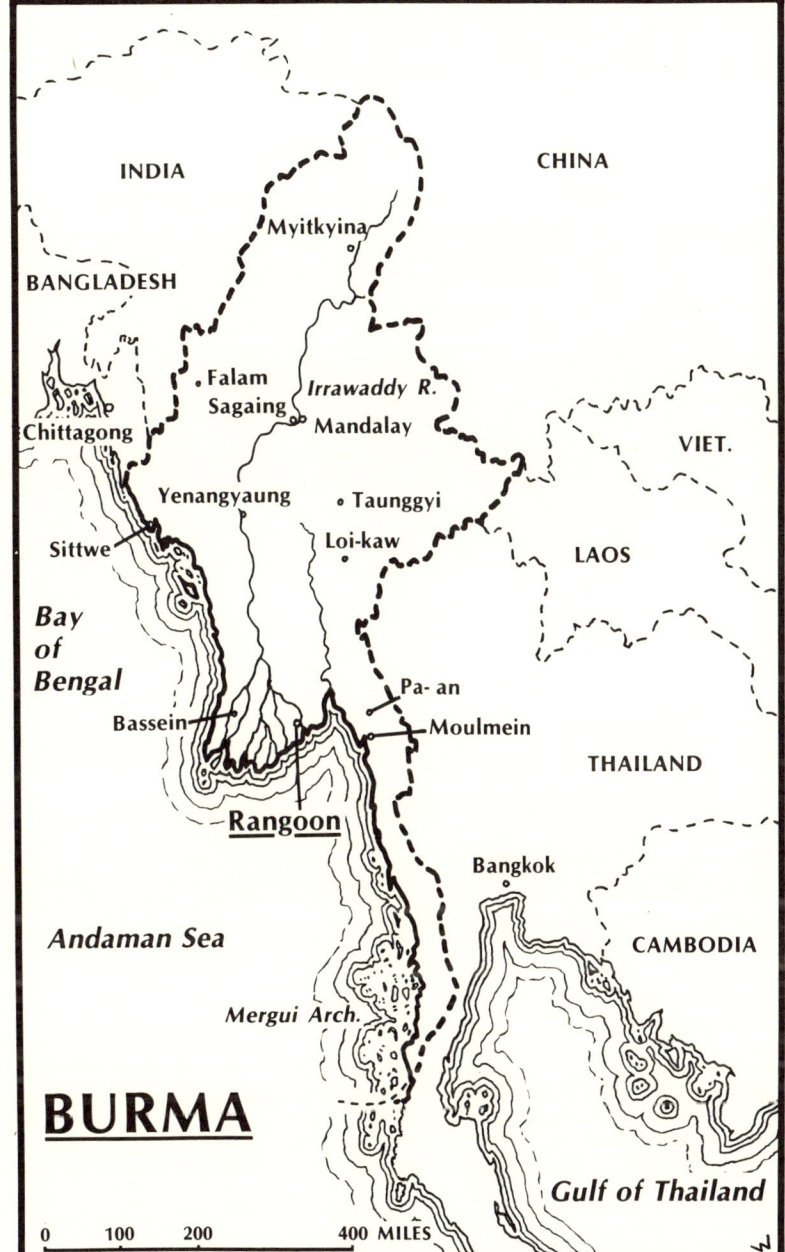

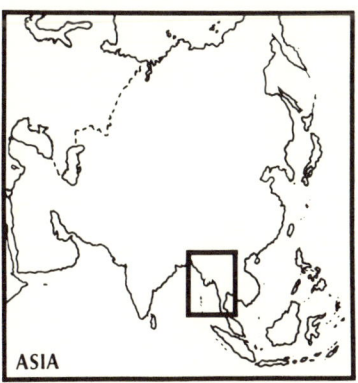

Burma, the largest country on the mainland of Southeast Asia, is isolated from the rest of the world and torn by internal unrest.

The country is bordered on the north, west, and east by mountains. On the Chinese border, these rise as high as 15,000 feet.

The Irrawaddy River runs up the center of Burma and is its most important transportation route.

The climate is tropical and the average annual temperature is 80 degrees F in the south and 75 in the interior. The maximum temperature during the hot season frequently exceeds 100 degrees F.

Rainfall ranges from 200 inches a year on the coast to less than 35 inches annually in the central portion of the country.

The ancestors of the Burmese came to the area from Tibet and established a Buddhist monarchy by the 11th century AD. From the 13th to 16th centuries Burma was under Chinese control.

Early in the 1800s, the British began to make their influence felt, and after some periods of warfare they ruled Burma as part of India. In 1937, the country was given a measure of self-government.

During World War II, the Japanese invaded and occupied Burma from March 1942 to March 1945 and it was the scene of some bitter fighting.

In 1942, the Burma Independence Army controlled the Irrawaddy delta

area and, with Japanese permission, issued stamps overprinted with the Burmese peacock emblem.

Following the liberation of Burma, the country became an independent nation outside the British Commonwealth on Jan. 4, 1948.

Socialization of the economy was imposed and the country became poor, despite considerable mineral resources.

In recent years, the government has attempted to reverse the trend to economic chaos by opening the country and is now doing more to encourage foreign investment.

The first Burmese stamps issued in 1937 were Indian stamps overprinted "BURMA."

Since independence, there have been few stamps and the country is one of the world's most conservative stamp-issuing areas.

Philatelic Bureau: Myanama Export Import Corp., Export Division, Philatelic Section, Rangoon, Burma.

CAMBODIAN PEOPLE'S REPUBLIC (KAMPUCHEA)

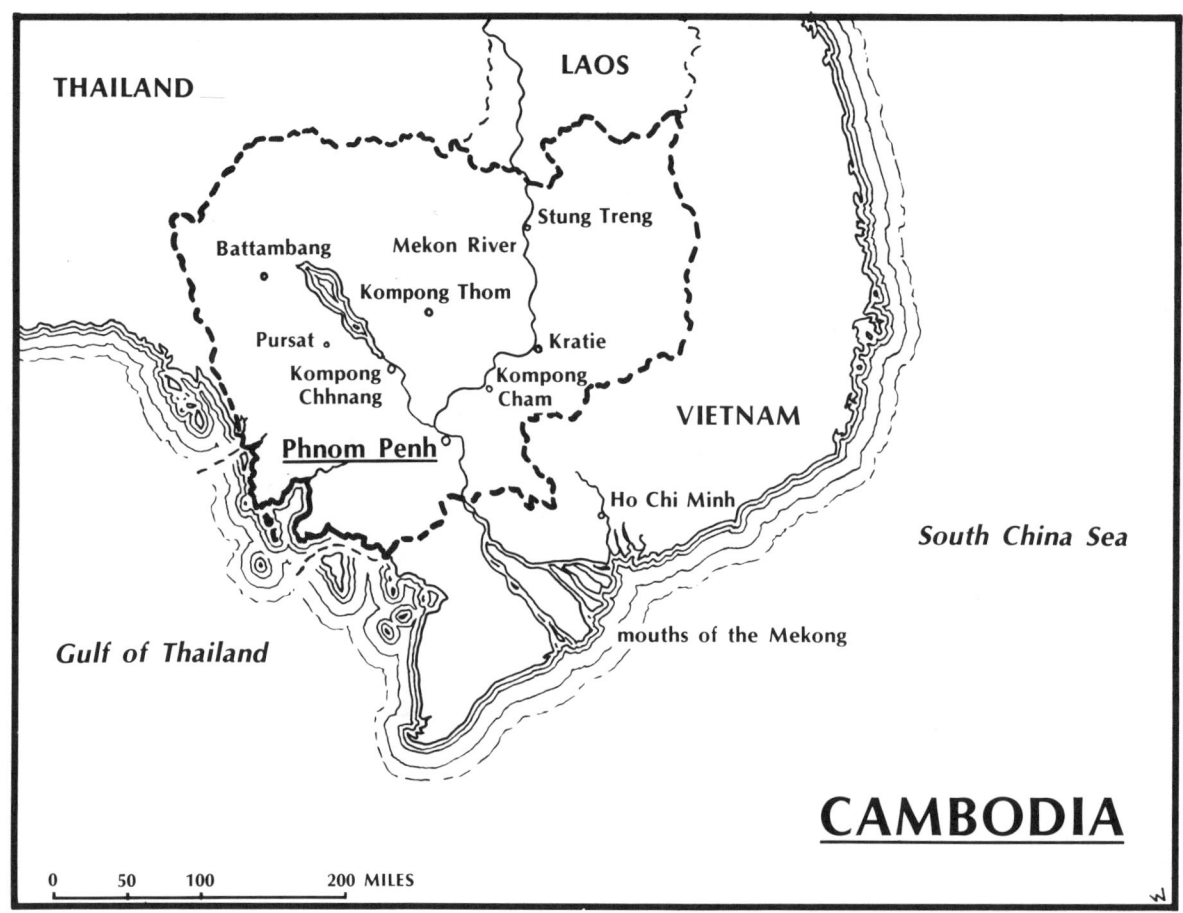

CAMBODIA

Area: 69,900 sq. miles
Population: 6,300,000
Capital: Phnom Penh
Currency: Riel (100 cents)

A land of forest and rice paddies, most of Cambodia comprises the drainage basin of the Mekong River. The large lake, Tonle Sap, is in this

area. The highest point is 5,740-foot Phnom Aural in the western mountains.

The temperature is between 65-100 degrees F year round and rainfall at Phnom Penh is about 60 inches a year.

The country's history includes a period as part of the Khmer Empire prior to the 13th century.

Its modern history began in the mid-1800s with the establishment of a French protectorate. It remained a part of French Indo China until the end of World War II, when it was made an associated state within the French Union, under the name of Cambodia. Full independence came in 1955.

In 1963, Cambodia accused the US Central Intelligence Agency of fomenting revolution in the country. Relations with the United States were broken in 1965 and restored in 1969.

Civil war broke out in 1970 between the government and the rebel Khmer Rouge. Despite massive US military and economic aid, the rebels gained control of the country and a reign of terror began that is unmatched in recent years.

More than one million people are estimated to have been murdered by the government, either by execution or being worked and starved to death.

In 1978, Vietnamese forces invaded Cambodia and toppled the government.

The fighting has driven thousands of refugees into Thailand and Thailand has accused Vietnam of using poison gas against Cambodians. The economy is poor and the war continues.

There is no significant industry and food production is insufficient to prevent widespread starvation.

The 1984 per capita income was $100 and the literacy rate is 48%.

Stamps of Cambodia have been forbidden entry into the United States since April 17, 1975.

Philatelic Bureau: Agence Philatelique, Direction Generale des PTT, Phnom Penh, Cambodia.

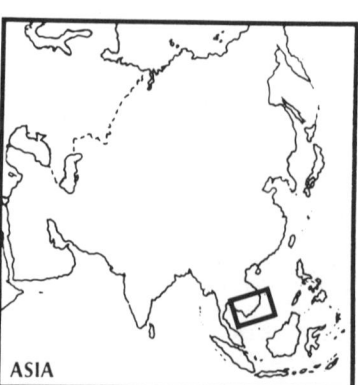

CHINA, REPUBLIC OF (TAIWAN)

Area: 13,850 sq. miles
Population: 19,117,000 (1984)
Capital: Taipei
Currency: Dollar (100 cents)

Named Formosa, meaning "beautiful," by the Portuguese, Taiwan is the island home of the Nationalist Government of China that was forced from the mainland in 1949 by the Communists.

It is located about 120 miles off the central coast of China.

The backbone of the island is a range of mountains that runs down the center. Its highest point is Yu Shan, which rises to 13,110 feet above sea level.

Situated on the Tropic of Cancer, the island has a semitropical climate. The average January temperature at Taipei is 58 degrees F. Summers are hot and humid. In the south, both winters and summers are hot.

Low lying areas get about 40 inches of rain each year, while in the mountains up to 200 inches can fall.

The Chinese did not settle on the island until early in the 17th century.

In 1895, after a war with Japan, China gave up Taiwan and the Pescadores. They remained a Japanese possession until 1945, when they reverted to China.

When Chinese Nationalist forces were defeated on the mainland by the Communists, about two million Nationalists under General Chiang Kai-shek, fled to Taiwan and established the Republic of China.

The republic comprises the island of Taiwan, the Pescadores (Penghu Islands) off the southwest coast, the islands of Quemoy and Matsu just off the Chinese coast, plus

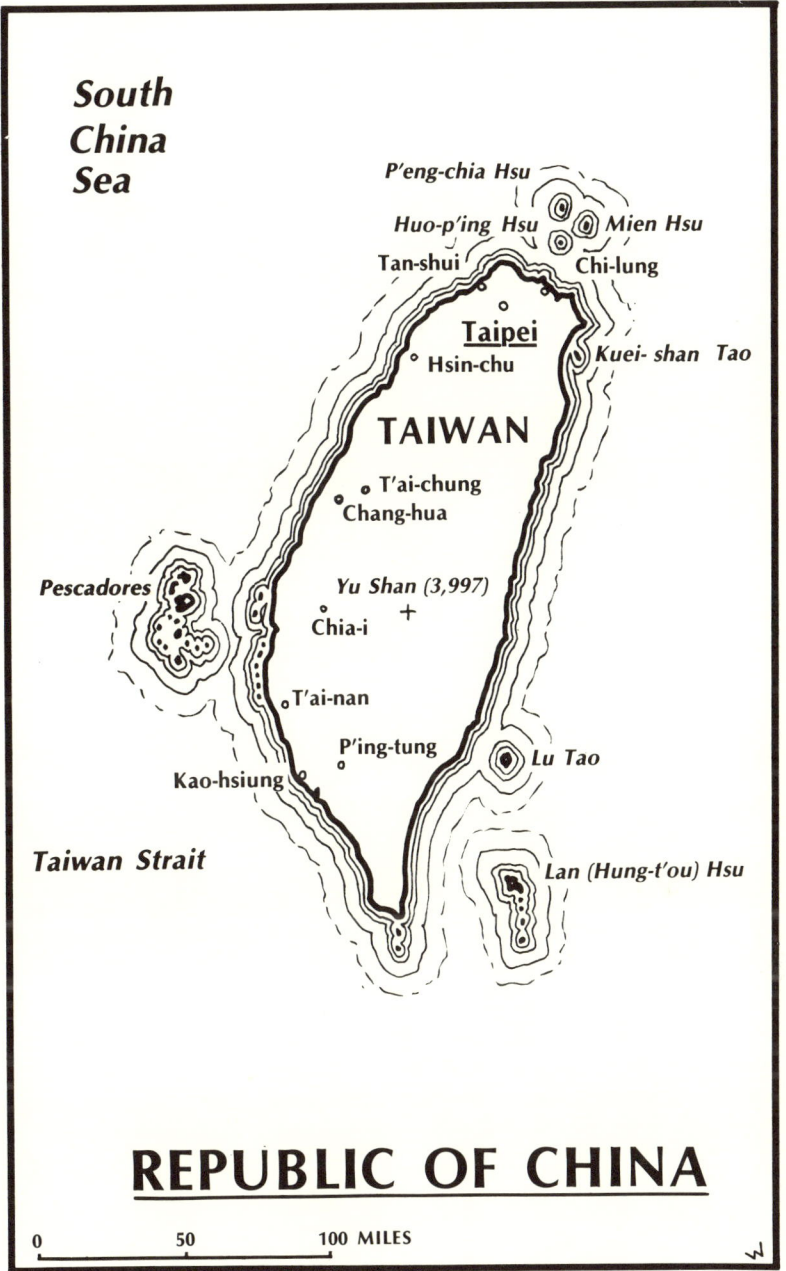

several other small islands off Taiwan.

The United States had always favored the Taiwan regime, but the fact of the People's Republic of China's existence could not continue to be ignored, and on Jan. 1, 1979, the US established diplomatic relations with the PRC and ended relations with the Republic of China. However, friendship and business ties remain strong.

The country has a varied and healthy economy, both industrial and agricultural.

The 1984 per capita income was $3,000 and the 1983 literacy rate was 83%.

The country has followed a conservative stamp-issuing policy and it is popular with the world's collectors.

Philatelic Bureau: Philatelic Department, Directorate General of Posts, Taipei 106, Taiwan, Republic of China.

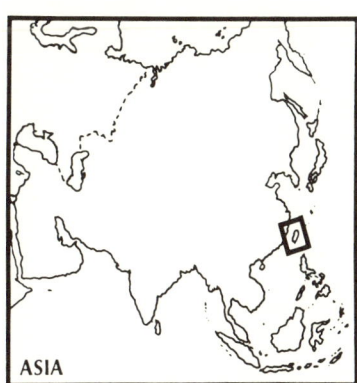

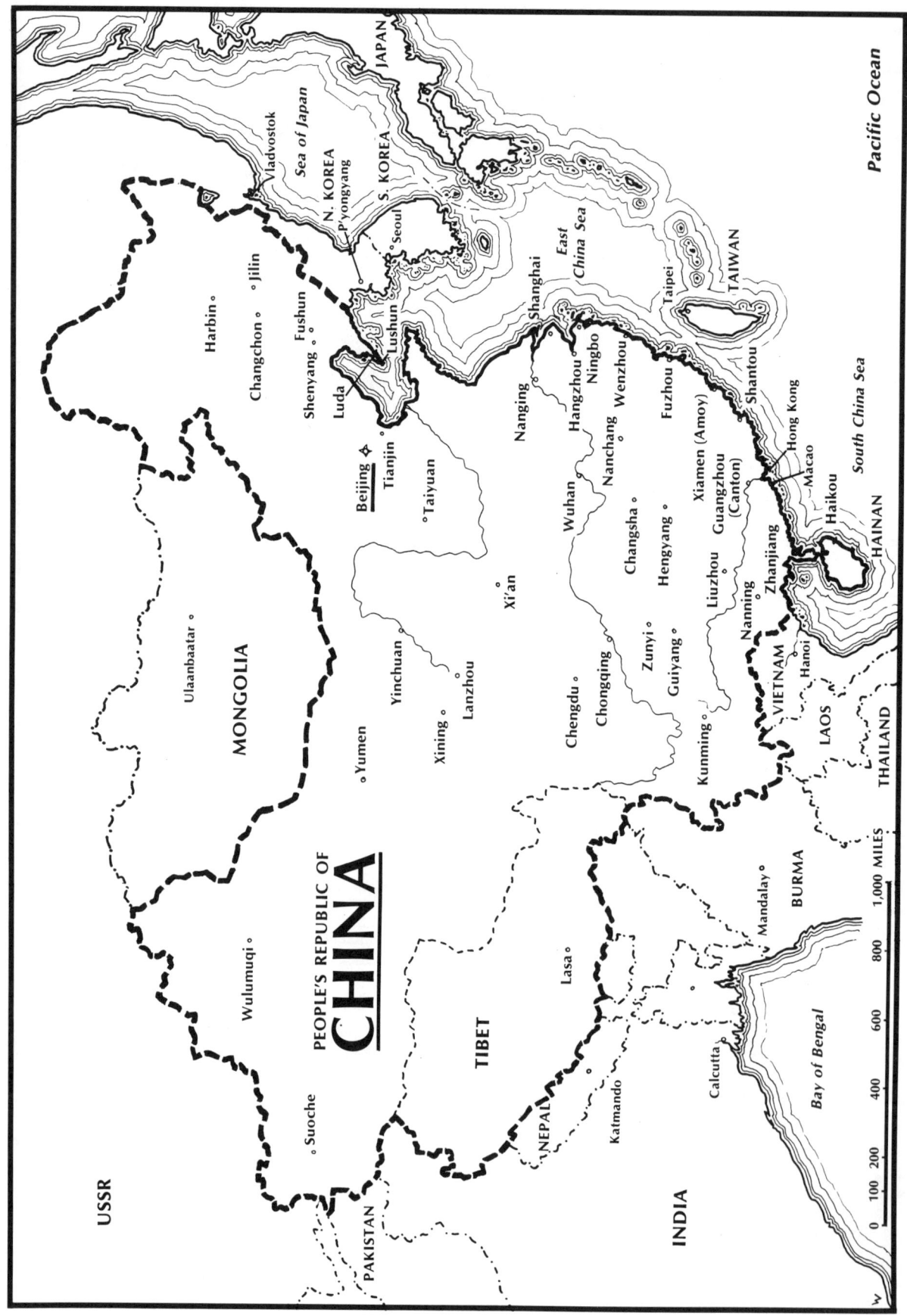

CHINA, PEOPLE'S REPUBLIC OF

Area: 3,691,520 sq. miles
Population: 1,034,907,000 (1984)
Capital: Beijing (Peking)
Currency: Yuan (100 fen)

The People's Republic of China is the world's third-largest country after the Soviet Union and Canada. More than 60% of China's area is mountainous or semidesert and 90% of the country's population lives on about 15% of the land, mostly in the east and in coastal regions.

The climate of the largest part of China is temperate, except for northern Manchuria, where winters are cold and long, and the tropical south coast.

Along the south coast, there is a year-long growing season, with high temperatures. Coastal areas are subject to destructive typhoons during summer and fall. The concentration of rainfall into short periods often results in massive flooding of the large rivers of China. These natural disasters have caused many millions of deaths.

China's civilization goes back far beyond that of most other areas. A culture under the Shang, or Yin, Dynasty was known as early as 1,500 BC, although even earlier cultures are believed to have existed.

Because of European misunderstanding of the Chinese philosophy, considerable friction arose between the Chinese and those they perceived as "barbarians." This friction finally gave way to conflict when the so-called "Opium War" broke out in 1840, sparked by the Chinese desire to prevent the trade in the drug.

The Boxer Rebellion of 1900 was a reaction to the growing foreign domination of a weakened China. The slogan of the Boxers was "Exterminate the Foreigners," and it took the combined forces of Japan, Russia, Britain, the United States, and France to restore peace in 1901.

A successful revolution led by Dr. Sun Yat-sen soon followed against the faltering Manchu Dynasty, which resulted in him becoming president of a new Republic of China in 1912.

The first half of the 20th century was largely one of war against an aggressive Japan. The island of Formosa (Taiwan) had been given up in 1895 and Manchuria was lost in 1931.

In 1937, Japan extended its war by invading Chinese mainland territory. During this period, internal unrest was sparked by Communist factions, who were unwittingly aided by the repressive policies of the Nationalist government. The Communists gained much strength. Soon after the defeat of Japan in 1945, much of China came under Communist control. General Chiang Kai-shek and his Nationalists were driven from the mainland to take refuge on Taiwan, where they formed the Republic of China.

In 1949, the Communists under Mao Tse-tung proclaimed the People's Republic of China.

Britain and France recognized the new government, but the United States refused and continued to regard the Taiwan regime as the Chinese government.

In 1951, China invaded and took over Tibet. Chinese troops intervened in the Korean conflict on the side of the North Koreans, which led to that war's stalemate.

The United Nations accepted China as a member in 1971 and expelled the Republic of China (Taiwan). The United States also began to relax its position and when President Nixon went to China in 1972, the barriers began to fall.

On Jan. 1, 1979, the US established diplomatic relations with the Communist nation and withdrew recognition from the Republic of China.

In recent years, following the recovery from the Cultural Revolution's reign of terror in the late 1960s, the country has made considerable technological and economic progress.

Industry is varied, but still primitive by Western standards, and there are large natural resources. The nation's greatest problem, its mushrooming population, is being solved with severe restrictions on family size.

The 1980 per capita income was $565 and the 1984 literacy rate was 75%.

Since the Communist state was formed, the designs of the country's many stamps have been largely political, but Chinese art, sports, and scenery are also widely featured.

Philatelic Bureau: China National Stamp Corp., 28 Dong An Men, Beijing, People's Republic of China.

A few of China's many beautiful stamps.

CHRISTMAS ISLAND (INDIAN OCEAN)

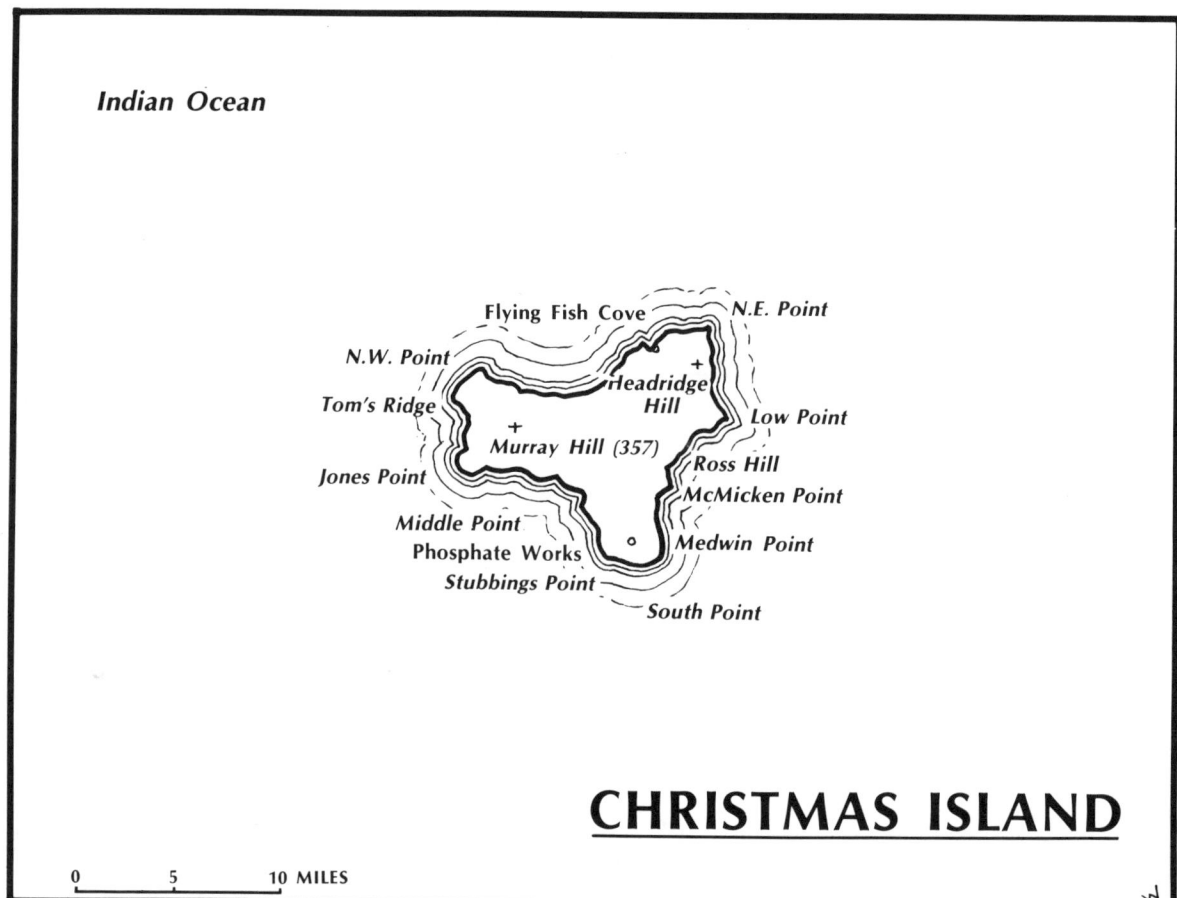

Area: 52 sq. miles
Population: 3,018 (1982)
Currency: Australian dollar

Christmas Island, in the Indian Ocean, is one of several islands in the world bearing that name.

It is situated about 225 miles south of the western end of Java, Indonesia.

The island consists generally of a plateau at an altitude of about 1,000 feet above sea level and is actually the tip of a large mountain that rises

about 15,000 feet from the bed of the ocean.

It had been known since 1650, although it was not annexed by Great Britain until June 1888.

The first inhabitants were Chinese and Malays brought in to work the extensive phosphate deposits.

In 1889, Christmas Island became

part of the Straits Settlements and was incorporated into the colony of Singapore in 1900.

The Japanese invaded the island during World War II and occupied it from 1942 until its liberation in 1945.

On Oct. 15, 1958, Christmas Island was ceded to Australia, which continues to administer it as an external territory.

The island received its first stamps on the date it became an Australian dependency. They consisted of Australian stamps overprinted "CHRISTMAS ISLAND" and surcharged in the decimal currency of Malaya. Australian currency is now used on the island.

Since then, a modest number of stamps have been issued, most of which have an island theme. Sets have featured famous visitors to the island, ships with an island connection, the phosphate industry, and the island's flora and fauna.

Philatelic Bureau: Philatelic Bureau, Christmas Island, Indian Ocean.

COCOS (KEELING) ISLANDS

Area: 5.5 sq. miles
Population: 569 (1981)
Currency: Australian dollar

Located in the Indian Ocean to the south of the Indonesian island of Sumatra, the Cocos (Keeling) Islands are about 1,700 miles northwest of Perth, Australia.

The islands comprise a group of five major islands plus several smaller islets, and uninhabited North Keeling Island about 16 miles to the north.

The climate is pleasant, with a high temperature range of 70-90 degrees F. Southeast trade winds blow during much of the year, although storms can occur during January-April.

The islands were discovered in 1609 by the British sailor William Keeling. They were not settled until 1823, when Alexander Hare, an English adventurer, is reported to have established a harem and imported slaves from Malaya.

In 1827, Captain John Clunies-Ross, a Scot, settled with his family on Direction Island. Hare returned to Malaya in 1831, and Clunies-Ross, left in sole possession, devoted himself to establishing a copra business.

Captain Fremantle of the Royal Navy, commanding HMS *Juno*, claimed the islands for his queen in 1857, setting to rest the concerns of Clunies-Ross that a foreign nation might take possession of the islands.

In 1878, the government of Ceylon was made responsible for the

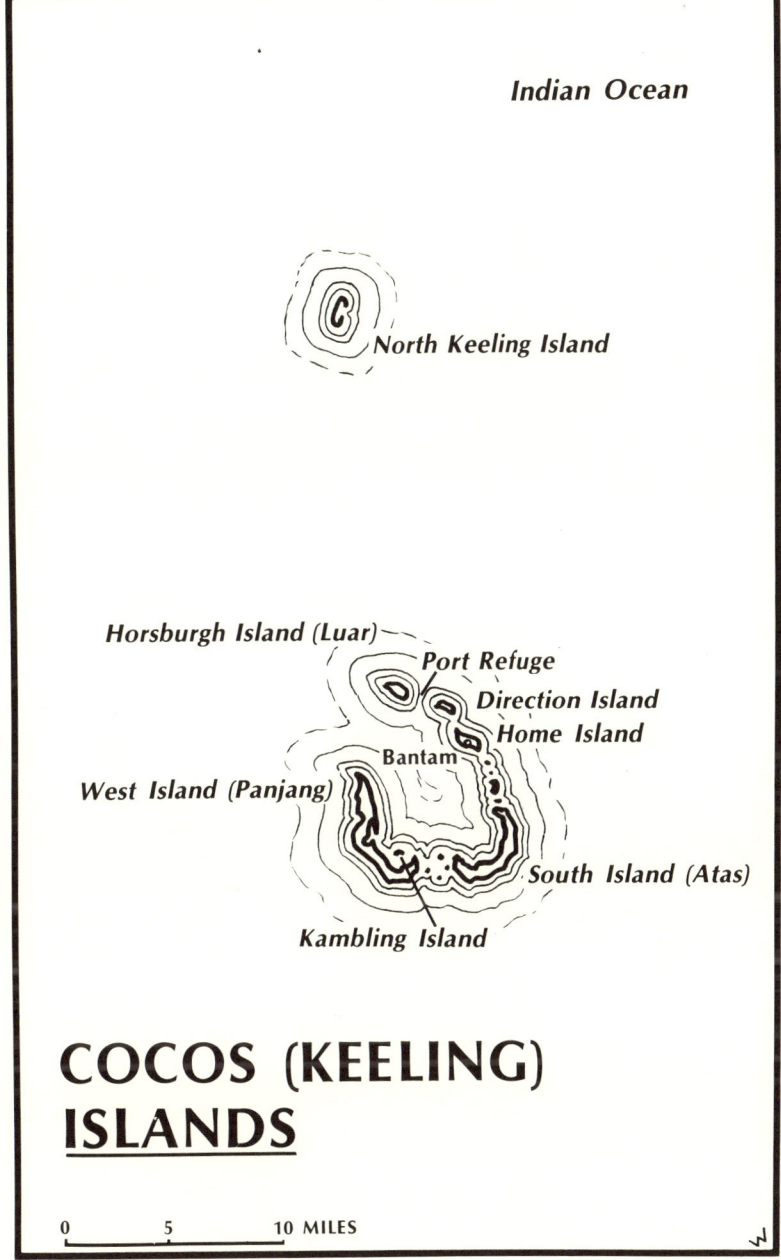

islands, but they were transferred to the Straits Settlements in 1886. The Settlement of Singapore became responsible in 1903.

The Australian government purchased the World War II airstrip on West Island in 1951, and used it as a refueling stop for Qantas aircraft until the introduction of long-range jet aircraft made the stop unnecessary. It continues to be an important weather-reporting station.

On Nov. 23, 1955, Great Britain handed the islands over to Australia with the provision that the property rights of the Clunies-Ross family be respected. Since then, they have been administered as an Australian territory.

Stamps were first issued by the Australian Post Office June 11, 1963.

On Sept. 3, 1979, the newly formed Cocos (Keeling) Island Council established a postal service of its own, independent from that of Australia.

Philatelic Bureau: Philatelic Bureau, Post Office, Cocos (Keeling) Islands, Indian Ocean.

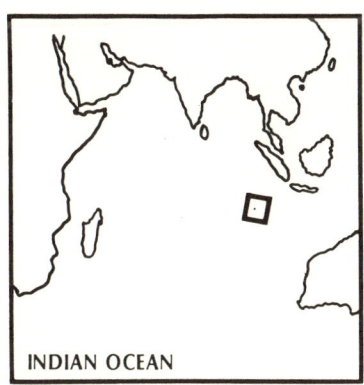

INDIA, REPUBLIC OF

Area: 1,269,420 sq. miles
Population: 746,388,000 (1984)
Capital: Delhi
Currency: Rupee (100 paise)

The three major regions of India are the Himalaya Mountains that run along the northern part of the country, the northern plains, and the peninsula. The latter area includes the Deccan Plateau.

The Himalayas, with an average elevation of 19,000 feet, tend to isolate India climatically from the rest of Asia to the north.

The Indian climate is dominated by the annual monsoon, a period when moisture-laden air sweeps in from the ocean and deposits heavy rain on coastal and eastern areas. In the west, the amounts reduce sharply as distance from the coast increases.

On the coast and in the east annual rainfall exceeds 80 inches a year, and in some regions more than 400 inches can fall in a season.

Much of the west receives 20-40 inches a year, with the northwest, bordering on Pakistan, receiving 5-20 inches.

The monsoon months are June-October, tapering off in November and December.

Temperatures in southern India tend to be fairly constant. At Trivandrum, in the far south, the year round monthly average is 78-82 degrees F.

In the north, much greater variation occurs, with lows in the cool months as much as 30 degrees F below those in the south.

The climate in the north is Mediterranean in character, with blue sky and dry weather from November to February. In March, the hot season begins and temperatures increase until the coming of the monsoon in June.

Because the 1947 partition of the subcontinent into India and Pakistan is so recent, it is impossible to apply a similar separation to the area's history.

The subcontinent can boast one of the world's oldest cultures, the 5,000-year-old Indus Valley civilization.

Buddhism was introduced to India prior to the third century by the Kushans from central Asia, and by the eighth century, Arabs had obtained a Moslem foothold in the west. In the areas into which Buddhism had found its way, Hinduism eventually won majority support.

By the 1200s, Turks controlled the north of India, but the Mogul emperors ruled from the early 1500s to the beginning of the 18th century.

At the beginning of the 1400s, the Portuguese set up trading posts on the Indian coast, which lasted until the Republic of India regained them in 1961.

The Dutch also established trading settlements on the Coromandel coast, as well as in Gujarat and Bengal. These were eventually eliminated by the growing British presence.

Permission for the first permanent British settlement at Surat was obtained in 1613. In 1687, Bombay replaced Surat as headquarters on the west coast of the East India Company. By the end of the century, settlements existed around the coast as far as Calcutta.

In 1664, the French decided to give the British some competition in India and formed a trading company of their own. Between 1666 and 1721, France set up posts at Surat, Pondicherry, Chandernagore (near Calcutta), Calicut, and Mahe.

As British power expanded, the French were restricted to their coastal settlements. The French government took over the remaining five in 1769 and retained them until the 1950s, when they became part of the Republic of India.

By the 1850s, the British government had taken over the administration of India from the East India Company and controlled virtually the entire subcontinent.

Queen Victoria was made Empress of India and it became the prime jewel in the crown of the British Empire.

As the 20th century dawned, the voice of nationalism began to be heard in the land and following World War I, there was considerable unrest.

Weakened by World War II, Britain no longer had the will to remain responsible for an enormous population clamoring for self-government. In 1947, it split India into the dominions of Pakistan and India. This assumption of self-government and the withdrawal of the British administration left a void in which massive population relocation and brutal religious conflict swept the country.

Neither India nor Pakistan has fully recovered from the turmoil of those days and both countries are poor.

India, in particular, has suffered greatly from overpopulation and poor sanitary conditions, the latter in large measure perpetuated by its veneration of the cow. Although the industrial base is broad and varied, food production to feed the mushrooming population has lagged, despite 70% of the labor force being engaged in agriculture.

The latest available per capita income figure is only $150 and the 1981 literacy rate was 36%.

India's stamp-issuing history is long and interesting. Stamp issues have not been excessive considering the volume of mail. However, production quality of stamps has been low and they are mostly not attractive.

Philatelic Bureau: Philatelic Bureau, GPO, Bombay 400001, India.

Stamps marking the first airplane mail.

HONG KONG, COLONY OF

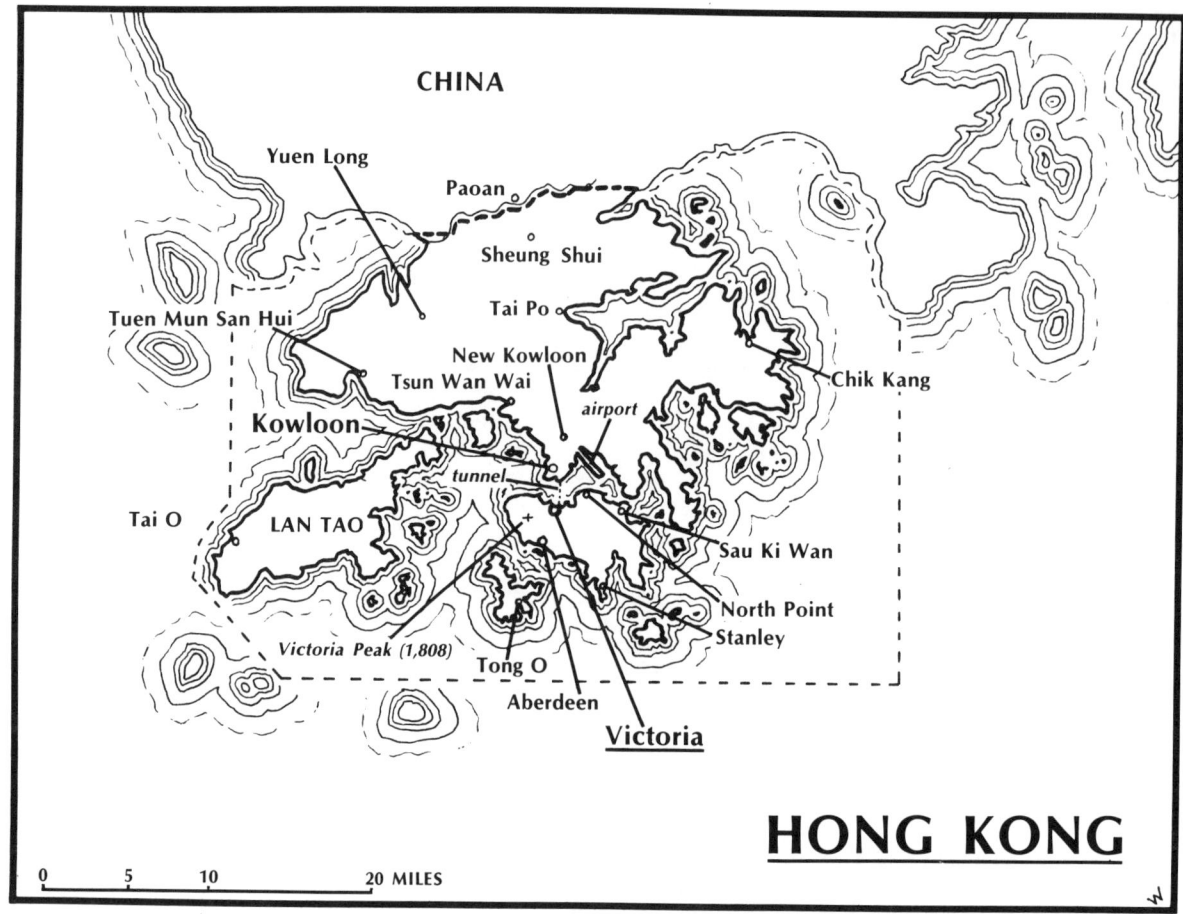

Area: 409 sq. miles
Population: 5,287,000 (1983)
Capital: Victoria
Currency: Dollar (100 cents)

The British colony of Hong Kong is located on the southern coast of China, adjoining the Chinese province of Kwangtung.

It comprises two large islands, an area on the mainland, and many smaller islands. The islands are hilly, although there is some level land suitable for agriculture on the mainland.

The climate is subtropical. It is generally warm and humid for half the year and cool and dry during the other half. Average temperatures range from 55-65 degrees F in February and 75-85 in July.

The average annual rainfall is 85 inches, most of which falls in the summer. Typhoons can occur during the same period.

The first foreign settlement on the Chinese coast was by the Portuguese at nearby Macao in 1557.

Hong Kong Island was granted to Britain as a result of the Opium War of the 1840s and the Treaty of Nanking. During the Anglo-French campaign against China of the 1850s, the British occupied the Kowloon Peninsula. Its possession by China had been seen as a threat to the security of Hong Kong and its harbor. The 1860 Treaty of Peking made it permanent British property.

Lan Tao Island and a large area on the mainland, some 365 square miles in area, was leased to the British in 1898 for 99 years.

The People's Republic of China has indicated its intention to reclaim all of Hong Kong when the lease expires in 1997.

After the WWII Japanese invasion and occupation of 1941-45, Hong Kong became one of the most important trade, financial, and tourist centers of the Far East.

Industries include textiles and the making of clothes, shipbuilding, steel making, electronics and other light industries.

Cantonese is the Chinese dialect spoken by most of the population although English is the official language.

The first stamps were issued in 1862. However, it was not until 1941 that any Hong Kong scene was depicted.

Philatelic Bureau: Philatelic Bureau, GPO, Hong Kong.

INDONESIA, REPUBLIC OF

Area: 741,100 sq. miles
Population: 169,442,000 (1984)
Capital: Jakarta
Currency: Rupiah (100 sen)

Columbus sought the spice islands of Indonesia when he set out on his 1492 voyage and bumped into the New World in the process.

The Republic of Indonesia comprises an archipelago of more than 13,500 islands stretching from the Southeast Asian mainland to the coast of New Guinea. It includes what was the Dutch East Indies, Portuguese Timor, and the western half of New Guinea.

The climate is tropical, although the upland areas of the larger islands are more temperate than the hot, humid coastal lands.

Rainfall varies from more than 320 inches a year in the mountains of Sumatra and Java to less than 20 inches a year in the western Celebes and Lesser Sundas Islands. The average rainfall for the archipelago is 80 inches.

By 1750, Java was a Dutch island, but they did not achieve control over the entire area until the 20th century.

After World War II, nationalists took over and proclaimed a republic. In 1963, the western part of New Guinea was added, and in 1976 Portuguese Timor was annexed.

The 1982 per capita income was $560 and the 1981 literacy rate was 64%.

Philatelic Bureau: Philatelic Subdivision, State Enterprise Post and Giro, 34 Jalan Jakarta, Bandung, Indonesia.

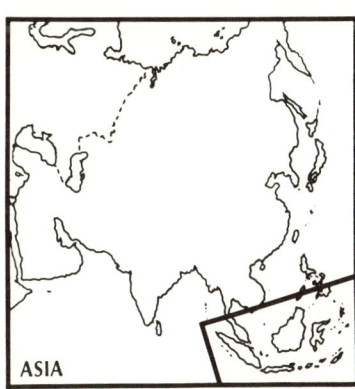

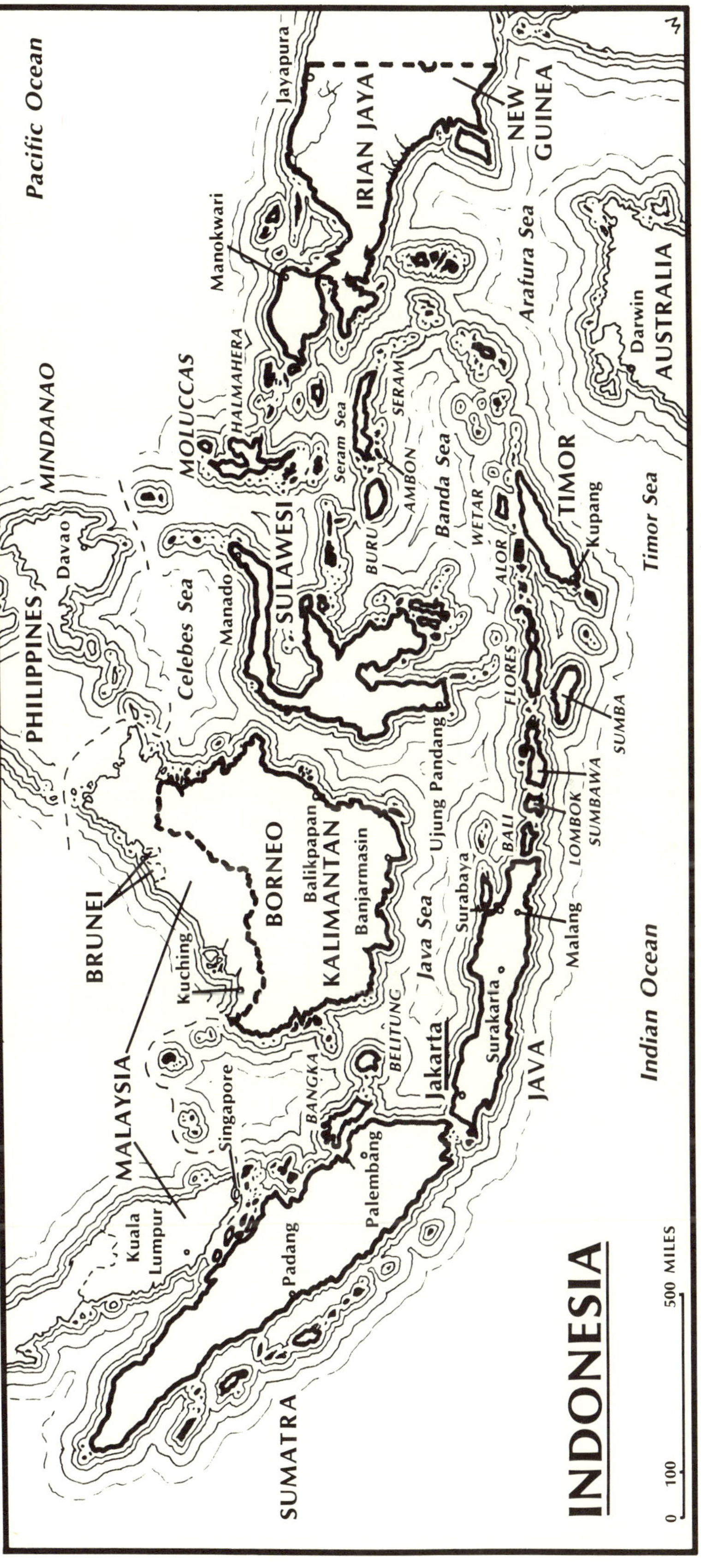

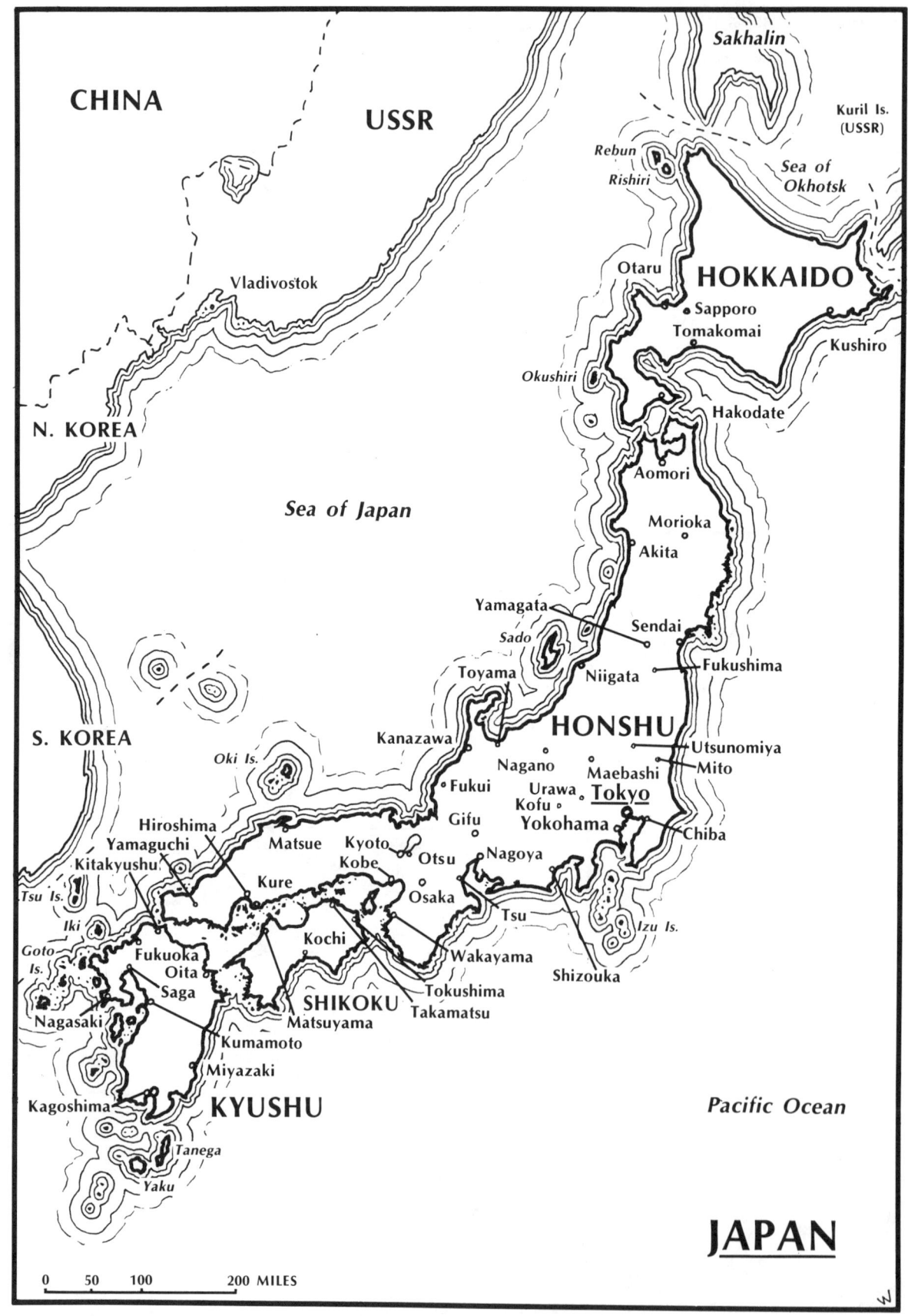

JAPAN

Area: 147,470 sq. miles
Population: 119,896,000 (1984)
Capital: Tokyo
Currency: Yen (100 sen)

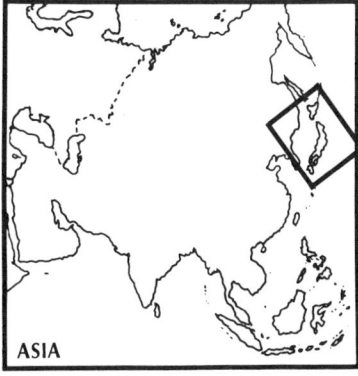

Japan is a constitutional monarchy consisting of a chain of mountainous islands running northeast to southwest off the coast of Asia, opposite the Soviet Union and the Korean Peninsula.

There are four main islands. From the north these are Hokkaido, Honshu, Shikoku, and Kyushu. There are also more than 3,300 smaller islands including the Ryukyu, Bonin, and Volcano groups.

The country's deeply indented coastline measures 16,470 miles in length.

There are many volcanoes in the various mountain ranges, mostly extinct or dormant, including the beautifully symmetrical, 12,388-foot Mount Fuji overlooking Tokyo.

Geologically, Japan is unstable and subject to frequent earthquakes. There is an average of four seismic occurrences daily, with major earthquakes coming on an average of once every six years.

Japan's climate ranges from the subtropical weather of Kyushu in the south, to the bitterly cold winters of Hokkaido in the north.

Temperatures vary widely from a January average in central Hokkaido of 14 degrees F to one of 45 degrees F in southern Kyushu.

Average temperatures for August are 79 degrees F in Kagoshima, 81 in Osaka, 77 in Tokyo, and 69 in Sapporo.

Located between the pressure differences over mainland Asia and the Pacific Ocean, Japan is subject to heavy precipitation and violent typhoons that can do massive damage, especially in the southern islands.

Most of the country receives more than 40 inches of precipitation each year. Along the west coast of central Honshu, 100-200 inches annually is not unusual.

The country's Japanese name, Dai Nippon, translates as the Land of the Rising Sun.

Legend records that the Japanese Empire was founded in 660 BC by the Emperor Jimmu, who claimed descent from the Sun Goddess. The Japanese court adopted the Chinese writing system about AD 400. During the sixth century Buddhism came to Japan.

Emperors of the Yamato Dynasty ruled from 710 to 1867, although the real power was held by families of shoguns, or military dictators.

The Portuguese, in 1542, became the first Europeans to visit Japan. In the years that followed, traders from the major European nations arrived, together with various missionaries.

A Japanese suspicion that these visitors were the forerunners in an attempt at military conquest caused the government to deport all foreigners and cut off relations with the outside world.

Not until 1854, when Commodore Matthew Perry of the US Navy negotiated the Convention of Kanagawa, did Japan again become open to the world.

This caused considerable changes in Japanese society. The feudal system was abolished and a number of Western institutions adopted, including constitutional government and a new legal system, based on that of the West.

Japan took only a few years to move from the Middle Ages and to achieve the status of a world power.

To be a world power, to the Japanese, meant going to war, and the country became involved in war with China in the mid-1890s and with Russian in 1904-05. These wars gained Japan part of Manchuria, the island of Formosa (Taiwan), and southern Sakhalin, plus a free hand in Korea, which it annexed in 1910.

World War I gained Japan a League of Nations mandate over the former German Pacific island colonies and new status as one of the major nations. Growing military influence brought about a policy of aggressive expansion during the interwar years. It invaded Manchuria and installed a puppet regime.

International criticism of its aggressions led to Japan's resignation from the League of Natons in 1933.

All-out war against China was begun in 1937 and tensions rose, culminating in the Japanese attack on Pearl Harbor in December 1941, made without declaration of war.

World War II was for Japan, a war that could not be won. Resources were insufficient to sustain the country against the growing power of the Allies. When the Allies pounded the country from the air, including the first use of atomic weapons in an attempt to avoid the massive casualties expected during an invasion of Japan, the country surrendered.

On Sept. 2, 1945, Japan formally surrendered and lost all the territory it had conquered, although the Ryukyu, Bonin, and Volcano islands were returned to Japan in 1972.

Since the war, Japan has engaged in another kind of conflict — economic war. Today, its products, automobiles, electronic equipment, computers, cameras, etc. have a large share of the world's markets, although it retains considerable control over imports to protect its own industries.

Japan's first stamps were issued in 1871. In recent years, its stamps have been numerous but are widely collected throughout the world.

Philatelic Bureau: Philatelic Section, GPO Box 888, Tokyo 100-91, Japan.

KOREA, DEMOCRATIC PEOPLE'S REPUBLIC OF

Area: 47,000 sq. miles
Population: 19,630,000 (1984)
Capital: Pyongyang
Currency: Won (100 chon)

The Democratic People's Republic of Korea (or North Korea) occupies the northern part of the Korean Peninsula. It borders on the People's Republic of China, with a short border on the Soviet Union.

The country is mostly mountainous, especially in the north and on the east coast. There are many deep, narrow valleys and some flat areas of cultivation.

The climate is continental, with cold winters and hot summers. The average temperature in August at Pyongyang is 85 degrees F, while in January it is 18 degrees F.

Precipitation mostly falls in the summer as rain. Although snowfall is generally light in winter snow can cover the ground for long periods, and temperatures can fall below 0 degrees F.

Since the Korean Peninsula was not politically divided until the end of World War II, it is difficult to separate the prior history of today's two countries.

Various attempts were made to open the country in the 19th century, but it was not until the 1890s that Japan began to take over the country, despite agreements with China and Russia to respect Korea's independence.

During the Russo-Japanese War of 1904-05, Japan mounted an invasion of Korea and occupied the peninsula. The takeover was completed in 1910, when the country was annexed by Japan.

Japan ruled by force, ruthlessly

putting down nationalism whenever it appeared. By 1941 there was one policeman in Korea for every 400 inhabitants. In 1942, Korea was made part of Japan.

World War II ended the Japanese presence in Korea and the Allies occupied the country, with Soviet forces taking over that portion north of the 38th parallel. Despite prior agreements that Korean independence should be restored, the Soviet Union refused to leave. It set up a puppet government in the area it controlled, and ignored all attempts to make it live up to its agreements.

In December 1948, the present Communist state was formed.

The economy is varied, although not strong. The 1978 per capita income was $570 and the literacy rate is 99%.

Philatelic Bureau: Korea Stamp Corp., Pyongyang, North Korea.

KOREA, REPUBLIC OF

Area: 38,210 sq. miles
Population: 42,000,000 (1984)
Capital: Seoul
Currency: Won (100 chun)

The Republic of Korea (South Korea) is located in the southern portion of the Korean Peninsula. It is mountainous, especially on the east coast, although not as rugged as in the northern peninsula.

The west and south coasts are indented, with many islands and numerous good harbors.

The climate is more moderate than that of the north. Average January temperatures on the south coast are above freezing. In Seoul, summer temperatures can reach 95 degrees F.

The country's pre-World War II history is outlined under "Korea, Democratic People's Republic of."

Following the Soviet Union's refusal to leave its World War II occupation zone or to permit the reunification of the country to which it had previously agreed, the Republic of Korea was formed on Aug. 15, 1948 in that part of the peninsula south of the 38th parallel.

On June 25, 1950, North Korea invaded the south and for three years the Korean War raged between United Nations forces, mostly US, and North Korea, supported by China and the Soviet Union.

An armistice signed on July 27, 1953, restored the two countries to just about what they had been before the invasion.

Despite periods of political unrest and harassment by Communist North Korea, South Korea has made great economic strides.

Industries include electronics, motor vehicles, shipbuilding, textiles, and clothing. The 1978 per capita income was $1,187 and the 1983 literacy rate was 92%.

Stamps were first issued for all of Korea in 1885.

Since independence, a considerable number of stamps has been issued.

Philatelic Bureau: Korean Philatelic Center, Division of Bando Sangsa Co. Lt., CPO Box 1899, Seoul, South Korea.

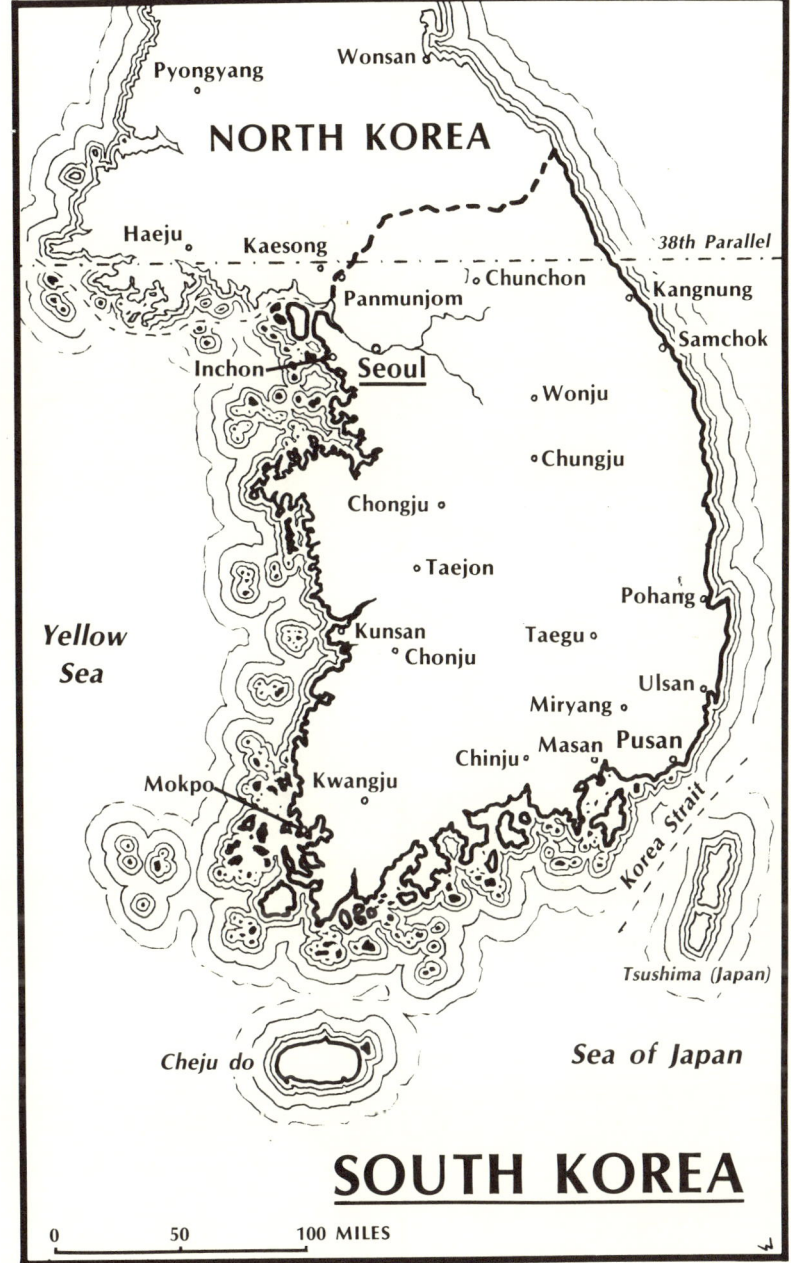

A traditional Korean wedding.

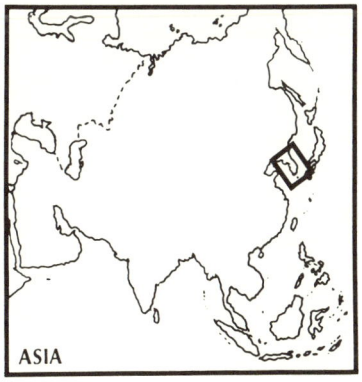

LAOS (LAO PEOPLE'S DEMOCRATIC REPUBLIC)

Area: 91,430 sq. miles
Population: 3,732,000 (1984)
Capital: Vientiane
Currency: New kip (100 cents)

Landlocked in Southeast Asia, Laos has long borders with Thailand and Vietnam, as well as shorter ones with China and Cambodia.

The border with Vietnam is formed by a rugged mountain range, peaks of which rise above 9,000 feet. Much of the border with Thailand is formed by the Mekong River.

Most of the country is covered by dense rain forest.

Heavy rains fall from May to September and there is a cool, drier period through January. The weather is hot and dry from February to April.

The annual temperature range at Vientiane is 55-95 degrees F.

Laos was part of French Indo China until World War II, when the Japanese invaded and occupied it.

After attempts by the French to reassert their control of Laos after the war, they finally recognized the country's independence within the French Union on July 19, 1949.

Under the 1954 Geneva Agreement, France removed most of its troops from Laos and the North Vietnamese, who had troops there, were supposed to do likewise. However, they did not and they have been in the country ever since.

After several years of political turmoil and numerous changes of government a second Geneva con-

ference was held in 1962. Again, the North Vietnamese refused to honor the agreement, making only a token withdrawal, and the unrest continued.

The Communists continued their efforts to gain control of the country and succeeded in abolishing the monarchy, proclaiming the Lao People's Democratic Republic on Dec. 2, 1975.

The country is poor and the economy almost nonexistent. The latest available per capita income figure is $85 and the literacy rate in 1978 was 28%.

Many early stamps of Laos are extremely beautiful, with fine engraving and rich colors. Under the Communist regime, stamps are less attractive. Their subjects are propagandistic, or follow topical themes popular with Western collectors.

Philatelic Bureau: Service Philatelique des PTT, Vientiane, Laos.

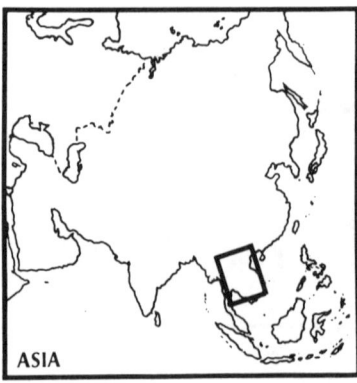

MACAO

Area: 6 sq. miles
Population: 400,000 (1984)
Capital: Macao
Currency: Pataca (100 avos)

The oldest European settlement in the Far East, Macao is located on the coast of China, 40 miles across the mouth of the Pearl River from Hong Kong.

It is a Portuguese overseas province comprising a peninsula and two small islands. Canton is 70 miles up river from Macao.

Macao has a subtropical climate, with about 80% of the average 80 inches annual rainfall coming in May to September. Winters are cool, with an average December temperature of 59 degrees F.

The area was used as a way station on the route to Japan by Portuguese traders as early as 1516.

China agreed to a Portuguese settlement there in 1557, but it was more than 300 years before the question of sovereignty was settled. The Portuguese government paid rent to China for the peninsula until 1849, when it declared Macao to be independent of Chinese authority.

In 1887, China finally recognized Portugal's sovereign rights in Macao in the agreement known as the Protocol of Lisbon. In it, Portugal promised never to hand Macao over to a third power without China's permission.

During World War II, Macao was the only neutral port in South China. The Japanese tried to interfere with the area, but did not occupy it.

Macao is represented in the Portuguese parliament by a member who is elected for a four-year term.

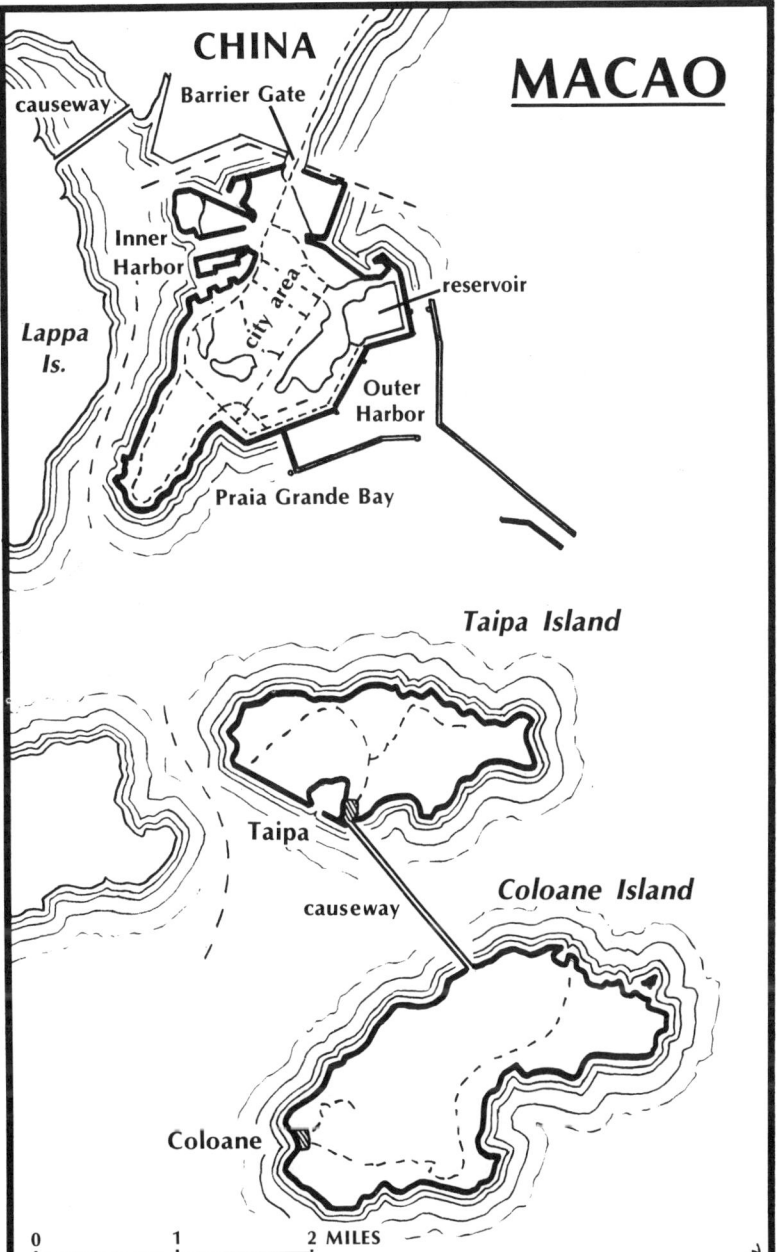

Macao's economy is based on light industry, including textiles and fireworks. Trade and tourism are important and there is a growing number of tourists and visitors from Hong Kong who are attracted by the casinos.

The port facilities of Macao are limited by heavy silting and ocean-going vessels must lie offshore.

Access to Macao is by ferry from Hong Kong or Canton, or by road from China. There is a fast hydrofoil service from Hong Kong.

Macao is a picturesque city extending up a hillside overlooking the harbor. Its buildings of many colors are a mixture of Oriental and European styles and many date from the early days of the Portuguese settlement.

It issued its first stamps in 1884 and these have followed the usual Portuguese colonial pattern. Few stamps have been issued in recent years.

Philatelic Bureau: Divisao de Filatelia, Largo do Senado, Macao.

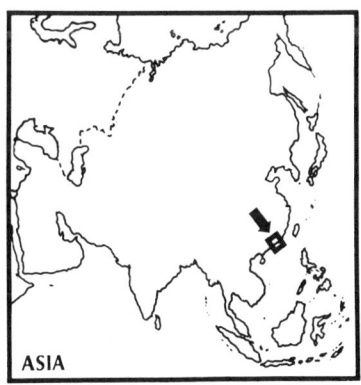

MALAYSIA

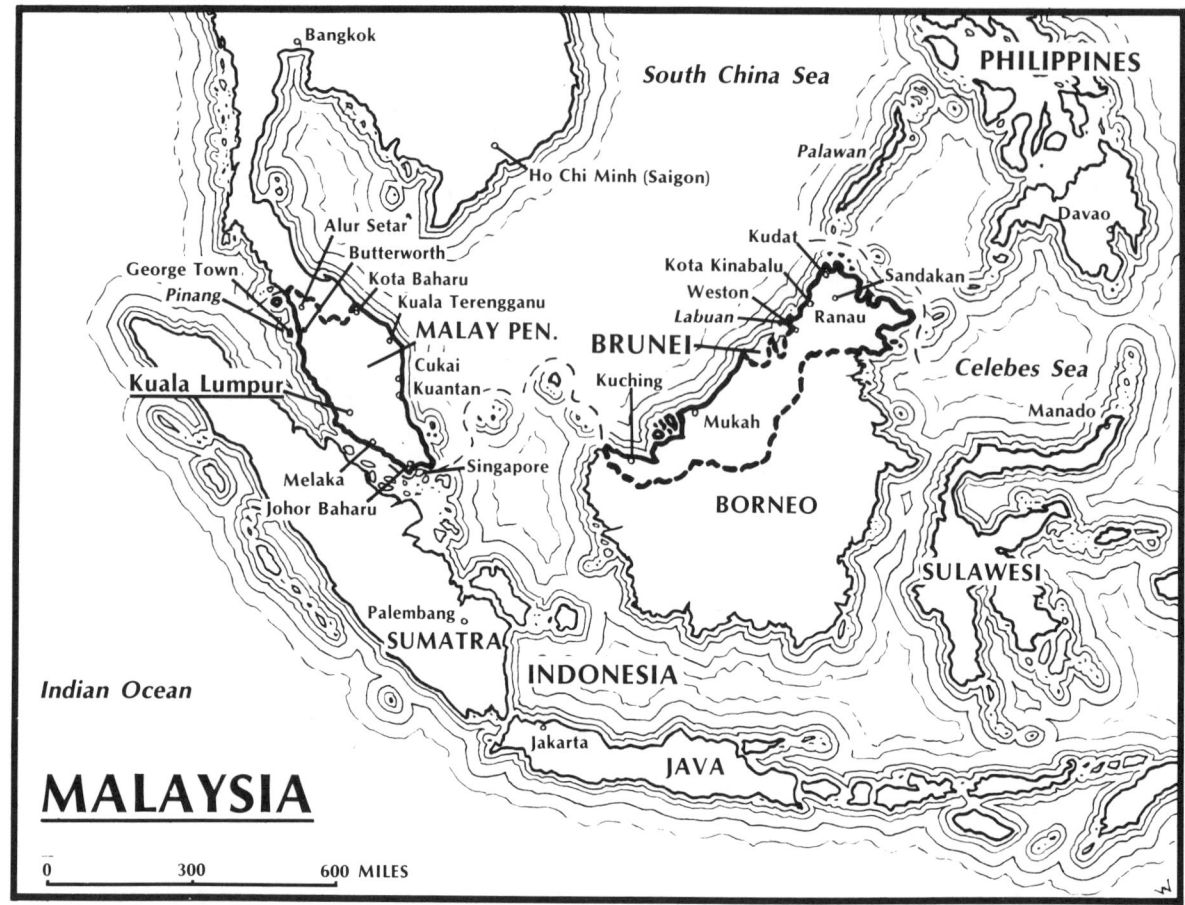

Area: 127,316 sq. miles
Population: 15,330,000 (1984)
Capital: Kuala Lumpur
Currency: Ringgit (100 cents)

Malaysia comprises two large and separate areas; the southern part of the Malay Peninsula and the northern portion of the island of Borneo. A 400-mile stretch of the South China Sea lies between them.

The country includes the former stamp-issuing areas of the Malay States, Sarawak, Sabah, and the island of Labuan. Singapore was part of the federation until 1965.

The climate is tropical with a year-round average temperature on the Malay Peninsula of 81 degrees F. Rainfall ranges from 90-120 inches a year, depending on location. The heaviest is generally on the coast.

On Borneo, temperatures range from 65-90 degrees F. Annual rainfall is from 60 inches on the coast to 180 inches in the interior.

Both areas are characterized by low-lying, swampy coastal strips, rising to rain forest covered hills.

The mountains are more rugged in northern Borneo, culminating in 13,455-foot Mount Kinabalu, the highest peak in southeast Asia.

The country was formed on Sept. 16, 1963.

The area has a long history of colonial development. The Portuguese were first in 1511, when they formed a settlement at Malacca. The British eventually came to control the Malay Peninsula after occupying Penang in 1786.

The British Straits Settlements was formed in 1826 from Malacca, Penang, and Singapore. In 1895, the Federated Malay States came into being.

Sarawak, on Borneo, had been founded in 1839 when James Brooke received it as a gift from the Sultan of Brunei.

Sabah, formerly North Borneo, had been administered by the British North Borneo Company from 1877 and Labuan, an island off the coast, had been a British crown colony since 1846.

With a varied economy and considerable natural resources, the country is stable and relatively prosperous. The latest per capita income figure is $714 and the literacy rate is 75%.

The country's first stamp was issued on Independence Day and since then its issue policy has been restrained.

Philatelic Bureau: Director General of Posts, Post Office Headquarters, Kuala Lumpur, Malaysia.

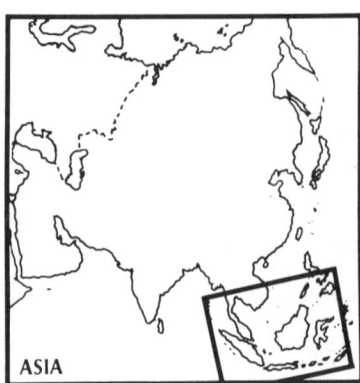

MALDIVES, REPUBLIC OF

Area: 115 sq. miles
Population: 173,000 (1984)
Capital: Male
Currency: Rufiyaa (100 Larees)

The Maldive Islands form a chain of about 2,000 coral islands arranged in a series of atolls, extending south from the tip of the Indian subcontinent.

Few exceed 5-6 feet in elevation and none covers an area of more than five square miles.

The climate is hot, with only slight year-round variation in temperature. The average high temperature is 80 degrees F. Rainfall is about 100 inches a year in the north rising to 150 inches in the south.

Legend has it that the history of the Maldives began when a Sinhalese prince from Ceylon named Koimala was becalmed in a Maldive lagoon with his bride. Believing himself to be in paradise, he stayed to become the islands' first sultan!

It is recorded that the islands were ruled as a sultanate from AD 1100 until Nov. 11, 1968, when the present republic was formed. The first sultan had introduced Islam to the islands.

The Portuguese established themselves on the islands for a brief period in the 1500s, before the Dutch arrived.

Early in the 19th century, the British gained the Maldives, when they took over Ceylon (Sri Lanka) from the Dutch, and for many years the economy of the islands was tied to that of Ceylon.

The British signed an agreement with the sultan in 1887, which provided that Britain would protect the islands.

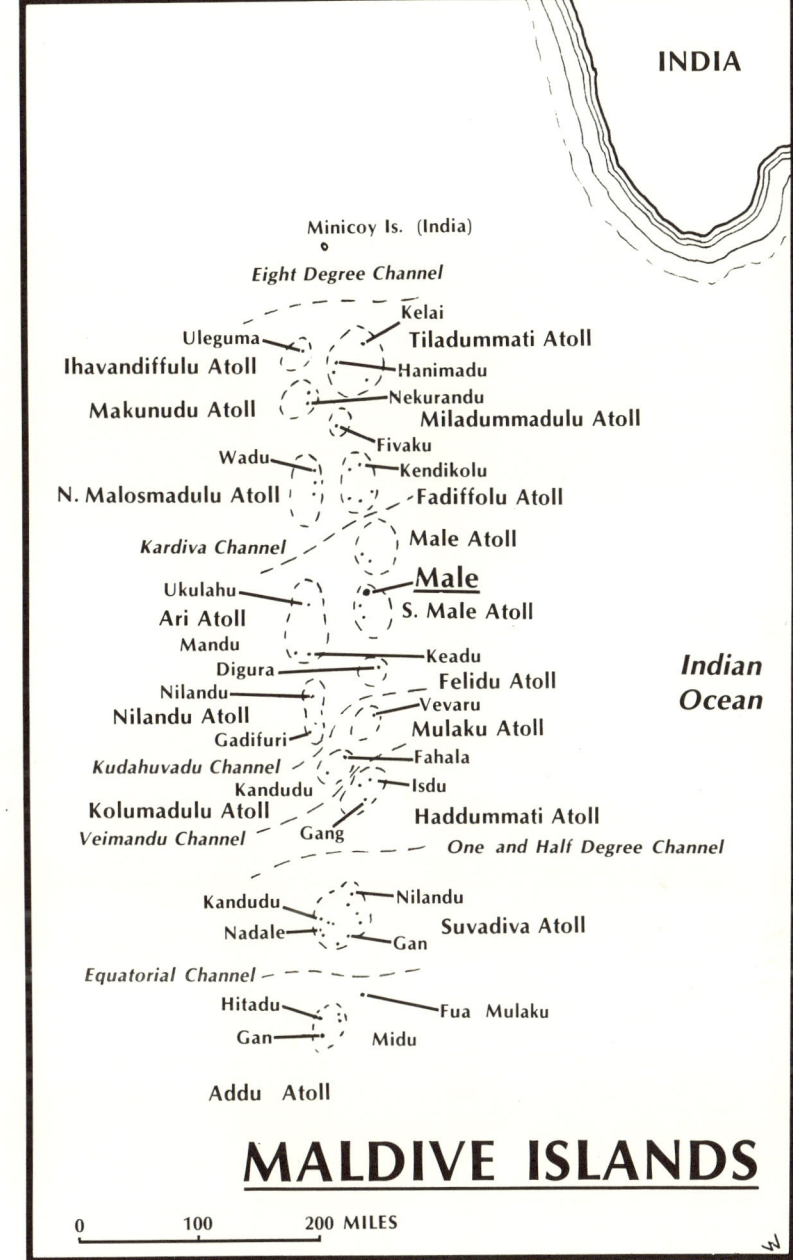

The islands became independent on July 26, 1965.

A treaty in that year gave Britain the use of Gan Atoll as an air base in return for British aid. It was terminated in 1976, when the British closed the base.

A poor country, the Maldives rely on fishing and small-scale agriculture for much of its income. Coconuts are extensively grown and constitute the main crop.

In recent years, tourism, particularly from Europe, has assumed greater importance as a source of revenue and the magnificent beaches and good climate offer considerable possibilities for future development.

The 1982 per capita income was $373 and the 1984 literacy rate is claimed by the government to be 85%.

Philatelic Bureau: Philatelic Bureau, GPO, Male, Maldives, Indian Ocean.

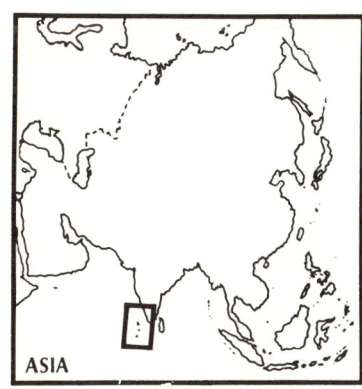

MONGOLIA (MONGOLIAN PEOPLE'S REPUBLIC)

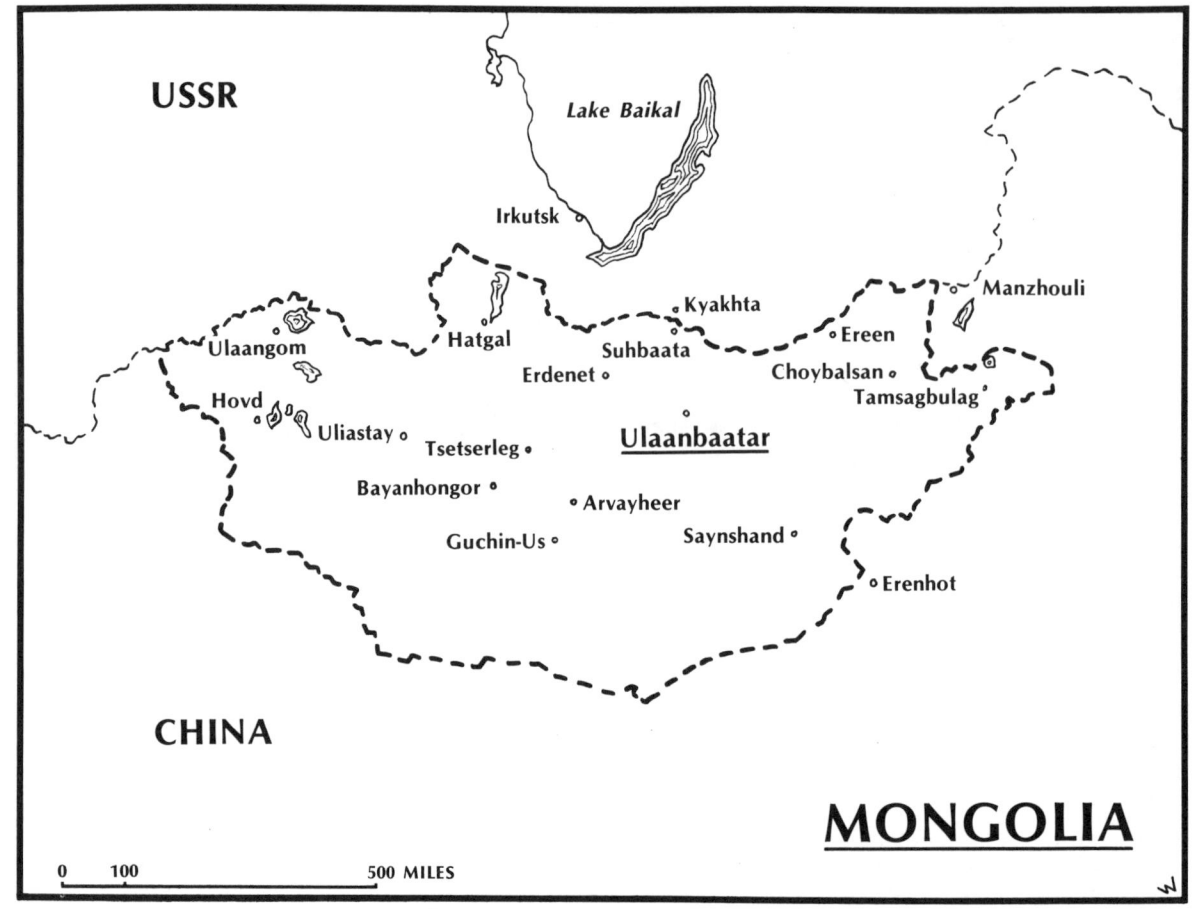

Area: 604,247 sq. miles
Population: 1,860,000 (1984)
Capital: Ulaanbaatar
Currency: Tugrik (100 mung)

Often labeled "Outer Mongolia" to distinguish it from Inner Mongolia (an autonomous region in the People's Republic of China), Mongolia lies sandwiched between the Soviet Union and China. Its modern history has been largely influenced by events in those countries.

Its topography ranges from the arid Gobi Desert in the southeast to mountains in the west rising to more than 13,000 feet. The north, with its grass plains stretching across the high plateau landscape, contains most of the population and is reasonably well watered.

The climate is continental, with long, cold winters and short, warm summers. The average January temperature at Ulaanbaatar is -17 degrees F. In July it is 64 degrees F. Recorded extremes are -54 degrees F and 102 degrees F.

Mongolia has had an influence far out of proportion to its present importance. Its greatest glory came in the 13th century when Genghis Khan and his successors ranged as far to the west as Hungary.

Later, as Mongol power waned, what remained of its vast empire came under Chinese control.

In 1911, as China became weakened by revolution, Mongolia proclaimed its independence. Its freedom did not last and by 1921, a Soviet Communist puppet regime was established. Now the country is firmly under Soviet domination and many Soviet troops are stationed there.

The economy is based on food processing, textiles, and chemicals.

Considerable grain is grown. The per capita income is estimated at $750 and the literacy rate is 80%.

The first stamps were issued in 1924. Since then, Mongolia's stamps have followed the usual Communist pattern with political figures and propaganda themes predominating.

Philatelic Bureau: Directeur de Bureau des Philatelistes, PO Box 175, Ulaanbaatar, Mongolia.

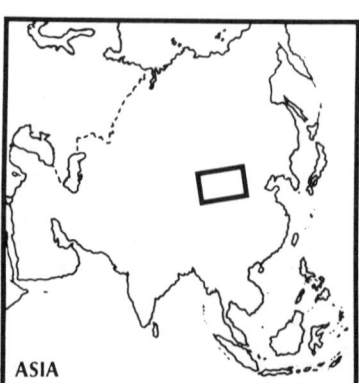

NEPAL, KINGDOM OF

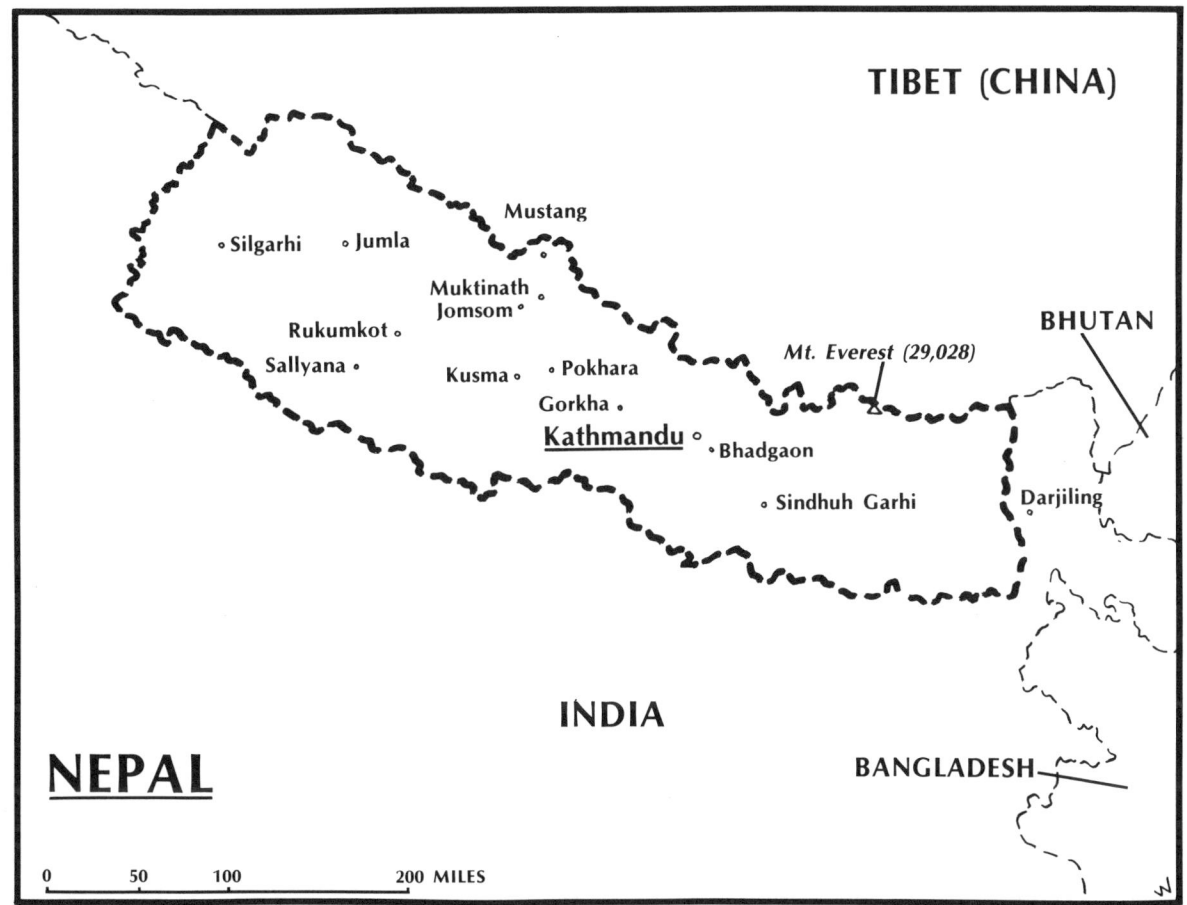

Area: 56,136 sq. miles
Population: 16,578,000 (1984)
Capital: Kathmandu
Currency: Rupee (100 paisa)

Hidden away in the Himalayas, to the north of India, Nepal was, until quite recently, a country of mystery with few contacts with the outside world.

There are three main geographic regions, which run from east to west. In the south is a level, fertile

strip that is part of the Ganges Basin. Across the center of the country there is a region of Himalayan foothills, while to the north is the dramatic range of the Himalayas.

In this range are eight of the world's 10 highest mountains, including Mount Everest; at 29,028 feet, the world's tallest mountain.

The climate varies from subtropical in the south to one of cool summers and severe winters in the north.

At Kathmandu, the average temperature in May is 86 degrees F. In December it is 35 degrees F. The city's annual rainfall is from 30-60 inches.

Until the early 1950s, Nepal was ruled by hereditary premiers of the Rana family. They had reduced the monarch to a figurehead who did not play any significant role in government.

Nepal came late into the modern world and did not abolish child marriage, polygamy, and the caste system until 1963. Now, there is commercial air service and roads link Nepal with Pakistan, India, and Tibet.

The land is the home of the Gurkhas, the legendary soldiers of the British Army, who gained a reputation for bravery in both World Wars I and II. Agreements with Britain and India continue to permit their recruitment into those country's armies.

Tourism is of growing importance in Nepal's economy, which is poor. Hides are processed, but 93% of the labor force is engaged in agriculture.

The 1982 per capita income was $140 and the 1981 literacy rate was 20%.

Stamps were first issued in 1881.

Philatelic Bureau: Officer-in-charge, Nepal Philatelic Bureau, Sundhara, Kathmandu, Nepal.

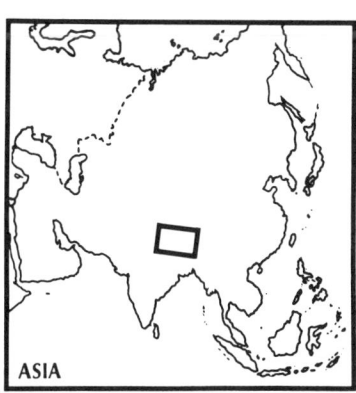

PHILIPPINES, REPUBLIC OF THE

Area: 115,830 sq. miles
Population: 55,528,000 (1984)
Capital: Quezon City
Currency: Peso (100 sentimos)

The Philippines comprise a large group of about 7,100 islands located between the southern tip of Taiwan and the northern part of Borneo. Eleven of the islands are home to 95% of the population.

The islands are mountainous, but most have a flat coastal belt. The most extensive agricultural area is the central plain of Luzon.

The climate is tropical. Low-lying areas have only a slight variation in the average annual temperature of 80 degrees F.

Rainfall varies widely. On Luzon the variation can be from 35-220 inches a year. Manila receives about 80 inches a year.

The islands are subject to frequent typhoons and there are an average of 15 each year, several of which may cause major damage.

The first inhabitants of the islands are thought to have come from Borneo or directly across the South China Sea, perhaps as long as 30,000 years ago.

Arabs brought Islam to the islands in the 14th century.

Magellan claimed the islands in 1521 and named them for King Philip II of Spain. For the next 377 years they were a Spanish possession.

The United States occupied the Philippines at the end of the 1898 Spanish-American War.

In 1935, the Philippines became a self-governing commonwealth and Manuel Quezon was elected president. Before independence could be granted, the Japanese invaded and the islands were occupied from 1941 until 1945.

On July 4, 1946 the independent Republic of the Philippines was created. The years since have been marked by harassment from Communist terrorists and considerable political unrest, culminating in the repressive regime of Ferdinand Marcos. The murder of Benigno S. Aquino led to growing demands for the ouster of Marcos and this was achieved in 1986 amid charges of massive corruption. He was replaced as president by the widow of the murdered Aquino in a peaceful coup, after losing an election and refusing to step down.

There is little industry and the economy remains in poor shape. The 1982 per capita income was $771 and the 1983 literacy rate was 88%.

Stamps were first issued under the Spanish administration.

Philatelic Bureau: Stamp and Philatelic Division, Bureau of Posts, Manila, Philippines.

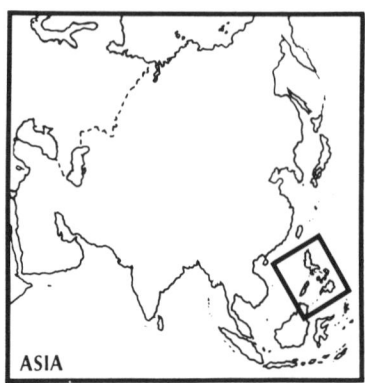

SINGAPORE, REPUBLIC OF

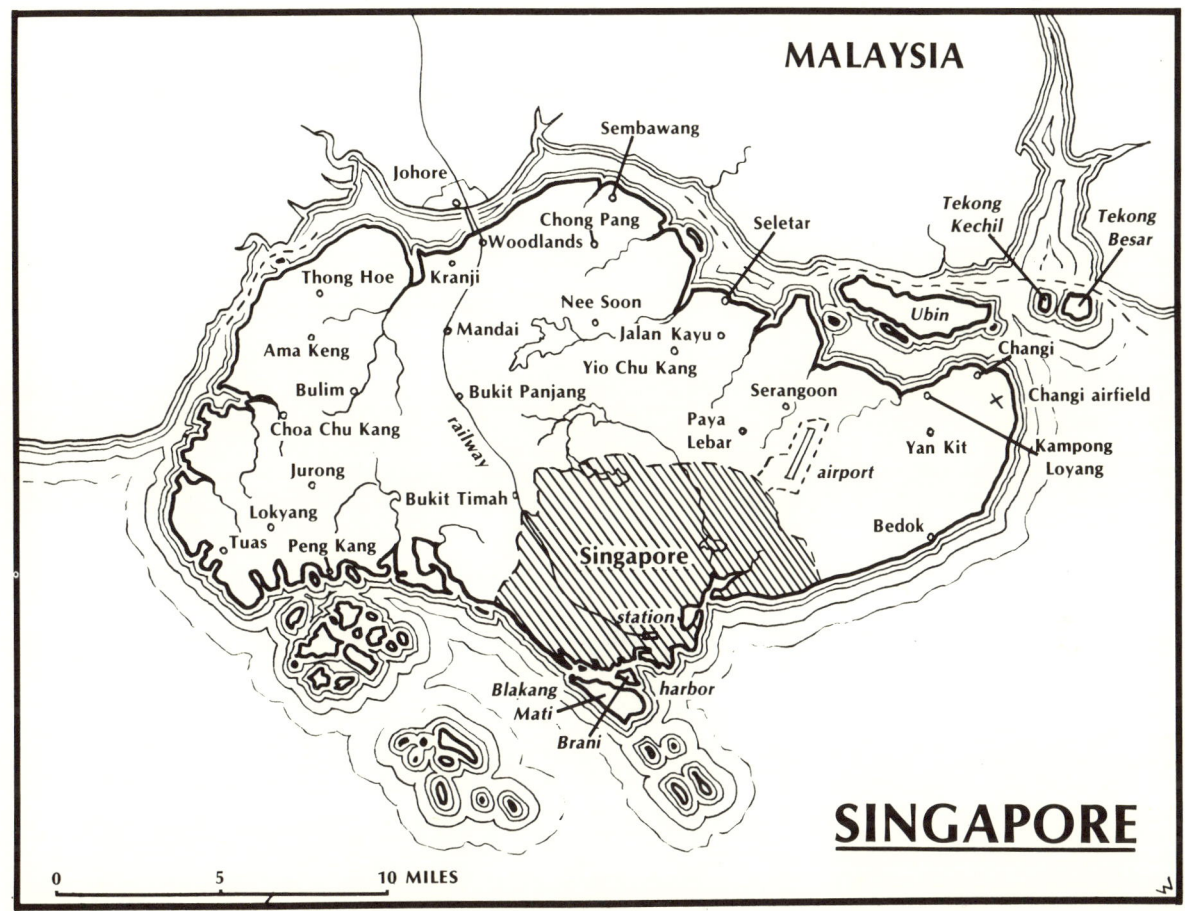

Area: 239 sq. miles
Population: 2,531,000 (1984)
Capital: Singapore
Currency: Dollar (100 cents)

The world's fourth-largest port, Singapore is located on an island at the tip of the Malay Peninsula. The country comprises one large island plus about 55 adjacent islets.

The island is low lying, with the highest point being 581-foot Bukit Timah.

The main urban area is at the south of the island occupying considerable areas of reclaimed swamp.

The climate is hot and humid with little year-round variation of the high temperature that averages 82 degrees F. The annual rainfall of about 95 inches is evenly spread throughout the year.

Sir Thomas Stamford Raffles landed at the site of Singapore on Jan. 28, 1819 and obtained land for a settlement. In 1824, a treaty with the Dutch made Malaya and Singapore a British sphere and in August of that year, the whole of Singapore Island was ceded to the British by the Sultan of Johore.

Singapore, Penang, and Malacca were combined in the Straits Settlements in 1826.

The opening of the Suez Canal in 1869 and the advent of the steamship led to prosperity for Singapore and a steady growth as a port serving Malay States and a large area of southeast Asia. The port became a British naval base in 1921.

Following the military disaster of 1942 and the Japanese occupation, Singapore was not liberated until September 1945.

After the war, economic progress was rapid. Following a period as part of the Federation of Malaya and later, Malaysia, its largely Chinese population proved incompatible with that of Malaya and Singapore broke away to become independent on Aug. 9, 1965.

Today, the country rivals Hong Kong as a trade, shipping, and financial center of the East. Highly industrialized, its 1983 per capita income was $6,526 and the 1984 literacy rate was 85%.

Its stamps are attractive and new issue policies are moderate.

Philatelic Bureau: Postal Services Department, 8th Floor, World Trade Center, Maritime Square, Singapore 0409, Singapore.

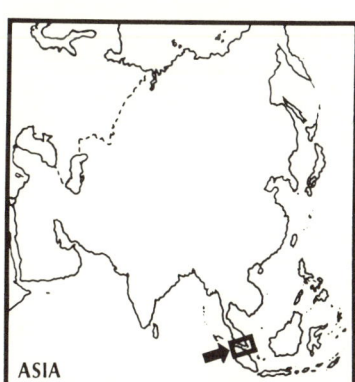

SRI LANKA, DEMOCRATIC SOCIALIST REPUBLIC OF

Area: 25,332 sq. miles
Population: 15,925,000 (1984)
Capital: Colombo
Currency: Rupee (100 cents)

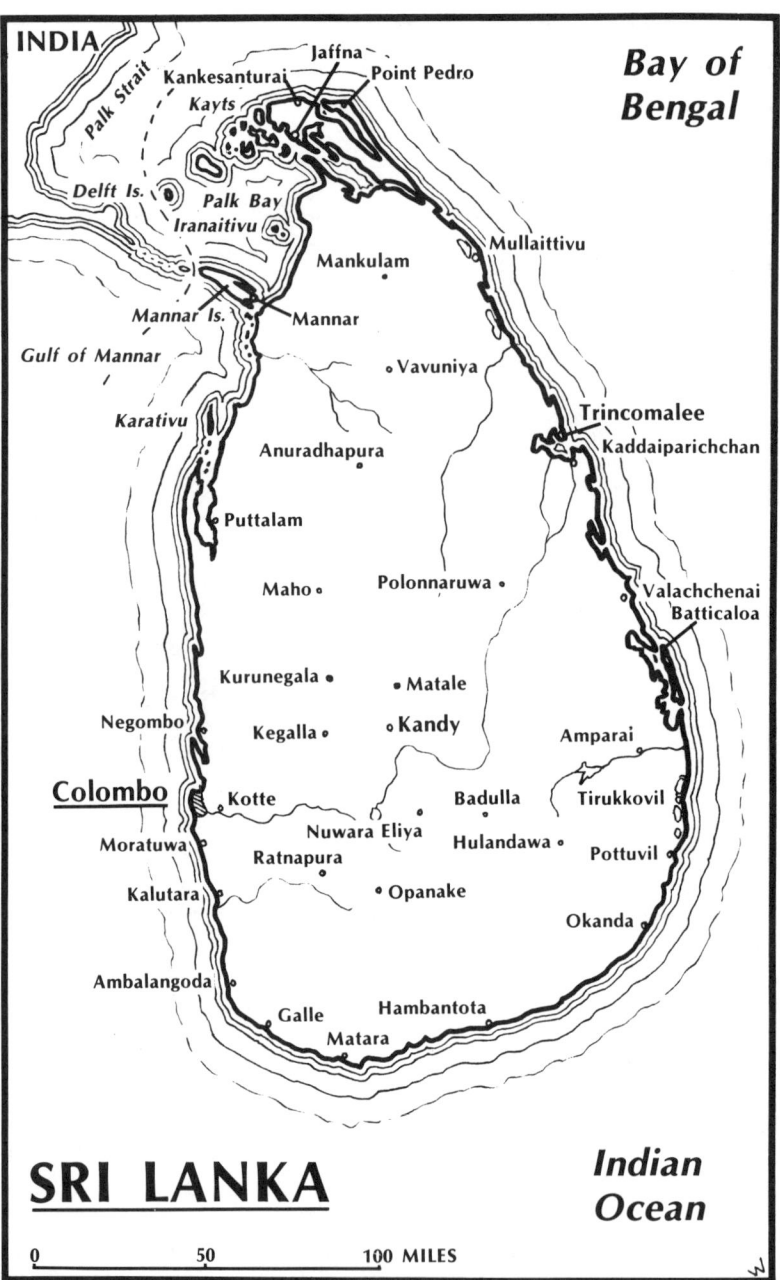

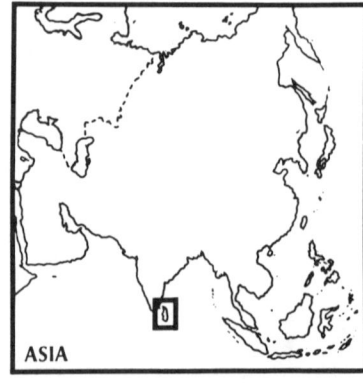

Falling like a teardrop from the subcontinent of India, the island nation of Sri Lanka was once the British colony of Ceylon, noted for its tea and elephants.

Separated by an 18-mile strait from India, the northern portion of the island is a low, flat plain that continues around the coast of the southern part.

The south central area is mountainous, with peaks reaching 7,000 feet in elevation.

Its climate is hot, although the higher mountain area offers some temperature relief.

The humidity is above 75% year round and the temperature averages 80 degrees F. There is little daily or seasonal variation.

Rainfall ranges from about 50 inches a year in the north to 200 inches in the southwest.

For almost 150 years the Portuguese controlled the area until replaced by the Dutch, who also wanted the spice trade.

By 1815, the British brought the entire island under control and it remained a British colony. They introduced a plantation economy growing rubber, coconuts, and especially tea, which became world famous.

Gradually, the British extended self-government and, with growing nationalist sentiment, made the island independent on Feb. 4, 1948.

In recent years, there has been

considerable political unrest. More recently the "teardrop" simile may be coming sadly more apt as conflict between the Sinhalese and the Tamil minority breaks into outright civil war.

The people of Sri Lanka are fast losing their gentle reputation. Their island paradise seems in danger of being torn apart by violence as bombings and other terrorist acts plus clashes with the army, escalate.

With basically an agricultural economy employing 46% of the labor force, the country is not prosperous. The 1982 per capita income was $266 and the 1983 literacy rate was 84%.

The first stamps were issued in 1857 and the colonial period saw some of the British Commonwealth's more attractive issues. Since independence a policy of moderation has been followed and stamps have Sri Lankan themes.

Philatelic Bureau: Philatelic Bureau, Ceylinco House, Colombo 1, Sri Lanka.

THAILAND, KINGDOM OF

Area: 198,500 sq. miles
Population: 51,725,000 (1984)
Capital: Bangkok
Currency: Baht (100 satangs)

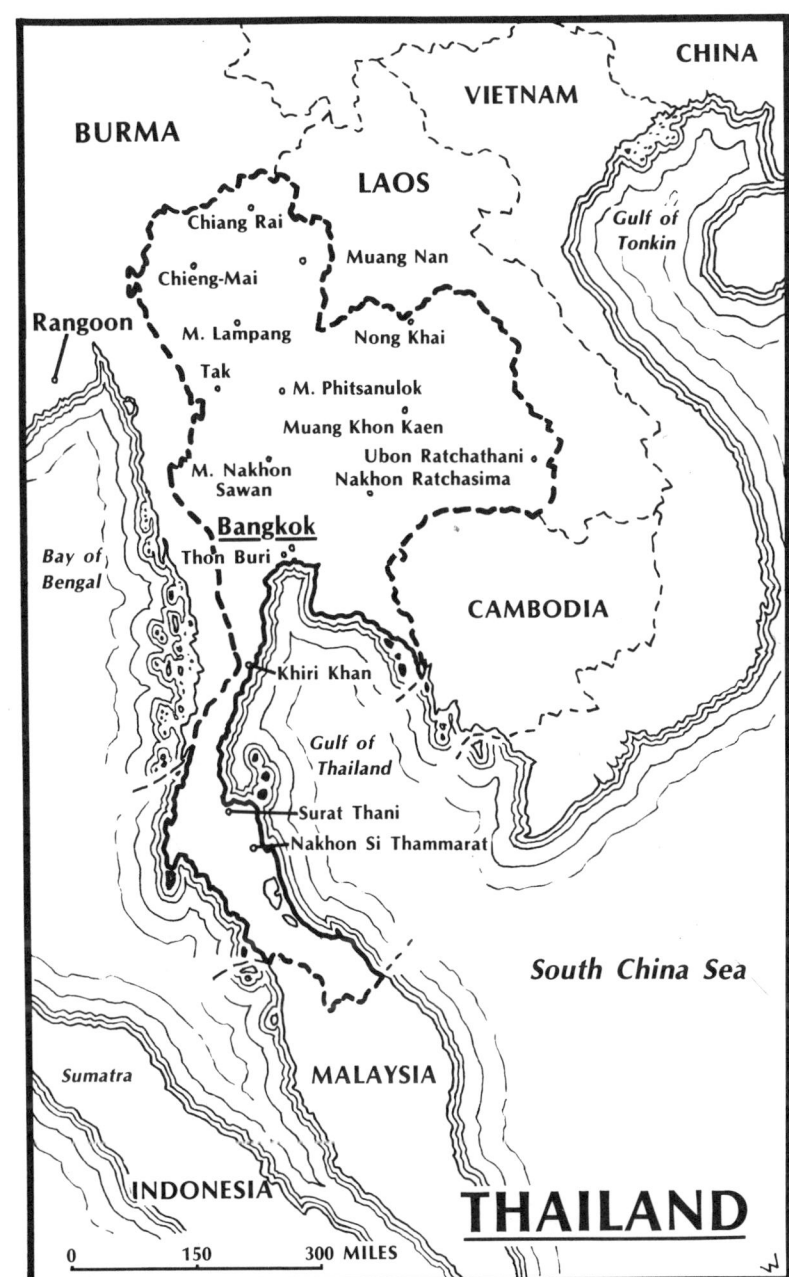

Once known as Siam, Thailand is located partly on the peninsula of southeast Asia and partly on the Malay Peninsula.

There are four main topographical regions; the agricultural and well-watered central region with its network of canals and irrigation schemes; the northeast plateau, with an average height of 1,000 feet; the mountainous north, which has narrow but fertile valleys; and the southern region extending down the Malay Peninsula to the border with Malaysia.

Thailand's climate is tropical, with both temperature and humidity being high. Much of the country is in the rain shadow of the mountains that run along the border with Burma and only about 50 inches a year falls, compared with more than 100 inches that falls on the Burmese side.

On the Malay Peninsula there is tropical rain forest and higher rainfall.

Frost does not occur except rarely in the northern mountains.

A Thai kingdom was established by 1350 and it flourished for the next 400 years, until the Burmese invaded the country. But the incursion was brief.

In 1826, Britain and Thailand signed a commercial treaty, and British influence remained strong throughout the 19th century.

In World War I, Thailand sided with the Allies. In the second worldwide conflict, it declared war

on the United States and Britain when Japan attacked Pearl Harbor on Dec. 7, 1941.

The military took over the government in 1976 and there has been political unrest since, mainly because of skyrocketing inflation.

In recent years, there have been incursions by Vietnamese forces into Thailand, although these have been repulsed.

There is some industry, mainly automobile assembly, drugs, textiles, and electrical products, but 76% of the labor force is employed in agriculture.

The 1981 per capita income was $758 and the 1983 literacy rate was 84%.

Its first stamps were issued in 1883 and featured King Chulalongkorn.

Philatelic Bureau: Philatelic Promotion Center, Commercial Division, The Communications Authority of Thailand, Bangkok, Thailand.

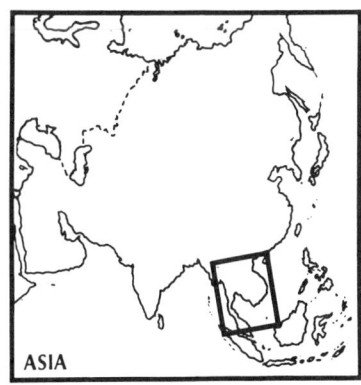

VIETNAM, SOCIALIST REPUBLIC OF

Area: 127,207 sq. miles
Population: 59,030,000 (1984)
Capital: Hanoi
Currency: Dong (100 xu)

Located on the South China Sea, Vietnam stretches from the Chinese border south to the tip of the southeast Asian peninsula.

Although much rice is grown in the north along the Red River and in its delta area, the rich Mekong Delta in the south is the agricultural center of the country.

The central part and much of the north is highland or mountainous, often covered with rain forest.

While the north and the south have a tropical climate with little year round temperature variation, the central area and the mountain regions can experience temperatures as low as 50 degrees F.

The area that is now Vietnam was under the control of China from 111 BC to AD 939. Modern history in Vietnam dates from 1858, when the French began their penetration of Indo-China. The country remained part of French Indo-China until World War II, when Japan invaded and occupied most of southeast Asia.

After the war, the French tried to reestablish their dominence over the area, but following the French defeat at Dienbienphu on May 8, 1954, the country became split between the southern part under Bao Dai and the Communist north under Ho Chi Minh.

This set the scene for the long, costly, and unsuccessful struggle

to avert a Communist takover of the entire country. Gradually, the United States became involved.

In 1964, US air strikes against North Vietnam began and US troops became directly involved in the fighting. By April 1969, there were 543,400 US troops in Vietnam.

A series of North Vietnamese offensives led to retreat by the South, which turned into a rout and on April 30, 1975, South Vietnam surrendered. US forces withdrew and on July 2, 1976, the Communists declared all of Vietnam to be unified.

There is little industry and 70% of the labor force is engaged in agriculture. The 1982 per capita income was $189 and the literacy rate was 78%.

The US Treasury Department bans the importation into this country of stamps of North Vietnam and the present Socialist Republic of Vietnam.

Philatelic Bureau: Xunhasaba, Philatelic Department, 32 Hai Ba Trung St., Hanoi, Vietnam.

AUSTRALASIA & PACIFIC

Stamp-issuing areas:

1. Aitutaki
2. Australia
3. Cook Islands
4. Fiji
5. French Polynesia
6. Kiribati
7. Marshall Islands
8. Micronesia
9. Nauru
10. New Caledonia
11. New Zealand
12. Niuafo'ou
13. Niue
14. Norfolk Island
15. Palau
16. Papua New Guinea
17. Penrhyn
18. Pitcairn Islands
19. Samoa
20. Solomon Islands
21. Tokelau Islands
22. Tonga
23. Tuvalu (incl. Funafuti, Nanumaga, Nanumea, Niutao, Nui, Nukufe, Nukulaelae, and Vaitupu)
24. Vanuatu
25. Wallis and Futuna Islands

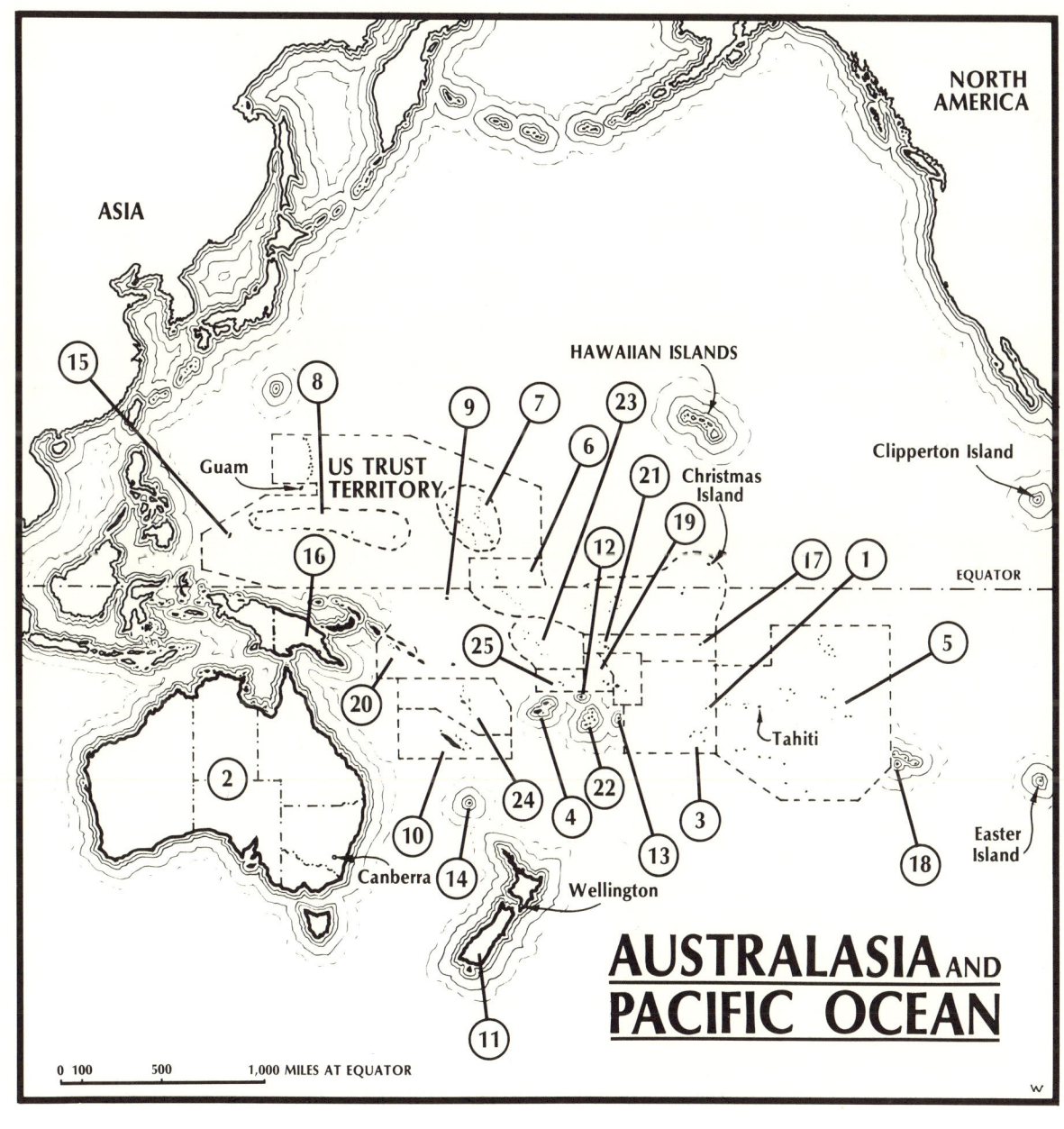

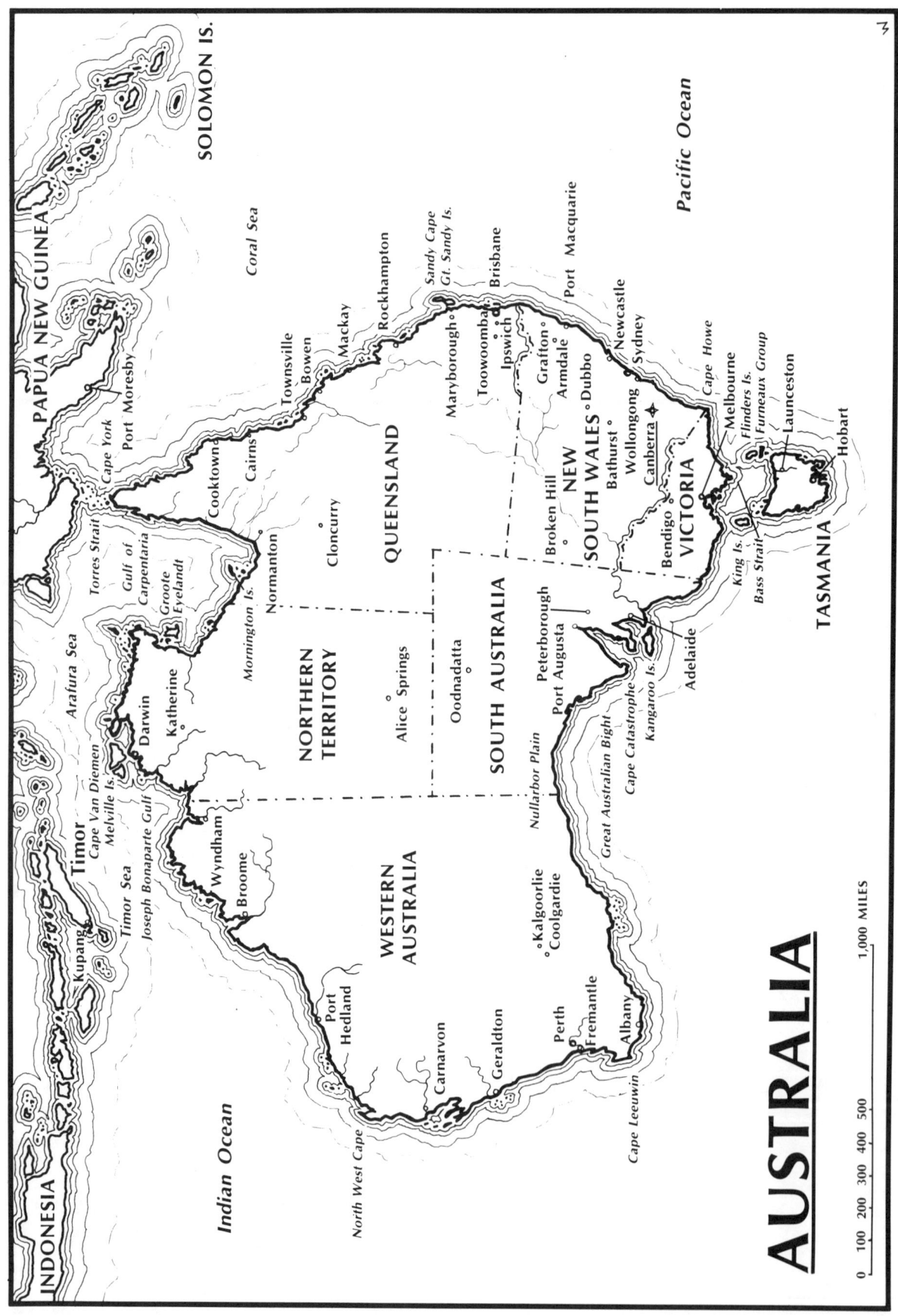

AUSTRALIA, COMMONWEALTH OF

Area: 2,966,200 sq. miles
Population: 15,462,000 (1984)
Capital: Canberra
Currency: Dollar (100 cents)

Occupying the smallest of the continents, Australia is almost as large as the continental United States, excluding Alaska.

Mostly it is plateau, except for areas of low mountains along the east coast, in the center, and in the west. The highest point is 7,314-foot Mount Kosciusko, located in the southeast.

The mainland comprises the states of New South Wales, Queensland, South Australia, Victoria, and Western Australia, plus the Northern Territory. Tasmania occupies a large island off the southeast corner of the continent.

There are a number of rivers, but most are short and few are navigable for any distance. The longest is the Murray. Much of its 1,609 miles form the border between New South Wales and Victoria.

One third of Australia is desert and much of the rest is only marginally useful for grazing. There are periods of severe drought.

On the coast, rainfall is adequate, but most of the inland areas receive less than 10 inches a year. In the north, which is tropical, rainfall can be as high as 100 inches a year. In the southeast and southwest it averages 40 inches each year.

Being south of the equator, the seasons are reversed from those in the United States. In the center and northern portion July averages 75 degrees F. In January, the average is 85 degrees F. Similar ranges in the south are 50-75 degrees F. In Tasmania it can fall below 45 degrees F during July.

The interior climate is more extreme and there can be a 30-degree range.

Abel Janszoon Tasman led a 1642 Dutch expedition to seek out land to the south on behalf of the governor general of the Dutch East Indies.

Tasman sailed to the south and discovered what is now Tasmania and which he named Van Diemen's Land, for his governor general. He went on to find New Zealand and then returned to Batavia via the north of New Guinea.

On April 20, 1770, James Cook became the first European to visit the east coast of Australia. This and two subsequent voyages led quickly to the first European settlement.

At first, Britain used Australia as a place of transportation for criminals and the first settlement was a penal one established at Port Jackson on Jan. 26, 1788. It was soon moved to nearby Sydney. By 1830, about 75,000 prisoners had been sent there and to Tasmania.

In 1829, Britain claimed the entire continent and colonies were founded around the coast, eventually conforming to today's states.

With the end of the penal colonies, immigration from overcrowded Britain began and settlements spread. By August 1850, there was a British population of 405,000.

On Jan. 1, 1901, after long negotiations, the colonies federated to form the Commonwealth of Australia.

A member of the British Commonwealth, Australia fought in both World Wars I and II and the Australian troops soon became noted for their fighting quality. Australians also fought in Korea and Vietnam.

Growing in wealth and prosperity over the years, Australian society was enriched by a large infusion of European immigrants after World War II.

Today, the country is one of the world's top exporters of meat, wool, and grain. Its industrial economy is varied and employs 30% of the labor force.

The 1983 per capita income was $9,960 and the literacy rate is 99%.

Although the Commonwealth was formed in 1901, not until 1913 did it issue stamps. The new country inherited a rich philatelic history in the form of the many beautiful classic stamps of the six colonies.

The stamps of Australia and those of the territories it administers, including Norfolk Island, Cocos (Keeling) Islands, Christmas Island, and the Australian Antarctic Territory, have always been popular.

Philatelic Bureau: Philatelic Bureau, GPO Box 9988, Melbourne, Victoria 3001, Australia.

The varied architecture of Australia's post offices.

AITUTAKI

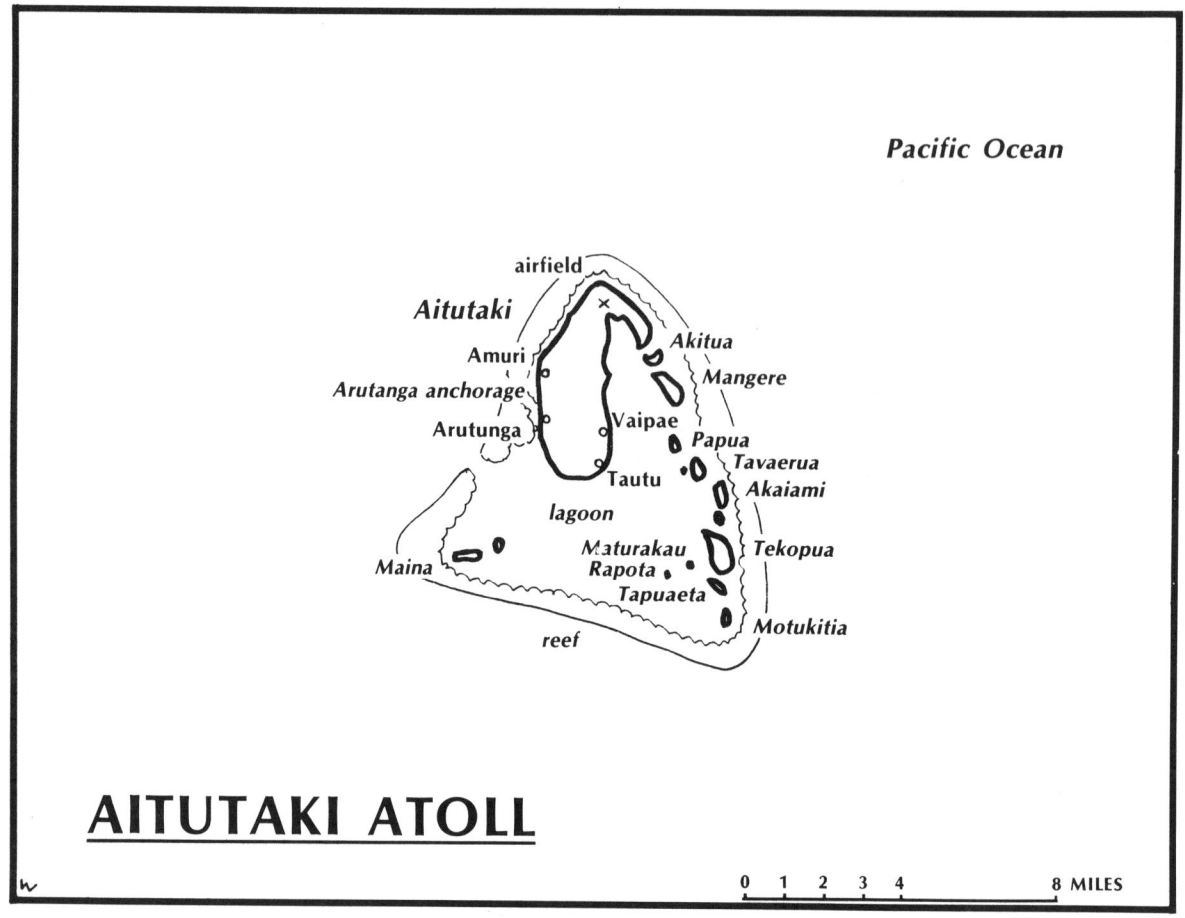

AITUTAKI ATOLL

Area: 7 sq. miles
Population: 2,900
Capital: none
Currency: Dollar (100 cents)

Aitutaki is an atoll in the lower, or southern, Cook Islands.

It comprises a volcanic main island, with a number of small

islands to the east and south in a large lagoon enclosed by a barrier reef.

It is located about 140 miles north of Rarotonga.

The island has a plateau area rising to a hill in the north that is 390 feet in height. The land is fertile, but the island experiences occasional water shortages. Vegetation is lush and breadfruit and coconuts flourish.

Offshore fishing is excellent. Tuna, marlin, wahoo, and barracuda are caught. Sharks are numerous.

Arutunga is the main settlement. It is located on the west coast and can be approached from the sea by way of a pass in the reef suitable for shallow-draft vessels, which can tie up at a cargo wharf.

There is an airstrip, built during World War II, that makes possible air service to Rarotonga. The climate is mild year round, with an average high temperature of 76 degrees F.

Credit for the island's discovery is given to Captain James Cook. Some sources give that honor to Captain Bligh, commanding HMS *Bounty,* who is said to have discovered the island on April 11, 1789, shortly before the famous mutiny.

Aitutaki's first stamps came in 1903, when the current issue of New Zealand was overprinted "AITUTAKI" plus the denomination in the native language. Overprinting was by the Government Printing Office, Wellington, New Zealand.

The low catalog prices of these stamps belie the quantities in which they exist. These range from 62,400 for the ½d and 1d, down to 11,280 for the 1/- denomination, according to Robson Lowe's *Encyclopedia* (Volume IV).

From 1932 to 1972, when it once more issued its own stamps, Aitutaki used stamps of the Cook Islands, of which it is a part. Since then a vast number of stamps have been issued.

Philatelic Bureau: Aitutaki Post Office, Aitutaki, Cook Islands, South Pacific.

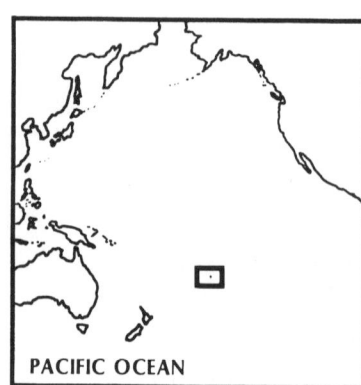

COOK ISLANDS

Area: 93 sq. miles
Population: 16,900 (1983)
Capital: Avarua (Rarotonga)
Currency: Dollar (100 cents)

Once administered by New Zealand, the Cook Islands have self-government in free association with that country.

They comprise 15 islands scattered over a broad expanse of the Pacific Ocean to the west of Polynesia and east of Samoa.

There are two main groups, the southern, or Lower Cooks and the Northern Cooks. The southern group is of mixed volcanic and coral origin. Most are hilly with a fringing coral reef.

Rarotonga is part of this group. It is 2,140 feet at its highest point and has an area of 26 square miles. The chief town, Avarua, is the seat of government.

The northern group consists of low coral atolls with the population being mostly on Penrhyn, the largest island. It has an area of 3.8 square miles.

The Cook Islanders are Polynesians and closely related to New Zealand's Maoris, with whom they share language, many traditions, and customs. The islands were discovered by James Cook in the 1770s. William Bligh visited the islands in 1789.

In 1823, John Williams of the London Missionary Society, came to the Cook Islands. The society gained a strong position in the islands and soon became an important factor in government and law making.

Britain proclaimed a protectorate over the islands in 1888 and they

were annexed to New Zealand in 1901. Independence was granted in 1965.

Chief exports are citrus fruits, copra, clothing, jewelry, pearl shell, and, in recent years, postage stamps. Most trade is with New Zealand.

On June 11, 1980, the United States signed a treaty with the Cook Islands, under which it agreed to relinquish its claim to the atolls of Danger, Manihiki, Penrhyn, and Rakahanga.

The Cook Islands first issued stamps in 1892. From 1919 to 1932, they were inscribed "Rarotonga."

Following independence in 1965, the rate of stamp issues increased.

The islands of Aitutaki and Penrhyn, which had their own stamps from 1903 to 1932 and 1902 to 1932 respectively, began to release their own stamps again in 1972 and 1973.

Philatelic Bureau: Philatelic Bureau, PO Box 200, Rarotonga, Cook Islands, South Pacific.

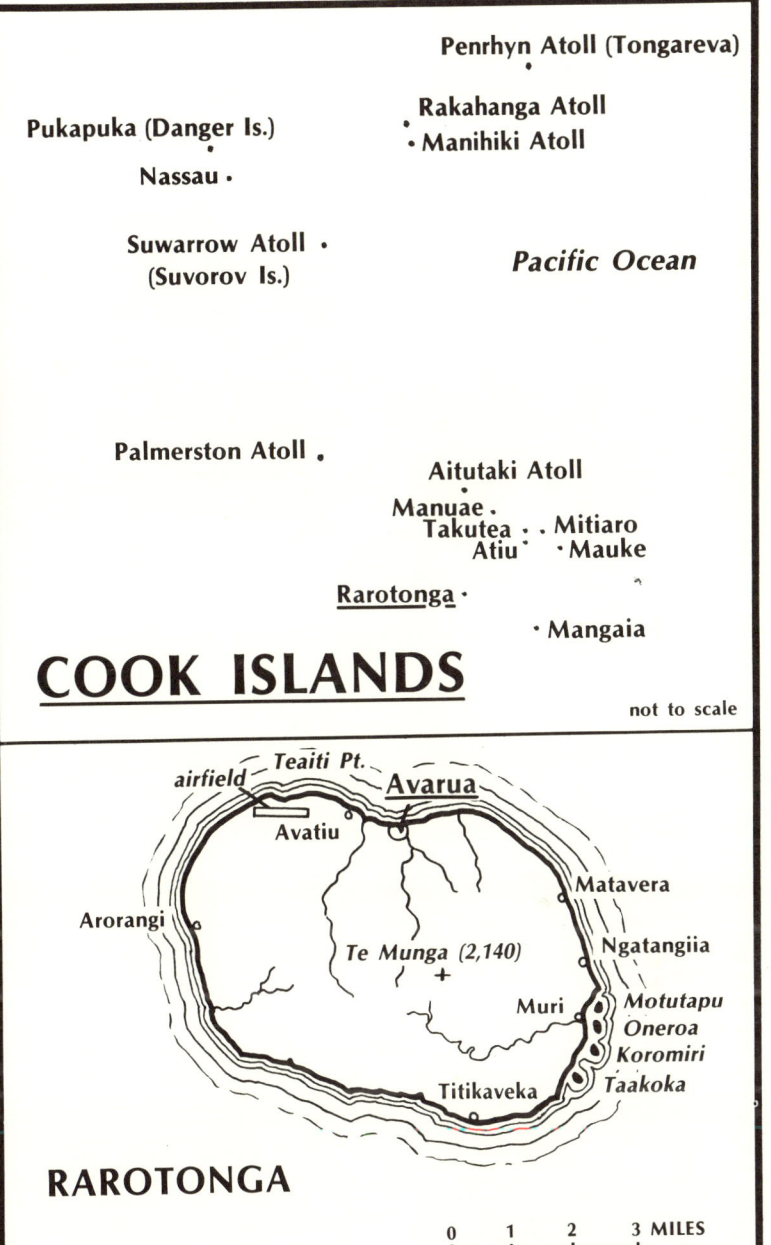

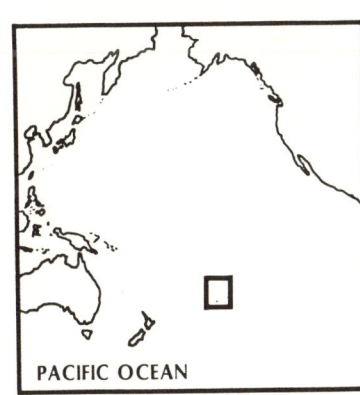

FIJI, DOMINION OF

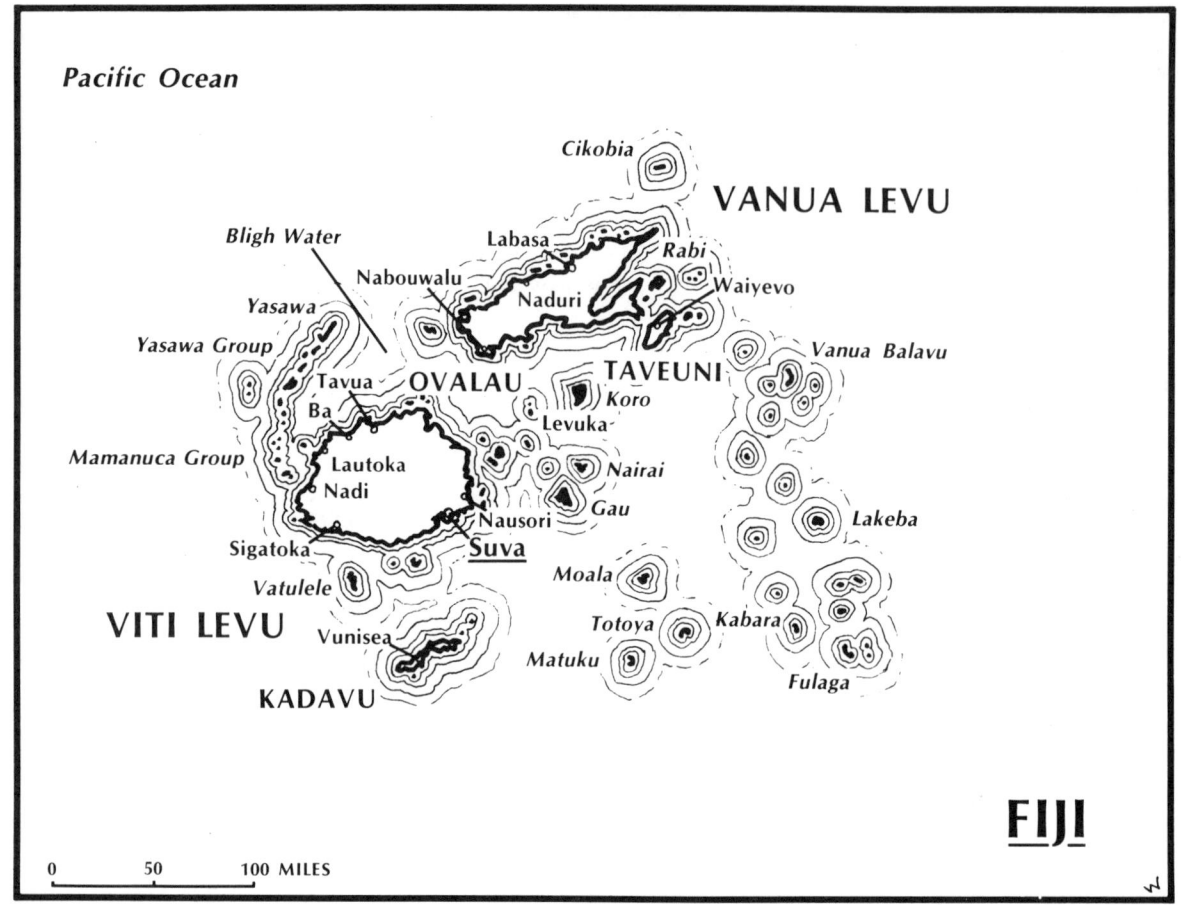

Area: 7,055 sq. miles
Population: 686,000 (1984)
Capital: Suva
Currency: Dollar (100 cents)

Fiji is a group of some 840 volcanic islands and islets in the South Pacific, southwest of Samoa and northeast of New Caledonia.

Only about 100 of the islands are inhabited and many are mere rocks a few square yards in area.

The island of Viti Levu is the largest and contains the highest

point in the group; 4,341-foot Mount Victoria (Mount Tomaniivi).

The climate is temperate considering the islands' tropical location. The temperature does not often fall below 60 degrees F, or rise above 90 degrees F.

At Suva, which is situated on a windward coast, the rainfall averages 125 inches a year. On the leeward coasts, this is reduced to about 70-90 inches annually. Hurricanes usually occur each year.

The friendly Fijians of today make it difficult to believe that their ancestors earned for the islands the name of "Cannibal Islands." Now, tourism is one of the major income producers for the islands and visitors stand little chance of ending up as a main course.

Abel Tasman, in 1643, was the first European to sight the islands.

By the early years of the 19th century the islands contained a strange mixture of missionaries, traders, and sailors deserted from their ships. This mixture corrupted the native inhabitants and the period was one of conflict and unrest.

Finally, in an attempt to achieve peace, a conference of chiefs ceded the islands to Great Britain on Oct. 10, 1874.

As a British colony, Fiji prospered and was groomed for independence, which came on Oct. 10, 1970. The country is a fully independent nation within the British Commonwealth.

The economy is based on sugar, light industry, and increasing tourism. The 1982 per capita income was $1,852 and the literacy rate is 75%.

Although the first stamps were issued in 1870, not until 1938 were the first pictorial stamps showing Fijian scenes released.

Philatelic Bureau: Philatelic Bureau, GPO Box 40, Suva, Fiji.

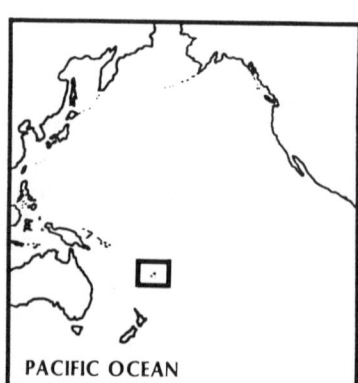

FRENCH POLYNESIA

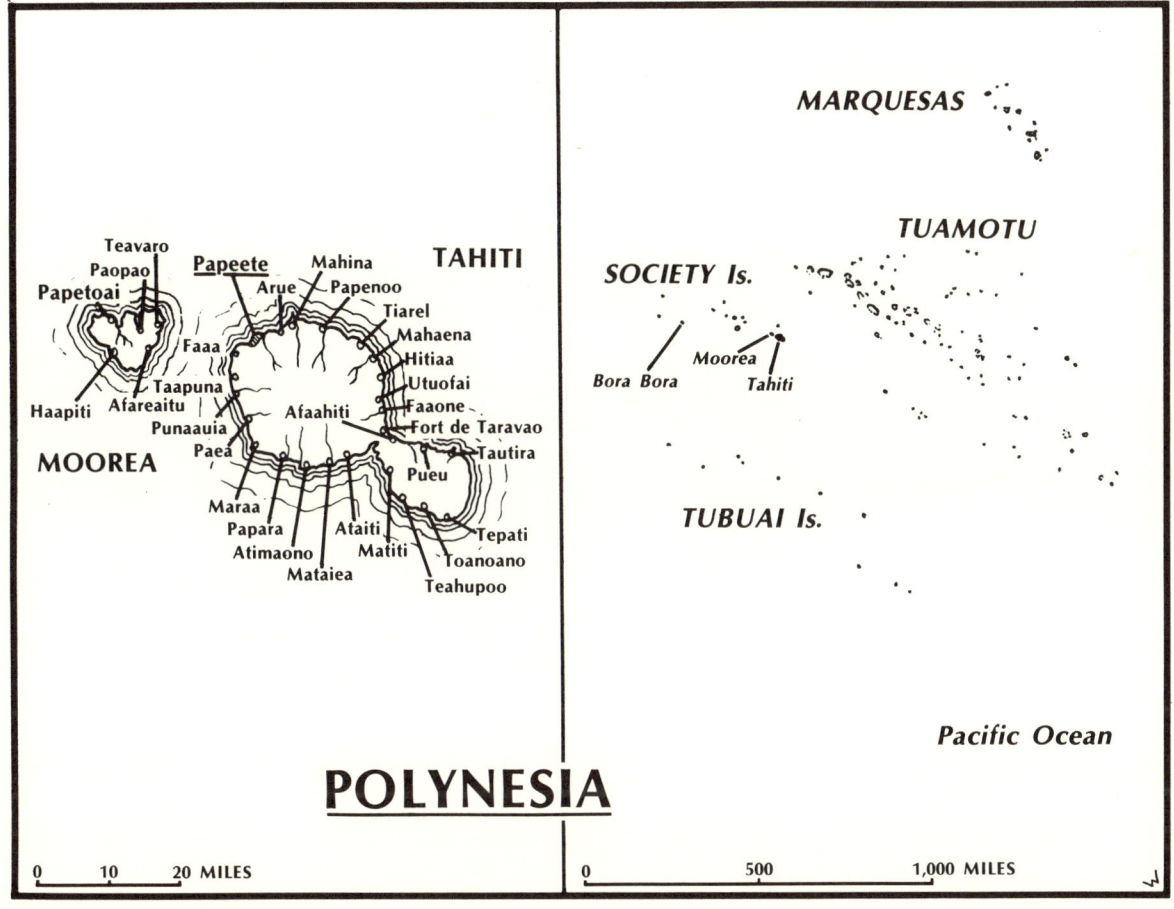

Area: 1,544 sq. miles
Population: 148,000 (1983)
Capital: Papeete
Currency: Franc (100 centimes)

An overseas territory of France, French Polynesia was known as French Oceania until 1957. It comprises a number of island groups spread over a wide area of the South Pacific.

The principal island is Tahiti in the Society Islands. Its chief town is Papeete, the territory's capital.

The island consists of two volcanic cones with surrounding lesser peaks. The highest point is 7,618-foot Tahiti Nui. There is a coastal plain and the island is surrounded by a coral reef. Its area is 388 square miles.

Located in the eastern trade wind belt, the island has a distinct wet side and a dry side. Rainfall averages 107 inches and 72 inches respectively.

Temperatures range from an average January-February high of 85 degrees F to a July-August average of 75 degrees F.

The various groups of islands making up Polynesia consist of two types; the so-called high islands and low islands. The high islands are rugged volcanic peaks and the low islands are coral and limestone atolls rising only a few feet above sea level. Both types are generally surrounded by a barrier reef.

A number of explorers discovered the various islands at different times in the 16th-18th centuries. James Cook named the Society Islands in 1769 for the Royal Society that had sponsored his expedition.

They became a French protectorate in 1842 and a colony in 1888. The other groups gradually came under French control.

Admired for their beauty, climate, and friendly people, the islands have attracted a number of famous people, most notable of whom was the artist Gauguin, whose works appear on several Polynesian stamps.

Tourism is important to the economy of the islands.

Crops grown include copra, bananas, oranges, sugar, and vanilla.

Stamps were first issued in 1882.

Philatelic Bureau: Centre Philatelique, Papeete, Tahiti, French Polynesia.

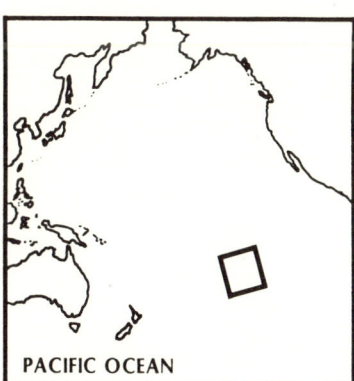

KIRIBATI, REPUBLIC OF

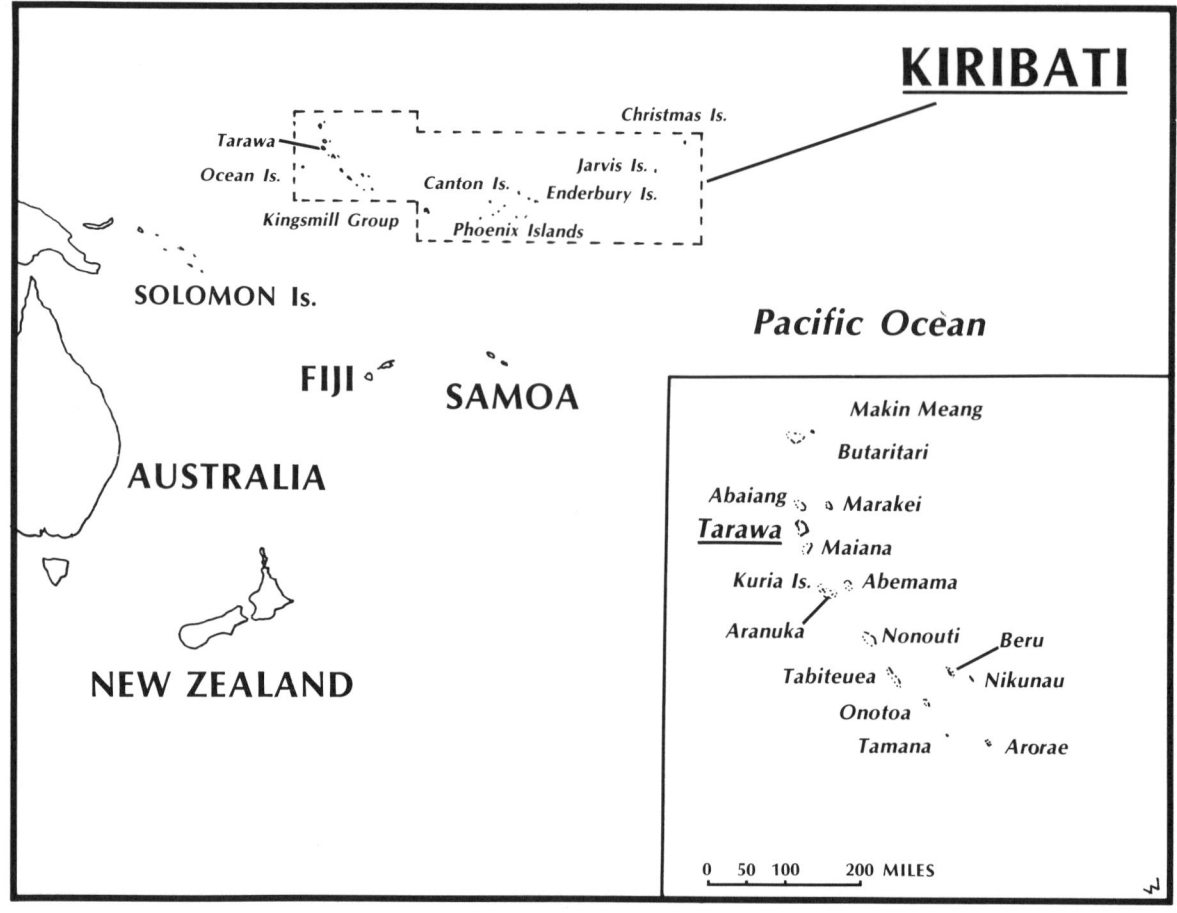

Area: 266 sq. miles
Population: 61,000 (1984)
Capital: Betio (Tarawa)
Currency: Dollar (100 cents)

The Republic of Kiribati (pronounced Kiribass) was formerly the Gilbert Islands and part of the British colony of the Gilbert and Ellice Islands. The latter group is now the country of Tuvalu.

Kiribati also includes the Line and Phoenix groups, and Ocean Island. They cover an area of more than two million square miles of the Pacific Ocean at the point where the International Date Line crosses the equator.

The islands are generally low-lying coral islands surrounded by a protecting reef. Many rise no more than about 12 feet above sea level. Most are thickly planted with coconuts and some pandanus.

Rainfall varies from 80-100 inches a year in the northern islands to 50 in the southern islands. It is often erratic and there are periods of drought.

Temperatures year round during the day are about 80-90 degrees F. At night, temperatures usually remain above 70 degrees F.

Sailors of various nations sighted or discovered various of the islands, mostly during the 1700s.

Britain established a protectorate over the islands in 1892 and at the request of the inhabitants, annexed them as a colony in 1915.

During World War II, the Japanese invaded and occupied the Gilberts and Ocean Island. They were driven out of the Gilberts in 1943 and from Ocean Island in 1945. Tarawa was the scene of especially bitter fighting.

In 1976, the Gilbert and Ellice Islands colony was split. The Gilberts continued under that name for a while, but on July 11, 1979 they became independent as the Republic of Kiribati.

Copra and fishing are the economic mainstays of the economy. Great Britain is the chief trading partner, handling 89% of the country's commerce.

Since independence, Kiribati has followed a moderate and responsible stamp-issuing policy. Stamp themes are generally related to the islands.

Philatelic Bureau: Philatelic Bureau, Box 494, Betio, Tarawa, Kiribati.

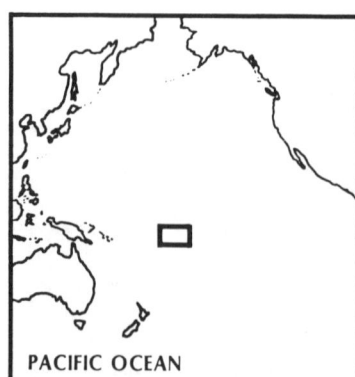

MARSHALL ISLANDS

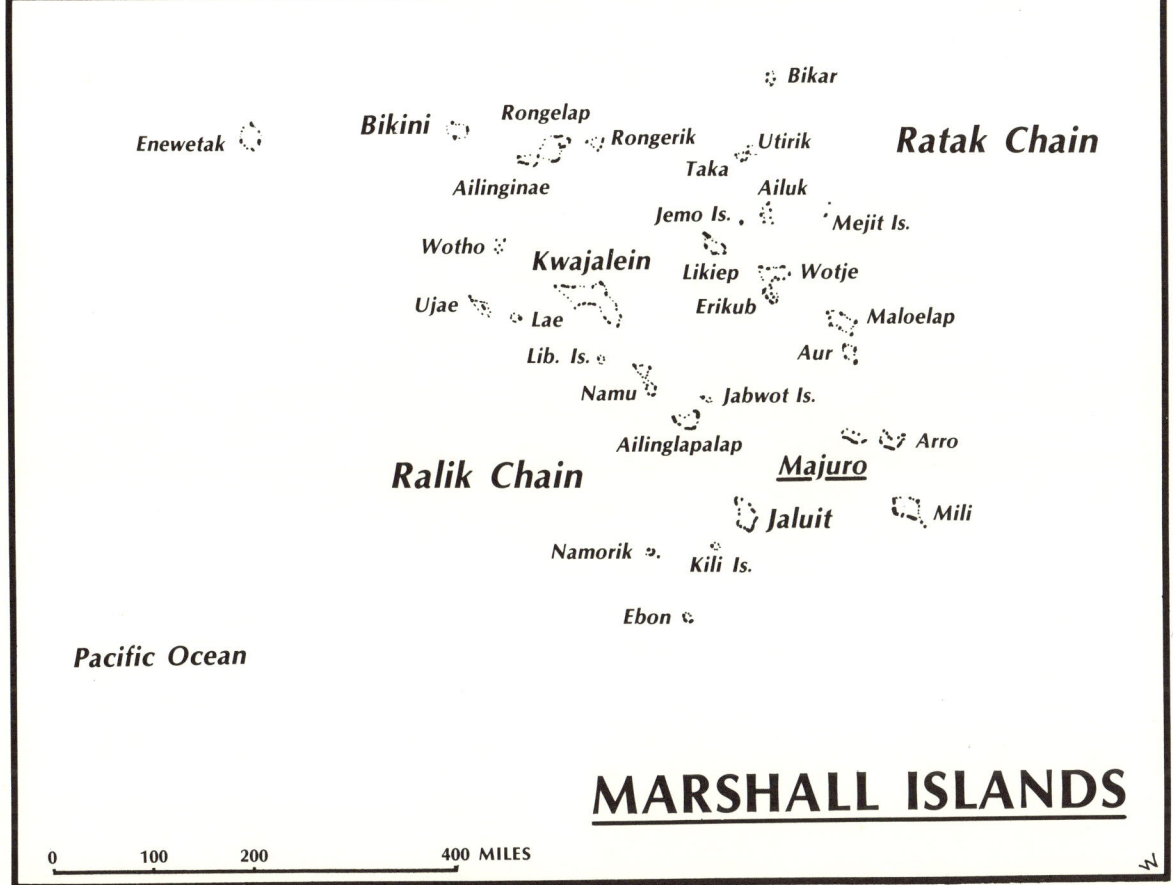

Area: 70 sq. miles
Population: 31,042 (1980)
Capital: Majuro
Currency: Dollar (100 cents)

Two chains of islands, the Ratak chain to the east and the Ralik chain on the west, make up the Marshall Islands.

They are located in the United States Trust Territory of the Pacific, east of the Caroline Islands and north of Kiribati.

The islands are coral caps on

dome volcanos that rise 18,000 feet from the floor of the ocean. Generally they do not exceed an elevation of 20 feet above sea level and are enclosed by protective reefs.

With a reef-enclosed lagoon covering an area of 840 square miles, Kwajalein, in the Ralik chain, is the world's largest coral atoll.

Spanish explorers visited the islands in the 16th century. Finding no riches, they did not linger.

Captain Marshall explored the islands in 1788, but it was the Russians, Adam Ivan Krusenstern in 1803 and Otto von Kolzebue in 1815 and 1823, who did most of the early mapping of the area. The islands became a Spanish colony until being sold to Germany following the 1898 Spanish-American War.

During World War I, Japan took the islands and received a League of Nations mandate over them at the end of the war.

They were a source of bitter fighting during World War II and in February 1944, Majuro became the first prewar Japanese possession to be taken. After the war the United Nations made the Marshall Islands a trusteeship of the United States.

Atomic bomb experiments were conducted in the late 1940s at Bikini and Eniwetok atolls after the populations had been removed. Hydrogen bomb tests were made there in 1952 and 1954. The islanders were not reimbursed for their enforced relocation until 1957.

Stamps were first issued for the Marshall Islands in 1897 under the German colonial administration, and lasted until Germany lost the colony during World War I.

Stamps were not issued again until May 2, 1984, when the Marshall Islands assumed responsibility for its own internal postal service.

Philatelic Bureau: Philatelic Bureau, Box 59648, Washington, DC 20012.

MICRONESIA, FEDERATED STATES OF

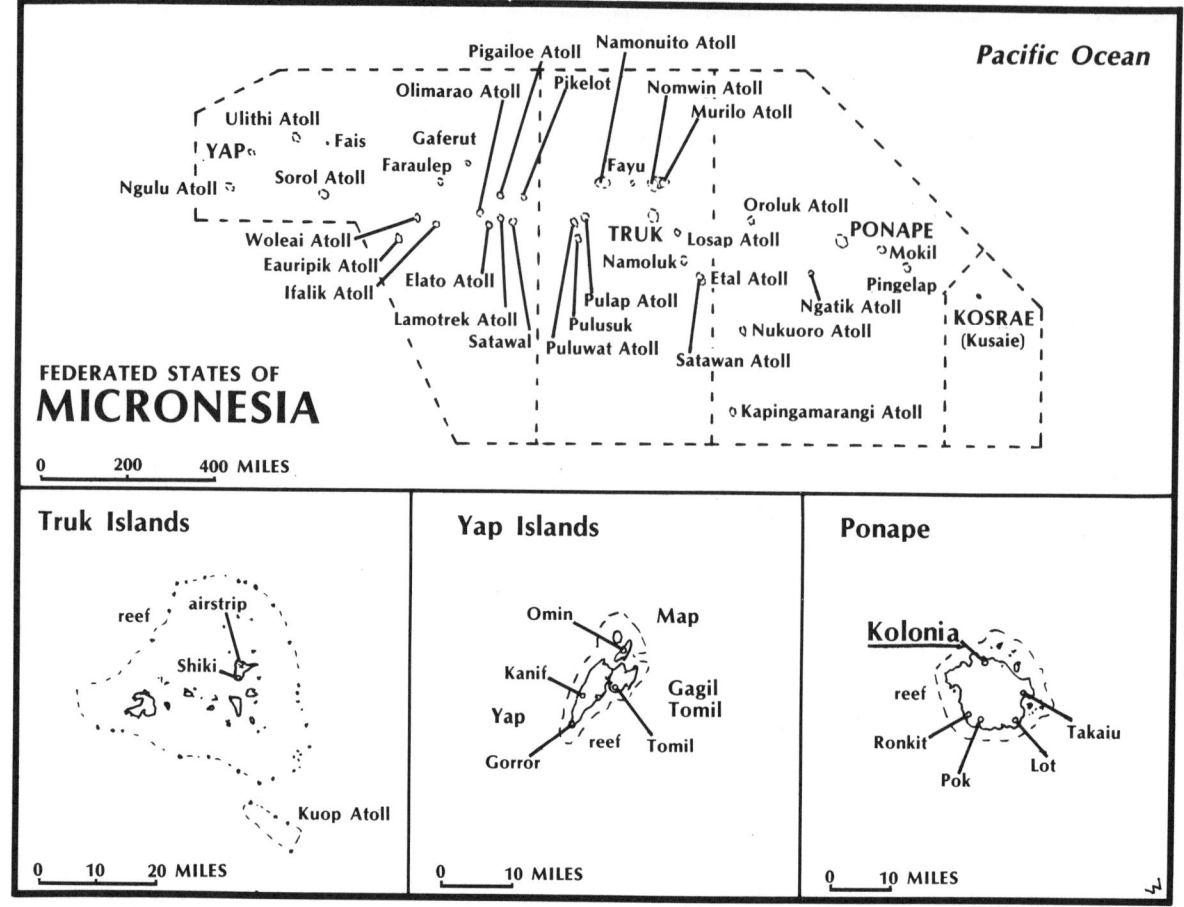

Area: 270 sq. miles
Population: 73,750 (1980)
Capital: Kolonia (Ponape)
Currency: Dollars (100 cents)

Formerly known as the Caroline Islands, the Federated States of Micronesia are part of the United States Trust Territory of the Pacific.

They comprise four states including the island groups of Yap, Truk, and Ponape, and the island of Kosrae. Palau, once included in the Caroline Islands is now the independent Republic of Palau.

A geologic division running between Truk and Yap, separates the islands into oceanic islands on the east and continental islands on the west. The oceanic islands are volcanic mountains, while the continental islands result from folds in the earth's crust. Most minerals, including copper, iron, bauxite, and manganese, are found on the continental islands.

The climate is warm and monthly average temperatures range from 80-85 degrees F. Rainfall can be heavy in some high islands, as much as 200 inches a year in some cases, although it is variable.

Settlements existed on Yap as early as the second century AD and even earlier settlements are thought to have been established on the islands to the east.

There is a great diversity of cultures and 12 languages plus several dialects are spoken there.

Although the Spanish explored the islands in the 16th century, they did not settle until the 19th century. Following the Spanish-American War of 1898, they were sold to Germany. Taken by Japan in World War I, that country was granted a mandate over them by the League of Nations after the war. Between the two world wars the islands were fortified and turned into military bases by the Japanese.

Liberated by the United States in World War II, they became a US trust territory on July 19, 1947.

The first stamps were issued by Germany in 1900.

In 1984, the new Federated States of Micronesia issued its first stamps, although they remain a trust territory and the US Postal Service is responsible for carrying mail to and from the islands.

Philatelic Bureau: Philatelic Bureau Manager, Box 1270, Ponape, Eastern Caroline Islands 96941, Federated States of Micronesia.

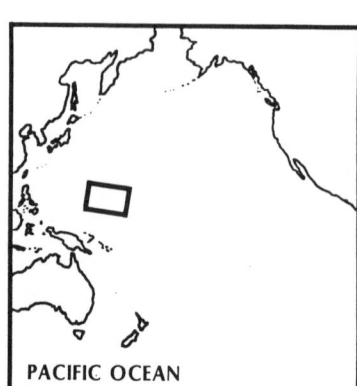

NAURU, REPUBLIC OF

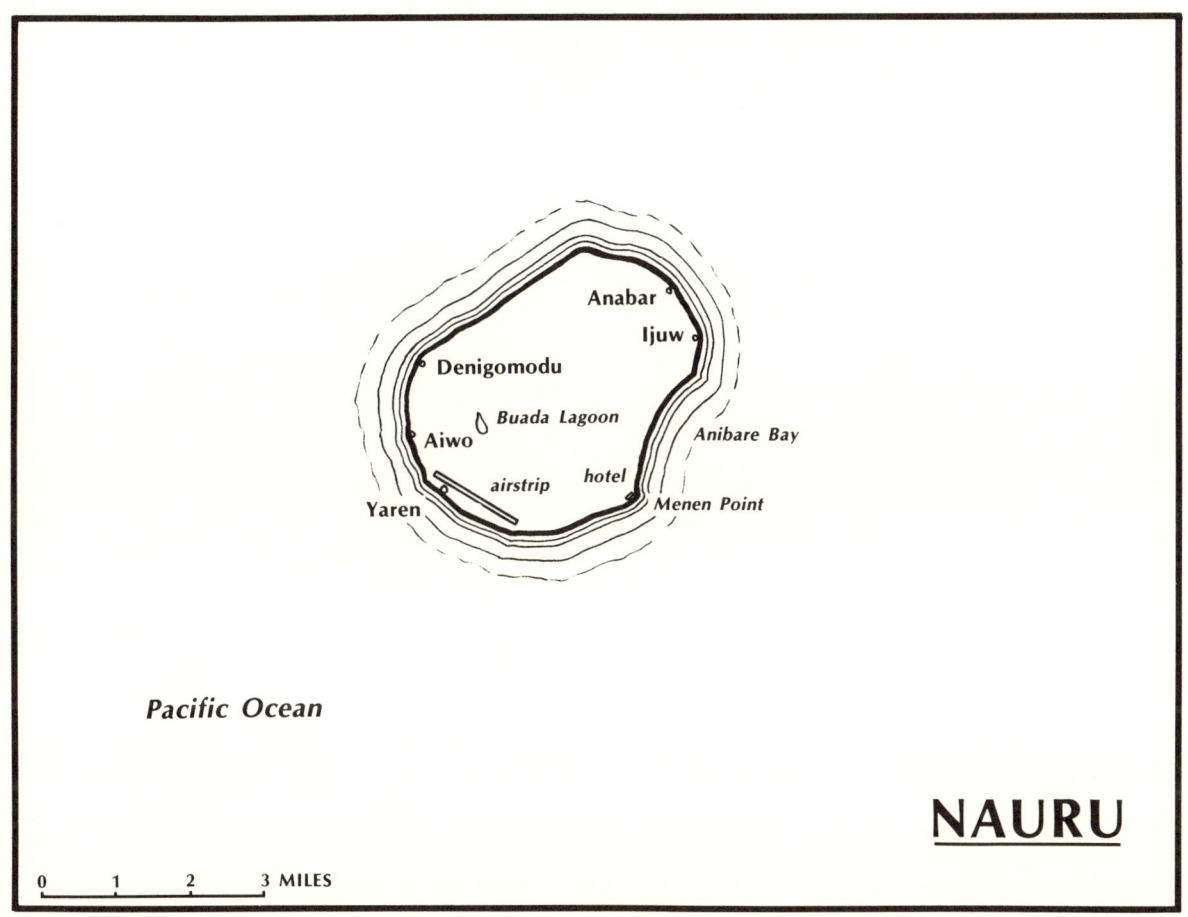

Area: 8 sq. miles
Population: 8,000 (1984)
Capital: Yaren
Currency: Dollar (100 cents)

Only 33 miles south of the equator, tiny Nauru is a phosphate-rock island whose inhabitants are among the world's richest populations.

There is a fertile coastal strip around the island from which rise 200-foot cliffs to a plateau containing one of the highest grade deposits of phosphate in the world.

The climate is hot, with temperatures up to 95 degrees F. The average low is about 75 degrees F. The humidity is about 70-80% and rainfall averages 18 inches a year. This is extremely variable and records show that, while only 12 inches fell in 1950, a total of 180 inches was dumped on the island in 1940!

Germany annexed Nauru in 1888. The phosphate deposits were discovered in 1900 and a British company began to work them.

Surrendered to Britain during World War I, Nauru was mandated to Britain, Australia, and New Zealand by the League of Nations. Australia administered it on behalf of the other two countries.

The island was occupied by Japan during World War II. Some 1,200 of the 1,800 inhabitants were taken as slave labor to Truk. Treated with barbarity by the Japanese, only 737 survived to return home in January 1946.

Australia continued to administer the island until it granted self-government in 1966. Full independence came on Jan. 31, 1968.

The phosphate deposits are the sole source of revenue for the country, and provided a per capita income of $21,400 in 1981. There are no taxes and $4.50 out of every $6 of revenue is invested in a fund to provide for the country's population when the phosphate runs out in a projected 15 years.

Everything must be imported, including water, which is brought to the island as ballast by ships that pick up cargoes of phosphate.

The British issued the island's first stamps during their World War I occupation. Since independence a number of attractive stamps have been issued and issue policies have been moderate.

Philatelic Bureau: Officer-in-Charge, Philatelic Bureau, Republic of Nauru, Central Pacific.

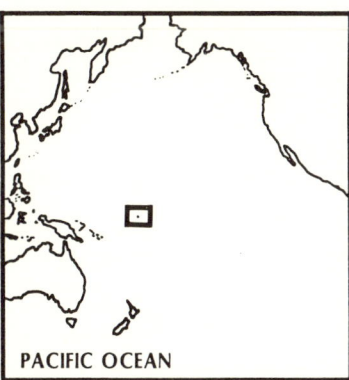

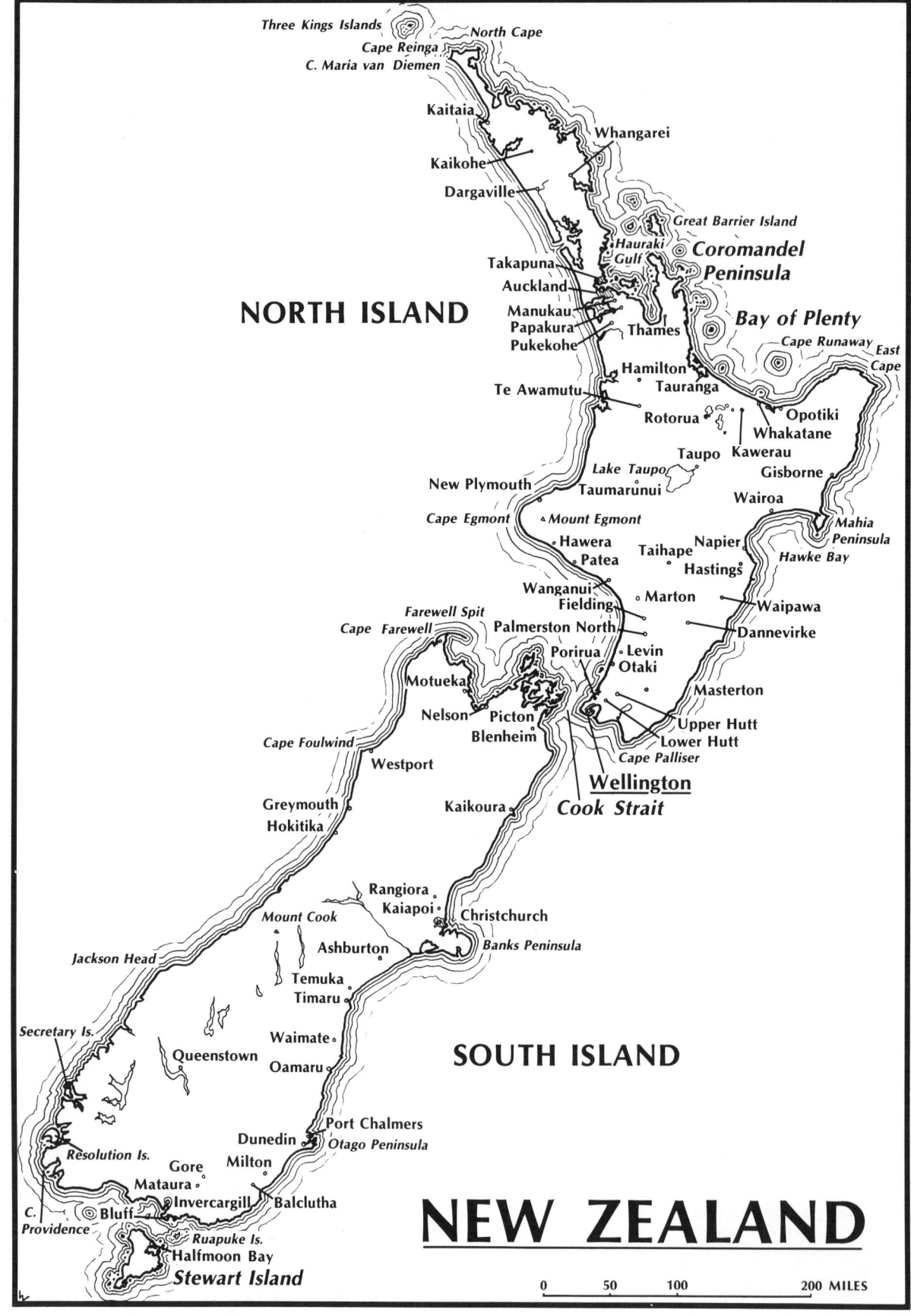

NEW ZEALAND

Area: 103,883 sq. miles
Population: 3,238,000 (1984)
Capital: Wellington
Currency: Dollar (100 cents)

New Zealand is an independent member of the British Commonwealth located about 1,200 miles to the southeast across the Tasman Sea from Australia.

A large portion of the two main islands is mountainous. The main area of plain suitable for agriculture is located on the central east coast of South Island. Most of the other plains areas are located in the eastern portions of both islands.

About two thirds of New Zealand is hilly or mountainous and has an elevation varying from 650-3,500 feet. There is a volcanic plateau in the center of North Island.

The main mountain range runs along the western part of South Island and there are 15 peaks rising above 10,000 feet. The highest point is 12,349-foot Mount Cook.

There are few rivers of importance and the country is drained by numerous short, fast-flowing rivers and streams. Few are suitable for navigation.

The longest river is the 270-mile Waikato, which drains a large area of North Island to the Tasman Sea.

Many of the fast-flowing streams are suitable for hydroelectric development and generating plants have been built.

New Zealand has a temperate climate with both adequate rainfall and a large amount of sunshine. Most of the northern peninsula is frost free at sea level, but frost occurs with increasing frequency towards the south.

The average temperature in Auckland ranges from 45-75 degrees F. For Wellington and Christchurch they are 41-68 degrees F and 34-72 degrees F respectively.

Average rainfall for the country is 51 inches a year, but this varies widely from 13 inches a year in the center of South Island to 250 inches in the mountains.

Being south of the equator, the seasons are reversed from those in the Northern Hemisphere.

The Dutch navigator Abel Tasman, was the first European to sight New Zealand in 1642 and named it during his circumnavigation of Australia, but James Cook claimed

New Zealand's beautiful first stamp design.

it for Britain in 1769.

Waiting on the shore for Cook were the islands' first settlers, the Maoris, who had sailed down from the Pacific islands in their large canoes about the 14th century.

At first made a dependency of the Australian colony of New South Wales, the new settlement belied it current peaceful state, as the Maoris took a rather dim view of the newcomers taking over their land. The 19th century was marked by a number of clashes between Europeans and Maoris.

These serious clashes caused the colonial authorities to develop some consideration for the original settlers and encouraged them to pursue the wiser course of fair treatment rather than the extermination practiced by the Spanish in their Central and South American colonies much earlier, and in many cases by the early settlers in the American West.

This wisdom eventually resulted in a lasting peace.

New Zealand claims the honor of being the first country to grant women suffrage, which was done in 1893. It became a self-governing dominion in 1907.

The country later contributed heavily to the Allied cause in both World Wars I and II. New Zealand also sent troops to fight in Vietnam during the war in that Southeast Asian country. Troops are currently stationed in Singapore and Malaysia as a result of a defense treaty with those countries.

New Zealand's refusal to allow US ships with nuclear weapons to use its port facilities has caused some strain in relations between the two countries in recent years and endangered treaty obligations.

Although industry has gained in importance in New Zealand in recent years, the country's economy is still based on agricultural products. It is the world's largest exporter of lamb, mutton, and dairy products and second only to Australia as an exporter of wool.

The 1982 per capita income was $7,916 and the literacy rate is 99%. New Zealand handles foreign affairs for the Cook Islands, Niue, and the Tokelau Islands.

Ross Dependency, administered by New Zealand since 1923, covers an area of 160,000 sq. miles in Antarctica.

New Zealand entered the stamp-issuing world in 1855 with the magnificent Chalon Head design, that put to shame the often ugly issues that succeeded it. Fortunately, a period began in the 1930s when its stamps were finely engraved and well printed.

Recently, many of the photogravure printed issues have not maintained that high design and production standard, although the lithographic process used for many contemporary issues is an improvement.

A popular aspect of New Zealand philately is the annual Health stamps, which are semi-postal stamps intended to raise money to fund holiday camps for children.

Philatelic Bureau: Post Office Philatelic Bureau, Private Bag, Wanganui, New Zealand.

NEW CALEDONIA

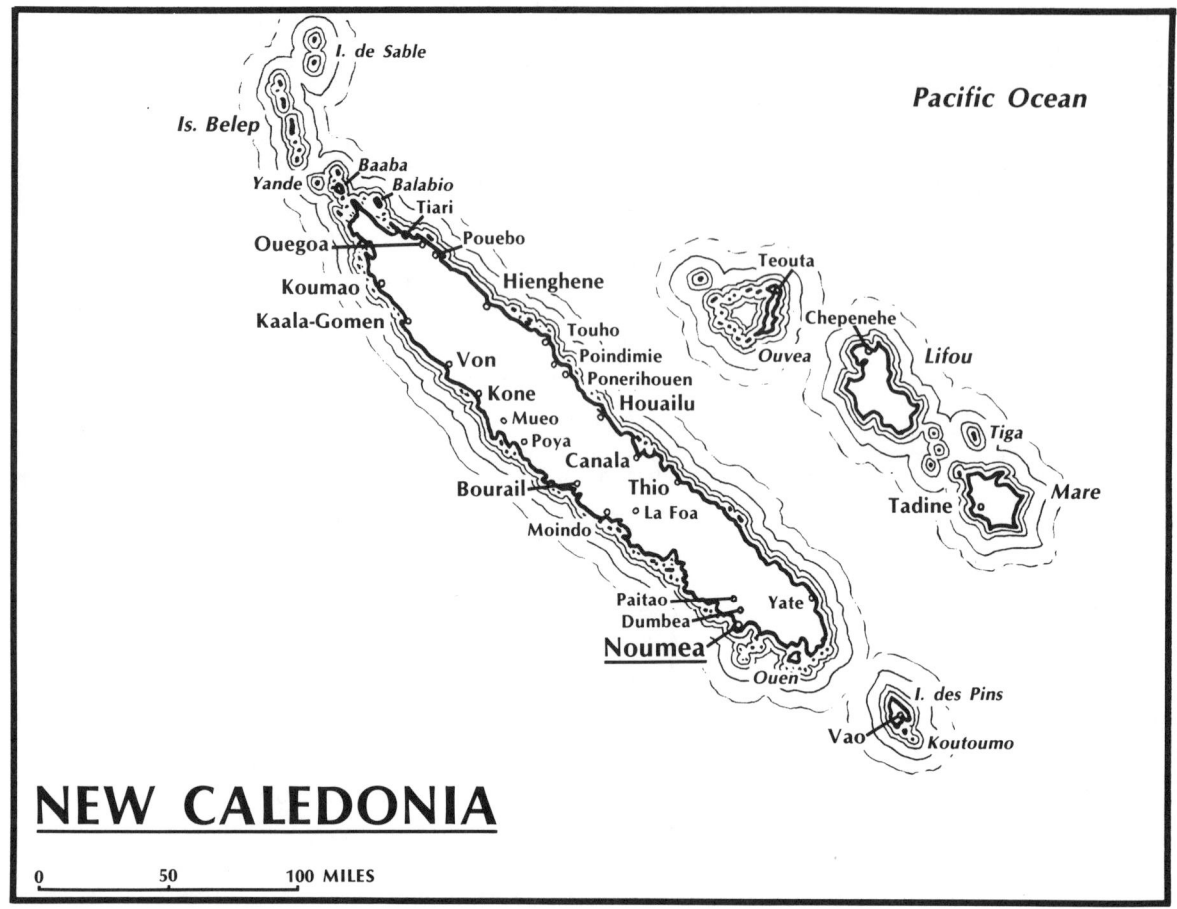

Area: 8,548 sq. miles
Population: 142,500 (1981)
Capital: Noumea
Currency: Franc (100 centimes)

In addition to the 6,530-square-mile main island, New Caledonia comprises the Isle des Pins and the Loyalty Islands, which include Mare, Lifou, and Ouvea, plus numerous smaller islands.

The main island is mountainous, with a range running down the center. The highest peak is 5,410-foot Mount Panie.

The climate is subtropical, with an average monthly temperature range of from 63-90 degrees F. Rainfall is about 80 inches a year on the east coast and generally less than 40 inches in the west.

The island was discovered and named by James Cook in 1774. In 1843 French Roman Catholics established a mission and the islands came under French control in 1853. The capital city of Noumea was founded in the following year.

The islands were used as a penal colony for a number of years.

Rich in minerals, New Caledonia is the world's third largest supplier of nickel. Other minerals include chrome, iron, cobalt, manganese, silver, gold, lead, and copper.

The chief agricultural crops are coffee, coconuts, coffee, tobacco, bananas, and pineapples. Stock breeding is a major occupation and includes both cattle and goats.

Noumea is the chief port and industrial center, with a nickel smelter, meat-packing plants, and timber mills.

The first stamp was issued in 1859. The design, by a French soldier stationed on the island, features a primitive profile of Napoleon III and as the stamps forming the sheet of 50 were all individually drawn on the lithographic stone, there are actually 50 different stamps in each sheet!

Since the war, there has been a moderate number of attractive stamps, which provide a good picture of the islands, their culture, and history.

Philatelic Bureau: Philatelic Bureau, Recette Principale des Postes, Noumea, New Caledonia.

NIUAFO'OU

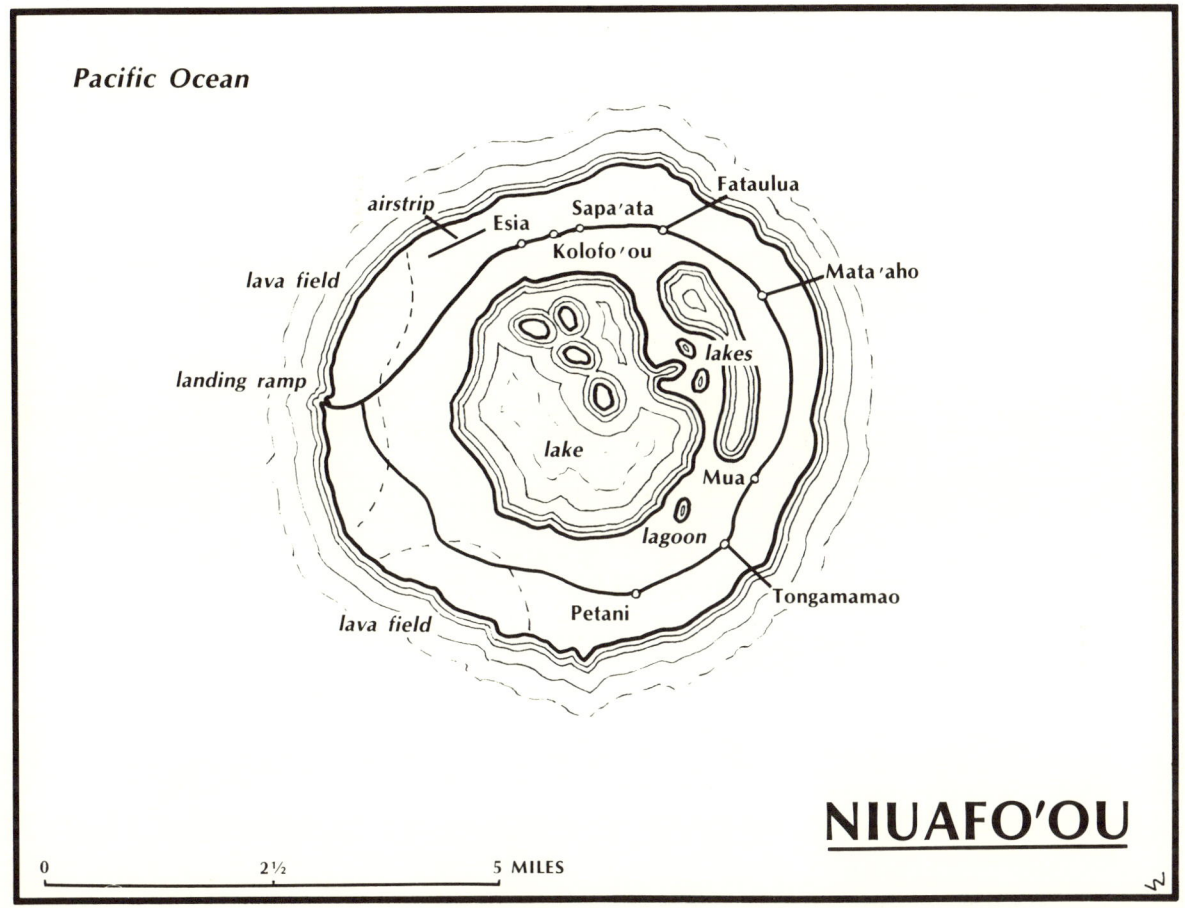

Area: 6 sq. miles
Population: 900 (1983 est.)
Capital: Kolofo'ou
(chief settlement)
Currency: Pa'anga (100 seniti)

Better known as Tin Can Island, for its unusual mail service, Niuafo'ou is part of the Kingdom of Tonga. It is located about 400 miles north of Tongatapu, between Fiji and Samoa.

The island is about 3½ miles by 3 miles. The land rises from the shore

to a rim surrounding a large water-filled crater in the center.

It is subject to considerable volcanic activity and there have been eruptions in 1814, 1840, 1853, 1867, 1886, 1912, 1926, 1935-36, 1943, and 1946. This last eruption destroyed the main settlement of Angaha and forced the evacuation of the population for about six years.

Because there were no landing places and ships had to lie well offshore, problems existed in getting mail to and from the island. The so-called Tin Can Mail Service solved this. Mail was sealed in cans and either towed by swimmers or carried by canoes.

The best known of the tin can mailmen and the one who made it famous, was Walter George Quensell, who created thousands of colorful covers during the 1930s and early 1940s.

The island boasts another unusual mail service. For a few years during the early 1900s, ships attempted to get mail ashore using rockets. The experiments were not entirely successful and it is reported that much mail was lost in the sea and in the dense jungle on the island.

There is now an airstrip on Niuafo'ou and South Pacific Island Airways operates Twin Otter service. The interisland ferry *Olavaha* also calls at the island.

Now, the tin can mail is no more. It had been revived briefly in the 1960s by the Matson Line as a tourist gimmick.

On May 11, 1983, the island began to issue its own stamps and these continue.

Philatelic Bureau: Box 164, Nuku'alofa, Tonga.

NIUE

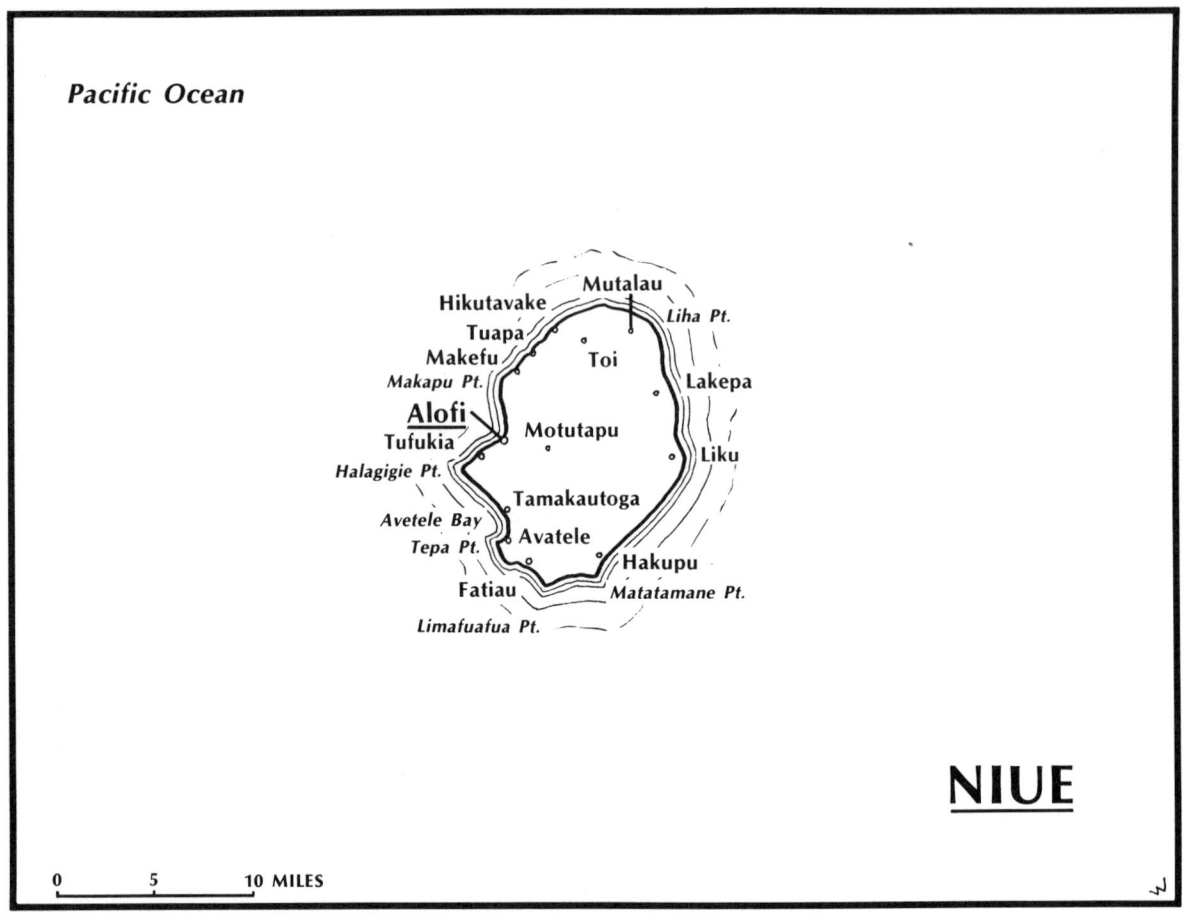

Area: 100 sq. miles
Population: 3,400 (1981)
Capital: Alofi
Currency: Dollar (100 cents)

Niue was once called Savage Island and is a self-governing island in association with New Zealand.

It is located in the Pacific Ocean about 400 miles west of the Cook Islands and east of Tonga.

The island, which has a circumference of 40 miles, comprises an old upheaved coral reef honey-

combed with caves and fissures. The plentiful rainfall tends to drain quickly into these cavities, which are connected with the ocean.

Comprising a central plateau with a maximum altitude of 200 feet, the island has fertile soil and exports copra and some bananas.

Captain James Cook discovered Niue in 1774. New Zealand annexed it in 1901. The island achieved self-governing status from that country in 1974, but continues in association with it.

The native population is of mixed Polynesian and Melanesian descent.

Stamps of the Cook Islands were used in Niue beginning in 1892 and continued until 1902, when stamps of New Zealand were overprinted "NIUE" and placed in use. These were used until 1920.

On Aug. 23, 1920, an attractive set of pictorial stamps was released and Niue has had its own stamps since then.

Until the 1960s, the island's stamps were intaglio printed and beautifully engraved in rich colors. Since then, most have been lithographed or photogravure produced.

In the late 1970s, Niue's stamps began to look very much like those of the Cook Islands. The policy of releasing large numbers in a variety of formats, with varying denominations, and bearing designs popular with topical collectors, but often having no connection with the island, indicates that the maximization of philatelic sales is a prime motive.

Philatelic Bureau: Philatelic Bureau, Box 150, Niue Post Office, Government of Niue, Alofi, Niue, South Pacific (via New Zealand).

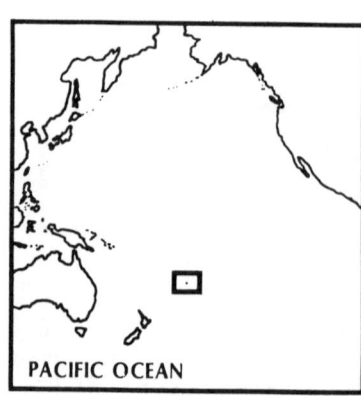

NORFOLK ISLAND

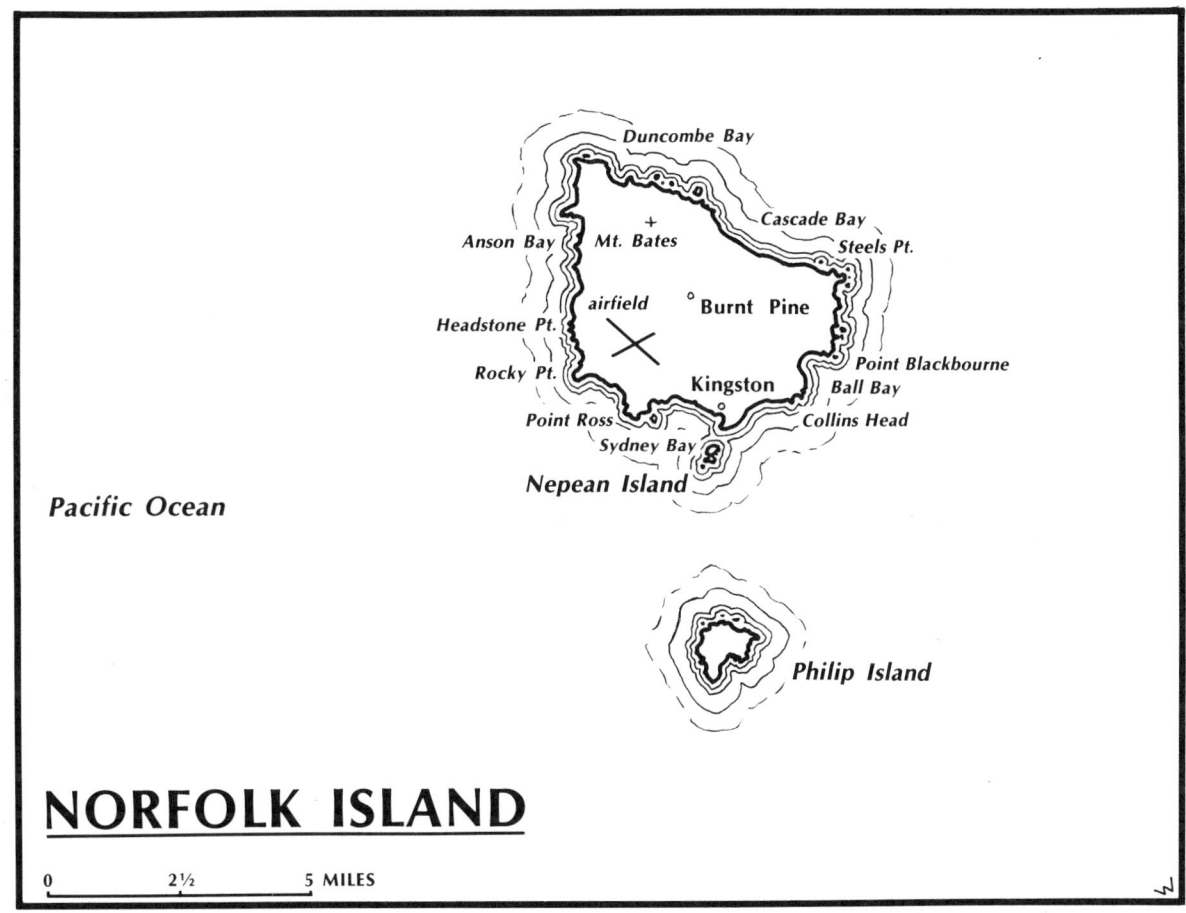

Area: 13.5 sq. miles
Population: 1,800 (1981)
Capital: Kingston
Currency: Dollar (100 cents)

Named for the Duchess of Norfolk, uninhabited Norfolk Island was discovered by Captain James Cook on Oct. 10, 1774.

The island is six miles long at its broadest point and lies some 400 miles north northwest of New Zealand and 930 miles east northeast of Sydney, Australia.

It has a subtropical climate and is best known as the home of the Nor-

folk Island pine, now a popular houseplant in North America. Some bananas, citrus fruit, and coffee are grown.

In contrast to its present tranquil state, Norfolk Island has a violent, bloody past. In 1788, a penal settlement was established at Kingston. Closed in 1814, it re-opened in 1826 as a dumping ground for the worst criminals of the penal colonies on Tasmania and in New South Wales.

Conditions became so bad, with riots, murders, and hangings common, that even in those harsh days, people became appalled. In 1856, the convicts were evacuated and the settlement closed. Today, only the remains of the buildings remind the inhabitants of those unhappy days.

In the same year that the convicts left, a group of people from Pitcairn Island arrived and this island turned from a violent to a peaceful settlement. Many of today's Norfolk islanders are descended from those settlers and have ancestors who were *Bounty* mutineers.

From 1856, the island was governed by the Australian colony of New South Wales and 1913 it became a federal territory of the Commonwealth of Australia. Norfolk Island received a measure of self-government in 1978.

The island's first stamps were issued in 1947 and depict a stand of Norfolk Island pines. Since then a moderate number of stamps have been released. They virtually all bear designs featuring some aspect of Norfolk history or flora and fauna.

Philatelic Bureau: Senior Philatelic Officer, Norfolk Island 2899, South Pacific.

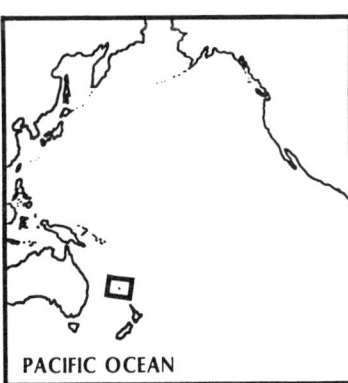

PALAU, REPUBLIC OF

Area: 179 sq. miles
Population: 16,000 (1983)
Capital: Koror
Currency: Dollar (100 cents)

The Republic of Palau comprises a group of some 100 islands that was once the most westerly group in the Caroline Islands.

It is located in the western Pacific Ocean, about 1,060 miles southeast of Manila and the same distance southwest of Saipan.

Until sold to Germany in 1899, the islands were part of the Spanish colony of the Caroline Islands.

During World War I, Japan took the islands and received a League of Nations mandate over them in 1919.

The islands of Angaur and Peleliu were invaded by US forces in 1944 and were liberated after some of the bloodiest fighting of the Pacific campaign.

Subsequently, Palau became part of the US Trust Territory of the Pacific.

On March 10, 1983, the islands began to issue their own stamps as the Republic of Palau, although the US Postal Service continues to carry mail to and from the islands.

Philatelic Bureau: Palau Philatelic Bureau, Box 59628, Washington, DC 20012.

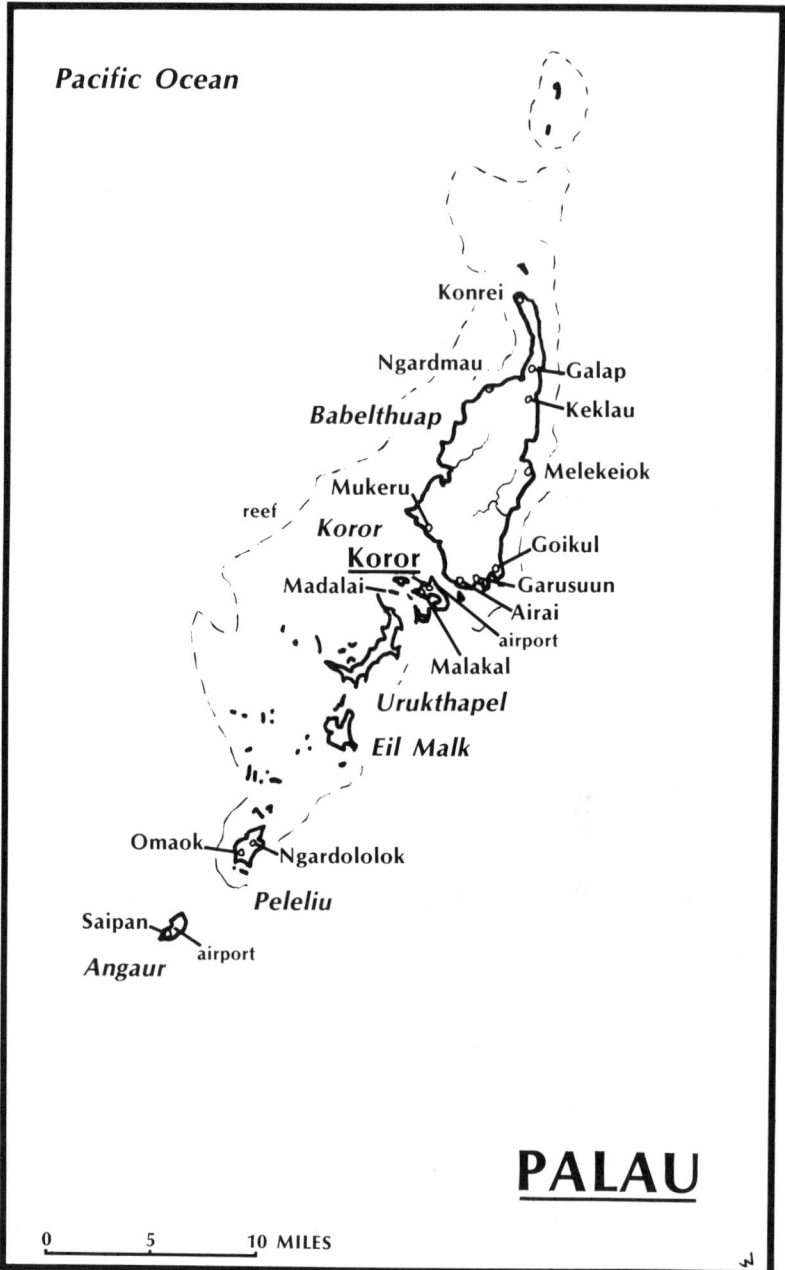

Strip of three memorial stamps honoring the murdered president of Palau.

PAPUA NEW GUINEA

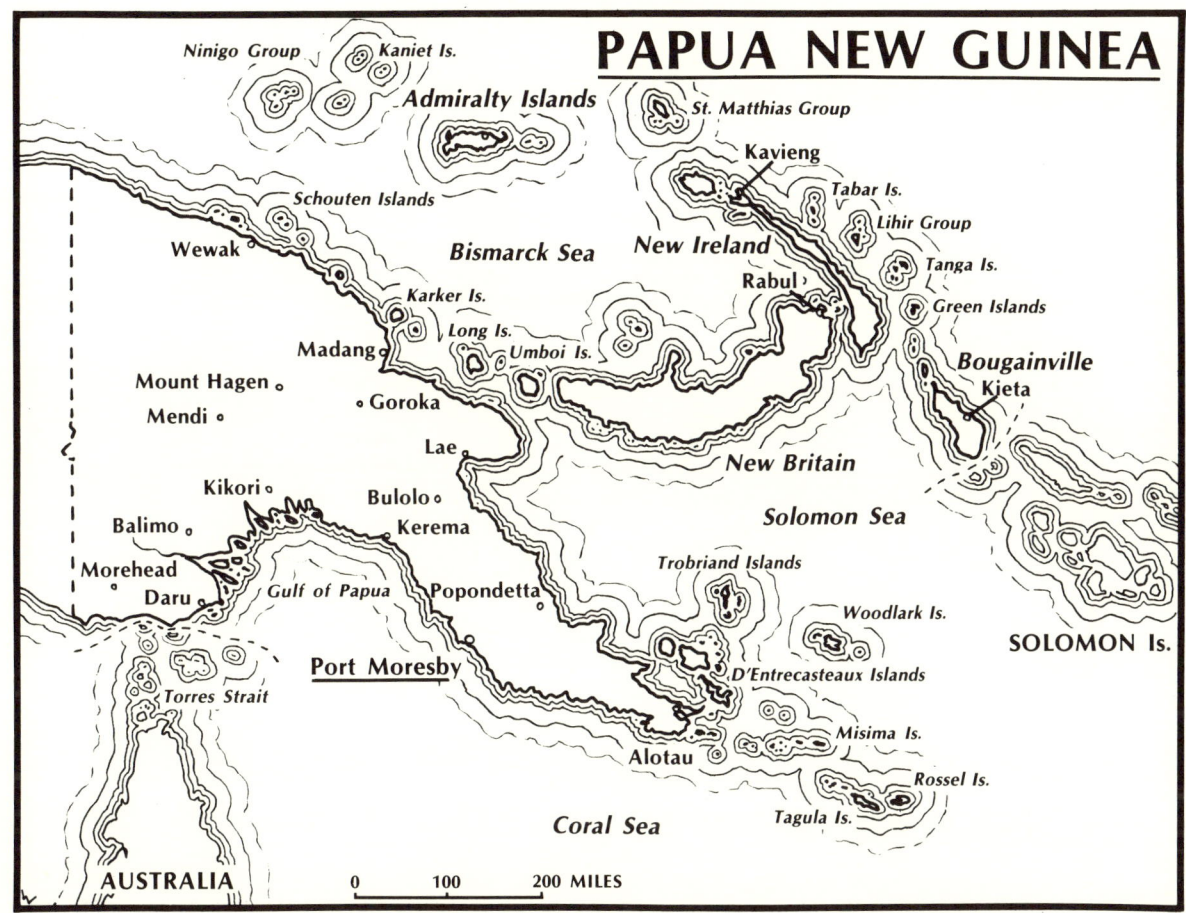

Area: 178,704 sq. miles
Population: 3,353,000 (1984)
Capital: Port Moresby
Currency: Kina (100 toea)

Sharing the island of New Guinea with Indonesia and including the Bismarck Archipelago, Bougainville and Buka in the western Solomons, plus a number of island groups off the eastern tip of New Guinea, Papua New Guinea lies to the north of Australia.

Its portion of New Guinea island is divided into Papua in the south and New Guinea in the north. It is mountainous with steep ranges running from the eastern tip to the western border with Indonesia.

Peaks rise to 15,000 feet and there are small plateau regions from 5,000-10,000 feet high. The islands are also mountainous.

Much of the country is covered by dense tropical rain forest and a wide variety of spectacular flora.

The climate is hot and the average daily sea-level temperature is 80 degrees F. Temperatures reduce with altitude and seasonal variation is slight.

The early explorers sighted New Guinea and it received its name in 1545 from the Spanish sailor Ynigo Ortis de Retez, because of a supposed resemblance between the inhabitants and those of the African area of Guinea. Not until the late 19th century did settling or trading take place.

In 1884, Germany took the northern part of the eastern half of New Guinea and the adjacent islands and in 1889 it became German New Guinea.

Also in 1884, Britain had proclaimed a protectorate over Papua, making it British New Guinea in 1888.

Australian forces took German New Guinea during World War I.

After the Japanese WWII occupation ended in 1945, the area was united and eventually assumed its present form. Independence came Sept. 16, 1975.

Coffee, coconuts, and cocoa are the chief crops but minerals provide the bulk of the revenue and include gold, copper, and silver.

The 1978 per capita income was $480 and the 1984 literacy rate was 25%.

Philatelic Bureau: Philatelic Bureau, PO Box 160, Port Moresby, Papua New Guinea.

PENRHYN (TONGAREVA)

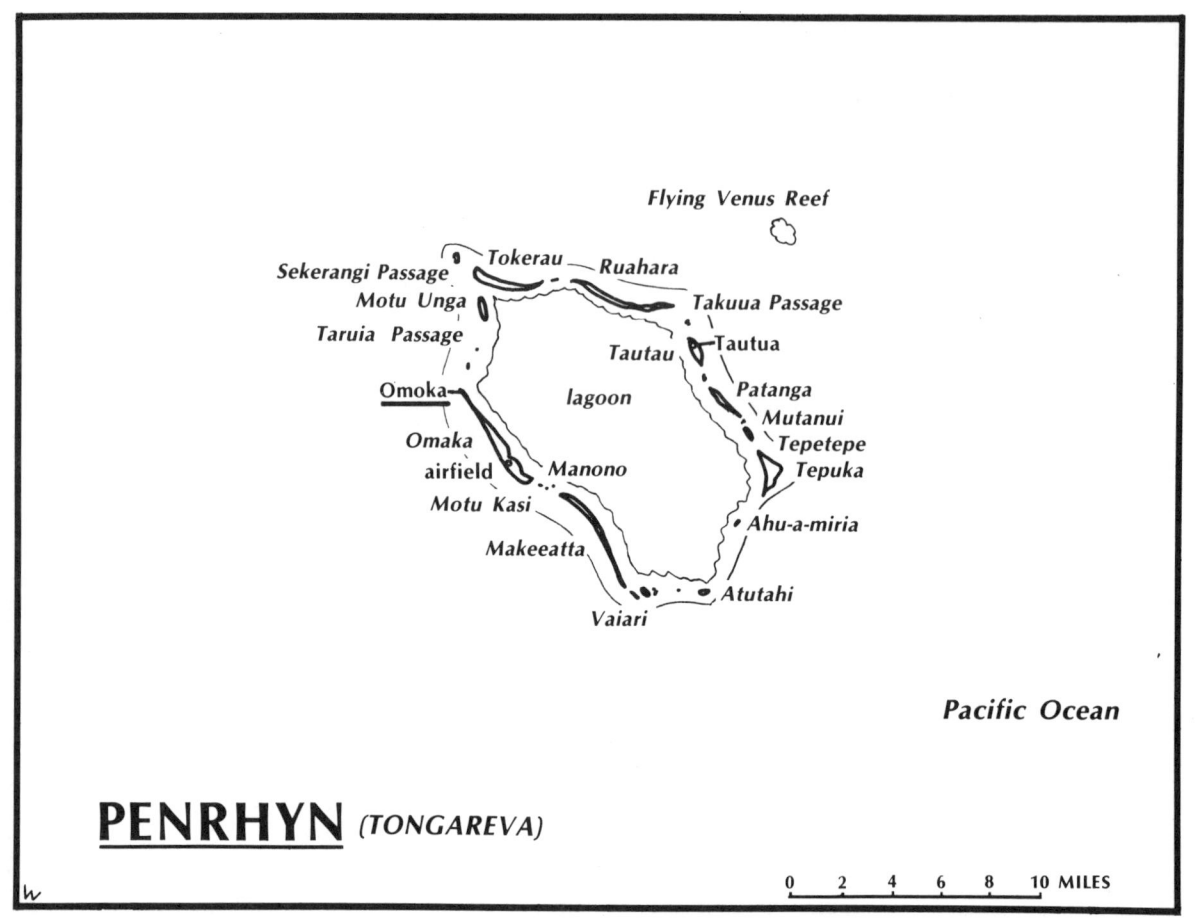

PENRHYN (TONGAREVA)

Area: 3.8 sq. miles
Population: 2,000 (1975)
Capital: Omoka
Currency: Dollar (100 cents)

Penrhyn is the largest and most northerly atoll in the Northern Cook Islands, of which country it is a part.

Its several islands are enclosed by a barrier reef and surround a 108-square-mile lagoon.

There are passages through the reef permitting quite large vessels to enter and tie up at the wharf at Omoka, the main settlement of Penrhyn.

Stamps of New Zealand overprinted "PENRHYN ISLAND" were first issued in 1902 and continued in various forms until 1920, when a set of pictorial stamps was issued inscribed for the atoll.

In 1973 stamps for Penrhyn were resumed and since then, a large number of stamps have appeared, many also bearing the inscription "NORTHERN COOK ISLANDS." Presumably this indicates that the stamps are also valid for postage in the other Northern Cook Islands of Pukapuka, Nassau, Rakahamga, Manihiki, and Suwarrow.

Like the stamps of the Cook Islands, and Aitutaki, Penrhyn's stamps have been issued in various formats and with denominations varied.

Philatelic Bureau: Penrhyn Post Office, Penrhyn Island, Northern Cook Islands, South Pacific Ocean.

Stamp issued by Penrhyn in 1986 marking the return of Halley's Comet.

PACIFIC OCEAN

PITCAIRN ISLANDS

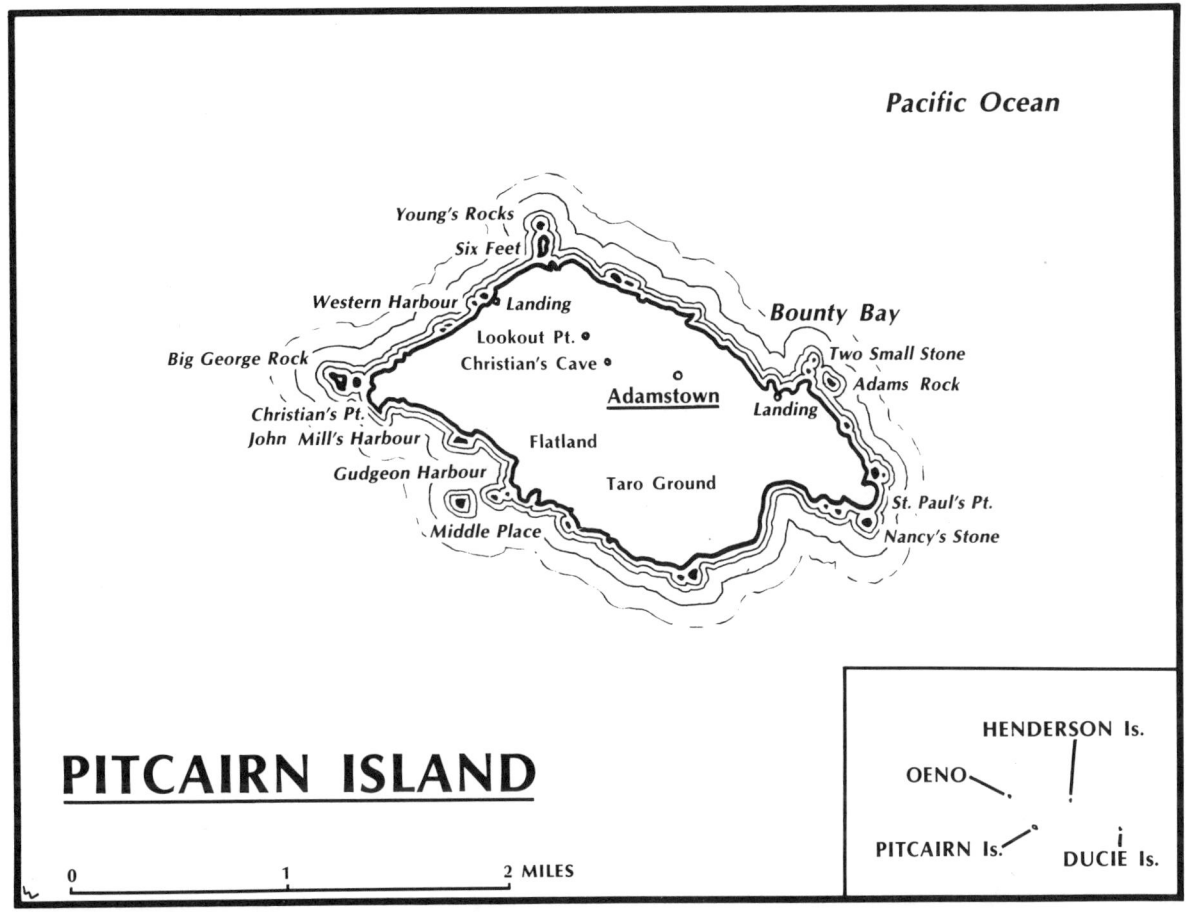

Area: 1.75 sq. miles
Population: 61 (1983)
Capital: Adamstown
Currency: Dollar (100 cents)

Tiny, remote Pitcairn is 5,325 miles from Australia, 4,650 miles from Los Angeles, Calif., and 4,000 miles from the South American coast.

The uninhabited islands of Henderson (12 square miles), Oeno (two square miles), and Ducie (2.5 square miles) are grouped to form the British colony of Pitcairn Islands.

Pitcairn is hilly, its highest point rising to 1,000 feet. The coast is rugged and landing from the sea is difficult.

The climate is described as excellent and there is no seasonal variation.

Discovered in July 1767 by Captain Philip Carteret commanding HMS *Swallow,* the island was named for the son of Major Pitcairn, who first sighted it. Because of rough conditions no landing was made.

The island remained deserted until Jan. 15, 1790, when a party of mutineers and native women arrived aboard HMS *Bounty.* Burning the ship, they established a settlement.

Disputes over the women arose and by 1800, only one of the mutineers remained alive. He was John Adams and he became leader of the population of women and children.

Although visiting ships had taken word to England, the British took no action and the settlement was left in peace to grow. In 1831, a move to Tahiti proved a mistake and the population returned to Pitcairn. By 1856, the population had grown so much that another move seemed necessary and the population was taken to Norfolk Island where most stayed. Some eventually returned to Pitcairn and their descendents form today's dwindling community.

The islands were formally annexed to the British Crown in 1902.

Subsistance agriculture and handicrafts are the main occupations.

The sale of postage stamps, first issued in 1940, is an important source of revenue.

The colony is administered by a British representative located in New Zealand.

Philatelic Bureau: Postmaster, Philatelic Bureau, GPO Box 40, Suva, Fiji.

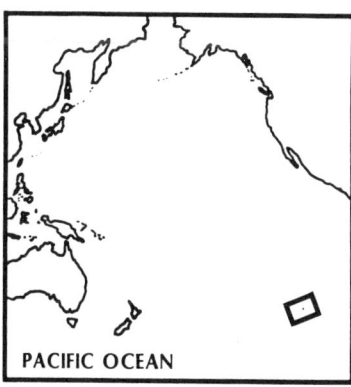

SAMOA, INDEPENDENT STATE OF WESTERN

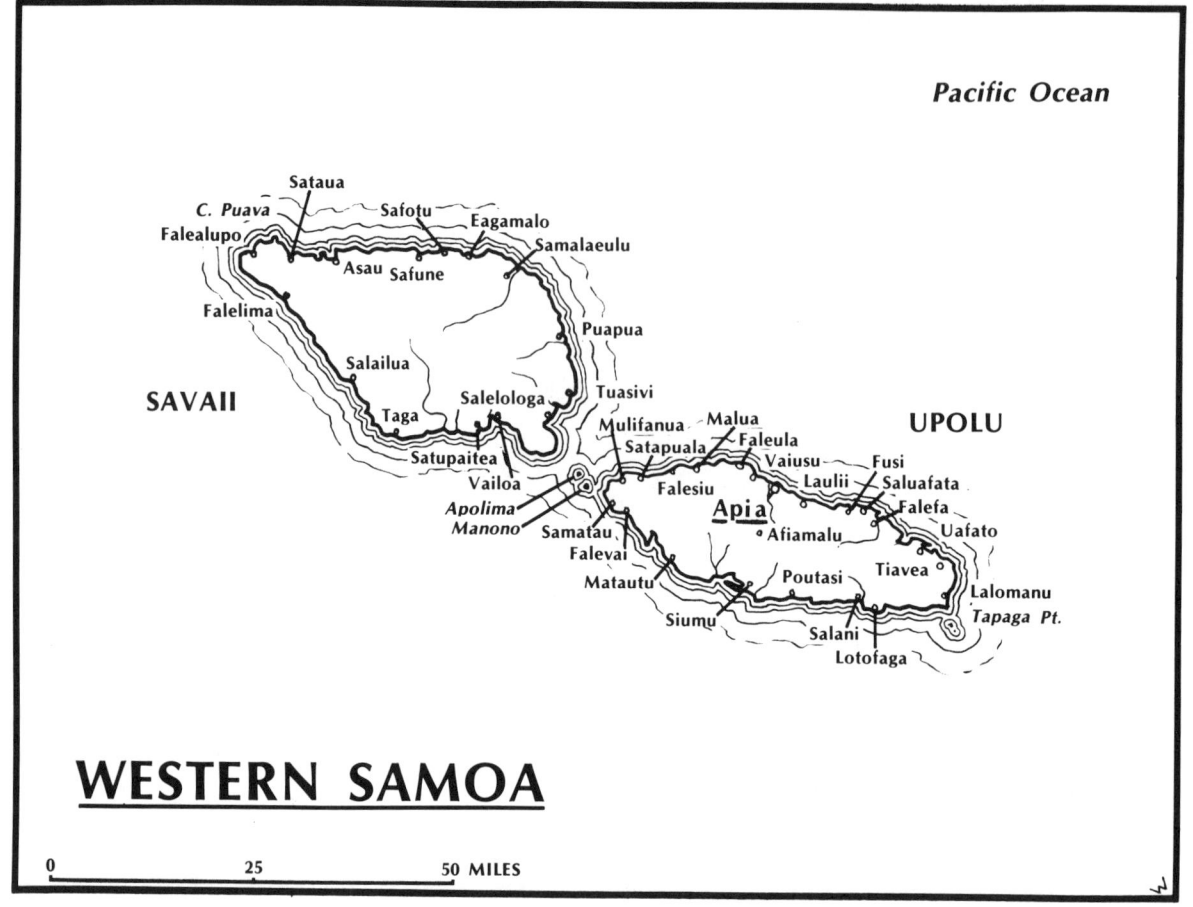

Area: 1,133 sq. miles
Population: 162,000 (1984)
Capital: Apia
Currency: Tala (100 sene)

Western Samoa is located about 1,600 miles northeast of Auckland, New Zealand and to the west of American Samoa.

It is composed of two islands formed from a range of extinct volcanoes, plus several small islands.

The highest point is 6,095 feet on the island of Savaii.

The climate is tropical and the average daily temperature is 80 degrees F. Rainfall averages 113 inches a year. Although located out of the normal typhoon track, there have been violent storms.

Samoa was a native kingdom until competition between the United States, Germany, and Great Britain led to tense situations. On March 15-16, 1889, warships of the three nations were in Apia harbor. A dangerous confrontation was only averted by a violent storm that destroyed all six US and German warships. The single British cruiser escaped.

Eventually an agreement was worked out following the death of the native king in 1898, whereby the United States annexed eastern Samoa and Germany took over what is now Western Samoa. Britain had given up its claim in exchange for recognition of its rights in other Pacific areas.

New Zealand forces took German Samoa in 1914, shortly after the outbreak of World War I.

New Zealand was granted a League of Nations mandate over the islands at the end of the war, and the United Nations made it a New Zealand trust territory after World War II. The country became independent Jan. 1, 1962.

Samoa's economy is based on copra, coffee, cocoa, and bananas. There is some hardwood production and commercial fishing.

The latest per capita income figure is $400 and the 1983 literacy rate was 90%.

The first stamps were issued under the Kingdom of Samoa in 1877 and are the famous Samoa Express stamps.

Philatelic Bureau: Supervisor, Philatelic Bureau, GPO, Apia, Western Samoa, South Pacific.

SOLOMON ISLANDS

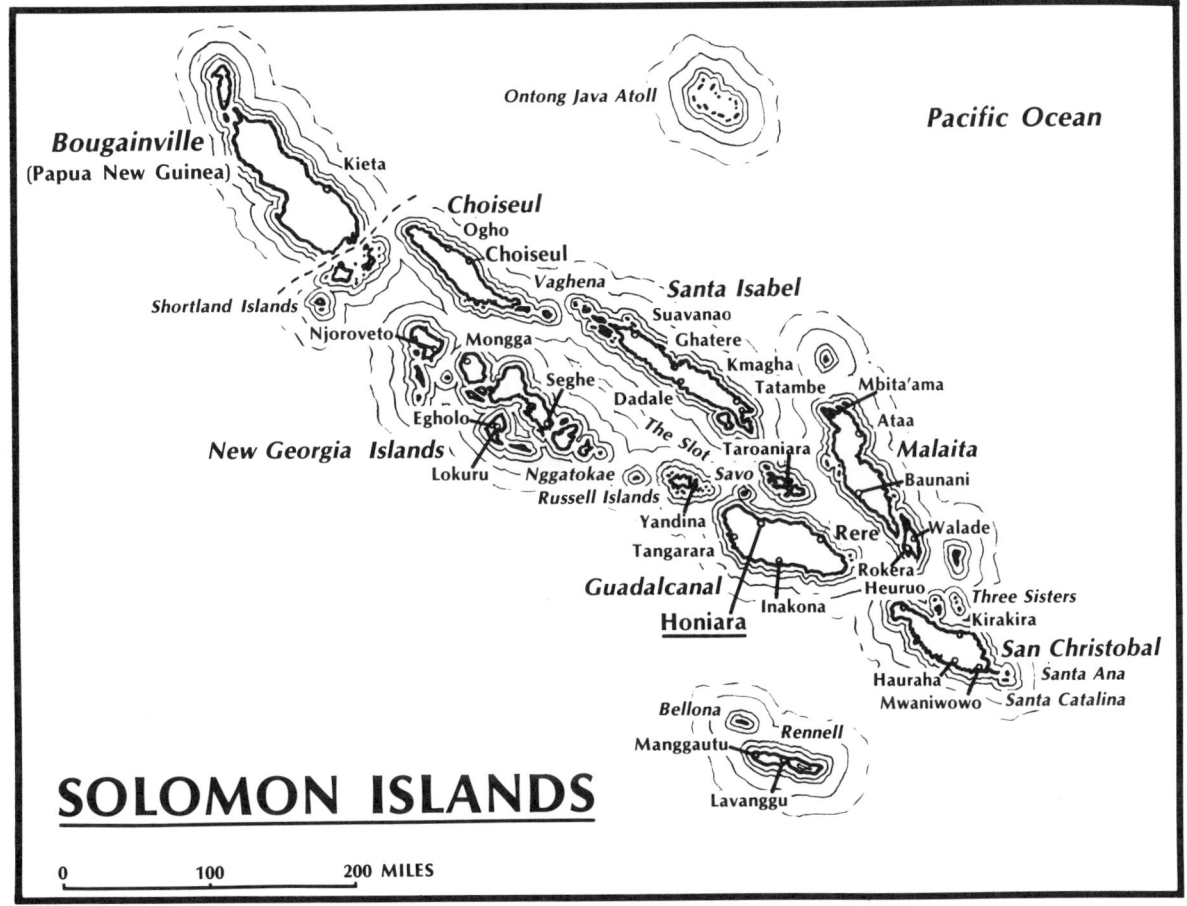

Area: 10,640 sq. miles
Population: 263,000 (1984)
Capital: Honiara
Currency: Dollar (100 cents)

Stretching in a 900-mile chain of islands from the eastern end of New Guinea, the Solomon Islands march to the southeast in double file, separated by a body of water well known to those who served there in World War II as The Slot.

The islands are mountainous and

of volcanic origin. Covered with rain forest, they are cut with deep valleys and fringed with coastal strips of coconut palms and mangrove swamps. There is usually a surrounding reef.

The area is geographically unstable and tremors are frequent.

The climate is pleasant with an average year round temperature of 80 degrees F. Annual rainfall is about 120 inches, mostly falling from November to April.

The flora is varied and more than 230 varieties of orchids and other tropical flowers abound.

The islands were discovered by the Spanish explorer Alvaro de Medana in 1568, but not until the 18th century did Europeans make any detailed exploration.

Great Britain declared a protectorate over the islands in 1893 and Germany took the islands of Bougainville and Buks immediately to the west.

Occupied by the Japanese, the islands suffered greatly in bloody fighting during World War II.

With postwar recovery, self-government came in 1976 and independence was achieved on July 7, 1978.

Copra is the basis of the economy, although fishing and forest products are important. The latest per capita income figure is $440.

The first stamps were issued in 1907. Since independence stamps-issuing policies have been moderate and responsible. The 1986 America's Cup issue may indicate a change. The issue contains 50 different stamps with a total face value of $26.60!

Philatelic Bureau: Philatelic Bureau, GPO, Mendana Avenue, Honiara, Solomon Islands.

TOKELAU ISLANDS

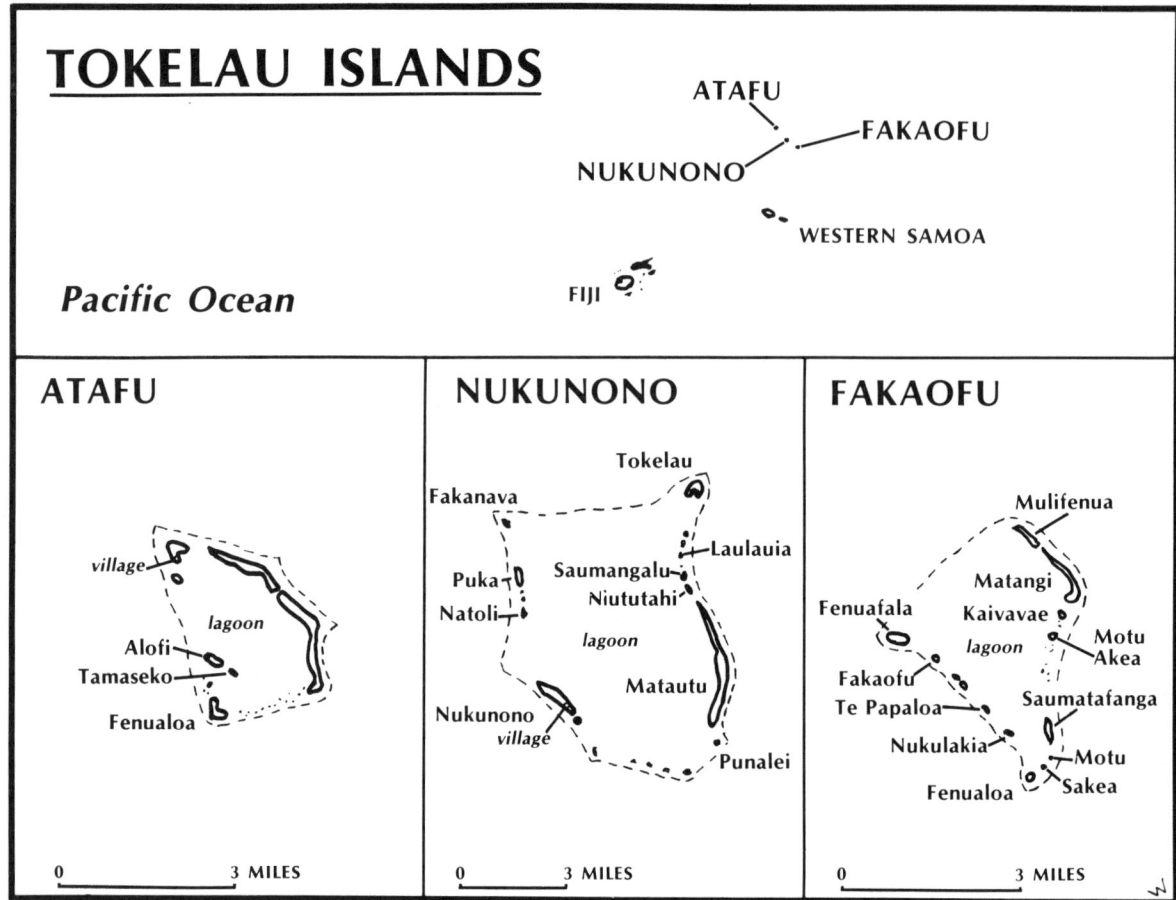

Area: 4 sq. miles
Population: 1,600 (1981)
Capital: none
Currency: Dollar (100 cents)

The Tokelau Islands are located about 300 miles north of Samoa and were once considered as part of the Ellice group.

Formerly called the Union Islands, their present name was adopted in 1946.

The group includes the three atolls of Atafu, Nukunono, and Fakaofu. The population is of Polynesian stock.

The islands were discovered in 1765 by a British ship, but did not come under British protection until 1877.

Once part of the Gilbert and Ellice Islands colony, on Nov. 4, 1925, they were transferred to New Zealand administration, and the group is now a dependency of that country.

The growing and export of copra and fishing are the main occupations of the islanders. The making of handicrafts, including carving and weaving, and the building of canoes are also widely practiced.

Stamps were first issued for the Tokelau Islands on June 22, 1948. It is an attractive intaglio printed set, finely engraved, and depicting a scene and map of each of the three atolls.

Since then, the island group has proven to be one of the world's most restrained stamp-issuing entities.

Up to 1984, only 103 stamps had been released. This grand total for 36 years is just about one third of the output of the nearby Tuvalu group for the year of 1984 alone!

Philatelic Bureau: Post Office Philatelic Bureau, Private Bag, Wanganui, New Zealand.

First Tokelau issue.

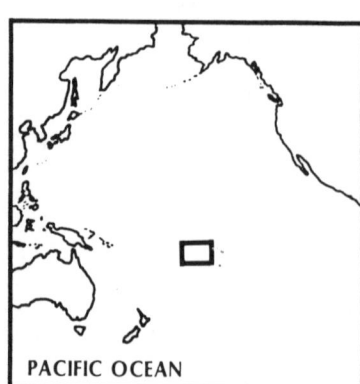

PACIFIC OCEAN

TONGA, KINGDOM OF

Area: 270 sq. miles
Population: 106,000 (1984)
Capital: Nuku'alofa
Currency: Pa'anga (100 seniti)

Located to the south of Samoa in the southern Pacific Ocean, Tonga is an archipelago of 150 islands and islets, 45 of which are inhabited. There are two types of island; those of coral on a limestone base and those of limestone on a volcanic base.

The climate is subtropical. The average daily temperature on Tongatapu, the main island, is 74 degrees F. This rises to 80 degrees F in the north. Rainfall likewise increases as one approaches the equator, from 65 inches to 118 inches a year.

Tonga's history is long. It has preserved the names of its monarchs for at least 1,000 years. At one time, the country was more powerful than at present and extended its influence as far north as Hawaii.

In 1643, Abel Tasman became the first European to visit Tongatapu. Captain James Cook arrived in 1773 and began contact with the Tongans.

Although Cook named them the Friendly Islands, from the reception he received, they became torn by civil war as various rulers struggled for power.

Eventually one assumed control. He converted to Christianity taking the name of George, with his queen assuming the name of Salote (Charlotte) in honor of the British monarchs. He united the country in 1845 and became King George I of Tonga.

In 1900, the islands came under British protection, retaining their independence, with Britain assuming responsibility for foreign affairs and defense.

On June 4, 1970, Tonga became completely independent as a member of the British Commonwealth.

The country's chief exports are coconut products and bananas, although tourism is one of the most important sources of income.

The most recent per capita income figure is $430.

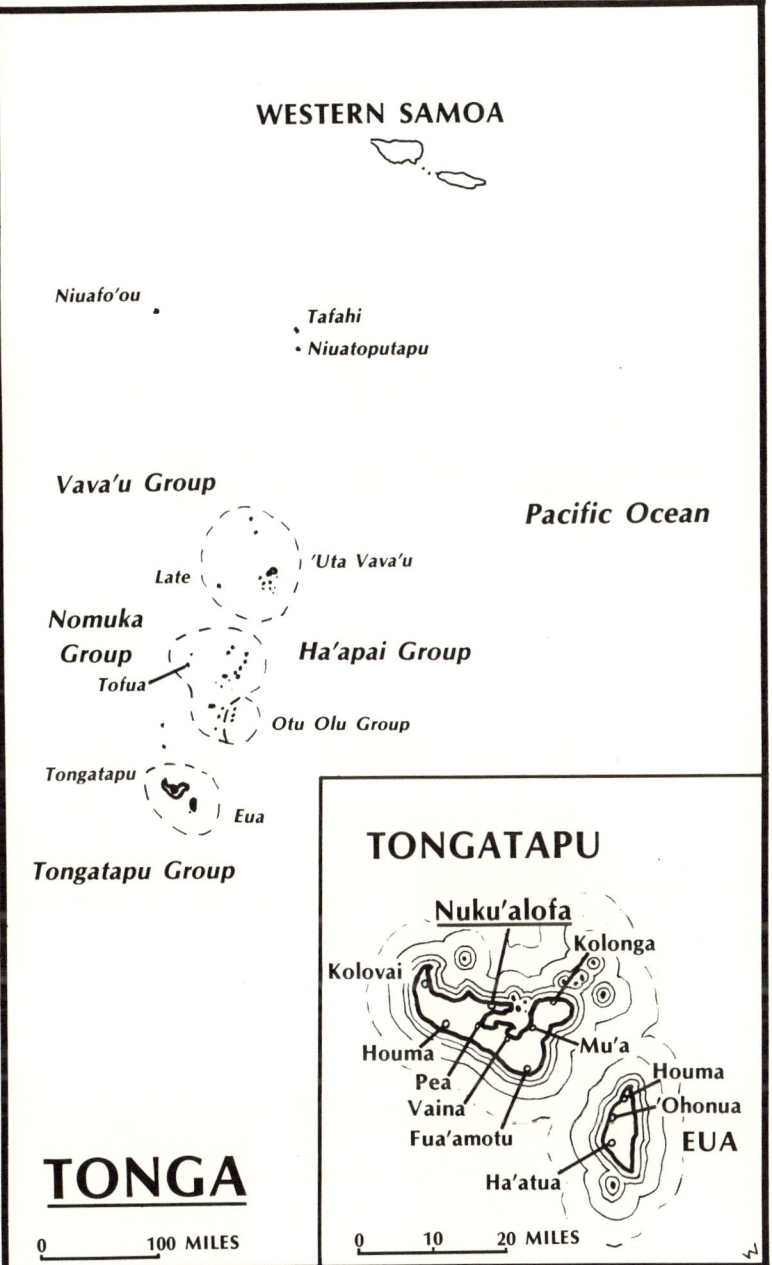

Until 1950, the country's stamps were inscribed "TOGA." This was then changed to "TONGA."

Beginning in 1963, the country issued a stream of free-form stickers in every shape, size, and subject that merchandising imagination could devise.

Current stamp-issuing policies are moderate.

Philatelic Bureau: The Stamp Section, Treasury Building, Nuku'alofa, Tonga.

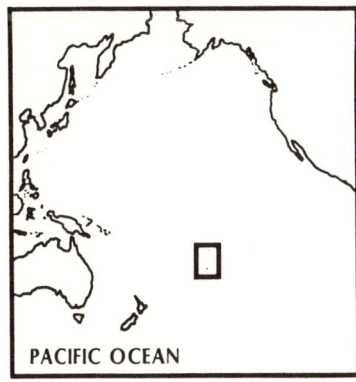

TUVALU

Area: 10 sq. miles
Population: 8,183 (1985)
Capital: Funafuti
Currency: Dollar (100 cents)

Tuvalu is composed of the nine islands that made up the Ellice Islands in the British colony of the Gilbert and Ellice Islands.

They are located north of Fiji, south southeast of Kiribati (formerly the Gilbert Islands), and west of the International Date Line.

The chief settlement and administrative center is on Funafuti.

The nine islands and their 1985 populations are Funafuti (2,810), Nanumaga (672), Nanumea (879), Niulakita (74), Niutao (904), Nui (604), Nukufetau (694), Nukulaelae (315), and Vaitupu (1,231).

The most southerly island of Niulakita was not known to the early inhabitants of the islands, according to Brian Cannon, writing in the journal of the Tuvalu and Kiribati Philatelic Society. This, notes Cannon, explains the native name of Tuvalu, which means "group of eight." "The Europeans found it for us," said an inhabitant of the islands.

The climate of Tuvalu is tropical. Temperatures range from 80-90 degrees F. At night it seldom falls below 70 degrees F. Rainfall is about 120 inches a year.

At one time, the population was Melanesian, but in the 16th century the islands were invaded by Samoans, who established the Polynesian race there.

The Spanish explorer Alvaro de Mendana is believed to have been the first European to sight the islands in 1568.

Britain established a protectorate over the islands in 1892 and annexed them in 1915 at the request of the inhabitants, forming the colony of the Gilbert and Ellice Islands.

Following the breakup of the colony, the Ellice Islands became the independent country of Tuvalu on Oct. 1, 1978.

Until the 1980s, the country followed a relatively conservative new stamp policy, but then began issuing an enormous number of stamps including issues inscribed for each one of the islands except for Niulakita.

Philatelic Bureau: Tuvalu Philatelic Bureau, Funafuti, Tuvalu, Central Pacific Ocean.

VANUATU, REPUBLIC OF

Area: 5,700 sq. miles
Population: 130,000 (1984)
Capital: Port-Vila
Currency: Vatu

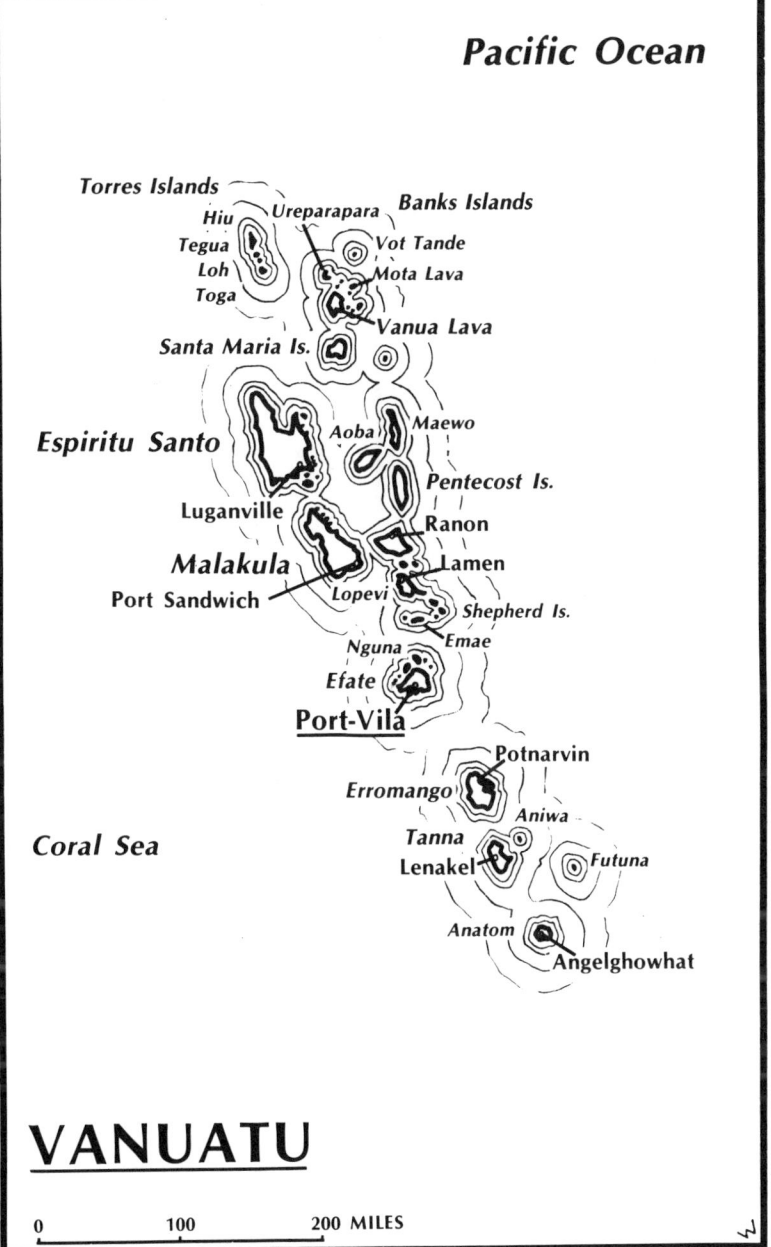

For many years, the Republic of Vanuatu was the Anglo-French Condominium of the New Hebrides.

It is a chain of islands some 500 miles west of Fiji and 250 miles northeast of New Caledonia.

The larger islands are volcanic, while many of the smaller ones are coral. The area is geologically unstable and there are frequent earthquakes. There are three active volcanoes in the group.

The highest point is 6,195 feet on the island of Espiritu Santo.

Vanuatu has a hot and humid climate. The year-round average temperature is 70 degrees F. Rainfall averages 95 inches a year, although the eastern slopes receive less rain than do those on the west.

The Portuguese navigator Pedro Fernandez de Quiros discovered the islands, but they were neglected until 1768, when the French explorer Louis de Bougainville re-discovered them.

Captain James Cook charted the islands in 1774. Commercial contact was exclusively with the British until the 1870s, when French interests developed.

The desires of both countries to influence the area led to the joint administration formalized in 1906, known as a condominium. It governed the islands until they achieved independence on July 30, 1980.

The condominium was a strange contraption. The administration was not just a joint one by the two countries — it was a duplicate one! The two governments exercised separate control over their nationals

and jointly over the native population, who, with some justification, felt a bit left out of the picture in their own land.

Fish and meat processing are major occupations and, together with the production of copra, form the basis of the economy. Tourism is of growing importance.

The first stamps were issued in 1908, and as might be expected, under the condominium arrangement there were also separate but equal stamp issues!

Designs were usually similar, but in one case the inscription was in French and the other in English.

Now that the country is running its own affairs, things are less complicated. Since independence, stamp issues have been moderate and most issues have themes relating in some way to the islands.

Philatelic Bureau: Philatelic Section, Post Office, Port-Vila, Vanuatu, South Pacific.

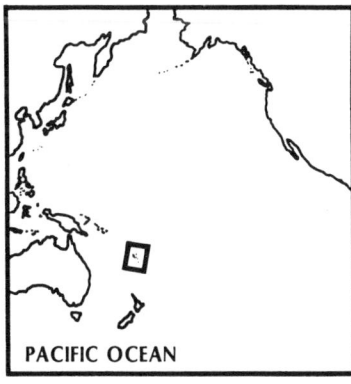

WALLIS AND FUTUNA ISLANDS

Area: 64 sq. miles
Population: 11,943 (1982)
Capital: Mata Utu
Currency: Franc (100 centimes)

The Wallis and Futuna Islands is a French overseas territory located in the Pacific Ocean west of Samoa and northeast of Fiju.

It comprises the island of Wallis (Uvea) and, 120 miles to the west southwest, the Horn Islands, consisting of Futuna and uninhabited Alofi.

Wallis is an island surrounded by a lagoon in which there are several other islets, all enclosed by a reef. Its total area is 29 square miles. Futuna and Alofi have a combined area of 35 square miles.

The climate is hot and humid.

The English explorer Samuel Wallis discovered Wallis in 1767 and the Horn Islands were first sighted by J. Lemaire and W.C. Schouten in 1616.

Both groups were placed under French protection in 1888. They were administered from New Caledonia until 1959. During World War II, the islands were used as an Allied base for the war against Japan.

On July 29, 1961, the islands were made an overseas territory of France.

The chief products of the islands are copra, yams, taro roots, and bananas.

The first stamps of the Wallis and Futuna Islands were issued in 1920. They consisted of stamps of New

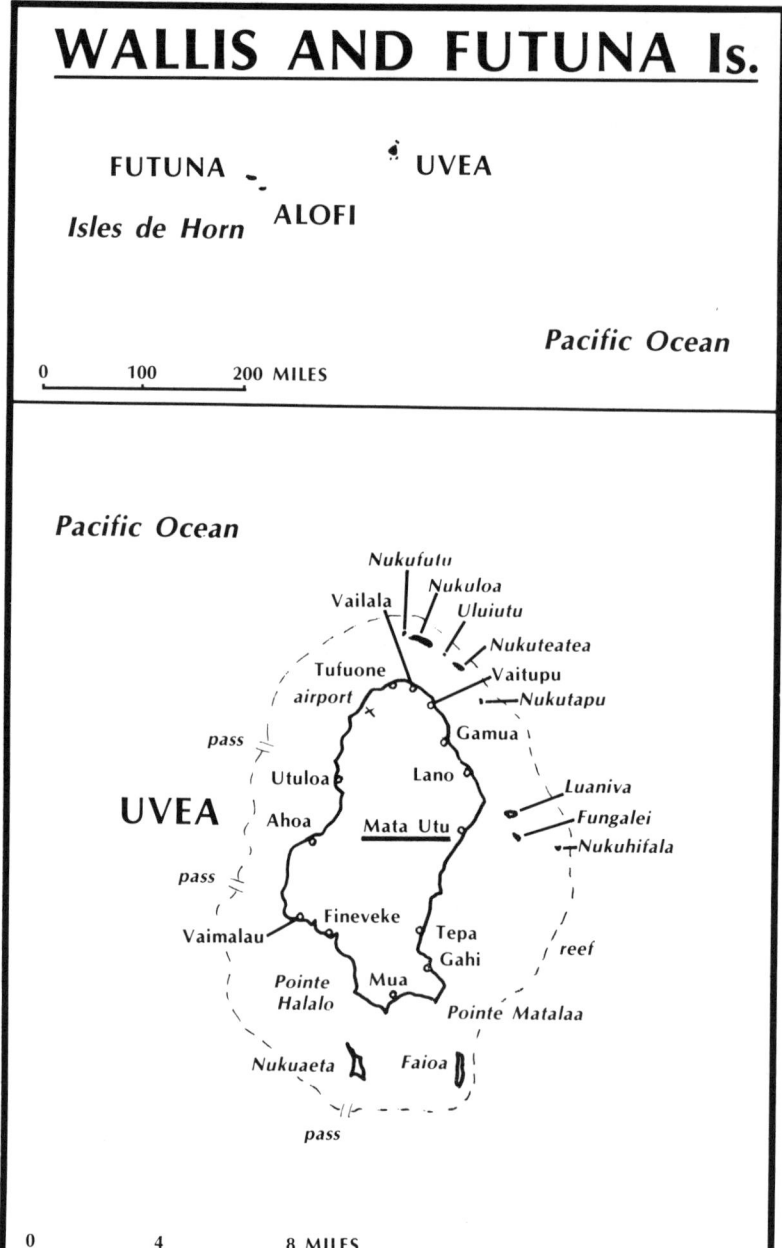

Caledonia overprinted "ILES WALLIS/ et/ FUTUNA."

The first stamps especially designed for the islands were issued in 1944, under the Free French administration. They feature a native bone carving.

In 1957, stamps depicting island scenes, culture, and history began and have continued in moderation since then. Most stamps are in large format. Many are well engraved and intaglio printed.

Philatelic Bureau: Service Philatelique, Direction Generale des PTT, Futuna, Wallis and Futuna Islands, South Pacific.

ANTARCTICA

Stamp-issuing areas:

1. Australian Antarctic Territory
2. British Antarctic Territory
3. French Southern and Antarctic Territory
4. Ross Dependency
5. South Georgia and South Sandwich Islands (formerly known as Falkland Island Dependencies)

Antarctica has an area of about 5.5 million square miles. The continent is divided into two geographic areas; West Antarctica, facing on the Pacific Ocean and East Antarctica, opposite the Southern Ocean.

It is a continent covered with ice to an average depth of one mile. The maximum ice depth discovered so far is 14,000 feet in West Antarctica.

The continent is also the highest of all the continents, having an average altitude of 8,000 feet. Its highest point is the Vinson Massif at 16,860 feet.

The existence of coal deposits indicate that the area may not have been as cold in the past as it is at present. And it is a cold place.

The average low temperature in winter in the interior ranges from -94 to -40 degrees F. On the coast it runs from -25 to -4 degrees F.

The average temperature during the warmest month of the year on the coast is right on the freezing mark at 32 degrees F.

Although the antarctic continent has segments claimed by various nations, a 1959 treaty established the entire continent as a demilitarized zone. The United States recognizes no claim of sovereignty, either for itself or any other nation.

Nations making territorial claims in the area include Argentina,

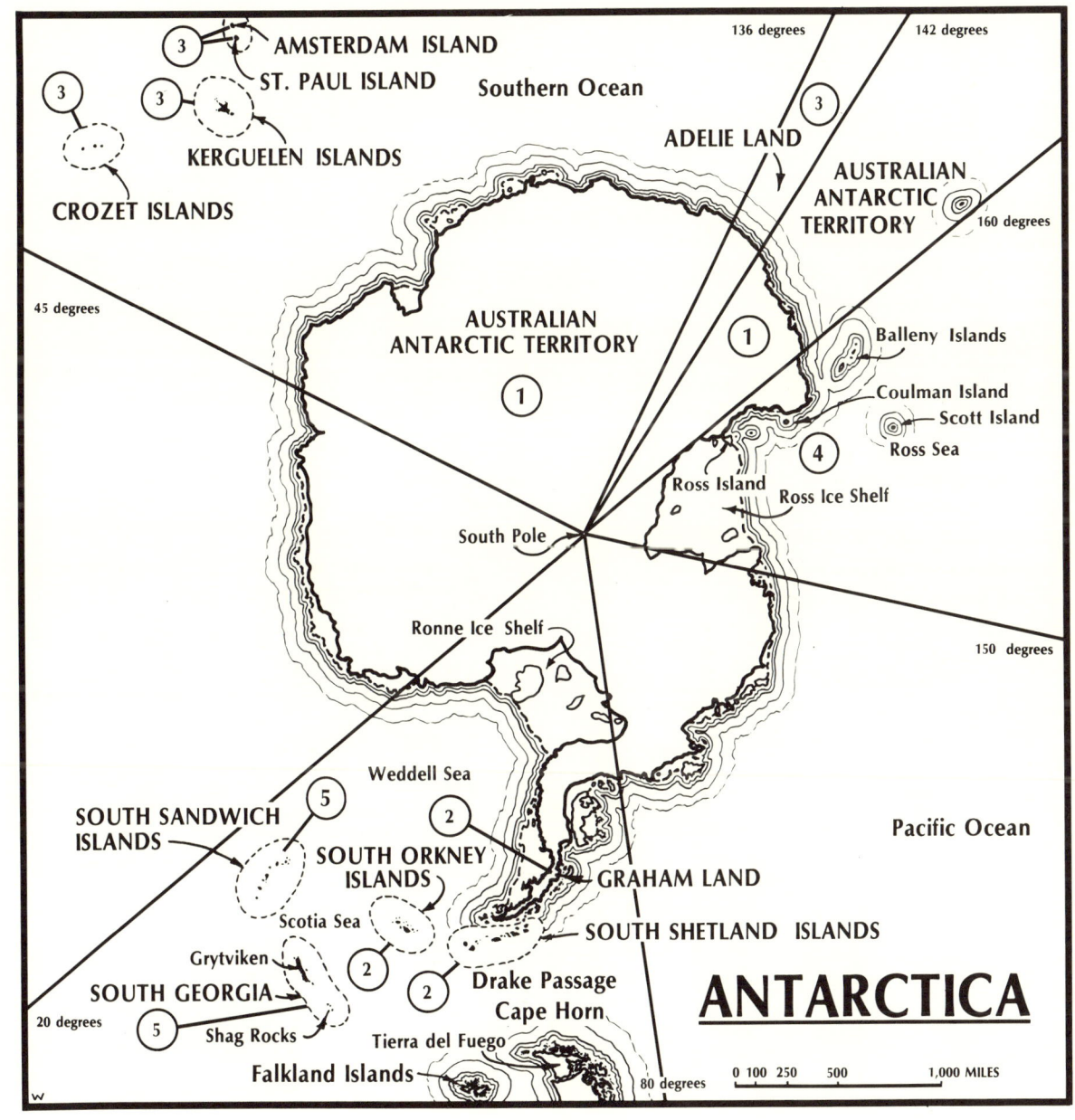

ANTARCTICA

Australia, Chile, France, Great Britain, New Zealand, and Norway.

Areas administered by Australia, France, Great Britain, and New Zealand have released stamps. These are regarded more as evidence of political claim rather than serving any real postal purpose.

It has long been an area attracting explorers and Roald Amundsen was the first to reach the South Pole on Dec. 17, 1911. Today's explorers are scientists seeking to unlock the mysteries of earth in one of its least-known places.

Australian Antarctic Territory

The Australian Antarctic Territory is located south of latitude 60 degrees South and between 160 degrees East longitude and 45 degrees East longitude, except for the Adelie Land area, which is part of French Southern and Antarctic Territory.

It covers an area of about 2,360,000 square miles.

The first stamps were issued in 1957. They are also valid for use throughout Australia.

Philatelic Bureau: Philatelic Bureau, GPO Box 9988, Melbourne, Victoria 3001, Australia.

British Antarctic Territory

The British Antarctic Territory comprises an area south of latitude 60 degrees South and between 80 degrees West longitude and 20 degrees West longitude.

It covers about 652,000 square miles and includes the South Shetland Islands, the South Orkney Islands, Graham Land on the Antarctic Peninsula, and an area extending to the Pole. The territory is administered from the Falkland Islands.

Stamps were first issued on Feb. 1, 1963.

Philatelic Bureau: Postmaster for British Antarctic Territory, c/o GPO, Port Stanley, Falkland Islands.

French So. and Antarctic Terr.

The French Southern and Antarctic Territory includes Adelie Land on continental Antarctica, plus the Indian Ocean islands of Amsterdam, St. Paul, the Kerguelen Islands, and the Crozet Islands.

Adelie Land has a 185-mile coastline and tapers 1,240 miles to the South Pole. The islands were discovered during the 1700s and contain research stations.

A French overseas territory established in 1955, it issued its first stamp on Oct. 1 of that year. It is an overprint on a stamp of Madagascar.

Since then a considerable number of attractive stamps have been issued.

Philatelic Bureau: Agence Comptble des Timbres Poste d'Outremer, 85 Avenue de la Bourdonnais, Paris 75007, France.

Ross Dependency

The Ross Dependency is administered by New Zealand and consists of antarctic land south of latitude 60 degrees South and between 160 degrees East longitude and 150 degrees West longitude, plus the Balleny Islands, Coulman Island, Ross Island, Scott Island, King Edward VII Peninsula, and part of Victoria Land.

It has an area of 160,000 square miles of land and 130,000 square miles of ice shelf.

Stamps were first issued on Jan. 11, 1957. There have been few issued since.

Philatelic Bureau: Post Office Philatelic Bureau, Private Bag, Wanganui, New Zealand.

S. Georgia and S. Sandwich Is.

Formerly known as the Falkland Island Dependencies, South Georgia and South Sandwich Islands comprise the island of South Georgia and the group known as the South Sandwich Islands. It assumed its new name in 1985.

South Georgia has an area of 1,450 square miles and a small population last reported at about 500. Its highest point is 9,625 feet.

The island was claimed for Britain by Captain James Cook during his 1772-75 voyage.

The South Sandwich Islands are uninhabited. They have an area of 120 square miles and are located about 1,350 miles east southeast of Cape Horn.

Stamps were first issued for the areas separately in 1944 and have been issued under various groupings since then.

A postmarker bearing the new name went into use Oct. 3, 1985 and stamps followed.

Philatelic Bureau: South Georgia and South Sandwich Islands Philatelic Bureau, GPO, Port Stanley, Falkland Islands.

Some stamps of Antarctica.

New names for old

This is a worldwide, cross-referenced list of cities and towns that have had one or more name changes, or that have a local spelling less familiar to English-speaking collectors.

Each place is listed under each of its variations, which means that any name you check will give the desired information.

The list will help to identify place names on old postal markings that no longer exist under those names.

The place name currently in use is shown in capital letters, and the country in which it is now located is given.

Where both names are in capitals, it means either that one is a local spelling and the other the English-language version, or that both names appear to be in current use.

AACHEN (Aix-la-Chapelle), West Germany.
ABENRA (Apenrade), Denmark.
Abercorn (MBALA), Zambia.
Abo (TURKU), Finland.
ABU DHABI (ABU ZABI), United Arab Emirates.
ABU ZABI (ABU DHABI), United Arab Emirates.
ACHALPUR (Ellichpur), India.
Acre (AKKO), Israel.
ADANA (Seyhan), Turkey.
AD DAKHLA (Villa Cisneros), Morocco.
AD DAWHAH (DOHA), Bahrain.
ADDIS ABABA (ADIS ABEBA), Ethiopia.
ADIS ABEBA (ADDIS ABABA), Ethiopia.
Adrianople (EDIRNE), Turkey.
Affreville (KHEMIS MIL), Algeria.
Agram (ZAGREB), Yugoslavia.
Aix-la-chapelle (AACHEN), West Germany.
AKKO (Acre), Israel.
Akyab (SITTWE), Burma.
AL BASRAH (BASRA), Iraq.
Aleppo (HALAB), Syria.
Alexandretta (ISKENDERUN), Turkey.
ALEXANDRIA (EL ISKANDARIYA), Egypt.
ALEXANDROUPOLIS (Dedeagh), Greece.
ALGER (ALGIERS or EL DJEZAIR), Algeria.
ALGIERS (ALGER or EL DJEZAIR). Algeria.
AL HUDAYDAH (Hodeida), Yemen Arab Republic.
AL KHUMS (HOMS), Libya.
AL KUWAYT (KUWAIT), Kuwait.
AL LADHIQIYAH (Latakia), Syria.
Allenstein (OLSZTYN), Poland.
AL MADINAH (MEDINA), Saudi Arabia.
AL MANAMAH (MANAMA), Bahrain.
AL MUKHA (Mocha), Yemen Arab Republic.
AMOY (XIAMEN), People's Republic of China.
Angora (ANKARA), Turkey.
ANKARA (Angora), Turkey.
ANNABA (Bone), Algeria.
ANTAKYA (Antioch or Hatay), Turkey.

ANTANANARIVO (Tananarive), Madagascar.
Antioch (ANTAKYA or Hatay), Turkey.
ANTSERANANA (Diego-Suarez), Madagascar.
ANTWERP (ANVERS), Belgium.
AN UAIMH (NAVAN), Ireland.
ANVERS (ANTWERP), Belgium.
Apenrade (ABENRA), Denmark.
Argyrokastron (GJIROKASTER), Albania.
AR RIYAD (RIYADH), Saudi Arabia.
Asmara (ASMERA), Ethiopia-Eritrea.
ASMERA (Asmara), Ethiopia-Eritrea.
Astrida (BUTARE), Rwanda.
ATHENS (ATHINAI), Greece.
ATHINAI (ATHENS), Greece.
Auschwitz (OSWIECIM), Poland.

Bahia (SALVADOR), Brazil.
BAILE ATHA CLIATH (DUBLIN), Ireland.
BANGHAZI (BENGHAZI or Bengasi), Libya.
BANGKOK (KRUNG THEP), Thailand.
BANJUL (Bathurst), The Gambia.
Banzyville (MOBAYI MBONGO), Zaire.
Baroda (VADODARA), India.
BASEL (BASLE), Switzerland.
BASLE (BASEL), Switzerland.
BASRA (AL BASRAH), Iraq.
Batavia (JAKARTA), Indonesia.
Bathurst (BANJUL), The Gambia.
BEIHAI (Pakhoi), People's Republic of China.
BEIJING (Peking or Peiching), People's Republic of China.
BEIRUT (BEYROUTH), Lebanon.
BELEM (Para), Brazil.
BELGRADE (BEOGRAD). Yugoslavia.
Benares (VARANASI), India.
Bengasi (BANGHAZI or BENGHAZI), Libya.
BENGHAZI (BANGHAZI or Bengasi), Libya.
BEOGRAD (BELGRADE), Yugoslavia.
Berlin (KITCHENER), Ontario, Canada.
BERN (BERNE), Switzerland.
BERNE (BERN), Switzerland.
BEYROUTH (BEIRUT), Lebanon.
BIR MOGHREIN (Fort Trinquet), Mauritania.

BITOLA (Monastir), Yugoslavia.
Bjorneborg (PORI), Finland.
Bone (ANNABA), Algeria.
BRATISLAVA (Pressburg or Pozsony), Czechoslovakia.
BRAUNSCHWEIG (BRUNSWICK), West Germany.
Breslau (WROCLAW), Poland.
BRNO (Brunn), Czechoslovankia.
Broken Hill (KABWE), Zambia.
Bromberg (BYDGOSZCZ), Poland.
BRUGES (BRUGGE), Belgium.
BRUGGE (BRUGES), Belgium.
Brunn (BRNO), Czechoslovakia.
BRUNSWICK (BRAUNSCHWEIG), West Germany.
BRUSSELS (BRUXELLES), Belgium.
BRUXELLES (BRUSSELS), Belgium.
BUCHAREST (BUCURESTI), Romania.
BUCURESTI (BUCHAREST), Romania.
Budweis (CESKE BUDEJOVICE), Czechoslovakia.
BUKAVU (Costermansville), Zaire.
BUSHEHR (Bushire), Iran.
Bushire (BUSHEHR), Iran.
BUTARE (Astrida), Rwanda.
BYDGOSZCZ (Bromberg), Poland.
Bytown (OTTAWA), Canada.

CAERNARFON (Carnarvon), Wales.
CAIRO (EL QAHIRA), Egypt.
Candia (IRAKLION), Crete, Greece.
Canea (KHANIA), Crete, Greece.
CANTON (GUANGZHOU or KWANGCHOW), People's Republic of China.
CAPE TOWN (KAAPSTAD), South Africa.
Carnarvon (CAERNARFON), Wales.
CASABLANCA (DAR EL BEIDA), Morocco.
Cattaro (KOTOR), Yugoslavia.
Cavalle (KAVALLA), Greece.
CAWNPORE (KANPUR), India.
CEANANNAS MOR (KELLS), Ireland.
Ceara (FORTALEZA), Brazil.
CESKE BUDEJOVICE (Budweis), Czechoslovakia.
CETINJE (Cettinge), Yugoslavia.
Cettinge (CETINJE), Yugoslavia.
Chemnitz (KARL-MARX-STADT), East Germany.

Chengchow (ZHENGZHOU), People's Republic of China.
CHENGDU (Chengtu), People's Republic of China.
Chengtu (CHENGDU), People's Republic of China.
CHERNOVTSY (Czernowitz), USSR.
CH'I-CH'I-HA-ERH (Tsitsihar), People's Republic of China.
CHI-LIN (Kirin), People's Republic of China.
Chimarra (HIMARE), Albania.
Chinhau (JINHUA), People's Republic of China.
CHIPATA (Fort Jameson), Zambia.
CHISIMAIO (Kismayu), Somali Republic.
Chkalov (ORENBURG), USSR.
CHONGQING (Chungking), People's Republic of China.
Chuanchou (QUANZHOU), People's Republic of China.
Chuchi (SHANGQIU), People's Republic of China.
Chuhsien (QUZHOU), People's Republic of China.
Chungking (CHONGQING), People's Republic of China.
Ciudad Trujillo (SANTO DOMINGO), Dominican Republic.
CLU-NAPOCA (Klausenburg or Kolozsvar), Romania.
COBH (Queenstown), Ireland.
COLMAR (Kolmar), France.
COLOGNE (KOLN), West Germany.
Constance (KONSTANZ), West Germany.
Constantinople (ISTANBUL), Turkey.
Conway (CONWY), Wales.
CONWY (Conway), Wales.
COPENHAGEN (KOBENHAVN), Denmark.
Coquilhatville (MBANDAKA), Zaire.
CORCAIGH (CORK), Ireland.
CORDOBA (Cordova), Spain.
Cordova (CORDOBA), Spain.
Corfu (KERKIRA), Greece.
CORK (CORCAIGH), Ireland.
Corunna (LA CORUNA), Spain.
Costermansville (BUKAVU), Zaire.
Cracow (KRAKOW), Poland.
Czernowitz (CHERNOVTSY), USSR.

Dacca (DHAKA), Bangladesh.
Dairen (DALIAN), People's Republic of China.
DALIAN (Darien or Luda), People's Republic of China.
DAMAS (DAMASCUS), Syria.
DAMASCUS (DIMASHQ, ESH SHAM, DAMAS), Syria.
DA NANG (Tourane), Vietnam.
Danzig (GDANSK), Poland.
DAR EL BEIDA (CASABLANCA), Morocco.
Darjeeling (DARJILING), India.
DARJILING (Darjeeling), India.
DARNAH (Derna), Libya.
DAUGAVPILS (Dunaburg), USSR.
Dedeagh (ALEXANDROUPOLIS), Greece.
Derna (DARNAH), Libya.
DHAKA (Dacca), Bangladesh.
Diedenhofen (THIONVILLE), France.
Diego-Suarez (ANTSERANANA), Madagascar.
DIMASHQ (DAMASCUS), Syria.
DOHA (AD DAWHAH), Qatar.
Dorpat (TARTU), Estonia — now USSR.
DROGHEDA (DROICHEAD ATHA), Ireland.
DROICHEAD ATHA (DROGHEDA), Ireland.
DUBAI (DUBAYY), United Arib Emirates.
DUBAYY (DUBAI), United Arab Emirates.
DUBLIN (BAILE ATHA CLIATH), Ireland.
DUBROVNIK (Ragusa), Yugoslavia.
Dunaburg (DAUGAVPILS), USSR.
DUNDALK (DUN DEALGAN), Ireland.
DUN DEALGAN (DUNDALK), Ireland.
Durazzo (DURRES), Albania.
DURRES (Durazzo), Albania.
Duzdab (ZAHEDAN), Iran.

EDIRNE (Adrianopel), Turkey.
Ekaterinodar (KRASNODAR), USSR.
Elbing (ELBLAG), Poland.
ELBLAG (Elbing), Poland.
EL DJEZAIR (ALGER or ALGIERS), Algeria.
Elisabethville (LUMBUMBASHI), Zaire.
EL ISKANDARIYA (ALEXANDRIA), Egypt.
ELK (Lyck), Poland.
Ellichpur (ACHALPUR), India.
EL QAHIRA (CAIRO), Egypt.
English Bazar (INGRAJ BAZAR), India.
ER RACHIDIA (Ksar es Souk), Morocco.
ESFAHAN (Isfahan), Iran.
ESH SHAM (DAMASCUS), Syria.
Espirito Santo (VILA VELHA), Brazil.

FDERIK (Fort Gouraud), Mauritania.
FIRENZE (FLORENCE), Italy.
Fiume (RIJEKA), Yugoslavia.
FLORENCE (FIRENZE), Italy.
Foochow (FUZHOU), People's Republic of China.
FORTALEZA (Ceara), Brazil.
Fort Dauphin (TAOLANARO), Madagascar.
Fort Gouraud (FDERIK), Mauritania.
Fort Jameson (CHIPATA), Zambia.
Fort Lamy (NDJAMENA), Chad.
Fort Rosebery (MANSA), Zambia.
Fort Rousset (OWANDO), People's Republic of the Congo.
Fort Trinquet (BIR MOGHREIN), Mauritania.
Fort William (THUNDER BAY), Canada.
Fort Victoria (MASVINGO), Zimbabwe.
FREDERIKSHAB (PAAMIUT), Greenland.
Friedrich Wilhelmshafen (MADANG), Papua New Guinea.
FU-CHOU (Foochow), People's Republic of China.
Funfkirchen (PECS), Hungary.
FUZHOU (Foochow), People's Republic of China.

GAILLIMH (GALWAY), Ireland.
GALATI (Galatz), Romania.
Galatz (GALATI), Romania.
Gallipoli (GELIBOLU), Turkey.
GALWAY (GAILLIMH), Ireland.
Gand (GENT), Belgium.
GATOOMA (KADOMA), Zimbabwe.
GDANSK (Danzig), Poland.
GELIBOLU (Gallipoli), Turkey.
GENEVA (GENEVE), Switzerland.
GENEVE (GENEVA), Switzerland.
GENOA (GENOVA), Italy.
GENOVA (GENOA), Italy.
GENT (Gand), Belgium.
Ghadames (GHUDAMIS), Libya.
GHENT (GENT), Belgium.
GHUDAMIS (Ghadames), Libya.
GIRESUN (Kerassunde or Kerason), Turkey.
GISENYE (Kisenyi), Rwanda.
GJIROKASTER (Argyrokastron), Albania.
GODHAVEN (QEQERTARSUAQ), Greenland.
GODTHAB (NUUK), Greenland.
GORKIY (Nizhniy Novgorod), USSR.
GOTEBORG (GOTHENBURG), Sweden.
GOTHENBURG (GOTEBORG), Sweden.
Gratz (GRAZ), Austria.
Graudenz (GRUDZIADZ), Poland.
GRAZ (Gratz), Austria.
GRUDZIADZ (Graudenz), Poland.
GUANGZHOU (CANTON or KWANGCHOW), People's Republic of China.
GUIYANG (Kweiyang), People's Republic of China.
GWELO (GWERU), Zimbabwe.
GWERU (GWELO), Zimbabwe.

HABANA (HAVANA), Cuba.
Hadersleben (HADERSLEV), Denmark.
HADERSLEV (Hadersleben), Denmark.
Haerhpin (HARBIN), People's Republic of China.
HAI-K'OU (Hoihow), People's Republic of China.
HAGUE, THE (s'GRAVENHAGE), The Netherlands.
HALAB (Aleppo), Syria.
Hangchow (HANGZHOU), People's Republic of China.
HANGZHOU (Hangchow), People's Republic of China.

Hankow (WUHAN), People's Republic of China.
HANNOVER (Hanover), West Germany.
Hanover (HANNOVER), West Germany.
HARARE (Salisbury), Zimbabwe.
HARBIN (Haerhpin), People's Republic of China.
Hatay (ANTAKYA or Antioch), Turkey.
HAVANA (HABANA), Cuba.
Helsingfors (HELSINKI), Finland.
HELSINKI (Helsingfors), Finland.
Herbertshohe (RABAUL) Papua New Guinea.
HIMARE (Chimarra), Albania.
Hirschberg (JELENIA-GORA), Poland.
HO CHI MINH (Saigon), Vietman.
Hodeida (AL HUDAYDAH), Yemen Arab Republic.
Hoihow (HAI-K'OU), People's Republic of China.
Hollandia (JAYAPURA), Indonesia.
HOLSTEINSBORG (Sisimiut), Greenland.
HOMS (AL KHUMS), Libya.
Hsuchang (XUCHANG), People's Republic of China.
Hsuchou (XUZHOU), People's Republic of China.
HWANGE (WANKIE), Zimbabwe.

IASI (Jassy), Romania.
ILEBO (Port Francqui), Zaire.
INGRAJ BAZAR (English Bazar), India.
IOANNINA (Yannina), Greece.
IRAKLION (Candia), Crete, Greece.
Isfahan (ESFAHAN), Iran.
ISKENDERUN (Alexandretta), Turkey.
ISTANBUL (Constantinople), Turkey.
IVANO FRANKOVSK (Stanislav), USSR.
IZMIR (Smyrna), Turkey.

Jaffa (YAFO), Israel.
JAKARTA (Batavia), Indonesia.
JAKOBSTAD (Pietarsaari), Finland.
Jassy (IASI), Romania.
JAYAPURA (Hollandia or Sukarnapura), Indonesia.
JEDDA (JIDDAH), Saudi Arabia.
JELENIA-GORA (Hirschberg), Poland.
Jesselton (KOTA KINABALU), Malaysia.
JIDDAH (JEDDA), Saudi Arabia.
JINHUA (Chinhua), People's Republic of China.
Joppa (YAFO), Israel.
JULIANEHAB (QAQORTOQ), Greenland.

KAAPSTAD (CAPE TOWN), South Africa.
KABWE (Broken Hill), Zambia.

KADOMA (GATOOMA), Zimbabwe.
KALININGRAD (Konigsberg), USSR.
KANPUR (CAWNPORE), India.
KARL-MARX-STADT (Chemnitz), East Germany.
KAUNAS (Kovno), USSR.
KAVALLA (Cavalle), Greece.
KELLS (CEANANNAS MOR), Ireland.
Kerason (GIRESUN), Turkey.
Kerassunde (GIRESUN), Turkey.
KERKIRA (Corfu), Greece.
KHANIA (Canea), Crete, Greece.
KHEMIS MIL (Affreville), Algeria.
KIEV (KIYEV), USSR.
KIN-MEN (Quemoy), Republic of China — Taiwan.
KINSHASA (Leopoldville), Zaire.
Kirin (CHI-LIN), People's Republic of China.
KISANGANI (Stanleyville), Zaire.
Kisenyi (GISENYE), Rwanda.
Kismayu (CHISIMAIO), Somali Republic.
KITCHENER (Berlin), Ontario, Canada.
KIYEV (KIEV), USSR.
KLAIPEDA (Memel), USSR.
Klausenburg (CLU-NAPOCA or Kolozsvar), Romania.
KOBENHAVEN (COPENHAGEN), Denmark.
Kolmar (COLMAR), France.
KOLN (COLOGNE), West Germany.
Kolozsvar (CLU-NAPOCA or Klausenburg), Romania.
Konigsberg (KALININGRAD), USSR.
KONSTANZ (Constance), West Germany.
KORCE (Koritsa), Albania.
Koritsa (KORCE), Albania.
KOTA KINABALU (Jesselton), Malaysia.
KOTOR (Cattaro), Yugoslavia.
Kouang Tcheou (ZHANJIANG), People's Republic of China.
Kovno (KAUNAS), USSR.
KRAKOW (Cracow), Poland.
KRASNODAR (Ekaterinodar), USSR.
Kristiania (OSLO), Norway.
KRUNG THEP (BANGKOK), Thailand
Ksar es Souk (ER RACHIDIA), Morocco.
KUCHING (Kucing), Malaysia.
Kucing (KUCHING), Malaysia.
KUNMING (Yunnan), People's Republic of China.
KUWAIT (AL KUWAYT), Kuwait.
KWANGCHOW (CANTON or GUANGZHOU), People's Republic of China.
Kweiyang (GUIYANG), People's Republic of China.
KWEKWE (QUE QUE), Zimbabwe.
KWIDZYN (Marienwerder), Poland.

LA CORUNA (Corunna), Spain.
Laibach (LJUBLJANA), Yugoslavia.
Laojunmiao (YUMEN), People's Republic of China.
La-sa (LHASA), Tibet — People's Republic of China.
Latakia (AL LADHIQIYAH), Syria.
Lefkosa (NICOSIA), Cyprus.
Leghorn (LIVORNO), Italy.
LEGNICA (Liesnitz), Poland.
Lemberg (L'VOV), Poland.
LENINGRAD (St. Petersburg or Petrograd), USSR.
Leopoldville (KINSHASA), Zaire.
LHASA (La-sa), Tibet — People's Republic of China.
Liesnitz (LEGNICA), Poland.
LIMERICK (LUIMNEACH), Ireland.
LISBOA (LISBON), Portugal.
LISBON (LISBOA), Portugal.
LIVINGSTONE (MARAMBA), Zambia.
LIVORNO (Leghorn), Italy.
LJUBLJANA (Laibach), Yugoslavia.
LOANDA (Luanda), Angola.
Lourenco Marques (MAPUTO), Mozambique.
LUANDA (LOANDA), Angola.
LUCERNE (LUZERN), Switzerland.
Luda (DALIAN), People's Republic of China.
Lugansk (VOROSHILOVGRAD), USSR.
LUIMNEACH (LIMERICK), Ireland.
LUMBUMBASHI (Elisabethville), Zaire.
LUSHUN (Port Arthur), People's Republic of China.
LUZERN (LUCERNE), Switzerland.
L'VOV (Lemberg), Poland.
Lyck (ELK), Poland.

Maarianhamina (MARIEHAMN), Aland Islands, Finland.
MADANG (Friedrich Wilhelmshafen), Papua New Guinea.
Mafeking (MAFIKENG), South Africa.
MAFIKENG (Mafeking), South Africa.
MAHAJANGA (Majunga), Madagascar.
Mahrisch Ostrau (OSTRAVA), Czechoslovakia.
Majunga (MAHAJANGA), Madagascar.
Makassar (UJUNG PANDANG), Indonesia.
MAKKAH (MECCA), Saudi Arabia.
MALABA (Sta. Isabel), Equatorial Guinea.
MALBORK (Marienburg), Poland.
MANAMA (AL MANAMAH), Bahrain.
Manitsoq (SUKKERTOPPEN), Greenland.
MANSA (Fort Rosebery), Zambia.
MAPUTO (Lourenco Marques), Mozambique.
MARAMBA (LIVINGSTONE), Zambia.
MARIEHAMN (Maarianhamina), Aland Islands, Finland.
Marienburg (MALBORK), Poland.
Marienwerder (KWIDZYN), Poland.
MASHHAD (Meshed), Iran.
MASQAT (MUSCAT), Oman.
MASVINGO (Fort Victoria), Zimbabwe.
MBALA (Abercorn), Zambia.

MBANDAKA (Coquilhatville), Zaire.
MECCA (MAKKAH), Saudi Arabia.
MEDINA (AL MADINAH), Saudi Arabia.
Memel (KLAIPEDA), USSR.
Meshed (MASHHAD), Iran.
MILAN (MILANO), Italy.
MILANO (MILAN), Italy.
MOBAYI MBONGO (Banzyville), Zaire,
Mocamedes (NAMIBE), Angola.
Mocha (AL MUKHA), Yemen Arab Republic.
Mogadiscio (MUODISHO), Somalia.
Mogadishu (MUODISHO), Somalia.
Molotov (PERM), USSR.
Monastir (BITOLA), Yugoslavia.
MORBI (Morvi), India.
Morvi (MORBI), India.
MOSCOW (MOSKVA), USSR.
MOSKVA (MOSCOW), USSR.
Mukden (SHENYANG), People's Republic of China.
Mulhausen (MULHOUSE), France.
MULHOUSE (Mulhausen), France.
MUNCHEN (MUNICH), West Germany.
MUNICH (MUNCHEN), West Germany.
MUODISHO (Mogadishu or Mogadiscio), Somalia.
MUSCAT (MASQAT), Oman.
MUTARE (UMTALI), Zimbabwe.
MYMENSINGH (Nasirabad), Bangladesh.

Nagyvarad (ORADEA), Romania.
NAMIBE (Mocamedes), Angola.
NANJING (Nanking), People's Republic of China.
Nanking (NANJING), People's Republic of China.
NAPLES (NAPOLI), Italy.
NAPOLI (NAPLES), Italy.
Nasirabad (MYSENSINGH), Bangladesh.
NAVAN (AN UAIMH), Ireland.
NDJAMENA (Fort Lamy), Chad.
NEUCHATEL (NEUENBURG), Switzerland.
NEUENBURG (NEUCHATEL), Switzerland.
New Amsterdam (NEW YORK), United States.
NEW YORK (New Amsterdam), United States.
NICOSIA (Lefkosa), Cyprus.
Nizhniy Novgorod (GORKIY), USSR.
Nossi-Be (NOSY BE), Madagascar.
NOSY BE (Nossi-Be), Madagascar.
NOSY BORAHA (Sainte-Marie), Madagascar.
NOUADHIBOU (Pt. Etienne), Mauritania.
NUREMBERG (NURNBERG), West Germany.
NURNGERG (NUREMBERG), West Germany.
NUUK (GODTHAB), Greenland.

Oldenburg (SOPRON), Hungary.
OLSZTYN (Allenstein), Poland.
OPORTO (PORTO), Portugal.
ORADEA (Nagyvarad), Romania.
ORAN (OUAHRAN), Algeria.
ORENBURG (Chkalov), USSR.
OSLO (Kristiania), Norway.
OSTRAVA (Mahrisch Ostrau), Czechoslovakia.
OSWIECIM (Auschwitz), Poland.
OTTAWA (Bytown), Canada.
OUAHRAN (ORAN), Algeria.
OULU (Uleaborg), Finland.
OWANDO (Fort Rousset), People's Republic of the Congo.

PAAMIUT (FREDERIKSHAB), Greenland.
Pakhoi (BEIHAI), People's Republic of China.
Para (BELEM), Brazil.
PECS (Funfkirchen), Hungary.
Peiching (BEIJING), People's Republic of China.
Peihoi (BAIHAI), People's Republic of China.
Peking (BEIJING), People's Republic of China.
PERM (Molotov), USSR.
Pernambuco (RECIFE), Brazil.
Petrograd (LENINGRAD), USSR.
Philippeville (SKIKDA), Algeria.
Philippopolis (PLOVDIV), Bulgaria.
Pietarsaari (JAKOBSTAD), Finland.
Pilsen (PLZEN), Czechoslovakia.
PIRAEUS (PIRAIEVS), Greece.
PIRAIEVS (PIRAEUS), Greec.
PLOVDIV (Philippopolis), Bulgaria.
PLZEN (Pilsen), Czechoslovakia.
Pola (PULA), Yugoslavia.
Ponthierville (UBUNDU), Zaire.
POONA (PUNE), India.
PORI (Bjorneborg), Finland.
Port Arthur (THUNDER BAY), Canada.
Port Arthur (LUSHUN), People's Republic of China.
Port Francqui (ILEBO), Zaire.
PORT LAIRGE (WATERFORD), Ireland.
PORTO (OPORTO), Portugal.
Posen (POZNAN), Poland.
POZNAN (Posen), Poland.
Pozsony (BRATISLAVA), Czechoslovakia.
PRAGUE (PRAHA), Czechoslovakia.
PRAHA (PRAGUE), Czechoslovakia.
Pressburg (BRATISLAVA), Czechoslovakia.
Pt. Etienne (NOUADHIBOU), Mauritania.
PULA (Pola), Yugoslavia.
PUNE (POONA), India.

QAQORTOQ (JULIANEHAB), Greenland.
QEQERTARSUAQ (GODHAVN), Greenland.
QINGDAO (Tsingtao), People's Republic of China.
QUANZHOU (Chuanchou), People's Republic of China.
Queenstown (COBH), Ireland.
Quemoy (KIN-MEN), Republic of China — Taiwan.
QUE QUE (KWEKWE), Zimbabwe.
QUZHOU (Chuhsien), People's Republic of China.

RABAUL (Herbertshohe), Papua New Guinea.
Ragusa (DUBROVNIK), Yugoslavia.
Ratisbon (REGENSBURG), West Germany.
RECIFE (Pernambuco), Brazil.
REGENSBURG (Ratisbon), West Germany.
Revel (TALLINN), Estonia — USSR.
RHODES (RODHOS), Greece.
RIJEKA (Fiume), Yugoslavia.
RIYADH (AR RIYAD), Saudi Arabia.
RODHOS (RHODES), Greece.
ROMA (ROME), Italy.
ROME (ROMA), Italy.
Ruschuk (RUSE), Bulgaria.
RUSE (Ruschuk), Bulgaria.

SAIDA (SIDON), Lebanon.
Saigon (HO CHI MINH), Vietnam.
Sainte-Marie (NOSY BORAHA), Madagascar.
St. Petersburg (LENINGRAD), USSR.
Salisbury (HARARE), Zimbabwe.
Salonika (THESSALONIKI), Greece.
SALVADOR (Bahia), Brazil.
SANTO DOMINGO (Ciudad Trujillo), Dominican Republic.
SARAGOSSA (ZARAGOZA), Spain.
Scutari (SHKODER), Albania.
SEOUL (SOUL), South Korea.
Seyhan (ADANA), Turkey.
'S-GRAVENHAGE (THE HAGUE), The Netherlands.
SHABANI (ZVISHAVANE), Zimbabwe.
SHANGQIU (Zhuji or Chuchi), People's Republic of China.
SHANTOU (Swatow), People's Republic of China.
SHENYANG (Mukden), People's Republic of China.
SHKODER (Scutari), Albania.
Sian (XIAN), People's Republic of China.
SIDON (SAIDA), Lebanon.
SINOP (Sinope), Turkey.
Sinope (SINOP), Turkey.
SIRACUSA (SYRACUSE), Italy.
Sisimiut (HOLSTEINSBORG), Greenland.
SITTWE (Akyab), Burma.
SKIKDA (Philippeville), Algeria.
SKOPJE (Uskub), Yugoslavia.
Smyrna (IZMIR), Turkey.
SOFIA (SOFIYA), Bulgaria.
SOFIYA (SOFIA), Bulgaria.
SOPRON (Oldenburg), Hungary.
SOUL (SEOUL), South Korea.

SOUR (Tyre), Lebanon.
SOVETSK (Tilsit), USSR.
Spalato (SPLIT), Yugoslavia.
SPLIT (Spalato), Yugoslavia.
Sta. Isabel (MALABA), Equatorial Guinea.
Stalingrad (VOLGOGRAD), USSR.
Stanislav (IVANO FRANKOVSK), USSR.
Stanleyville (KISANGANI), Zaire.
Stettin (SZCZECIN), Poland.
STRASBOURG (Strassburg), France.
Strassburg (STRASBOURG), France.
Stuhlweissenburg (SZEKESFEHERVAR), Hungary.
Sukarnapura (JAYAPURA), Indonesia.
SUKKERTOPPEN (Manitsoq), Greenland.
Swatow (SHANTOU), People's Republic of China.
SYRACUSE (SIRACUSA), Italy.
SZCZECIN (Stettin), Poland.
SZEKESFEHERVAR (Stuhlweissenburg), Hungary.

TALLINN (Reval), Estonia — USSR.
Tamatave (TOAMASINA), Madagascar.
Tammerfors (TAMPERE), Finland.
TAMPERE (Tammerfors), Finland.
Tananarive (ANTANANARIVO), Madagascar.
TANGER (Tangiers), Morocco.
Tangiers (TANGER), Morocco.
TAOLANARO (Fort Dauphin), Madagascar.
TARABULUS (TRIPOLI), Libya.
TARFAYA (Villa Bens), Morocco.
TARTU. (Dorpat), Estonia — USSR.
Tashi Chho (THIMBU), Bhutan.
TBILIS (Tiflis), USSR.
TEHERAN (TEHRAN), Iran.
TEHRAN (TEHERAN), Iran.
Temesvar (TIMISOARA), Romania.
TETOUAN (Tetuan), Morocco.
Tetuan (TETOUAN), Moroco.
THE HAGUE ('S-GRAVENHAGE), The Netherlands.
THESSALONIKI (Salonika), Greece.
THIMBU (Tashi Chho), Bhutan.
THIONVILLE (Diedenhofen), France.
Thorn (TORUN), Poland.
THUNDER BAY (Fort William and Port Arthur), Canada.
TIANJIN (Tientsin), People's Republic of China.
Tientsin (TIANJIN), People's Republic of China.
Tiflis (TBILIS), USSR.
Tilsit (SOVETSK), USSR.
Timbuktu (TOMBOUCTOU), Mali.
TIMISOARA (Temesvar), Romania.

Tirana (TIRANE), Albania.
TIRANE (Tirana), Albania.
TOAMASINA (Tamatave), Madagascar.
Tobruch (TUBRUQ), Libya.
Tobruk (TUBRUQ), Libya.
TOLIARA (Tulear), Madagascar.
TOMBOUCTOU (Timbuktu), Mali.
Tongshan (XUZHOU), People's Republic of China.
TORINO (TURIN), Italy.
TORUN (Thorn), Poland.
Tourane (DA NANG), Vietnam.
TRABLOUS (TRIPOLI), Lebanon.
TRABZON (Trebizond), Turkey.
TRAIGHLI (TRALEE), Ireland.
TRALEE (TRAIGHLI), Ireland.
Trebizond (TRABZON), Turkey.
Trent (TRENTO), Italy.
TRENTO (Trient), Italy.
TREVES (TRIER), West Germany.
Trient (TRENTO), Italy.
TRIER (TREVES), West Germany.
TRIPOLI (TRABLOUS), Lebanon.
TRIPOLI (TARABULUS), Libya.
Tsingtao (QINGDAO), People's Republic of China.
Tsitsihar (CH'I-CH'I-HA-ERH), People's Republic of China.
TUBRUQ (Tobruk or Tobruch), Libya.
Tulear (TOLIARA), Madagascar.
Tunchi (TUNXI), People's Republic of China.
TUNXI (Tunchi), People's Republic of China.
TURIN (TORINO), Italy.
TURKU (Abo), Finland.
Tyre (SOUR), Lebanon.
Tzaritzin (VOLGOGRAD), USSR.

UBUNDU (Ponthierville), Zaire.
UJUNG PANDANG (Makassar), Indonesia.
ULAANBAATAR (Ulan Bator or Urga), Mongolia.
Ulan Bator (ULAANBAATAR), Mongolia.
ULEABORG (OULU), Finland.
UMTALI (MUTARE), Zimbabwe.
Urga (ULAANBAATAR), Mongolia.
Urumchi (URUMQI), People's Republic of China.
URUMQI (Urumchi), People's Republic of China.
Uskub (SKOPJE), Yugoslavia.

VAASA (Vasa), Finland.
Valona (VLORE), Albania.
VARANASI (Benares), India.
Vasa (VAASA), Finland.
VASDODARA (Baroda), India.
VENEZIA (VENICE), Italy.

VENICE (VENEZIA), Italy.
VIENNA (WIEN), Austrai.
VILA VELHA (Espirito Santo), Brazil.
Villa Bens (TARFAYA), Morocco.
Villa Cisneros (AD DAKHLA), Morocco.
VLORE (Valona), Albania.
Vohemar (VOHIMARINA), Madagascar.
VOHIMARINA (Vohemar), Madagascar.
VOLGOGRAD (Stalingrad or Tzaritzin), USSR.
VOROSHILOVGRAD (Lugansk), USSR.

WALBRZYCH (Waldenburg), Poland.
Waldenburg (WALBRZYCH), Poland.
Walfisch Bay (WALVIS BAY), South Africa.
WALVIS BAY (Walfisch Bay), South Africa.
WANKIE (HWANGE), Zimbabwe.
WARSAW (WARSZAWA), Poland.
WARSZAWA (WARSAW), Poland.
WATERFORD (PORT LAIRGE), Ireland.
WEIN (VIENNA), Austria.
WROCLAW (Breslau), Poland.
WUHAN (Hankow), People's Republic of China.

XIAMEN (Amoy), People's Republic of China.
XIAN (Sian), People's Republic of China.
XUCHANG (Hsuchang), People's Republic of China.
XUZHOU (Tongshan or Hsuchou), People's Republic of China.

YAFO (Jaffa or Joppa), Israel.
Yannina (IOANNINA), Greece.
YUMEN (Laojunmiao), People's Republic of China.
Yunnan (KUNMING), People's Republic of China.

ZADAR (Zara), Yugoslavia.
ZAGREB. (Agram), Yugoslavia.
ZAHEDAN (Duzdab), Iran.
Zara (ZADAR), Yugoslavia.
ZARAGOZA (SARAGOSSA), Spain.
ZHANJIANG (Kouang Tcheou), People's Republic of China.
ZHENGZHOU (Chengchow), People's Republic of China.
Zhuji (SHANGQIU), People's Republic of China.
ZVISHAVANE (SHABANI), Zimbabwe.

References

Atlases

Britannica Atlas, Encyclopedia Britannica, Inc., Chicago, 1970.
Goode's World Atlas, 17th Edition, Rand McNally, Chicago, 1986.
National Geographic Society maps, National Geographic Society, Washington, D.C.
Nock, O.S., *World Atlas of Railways,* Bonanza Books, London, 1983.
Oxford Atlas, Oxford University Press, London, 1970.
Road Atlas of Britain and Ireland, Wm. Collins Sons, Glasgow, 1980.
Road Book of Europe, Automobile Association of Great Britain, 1976.
Times Atlas of the World, Fifth Comprehensive Edition, Times Books Ltd., New York, 1975.
Times Atlas of the World, Seventh Comprehensive Edition, Times Books Ltd., New York, 1985.
Wood, Kenneth A., *Where in the World,* Van Dahl Publications, Albany, Ore., 1983.

General references

Baedeker's Great Britain, Automobile Association of Great Britain, 1982.
Edwards, C.B., *Instant World Facts,* Tutor Press, Toronto, Canada, 1980.
Encyclopedia Britannica, 200th Anniversary Edition, 1970.
Encyclopedia of World Rivers, Rand McNally & Co., 1980.
Encyclopedia of World Travel, Doubleday & Co., Inc., New York, 1973.
Hawthorne, A.J., *Countries of the World,* Coles, Toronto, Canada, 1981.
Linn's World Stamp Almanac, Fourth Edition, Amos Press, Sidney, Ohio, 1982.
Slater, Mary, *The Caribbean Islands,* Viking Press, New York, 1968.
Standard Reference Encyclopedia, Funk and Wagnalls Co., 1970.
Status of the World's Nations, US Department of State, Bureau of Intelligence and Research, 1983.
Webster's New Geographical Dictionary, G.&C. Merriam & Co., Springfield, Mass., 1980.
Wood, Kenneth A., *Post Dates,* Van Dahl Publications, Albany, Ore., 1985.
World Almanac, 1987 Edition, Newspaper Enterprise Association, Inc., New York.

Catalogs

Sources include catalogs published by:
Gibbons — Stanley Gibbons Publications Ltd., London, England.
Michel — Schwaneberger Verlag GmbH, Munich, Federal Republic of Germany.
Minkus — Minkus Publications Inc., New York, N.Y.
Scott — Scott Publishing Co., Sidney, Ohio.
Yvert — Yvert & Tellier, Amiens, France.
Zumstein — Zumstein & Cie., Bern, Switzerland.

Index

Abu Dhabi (see United Arab Emirates)
Abyssinia (see Ethiopia)
Aden (see Yemen, People's Democratic Republic of)
Afars and Issas (see Djibouti)
Afghanistan, 172
Aitutaki, 222
Ajman (see United Arab Emirates)
Aland Islands (see Finland)
Albania, 57
Alderney, 105
Algeria, 114
Andorra, 58
Angola, 115
Anguilla, 23
Anjouan (see Comoros)
Annobon (see Equatorial Guinea)
Antigua, 24
Argentina (see Argentine Republic)
Argentine Republic, 42
Aruba (see Netherlands Antilles)
Ascension, 116
Australia, 220
Australian Antarctic Terr., 248
Austria, 59
Austro-Hungarian Empire (see Austria)
Azores, 91

Bahamas, 2
Bahrain, 173
Bangladesh, 190
Barbados, 25
Barbuda (see Antigua)
Basutoland (see Lesotho)
Bechuanaland Protectorate (see Botswana)
Belgian Congo (see Zaire)
Belgium, 60
Belize, 12
Benin, 117
Bequia (see St. Vincent)
Berlin, West, 72
Bermuda, 3
Bhutan, 191
Biafra (see Nigeria)
Bohemia and Moravia (see Czechoslovakia)
Bolivia, 43
Bonaire (see Netherlands Antilles)
Bophuthatswana (see South Africa)
Botswana, 118
Brasil (see Brazil)
Brazil, 44
British Antarctic Terr., 248
British Guiana (see Guyana)
British Honduras (see Belize)
British India (see India and Pakistan)
British North Borneo (see Malaysia)
British Virgin Islands, 40
Brunei, 192
Bulgaria, 61
Burkina Faso, 119
Burma, 193
Burundi, 120

Caicos Islands (see Turks and Caicos Islands)
Cambodia, 194
Cameroon, 121
Cameroun (see Cameroon)
Canada, 5
Cape of Good Hope (see South Africa)
Cape Verde, 122
Caroline Is. (see Micronesia)
Cayes of Belize (see Belize)
Cayman Islands, 13
Central African Empire (see Central African Republic)
Central African Republic, 123
Ceylon (see Sri Lanka)
Chad, 124
Channel Islands (see United Kingdom)
Chile, 46
China, People's Republic of, 196
China, Republic of (Taiwan), 195

Christmas Island, 198
Ciskei (see South Africa)
Cocos (Keeling) Islands, 199
Colombia, 47
Comoros, 125
Congo, 126
Congo Democratic Republic (see Zaire)
Cook Islands, 223
Corisco (see Equatorial Guinea)
Costa Rica, 14
Cuba, 15
Curacao (see Netherlands Antilles)
Cyprus, 62
Cyprus, Turkish (see Cyprus)
Cyrenaica (see Libya)
Czechoslovakia, 63

Dahomey (see Benin)
Denmark, 64
Djibouti, 127
Dominica, 26
Dominican Republic, 27
Dubai (see United Arab Emirates)
Dutch East Indies (see Indonesia)
Dutch Guiana (see Suriname)

East Germany (see German Democratic Republic)
East Pakistan (see Bangladesh)
Ecuador, 48
Egypt, 128
Eire (see Ireland)
Elobey (see Equatorial Guinea)
El Salvador, 16
England (see United Kingdom)
Equatorial Guinea, 129
Ethiopia, 130

Falkland Islands, 49
Faroe Islands, 65
Federated Malay States (see Malaysia)
Federation of Mali (see Mali)
Federation of Rhodesia and Nyasaland (see Malawi, Zambia, and Zimbabwe)
Fernando Po (see Equatorial Guinea)
Fiji, 224
Finland, 66
Formosa (see Republic of China, Taiwan)
France, 68
French Morocco (see Morocco)
French Oceania (see French Polynesia)
French Polynesia, 225
French Somali Coast (see Djibouti)
French Southern and Antarctic Terr., 248
French Sudan (see Mali)
Fujeira (see United Arab Emirates)
Funafuti (see Tuvalu)

Gabon, 131
Gambia, The, 132
German Democratic Republic 72
German East Africa (see Tanzania)
Germany, Federal Republic of, 71
Ghana, 133
Gibraltar, 73
Gilbert Islands (see Kiribati)
Gold Coast (see Ghana)
Grand Comore (see Comoros)
Great Britain (see United Kingdom)
Greece, 74
Greenland, 76
Grenada, 28
Grenada Grenadines (see Grenada)
Guatemala, 17
Guernsey, 105
Guinea, 134
Guinea-Bissau, 135
Guyana, 50

Haiti, 30

Hejaz (see Saudi Arabia)
Hellenic Republic (see Greece)
Holland (see The Netherlands)
Honduras, 18
Hong Kong, 202
Hungarian People's Republic (see Hungary)
Hungary, 77

Iceland, 78
India, 200
India, British (see India and Pakistan)
Indo China, French (see Cambodia, Laos, Vietnam)
Indonesia, 203
Iran, 174
Iraq, 175
Ireland, 79
Irish Republic (see Ireland)
Isle of Man, 107
Israel, 176
Italian Somaliland (see Somali Democratic Republic)
Italy, 80
Ivory Coast, 136

Jamaica, 19
Japan, 204
Jersey, 106
Jordan, 177
Jugoslavia (see Yugoslavia)

Kalaallit Nunaat (see Greenland)
Kamerun (see Cameroon)
Kampuchea (see Cambodia)
Kenya, 137
Kiribati, 226
Korea, North, 206
Korea, South, 207
Kuwait, 178

Labuan (see Malaysia)
Lao People's Democratic Republic, 208
Laos, 208
Lebanon, 179
Leeward Islands (see British Virgin Islands, St. Kitts-Nevis, Anguilla, Antigua, Montserrat, and Dominica)
Lesotho, 138
Liberia, 139
Libya, 140
Liechtenstein, 82
Lower Canada (see Canada)
Luxembourg, 83

Macao, 209
Madagascar, 141
Madeira, 92
Malagasy (see Madagascar)
Malawi, 142
Malaysia, 210
Maldives, 211
Mali, 143
Malta, 84
Malvinas Islands (see Falkland Islands)
Marshall Islands, 227
Mauritania, 144
Mauritius, 145
Mesopotamia (see Iraq)
Mexico, 6
Micronesia, 228
Middle Congo (see Congo)
Modena (see Italy)
Moheli (see Comoros)
Moldavia (see Romania)
Monaco, 85
Mongolia, 212
Montserrat, 31
Morocco, 146
Mozambique, 147

Mozambique Company (see Mozambique)
Muscat and Oman (see Oman)

Namibia, 148
Nanumaga (see Tuvalu)
Nanumea (see Tuvalu)
Natal (see South Africa)
Nauru, 229
Nejd (see Saudi Arabia)
Nepal, 213
Netherlands Antilles, 32
Netherlands, The, 88
Nevis (see St. Kitts-Nevis)
New Caledonia, 232
Newfoundland (see Canada)
New France (see Canada)
New Hebrides (see Vanuatu)
New South Wales (see Australia)
New Zealand, 230
Nicaragua, 20
Niger, 149
Nigeria, 150
Niuafo'ou, 233
Niue, 234
Niutao (see Tuvalu)
Norfolk Island, 235
Northern Ireland, 108
Northern Rhodesia (see Zambia)
North German Confederation (see Germany)
Norway, 86
Nui (see Tuvalu)
Nukufetau (see Tuvalu)
Nukulaelae (see Tuvalu)
Nyasaland Protectorate (see Malawi)
Nyassa (see Mozambique)

Obock (see Djibouti)
Oman, 180
Orange River Colony (see South Africa)
Outer Mongolia (see Mongolia)

Pakistan, 181
Palau, 236
Palestine (see Israel)
Panama, 21
Papua New Guinea, 237
Paraguay, 51
Parma (see Italy)
Penrhyn, 238
Persia (see Iran)
Peru, 52
Philippines, 214
Pitcairn Is., 239
Poland, 89
Portugal, 90
Portuguese Guinea (see Guinea-Bissau)
Prussia (see Germany)

Qatar, 182
Queensland (see Australia)

Rarotonga (see Cook Islands)
Ras al Khaima (see United Arab Emirates)
Redonda (see Antigua)

Rhodesia (see Zimbabwe)
Rio Muni (see Equatorial Guinea)
Romagne (see Italy)
Romania, 93
Ross Dependency, 248
Ruanda-Urundi (see Burundi and Rwanda)
Russia (see USSR)
Rwanda, 151

Saba (see Netherlands Antilles)
St. Christopher (see St. Kitts-Nevis)
St. Eustatius (see Netherlands Antilles)
St. Helena, 152
St. Kitts-Nevis, 34
St. Kitts-Nevis-Anguilla (see St. Kitts-Nevis)
St. Lucia, 35
St. Maarten (see Netherlands Antilles)
St. Pierre and Miquelon, 10
St. Thomas and Prince, 153
St. Vincent, 36
St. Vincent Grenadines (see St. Vincent)
Salvador (see El Salvador)
Samoa, 240
San Marino, 98
Sao Tome and Principe (see St. Thomas and Prince)
Sardinia, Kingdom of (see Italy)
Saudi Arabia, 183
Scotland, 109
Senegal, 154
Seychelles, 155
Sharjah (see United Arab Emirates)
Shqiperi (see Albania)
Siam (see Thailand)
Sierra Leone, 156
Singapore, 215
Slovakia (see Czechoslovakia)
Solomon Is., 241
Somali Democratic Republic, 157
Somaliland Protectorate (see Somali Democratic Republic)
South Africa, 158
South Australia (see Australia)
Southern Rhodesia (see Zimbabwe)
South Georgia and South Sandwich Is., 248
South West Africa (see Namibia)
Spain, 94
Spanish Morocco (see Morocco)
Spanish Sahara (see Morocco)
Sri Lanka, 216
Straits Settlements (see Malaysia)
Sudan, 160
Sudanese Republic (see Mali)
Surinam (see Suriname)
Suriname, 53
Swaziland, 161
Sweden, 96
Switzerland, 99
Syria, 184

Tahiti (see French Polynesia)
Tanganyika (see Tanzania)
Tanzania, 162
Tasmania (see Australia)
Tchad (see Chad)
Thailand, 217
The Gambia, 132

The Netherlands, 88
Tobago (see Trinidad and Tobago)
Togo, 163
Tokelau Is., 242
Tonga, 243
Transjordan (see Jordan)
Transkei (see South Africa)
Transvaal (see South Africa)
Trinidad and Tobago, 38
Tripolitania (see Libya)
Tristan da Cunha, 164
Tunisia, 165
Turkey, 185
Turkish Republic of Northern Cyprus (see Cyprus)
Turks and Caicos Islands, 39
Turks Islands (see Turks and Caicos Islands)
Tuscany (see Italy)
Tuvalu, 244

Ubangi-Shari (see Central African Republic)
Uganda, 166
Umm al Qiwain (see United Arab Emirates)
Union (see St. Vincent)
Union of Soviet Socialist Republics (see USSR)
United Arab Emirates, 186
United Kingdom, 102
United States, 8
Upper Canada (see Canada)
Upper Volta (see Burkina Faso)
Uruguay, 54
USSR, 100

Vaitupu (see Tuvalu)
Van Diemen's Land (see Australia)
Vanuatu, 245
Vatican, 111
Venda (see South Africa)
Venezuela, 55
Victoria (see Australia)
Vietnam, 218
Virgin Islands (see British Virgin Islands)

Walachia (see Romania)
Wales, 110
Wallis and Futuna Is., 246
Western Sahara (see Morocco)
West Germany (see Germany, Federal Republic of)

Yemen Arab Republic, 187
Yemen, People's Democratic Republic of, 188
Yugoslavia, 112

Zaire, 167
Zambia, 168
Zanzibar (see Tasmania)
Zil Eloigne Sesel (see Zil Elwannyen Sesel)
Zil Elwagne Sesel (see Zil Elwannyen Sesel)
Zil Elwannyen Sesel, 169
Zimbabwe, 170